A History of
The Expansion of Christianity

Volume IV

THE GREAT CENTURY
IN EUROPE AND THE UNITED
STATES OF AMERICA
A.D. 1800-A.D. 1914

A History of
THE EXPANSION OF CHRISTIANITY

(*Volume IV*)

THE
GREAT CENTURY
IN EUROPE AND THE UNITED
STATES OF AMERICA
A.D. 1800-A.D. 1914

by

KENNETH SCOTT LATOURETTE

THE PATERNOSTER PRESS

ISBN: 0 85364 117 X

THE GREAT CENTURY

Copyright © 1941, 1969 by Harper and Row, Publishers
Published by special arrangement with Harper and Row, Publishers,
New York
Printed in the United States of America
This edition is distributed by The Paternoster Press
Paternoster House, 3 Mount Radford Crescent
Exeter, Devon, by arrangement with
The Zondervan Publishing House, Grand Rapids, Mich., U.S.A.

This Edition 1971

AUSTRALIA:
Emu Book Agencies Pty., Ltd., 511 Kent Street, Sydney, N.S.W.

SOUTH AFRICA:
Oxford University Press, P.O. Box 1141, Oxford House,
11, Buitencingle Street, Cape Town

In memory of

HARLAN PAGE BEACH

1854–1933

Contents

Chapter I

BY WAY OF INTRODUCTION.   I

Chapter II

THE MOVEMENTS WHICH CHARACTERIZED THE NINETEENTH CENTURY AND IN THE
MIDST OF WHICH THE EXPANSION OF CHRISTIANITY WAS ACCOMPLISHED.   9

Chapter III

THE NEW MOVEMENTS WITHIN CHRISTIANITY THROUGH WHICH THE EXPANSION
OF THE FAITH WAS CHIEFLY ACCOMPLISHED.   22

Chapter IV

THE PROCESS BY WHICH CHRISTIANITY SPREAD. General Features: Roman Catholic organization and methods: Protestant organization and methods: The
Russian Orthodox Church.   47

Chapter V

EUROPE: Jews: Pagans: Moslems: Missions of Christians among other Christians: holding Christians to their faith: the effect upon the environment:
the effect of the environment.   110

Chapter VI

THE UNITED STATES OF AMERICA. Introductory. The older American stock on
the frontier.   175

Chapter VII

THE UNITED STATES OF AMERICA. Winning the immigrants: Roman Catholics:
Eastern Churches: Protestants.   224

CONTENTS

Chapter VIII

THE UNITED STATES OF AMERICA. Efforts to win the Indians: Roman Catholic: Russian Orthodox: Protestant.   299

Chapter IX

THE UNITED STATES OF AMERICA. The Negroes.   325

Chapter X

THE UNITED STATES OF AMERICA. Shifting populations and changing social conditions.   367

Chapter XI

THE UNITED STATES OF AMERICA. The effect of Christianity upon its environment.   381

Chapter XII

THE UNITED STATES OF AMERICA. The effect of the environment upon Christianity.   424

Chapter XIII

BY WAY OF SUMMARY AND ANTICIPATION.   457

BIBLIOGRAPHY.   493

INDEX.   497

MAPS.

I EUROPE   Front End Paper

II THE UNITED STATES   Back End Paper

The author wishes to record his appreciation and gratitude for the helpful suggestions of Professor Ralph H. Gabriel and Dean Luther A. Weigle. Each of these most generously took time from a summer vacation to read the manuscript. As in the case of the preceding volumes, Mrs. Charles T. Lincoln turned a difficult first draft into neat typescript and at the same time made valuable suggestions as to style. The officers and librarians of the Congregation for the Propagation of the Faith graciously gave the author free access to their invaluable library and, equally important, of their counsel. As ever, the libraries of Yale University and particularly Professor Raymond P. Morris, Librarian of the Yale University Divinity School and its Day Missions Library were unfailingly helpful. Professor Harlan P. Beach, although he did not live to see the inception of this volume, through his years as Librarian of the Day Missions Library accumulated much of the collection without which the work could hardly have been written. To these chiefly, but also to many others, too numerous to catalogue, who in one way or another have consciously or unconsciously helped, the author would express his thanks.

A History of
The Expansion of Christianity

Volume IV

THE GREAT CENTURY
IN EUROPE AND THE UNITED
STATES OF AMERICA
A.D. 1800-A.D. 1914

Chapter I

BY WAY OF INTRODUCTION

AS OUR story moves into the nineteenth century we come to the age of the most extensive geographic spread of Christianity.

By the close of the eighteenth century Christianity was represented in all the five continents. Never before had any religion been planted over so large a proportion of the earth's surface. In Europe it was the professed faith of the large majority of the population. Scattered Christian constituencies were to be found in Asia. Some of these were in the western part of the continent, remnants of the older Eastern churches, on the stubborn defensive against the long dominant Islam and slowly yielding ground to it. From most of them zealous missionaries from Europe had gathered groups into union with Rome. In India, largely along its southern coasts, Christian communities existed, part of them dating back to the early Christian centuries, and others of them the fruits of more recent Roman Catholic and Protestant missions. In Ceylon Christianity was introduced and became proportionately much stronger than in India. Burma and Siam contained a few handfuls of Roman Catholic Christians. In what in the nineteenth century became French Indo-China rather larger numbers had been won by Roman Catholic missionaries. In China several tens of thousands of Christians, Roman Catholics, existed, divided into many small clusters in most of the provinces and on the northern borders of China proper, and subject to chronic persecution. Tibet had seen Roman Catholic missionaries. Through contacts with China, Roman Catholicism had spread to Korea. Russian Christianity had been planted in various centres across Siberia and possessed an outpost in Peking. Japan contained a few hidden remnants of the Roman Catholic communities which had flourished before determined proscription by the state had decimated them and had reduced them to a clandestine existence. The majority of 'the Filipinos were Roman Catholics. In the Netherlands East Indies Dutch Protestantism had several footholds. In Africa, in Egypt and Abyssinia, were well-entrenched churches, survivals from a more prosperous pre-Islamic age. Along the shores of Africa were numbers of Christian groups, all of them small, from the captives held by the Moslems on the southern borders of the Mediterranean,

1

through several posts on the West Coast, to the Dutch settlements at the Cape of Good Hope and the Portuguese possessions on the East Coast. The Azores, the Madeiras, and the Cape Verde Islands to the west of Africa, and Réunion and Mauritius on the east contained Christians. In the Western Hemisphere the majority of the population were professedly Christian. There most of the whites retained the faith of their European progenitors and the indigenous peoples in the more thickly settled centres and some of the Negroes had been won. In the Americas the larger part of the Christians were Roman Catholics, but on the east coast of North America, in the West Indies, in Surinam, and in Greenland Protestants were strong, and in Alaska the Christianity was of the Russian Orthodox variety, brought over by way of Siberia.

In most of these areas Christianity had been planted by the great missionary movement of the sixteenth, seventeenth, and eighteenth centuries. In A.D. 1800, to be sure, the overwhelming majority of Christians were the descendants of those who had been won before A.D. 1500. However, the larger proportion of the regions in which Christian communities were found had been brought within the orbit of the faith by the expansion in the three centuries between these two dates. This expansion was in connexion with phenomenal explorations, commercial enterprises, and conquests by Christian Europeans, in themselves also on a scale unprecedented in human history. It had not automatically accompanied them, but had arisen out of the religious awakenings in Western Europe in these centuries—awakenings which for potency were without equal in previous Christian history. The questions as to whether the secular activities of Europeans in this period were the results of Christianity, whether both secular and religious activity were due to a common cause, or whether several factors, including Christianity, co-operated to produce the remarkable burst of energy in European life have been discussed in the preceding volume. While the answers must be tentative and disappointingly hesitant, the indubitable fact remains of the vast extension of Christianity among non-European peoples and in territories outside of Europe.

Now, in the nineteenth century, came a further expansion of Christianity. Not so many continents or major countries were entered for the first time as in the preceding three centuries. That would have been impossible, for on all the larger land masses of the earth except Australia and among all the more numerous peoples and in all the areas of high civilization Christianity had been introduced before A.D. 1800. What now occurred was the acquisition of fresh footholds in regions and among peoples already touched, an expansion of unprecedented extent from both the newer bases and the older ones, and the entrance of Christianity into the large majority of such countries, islands, peoples, and tribes as had previously not been touched. In the Americas almost all the indigenous tribes which had not been reached were approached, the majority of the Negroes were won, and among the rapidly increasing white population of the United States, the land which, among all others in this century, experienced the largest growth in population, the proportion of those having a formal membership in the Church mounted. Among those of European stock in Latin America the traditional hold of Roman Catholic Christianity was somewhat shaken, but this loss was partly offset by the growth of Protestantism in this region, and for Christianity as a whole it was more than compensated by the growth of the churches in the United States and Canada. To the west of the Americas, in the islands of the Pacific, Christianity also had a phenomenal growth. The majority of the native peoples of Polynesia and Micronesia were brought to accept the faith, in the new nations of European blood which arose in Australia and New Zealand Christianity had a large place, and in the Netherlands East Indies and in the non-Dutch portions of Borneo and New Guinea missionaries planted the Christian faith. On the northern shores of Africa west of Egypt French and Italian immigration was accompanied by the rise of Christian churches stronger than any which that area had known since the Moslem conquest. Africa south of the Sahara was criss-crossed with mission stations. In this Negro Africa hundreds of thousands of converts were made, and on the southern extremity of the continent a new nation arose, with those of European descent as the controlling element, in which Christianity was the prevailing religion. In Asia Christianity became more widespread than ever before, and, when the continent is considered as a whole, the faith that had begun on its western fringes, had been disseminated so widely in it, and then had suffered such disastrous reverses, largely at the hands of Islam, now become more prominent and influential than ever before. In Western Asia, Christianity, while it enjoyed no great increase in numbers, through its schools and hospitals made itself felt in moulding ideals and life as it had not done since the early centuries of the Moslem conquest. In India, Ceylon, Burma, Siam, Malaya, what became French Indo-China, China, Korea, and, possibly, Japan Christians became more numerous than at any previous time and upon the cultures of most of these lands Christianity had more profound effects than the numerical strength of the churches would have led one to expect. In Siberia churches multiplied. Indeed, in Asia as a whole, while its formal adherents, even after the increases of the century, still numbered no more than one per cent. of the total population, Christianity was effecting a mass permeation of culture and was shaping ideals, customs, and institutions as in no other previous period.

In spite of this extensive spread, Christianity continued to have its chief strength in Europe and among peoples of European descent. It remained primarily the religion of the Occident. Yet it was already overpassing its Occidental bounds. Moreover, in some of the new nations founded by Europeans is was beginning to take on features peculiar to those areas and among some non-European peoples was showing the tinge of its surroundings. Never before had Christianity, or any other religion, been introduced among so many different peoples and cultures.

The nineteenth century spread of Christianity was due primarily to a new burst of religious life emanating from the Christian impulse. As in the three centuries before A.D. 1800, so in the nineteenth century, the expansion of Christianity was closely associated with the migrations, the commerce, and the conquests of peoples of European stock. However, as had been the case in the centuries between A.D. 1500 and A.D. 1800, it did not automatically accompany the extension of European economic and political power and even less than in those centuries was it ancillary to European secular ambitions. Never in any corresponding length of time had the Christian impulse given rise to so many new movements. Never had it had quite so great an effect upon Western European peoples. It was from this abounding vigour that there issued the missionary enterprise which during the nineteenth century so augmented the numerical strength and the influence of Christianity.

The revival of Christianity showed itself primarily in Protestantism. Protestantism now became more prominent in the total stream of the Christian movement than at any previous time. Yet Roman Catholicism also displayed renewed life and spread more widely than ever before. The Russian Orthodox Church and some of the other Eastern churches, while by no means exhibiting so much vitality, had some extension, notably by migration.

The vigour and expansion of nineteenth century Christianity were preceded by a period when the faith appeared to be at a low ebb and when its future seemed dubious. In the second half of the eighteenth century Christianity suffered several severe blows. The nations chiefly responsible for its expansion in the sixteenth and seventeenth centuries, Spain and Portugal, were obviously in decay and could no longer accord missions the energetic support which they had once given. One of the chief missionary agencies, the Society of Jesus, was dissolved. In China persecution was being intensified and in Japan it succeeded in obliterating all surface traces of once flourishing Christian communities. In Europe among intellectual circles the Church was being attacked, "revealed religion" was being discounted as obsolete, and praise was reserved for "natural religion" and a cold Deism. Even within the Church a strong tendency was seen to stress human reason and to decry enthusiasm and the emotions. In the British Thirteen Colonies of North America the Revolutionary War, the political agitation which preceded it, and the disorganization which immediately followed it checked the rising tide of religious fervour which was the fruit of the Great Awakening. Beginning with 1789 all Western Europe was distraught by the French Revolution and by the wars of Napoleon. In some of its phases the French Revolution was avowedly and militantly anti-Christian. Especially did the Roman Catholic Church suffer,[1] and it was through Roman Catholicism that in the preceding three centuries Christianity had had most of its expansion. Between 1789 and the downfall of Napoleon in 1815, few new missionaries could be sent and only meagre support could be accorded those already at work. For a time, for instance, the Société des Missions-Étrangères of Paris was forced to seek headquarters outside of France,[2] and Napoleon later sought to consolidate it with the Lazarists and the Holy Ghost fathers and make of the combined missions a tool for his imperialism.[3] In 1798 the central bureau for the supervision of Roman Catholic missions, the Congregation for the Propagation of the Faith, was driven out of Rome by revolutionary upheavals, and from 1810 to 1814 Napoleon placed it under an administration through which he endeavoured to make Roman Catholic missions subserve his ambition.[4] In the Spanish possessions in America the upheavals during the initial three decades of the nineteenth century which ended in the independence of all the colonies of the mainland were accompanied by distress to the church and to missions. The old order was being brought abruptly to a close and the church which had been so intimately associated with it inevitably suffered.

The reverse which overtook Christianity at the close of the eighteenth century differed somewhat from the major ones which followed the fifth century and which came in the fifteenth century. In these earlier ones the menace was from both within and without. In the more severe of the two, that which began in the fifth century and which in the ninth and tenth centuries brought Christianity to the lowest point in its history, the threat came partly from the collapse of the civilization with which Christianity had been so

---

[1] Out of the immense literature on the subject, see, as a good summary, Aulard, *Christianity and the French Revolution, passim.*
[2] Launay, *Histoire Générale de la Société des Missions-Étrangères,* Vol. II, pp. 257ff.
[3] Launay, *op. cit.,* Vol. II, pp. 419ff.
[4] Schmidlin, *Die Propaganda während der napoleonischen Invasion,* in *Zeitschrift für Missionswissenschaft,* Vol. XII, pp. 112-115.

closely intertwined, that of the Græco-Roman world, and partly from the foreign invasions by non-Christian peoples which, pressing in from all sides, seemed about to eliminate Christianity. The recession of the fifteenth century was due partly to an inward decay in Latin Christianity, and partly to a series of irruptions of non-Christian peoples, most of whom championed a resurgent and triumphant Islam. In contrast with the earlier reverses, the decline at the end of the eighteenth century was the product almost exclusively of internal factors. It was from within so-called Christendom, the regions in which Christianity was the official religion of the community, that the menace issued. This was serious, for it might indicate that Christianity was incapable of holding permanently the allegiance of races which had longest embraced it. Indeed, some declare that the eighteenth century departure from Christianity was a continuation of a rejection which had begun with the Renaissance.[5] If that interpretation were true, it would seem that beginning with the decline of mediaeval culture Christianity had been playing a diminishing rôle among Western European peoples. This hypothesis, however, fails to take account of the fact that never before had Western Christianity given rise to so many new movements and never had it influenced human civilization so profoundly as in the sixteenth, seventeenth, and eighteenth centuries. It also ignores the fact that in the eighteenth century, even in the face of many adverse circumstances, in Protestantism the tides of life were beginning to rise. We must also note a phenomenon to which we are to recur again and again, that never in any one century had so many movements emerged from within Christianity as in the nineteenth century, and that never before had the Christian movement exerted so great an influence upon mankind. The blows dealt Christianity at the end of the eighteenth century, and the disintegration within it, did not reduce it to such straits as in the preceding two major periods of decline.

The threat to Christianity did not cease with the coming of the nineteenth century. Most of the forces within the Occident which in the eighteenth century worked for the rejection of Christianity continued into the succeeding period. Indeed, some of them became more potent and to them others were added. We are to meet them in many pages of our story.

The nineteenth century witnessed contradictory trends. On the one hand, among Western European peoples denial and rejection of Christianity took place more openly and more formally than at any other time since the faith had been made the community religion of the Occident. Movements to deprive the Church of the support of the state or to create new governments among

[5] Nicholas Berdyaev, *The End of Our Time* (New York, Sheed and Ward, 1933, pp. 258), p. 32.

peoples of European stocks in which the Church should have no assistance from the state increased in number. On the other hand, never had Christianity shown such vigour.

For what we have termed the nineteenth century the boundary dates are not A.D. 1800 and A.D. 1900. For the United States the new era began with the War of Independence. For most of Europe it could be dated either from 1789, the outbreak of the French Revolution, or from 1815, the end of the Napoleonic Wars. In general, 1815 was the more pivotal year in introducing a period through which certain general features persisted. In the several sections of the world we will, however, be forced to commence our story at somewhat different dates and to describe movements some of which began before and some after 1815. The terminal date, 1914, is more precisely defined. The outbreak of the World War of 1914-1918 marked the end of one age and the beginning of another. Yet 1914 saw no sharp severance of the human race with its past. Many nineteenth and pre-nineteenth century forces and movements continued. Indeed, it was the coming to fruition of previously existing movements rather than the injection of new ones which brought about the transition.

To the nineteenth century as so delimited we must devote as much space as to all the preceding eighteen centuries. This is not primarily because the material from which to construct our story is so much more abundant, although it is so mountainous as to dismay even the most stout-hearted. Nor is it because, being so much nearer our own time, we have in it the special interest which centres about those events having directly to do with ourselves. It is, rather, because Christianity was now taken to more peoples than ever before and entered as a transforming agency into more cultures than in all the preceding centuries. The scene is no longer confined, as in the first five centuries, solely to the basin of the Mediterranean and to a few peoples outside that basin touched by Mediterranean culture. Nor is it restricted mainly to Europe with a few excursions to Asia and Africa, as in the succeeding thousand years, or chiefly to Europe and America, with some extensions to Asia and Africa, as in the three centuries between A.D. 1500 and A.D. 1800. It is now expanded to include all the globe and all peoples, nations, races, and cultures. It demands, therefore, a much larger canvass. Indeed, even more than in preceding volumes our problem is one of condensation. So many were the movements, so numerous were the individuals and organizations which brought about the spread of Christianity, and so abundant the records that we must be even more rigid than heretofore in avoiding unnecessary details and more ruthless in our omissions. We must confine ourselves for the most part to major events and outstanding leaders.

In the present volume we are to deal with Europe and the United States. These lands belong together, for in them European peoples predominated in numbers as well as in culture and in economic and political control. In the next volume we are to cover Canada, Greenland, the West Indies, Latin America, the islands of the Pacific, including Australia and New Zealand, and Africa. These follow logically after the chapters on the United States, because here Christianity was confronted by non-European peoples of primitive cultures and animistic faiths and it also met the problem of retaining and if possible strengthening its hold upon migrant Europeans who founded new nations. The third volume on the nineteenth century, the sixth in our series, will be devoted to Asia, where Christianity had begun and where it had as its chief field vast populations moulded by ancient and highly developed cultures. To this sixth volume will be added summaries of the nineteenth century.

In the present volume, before entering upon the details of the progress of Christianity in Europe and the Americas, we must speak of those general movements, all of them having their origin in the Occident, which conditioned the nineteenth century spread of Christianity, and we must describe the main characteristics of the expansion of Christianity in that period and give an account of the organizations through which that expansion was accomplished. This will provide an answer to one of the questions which we propounded at the outset of our study: What was the Christianity which spread? It will also give partial answers to two other questions: Why did Christianity spread, and by what processes did it spread? As we go on with our story we shall wish to seek in each major area answers not only to these three questions but also to the four other questions with which we introduced our survey: Why in some places did Christianity fail to spread; what effect did Christianity have upon its environment; what effect did the environment have upon Christianity; and what bearing did the processes by which Christianity spread have upon the effect of Christianity upon its environment and of the environment upon Christianity?

Chapter II

THE MOVEMENTS WHICH CHARACTERIZED THE NINE-TEENTH CENTURY AND IN THE MIDST OF WHICH THE EXPANSION OF CHRISTIANITY WAS ACCOMPLISHED

IF WE are to understand the expansion of Christianity in the nineteenth century we must see it in its setting. We must know the contemporary movements which modified it. Some of these aided the spread of Christianity, some hindered it, and others both assisted and opposed it. Here, at the outset of our account of the century, we must confine ourselves to the main features of the Occident of the time, as the region from which Christianity spread, and to trends of world-wide scope which affected the course of Christianity in all lands. The descriptions of environments peculiar to particular areas and countries must be reserved for the appropriate places in the narrative as it proceeds in its geographic course. So well known are these general movements and so much a commonplace in the history of the period are they that here they need only a brief summary with some indication of their bearing upon the spread of Christianity.

First of all, the nineteenth century was marked by a phenomenal growth of man's knowledge of the physical universe. This knowledge man classified under various headings. In the realms of physics and chemistry he discovered something of the nature, composition, and structure of matter, talked of molecules and atoms, and began to learn that the atom itself could be resolved into other constituents. In the astronomical field he came to know more about the stars and the planets. With his telescopes, his spectroscopes, his mathematics, and what he had learned through physics and chemistry he penetrated to distances of appalling magnitude, he weighed the stars, ascertained their chemical composition, made estimates of their age and of their motions, and began to be aware that not only is the earth a relatively minor object in a vast solar system, but that the solar system itself is also only an insignficant member of a family of unnumbered stars and of an unimaginably greater stellar system. Under geology he opened up a hitherto undreamed of vista of the history of the earth and of the development of life on the planet. Through biology he dipped into life itself and acquired an extensive fund of information

9

concerning the many manifestations of life and of the structure and functions of living bodies. Under physiology he investigated his own body and under psychology he sought to learn more of the nature and operation of his own brain. By subdividing these sciences and through specialization, man further explored the physical universe in the midst of which he was set.

In the second place, hand in hand with the growth in man's knowledge a startling increase occurred in the mastery by man of his physical environment. Man invented new machines, produced them in great numbers, and harnessed them to steam, water, and electricity in a fashion that would have seemed to his forefathers magical. Through these machines thus driven by inanimate power he multipled food, shelter, and raiment for himself, transported them and himself over the vast continents and the seven seas with a rapidity and to an extent without parallel in his history, and flashed the news of his deeds around the world. The innovations had begun in the eighteenth century, but in the nineteenth century they increased with accelerated rapidity. The factory, the railway, the steamship, the automobile, the telegraph, and the telephone augmented man's necessities and comforts and brought mankind physically together to an extent beyond even the wildest fancy of earlier generations.

A third feature of the nineteenth century, and one which made possible the two just mentioned, was the development of the scientific method. By this was meant the determination of facts by observation, the discovery of what was believed to be the relationship between these facts, the disclosure of what were called natural laws, the classification of the facts according to these relationships and laws, and the use of these relationships or hypotheses concerning these relationships to uncover additional facts. The scientific method antedated A.D. 1800, but in the nineteenth century it enjoyed a rapid growth. More and more the scientific method and the attitude of mind associated with it characterized those who were affected by the nineteenth century climate of opinion.

An essential feature of the scientific method was an emphasis upon objectivity and an insistence that the individual mind must be transparently honest and unhampered by prejudices and bias. This necessitated freedom of thought for the individual and an absence of any coercion which would curb the search for truth.

The first three developments were chiefly responsible for a fourth, a series of alterations in the structure of man's life. Never before in so brief a time had human society been changed so profoundly and in such a variety of ways. What was termed the industrial revolution became a major factor in producing a revolution in all phases of civilization. Wealth rapidly mounted. What had once been the luxuries of the rich were placed within reach of all and were esteemed indispensable. The factory system appeared. Population increased. Great cities arose which dwarfed the urban centres of previous ages. Curricula and methods of education were transformed to admit the new branches of learning and to take advantage of the scientific method. Universal primary education was made possible by the increase in riches and became essential if human beings were to take their part in the machine age. In industrial communities the family ceased to be as important as formerly as a social and economic unit and tended to disintegrate. Machines augmented the destructiveness of war and by permitting the more rapid and complete concentration of the efforts of a nation upon fighting speeded up the dislocation of normal life and the exhaustion which accompany armed conflict. In time distances the earth shrank to a mere fraction of its former size and once distant nations and cultures were brought into intimate contact.

Partly as a feature of the revolution wrought by the machine and by the scientific method, and partly as a development from ideas earlier present in the Occident came a fifth set of changes, attempts at the reorganization of society on the basis of ideologies. Several of the latter were reciprocally contradictory and led to conflicts. In its initial stages and through most of its nineteenth century development the machine age was intimately associated with marked individualism, *laissez-faire* economics, and a capitalism which thrived on free competition. These were closely, although by no means necessarily, affiliated with political democracy. The nineteenth century, indeed, was the era of a democracy which sought to embody the conviction that the welfare of mankind could be best furthered by giving to each individual the greatest possible opportunity and liberty. In part as a reaction against extreme expressions of *laissez-faire* individualism came various programmes for socialism and communism. Fundamentally they arose out of the aspirations which underlay the political and economic philosophies which they opposed, for they professed to have as an ideal more opportunity for the abundant life for every human being than was being realized through the types of democracy and individualism which were popular in the nineteenth century Occident.

Added to the nineteenth century scene was a sixth set of factors, several intellectual currents, some of them at counter-purposes with one another. The rationalism which had been so strong in the eighteenth century persisted and had friendly kinship to the scientific method. Romanticism, which had also been prominent in the eighteenth century, continued, and had much in it which was opposed to rationalism. The belief in the evolution of higher from lower forms of life and the closely allied confidence in the progress of the human race towards ever higher levels of civilization and well-being widely permeated the Western mind.

A seventh characteristic of the nineteenth century was a mounting nationalism. Like so many of the movements which had their most striking developments in the nineteenth century, it first became prominent in the eighteenth century.[1] In the nineteenth century it contributed powerfully to the political unification of Italy and Germany and to the defeat of the internal efforts to sever the bonds which held the United States together.

An eighth feature of the nineteenth century was peace. He would be obtuse to the most obvious facts who would say that wars had ceased. Several were fought in Europe and in the Americas, and they were frequent in other parts of the world. However, no such prolonged and exhausting struggles wracked the Occident as had been almost chronic in the sixteenth, seventeenth, and eighteenth centuries. Between 1815 and 1914 no general European war broke out, in no war were more than five European powers engaged, and all wars in Europe were brief. In Latin America the wars of independence were over before the first third of the century had passed. Of the conflicts in the Occident the American Civil War involved the largest forces, but even it was only an interlude in the growth of the United States. In the process of their expansion, Occidentals waged many wars against non-European peoples, but while several of these proved disruptive to non-Occidental cultures, few were long and none brought exhaustion either to an Occidental or to a major non-Occidental nation. The latter part of the century was especially a time of peace. After the Franco-Prussian conflict of 1870, no war was fought in Western Europe until 1914. Russia and Turkey came to blows, Spain and the United States had a brief struggle, in South Africa the British defeated the Boer republics, the Japanese checked the Russian advance in the Far East, and, on the eve of 1914, Italy took lands from Turkey, and the Balkan states fought Turkey and one another. However, the last generation of the hundred years was more nearly free from major disturbances than even the first fifty-five years had been. This period of comparative peace coincided with a rapidly mounting material prosperity in the Occident. Never since the fourth century, and possibly never since the dawn of recorded history, had the world been so nearly free for so long a period from major and exhausting armed conflicts as in the ninety-nine years from Waterloo to Sarajevo.

A ninth characteristic of the nineteenth century Occident was an abounding optimism. The optimism was not without a parallel pessimism. Again and again men were dismayed by rapid changes in culture and institutions, were

[1] Hayes, *The Historical Evolution of Modern Nationalism*, pp. 13ff.

terrified by fears of impending doom, and were thrown into despair by periodic financial depressions. Yet, in general, the dominant note of the century was one of confidence and hope. Rapidly increasing wealth, new discoveries in the realm of the natural sciences, fresh inventions, the rapid expansion of trade and of colonies, and the opening and development of virgin lands brought an exhilarating sense of expectancy and accomplishment. If society was not perfect, so it was declared, it was on the way to perfection. If man had not yet mastered fully the powers of nature and made them serve his happiness, he was in process of doing so. Human intelligence and will, so it was held, were so rapidly surmounting the obstacles to human happiness that there was every reason to believe that in the not too distant future they would abolish the ills which from time immemorial had dogged the steps of the race. The multiplication of physical comforts and luxuries, the rapid strides made by medicine, hygiene, and public health, the multiplication of schools and universities, and the many plans put forward for world peace appeared about to remove the chronic enemies of man—famine, poverty, disease, ignorance, and war.

The movements and characteristics we have so far mentioned had their origin in the Occident and in it displayed their most extensive developments. However, before 1914 they had attained world-wide significance, for a tenth feature of the nineteenth century was the expansion of Western and Northern European peoples. This had begun in the fourth century with the Teutonic invasions of the Roman Empire. It had continued in the Crusades and in the commerce and missions of the thirteenth and fourteenth centuries. In the fifteenth, sixteenth, seventeenth, and eighteenth centuries it had sprinkled Westerners along most of the African littoral, it had carried them to India and the Far East, it had settled them in the Americas, and it had brought Siberia and Alaska under Russian influence. Now, in the nineteenth century, Europeans explored and subjugated Africa, they completed the conquest of India and Ceylon, they blasted open the doors of China and threatened to partition that empire among themselves, they induced the Japanese to admit their merchants, diplomats, and missionaries, they made themselves masters of the islands of the Pacific and in Australia and New Zealand built new nations of European stock, they further developed Siberia, and they completed their occupation of the Americas. By A.D. 1914 all the land surface of the world was politically subject to European peoples except a few spots in Africa, some of the Asiatic states, Japan, a little corner of South-eastern Europe, and the jungles in the interior of some of the largest of the islands of the Pacific. Even the lands which had not submitted politically had been touched by the commerce of Europeans and most of them had been modified by European culture.

As a result of the expansion of Europe came an eleventh feature, the disintegration or transformation of non-European cultures under the impact of the culture of the Occident. As a rule, the cultures of primitive tribes succumbed quickly. The higher civilizations of the Near East, India, Ceylon, Burma, Siam, Indo-China, China, and Japan yielded less readily, but before A.D. 1914 even they were in revolution. The resulting changes were made the more drastic and confusing by the fact that the civilization which was producing the alterations, that of the Occident, was itself in rapid transition. Non-European cultures were undergoing a double revolution. They were disappearing or being reshaped under the pressure of the West, and they were sharing in the sweeping transformations in the civilization of the Occident.

In their adoption of Western civilization, non-European peoples did not necessarily reproduce exactly their Occidental models. They tended to take over only what seemed to them most desirable. This was usually the machines which appeared to them to have given the Westerner his riches and his power and the scientific techniques by which the machines had been constructed. It was the materialistic side of the Occident rather than the spiritual bases of Occidental life which most impressed them and which they endeavoured to emulate.

Out of the world-wide expansion of Europe and the transformation of non-European cultures through contact with the West came a twelfth feature of the nineteenth century—the beginning of a world culture. This world culture was really an extension of the civilization of Europe. The most prominent characteristics of the cosmopolitan culture were the most obvious features of the nineteenth century Occident—the machine, the products of the machine, and the types of education which enabled men to build and operate machines.

As a thirteenth distinguishing mark of the nineteenth century we must note that the period was one in which English-speaking peoples were outstanding. It was Great Britain which was the first land to develop the machine and to become industrialized. On the seas the British navy was supreme. The British had the lion's share of the commerce of the world. The British Empire grew apace and in extent surpassed any which the world had seen. In the Western Hemisphere the United States increased enormously in territory, in wealth, in population, and in power. Of the continental European nations, France and Russia were the most prominent as empire-builders. In commercial and naval power the French were far behind the British, but they built up, principally in Africa, an overseas empire which was second in extent only to that of Great Britain. Russia did not extend her boundaries beyond the Euro-Asiatic continent. Indeed, she sold out her holdings in the Americas to the United

States. However, she advanced her frontier south of the Aral to include what became Russian Turkestan, she acquired from China land north of the Amur and east of the Ussuri, and she tightened her hold on Siberia. The nations which profited most by the expansion of the nineteenth century, then, were Great Britain, the United States, France, and Russia, in about the order named.

To Christianity these outstanding features of the nineteenth century proved both a hindrance and a help. In the main they greatly assisted in the spread of the faith. Yet never was that faith undisputed. Throughout the century, when as never before it was giving rise to new movements, moulding civilization, and expanding geographically, its very existence was chronically threatened in the very areas and among the very peoples where it had traditionally been strongest, and by phases of some of the very movements which were assisting in its dissemination.

On these threats to Christianity we must not take the space or the time to pause long. That is not because they were unimportant. On the contrary, they were highly significant. Throughout the nineteenth century they were present, and, on the whole, for those who had eyes to see, were increasingly ominous. After A.D. 1914 they brought to Christianity one of those major periods of crisis by which that faith had periodically been threatened. Like the one at the close of the eighteenth century, moreover, the recession came about as the result of factors within Christendom and not through attacks from outside. While we will not elaborate these threats, we must summarize them and must occasionally remind ourselves of their presence. When we come to the period for which A.D. 1914 was the opening year we shall be forced to take fresh cognizance of them.

Man's increased knowledge of the physical universe brought its menace. In some of its features the intellectual garb with which past thinkers had clothed Christianity was rendered obsolete by the exhilarating but terrifying vistas which were now opened. Its familiar thought forms being in part outmoded, Christianity itself appeared to many to be untenable. Now that the chronology of creation which arose out of accepted interpretations of the first chapters of Genesis had been disproved, could men retain any confidence in the Biblical accounts of the origin of the universe? Did evolution leave any place for the creative activity of God? Had it not bowed out of court the belief in the fall of man and with it the doctrine of original sin which was so integral a part of much of Christian theology? Many wondered whether, even if there were a God, the Being who created and sustained the vast stellar universe disclosed by the new astronomy really concerned himself, as Christians declared that he did, with each of the hundreds of millions of ephemeral mites who inhabited one of the least of the planets of one of the middle-sized stars. To many it seemed preposterous that this Being should have incarnated himself in one of these minute and apparently insignificant creatures—and so for them a central conviction of the Christian faith was shattered. Many sensitive and thoughtful souls felt their inherited Christian faith to be hopelessly undermined and thousands of less thoughtful spirits blithely derided or ignored it.

Man's increasing utilization of the physical universe also brought its dangers. In the first flush of the achievements of the age when an era of magic appeared to have dawned, many became self-confident and believed man able by his own endeavours, unassisted by any Divine Power, to solve his problems and make himself master of his own environment. The machine seemed to be producing numbers of the goods which man had traditionally looked to religion to supply. No longer did it appear necessary to ask in prayer one's daily bread when the machine, if properly used, could supply it. The intoxicating vistas of wealth opened by the new processes did for thousands what Jesus had said wealth would do and lured them from the path which Jesus declared was the road to true life. The grinding mass poverty in fetid slums which became the lot of multitudes under the new industrialism threatened to stifle any Christian faith in those who suffered from it.

The scientific method had for some a dulling effect upon Christian faith. Men seemed unable to discover the God of Jesus by the processes which science advocated. Indeed, science appeared to leave no room for God or at most to make possible only an uncertain belief in a Being whom men with all their searching could never unveil. Moreover, when men applied to the Bible the exacting tests of the historical method which had been developed in connexion with science, many of the traditional beliefs about that collection of writings were thrown into question and, as an inevitable consequence, confidence was undermined. Thousands came to feel that science and religion were incompatible. Historically, as we saw in the preceding volume,[2] the scientific approach had been made possible by a trust in the orderliness and dependability of the universe which was an outgrowth of the Christian faith. Now it looked as though the child had found the parent unnecessary and even a hindrance.

The revolution in man's life which came as a result of the machine disturbed established institutions and customs. Since Christianity and the Church were closely intertwined with the social structure, when the latter was altered so profoundly the former were also shaken. Into the great cities which sprang up millions moved from rural communities and small towns, and in doing so left the Church behind. Attempts were made, as we are to see, to bring the

[2] Vol. III, Chap. 16.

Church to them, and with some success. However, a large proportion of the labourers in the mines and factories of the new industrial order lost contact with the Church, and Christianity all but dropped out of their consciousness. It was in the rural districts, in the towns, and in the smaller cities, where the social upheaval was less marked and where more of the old order persisted, that Christianity remained strongest.

Some of the new programs for the reorganization of society made little room for Christianity and even regarded the Church as an enemy. Several of them had Christian origins and all were indebted to Christianity for attitudes towards the value of the individual. As we are to see, some schools of socialism were inaugurated by earnest Christians. However, much of socialism and communism was indifferent to the Church and numbers of socialists and communists denounced it and its religion as an obstacle to human welfare. Many of the political leaders of the century were anti-clerical and thought they saw in the Church a major barrier to human advance. The antagonism was directed more against the Roman Catholic Church than against the Protestant bodies. It led to the confiscation of much of the property of the Church and, notably in France, to disestablishment.

Of the main intellectual currents of the nineteenth century, romanticism in general assisted Christianity,[3] but rationalism opposed it.

Until A.D. 1914 nationalism did not become a major menace to Christianity. Indeed, some of the outstanding leaders in nationalistic movements—Bismarck in Germany[4] and Lincoln in the attempt to preserve the integrity of the United States[5]—were profoundly influenced by Christianity and were committed to it. Yet several of the nationalistic leaders—Mazzini, for instance[6]— believed Christianity to be outworn. Moreover, the exaltation of the nation tended to place loyalty to the state above loyalty to God and to make the Church a tool of the state.

In the expansion of Europe the resentment aroused among non-European peoples by Western aggression and imperialism was directed in part against the religion which the white man was assumed to represent.

[3] Some of the teachings of Rousseau, who did so much to give impulse to the Romantic movement, stimulated affection for Christianity.—Collins, *Catholicism and the Second French Republic*, pp. 20-24.
[4] Dawson, *Bismarck and State Socialism*, pp. 23, 24, gives excerpts from addresses of Bismarck from 1847 to 1882, in which Bismarck declared that Germany as a Christian state must seek to realize Christian teachings in its collective life.
[5] See, for instance, Lincoln's second inaugural address.
[6] *Mazzini's Letters*. Translated from the Italian by Alice de Rosen Jervis, with an introduction by Bolton King (London, J. M. Dent and Sons, 1930, pp. xvi, 211), p.x. See also Giuseppe Calabro, *La Dottrina Religioso-Sociale nelle Opere di Giuseppe Mazzini* (Palermo, Libreria Int. A. Reber, 1912, pp. 376), *passim*.

Although much in the movements which characterized the nineteenth century was opposed to Christianity, yet, on the whole, the aid given was greater than the hindrances raised.

Since peoples supposedly Christian were the initial possessors of the machines of the new day and of the knowledge and the scientific method which made them possible, Christianity acquired a certain amount of prestige. More important was the fact that in many regions Christian missionaries were the first to conduct schools in which the new learning could be acquired. Christianity became the vehicle for the new knowledge and some of the new methods and machines, much as it had been many centuries before in the introduction of Græco-Roman learning into Northern Europe and as Buddhism had been in bringing to Japan the culture of the adjoining continent. Since what it brought proved desirable, frequently Christianity was also adopted.

By making travel easier and more rapid and by accelerating communication, the new mechanical appliances assisted the more rapid spread of ideas. The surging currents of life within Christianity found ready to hand the physical appliances for making themselves felt the world around. Railways and steamships carried not only merchants, but also missionaries. The cable, the telegraph, the improved postal systems, and the printing press provided quick communication between missionaries and their supporting constituencies in the Occident, facilitated the raising of funds for the support of missions, and aided the dissemination of Christian ideas.

The wealth which mounted so spectacularly through the machine made possible the financing of missions on an unprecedented scale. Only a very small fraction of this wealth was thus contributed, but that fraction was, as we shall see, enough to support an extensive enterprise.

The individualism of the nineteenth century found partial expression in the courageous initiative of missionaries who single-handed or by twos and threes dared to bring their faith to areas heretofore untouched by Christianity. The spirit of enterprise and adventure which impelled Europeans to penetrate jungles, cross deserts, scale the highest mountains, seek the North and South Poles, span continents with railways, and delve into the mysteries of the heavens and of the atom also drove others to carry the Christian message to peoples who had not known it and to dream of moulding vast nations and cultures according to the principles of their faith.

In the atmosphere of abounding optimism and achievement which characterized the Occident of the period, it was natural for Christians to plan for "the evangelization of the world in this generation," a slogan which meant that Christians of each generation should give to every contemporary member of the human race a knowledge of the Christian faith.[7]

It is significant that the Christian faith spread chiefly from those peoples and sections of the Occident which were most affected by the new movements. It was Protestant Great Britain which took the lead in the industrial revolution and, next to Great Britain, it was the United States, where Protestantism was more prominent than Roman Catholicism, which, through the new machines, expanded most rapidly in population, in territory, and in wealth. It was Protestantism which proportionately grew the most rapidly in its share in the propagation of Christianity, and it was from Great Britain and the United States that the majority of the Protestant missionaries came. Within the Roman Catholic portion of Europe it was from France, Belgium, Germany, and Northern Italy, countries or areas which led the others in the adoption of the machines and profited most by them, that the majority of the new organizations, personnel, and funds of nineteenth century Roman Catholic missions were derived. The new life which expressed itself in learning, industry, commerce, and territorial expansion also showed itself in the propagation of the Christian faith. This was probably because that new life had in part (although by no means fully) Christian origins. It was also because the temper of mind begotten of the age favoured the spread of the religion professed by the peoples and sections which were the first to feel and give expression to the new life.

The relative peace also assisted the spread of Christianity. Because of it, missionaries could travel with comparative safety, funds could be sent them expeditiously, Christian communities could grow uninterruptedly, and fellowship could be maintained and strengthened between the new churches and those which had founded them.

The fact that the era of greatest peace, the generation immediately before 1914, coincided with the period of greatest prosperity and of the furthest extension of European imperialism was of significance for the spread of Christianity. From 1870 to 1914 conditions were peculiarly favourable for the expansion of the faith. Equipped with facilities given by the growing wealth and

---

[7] As one example of this, see Wayland, *The Moral Dignity of the Missionary Enterprise,* a sermon delivered Nov. 4, 1824, before the Boston Missionary Society, where, on p. 26, it is declared that "Our field is the world. Our object is to effect an entire moral revolution in the whole human race." The fact that the sermon so soon crossed the sea and so quickly went into its sixth edition indicated the popularity of its views. See also, as other examples, John Griffin, *A Retrospect of the Proceedings of the London Missionary Society* (Portsea, Samuel Griffin, 1827, pp. 80), pp. 13ff., and John R. Mott, *The Evangelization of the World in This Generation* (New York, Student Volunteer Movement for Foreign Missions, 1900, pp. 245), especially Chaps. 5 and 6.

encouraged by the prevailing peace and optimism, the tide of religious interest and activity which had been rising since the dawn of the nineteenth century reached a new highwater mark. Inevitably it overflowed into the lands touched by Occidental peoples.

The expansion of European peoples made powerfully for the spread of Christianity. A large proportion of the millions who migrated to the Americas, Australia, New Zealand, and South Africa held to their ancestral faith. The exploration, the commerce, and the colonial administration of non-Europeans by European nations helped to open the way for the missionary. Merchants, soldiers, and officials from the Occident were often scornful and even hostile to the missionary, and by their conduct frequently raised barriers of prejudice against Christianity. Missions received less active support from European governments than at any time since the fourth century. Yet the presence of Western commerce greatly aided the physical entrance of the missionary even when it raised barriers to his spiritual message, and it facilitated communication between the missionary and his supporters in the West. European governments protected missionaries none the less effectively because they did it for them not as missionaries but as citizens. Much financial support was given by European colonial administrations to mission schools, and although it was contributed because the schools were schools and not because they were Christian, it was of substantial assistance in the spread of Christianity. Then, too, the general spirit of expansion which was abroad among Western peoples helped to prepare the way for the birth and growth of enterprises for the propagation of Christianity. When merchants were dreaming in terms of new markets and enlarging foreign trade and when statesmen were planning fresh colonial adventures, it was natural for the more earnest among the Christians to seek to parallel these movements with others for the world-wide extension of their faith.

The disintegration of non-European cultures under the impact of the expanding Occident also aided the spread of Christianity. So long as these cultures were intact they made difficult the acceptance of Christianity, for in many of their features, not only in the realm of religion but also in family, political, and economic institutions, they were antagonistic to Christianity. The adoption of the faith would necessitate recasting the entire structure of civilization. Now that these cultures were collapsing under the economic and political pressure of the West, much less resistance was offered to Christianity. In many instances the missionary contributed to the disappearance of the old life. Everywhere, however, it would sooner or later have occurred without him. What the missionary did was to take advantage of the situation to present his faith and to help determine the character of the new structures which succeeded the old.

The fact that the emerging world culture had its origins in the Occident was of advantage to Christianity. Because of the Western source of that culture and because Christianity was traditionally the religion of the West, the way was opened for the Christian impulse to become a constituent part of that culture and to help shape it.

In the main, then, the new movements of the nineteenth century furthered more than they retarded the expansion of Christianity.

Chapter III

THE NEW MOVEMENTS WITHIN CHRISTIANITY THROUGH WHICH THE EXPANSION OF THE FAITH WAS CHIEFLY ACCOMPLISHED

THE remarkable expansion of Christianity·in the nineteenth century was not simply or even primarily the result of a favourable environment. It was due to an upsurging, creative impulse within Christianity itself. As we saw in the preceding chapter, the environment aided more than it hindered, but the chief cause of the unprecedented spread of Christianity in this era was an innate energy within the faith itself. This vigour gave rise to more new movements than in any preceding period of equal duration.

The nineteenth century had in it much of religious scepticism. Never since the conversion of Western Europe had what was known as Christendom contained so much open and reasoned departure from the faith of the community. Previous centuries had had fully as much if not more practical scepticism. Men had derided the Church, had parodied its services, or in their deeds had ignored or flouted its teachings. However, the vast majority in Western Europe had formally been members of it. Even eighteenth century rationalists who professed to have discarded "revealed religion" had for the most part preserved a formal connexion with it. Voltaire wished to destroy the despotic power of the Church and to bring in more religious liberty, but he did not advocate the immediate separation of Church and state.[1] When "revealed religion" was denied, "natural religion" remained, with a God who was in some respects so similar to the Christian God that many "Deists" remained fairly comfortably in the Church. Now, in the nineteenth century, some of the most influential among the intellectuals actively advocated views which, while giving evidence of a Christian background even in their reaction from it, completely dethroned the Christian God. Comte elevated humanity to the vacant place. Some did not go quite to that extreme, but moved farther in that direction than had most of the eighteenth century radicals. In the seat of the great first cause which the Deists believed that reason disclosed, Herbert

[1] Aulard, *Christianity and the French Revolution*, pp. 38, 39.

22

Spencer placed a vague, unknowable power. While rejecting positive atheism[2] and consenting to the christening of his infant son,[3] Huxley held that underlying the thin veil of phenomena was the passionless impersonality of the unknown and the unknowable.[4] Agnosticism, a term coined to express the conviction that the evidence did not warrant either the affirmation or the denial of the existence of God, became the attitude of many of the educated. In a widely read book Guyau declared religion to be in the process of being discarded.[5] In the United States agnosticism became militant under the leadership of the persuasive and eloquent Robert Green Ingersoll. To Ingersoll, underlying nature was impersonal and inexorable law. The application to the Bible of the new methods of historical criticism brought much doubt concerning the reliability of a book which Christians had traditionally regarded as authoritative. The divergence of many intellectuals and pseudo-intellectuals in Christendom from Christianity became more openly pronounced than at any previous time.

States, too, instead of dominating the Church, as they had done in the preceding three centuries, began separating themselves entirely from it. From its very outset, the National Government of the United States, while maintaining a friendly attitude towards Christianity, formally renounced any intention of establishing any form of religion. In 1905, as a climax of a prolonged and mounting anti-clerical sentiment, the French concordat with the Holy See was terminated. These are outstanding examples of a fairly general trend.

Yet, paralleling what seemed to be a growing renunciation of the traditional faith of Western European peoples came a rising tide of vitality within the Christian churches. This was found in both Roman Catholicism and Protestantism.

Roman Catholicism exhibited a marked revival. Through the scepticism of the eighteenth century and during the turmoil of the French Revolution and the wars of Napoleon it had suffered severely, more so than had Protestantism. Before 1815 recovery had begun. Although Napoleon dealt masterfully with the Church and had the Pope arrested and for a time kept in confinement, and although the Pope excommunicated Napoleon and his supporters, the concordat of 1801, while imposing harsh terms on the Church, was more favourable to Christianity than the aggressively anti-Christian policy of the Revolution

---

[2] Leonard Huxley, *Life and Letters of Thomas Henry Huxley*, Vol. II, p. 172.
[3] Huxley, *op. cit.*, Vol. I, p. 240.
[4] Huxley, *op. cit.*, Vol. I, p. 260.
[5] See an English translation, Marie Jean Guyau, *The Non-Religion of the Future. A Sociological Study* (New York, Henry Holt and Co., 1897, pp. xi, 543).

in much of the preceding decade.[6] Moreover, in 1802 there was published Chateaubriand's *Génie du Christianisme, ou Beautés de la Religion Chrétienne.* The book had its source in part in the romantic movement and was an indication that this rising stream was contributing to the renewal of the tide towards Roman Catholicism. It helped to make Roman Catholicism intellectually respectable and emotionally attractive.[7] In Germany the conversion to Roman Catholicism of the poet Friedrich Leopold Stolberg (1800) and one of the prominent poets and critics of the romantic school, Friedrich von Schlegel (1808), both of whom had been reared as Protestants, gave indication of the direction in which the current was setting.[8]

The end of the Napoleonic wars and the partial restoration of the old order which had been toppled over by the French Revolution brought with them, as was natural, something of a re-establishment of the former status and privileges of the Church. In France the clergy rallied to the revived Bourbon throne. Throughout much of the country missions were preached which denounced the anti-clerical acts of the Revolution and had their climax in the mass renewal of baptismal vows.[9] In Spain, immediately after the restoration, the ecclesiastical decrees of the Cortes of 1812 were suspended and the concordat of 1782 was again put into effect. Sardinia followed Spain, and in the Kingdom of Naples, Roman Catholicism was declared to be the only faith recognized by law.[10] In the Russian portions of Poland the deeply religious Tsar Alexander I richly endowed the Roman Catholic Church.[11]

If the revival of Roman Catholicism had depended simply upon the rebound of public sentiment from the radicalism of the French Revolution, it would not have had a long life. The reaction lasted scarcely a generation and the strong undercurrent of political and social liberalism could not be permanently repressed.

However, springs of life were also welling up within the Roman Catholic Church itself. Notably in Germany and France, the romanticism which represented a revulsion from the cold rationalism of much of the eighteenth century, and which captured numbers of the intellectuals, stimulated in many a passionate attachment to the Church. Christianity as seen in the Roman Catholic Church profoundly appealed to at least a minority of the high-minded and

[6] Phillips, *The Church in France, 1789-1848*, pp. 42, 62, 93ff.
[7] Phillips, *op. cit.*, p. 42; Vidler, *The Modernist Movement in the Roman Church,* pp. 17-19.
[8] Vidler, *op. cit.*, p. 32; Goyau, *L'Allemagne Religieuse. Le Catholicisme*, Vol. I, pp. 180, 188.
[9] Phillips, *op. cit.*, pp. 150-155.
[10] Nippold, *The Papacy in the 19th Century*, p. 58.
[11] Nippold, *op. cit.*, p. 61.

enthusiastic spirits of the time. In Italy Alessandro Manzoni, an outstanding literary figure of the first half of the century and a warm champion of a united Italy and of the labouring classes, was a devout and pronounced Roman Catholic.[12] In France a movement which sought to combine many liberal principles with an ardent attachment to Roman Catholicism, and of which Lammenais, Lacordaire, and Montalembert were outstanding exponents, attained prominence.[13] It was years before the rural parishes were supplied with priests, but after 1830 the seminaries began to be filled, and that in spite of the fact that no such prestige attached to the priesthood as formerly.[14] In Germany scholarly centres of the new life were developed at Munich and Tübingen.[15] These wished to effect a reconciliation between the traditional teaching of the Church and the findings of modern historical and scientific research.[16]

As the century wore on, many Roman Catholics were stirred by their faith to concern themselves with the social ills and problems brought by the advent of the factory. The labourers in the new industries had tended to drift away from the Church, but movements arose among Roman Catholics to win them and to seek on the basis of Christian ideals to find a solution for some of the social problems of the day. In France efforts were made in that direction.[17] In Germany organizations were formed to help relieve the unhappy lot of peasants and industrial workers.[18] In Italy the priest John Bosco gave himself with imagination and devotion to the underprivileged boys of the rapidly growing city of Turin, and the order which he founded, the Salesians of Don Bosco, multiplied his ministry in other centres.[19] Giuseppe Toniolo, the holder of a chair of political economy at Pisa, a close friend of Pope Leo XIII, became the outstanding exponent of a Christian school of social science[20] and the creator and first president of the *Unione Popolare*, through which he sought to put some of his convictions into action.[21] Leo XIII showed himself sympathetic with labour and in his encyclical *Rerum Novarum* (1891) won for himself the appellation "the workingman's Pope."[22]

[12] Hughes, *The Catholic Revival in Italy*, pp. 3ff.
[13] Vidler, *op. cit.*, pp. 20-22; Phillips, *op. cit.*, pp. 206ff.
[14] Phillips, *op. cit.*, p. 282.
[15] Goyau, *op. cit.*, Vol. II, pp. 56ff.; Vidler, *op. cit.*, p. 32.
[16] Phillips, *op. cit.*, p. 264.
[17] Phillips, *The Church in France, 1848-1907*, pp. 224, 225.
[18] Goyau, *op. cit.*, Vol. III, pp. 116ff.
[19] Ghéon, *The Secret of Saint John Bosco, passim*; Hughes, *op. cit.*, pp. 49ff.
[20] Hughes, *op. cit.*, pp. 67ff.
[21] Hughes, *op. cit.*, p. 102.
[22] Eduardo Soderini, *Il Pontificato di Leone XIII* (Milan, A. Mondadori, 3 vols., 1932, 1933), Vol. I, pp. 243ff., especially pp. 406ff.

The revival in the Roman Catholic Church expressed itself in part in the emergence of new orders and congregations and in the renewal of old orders. One of the indications of vitality in a religion is the movements to which it gives rise. The periods of greatest vigour in Christianity have been times when the impulse within it has issued in fresh organizations. Judged by this standard, the nineteenth century marked a high point in the Roman Catholic form of Christianity. In the hundred years after 1815 more new orders and congregations came into existence through which men and women devoted themselves to the Church than in any previous period of equal length.[23] Among those for men the following are selected almost at random: The Picpus Fathers, or the Society of the Holy Hearts of Jesus and Mary, founded in 1805 and receiving Papal approval in 1817, for the conversion and religious training of both sexes;[24] the Oblates of the Immaculate Virgin Mary, founded in 1816;[25] the Society of Mary, or the Marists, also founded in 1816;[26] the Congregation of the Precious Blood;[27] the Salesians of Don Bosco, already mentioned, founded in 1855;[28] The Fathers of the Holy Heart of Jesus of Issoudun;[29] the Pallotti Fathers, who arose from the zeal of a native of Rome who spent his life in self-denying devotion to the poor and sick;[30] and the Society of Saint Vincent de Paul, an association of laymen for the care of the poor, founded by Antoine Frédéric Ozanam (1813-1853), a warm friend and admirer of Lacordaire and a professor in the Sorbonne, who at the early age of twenty stimulated some of his fellow students to join with him in personal service of the destitute.[31] A large number of teaching brotherhoods came into being.[32]

Especially numerous were the congregations of women. Through them women celibates became more prominent in the life and work of the Church than ever before. Some dedicated themselves to the contemplative life of prayer. Perpetual adoration of the reserved sacrament was emphasized.[33] Others were primarily engaged in an active life of nursing, teaching, or the

[23] For a partial list, see Heimbucher, *Die Orden und Congregationen der katholischen Kirche*, Vol. II, pp. 384ff.
[24] Heimbucher, *op. cit.*, Vol. II, p. 384.
[25] Heimbucher, *op. cit.*, Vol. II, p. 385.
[26] Heimbucher, *op. cit.*, Vol. II, p. 387.
[27] Heimbucher, *op. cit.*, Vol. II, p. 388.
[28] Ghéon, *op. cit., passim*; Heimbucher, *op. cit.*, Vol. II, pp. 405ff.
[29] Heimbucher, *op. cit.*, Vol. II, p. 389.
[30] Heimbucher, *op. cit.*, Vol. II, p. 397.
[31] Phillips, *The Church in France, 1789-1848*, p. 267.
[32] Heimbucher, *op. cit.*, Vol. II, pp. 418ff.
[33] Phillips, *The Church in France, 1848-1907*, pp. 320, 321.

care of orphans. An incomplete list records over a hundred such congregations founded in the nineteenth century.[34]

This women's movement within the Roman Catholic Church paralleled roughly an increasingly prominent share by women in the organized activities of the Protestant forms of Christianity, campaigns for legal equality of women with men in secular life, and an enhanced participation by women in lay occupations traditionally reserved for men. Never had women taken so outstanding a part in institutional Christianity or in the entire gamut of the activities of civilized life.

The Society of Jesus was revived. After its formal dissolution by the Pope (1773) it had persisted in Russia and Prussia and even, partially disguised under other names, in Belgium, Italy, and France. In 1801 Pope Pius VII permitted the Society to reconstitute itself in Russia, and in 1804 restored it in the Kingdom of Naples. In 1814 he permitted it again a full legal existence. Fairly rapidly the Jesuits re-entered various countries where they had once flourished.[35] They quickly regained the prominence in the life of the Church that had once been theirs.

In France several of the older orders which had been driven out by the Revolution returned. Among them were the Benedictines, the Dominicans, the Franciscans, the Carmelites, and the Eudists.[36]

The re-awakening of devotion through the celibate life was paralleled by augmented devotion on the part of the laity who continued in secular pursuits. Frequent communion became more common.[37] Eucharistic Congresses, for emphasis upon the Eucharist, began in the last quarter of the nineteenth century and quickly assumed vast proportions.[38] The cults of the Sacred Hearts of Jesus and Mary and of the Immaculate Conception became more and more popular. In the latter half of the century through official encouragement from Rome they enjoyed a rapid growth.[39] Reports of the appearance of the Virgin Mary gave rise to local cults, notably at Lourdes.[40] Popular piety took on fresh enthusiasm.

---

[34] Heimbucher, op. cit., Vol. II, pp. 450ff.
[35] Nippold, The Papacy in the 19th Century, pp. 31-50; Heimbucher, op. cit., Vol. II, pp. 114ff.
[36] Phillips, The Church in France, 1789-1848, pp. 275, 283.
[37] Underhill, Worship, p. 261.
[38] The Catholic Encyclopedia, Vol. V, pp. 592-594.
[39] Phillips, The Church in France, 1789-1848, p. 284. On the cults of the Sacred Heart of Jesus and the Sacred Heart of Mary, see The Catholic Encyclopedia, Vol. VII, pp. 163-166, 168, 169. On the immaculate conception, see The Catholic Encyclopedia, Vol. VII, pp. 674-680.
[40] Phillips, The Church in France, 1789-1848, p. 284; Phillips, The Church in France, 1848-1907, p. 79.

It must be noted that the new life in Roman Catholic Christianity did not express itself in any great intellectual statement of the faith. Theologically the Church was content with the achievements of earlier ages. Leo XIII gave impetus to the study of Thomas Aquinas, but he and the other pontiffs of the century discouraged any creative thinking which would do what Aquinas had done for his age and produce an elaboration of Christian beliefs in the intellectual forms of the day. It was in personal piety, in the multiplication of new organizations, in social activities, largely in channels through which Roman Catholic benevolence had been accustomed to find expression, and in the propagation of the faith that the renewed energy was seen.

The rising tide of life within the Roman Catholic Church, as we have suggested, went side by side with indifference and active opposition. The currents which in the French Revolution broke out into violence against the Church were still present, running deep and strong. From time to time, and with mounting frequency, they made themselves felt. In France the Revolution of 1830[41] and the Commune in Paris in 1871[42] were marked by irruptions against the Church. For decades the majority of leading Roman Catholics were opposed to the Third Republic.[43] In the first decade of the twentieth century anti-clericals in the government drastically restricted the share of the Church and of members of religious orders and congregations in education and brought about the separation of Church and state. In Italy, the Papal States were incorporated in the new Kingdom of Italy, the Pope became the intransigent "prisoner of the Vatican," and much of the property of religious bodies was confiscated. In Germany, Bismarck and the Church engaged in the *Kulturkampf*. In Spain, the Church suffered from its involvement in the prolonged internal political dissensions. For a time it was despoiled of much of its property and religious orders were vigorously curtailed.[44]

As a result of the conflict between the revived Church on the one hand and the main stream of liberal and radical elements on the other hand, two tendencies developed.

On the one side more and more of life in lands and regions traditionally Roman Catholic went its way without reference to the Church. The drift was towards removing from the Church functions which it had performed for more than a thousand years, the control of education and of marriage. Increasingly children were trained in state schools in which religion was either

[41] Collins, *Catholicism in the Second French Republic*, p. 17.
[42] Phillips, *The Church in France, 1848-1907*, p. 169.
[43] Phillips, *op. cit.*, pp. 178-183.
[44] On France, see Phillips, *op. cit.*, pp. 263ff. On Spain, see Peers, *Spain, the Church and the Orders*, pp. 62, 68, 72, 86.

less prominent than formerly or from which it was entirely excluded. The movement was towards the regulation of marriage by civil rather than by canon law and even to the performance of the ceremony by civil rather than by clerical officials. With the weakening of its control over the young and over the basic social institution of the family, the Roman Catholic Church seemed about to be ushered out of European life. In the great new industrial cities the masses had little contact with it. It appeared to be progressively restricted to areas and classes in which traces of the old order persisted—the country districts, the small towns, and the old aristocracy. Yet the very liberalism which saw in the Roman Catholic Church an enemy, also, out of conviction, worked for religious freedom, the principle that each individual must be allowed to choose his own faith, and in doing so gave to that church an opportunity for life and for growth.

On the other side, among those, still a very considerable proportion of the population, who were known as practising Catholics, loyalty to the Church was stronger than ever and religious duties more faithfully observed. In morals and in training the level of the parish clergy was probably as high as at any previous time and, perhaps, higher. Orders and congregations had never been so numerous and, probably, the total of those who by joining them followed the traditional fashion of giving themselves fully to the Christian way of life had never been so great.

Over the Roman Catholic Church the Pope exercised more absolute dominion than ever before. This was due to two movements, arising from contradictory motives, but leading to the same result. The political liberalism of the time, anti-clerical as most of it was, wished to free the state from any control by the Church. Among earnest Roman Catholics an ultramontanism prevailed with a strong insistence that the Church must be free from that domination by the state which had been the rule since the rise of the absolute monarchies in the fifteenth and sixteenth centuries. The Gallicanism which had made the French Church so nearly independent of Rome was slow to die, but even in France ultramontanism had been prominent since early in the nineteenth century and before the end of the century it had triumphed.[45] Between 1839 and 1875 the Roman rite was adopted in all the dioceses of France, replacing the Gallican liturgy.[46] The Vatican Council of 1870 crowned the authority of the Pope over the Roman Catholic Church. Contrary to previous custom, to this Council lay princes of that faith were not invited,[47] thus marking the exclu-

[45] Phillips, *The Church in France, 1848-1870,* pp. 1-17.
[46] Phillips, *op. cit.,* pp. 20, 21.
[47] Bury, *History of the Papacy in the 19th Century,* p. 60.

sion of the secular arm. The chief act of the Council was the formal definition and affirmation of Papal infallibility.[48]

The Roman Catholic Church, more effectively regimented under one head than ever before, set itself resolutely against all trends which might weaken its traditional doctrines. The French liberal Roman Catholic movement of the first half of the century, which, led by Lamennais, had endeavoured to combine many of the progressive principles of the day with the ancient faith, was condemned by the Pope. While some acquiesced, Lamennais, after first submitting, later withdrew from the Church.[49] In 1864 a Papal encyclical and an accompanying Syllabus of Errors anathematized many of the prevailing liberal beliefs and practices, such as the assumption by the state of the education of children, the belief that divine revelation is imperfect and therefore subject to a continuous and indefinite progress corresponding to the advance of human knowledge, the contention that it is lawful for any individual to accept and profess any religion which, guided by the light of reason, he considers true, the separation of Church and state, and the superiority of the civil power in case of a conflict between it and the Church. Socialism, communism, secret societies, and societies of liberal clergy were denounced.[50] In Germany after the Vatican Council a large proportion of those who had sought to apply modern critical methods to the history and traditions of the Church hived off into the Old Catholic Church.[51] Late in the nineteenth and early in the twentieth century another tendency arose, denominated modernism, which strove to reconcile current thought with Roman Catholic faith and to apply to the study of the Bible and the documents of Christian history the technique of contemporary scholarship. However, Rome again spoke with no uncertain voice (especially in the Papal encyclical *Pascendi*, in 1907), in condemnation of the innovations.[52]

It is true that under Leo XIII the Papacy seemed to take a less uncompromising attitude, for it urged the faithful in France to accept the Republic

---

[48] Bury, *op. cit.*, pp. 47ff. On the Vatican Council, see also Johann Friedrich, *Geschichte des vatikanischen Konzils* (Bonn, P. Neusser, 3 vols., 1877-1887), *passim*.

[49] Phillips, *The Church in France, 1789-1848*, pp. 206, 245-259.

[50] Bury, *op. cit.*, pp. 1-46. See also the encyclical of Pope Leo XIII, *Immortale Dei*, Nov. 1, 1885. An English translation is in John A. Ryan and F. X. Millar Moorhouse, *The State and the Church* (New York, The Macmillan Co., 1922, pp. vi, 331), pp. 1-25. While reaffirming the Papal condemnation of popular sovereignty and of the right of the individual to judge in matters of religion, and insisting upon the duty of the state to support the Roman Catholic faith, it affirmed the divine origin and authority of the state, declared that since all truth is one, the Church welcomes the investigation of nature, and insisted that the Church encouraged the arts and crafts.

[51] Bury, *op. cit.*, p. 159.

[52] Phillips, *The Church in France, 1848-1907*, pp. 290-318. See a brief bibliography of modernism in Phillips, *op. cit.*, p. 293.

and it showed its sympathy with the labouring classes and outlined a programme for meeting the social ills of an industrial age. Yet on matters which it believed essential to the Christian faith the Papacy was adamant even when, as often, this position placed it in opposition to some of the main convictions of the age and led its critics to denounce it as reactionary and an anachronism.

Here was a militant ecclesiastical organization, increasingly closely knit and directed from one centre, supported by the devotion of a growing body of adherents which, though in most countries a minority, yet totalled millions, and holding to its traditional beliefs even when these seemed to set it against the main intellectual, political, and social currents of its time. In its ancient strongholds the Roman Catholic Church was a far more vigorous institution in the nineteenth century, and especially in the latter part of the nineteenth century, than it had been in the eighteenth century. It was making gains in what had long been overwhelmingly Protestant countries. In Great Britain the first half of the nineteenth century saw the removal of the legal disabilities under which Roman Catholics had long suffered, and the Oxford Movement led a number, among them the extraordinarily brilliant Newman and the able Manning, from the Church of England into communion with Rome. In 1850 the Roman Catholic hierarchy was reconstituted in England and in 1878 in Scotland.[53] We are to note later the remarkable extension in the United States and Canada.

While the Roman Catholic Church was making its difficult and not always successful adjustment to the new era in its traditional strongholds in Europe, in Latin America it was having to face a political and intellectual revolution, in the United States and to a less degree in Canada and Australia it was confronted with a vast immigration, by heredity Roman Catholic, which must be held to the faith, and in almost every land opened by the expansion of European peoples doors of opportunity were opened to it. That, under these hard and challenging circumstances, in Europe the Roman Catholic Church was able to set its house in order and to end the century stronger than when it entered it, that in Latin America it retained at least part of its hold, that in the United States, Canada, and Australia it kept pace with the immigrant flood, that at the same time it strengthened its forces in lands in Asia where it had been previously represented and entered for the first time new lands in Africa and the Pacific, and that at the end of the century it was more widely extended than ever before, is evidence of an extraordinary inward vitality. Far from being a spent force, as many in the eighteenth century believed it to be,

[53] Williams, *The Catholic Church in Action*, p. 56; Nippold, *The Papacy in the 19th Century*, pp. 253ff.

Roman Catholic Christianity proved that within it was an unsuspected power of renewal. In numbers of new organizations and in geographic spread the nineteenth century was the greatest era which it had thus far had.

From the standpoint of the manner of its expansion, it is important to note that in the nineteenth century Roman Catholic Christianity became less a community or group faith than at any time since Constantine. More and more it was the religion of a minority into which men and women entered one by one or at best in small groups. It did not completely lose its character as a community faith, but its spread henceforth was more by individual and less by group conversions than in any period since the fourth century. Not only in Europe but also elsewhere it increasingly took on the character of a minority religion. It was continually more widespread and it was more aggressive than on the defensive, but it was a minority with a record of persecution and martyrdom. This fact affected both the method of expansion and the mental attitude of the leaders and of much of the rank and file of the membership. The outlook of the martyr was combined with an enthusiastic confidence in the absolute truth of the faith to which the Church witnessed.

If the nineteenth century saw a revival in the Roman Catholic form of Christianity it was marked by an even greater growth of the varieties which are embraced under the term Protestantism. Protestantism had not suffered so much from the scepticism of the eighteenth century or from the French Revolution as had Roman Catholicism. Both of these movements had affected it, but through the Great Awakening in the Thirteen Colonies in British America and through the Wesleyan revival in Great Britain new springs of life had welled up earlier in Protestantism than in the old church. In the United States and Great Britain, where these were strongest, the French Revolution had not proved to be so destructive to established institutions as on the continent of Europe. Moreover, the prevailing currents of the nineteenth century did not prove quite so antagonistic to Protestantism as to Roman Catholicism. To be sure, in Protestant as in Roman Catholic lands the paradox was seen, on the one hand, of a more open rejection of the traditional community faith of Western European peoples than had occurred since the Islamic invasions of the eighth century paralleled, on the other hand, by a renewal of vigour in the churches. However, Protestantism was more flexible than Roman Catholicism and more readily adjusted itself, although not without pain and never completely, to the new intellectual climate and to the fresh social conditions. Then, too, much of the genius of Protestantism, especially in its more radical forms, was akin to the political liberalism and especially to the democracy which were so strong in the nineteenth century. The emphasis upon individual freedom of thought had one of its sources in Protestantism. The closely allied political democracy, as we saw in the preceding volume,[54] to no small degree owed its origin to the Christian impulse as expressed in some of the phases of Protestantism. We must remind ourselves, too, that the power which held the lead in commerce and industry and whose empire displayed the greatest territorial growth in the nineteenth century, Great Britain, was predominantly Protestant, and that in the nation which showed the largest aggregate increase in population and which vied with Great Britain in the rapid accumulation of wealth, the United States, the religious faith of the majority, so far as that majority had a religion, was by tradition Protestant Christianity. It is not surprising, therefore, that the new life which had become apparent within Protestantism in the eighteenth century swelled to flood tide and that it was reinforced by other currents. Nor is it strange that in the total stream of Christianity Protestantism became more prominent than at any previous time. The nineteenth century was the Protestant century. In that period the impulse derived from Jesus gave rise to more different and varied movements within Protestantism than in any other type of Christianity. In the course of that century the expansion of Christianity took place more through Protestantism even than through Roman Catholicism.

As in the case of the Roman Catholic Church, so in Protestantism, the growth in the nineteenth century was not due entirely or even primarily to favourable external conditions, but chiefly to internal vigour. In the nineteenth century Protestantism became more purely religious than ever before. In the course of that century the Christian impulse within Protestantism was less mixed with other, often inimical elements than in previous generations. At its outset and for generations Protestantism had sometimes been even more a political and a nationalistic than a religious movement. It was indelibly stamped with the profound religious experiences and convictions of a Luther, a Calvin, and many another devout soul, but it was also made possible by the resentment of Germans against exploitation for the benefit of Rome and by the desire of princes to control the church within their domains. In lands such as England and Scandinavia the Reformation at its inception was transparently more from the political ambitions and personal desires of the reigning monarchs, who saw in it a means of furthering their own ends, than from motives derived from Jesus. In the nineteenth century, particularly in Great Britain and the United States, countries which were playing an increasingly important part in the history of mankind, movement after movement arose within Protestantism primarily from a desire to be loyal to Jesus and to the primitive

[54] Vol. III, Chap. 16.

Christian faith. These profoundly altered Protestantism. It was not that they brought in ideals radically different from those which Protestantism had professed from the beginning. They did not. In the principles to which it had avowed its allegiance Protestantism was very little altered. The change came rather in the mounting number of those who entered into experiences similar to those of the leaders of the religious elements in Protestantism and in the active loyalty of a growing proportion of Protestants to the full claims of their Christian profession. In some lands Protestantism remained the official faith of the state, and the Church and the state were connected. However, for Protestantism as for Roman Catholicism trends were abroad both in the churches, from religious motives, and in the state, at times from a coolness towards Christianity, which in some countries weakened and in some others severed the legal bond between Church and state. Thus, as in the Roman Catholic form of Christianity, the tendency was away from the acceptance of Protestant Christianity by the community as a whole and towards a tension between the Church and its teachings on the one hand and the world in which it was set on the other. To a certain degree the tension had always been present. It is possible, too, to exaggerate the degree to which it was accentuated in the nineteenth century. Taken as a whole, however, Protestantism was more religious and was more earnest in giving embodiment to the Christian impulse than in any previous century.

As in Roman Catholicism, so in Protestantism, the renewed vigour expressed itself in a large number of new movements. In Protestantism these were even more varied than in Roman Catholicism. Moreover, as the nineteenth century progressed, the current of life in Protestantism ran with increasing strength and its expressions multiplied in diversity, in potency, and in geographic extent.

One type of movement was what were known as revivals. These were particularly marked in the United States and in the British Isles. In the United States the impulse of the Great Awakening did not completely die out, although disturbances associated with the American Revolution proved antagonistic to it. With the re-establishment of peace, revivals again began in several parts of the country[55] and throughout the nineteenth century were an outstanding feature of American Protestantism, particularly the Protestantism of Americans of Anglo-Saxon stock and of the Negroes. The revival which broke out on the frontier in Kentucky and Tennessee in 1800 was famous.[56] Indeed, in the years immediately before and after 1800 most of the United States was swept by a series of revivals which had even greater effect than had the Great

[55] Beardsley, *A History of American Revivals*, pp. 84ff.
[56] Beardsley, *op. cit.*, pp. 84ff.; Weigle, *American Idealism*, pp. 151-153.

Awakening. They gave an impulse and set a pattern of religious life which persisted through much of the nineteenth century and had great importance in the spread of Protestant Christianity. From the 1820's until past the middle of the century Charles G. Finney was the best known of the preachers of revivals.[57] In the second half of the century Dwight L. Moody was the most influential of the itinerant "evangelists."[58] Both Finney and Moody extended their labours to Great Britain. Moody especially had a profound effect in the British Isles and men inspired by him carried his methods and his message to the continent of Europe. Finney and Moody were simply the most prominent among hundreds of these travelling preachers. Somewhat like the Franciscans and the Dominicans of the thirteenth century they went forth, the majority of them Americans and British, many of them laymen, some of them from the upper classes but most of them from the common walks of life,[59] telling, in the language of everyday life, the Christian message and calling their fellows to repentance and faith. They were at once the inspirers and the leaders of a mass movement towards a more earnest Christian life among populations which had, through inheritance, a mild tincture of Christianity.

Closely allied to the revivals and in large part as an outgrowth of them, organizations arose to serve particular groups. As early as the eighteenth century Protestant students had formed societies for the cultivation of the religious life. In the nineteenth century these multiplied.[60] They were given a great impulse by Moody and by his friend, Henry Drummond, a cultivated Scot, who did much to help persons of education to effect a harmony between the Christian faith and the scientific thought of the time.[61] In the last quarter of the nineteenth century and in the first decade of the twentieth century student Christian societies rapidly increased in numbers and in influence. Largely through the genius of an American, John R. Mott, who had been nurtured in them and had been profoundly influenced by the Moody movement, they were bound together through the World's Student Christian Federation.[62]

[57] The best comprehensive biography is G. Frederick Wright, *Charles Grandison Finney* (Boston, Houghton Mifflin and Co., 1893, pp. 329). See also *Memoirs of Charles G. Finney Written by Himself* (New York, A. S. Burnes & Co., 1870, pp. xii, 477).

[58] The most conscientious and careful biography is by a son, William R. Moody, *D. L. Moody* (New York, The Macmillan Co., 1930, pp. 556). Somewhat more readable is Gamaliel Bradford, *D. L. Moody, A Worker in Souls* (Garden City, N. Y., Doubleday, Doran and Co., 1928, pp. 320).

[59] On some of these in Scotland, see Fleming, *A History of the Church in Scotland, 1843-1874*, pp. 111-114.

[60] Shedd, *Two Centuries of Student Christian Movements, passim.*

[61] George Adam Smith, *The Life of Henry Drummond* (New York, Doubleday and McClure Co., 1898, pp. xi, 541), *passim.*

[62] Shedd, *op. cit.,* pp. 355ff.

From these student Christian organizations came a large proportion of the men and women who led the churches in the twentieth century.

For the underprivileged dregs of the great cities of the new age the Salvation Army came into existence. Its founder, William Booth (born April 10, 1829), had himself been reared in poverty, at the age of fifteen had entered into a transforming religious experience in a Methodist meeting, was for a time a Methodist preacher, later was an itinerant evangelist with no ecclesiastical connexion, still later gave himself to the poor in the East End of London, and in 1865 organized what soon was called the Salvation Army. This organization spread rapidly through the English-speaking world and even beyond its borders.[63]

The Salvation Army was by no means the only agency developed for rehabilitating the derelicts of the expanding urban industrial civilization. What were known as missions or rescue missions also arose in large numbers, sometimes with ecclesiastical connexions, sometimes quite independently of them.[64] Somewhat akin to the rescue missions were institutions for sailors in which religious gatherings were held and provision made for wholesome living quarters for seamen when ashore.[65]

For the young men in the cities, largely for the clerks or the lower income groups of what colloquially were known as the white collar class, the Young Men's Christian Associations sprang up. Organizations for a somewhat similar purpose arose on the continent of Europe in the first half of the nineteenth century, but the first group which bore the name was initiated in London in 1844 by George Williams, himself at that time still in his twenties. Similar groups quickly came into being elsewhere in the British Isles. In the following decade the movement spread to the United States and Canada, and by 1853 twenty-seven Associations were in existence in these two countries. In 1854 a confederation of the Associations was formed for North America, and in 1855, in Paris at the time of the Industrial Exhibition, the World's Alliance of the Young Men's Christian Associations was constituted by representatives from

[63] St. John Ervine, *God's Soldier: General William Booth* (London, William Heineman, 2 vols., 1934), *passim*.

[64] See the story of one of the most famous of these missions in *Jerry McAuley: His Life and Work* (with an introduction by S. I. Prime and personal sketches by A. S. Hatch, edited by R. M. Offord, New York, The New York Observer, 2d ed., 1885, pp. xi, 227), *passim*.

[65] As an example of one of these, see Gilbert Haven and Thomas Russell, *Father Taylor. The Sailor Preacher. Incidents and Anecdotes of Rev. Edward T. Taylor for over Forty Years Pastor of the Seaman's Bethel, Boston* (First published 1871. The present edition, Boston, The Boston Port and Seaman's Aid Society, 1904, pp. lxxxv, 472), *passim*.

both sides of the Atlantic.[66] The Young Men's Christian Associations had their richest flowering in the United States. They there developed a multiform programme for the intellectual, social, spiritual, and physical development of boys and young men and for these purposes created a professional, specialized secretariat and erected numerous buildings, some of them large. At the outset they were unhampered by traditions and were free to adapt themselves to current needs. They appealed to an able leadership which was attracted in part by the opportunity to create new devices for meeting unselfishly the needs of young men in the cities. They branched out into the colleges and universities and until after 1914 provided the usual channel for the voluntary religious activities of students. Within two generations they became institutionalized and stereotyped, but in the meantime they had achieved an accepted place in urban life.

Slightly later than the Young Men's Christian Associations, Young Women's Christian Associations began to appear. These were for the young women who were earning their living in the cities. They first arose in the 1850's in Germany and Great Britain, but in the following decade they began to be organized in the United States as well. Like their brother institutions, they had their most extensive development in the United States and there spread to college and university campuses as well as to the cities. Like them, too, they addressed themselves to the entire range of the life and interests of those to whom they ministered. Eventually (1894) there came into existence the World's Young Women's Christian Association, bringing together the various national coordinating organizations.[67]

In 1881, through the efforts of a youthful Congregational pastor in New England, Francis E. Clark, the Young People's Society of Christian Endeavour was initiated. It sought to call youth to a more thoroughgoing devotion to the Christian purpose and to afford it an opportunity to take more part in the activities of the Church. The idea proved contagious, what was known as the United Society of Christian Endeavour was organized, and in 1895 the World's Christian Endeavour Union was launched.[68] The Young People's Societies of Christian Endeavour were not limited to any one Christian denomination, but somewhat similar to them in general purpose were various denominational organizations, such as the Epworth League, the Baptist Young People's Union, and the Luther League.

[66] Laurence L. Doggett, *History of the Young Men's Christian Association* (New York, Association Press, 1922, pp. 405), *passim*.

[67] Sims, *The Natural History of a Social Institution—The Young Women's Christian Association*, pp. 2-5; *International Survey of the Young Men's and Young Women's Christian Associations*, pp. 33-45.

[68] L. A. Weigle in *Dictionary of American Biography*, Vol. IV, pp. 126, 127.

Another movement which spread to many lands and which assumed even larger numerical proportions than those which we have thus far mentioned was the Sunday School. What is usually denominated the first Sunday School was organized in 1780 in Gloucester, England, by Robert Raikes. The original purpose was to give religious and moral instruction to the very poor. At first this involved teaching many of the pupils to read. The need was clear, similar ideas were abroad elsewhere, and the Sunday School spread rapidly.[69] Indeed, one of the early London promoters of the enterprise professed as an ultimate goal teaching every one in the world to read the Bible.[70] Sunday Schools multiplied on both sides of the Atlantic and sprang up in Protestant circles in many lands. In time they became the most generally accepted means of giving to the young, whether rich or poor, instruction in Christian principles and so of perpetuating the Protestant forms of Christianity among peoples traditionally of that faith. Very early (1785) a Sunday School Society was formed in London for the purpose of extending the movement throughout the British Empire. In the United States, state Sunday School associations developed and national and then international conventions were held. In 1889 the first of a series of World's Sunday School Conventions assembled in London, and at the seventh of these, convened in Rome in 1907, the World's Sunday School Association was constituted. In their leadership and teaching staff the Sunday Schools were predominantly lay rather than clerical. The overwhelming majority of teachers served without salary. Superficial though much of the instruction was, the Sunday Schools were a popular religious movement unprecedented in their extensive enlistment of the rank and file of Christians in the teaching and study of the Bible.

Still another manner in which the new life within Protestantism expressed itself was in trends within existing churches or denominations.

Not all who had been touched by the spirit of the Evangelical movement, which had John Wesley and Whitefield as its outstanding leaders, separated from the Church of England. Many remained within it. The attitude which they represented continued into the twentieth century. It stressed individual conversion, it made little of ceremonies, it emphasized the cultivation of the spiritual life of the individual, it gave rise to great philanthropists, such as William Wilberforce and Lord Shaftesbury, it valued action rather than reflective scholarship, and it sought to spread the Christian message as widely

---

[69] On the history of the Sunday School, see Fergusson, *Historic Chapters in Christian Education in America, passim;* Rice, *The Sunday-School Movement 1780-1917, passim.* See also A. Black, in *The International Review of Missions,* Vol. XXVIII, pp. 252-258.

[70] Rice, *op. cit.,* p. 21.

as possible.[71] From the Evangelical movement arose much of the missionary and philanthropic activity of the Church of England, both at home and abroad. For instance, towards the end of the eighteenth century a group of prominent men who were influenced by it, called the Clapham Sect from the London suburb in which they lived, had a prominent share in the creation of the Church Missionary Society and in the anti-slavery campaign.[72] Cambridge became a strong centre of Evangelicalism. There one of its leading representatives, Charles Simeon, long had a marked influence over young men. He did much to train clergymen in sympathy with it and, by placing them in parishes, spread Evangelical convictions and practices.[73]

Partly as an outgrowth of Evangelicalism and partly from dissatisfaction with it and its individualism came the Oxford or Tractarian movement. It emphasized the Church as a continuing and universal institution, stressed the features which the Church of England had in common with the historic Catholic tradition, and protested against the subserviency of the Church of England to the state. Like much of the contemporary revival in Roman Catholicism, it was in part a reaction against the liberalism of the day and was indebted to romanticism.[74]

It was not only in the Church of England that new schools of thought and life developed. They also arose in many another church and nation, indications that Protestantism, far from being static and petrified, was pulsing with life.

Some of the life could not be confined within existing churches but created additional denominations, either by the disruption of an old one or by attracting adherents to an entirely fresh ecclesiastical organization. In Scotland the emergence of new denominations came about chiefly through secessions from the Church of Scotland. In England and the United States the birth rate of denominations was much higher than in Scotland and the new bodies arose both by fission and by independent generation. On the continent of Europe the new denominations were comparatively few, perhaps because of the stronger support of the established churches by the state.

In Scotland the major fresh body came through what was known as the Disruption. In the eighteenth century splits had occurred from the Church of Scotland, usually on the ostensible ground of the Church's undue sub-

---

[71] Binns, *The Evangelical Movement in the English Church*, pp. 76-84, 91.

[72] Binns, *op. cit.*, pp. 33-37.

[73] Binns, *op. cit.*, pp. 37ff.; Zabriskie in *Church History*, Vol. IX, pp. 103-119.

[74] Binns, *op. cit.*, p. 49; L. E. Elliott-Binns, *Religion in the Victorian Era* (London, The Lutterworth Press, 1936, pp. 526), pp. 92ff., 226ff. The bibliography on the Oxford movement is, of course, extensive. References to much of it are to be found in the footnotes of Yngve Brilioth, *The Anglican Revival. Studies in the Oxford Movement* (London, Longmans, Green and Co., 1933, pp. xv, 357).

serviency to the state.[75] The rising tide of economic prosperity in the nation was paralleled by a growing life in the Church. Many of the finest spirits were restive under the degree of control exercised over the Church by the state and by the laymen who through the right of patronage filled vacant pulpits. The protest was akin to that of the leaders of the Oxford movement on the other side of the border and to the increasing ultramontane sentiment in the Roman Catholic Church. It, like these others, sprang in part from the conviction that the Church must not be compromised through dictation by a secular power whose interests might seek to nullify the Christian message. As a result, in 1843, in a dramatic scene, a large proportion of the clergy and laymen withdrew from the Assembly of the Church of Scotland and organized the Free Church of Scotland.[76] Although the Free Church was cut off from the endowments and equipment of the parent body, so great was the devotion of its members that within its first year it erected about five hundred churches, and it supported its ministry, it established its own colleges, and, since every overseas missionary joined it, it bore the burden of foreign missions as well.[77]

In the United States many new denominations appeared. One of the most prominent of these was the Disciples of Christ, of which we are to hear more in a later chapter. It was mainly the outgrowth of revivals.[78] In New England the majority church broke apart. One wing, the Unitarian, more liberal in its theology, centred about Boston. The other, the orthodox Congregational, representing the more conservative elements, became the chief agent for spreading New England Christianity in other lands and among the new settlements on the frontier. The Methodist Episcopal Church came into being. Out of the revivals and especially from contact with Methodism came the United Brethren in Christ and the Evangelical Association. From the revivals sprang the Free Baptists. Out of immigration from Europe arose a number of Lutheran bodies. As strange offshoots of the New England stock, Christian Science and the Church of Jesus Christ of Latter Day Saints (the Mormons) came into being. The Seventh Day Adventists, although never a large body, were extraordinarily active as missionaries in many lands. Later we are to recur to these and are to mention a number of other denominations which

[75] See a list of these, in the form of a chart, in Slosser, *Christian Unity*, between pp. 152 and 153. For a brief summary of them, see Fleming, *The Church of Scotland 1843-1874*, pp. 10, 11, Buchan and Smith, *The Kirk in Scotland*, pp. 53-56, and Barr, *The United Free Church of Scotland*, pp. 52ff.

[76] Barr, *op. cit.*, pp. 83ff.; Buchan and Smith, *op. cit.*, pp. 72ff.; Fleming, *op. cit.*, pp. 19ff.

[77] Buchan and Smith, *op. cit.*, p. 79.

[78] Winfred Ernest Garrison, *Religion Follows the Frontier. A History of the Disciples of Christ* (New York, Harper & Brothers, 1931, pp. xiv, 317), *passim*.

sprang up in the United States and which helped to give to the Protestantism of the land its great variety.

The complete list of the new denominations with even the briefest account of their origin would prolong these pages unduly. Some were born of envy, strife, and personal ambition, but of the larger ones the great majority sprang primarily from fresh expressions of the Christian impulse. In Protestantism they corresponded roughly to the new orders and congregations in the Roman Catholic Church. The units in both of these wings of Christianity came into being primarily because of the contagious conviction of outstanding individuals who were impelled by experiences or beliefs born of contacts with Christianity.

The movements which we have thus far mentioned by no means embrace all of the expressions of the abounding life of nineteenth century Protestantism. To them one must add the many scores of societies for the propagation of Christianity in the Occident and among non-Occidental peoples and whose activities are to constitute much of the remainder of our story. One must also include within the current of Protestantism hundreds of agencies, large and small, for the promotion of the physical and intellectual welfare of mankind. Protestantism, and especially the Protestantism of the British peoples and the United States, expressed itself in part in a great variety of efforts for the present welfare of man. From it sprang peace societies, societies for the abolition of slavery, organizations for the betterment of the condition of the labouring classes, temperance societies, hospitals, orphanages, societies for the distribution of wholesome literature, and thousands of schools.

Although the nineteenth century was one of action and expansion rather than of the emergence of great philosophy and theology, Protestantism displayed a rich and varied intellectual life. In this German Protestantism led the way. The most influential theologians were Schleiermacher (1768-1834) and Ritschl (1822-1889). Out of Protestantism, too, came the philosopher Hegel. Scholars directed towards the Bible the current methods of historical study and criticism. There developed an intense study of the Christian Scriptures and of the records of the life of Jesus. The results were alarming to many of the orthodox, but they made of Jesus a more warmly human figure than he had been since the first century.

Multiform and fissiparous though Protestantism was, it also gave rise to efforts for union. These, too, were many and various. Some sought to merge similar denominations. Thus the United Free Church of Scotland was formed.[79]

[79] J. R. Fleming, *The Story of Church Union in Scotland. Its Origins and Progress 1516-1929* (London, James Clarke and Co., 1929, pp. 176), *passim*.

Others worked for *rapprochement* between Protestants and Roman Catholics, between Anglicans and Eastern Orthodox, or between dissimilar schools of Protestantism.[80] The Evangelical Alliance, formed in 1846, endeavoured to draw together in fellowship all those in the stream of the Protestant Reformation who held to the authority of the Bible, the incarnation, the atonement, salvation through faith, and the work of the Holy Spirit.[81] The movement for co-operation and union gathered momentum and had its main fruitage in the twentieth century, but it was already in existence before 1914 and even before 1900.

In the Eastern churches no such new life was apparent in the nineteenth century as in the Protestant and Roman Catholic folds. Changes occurred, some of them accompanied by new vigour. As the wave of Moslem Turkish rule receded from Europe, and Greece, Roumania, Serbia, and Bulgaria achieved their independence, the Orthodox Church in each of these lands became independent of the Œcumenical Patriarch of Constantinople, for that dignitary was still under the Sultan of Turkey. In some instances this led to a revival in the life of the Church.[82] In Russia a marked growth occurred among several of the groups which dissented from the state church. For instance, the Stundists arose from contact with foreign influences and spread widely,[83] and a few of the sects, instead of being confined to the lowly, began to acquire followers from the upper classes.[84] These dissidents from Orthodoxy, however, did little or nothing to spread the faith outside nominally Christian peoples. In the latter half of the nineteenth century something of a revival began within the Russian Orthodox Church. A few influential scholars and authors became dissatisfied with the rationalism which had entered from Western Europe and found inspiration in a return to the sources of Orthodoxy.[85] Under the energetic leadership of the reactionary but able Procurator of the Holy Synod, Pobiedonostsiev, improvement was made in the rural parishes and the priesthood, and parochial schools were strengthened.[86] Moreover, efforts to propagate Russian Orthodoxy arose spontaneously from inner religious conviction. In general, however, the state church remained formal and somnolent, an agent of the Tsar, and most of such spread of the faith

[80] Slosser, *Church Unity*, pp. 117ff.; Douglass, *Church Unity Movements in the United States*, pp. 47ff.

[81] Slosser, *op. cit.*, pp. 174ff.

[82] As in Bulgaria.—Adeney, *The Greek and Eastern Churches*, p. 350.

[83] Milukow, *Skizzen russischer Kulturgeschichte*, Vol. II, p. 145.

[84] Vernadsky, *A History of Russia*, p. 117.

[85] Visser 't Hooft, *Anglo-Catholicism and Orthodoxy*, pp. 81-83.

[86] Frere, *Links in the Chain of Russian Church History*, pp. 179, 180.

among non-Christians as took place was inside the Russian Empire and with strong assistance from the secular authorities.

With the past two chapters back of us, we are now in a position to give in summary answers for the nineteenth century to two of the questions to which throughout our survey of the expansion of Christianity we have from time to time recurred: What was the Christianity that spread and why did it spread?

In the nineteenth century the Christianity which spread was overwhelmingly Roman Catholicism and Protestantism. Of the two wings of Western European Christianity, in the nineteenth century Protestantism had the larger share in the propagation of the faith and displayed the greater proportionate growth.

The Roman Catholicism was that of a revival which expressed itself largely through celibate orders and congregations and through an enhanced religious devotion of those of the laity who remained true to the Church. Among the congregations, women's organizations became more prominent than formerly and, accordingly, women had an increasing share in the propagation of the faith. The Church was less under the domination of the secular state than at any time since the fourth century and was more closely integrated under the autocratic control of the Pope than ever it had been. The Roman Catholic Church was growing in numbers, in enthusiasm, and in geographic extent, but more and more it had the character of a minority which was set in opposition to the world about it and which was seeking not so much to win that world or to transform it as to draw into its fellowship individuals and groups from that world.

The Protestant Christianity which spread was that of a large number of denominations and churches. It was primarily from the British Isles, from peoples of European stock within the Empire, notably Canada, Australia, New Zealand, and South Africa, and from the United States. Germans, who had had the leading part in Protestant missions before the nineteenth century, were still prominent, and from several other countries on the continent of Europe Protestant missionaries were sent. However, the overwhelming majority of the Protestant missionaries of the nineteenth and twentieth centuries were from the British Isles and the United States. The kinds of Protestantism from which the major part of the expansion took place were those which were most affected by the Pietist tradition, the Wesleyan movement, and the revivals of the eighteenth and nineteenth centuries. They made much of the transformation of individuals through the Christian Gospel and they also gave rise to many efforts to better the physical and mental lot of men. To use more technical terms, they were evangelistic, in the sense of winning men and women one by one to the Christian faith, and they were philanthropic and humanitarian. They issued in efforts to present the Christian Gospel to every man and woman and in attempts to transform entire cultures.

This Protestantism was characterized by an abounding vitality and a daring unequalled in Christian history. Through it for the first time plans were seriously elaborated for bringing the Christian message to all men and to make the life of all mankind conform to Christian ideals. In the first century some Christians had believed it to be their obligation to "preach the Gospel to every creature." Buddhists, moreover, had held before themselves the salvation not only of all men but of every living being. Never before, however, had the followers of any faith formulated comprehensive plans covering the entire surface of the earth to make these purposes effective. Not even the Christians of the first century had hoped by their efforts to revolutionize all human society. Now, however, came projects for placing the Bible among all the population of a whole nation[87] and even of the entire world,[88] surveys of the earth's surface with the announced purpose of "carrying the Gospel to all the non-Christian world,"[89] and the adoption of the slogan "the evangelization of the world in this generation" as the "watchword" of the Student Volunteer Movement for Foreign Missions.[90] Now such hymns gained currency and voiced widespread aspiration as Thomas Hastings's "Hail to the brightness of Zion's glad morning" (written in 1832), with its vision of praise to Jehovah "ascending from all lands, from all isles of the ocean," and of the end of "war and commotion," and Reginald Heber's (who died in 1826) "From Greenland's icy mountains" with its call to take the Christian message to all peoples. To be sure, these aspirations were not entirely new. Since the early part of the eighteenth century Protestants of English speech, and especially Nonconformists, had been singing the hymn of Isaac Watts—"Jesus shall reign where'er the sun does his successive journeys run, his kingdom stretch from shore to shore till moons shall wax and wane no more." Yet the fact that they continued to sing it gave indication that it voiced their hopes. Now, in a widely circulated address before a missionary society the declaration was made, "Our field is the world. Our object is to effect an entire moral revolu-

[87] Dwight, *The Centennial History of the American Bible Society*, Vol. I, pp. 86, 131, Vol. II, pp. 369, 375.

[88] Dwight, *op. cit.*, Vol. I, pp. 113-118.

[89] *World Missionary Conference, 1910. Report of Commission I. Carrying the Gospel to All the Non-Christian World* (Edinburgh, Oliphant, Anderson and Ferrier, 1910, pp. viii, 452), *passim*.

[90] Wilder, *The Great Commission*, pp. 84-90.

tion in the entire human race."[91] It was this conception which led an able young New Englander, in 1836, in announcing his purpose to become a missionary, to say that he had reached his decision by way of the question: "How can I exert the most influence upon the ultimate conversion of the world?"[92]

Between the Roman Catholic and the Protestant forms of Christianity great differences existed which reflected themselves in the forms of their expansion. Roman Catholicism was authoritarian, highly centralized, dominated by the clergy, prized celibacy, and sought not to broadcast the Christian message or to transform entire peoples but to build up the Church as an institution. Protestantism, particularly in the types which were most active in the spread of the faith, tended to stress the individual, the conversion of the individual, and the right and duty of each Christian to think for himself. It was authoritarian in that it emphasized the Bible as the standard of faith, but it did not give to any central body the function of interpreting the Bible. It was divided organizationally, although with an increasing tendency to co-operation. In it the lay element was very strong and to a large degree it was a lay movement. It had little to say about celibacy, although many of its women missionaries were unmarried. In general it made much less of the sacraments than did Roman Catholicism. It sought to acquaint all men with the Christian message and in some of its manifestations endeavoured to transform entire societies. In practice, many Protestant groups subordinated the building of the Church to these other ends. The result was that in most lands to which it spread Christianity was represented by two very diverse strains. Between these there was almost no connexion except their common origin. Sometimes antagonism arose. More frequently each ignored the other.

The reasons for the spread of Christianity were many. Some of them were to be found in the general air of hope and expansion which permeated much of the Occident, notably Great Britain and the United States. Some came from the great increase in wealth in the lands where Christianity was strongest and which provided means for the support of missionaries. The striking improvements in communication and the rapid growth of the commerce and the empires of Western peoples were important factors. The breakdown of non-European cultures under the impact of Western peoples weakened the resistance to Christianity. All of these, however, would have been of no avail had they not been paralleled by the burst of new life within Christianity itself. It was this surge of vitality which was the primary cause of the daring vision, the comprehensive plans, and the offering of life and money which sent mission-

[91] Wayland, *The Moral Dignity of the Missionary Enterprise*, p. 26.
[92] Joseph P. Thompson, *Memoir of Rev. David Tappan Stoddard, Missionary to the Nestorians* (New York, Sheldon, Blakeman and Co., 1858, pp. vi, 422), pp. 55-57.

aries to all quarters of the globe—to the advancing frontiers of Europear settlement in the Americas, Australia, and New Zealand, to the Eskimos in the Arctic, to the jungles and plains of Africa, to the remotest islands of the Pacific, to all the provinces and dependencies of China, to the many district of India, and to the Siberian steppes. It is this which led to the reduction ol hundreds of languages to writing and to the translation of the Bible into a thousand tongues, to the erection of hospitals and the creation of new medica' professions, to the rise of educational systems for entire peoples, and to vast changes in the family system and in the status of women. When one traces it to its source, this vast outpouring of life is found to have its origin in the impulse which was as old as Christianity itself and which came through Jesus.

Chapter IV

THE PROCESSES BY WHICH CHRISTIANITY SPREAD. GENERAL FEATURES: ROMAN CATHOLIC ORGANIZATION AND METHODS: PROTESTANT ORGANIZATION AND METHODS: THE RUSSIAN ORTHODOX CHURCH

ONE of the aspects of our subject which has engaged our attention in each period of our study has been the processes by which Christianity spread. In the nineteenth century these had distinctive characteristics which helped to make the expansion of Christianity in that period different from that in any preceding era and, indeed, unlike the spread of any other religion at any time. Most of these features, as we are to see in the final volume, persisted into the twentieth century. They acquired added significance from the fashion in which they in part determined the effect of Christianity upon its environment from land to land.

One outstanding feature of the expansion of Christianity in this period was the comparative absence of active assistance by governments.

Ever since the Emperor Constantine adopted the labarum Christianity had spread chiefly through the dual activities of princes and missionaries. Again and again the propagation of Christianity had been utilized as a means of extending the authority or the prestige of a particular monarch or people. This had never been more marked than in the three centuries immediately preceding A.D. 1800, when the major part of the geographic extension of Christianity was accomplished under the direction of the Spanish, Portuguese, and Russian governments.

In the nineteenth century some of this policy persisted. The French Government, although frequently dominated by anti-clericals and seeking to curtail the Church at home, usually gave active endorsement to Roman Catholic missions abroad. Indeed, in the Near East, French Roman Catholic missions were a major channel for French political imperialism and even some non-French missions in that region were given financial assistance.[1] In the Far East it was through coming to the support of Roman Catholic missionaries that France laid the foundations for her territorial holdings. Portugal and Spain

---

[1] Schwager, *Die katholische Heidenmission der Gegenwart,* p. 27.

47

each sought to control the Roman Catholic Church in their diminished colonial possessions. Such expansion of the Russian Orthodox form of Christianity as occurred enjoyed the active assistance of the Tsar's government. British colonial regimes granted extensive subsidies to mission schools, and in the United States the Federal Government furnished large financial aid to Christian schools for the Indians.

However, none of the major colonial powers of the period accorded missions anything like as extensive support as had been given by Spain and Portugal in the preceding period, and none of them except Russia exercised so close and so autocratic a control over the Church and over missions as had the Portuguese and Spanish crowns or as had even the Dutch East India Company. The Government of France did not give such systematic financial subsidies as had those of Spain and Portugal or as had the Dutch trading company. We find, too, on the part of French Roman Catholics a conscious desire to use missions as a means of counterbalancing among primitive peoples the evils introduced by the advent of European colonial regimes.[2] The assistance to schools from the Governments of the British and of the United States was contributed not because the institutions were Christian but because they were schools. When, as sometimes happened, the diplomatic, naval, or military officials of Great Britain or the United States safeguarded missionaries, it was almost never because of the latters' religious errand or because they might prove a convenient opening wedge for political conquest, but because they were citizens and as such were, like other citizens, entitled to the protection of their respective governments. The weakening or the actual severance of the ties which since Constantine had bound together Church and state in lands in which Christianity was the faith of the community was accompanied by a lessening of the participation of the state in the spread of that religion.

A second distinctive feature of the expansion of Christianity in the nineteenth century was the extent to which Christian missions became an enterprise of the rank and file of the membership of the churches. As the support of governments declined, that of the average lay Christian increased. More nearly than ever before, the spread of Christianity became a popular movement. Heretofore, as a rule, the financial undergirding of missions had been provided by governments, princes, a few wealthy individuals, or the missionaries themselves. In the lands from which missionaries went, only an infinitesimal minority of the laymen and of the rank and file of the clergy had any concern for the spread of the faith in distant lands. Not even in the nineteenth

---

[2] André Boucher, President of the Propagation of the Faith at Paris, in Léon Derville, *Madagascar-Betsiléo. Ils ne sont que quarante. Les Jesuites chez les Betsiléos* (Paris, Dillen et Cie, 1930, pp. 126), p. 11.

century did the majority of professing Christians give active assistance to missions. However, now for the first time a substantial minority of laymen and clergy became interested and contributed of their means to make missions possible. What in the aggregate were large sums of money were provided by hundreds of thousands of givers. The large majority of those who gave were not people of wealth, but of modest incomes. Of the majority, moreover, it can be said that in aiding missions they had nothing to gain, either politically or commercially. Indeed, some of the most extensive missions, notably those of Protestants of the United States in the Near East, India, Burma, and the Congo, were in lands in which the nation from which they came had no political interest and with which its commerce was either meagre or almost non-existent. Much of the giving was accompanied by the prayers of the donors. While motives are seldom entirely unmixed, on a scale never before witnessed money was being contributed to a cause with a minimum of self-interest and primarily from a sense of duty or from a love for other human beings which had their source in the Christian impulse.

This broadening of the base of support of missions is evidence of the continuation of the process which we have noted in the two previous volumes as in progress since at least the thirteenth century, the permeation of the masses by the Christianity which had been adopted hundreds of years before under the leadership of the aristocracy. The fact that, in contrast with earlier periods when the spread of Christianity was through monks as active agents supported by princes and a few of the wealthy nobility, so many hundreds of thousands were willing to contribute to the propagation of their faith is additional indication that increasingly the large body of professing Christians were devoting themselves seriously to their faith and were not merely passive recipients of it. Even though millions were drifting away from the Church, the minority which was actively and devotedly allying itself with it was growing.

A third characteristic of the processes by which Christianity spread in the nineteenth century was the large part played by women. Heretofore only a small minority of professional Christian missionaries had been women. We hear of a number who in the eighth century assisted Boniface in Germany. However, the vast majority of those who carried the faith to new frontiers had been men. This was at least in part because men were better fitted physically to meet the dangers and the hardships of this type of pioneer effort. By 1914, in contrast, about half of the missionaries were women. This was true of Roman Catholic enterprises.[3] It was also true of the Protestant mis-

[3] Schwager, op. cit., pp. 219, 309, 445.

sionary body.[4] The change seems to have been due in some degree to the increasing peace and to the rapidly improving ease of travel and communication which characterized the nineteenth century, and so to the decreasing physical risk in the task of the missionary. It probably also was because of the growing share of women in the active work of the churches in the Occident and of the general trend in the Occident towards the entrance of women into occupations which had formerly been reserved for men.

A fourth feature of the spread of Christianity in the nineteenth century was the relatively high standards set by missionaries for admission to the Church. For more than a thousand years the amount of instruction given to converts before baptism had usually been comparatively slight. The majority of converts came in through group movements. Their numbers made difficult if not impossible the kind of pre-baptismal instruction which the Church in theory desired. In the nineteenth century requirements varied with the missionary agency. In many instances the instruction given and the ethical demands made of the neophyte were still meagre. In general, however, both Roman Catholics and Protestants established higher prerequisites for admission to the Church than had been customary since the first few centuries of the expansion of the faith.

Partly associated with this fourth characteristic was a fifth. Entrance to the Church now became chiefly an individual rather than a group decision. To this many exceptions can be cited. Among primitive peoples, notably in some of the islands of the Pacific, among several of the tribes of Asia and Africa, and among the outcastes of India, conversion was still largely by groups.[5] Yet the temper of the churches of the Occident, both Roman Catholic and Protestant, was against this method. The tendency to regard the Church as something in contradiction to the societies in which Christians were set, which was so marked in the nineteenth century, made for the winning of converts one by one or at most by families.

This, it must be noted, was markedly different from the process by which Christianity had spread in other eras. Then mass conversion had been the rule. It was also different from the group conversions by which other religions had acquired their followings.

The infrequency of mass movements partly accounts for a sixth characteristic, the fact that in most lands Christians constituted only a small percentage of

---

[4] Beach, *A Geography and Atlas of Protestant Missions*, p. 19.

[5] See, for instance, the accounts to be given in Vol. V of the progress of Protestant Christianity in the Pacific Islands, and methods of the Roman Catholics in New Pomerania as given in Schmidlin, *Catholic Mission Theory*, pp. 353-355.

the population. This was particularly the case among the more numerous non-Christian peoples, such as the Chinese, the Indians, and the Africans. In China in 1914 the number of professing Christians was only about one-half of 1 per cent. of the population.[6] In India at about the same time it was only slightly more than 1 per cent.,[7] and among the Negroes of Africa perhaps 1½ per cent.[8] While the proportion of Christians was increasing, outside of the Occident and the Near East, except for a few islands and tribes, when seen against the background of an entire people or nation, the Christian communities appeared almost negligible.

Over against the small size of the churches planted was a seventh feature of nineteenth century missions, the extraordinary effect of Christianity upon non-Christian peoples. As non-Occidental cultures weakened or collapsed under the pressure of the West, Christianity had a growing part in penetrating them and in shaping the new cultures which were beginning to emerge. The small Christian minorities exerted an influence all out of proportion to their size. A kind of mass permeation occurred. It could scarcely be called conversion, for no formal change of religion took place. However, some of the larger cultures, although avowedly non-Christian, were being modified fully as much as had been the civilization of the Græco-Roman world in the fourth and fifth centuries after the nominal conversion of the Roman Empire. Through schools, literature, medical care, famine relief, and many another channel Christian missions and missionaries were profoundly moulding culture after culture. The process was to be greatly accelerated after 1914.

In this permeation and transformation of cultures, Protestants had a larger share than Roman Catholics. While the latter conducted schools and prepared literature in many languages[9] and in some areas engaged in extensive agricultural operations,[10] they placed their chief emphasis upon building the Church. In contrast, as we suggested at the close of the last chapter, Protestants directed much of their energy into channels which only indirectly if at all helped in the creation of a continuing Christian community, but which issued in effects upon the life of a nation or tribe as a whole. Among these channels were the reduction of hundreds of languages to writing, broadcasting the

---

[6] Latourette, *A History of Christian Missions in China*, pp. 537, 680.

[7] Beach and St. John, editors, *World Statistics of Christian Missions*, p. 59; Streit, *Atlas Hierarchicus*, p. 103.

[8] Beach and St. John, *op. cit.*, p. 59; Streit, *op. cit.*, pp. 103, 104.

[9] Up to 1898 one of the orders, the Holy Ghost Fathers, had prepared literature in twenty-two different languages. During the first half century or less of its history the Society of the Divine Word had done something in a literary way in thirty-nine different tongues.—Berg, *Die katholische Heidenmission als Kulturträger*, Vol. II, p. 21.

[10] Schmidlin, *Catholic Mission Theory*, p. 302.

Christian message, a marked emphasis on schools, hospitals, and medical education, the creation of nursing professions, and measures to promote public health and to prevent famines. Protestantism was torn between two quite diverse methods. One was the winning of converts one by one. With its individualism, its emphasis upon the soul's direct access to God, this was quite natural. The other was the transformation of entire societies, even though this was not accompanied by their formal conversion. Many Protestants disavowed this latter purpose and, indeed, held it to be unscriptural. Yet even they, by their efforts to spread the Christian message broadcast to all men and by their medical service contributed to it.

In this mass modification the initiative came from foreigners. It remained a question whether, if once the missionary were to leave, the influence of Christianity would continue. Numerically the churches established were so weak that, if foreign assistance were withdrawn, they might have difficulty even in surviving and would probably have no such extensive effect upon the surrounding cultures as they had had when reinforced by missionaries.

Moreover, in spite of its contrasts with previous periods, this nineteenth century expansion of Christianity had this much in common with the spread of the faith in the preceding three centuries—it was under the direction of Occidental peoples. With a few exceptions, until the twentieth century the Christian communities established were under the supervision of Westerners and the new churches were dependent upon the Occident for leadership and funds. Nineteenth century Christian missions were largely a paternalistic enterprise, a kind of spiritual imperialism. It was a benevolent imperialism, but it was imperialism. Not until the twentieth century did there come a decided change.

We must now turn to a description of the organizations through which Christianity spread in the nineteenth century. Never before had Christianity, or, indeed, any other religion, developed such elaborate and extensive machinery for its propagation. This in itself was evidence of abounding vigour, for it arose spontaneously from religious conviction. In it ulterior motives such as economic and political imperialism had little or no part. This was true of both Roman Catholicism and Protestantism. First we must say something of the Roman Catholic organizations. Then we will deal with those of Protestantism.

Much of the Roman Catholic machinery for the propagation of the faith was either a continuation of that earlier in use or closely resembled it. As in all previous periods since the fourth century, the large majority of the missionaries were celibates associated in congregations, societies, or orders.[11] Some were regulars and some seculars. Some were priests, others lay brothers. Many, as we have suggested, were women. Numbers of the orders, congregations, and societies which for the past several centuries had borne the brunt of the load, notably the Jesuits, the Franciscans, the Société des Missions Étrangères of Paris, and the Lazarists,[12] continued. To these were added other similar bodies. Some were for work both in Christendom and abroad. Others were purely for the purpose of spreading the faith in non-Christian lands. Even to enumerate the new bodies would prolong these pages unduly. One list, for instance, contains twenty orders and congregations founded before the nineteenth century engaged in missions, seventeen founded in the nineteenth century which laboured both within Christendom and outside it, nine founded between 1789 and 1914 exclusively for service in non-Christian lands, two organizations of lay brothers founded before 1789 and ten between 1789 and 1914 which helped in foreign missions, and twenty-seven associations of sisters founded before 1789 and about one hundred and twenty-five founded between 1789 and 1914 which assisted within and outside the Occident.[13] While we cannot take the space even to name them all, we must mention a few of the more prominent.

First we must select, almost at random, a few of the bodies whose members served both inside and outside so-called Christendom. Not far from the middle of the nineteenth century the Missionaries of the Holy Heart were founded at Issoudun by Julius Chevalier. At first they confined their energies to domestic missions, but within less than a generation they had extended their efforts to islands in the Pacific.[14] The Assumptionists, inaugurated in 1845 in Nîmes, at the outset confined their efforts to the founding of a college for Southern France. Later they took a leading part in missions in the Near East.[15] The Oblates of St. Francis de Sales were begun in 1830 for the quickening of the religious life of France, but in 1845 they assumed responsibilities in India.[16] The Oblates of the Immaculate Heart of Mary also had as their initial scope

---

[11] On the difference between orders and congregations, see Schmidlin, *Catholic Mission Theory*, pp. 137-141.

[12] Coste, *La Congrégation de la Mission*, pp. 195, 196, enumerates twenty-five countries which the Lazarists entered between 1875 and 1914. On the Société des Missions Étrangères of Paris, see Adrien Launay, *Histoire Générale de la Société des Missions-Étrangères* (Paris, Pierre Téqui, 3 vols., 1894), *passim*, and Manceau, *L'Abbé Jean-Joseph Rousseille, Ancien Supérieur et Directeur du Séminaire des Missions Étrangères de Paris d'après sa Correspondance* (Paris, Victor Lecoffre, 1902, pp. xiv, 316), *passim*.

[13] Arens, *Handbuch der katholischen Missionen* (1920), pp. 32ff.

[14] Schwager, *Die katholische Heidenmission der Gegenwart*, p. 46.

[15] Schwager, *op. cit.*, p. 45.

[16] Schwager, *op. cit.*, p. 44.

work among the masses in Europe, but before the middle of the century they had spread to Ceylon and to the Canadian frontier, and eventually they extended their activities to several other parts of the world.[17] Out of the efforts of the amazing John Bosco arose the Salesians of Don Bosco, the Congregation of Daughters of Mary Help of Christians, and the Union of Salesian Co-operators.[18] The Little Brothers of Mary, founded in 1817 at Lavalle, France, by Benedict Champagnot, conducted schools in many countries, both in the Occident and in non-Occidental regions.[19] The Sisters of Providence of Portieux were the outgrowth of the devotion of a French priest of the eighteenth century, Jean Martin Moÿe (1730-1793), who had given himself to the poor, both in Europe and in China, and had done much to train women teachers. However, the movement initiated by him was disrupted by the French Revolution, and it was not until 1812 that the mother house of the congregation was opened. The members established hundreds of schools in Europe and in 1875 extended their labours to Manchuria and Cambodia.[20]

As we have suggested, numbers of the new orders and congregations had as their exclusive object the conversion of non-Christians outside Christendom. Thus the Fathers of the Holy Ghost were primarily for work among Negroes. They were the outgrowth of a merger of the Society of the Holy Heart of Mary, begun in 1839 by a converted Jew, Libermann, and of the Congregation of the Holy Ghost. They had extensive missions in the West Indies and Africa.[21] In the eighteen sixties Theophile Verbist founded in Belgium the Congregation of the Immaculate Heart of Mary. Its headquarters were placed at Scheutveld, a suburb of Brussels. Its first field was Inner Mongolia. Verbist himself went with its initial contingent and died before he could see the enterprise thoroughly established.[22] When the congregation celebrated its seventy-fifth anniversary it had over 700 missionaries in China, the Belgian Congo, the Philippines, and Celebes.[23] The Society of the Divine Word was started in 1875 by Arnold Janssen. The purpose was to bring into existence a German organization through which missionaries could be trained and sent.

---

[17] Schwager, op. cit., p. 43.

[18] Ghéon, The Secret of Saint John Bosco, passim; Heimbucher, Die Orden und Kongregationen der katholischen Kirche, Vol. II, pp. 407, 408.

[19] Fides News Service, Aug. 3, 1935.

[20] J. C. Bouchot, Un Cinquantenaire, 1876-1926. Les Sœurs de la Providence de Portieux dans la Mission de Phnôm-Penh Indochine (Paris, S. A. Gravure et Impressions, 1926, pp. 71), pp. 1-3.

[21] Döring, Vom Juden zum Ordensstifter, passim; Schwager, op. cit., p. 42.

[22] Joseph Rutten, Les Missionaires de Scheut et leur Fondateur (Louvain, Editions de l'Aucam, 1930, pp. 228), passim; Heimbucher, op. cit., Vol. II, p. 392; Missions du Chine et aux Congo, 1901, pp. 274-278.

[23] Fides News Service, Dec. 4, 1937.

Since the *Kulturkampf* was then in progress between the Government of the German Empire and the Roman Catholic Church, the headquarters of the society were placed at Steyl, in Holland, not far from the German border. Missions were first begun in Shantung Province, China, but were later undertaken in several other parts of the globe.[24] In England, where the Roman Catholic Church was being reorganized, the St. Joseph's Society of Mill Hill was founded on the outskirts of London by Herbert Vaughan, eventually Archbishop of Westminster and Cardinal, but drew its students largely from Holland.[25] In the United States, towards the close of this period, in 1911, the Catholic Foreign Mission Society of America was begun under the leadership of two priests, James A. Walsh and Thomas F. Price.[26] The establishment of the Roman Catholic Church in the United States had itself absorbed part of the missionary energy of Europe. Now that church was beginning to stand on its own feet and to be more active in the world-wide task of the Roman Catholic communion. The new society had the authorization of the hierarchy in the United States as well as the Papal blessing. At Maryknoll, north of New York City, a seminary was founded for the training of missionaries. Missionary sisters were soon added to the undertaking.

The largest community of missionary sisters[27] was the Franciscan Missionaries of Mary. These owed their existence and much of their importance to the force of character, determination, and extraordinary organizing and administrative ability of their foundress, Helene Marie Philippine de Chappotin (1839-1904), who is better known under her religious name, Mary of the Passion.[28] Mary of the Passion had gone to India in 1866 under the recently founded Society of Marie-Réparatrice and by 1870 had become the provincial of three houses of the Madura mission of that congregation. Differences developed between her and her superiors in Europe and she was deposed from

[24] H. Fischer, *Arnold Janssen, Gründer des Steyler Missionswerkes, ein Lebensbild* (Steyl, Missionsdruckerei, 1919, pp. v, 493), *passim;* Herm. auf der Heide, *Die Missionsgenossenschaft von Steyl. Ein Bilde der ersten 25 Jahre Ihres Bestehens* (Steyl, Missionsdruckerei, 1900, pp. 607), *passim.*
[25] Heimbucher, *op. cit.,* Vol. II, pp. 392-394; Schwager, *Die katholische Heidenmission der Gegenwart,* pp. 66, 67.
[26] George C. Powers, *The Maryknoll Movement* (Maryknoll, N. Y., The Catholic Foreign Mission Society of America, 1926, pp. xix, 167), *passim.*
[27] *Fides News Service,* Sept. 22, 1934.
[28] *Les Très Révérende Mère Marie de la Passion. Ouvrage Publié par l'Institut des Franciscaines Missionaires de Marie* (Paris, Imprimerie Franciscaine, 1914, pp. 553), *passim;* Marie-Bernard Hygonet, *Une Grande Ame. Une Grande Œuvre. La Très Révérende Mère Marie de la Passion, Fondatrice des Franciscaines Missionaires de Marie* (Paris, Tolra, 1922, pp. xxix, 358), *passim;* Dominic Devas, *Mother Mary of the Passion Foundress of the Franciscan Missionaries of Mary (1839-1904)* (London, Longmans, Green and Co., pp. 102), *passim.*

her office. With the nuns who remained loyal to her, she decided to found an independent institute. For this she obtained Papal permission. She attached her congregation to the Franciscans. After a period of intense opposition, beginning with the 1880's, houses multiplied rapidly and in many countries. Since their special purpose was the spread of the Christian faith among non-Christians, the Franciscan Missionaries of Mary were placed under the Congregation for the Propagation of the Faith.

Several institutions for training and sending secular priests as missionaries were begun, something after the pattern of the seminary which was the heart of the famous Société des Missions-Étrangères of Paris. One of these was founded at Milan, in Italy, in 1850, by Angelo Ramazotti, at that time Bishop of Pavia.[29] Another, bearing the names of Peter and Paul, was inaugurated in Rome.[30] Still another, at Lyons, was primarily for African Missions.[31]

Roman Catholic machinery for the propagation of Christianity was not confined to organizations which perpetuated earlier forms and traditions. Bodies of an entirely new kind sprang into being. Conviction and enthusiasm were sufficiently strong and inward vitality flexible enough to give rise to innovations. This was particularly apparent in the raising of money for the support of missions. As we have said, the funds for the missionary enterprise did not come primarily from governments or from a few of the wealthy, as earlier, but from the many. An increasing number of laymen and laywomen and of the secular clergy became actively concerned with missions. No longer was the extension of the faith among non-Christians the enterprise of a few specialists, but more and more it engaged the active attention of the great body of practising Roman Catholics, those who took their faith seriously.

The most prominent of the organizations for the raising of funds was the Society for the Propagation of the Faith.[32] It was begun in 1822 in Lyons,

[29] Heimbucher, op. cit., Vol. II, pp. 380, 381; Schwager, op. cit., p. 32.
[30] Schwager, op. cit., p. 32.
[31] Heimbucher, op. cit., Vol. II, p. 381.
[32] An excellent account of the Society for the Propagation of the Faith, with an extensive bibliography and voluminous footnote references to manuscript and printed sources, is Edward John Hickey, The Society for the Propagation of the Faith. Its Foundation, Organization and Success (The Catholic University of America Studies in American Church History, Vol. III, 1922, pp. x, 196). A much briefer account, by an official of the society, is Joseph Freri, The Society for the Propagation of the Faith and the Catholic Missions (New York, Press of the Society for the Propagation of the Faith, 1912, pp. 40). A standard biography of Pauline-Marie Jaricot, with warm partisanship for its subject, is M. J. Maurin, Vie Nouvelle de Pauline-Marie Jaricot, Fondatrice de la Propagation de la Foi et du Rosaire-Vivant (Brussells and Paris, Alfred Vromant et Cie, 1892, pp. xxii, 568. A German translation appeared at Trier in 1898). Another appropriate biography, but quite uncritical, is M. J. Maurin, Vie Complète de Marie Dubois, l'Inséperable Amie de Pauline-Marie Jaricot (no date or place of publication given, pp. 478). It is from these accounts, unless otherwise designated, that the material for this paragraph is drawn

one of the great industrial centres of France. Suggestions and preliminary steps which contributed to its formation were made by several persons, and apparently the credit for its foundation can be attributed to no single individual. In part it arose from the devotion and efforts of Pauline-Marie Jaricot (1799-1862), who in 1822 was in her early twenties and some time before had begun the collection of funds for missions to be contributed at the rate of one centime a week by each member of her circle. Suggestions, too, had come from the efforts of Bishop Du Bourg of New Orleans to raise funds for his work in the United States. Ideas were also early derived from other sources. The original rule outlined a purpose and method to which, in its main features, the society continued to adhere. The object was the extension of the Roman Catholic faith through assistance to missionaries in both hemispheres. Each member was to pray daily for missions and to contribute one centime a week. The society itself sent out no missionaries but aided those of other organizations. Here, in a city which was sharing in the prosperity of the machine age, began a movement through which tens of thousands, among them factory labourers, might contribute, even when their incomes were very small, to the spread of the Christian faith. The society early received Papal endorsement, and it regularly submitted to the Propaganda for approval its schedule of allocations to the missions which it aided. Throughout the nineteenth century it remained prevailingly French in leadership. Although subscriptions came from many lands, for decades more than half the funds were contributed by French Roman Catholics.[33] Since complaints were made that the organization was being used to further French interests,[34] eventually, but not until after 1914, the society was placed directly under Papal supervision and its headquarters were removed to Rome.[35]

A sister organization was the Association of the Holy Childhood. The purpose was the enlistment of the gifts of Christian children on behalf of non-Christian children outside of Christendom. The movement obviously took part of its inspiration from the Society for the Propagation of the Faith, for, like the latter, its members were to contribute one centime a week and were to pray for missions. Indeed, it is said that contact with Pauline-Marie Jaricot was the source of the suggestion which brought the Association into existence. The founder was Charles de Forbin-Janson, Bishop of Nancy, and 1843 was the year in which the first council of the organization was assembled. Like its sister society, the Association of the Holy Childhood was long French in

[33] Joseph Fréri, *Une Œuvre à Reformer La Propagation de la Foi* (printed for private circulation, c. 1919, pp. 28), pp. 5, 6.
[34] O'Connell, *Recollections of Seventy Years*, pp. 302-304.
[35] Lesourd, *L'Année Missionaire 1931*, pp. 301-304.

its leadership, but, also like the former, its supporting constituency was to be found in many lands, and eventually it was placed directly under Papal supervision. No missionaries were sent directly by the Association, and the funds which it raised were apportioned among various organizations. They were used to make possible the baptism of children in danger of death and to rear in the Christian faith such of the children so baptized as survived.[36] Here again was a popular movement enlisting the gifts of thousands in the propagation of the faith.

The Leopoldinen-Stiftung, or Leopoldine Association, was also akin to the Society for the Propagation of the Faith. Indeed, it adopted some of the essential principles and methods of the latter. The bulk of its funds, moreover, came from those in humble circumstances—labourers and servant girls. It drew its support, however, from Austria. It was organized in 1829. Thus, within less than a decade, the method initiated by the Society for the Propagation of the Faith had proved contagious and had spread outside of France. The organization was the direct outgrowth of an appeal from Frederic Rese, then Vicar-General of the see of Cincinnati, for help for the Roman Catholic Church in the United States. A leader in the formation of the Association was the Prince-Archbishop of Vienna, Leopold Maximilian, and the name was given in honour of the Archduchess Leopoldina, daughter of the Emperor Francis I of Austria and consort of the Emperor Pedro I of Brazil. The purpose was the assistance of missions not only in the United States but in other countries as well.[37]

Also similar to the Society for the Propagation of the Faith was the Ludwig-Missionsverein, an organization in Bavaria for the collection of funds. This, too, arose in response to the appeal of Frederic Rese for help for missions in the United States. The foundations were laid during a visit of Rese to Bavaria in 1828. However, the society was not formally organized until 1838. It had as its protector the King of Bavaria. The sums collected by it were to go to missions in North America and Asia, and to the Franciscans who were custodians of the Holy Sepulchre.[38]

L'Œuvre Apostolique, or the Apostolic Society, was initiated by Marie-Zoc du Chesne when, in 1838, she sent an altar ornament to the Gambier Islands, off the coast of Australia. From this modest beginning sprang an organization whose purpose it was to supply missionaries with objects necessary for their

---

[36] Lesourd, *op. cit.*, pp. 305-309; Schwager, *Die katholische Heidenmission der Gegenwart*, p. 37.

[37] Hickey, *op. cit.*, pp. 40-42.

[38] Roemer, *The Ludwig-Missionsverein and the Church in the United States*, pp. 2, 3; Hickey, *op. cit.*, pp. 42, 43.

ministry, such as vessels and vestments for the altar, crucifixes and medals, bicycles, and, later, automobiles. Mlle. Chesne headed the society until her death, in 1879, and by that time it had become so well established that it continued.[39]

L'Œuvre des Écoles d'Orient, or the Society of the Schools of the Orient, later l'Œuvre d'Orient, or the Society of the Orient, was founded at Paris in 1856. Its purpose was the assistance of missionary institutions in the Near East, chiefly schools, seminaries, and hospitals. By this aid it endeavoured to bring about the union with Rome of the non-Roman Catholic churches of the Near East. Its first director was the able and energetic Lavigerie, whom we are to meet again in a subsequent volume as Primate of Africa and Cardinal.[40]

The Society of St. Peter the Apostle was also French in origin. About 1889 the Vicar Apostolic of Nagasaki appealed to Madame Bigard for help in educating Japanese clergy. Mme. Bigard was a widow who after deep sorrows had dedicated herself and her daughter to the cause of missions. In this appeal these two women found their life work. Henceforth they gave themselves to finding funds for the preparation of a native clergy. After the death of Mme. Bigard, Mlle. Bigard suffered from a long illness and at her request the society was entrusted to the Franciscan Missionaries of Mary. They carried it on until 1919, when its headquarters were removed to Rome and it was placed directly under the Pope.[41]

The number of societies for raising funds for missions was very large. One list enumerates about 160 of them founded between 1815 and 1914.[42] Some had as their goal the assistance of missions in many countries and of many orders and congregations. Others confined their efforts to a particular country or to the support of a single organization. Of the last named type was one founded in 1899 in Lucerne for financial assistance to Capuchin missions. It undertook to have said each year four thousand masses for the living and the dead and to donate to the missions of the Capuchins the gifts arising from them.[43]

Taken together, these societies represented a movement of unprecedented proportions for the financial support of the spread of Roman Catholic Christianity by popular subscription. They were equalled only by a similar move-

---

[39] Lesourd, *op. cit.*, 322-325.

[40] Lesourd, *op. cit.*, pp. 325, 326.

[41] Lesourd, *op. cit.*, p. 309; *Fides News Service*, May 12, 1934; Devas, *Mother Mary of the Passion*, pp. 87-89.

[42] Arens, *Handbuch der katholischen Missionen* (1925 edition), pp. 306ff.

[43] *Statuten des seraphischen Messbundes zur Unterstützung der ausländischen Kapuziner-Missionen* (Uznach, Aberholzers Buchdruckerei [no date], pp. 8), *passim*.

ment among Protestants. Never before in human history had the spread of any set of ideas, religious or secular, been maintained by the voluntary gifts of so many millions of donors.

What the totals raised by these Roman Catholic societies were, we do not know. One estimate declares that in the nineteenth century they amounted to 1,606,370,500 marks, or, in the exchange of that day, not far from $400,000,000 or £80,000,000.[44] Another estimate suggests that somewhat more than half of this sum was spent upon Roman Catholic emigrants in various parts of the world. It also offers the conjecture that, since gifts greatly increased in the latter third of the century, by 1900 the amount given for work among non-Christians and Protestants was between 16,000,000 marks and 32,000,000 marks a year,[45] or, in the then rates of exchange, between $4,000,000 and $8,000,000 or £800,000 and £1,600,000 a year. In 1913 the receipts of the Society of the Propagation of the Faith are reported as 8,114,953 francs[46] and of the Association of the Holy Childhood as 4,150,820 francs,[47] or, at the current rates of exchange, about $1,600,000 and $800,000 (approximately £320,000 and £160,000) respectively.

Among the various nations the French had the leading share in the Roman Catholic missions of the nineteenth century. France took the place which in the preceding three centuries had been held by Spain and Portugal. It was in France that a major proportion of the new orders and congregations which gave themselves to the spread of the faith had their rise. It was a French-woman who founded the largest of the missionary sisterhoods, the Franciscan Missionaries of Mary. It was in France that the chief organizations for the raising of money, the Society for the Propagation of the Faith and the Association of the Holy Infancy, were begun and until after 1914 had their head-quarters. Until after 1914 the French contributed a higher proportion of the funds of these two societies than did any other people.[48] More Roman Catholic missionaries came from France than from any other one country. Indeed, in 1900 about seventy per cent. of the Roman Catholic missionaries were French.[49] It is interesting that the greatest age of French participation in the propagation of the faith was not the seventeenth and eighteenth centuries, when France was the outstanding Western European power and when the

[44] Baumgarten, *Das Wirken der katholischen Kirche auf dem Erdenrund*, pp. 406ff., cited in Schwager, *Katholische Heidenmission der Gegenwart*, p. 73.
[45] Schwager, *op. cit.*, p. 74.
[46] Lesourd, *L'Année Missionaire 1931*, pp. 301-304.
[47] Lesourd, *op. cit.*, pp. 305-309.
[48] Schwager, *op. cit.*, pp. 36-47, describes the place of France in Roman Catholic missions.
[49] C. J. H. Hayes, *France, a Nation of Patriots* (New York, Columbia University Press, 1930, pp. x, 487), p. 105.

monarchy was giving strong support to the Church, but the nineteenth century, when so much antipathy to the Church existed and when increasingly the Government was under the influence of the anti-clericals.

Part of the reason for French leadership is to be found in the colonial history of the period. The French acquired a larger colonial empire than did any of the other nations in which Roman Catholicism was the prevailing religion. Another cause was in the wealth which the introduction of machinery was bringing to the nation. However, these in themselves would not have been sufficient. It was the renewed life in the Church which was so actively manifested in France which was the major factor. Next to France as a source of nineteenth century Roman Catholic missionaries was Italy. During the fore part of the century Italy was again and again troubled by internal political disturbances. The annexation of the Papal States to the new Kingdom of Italy made necessary for the Church serious readjustments. It was not until late in the century that Italy had even a small colonial empire. In spite of these handicaps Italians were prominent in the spread of the faith. Most of the missionaries and the major part of the financial support came not from Southern but from Northern Italy. It was in the North that modern industry had its most extensive development.[50] As in other regions of other nations, this factor was important. The increased wealth and the augmented spirit of enterprise proved favourable to overseas religious expansion.

As the century wore on, Roman Catholics in several other countries took an increasingly active share in the propagation of their faith. This was true of Belgium. In 1830 the unnatural tie by which in 1815 the victorious Powers had bound the country to the Netherlands was severed and for the first time in modern history the land began an independent life. Belgium was overwhelmingly Roman Catholic and it was not surprising that the national spirit partly found vent in foreign missions. Then, too, the land, traditionally industrial and commercial, had its wealth rapidly augmented by the new machines and factories. In the 1880's the Congo Free State was brought under the administration of the King of the Belgians and in 1908 it was made the possession of Belgium and became the Belgian Congo. The acquisition of this huge colony gave a pronounced stimulus to Belgian missions.[51] In the Netherlands, Roman Catholics constituted a substantial minority. In 1853 Pope Pius IX restored the hierarchy, broken after the Protestant Reformation. Dutch Roman Catholics, encouraged by this step and by the colonial domains open to Dutch enterprise, rapidly grew in their participation in the foreign missions

[50] Schwager, *op. cit.*, pp. 30-34; Schmidlin-Braun, *Catholic Mission History*, pp. 569, 570.
[51] Schwager, *op. cit.*, pp. 47-50.

of their church. As was to be expected, some of their energy was directed to the Netherlands East Indies, but much of it also found vent in non-Dutch territory.[52]

In several parts of Germany and in Austria, as may be gathered from what was said a few paragraphs above, organizations arose to further missions.[53] The beginning of the acquisition of colonies by Germany in the 1880's was accompanied by a greatly increased enthusiasm in Germany for Roman Catholic missions. Many new local societies were formed for the support of missions. In 1914 German organizations had a little over two hundred thousand converts in German colonies and almost twice that number outside German territory.[54]

Roman Catholic Slavs and Magyars made relatively little effort to assist the spread of the faith. The Poles did more than any of the others, but Central Europeans had too scanty direct contact with non-Europeans and had too slight an industrial development to share in the currents of life which were impelling and enabling their Western European co-religionists to be active in propagating Christianity.[55]

Irish Roman Catholics had small part in spreading their faith among non-Christian peoples. Most of them were poor, and such resources as they possessed were almost entirely absorbed in assisting in the spiritual care of the huge Irish emigration to Great Britain, the United States, Canada, and Australia.[56] Spain and Portugal had sadly fallen from the leading place which had once been theirs in the expansion of Christianity. Both countries, especially Spain, suffered extensive losses of colonial possessions. In both lands civil disturbances and anti-clerical movements tended to focus the efforts of the Church upon self-preservation.[57] In 1837 a visitor found that a college in Valladolid which had prepared priests for the Philippines contained no students.[58] Yet in the second half of the century some recovery took place and new territories were entered. The Spanish Dominicans kept most of their missions in Asia. The Spanish Jesuits re-entered some of their former fields and made fresh efforts to prepare missionaries.[59] Beginning with the 1870's, when Africa was being explored and Portugal was expanding her African holdings, a re-

[52] Schwager, op. cit., pp. 50-52.
[53] Schwager, op. cit., pp. 52-63.
[54] F. S. Betten in Guilday, The Catholic Church in Contemporary Europe, 1919-1931, p. 113.
[55] Schwager, op. cit., p. 64.
[56] J. F. Kenney in Guilday, op. cit., pp. 160, 161.
[57] Schwager, op. cit., pp. 34, 35.
[58] Borrow, The Bible in Spain, p. 197.
[59] M. R. Madden in Guilday, op. cit., p. 309; Schwager, op. cit., pp. 34, 35.

vived interest awoke in Portuguese missions, seminaries were founded for the training of missionaries, and financial aid was accorded by the state.[60]

In Great Britain, Roman Catholics were too small a minority to assume much of the burden of the propagation of their faith.

In the United States the energies of Roman Catholics were so absorbed in making provision for the religious care of the increasing flood of immigrants of that faith that they could give little attention to other lands. Not until the opening decades of the twentieth century did they begin taking much independent share in foreign missions.

In every country participation or non-participation in the missionary enterprise of the Roman Catholic Church was dependent in large part upon such non-religious factors as the presence or absence of colonial possessions, of foreign trade, and of industrialization. However, we must remember that, while these were important, had it not been for inward spiritual life and deep religious conviction, colonies, commerce, and the mounting wealth accumulated through the machine would not have given rise to missions.

Over all this varied activity and over all these many organizations for the spread of the Roman Catholic form of the Christian faith, the Papacy exercised close and careful supervision. Never before, indeed, had the See of Peter had such complete and intimate direction of the propagation of Roman Catholic Christianity. In the Middle Ages time-distances had been too great to permit of much control, particularly on the far periphery. Moreover, kings and princes frequently took the lead and, when they recognized Rome at all, often paid only nominal allegiance to its authority. In the sixteenth, seventeenth, and eighteenth centuries, the autocratic rulers of the main countries from which missionaries went insisted upon such extensive dictation that as a rule Rome was constrained to give automatic approval to their ecclesiastical acts. Now, in the nineteenth century, largely because of the weakening of the tie between Church and state and the growth of ultramontanism with its enhanced submission of all the Roman Catholic Church to the Papacy, Rome successfully asserted its authority over every phase of the expansion of its form of the faith. In common with the other aspects of the Church's life, missions were more and more under the direction of the Vatican.

The chief instrument for this Papal direction was the Congregation for the Propagation of the Faith. The Propaganda, to give that organ its brief familiar name, had suffered severely under Napoleon I. In 1808, indeed, when Napoleon occupied the States of the Church, it was discontinued.[61] However, in 1814 it

[60] Schwager, *op. cit.*, p. 35.
[61] Schwager, *op. cit.*, p. 19.

was resumed and in 1817 much of its property was restored.[62] The Propaganda, too, suffered from confiscations by the new Kingdom of Italy.[63] Yet, thanks to the liberality of Popes and of dues which came to it automatically, it continued to enjoy a large income.[64] Moreover, some of the nineteenth century Popes showed it marked favour. Before his election to the Papacy, Gregory XVI (reigned 1831-1846) had been Prefect of the Propaganda. With the insight gained from that experience, as Pope he was able to give that Congregation intelligent support.[65] In 1908 Pope Pius X made important changes in the Propaganda. In a number of lands in which Protestants were in the majority, notably Great Britain, the United States, Canada, Newfoundland, and Holland, the Roman Catholic Church was deemed to have developed to a point where its supervision could be placed on a par with that in countries which were traditionally Roman Catholic, and the tutelage of the Propaganda was withdrawn.[66]

One of the objects of Roman Catholic missions was to bring the Church in each land to sufficient maturity to be served by its own clergy and to be governed by a hierarchy on an equality with that in nations where the Church was well established. In the development of a hierarchy four stages were normal. First was the foundation of mission stations, second the grouping of these mission stations into a prefecture apostolic, third the raising of the prefecture apostolic to a vicariate apostolic, and lastly the transformation of the vicariate into a diocese akin to dioceses in Roman Catholic countries.[67] Increasing efforts were made to call forth and rear an indigenous clergy. To this both Rome and local synods gave much attention.[68] In 1907, in Asia, Africa, and the islands of the Pacific, 135 seminaries with over 5,000 students were reported.[69] After 1914 the growth of a native clergy and hierarchy was to be greatly accelerated.

Protestant organization for the propagation of Christianity displayed an

[62] *Ibid.*
[63] *Ibid.*
[64] Lesourd, *L'Année Missionaire 1931*, p. 32.
[65] Baudrillart in Descamps, *Histoire Générale Comparée des Missions*, p. 513.
[66] Schmidlin, *Catholic Mission Theory*, p. 128; Williams, *The Catholic Church in Action*, p. 121.
[67] Schmidlin, *op. cit.*, pp. 285, 286. For a technical, well documented study of the functions, powers, and duties of vicars apostolic and prefects apostolic, see Francis Joseph Winslow, *Vicars and Prefects Apostolic* (Maryknoll, N. Y., The Catholic Foreign Mission Society of America, 1924, pp. iv, 141), *passim*.
[68] Huonder, *Der einheimische Klerus den Heidenländern*, pp. 4-6.
[69] Huonder, *op. cit.*, p. 269.

even more spectacular growth than did that of the Roman Catholics and showed greater flexibility in adapting itself to the conditions of the new age.

New societies and associations which helped to make the nineteenth century so memorable in the spread of the faith began earlier in Protestant than in Roman Catholic circles. In the latter they were not to have much of a beginning until after the Napoleonic Wars. In the former several of the leading ones arose during the stormy period of the French Revolution and the subsequent wars. Between 1789 and 1815 in Great Britain, the United States, and the Netherlands, some of what quickly became the leading organizations for Protestant foreign missions came into being. This was in spite of the fact that all of these lands were deeply involved in the wars and disturbances of the period. So great was the rising tide of life in Protestantism that it did not wait for the re-establishment of peace to undertake measures for the extension of the faith. In a crumbling world and in the face of widespread religious scepticism, earnest minorities within Protestantism were already building for a new day. While the French Revolution was destroying the old order in Europe, impelled by their Christian purpose, humble men and women were initiating movements which were to disseminate their faith more widely than even the ideals of the French Revolution were carried. The new Protestant missionary movement was largely the outgrowth of the awakenings of the seventeenth and especially of the eighteenth century and was to be reinforced by the many revivals of the nineteenth century. As we have suggested, it was chiefly an expression of the strain within Protestantism which is sometimes known as Evangelicalism. It was this strain which had so vivid a manifestation in Pietism and Moravianism, in the Great Awakening and the Wesleyan movement, and in the many revivals in the nineteenth century. It made much of the transformation of the individual through the Christian Gospel and it also gave rise to many efforts for the elimination of social ills and for the collective betterment of mankind.

It was in Great Britain that the first of the new societies had their origin. During the fore part of the nineteenth century the British held the leading place in the spread of the Protestant forms of Christianity. When the world as a whole is viewed, as far back as the seventeenth century they had the major share in the geographic extension of Protestantism. It was through them that the largest overseas Protestant enclaves, the Thirteen Colonies, were set up. The majority of the population of these colonies were of British stock. As we saw in the preceding volume, moreover, the British, either colonials or directly from the British Isles, had numerous missions among North American Indians and the Negroes of the West Indies and gave financial support to some of the continental missionaries in India. Yet in the eighteenth century continental Protestants, German, Dutch, and Danish, had more far-flung missions among non-Europeans than did the British. German Pietists and Moravians were particularly prominent. Now, in the course of the first half of the nineteenth century, the British became more outstanding. British Protestantism was dominant in the new nations which were being founded in Australia and New Zealand, and it was prominent in the white communities in South Africa and in Newfoundland and the rapidly growing Canada. From Great Britain more than from any other country issued Protestant missionaries to non-European peoples.

The reasons for this British leadership are obvious. It was in Great Britain that the Industrial Revolution first took effect, and it was Great Britain which first experienced the vast increase of wealth which the machine made possible. Great Britain led in the commerce and the empire building of the century. She was the greatest colonial power of the period. Not even the Spanish or the Portuguese colonial empires of the sixteenth, seventeenth, and eighteenth centuries equalled the nineteenth century British Empire in population and area or were so widely scattered. Never before had any one regime ruled over so many millions in so many different parts of the globe. This vast increase in material resources and this contact with non-European peoples were matched by a mounting tide of life in the churches. Great Britain was being stirred religiously by awakening after awakening and movement after movement. It is not strange that in the nineteenth century, and especially in the fore part of the century, the British had so prominent a part in the spread of the Protestant forms of Christianity.

The first of the organizations through which this enhanced participation of the British in the expansion of Christianity was effected was what eventually was called the Baptist Missionary Society. This body had its origin in the purpose of William Carey. William Carey (1761-1834) was born in Paulers Pury, a small village in Northampton in the English Midlands.[70] Both his

[70] A large number of lives of Carey have appeared. The best are: Eustace Carey, *Memoir of William Carey, D.D.*, with an introductory essay by Jeremiah Chaplin (Hartford, Canfield and Robins, 1837, pp. 468), containing a number of important letters and other writings of William Carey; John Clark Marshman, *The Life and Times of Carey, Marshman, and Ward, Embracing the History of the Serampore Mission* (London, Longman, Brown, Green, Longmans & Roberts, 1859, pp. xxvi, 511), containing very little on Carey's life before going to India; George Smith, *The Life of William Carey, D.D., Shoemaker and Missionary* (London, John Murray, 1885, pp. xiii, 463), based upon careful research, especially in India; F. Deaville Walker, *William Carey, Missionary Pioneer and Statesman* (London, Student Christian Movement, 1926, pp. 320), based upon careful research and devoting more than a third of its space to the pre-India years; S. Pearce Carey, *William Carey, D.D., Fellow of Linnaean Society* (New York, George H. Doran Co., preface 1923, pp. xvi, 428), by a great-grandson, a labour of love, very carefully done. The following sketch has used all of these lives.

father and grandfather had taught the village school and had been parish clerk. Carey was, therefore, reared in a family that knew something of books. He was accustomed to the reading of the Bible and to regular attendance at the parish church. He early developed an interest in the animal, plant, and insect life about him. He had, too, a great liking for reading and for books of travel. From this grew in part his study of geography and his passion to master other languages. Yet the family was in humble circumstances, and when Carey was fourteen he was apprenticed to a shoemaker and cobbler. While an apprentice, through contact with dissenters, especially a fellow apprentice, Carey came into an earnest religious experience and a little later joined himself to the Baptists. He married early, and earned a living for himself and his family by teaching school, by mending and making shoes, and by preaching. For a time he was pastor of the Baptist chapel, teacher, and shoemaker at Moulton, not far from Kettering. From there he moved to a pastorate in Leicester. He was an indefatigable student. He acquired several languages. He maintained his interest in travel and geography and read the *Voyages* of Captain James Cook which were then revealing the Pacific area to the English-speaking world and were arousing much discussion. The combination of his passion for geography and his warm religious conviction led to a growing concern for missions. He was profoundly influenced by John Eliot and David Brainerd, of whose efforts for the American Indians we have spoken in the preceding volume. These, with Paul, became his great heroes. He prepared *An Enquiry into the Obligations of Christians to Use Means for the Conversion of the Heathens.*[71] In this he maintained that the New Testament command to "preach the Gospel to every creature" was binding not only upon the original Apostles but also upon Christians of the present time. He gave an outline of the history of efforts of Christians to fulfil the command and a survey of the population of the entire world with the religions professed by the various peoples, he urged the practicability of doing something towards conveying the Christian message to non-Christians, and he suggested feasible steps. He continued to urge the project upon his fellow Baptist ministers. Finally, at a meeting of the Northampton Baptist Association at Nottingham in May, 1792, he presented his convictions in a sermon which had as its text the second and third verses of the forty-fourth chapter of Isaiah and which contained as central phrases words which his hearers were

---

[71] William Carey, *An Enquiry into the Obligations of Christians to Use Means for the Conversion of the Heathens. In which the Religious State of the Different Nations of the World, the Success of the Former Undertakings, and the Practicability of Further Undertakings are Considered* (Leicester, Ann Ireland, 1792, pp. 87). This was reprinted by photographic reproduction (London, Baptist Missionary Society, 1934).

not to forget: "Expect great things from God. Attempt great things for God."[72] As a result of the sermon and of Carey's perseverance a meeting was called at Kettering, October 2, 1792, at which was organized what was called the Particular Baptist Society for Propagating the Gospel amongst the Heathen,[73] a name which within a few years was superseded by the Baptist Missionary Society. The funds of the society were to be raised by subscription. Carey himself had proposed that they range from a penny a week up,[74] an interesting foreshadowing of the plan of the Roman Catholic Society for the Propagation of the Faith. Actually any person who contributed £10 or more in a lump sum or 10s 6d annually was to be considered a member.[75]

Carey became one of the original contingent sent by the society. Because of what he had learned in Cook's *Voyages* he had hoped to go to Tahiti, but through information supplied by an eccentric and enthusiastic physician, John Thomas, the enterprise was diverted to India.[76] In India Carey was to have a long and distinguished career. We are to trace his story further when, in a later volume, we reach that country.

The organization of the Baptist Missionary Society is usually called the inception of the modern Protestant foreign missionary enterprise. In one sense this is not in accord with the facts. As we saw in the preceding volume, more than two centuries before Carey Protestants had had missions among non-Christians, and the eighteenth century had been marked by a rising tide of Protestant efforts in many parts of the world to win pagans to the Christian faith. Yet in another sense Carey marks the beginning of a new era. He seems to have been the first Anglo-Saxon Protestant either in America or in Great Britain to propose that Christians take concrete steps to bring their Gospel to all the human race. His *Enquiry* endeavored to give a comprehensive survey of mankind.[77] While because of the divided state of the Church he advocated the formation of a denominational missionary society, he wished

---

[72] S. Pearce Carey, *op. cit.*, p. 83. When the present author was in Nottingham in June, 1936, he found that on the site of the chapel where Carey preached this sermon was a building bearing the name *Theosophical Hall*. Thus a cult professing to propagate a form of an Indian religion had been erected on the spot where a movement was begun which resulted in a mission to India.

[73] *Four Pages (in facsimile) From the Original Minutes of the Meeting held on October the Second, 1792, at Kettering Showing the Formation of the Baptist Missionary Society* (London, Baptist Missionary Society, no date) ; F. A. Cox, *History of the Baptist Missionary Society from 1792 to 1842* (London, T. Ward & Co., 2 vols., 1842), Vol. I, p. 17 ; S. Pearce Carey, *op. cit.*, pp. 88ff.

[74] Carey, *Enquiry*, Section V.

[75] *Periodical Accounts Relative to a Society formed among the Particular Baptists for Propagating the Gospel among the Heathen*, No. 1, p. 3.

[76] S. Pearce Carey, *op. cit.*, p. 96.

[77] Carey, *Enquiry*, pp. 30-62.

all Christians to recognize their responsibility for carrying the Gospel to all.[78] The first annual report of this Baptist society contained an address to fellow Christians at large calling upon them to engage in preaching the Gospel to those who in the vocabulary of the day were called "the heathen."[79] The idea of giving the Christian message to all mankind was as old as the New Testament itself. Zinzendorf and the Moravians had cherished it. Yet up to this time the various missionary societies organized by Anglo-Saxons in Great Britain and America had not seemed to share this dream. They had confined themselves to particular fields. Even the Society for the Propagation of the Gospel in Foreign Parts had had in mind only the British possessions,[80] and while the Society for Promoting Christian Knowledge had ventured outside the British domains, it was designed peculiarly for British territory[81] and appears not to have thought in world-wide terms. It was one of the distinguishing features of this humble shoemaker-teacher-clergyman of the Midlands that he dreamed and dreamed persistently of the needs of the entire human race and called upon his fellow Christians to make the dream come true. His vision proved contagious. He marks the beginning in British and American Protestantism of an enterprise which planned in terms of the globe. Protestants of the continent of Europe were also profoundly influenced. William Carey and the society which arose in response to his faith were in fact the beginning of an astounding series of Protestant efforts to reach the entire world with the Christian message.

Carey's hope that Christians of other denominations would join in spreading the Christian message was partly fulfilled in the formation of the Missionary Society, later called the London Missionary Society, in 1795. Indeed, it was Carey who was largely responsible for the undertaking. It was a letter of his from India which led to the calling of a meeting out of which came the new society.[82] In this movement no one man stood out as leader. A number had an active share.[83] The society was designed as an instrument through which Christians from many different denominations could join in propagating their faith. It was hoped that in it Dissenters, Methodists, and members of the Church of England would co-operate,[84] and it was early resolved "not to send

[78] Carey, *Enquiry*, Section V.
[79] *Periodical Accounts*, etc., No. 1, pp. 8-13.
[80] Pascoe, *Two Hundred Years of the S.P.G.*, Vol. I, pp. 1ff.
[81] Allen and McClure, *Two Hundred Years: The History of the Society for Promoting Christian Knowledge*, p. 22.
[82] Lovett, *The History of the London Missionary Society 1795-1895*, Vol. I, p. 5.
[83] See the biographies of these in Morison, *The Fathers and Founders of the London Missionary Society, passim.*
[84] Lovett, *op. cit.*, Vol. I, pp. 15, 16.

Presbyterianism or any other form of church government, but the glorious Gospel of the Blessed God."[85] However, the society was intended primarily for those of "evangelical sentiments,"[86] namely those who held in general to the beliefs represented by the Moravians, the Wesleyans, and those who had shared in the various revivals within Protestantism, particularly in the seventeenth and eighteenth centuries. While in practice the society drew chiefly from Congregational churches, others, notably Presbyterians, long had a part in it.[87] Like Carey, the London Missionary Society held the entire world in its purview. The sermon preached at the organization of the society spoke of the field as the world.[88] Actually, too, the society undertook missions in many different islands and countries.

In 1799 what eventually came to be called the Church Missionary Society[89] was begun. As its name suggests, it was a channel through which members of the Church of England could carry on missions to non-Christians. Since the older missionary agencies within the Established Church, of which the outstanding ones were the Society for Promoting Christian Knowledge and the Society for the Propagation of the Gospel in Foreign Parts, confined their efforts almost entirely to the British Empire, the need came to be felt for an organization which would reach out to non-Christians not only within but also outside British territories and particularly to Africa and Asia.[90] The founders were Evangelicals, namely, those representing the revivals of the eighteenth century who remained within the Church of England. The project was the outgrowth of a rising interest in missions. Already in Calcutta and Bengal beginnings had been made. Charles Grant, who was in the service of the East India Company, had been brought by the tragic death of two of his children to a warm Christian faith, and had made efforts to inaugurate efforts for non-Christians.[91] David Brown, a protégé of that Charles Simeon[92] who was to become famous as an Evangelical leader in Cambridge, was in charge of an orphanage in Calcutta.[93] Through Granville Sharp, who was associated

[85] Morison, op. cit., Vol. II, p. 1.

[86] Lovett, op. cit., Vol. I, pp. 15, 16, 19, 20.

[87] In 1890, for instance, several Presbyterian churches as well as Congregational unions were each invited to appoint a director of the Society.—Lovett, op. cit., Vol. II, p. 726.

[88] Lovett, op. cit., Vol. I, p. 27.

[89] On the name, see Hole, Early History of the Church Missionary Society, p. 41.

[90] Proceedings of the Church Missionary Society for Africa and the East, Vol. I (London, 1805, pp. 479), pp. 8, 9; Hole, op. cit., p. 37.

[91] Henry Morris, The Life of Charles Grant (London, John Murray, 1904, pp. xviii, 404), pp. 56-69, 92-143.

[92] On Charles Simeon see William Carus, editor, Memoirs of the Life of the Rev. Charles Simeon (New York, Robert Carter, 1847, pp. xxvii, 491), passim.

[93] Hole, op. cit., pp. 4-7.

with that intimate circle of Evangelicals who centered at Clapham,[94] was begun, in 1787, Sierra Leone, for freed Negroes from England.[95] The initiative in actually forming the new organization came from the Eclectic Society, which was composed of clergy.[96] While the founders were not unfriendly to the London Missionary Society (both societies, indeed, were inaugurated in the same hotel room),[97] it was their belief that members of the Church of England could best further the spread of the Christian faith through an organization which held to the principles of that church and which was connected with the Evangelical part of that communion.[98] William Wilberforce, who had been led by Evangelical convictions to devote his charm and his political ability to the fight against Negro slavery,[99] was asked to become president, but declined. However, he and such other members of the Clapham group as Charles Grant, now returned to England, and Samuel Thornton were among the vice-presidents.[100] The earliest missionaries were not English, but were obtained from a training school in Berlin.[101] When the Church Missionary Society was founded, the Evangelicals, on whom it depended, were still a minority in the Church of England and were bitterly opposed by many, even of the bishops.[102] However, as the decades passed the Evangelicals increased and became accepted, and the resources of the society were augmented. In time, too, it drew support from Ireland. There before 1814, several missionary societies had been organized, largely interdenominational.[103] In 1814, as the result of a deputation from the Church Missionary Society, the Hibernian Church Missionary Society was formed.[104]

In the year that the Church Missionary Society came into being, 1799, the Religious Tract Society was organized.[105] The man chiefly responsible for the latter was George Burder, the minister of an Independent congregation at Coventry. He had been writing and circulating religious pamphlets, or tracts,

[94] On Granville Sharp, see Stephen, *Essays in Ecclesiastical Biography,* Vol. II, pp. 203ff., pp. 178ff.; Colquhoun, *William Wilberforce, His Friends and His Times, passim.* On "the Clapham Sect," see Stephen, *op. cit.,* Vol. II.

[95] Hole, *op. cit.,* pp. 17, 18.

[96] Hole, *op. cit.,* p. 29.

[97] Stock, *The History of the Church Missionary Society,* Vol. I, p. 68.

[98] Hole, *op. cit.,* p. 29.

[99] Colquhoun, *op. cit.,* pp. 27ff.

[100] Stock, *op. cit.,* Vol. I, p. 69; Colquhoun, *op. cit.,* pp. 269, 308ff.; Morris, *The Life of Charles Grant,* pp 225ff

[101] Stock, *op cit.,* Vol. I, p. 82.

[102] Stock, *op. cit.,* Vol. I, pp. 38, 39.

[103] Bland, *How the Church Missionary Society Came to Ireland,* pp. 50, 82, 83.

[104] Bland, *op. cit.,* pp. 101ff.

[105] William Jones, *The Jubilee Memorial of the Religious Tract Society. Containing a Record of its Origin, Proceedings, and Results* A.D. *1799* to A.D. *1849* (London, The Religious Tract Society, 1850, pp. viii, 698), pp. 12ff., 71.

and felt the need for a body in which other like-minded men could join to further the spread of the Christian faith to the masses at home and abroad through this form of the printed page. In the new enterprise both Nonconformists and clergymen of the Church of England joined.

In 1804 came the formation of the British and Foreign Bible Society.[106] Several societies already existed for the distribution of the Scriptures.[107] However, the new one was to be far more inclusive in its scope. The initiative which led to the founding of the British and Foreign Bible Society came from Thomas Charles, an Evangelical who had left the Established Church and had become pastor of a Calvinistic Methodist congregation in Wales. He had been endeavouring to supply Bibles in Welsh to those without them in the principality. Out of this local effort came the larger one. Granville Sharp presided at the first meeting and Lord Teignmouth (John Shore), another of the Clapham circle, and who had begun, while in service in India, his rise from obscurity,[108] was the first president.[109] Charles Grant, William Wilberforce, and Henry Thornton were among the vice-presidents.[110] From the outset, the plans of the society were ambitious. Members of the Church of England, Nonconformists, and some Protestants of the continent of Europe joined in it.[111] Its first annual report showed interest in England, Scotland, Ireland, and the continent and told of a society formed at Nuremberg through the encouragement of its example.[112] Its activities were to extend to every continent.

Before the appearance of any of these new societies the Methodists had been engaged in spreading the faith. As we saw in the preceding volume, in the 1780's Thomas Coke, a close friend of John Wesley, had become active in propagating Methodism in America, including the West Indies. Until his death, in 1814, on his way to the East, Coke was the leader in Methodist missions to non-Occidental peoples.[113] Beginning in 1790,[114] the Wesleyan Con-

---

[106] Canton, *A History of the British and Foreign Bible Society*, Vol. I, pp. 1ff.; George Browne, *The History of the British and Foreign Bible Society* (London, 2 vols., 1859), Vol. I, pp. 2ff.

[107] John Owen, *The History and the Origin and First Ten Years of the British and Foreign Bible Society* (London, Tilling and Hughes, 2 vols., 1816), Vol. I, pp. 19ff., much fuller on the origin and background than Canton or Browne.

[108] Colquhoun, *op. cit.*, pp. 316ff.

[109] Canton, *op. cit.*, Vol. I, p. 19.

[110] Canton, *op. cit.*, Vol. I, p. 20.

[111] Canton, *op. cit.*, Vol. I, p. 15.

[112] *Reports of the British and Foreign Bible Society, with Extracts of Correspondence &c.*, Vol. I, 1805-1810 (London, pp. xvi, 399 +), pp. 11ff.

[113] Two biographies of Coke are Samuel Drew, *The Life of the Rev. Thomas Coke, LL.D.* (London, Conference Office, 1817, pp. xix, 391) and Warren A. Candler, *Life of Thomas Coke* (Nashville, Tenn., Publishing House M. E. Church, South, 1923, pp. 408).

[114] Findlay and Holdsworth, *The History of the Wesleyan Methodist Missionary Society*, Vol. I, p. 65.

ference gradually made organizational provision to assist him. In 1804 the Conference enlarged this to a Committee of Finance and Advice.[115] Beginning with 1813 auxiliary societies were formed, partly to keep for Methodist missions money which was being given by Methodists through the London Missionary Society.[116] Eventually, in 1817-1818, the Wesleyan Methodist Missionary Society was formed as an official organ of the Conference.[117]

The societies thus far mentioned, together with the older Society for Promoting Christian Knowledge and the Society for the Propagation of the Gospel in Foreign Parts, were the major organizations through which English Christianity was extended among non-Occidental peoples. The Society for the Propagation of the Gospel in Foreign Parts continued to give its attention chiefly to the British Empire. It worked in practically every British colony. Of the colonial, Indian, and missionary bishoprics planted by the Church of England the large majority were either an outgrowth of its labours or were aided by it.[118] The Society for Promoting Christian Knowledge also gave financial aid to many of these bishoprics.[119] The latter organization took active steps to provide religious ministrations for the flood of emigration which issued from the British Isles.[120] Both societies were reinforced by the new tide of life which came from the Oxford Movement.[121]

As time passed, other societies were founded, some of them by Nonconformists, some by adherents of the Church of England.[122] Among the most notable of the latter were the Colonial and Continental Church Society, begun in 1823,[123] the Church Pastoral Aid Society (for the purpose of increasing the number of working clergymen in the Church of England),[124] and the Colonial Bishoprics Fund, founded in 1841.[125]

Thanks partly to the generous assistance given from England, and in striking contrast with the absence of bishops in the Thirteen Colonies, bishoprics

---

[115] Findlay and Holdsworth, op. cit., Vol. I, pp. 36, 69.
[116] Findlay and Holdsworth, op. cit., Vol. I, pp. 36ff.
[117] Findlay and Holdsworth, op. cit., Vol. I, p. 72.
[118] Pascoe, Two Hundred Years of the S.P.G., p. x.
[119] Pascoe, op. cit., p. 753; Allen and McClure, Two Hundred Years: The History of the Society for Promoting Christian Knowledge, pp. 402-429, 513-527.
[120] Allen and McClure, op. cit., pp. 402-429.
[121] Morgan, The Catholic Revival and Missions, pp. 1-6; Giles, The Constitutional History of the Australian Church, p. 76.
[122] See a list, with dates of organization, in Beach and Fahs, World Missionary Atlas, pp. 34-42.
[123] Carpenter, Church and People, 1789-1889, p. 36.
[124] Ibid.
[125] Giles, op. cit., p. 141; Carpenter, op. cit., p. 431; Allen and McClure, op. cit., pp. 433, 434; Morgan, op. cit., p. 12.

of the Anglican communion were rapidly created in the leading British colonies.[126] Originally the overseas metropolitans were under the Archbishop of Canterbury, but eventually they were given an independent status.[127] In synods of the Anglican communion in the colonies, laymen were accorded active participation before that status was conceded to them in England.[128]

In Scotland formal efforts to spread the Christian faith in other lands did not take on large proportions quite so early as in England. Yet in 1796 the Scottish Missionary Society and the Glasgow Missionary Society were organized.[129] Even before that time Scotland had had a share, although a slight one, in the support of the spread of Christianity overseas. The Scotch Society for Propagating Christian Knowledge, begun near the outset of the eighteenth century, while having Scotland as its primary field, contributed to the mission among the North American Indians of which David Brainerd was the most famous member. Indeed, in 1762, long after the death of Brainerd, the General Assembly of the Church of Scotland authorized a collection on behalf of this mission.[130] Beginning with 1753, missionaries had gone from the General Associate Synod of the Secession Church, a body which had arisen in the seventeen-thirties by division from the Church of Scotland,[131] to settlers in Pennsylvania,[132] and, with 1765, to colonists in Nova Scotia.[133] Yet in 1796 the General Assembly of the Church of Scotland, after full debate, rejected suggestions from two of the synods that the Church take steps for "the diffusion of the Gospel over the world."[134] However, in 1821 the Glasgow Missionary Society began a mission in Kaffraria,[135] in 1823 the Scottish Missionary Society commenced work in India,[136] in 1824 the General Assembly of the Church of Scotland appointed a committee on foreign missions, and in 1831 the first missionary sent out under this committee, Alexander Duff, to whose distinguished career we shall recur in a later volume, arrived in India.[137]

---

[126] See a list of the earlier ones in Allen and McClure, *op. cit.*, pp. 430-452.

[127] Clarke, *Constitutional Church Government*, pp. 11, 12, 28; Morgan, *op. cit.*, pp. 14ff.

[128] Clarke, *op. cit.*, pp. 12, 13.

[129] Mackichan, *The Missionary Ideal in the Scottish Churches*, p. 74.

[130] Mackichan, *op. cit.*, pp. 69ff.

[131] Barr, *The United Free Church of Scotland*, pp. 52ff.

[132] M'Kerrow, *History of the Foreign Missions of the Secession and United Presbyterian Church*, pp. 5, 7.

[133] M'Kerrow, *op. cit.*, p. 37.

[134] Mackichan, *op. cit.*, pp. 74ff.

[135] Mackichan, *op. cit.*, p. 105.

[136] Mackichan, *op. cit.*, p. 107.

[137] Mackichan, *op. cit.*, pp. 112ff.; Robert W. Weir, *A History of the Foreign Missions of the Church of Scotland* (Edinburgh, R. and R. Clark, 1900. pp. xiv, 199), pp. 31ff.

From then onward, through various bodies,[138] the participation of the churches
of Scotland in the spread of Christianity fairly rapidly mounted.

Although it was in the British Isles that the first of the new societies arose
which led in the spread of Christianity in the nineteenth century, it was from
the United States that the majority of the missionaries and more than half of
the funds of the Protestant missionary enterprise eventually came.

At first thought it seems strange that the United States should have had so
prominent a part in the propagation of the Protestant forms of Christianity
the world around. Unlike Portugal, Spain, Holland, France, and Great Britain,
the countries which led in the spread of Christianity in the sixteenth, seventeenth, and eighteenth centuries, and unlike France and Great Britain, which
were so prominent in the expansion of the faith in the nineteenth century,
until 1898 the United States had no overseas possessions. Even after that year
its territories outside North America were comparatively small and the large
majority of its foreign missionaries were not in them. When, in the latter part
of the nineteenth century, missions from the United States became especially
prominent, they were found mostly in lands in which Americans had by no
means the leading place in foreign trade. In India, where missionaries from
the United States were second in numbers only to the British, and in the
Near East, where, in Protestant circles, they were dominant, commerce from
the United States was relatively unimportant and political control was entirely absent. Moreover, by the opening years of the twentieth century a very
large proportion of the personnel and funds of American Protestant missions
were coming not from the Atlantic seaboard, the region from which the bulk
of the foreign trade issued, but from the interior, the Mississippi Valley north
of the Ohio and the mouth of the Missouri, which apart from foreign missions
had almost no direct contact with the lands to which missionaries went. Then,
too, during the nineteenth century the United States was engrossed in westward expansion across North America and in developing the unimaginably
rich virgin resources of its huge continental domains. The churches in the
older states were engaged in a vast missionary enterprise to extend the Christian faith among the settlements on the frontier, the immigrants from Europe,
the Indians, and the millions of Negroes. It seemed unbelievable that any
energy could be available to spread the faith to other lands.

On second thought, however, the prominent part of the Protestants of the
United States in the world-wide expansion of Christianity is understandable.
The United States was growing rapidly in wealth, in population, and in terri-

[138] For a list of the societies see Beach and Fahs, *op. cit.*, pp. 43, 44. See also Fleming,
A History of the Church in Scotland 1843-1874, pp. 65, 66, 87, 144, 148.

tory. Expansion, pioneering, and adventure were in the air. In the course of the nineteenth century the American people occupied the Mississippi Valley, obtained possession of the vast area between the Mississippi and the Pacific, spanned the western prairies and the Rocky Mountains with roads and railways, and mounted in numbers from a little over five millions in 1800 to nearly seventy-six millions in 1900, and to nearly ninety-two millions in 1910. New mechanical appliances, many of which they invented, coupled with the natural resources of their land, piled up wealth. At the same time, a series of religious awakenings brought fresh life to the Protestant churches. By tradition the majority of the white population of the country were Protestant. The combination of the spirit of the nation, of mounting material resources, and of growing religious zeal brought the most remarkable spread of Christianity which the century was to see in connexion with any one nation. In the United States itself a home missionary movement more than kept pace with the rise in population. As we are to record in later chapters in this volume, about half of the huge Negro population was won to membership in Protestant communions, a large percentage of the widely scattered Indian population was similarly attracted, an increasing proportion of the older native white stock allied itself with the Protestant churches, and for the most part the newer immigration of Protestant background was held to the faith. At the same time Protestant missionaries from the United States went to all of the continents and to many of the islands of the sea. By 1914 the leadership and initiative in the Protestant foreign missionary enterprise were passing into the hands of Americans. British and continental Europeans still shared in that leadership, but the new movements for augmenting the missionary staff and for co-operation between Protestants on a world-wide scale were now becoming more and more indebted to the United States.

As between the Protestantism which spread from the United States and that which came from Great Britain, few if any striking differences existed. Both issued chiefly from what was known as Evangelicalism, fed by the religious awakenings of the eighteenth and nineteenth centuries. Both tended to seek the conversion of the individual rather than of the group. Both made much of education, the healing of the sick, and the preparation and distribution of literature, including especially the Bible. However, particularly as the century wore on, Protestant missions from America differed slightly from those from Great Britain. The Protestant Episcopal Church did not loom so large in missions from the United States as did the Church of England in those from Great Britain. Probably, too, American missionaries tended to work more for the transformation of society as a whole than did British missionaries. To this latter generalization, however, many exceptions could be cited.

Back of the emergence of new Protestant societies in the United States which were prominent in the expansion of Christianity in the nineteenth century was a long development of interest in missions and a rising tide of missionary activity. As we saw in the preceding volume,[139] many of the colonists had been zealous in spreading the faith among their fellows, among the Negroes, and among the Indians. American Moravians had participated in the support of the work of their church among non-Christians outside the Thirteen Colonies.[140] After the United States achieved its independence, the Protestants of the country became even more active in propagating their faith among non-Christians. Financial support was largely cut off from Great Britain.[141] The spirit of nationalism begot a new initiative. Baptists and Methodists experienced a remarkable growth.[142] In New England in 1797 what was sometimes known as the Second Great Awakening broke out among the Congregational churches, and continued for a number of years.[143] Throughout other parts of the land about the turn of the century notable revivals began. As we have seen and are to see again, this series of revivals had an even greater and more widespread effect than did the earlier Great Awakening. From it came a number of missionary societies. As early as 1773 an organization was formed at Newport, Rhode Island, by Samuel Hopkins and Ezra Stiles, for the education and support of Negroes as missionaries to Africa.[144] In 1787 American Moravians reorganized their Society for Propagating the Gospel among the Heathen (first constituted in 1745 but suspended during the American Revolution).[145] Not far from the same time a number of societies were formed whose avowed field was North America and which had in mind primarily the Indians and white settlers on the frontiers.[146] Thus in 1787 the Massachusetts Legislature gave a charter to the American Society for Propagating the

[139] Vol. III, Chap. 6.

[140] *Proceedings of the Society for Propagating the Gospel among the Heathen. Sesqui-Centennial Volume*, 1937, p. 1.

[141] For instance, in 1785 the Society for the Propagation of the Gospel in Foreign Parts withdrew its support.—Pascoe, *Two Hundred Years of the S.P.G.*, p. 79.

[142] Elsbree, *The Rise of the Missionary Spirit in America, 1790-1815*, pp. 28ff.

[143] Elsbree, *op. cit.*, pp. 36ff.

[144] E. A. Park, *Memoir of Samuel Hopkins*, p. 138, in *The Works of Samuel Hopkins*, Vol. I.

[145] *Proceedings of the Society for Propagating the Gospel among the Heathen. Sesqui-Centennial Volume*, 1937, p. 1.

[146] For accounts of the formation of several of these, see Elsbree, *op. cit.*, pp. 49-83. See also a list of several in Vail, *The Morning Hour of American Baptist Missions*, pp. 88ff., and in *The New-York Missionary Magazine*, Vol. IV, pp. 385ff.

Gospel among the Indians and Others in North America.[147] In 1796 an inter-denominational group founded the New York Missionary Society, primarily for the Indians.[148] In 1798 the Missionary Society of Connecticut was organized,[149] the outgrowth of earlier missions on the frontier carried on by Congregational churches through the General Association of Connecticut,[150] and with the new settlements and the Indians as its objectives.[151] The year 1799 saw the establishment of the Massachusetts Missionary Society with the United States as its field.[152] The Massachusetts Baptist Missionary Society came into existence in 1802, primarily for the new settlements on the frontier.[153] Magazines which circulated among the supporters of these organizations, moreover, were carrying news of the newly formed British societies and of the missions of these bodies in India and the South Seas.[154] Then, too, Samuel Hopkins (1721-1803), who was continuing and modifying the tradition of Jonathan Edwards and was to have a large influence upon religious thought, particularly upon what came to be known as the New England Theology and which was to mould Congregationalism and much of American Presbyterianism, was stressing what he called "disinterested benevolence." He taught that the true Christian must have "universal disinterested benevolence"[155] which must extend to "all beings which exist, capable of good, or that can be in any sense and degree, objects of good-will."[156] He looked forward to the time when "Christianity shall spread over the whole world" "forming men to a high degree of universal benevolence and disinterested affection," uniting "all mankind into one happy society, teaching them to love each other as brethren, each seeking and rejoicing in the public good and in the happiness of individuals."[157] Americans were sending money to aid the English Baptist Mission in India.[158] English missionaries were visiting the United States on their way to and from the East.[159] However, except for the Moravian society and

[147] The New-York Missionary Magazine, Vol. I, p. 427.
[148] The New-York Missionary Magazine, Vol. I, pp. 5ff.
[149] The New-York Missionary Magazine, Vol. I, pp. 169ff.
[150] Ibid.; Elsbree, op. cit., p. 56.
[151] The New-York Missionary Magazine, Vol. I, p. 170.
[152] The New-York Missionary Magazine, Vol. I, pp. 434, 435.
[153] The Massachusetts Baptist Missionary Magazine, Vol. I, pp. 5ff.
[154] See, for instance, The New-York Missionary Magazine, Vol. I (1800), pp. 153ff., 217ff., 231ff.; The Massachusetts Baptist Missionary Magazine, Vol. I (1805), pp. 97ff., 219ff.; The Connecticut Evangelical Magazine and Religious Intelligencer, Vol. II (1809), pp. 388ff.
[155] The Works of Samuel Hopkins, Vol. I, p. 389.
[156] The Works of Samuel Hopkins, Vol. III, p. 16.
[157] The Works of Samuel Hopkins, Vol. I, p. 399.
[158] Wayland, A Memoir of the Life and Labors of the Rev. Adoniram Judson, Vol. I, p. 45.
[159] Ibid.

the one founded at Newport by Hopkins and Stiles, until after 1800 no organization came into existence which actually took measures to spread Christianity outside of North America.

The society which marked the entrance of the Protestantism of the United States in any large way into participation in the spread of Christianity outside of the confines of the country was the American Board of Commissioners for Foreign Missions. This came into being in 1810 through action of the General Association of Massachusetts,[160] an organization of Congregational clergy of the Old Calvinist School.[161] The initiative was from a group of students at Andover Theological Seminary.[162] Andover Theological Seminary was then only about two years old. It had been founded in 1808 by the Old Calvinists and the followers of Samuel Hopkins because of dissatisfaction with the liberalism of Harvard.[163] It did much to raise the level of preparation for the Christian ministry in the United States. From this young school and issuing from the streams that combined the conservatism of New England Puritanism with that revival tradition of Edwards and his successors which sought the wide proclamation of the Christian message, came the movement which more than any other led Americans to attempt to spread their faith throughout the world. Of the students at Andover whose purpose brought about the American Board of Commissioners for Foreign Missions, the leaders were Samuel J. Mills and Adoniram Judson.

Samuel J. Mills was the child of a New England parsonage and of the New England revival movement.[164] He was born in 1783, the son of a Congregational clergyman in Litchfield County, Connecticut. When Mills was about fifteen, a revival swept across his home county. This was part of that Second Great Awakening which so shook New England in these years and of the tide of revivals which swept the United States in the closing decade of the eighteenth and the opening decades of the nineteenth century. To the sensitive spirit of Mills the first contact with the revival brought an overwhelming sense of sin and deep unhappiness, but the release and joy of the conversion experiences which were coming to others did not touch him. When, however, he was about eighteen, relief came. Soon there followed the conviction that

[160] Tracy, *History of the American Board of Commissioners for Foreign Missions,* pp. 25ff.
[161] Walker, *A History of the Congregational Churches of the United States,* pp. 333, 334.
[162] Tracy, *op. cit.,* p. 24.
[163] Walker, *op cit.,* pp. 348ff.
[164] For lives of Mills, see Gardiner Spring, *Memoirs of the Rev. Samuel J. Mills* (New York, The New York Evangelical Missionary Society, 1820, pp. 247), by a friend and containing extensive excerpts from the diary, letters, and reports of Mills, and Thomas C. Richards, *Samuel J. Mills* (Boston, The Pilgrim Press, 1906, pp. 275), based upon an extensive bibliography.

he should become a missionary. To prepare for that career, in 1806 he went to Williams College. At Williams he became a leader in a group of religiously minded students.[165] There, too, a few other kindred spirits joined him in his purpose of becoming a missionary. A meeting which was a landmark in the history of this latter group is said to have been held in the shelter of a haystack near the college.[166] Eventually the group formally organized themselves into a society which they called the Brethren. Its very existence was to be kept secret. Its object was declared to be "to effect in the persons of its members a mission or missions to the heathen."[167] Whether at the outset the vision of the little band ranged beyond North America is not clear. In the haystack meeting they are said to have considered Asia,[168] Mills is reported to have thought of Africa,[169] and it is recorded that Mills later declared to a fellow clergyman, "though you and I are very little beings, we must not rest satisfied till we have made our influence extend to the remotest corner of this ruined world."[170] However, a letter of Mills, presumably written after graduation from Williams, indicates that at the outset the purpose of the group was limited to the Indians on the western frontier.[171] Whatever the original scope intended by the "missions to the heathen," before many years the vision of the Brethren was geographically enlarged and the currents to which they contributed carried American Protestants to the other side of the globe.

For a brief time after graduating from Williams, Mills went to Yale to study theology and to foster an interest in missions.[172] From there he entered Andover Theological Seminary. Several others of the Society of the Brethren also went to Andover.[173] At Andover, indeed, the society perpetuated itself for many years.[174]

Adoniram Judson (1788-1850), the other outstanding figure in the Andover student group, had a somewhat different history.[175] He, too, was the son of

---

[165] Spring, op. cit., p. 23.

[166] Spring, op. cit., p. 29; Richards, op. cit., pp. 29-31. The entire story of the haystack meeting is somewhat uncertain. The year is in doubt and the details are debatable.

[167] The Constitution of the Brethren, Ms. in the Harvard-Andover Theological Library, cited in Shedd, Two Centuries of Student Christian Movements, p. 52.

[168] Richards, op. cit., p. 30.

[169] Tracy, op. cit., p. 23.

[170] Spring, op. cit., p. 25.

[171] See the letter in Richards, op. cit., pp. 97, 98. On this point, see also Wayland, A Memoir of Adoniram Judson, Vol. I, pp. 41-43, 53.

[172] Spring, op. cit., p. 31.

[173] Spring, op. cit., p. 33.

[174] R. P. Wilder, The Great Commission, p. 16, records that his father, Royal G. Wilder, was a member at Andover in the eighteen-forties. The Brethren continued through 1870.— Shedd, op. cit., p. 55.

[175] The best biographies of Judson are Francis Wayland, A Memoir of the Life and Labors of the Rev. Adoniram Judson (Boston, Phillips, Sampson and Co., 2 vols., 1853).

a New England Congregational parsonage. His father was noted for his espousal of the views of Samuel Hopkins. Judson had a brilliant mind, was precocious intellectually, and possessed marked vivacity and charm. He went to Brown (at the time of his entrance known as Rhode Island College) and graduated as the ranking scholar of his class. In contrast with Mills, in college he had no pronounced interest in religion and even for a time departed from the teachings in which he had been reared. Not many months after leaving college, however, the death of a sceptical college mate gave him pause, and in 1808, although not yet a convinced Christian or a candidate for the ministry, he entered Andover Theological Seminary. Within a few months his doubts melted, and he united with his father's church. Not long afterward, in September, 1809, he read a sermon, *The Star in the East,* by Claudius Buchanan, a clergyman of the Church of England of the Evangelical school. Buchanan had been a chaplain of the East India Company, and on his return to England had become an ardent advocate of missions to India.[176] In this sermon, preached for the benefit of the Church Missionary Society, he told of the progress of the faith in India and maintained that the time had come greatly to increase the spread of Christianity in the East.[177] It was this sermon which determined Judson to become a missionary and which made India his destination.[178]

Mills and others of the Brethren were indefatigable in creating a missionary interest. They sought, unsuccessfully, to establish similar groups in some of the other colleges.[179] In Andover they and Judson talked to their fellow students, to their teachers, and to prominent clergymen about their design.[180] In 1810 Mills, Judson, and two others formally brought to the attention of the General Association of Massachusetts their purpose to become missionaries, and asked for counsel.[181] The Association thereupon organized a Board of Commissioners for Foreign Missions and included men from Connecticut as well as from Massachusetts in the membership of the new body.[182]

by a personal friend and containing extensive excerpts from Judson's letters; Edward Judson, *The Life of Adoniram Judson* (New York, Anson O. F. Randolph & Co., 1883, pp. xii, 601), by a son; and Stacy Warburton, *Eastward! The Story of Adoniram Judson* (New York, Round Table Press, 1937, pp. xi, 240), very carefully done. The account in this paragraph is based upon these three books.

[176] On Buchanan, see Hugh Pearson, *Memoirs of the Life and Writings of the Rev. Claudius Buchanan* (New York, Kirk and Mercein, 1818, pp. 537), *passim.*

[177] See the text in *The Works of the Reverend Claudius Buchanan, LL.D.* (Boston, Samuel T. Armstrong, 6th American edition, 1812, pp. viii, 351), pp. 315ff.

[178] Letter of Judson in Wayland, *op. cit.,* Vol. I, p. 51.

[179] Tracy, *op. cit.,* p. 24.

[180] Tracy, *op. cit.,* pp. 24, 25. Judson did not join the Brethren until 1811, after he had graduated from Andover. Wayland, *op. cit.,* Vol. I, pp. 41, 51.

[181] See the text in Tracy, *op. cit.,* p. 26.

[182] Tracy, *op. cit.,* pp. 26, 27.

The prudential committee (the central executive group) of the new organization sent Judson to England to confer with the directors of the London Missionary Society to ascertain what its relation should be with the older body.[183] The London Missionary Society was friendly, but while offering to receive the Americans as their missionaries,[184] held that joint control from both sides of the Atlantic was impracticable and that the Board of Commissioners should be quite independent. The latter acquiesced and determined to assume support of its own missionaries.[185]

In 1812 the new organization, now legally incorporated under the name the American Board of Commissioners for Foreign Missions, sent out its first group of missionaries, with Asia as their goal.[186] Judson was one of the number, but Mills was detained in the United States, a decision which seems to have been made by the Brethren, and possibly because he seemed peculiarly fitted to foster an interest in missions.[187]

On the voyage to India Judson and his bride, knowing that they were to meet Carey, studied the point on which they differed from him, that of baptism. As a result, they reluctantly came to the conclusion that the baptism of infants and of unconverted servants in a family whose head was Christian was contrary to the New Testament, and that baptism should be only for those who consciously accepted the Christian faith and should be by immersion rather than by sprinkling.[188] They were, accordingly, immersed—by one of the Baptist missionaries in Calcutta.[189] Another of the initial band of missionaries, Luther Rice, also felt constrained to become a Baptist.[190]

This action of the Judsons and Rice led to the formation of an additional American society for foreign missions, that of the Baptists. Both Judson and his colleagues were convinced that in becoming a Baptist his connexion with the American Board of Commissioners for Foreign Missions must be severed.[191] Judson wrote to a Baptist clergyman in Massachusetts whom he knew, appealing through him to the Baptists of the United States for support.[192] Rice

[183] See letter of instructions to Judson in Wayland, *op. cit.,* Vol. I, pp. 63, 64.

[184] See extracts from minutes of the Directors of the London Missionary Society in Wayland, *op. cit.,* Vol. I, pp. 74-77.

[185] Tracy, *op. cit.,* p. 29.

[186] Tracy, *op. cit.,* p. 79.

[187] Richards, *Samuel J. Mills,* pp. 77, 78.

[188] Wayland, *op. cit.,* Vol. I, pp. 95ff.

[189] Warburton, *op. cit.,* p. 51.

[190] Taylor, *Memoir of Rev. Luther Rice,* pp. 98ff.; Pollard and Stevens, *Luther Rice,* pp. 18-20.

[191] Wayland, *op. cit.,* Vol. I, p. 110.

[192] Wayland, *op. cit.,* Vol. I, p. 111.

returned to America, partly for the purpose of presenting the plea in person.[193]
In the United States, Baptists had formed in the past few years several scores
of missionary societies, some of them bearing state names, others of them local,
some of them consisting of children, and many of them of women whose members contributed a cent a week.[194] They had, however, as their objectives missions among the whites and for North American Indians. Sums, too, had been
sent from time to time to assist the English Baptist missions in the East.[195] In
response to Judson's challenge, the Baptist Society for Propagating the Gospel
in India and other Foreign Parts was formed in Boston, and a request was
sent on its behalf to the English Baptist Missionary Society, asking that Judson be taken into the English mission in India.[196] The English, however, ad-
vised a separate American mission.[197] Rice went up and down the country,
organizing local missionary societies. In May, 1814, representatives from these
met in Philadelphia and formed the General Missionary Convention of the
Baptist Denomination in the United States of America for Foreign Missions.[198]
Under this title American Baptist efforts for missions outside the country were
continued until the withdrawal of the Baptists of the southern states in 1845.[199]

Forced out of India by the East India Company, Judson went to Burma
and there began a notable mission, the history of which we are to summarize
in a subsequent volume.

The resignation of Judson and Rice brought perturbation to the American
Board of Commissioners for Foreign Missions. Moreover, the East India Company seemed adamant against an Indian residence for those of the original
group who continued in the service of the Board. However, in 1813, permission was obtained to remain in Bombay.[200] Within a few years other missions
were established in Ceylon, in the Hawaiian Islands, and among the Cherokees.[201] The story of these missions we are to pursue later.

Samuel J. Mills, who had played so large a part in the movement which led
to the formation of the American Board of Commissioners for Foreign Missions, had a comparatively short career. In that brief time he had a share in
the initiation of several other enterprises which became channels for the rising

---

[193] Taylor, *op. cit.*, p. 119.
[194] Vail, *The Morning Hour of American Baptist Missions*, pp. 86ff.
[195] Vail, *op. cit.*, pp. 238ff.
[196] Wayland, *op. cit.*, Vol. I, pp. 122-124.
[197] Wayland, *op. cit.*, Vol. I, p. 125.
[198] Wayland, *op. cit.*, Vol. I, p. 126; Gammell, *A History of American Baptist Missions*,
pp. 17ff., giving the constitution of the Convention.
[199] Wayland, *op. cit.*, Vol. I, p. 126.
[200] Tracy, *History of the American Board of Commissioners for Foreign Missions*,
pp. 45-47.
[201] Tracy, *op. cit.*, pp. 56ff.

tide of interest in the United States in the spread of Christianity. While at Yale, Mills met a Hawaiian, Henry Obookiah, who had recently arrived in America and was being tutored by E. W. Dwight. In him Mills saw a potential missionary to Hawaii.[202] He was taken into the home of Mills's father and given further education.[203] Later he assisted in raising funds for a school at Cornwall, Connecticut, not many miles from the Mills home, for the preparation of North American Indians, Pacific Islanders, and Asiatics as missionaries to their respective peoples.[204] Through Obookiah, Mills made a contribution to the beginning of the important mission to the Hawaiian Islands which we are to describe in the next volume. Mills made two trips, in 1812-1813 and 1814-1815, to the new frontier in the Mississippi Valley to survey the religious needs of the region and there helped to bring into existence several local Bible societies.[205] Before 1814, although by no means entirely through the initiative of Mills, nearly one hundred local and state Bible societies had been organized for the circulation of the Scriptures.[206] Mills urged that a national society be formed to co-ordinate their efforts in meeting the needs of the frontier.[207] While probably that would have been done without his efforts, and although the suggestion did not originate with him and he was not one of the official delegates, it was in 1816, the year after his second journey through the West, that representatives of a number of societies constituted the American Bible Society and he was present at the meeting.[208] Mills seems to have been at least partly responsible for the plan for the United Christian Missionary Society, which was to afford a channel for the Presbyterian, Dutch Reformed, and Associate Reformed Churches.[209] This society was organized in 1817 "to spread the Gospel among the Indians of North America, the inhabitants of Mexico and South America, and in other portions of the heathen and anti-Christian world."[210] In 1826, since it was appealing to the same constituency as was the American Board of Commissioners for Foreign Missions, it transferred its property and mission stations to the latter organization.[211] The vision of Mills ranged far. He wished to extend his labours beyond the

[202] Spring, *Memoirs of the Rev. Samuel J. Mills,* pp. 47ff.
[203] E. W. Dwight, *Memoir of Henry Obookiah,* pp. 27ff.
[204] E. W. Dwight, *op. cit.,* pp. 88ff.; Spring, *op. cit.,* p. 55; Tracy, *op. cit.,* p. 65.
[205] Spring, *op. cit.,* pp. 59ff.
[206] H. O. Dwight, *The Centennial History of the American Bible Society,* Vol. I, pp. 15ff.
[207] H. O. Dwight, *op. cit.,* Vol. I, p. 17; Spring, *op. cit.,* p. 93.
[208] *Annual Reports of the American Bible Society,* Vol. I, pp. 5-8; H. O. Dwight, *op. cit.,* Vol. I, pp. 21ff.
[209] Spring, *op. cit.,* p. 100.
[210] Brown, *One Hundred Years,* p. 16.
[211] *Ibid.*

United States and, in spite of his Western travels, felt, as he said, "pestered in this pin-hole here."[212] He dreamed of a tour to South America to open the way there for Protestant missions.[213] For a time he did religious work among the poor of New York City.[214] He was interested in projects for the training of Negroes to go as missionaries to their own race in the Southern states and raised funds for a school for this purpose.[215] He became an earnest advocate of the project of settling freed Negroes in Africa, and was one of the two first agents to Africa of the American Colonization Society.[216] The American Colonization Society was organized in 1817 for the purpose of removing emancipated Negroes to Africa.[217] It was through it that Liberia came into existence. Mills was not the originator of the society, but he was enthusiastic about it and joined in promoting its organization. The object of the mission on which he embarked was to determine upon territories in Africa where the Negro emigrants could be settled and to obtain permission from the local authorities for the planting of the colonies. On June 15th, 1818, while on his way back to America from Africa, Mills died.[218]

From the foregoing paragraphs it must be clear that Mills, Judson, and their fellow students had a very important part in directing the energies of the Protestants of the United States to other lands. They were not the originators of the enterprises in the United States for the spread of Christianity. Long before their day their fellow-countrymen had been seeking to propagate their faith among the white settlements on the frontier and among the Indians, and had been contributing to the expansion of Christianity in other lands. In the last decade of the eighteenth century and in the opening years of the nineteenth century scores of local and state societies were springing up whose object it was to win all the population of the United States, white, Negro, and Indian, to the Christian faith and to give them religious instruction. Most of these were local. Here and there they were state-wide. All sought to enlist the financial support of the masses of Christians and opened their membership to regular contributors of comparatively small sums. Many were composed of women. Some were for the enlistment of children. Several were for the distribution of the Bible and of religious tracts. The movement was both stimulated by the similar one in Great Britain and in turn gave added impetus to it. It was an outgrowth of the rising tide of religious life in American and

212 Letter of Mills, Oct. 3, 1816, in Spring, *op. cit.,* p. 103.
213 Spring, *op. cit.,* pp. 102ff.
214 Spring, *op. cit.,* pp. 108ff.
215 Spring, *op. cit.,* pp. 114, 115, 123ff.
216 Spring, *op. cit.,* pp. 132ff.
217 Fox, *The American Colonization Society 1817-1840,* pp. 50ff.
218 Spring, *op. cit.,* pp. 132ff.

British Protestantism. Mills, Judson, and their confreres were in part the product of this burst of life and in part reinforced it. Yet beginning with the formation of the American Board of Commissioners for Foreign Missions new features appeared in the efforts of American Protestants to propagate their faith. Mills, Judson, and their fellows had the leading rôle in calling these into being. In the first place, the Protestants of the United States now became increasingly interested not only in winning the population of their own country to their faith, but also in spreading that faith outside their borders in distant parts of the earth. "Foreign missions" began to be a normal activity of American denominations. In the second place, national organizations arose for both domestic and foreign missions. Heretofore missionary societies had been local. It was now perceived that the task of spreading the Christian faith could better be accomplished by more inclusive bodies. Some of these, like the American Bible Society and the American Tract Society,[219] were undenominational and sought the assistance of all "Evangelical Christians." Some drew support from several denominations of similar theological outlook. Congregationalists, Presbyterians, and Dutch Reformed co-operated in more than one undertaking. Others were the organs of single denominations.

To tell of the origin of all even of the nationally organized societies in the United States would require the major part of a volume. The only considerable denomination (and it was a small minority) which declined to organize for the spread of its faith was the anti-mission Baptists. Almost all of its constituency was on the frontier. Its attitude arose from an extreme Calvinism, from the fear of the pioneer for the centralized authority represented by missionary societies, and from the distrust of the frontiersman for an educated, paid ministry.[220]

Usually separate societies or boards were conducted for "home" and "foreign" missions.[221] A few denominations placed both home and foreign missions in the charge of one society. For a time the term "foreign" was often made to include missions to Indians within the confines of the United States as well as undertakings in other lands. Frequently separate organizations were formed by women. Many of the national societies were undergirded by local "auxiliaries." In no other one land did Protestants have so many societies, national and local, for the spread of the faith. The number must have totalled many thousands. While in any one local congregation those actively inter-

[219] *First Annual Report of the American Tract Society Instituted in New York, 1825,* (New York, 1826, pp. 48), *passim.*
[220] Sweet, *Religion on the American Frontier. The Baptists, 1783-1830,* pp. 58-76.
[221] For the list of societies conducting foreign missions, see Beach and Fahs, *World Missionary Atlas,* pp. 18-31.

ested in "missions" were generally in the minority, and although much opposition was voiced by church members and indifference characterized the majority, in the aggregate, by the latter part of the century, the contributors to these societies numbered several hundreds of thousands.

A few of the denominational societies of national scope whose beginnings date back to the early decades of the nineteenth century must be mentioned. In 1819 the Missionary and Bible Society of the Methodist Episcopal Church in America was formed[222] and the following year received the endorsement of the General Conference.[223] Its first appointee was designated for the French in Louisiana[224] and for a time its field was expressly limited to the United States.[225] However, in 1832 a missionary was sent to Liberia[226] and in 1836 another to Rio de Janeiro.[227] Numerous auxiliaries were organized, the first of them being the Female Missionary Society of New York.[228] In 1821, in pursuance of action taken the preceding year by its General Convention, the Protestant Episcopal Church initiated its Domestic and Foreign Missionary Society.[229] In 1825 the American Tract Society was begun.[230] In 1826 the American Home Missionary Society was organized on the foundation of the United Domestic Missionary Society which had been brought into being in 1822 by Presbyterians and (Dutch) Reformed. The Presbyterian General Assembly gave approval and various local home mission bodies in New England became auxiliary to it. In 1837 the Old School Presbyterians withdrew endorsement. When, in 1861, the New School Presbyterians also discontinued their support, the society became wholly Congregational.[231] The Presbyterians were long in creating a society which was an official board of their General Assembly. The denomination had two wings, the Old School, in which those of Scotch descent predominated, and the New School, in which the New England element was strong. For a time Congregationalists and Presbyterians worked together closely. However, strains developed, the Old School wing of the Presbyterians withdrew, and eventually the New School united with the

[222] Reid, *Missions and Missionary Society of the Methodist Episcopal Church,* Vol. I, p. 17.

[223] Reid, *op. cit.,* Vol. I, p. 23.

[224] Reid, *op. cit.,* Vol. I, p. 84.

[225] Reid, *op. cit.,* Vol. I, p. 23.

[226] Reid, *op. cit.,* Vol. I, p. 183.

[227] Reid, *op. cit.,* Vol. I, p. 281.

[228] North, *The Story of the New York Branch of the Woman's Foreign Missionary Society of the Methodist Episcopal Church,* p. 10; Reid, *op. cit.,* Vol. I, pp. 21, 22.

[229] Emery, *A Century of Endeavor,* pp. 29-36.

[230] *First Annual Report of the American Tract Society Instituted at New York, 1825* (New York, 1826, pp. 48), *passim.*

[231] Walker, *A History of the Congregational Churches in the United States,* p. 328.

northern branch of the Old School wing. In 1831 the Synod of Pittsburgh, in which Old School elements were in the ascendant, constituted the Western Foreign Missionary Society with the hope that other Presbyterians, especially in the middle and western states, would join in its support.[232] In 1837 the name was changed to the Presbyterian Foreign Missionary Society.[233] That same year the General Assembly created a Board of Foreign Missions and the Presbyterian Foreign Missionary Society transferred its funds and missionaries to the new body.[234] In 1838 the formal schism occurred between the Old School and the New School. The Old School retained the Board of Foreign Missions and the New School co-operated with the American Board of Commissioners for Foreign Missions. The reunion of the two churches in 1870 brought most of the support of the New School to the Board of Foreign Missions.[235] In 1832 the American Baptist Home Mission Society was formed. From the outset its field was regarded as not merely the United States, but all of North America.[236] In 1837 the Foreign Missionary Society of the Evangelical Lutheran Church in the United States was organized.[237] In 1846 some who were opposed to slavery and were dissatisfied with several of the policies of the American Board of Commissioners for Foreign Missions formed the American Missionary Association.[238] The separation between the northern and southern elements in the Baptists,[239] Methodists,[240] and Presbyterians led to distinct denominational societies supported by the Southern churches, an organizational breach intensified by the Civil War and the post-war Reconstruction.

The societies which we have named, it must be reiterated, were only among the more prominent. Even a bare catalogue of all the regional and local organizations would extend these paragraphs to many hundreds of pages. We must also note the fact that most of this organized effort was among denominations

[232] Brown, *One Hundred Years,* pp. 21-24; see also T. C. Pears, Jr., *A Brief History of the Western Foreign Missionary Society,* in J. A. Kelso, editor, *The Centennial of the Western Foreign Missionary Society 1831-1931* (Pittsburgh, 1931, pp. 234), pp. 8-72.

[233] Brown, *op. cit.,* pp. 34, 35.

[234] Brown, *op. cit.,* pp. 38-40.

[235] Brown, *op. cit.,* pp. 41, 46.

[236] *One-Hundredth Annual Report of the American Baptist Home Mission Society* (New York City, 1932, pp. 180), p. 13.

[237] Drach (editor), *Our Church Abroad,* p. 23.

[238] Beard, *A Crusade of Brotherhood,* pp. 23-32.

[239] At the initial meeting of the Southern Baptist Convention, in 1845, a board for foreign missions and another for domestic missions were formed.—H. A. Tupper, *The Foreign Missions of the Southern Baptist Convention* (Philadelphia, American Baptist Publication Society, 1880, pp. xv, 512), p. 471.

[240] In 1846 the first General Conference of the Methodist Episcopal Church, South, constituted a missionary society for home and foreign missions.—Cannon, *History of Southern Methodist Missions,* p. 47.

whose constituencies were of predominantly British stock. Since British societies were so prominent and since the missionary bodies of the United States were so largely of British background, it is not surprising that the Protestant Christianity which spread in the nineteenth century was overwhelmingly Anglo-Saxon.

The awakening of missionary interest was also seen in Protestant circles on the continent of Europe. It came in part through contact with the British missionary movement, and in part through indigenous sources, largely of Pietist and Moravian origin. Much of this was delayed until the downfall of Napoleon brought a period of peace. However, it began even before 1815.

The first of the new continental Protestant societies for the spread of Christianity arose in Holland. It was the Netherlands Missionary Society (Nederlandsche Zendelinggenootschap) and was begun in Rotterdam in 1797, largely in connexion with the London Missionary Society.[241] The individual chiefly responsible for its founding was John Theodore Vanderkemp.[242] Vanderkemp had come by a devious and stormy road to a warm Christian faith and a missionary purpose. In his young manhood a proud army officer, he had led a dissolute life. Then love and a happy marriage had won him to rectitude, he completed a medical course, and in seeking to meet the religious needs of his wife and daughter he had begun to emerge from scepticism to a Christian experience. A tragic accident caused the sudden death of his wife and daughter. Through his anguish he was brought to a humble Christian faith. He offered himself to the London Missionary Society and eventually was sent by them to South Africa, where in the next volume we are to meet him again. Before going to Africa, he initiated a society in his native land. For a time this was almost an auxiliary of the London Missionary Society, but its membership was drawn largely from the Dutch Reformed Church. Even more than its English prototype, it was inclusive theologically. Until the middle of the nineteenth century it was the only missionary society in Holland. However, religious awakenings then brought dissatisfaction with the liberalism of the directors and several other societies were formed by groups of more conservative and intransigent views.[243]

In Germany the nineteenth century witnessed a marked development of

---

[241] E. F. Kruijf, *Geschiedenis van het Nederlandsche Zendelinggenootschap en zijne Zendingsposten* (Groningen, J. B. Wolters, 1894, pp. xv, 695), pp. 3ff.

[242] A biography of Vanderkemp, based largely on a manuscript autobiography and other manuscript sources, is A. D. Martin, *Doctor Vanderkemp* (Westminster, The Livingstone Press, no date; pp. ix, 195).

[243] Warneck, *Geschichte der protestantischen Missionen*, pp. 159, 160; Baron van Boetzelaer van Dubbledam in *The International Review of Missions*, Vol. XXII, pp. 233-239.

missionary interest. Towards the close of the eighteenth century the impulse which had been so fruitful in the Danish-Halle mission in India had ebbed. The East India Missionary Institute at Halle was gradually deserted and ceased to send out missionaries.[244] However, the old life was not dead. The Moravians continued. The Pietist tradition remained. From these, revivified and reinforced by contacts with the fresh missionary movements in England, the German Protestant nineteenth century missionary movement arose to much larger proportions than that of the eighteenth century.

In Berlin in 1800 Pastor Johann Jänicke founded a school to train youths for service as missionaries.[245] Jänicke was of Bohemian ancestry and was pastor of the Bethlehem Church in Berlin, which had been founded by Protestant refugees from Bohemia. Because of this connexion he had been in touch with the Moravians of Herrnhut. He also had contacts with Halle and with the Danish-Halle mission in India. The immediate impulse to the initiation of the institution came in part through the London Missionary Society. For his school Jänicke received financial assistance from England and from various sections of Germany. Most of those whom he prepared were Germans, but the majority of them served under the London Missionary Society, the Church Missionary Society, and the Netherlands Missionary Society. Their fields were widely scattered—India, Ceylon, South Africa, Sierra Leone, the Dutch East Indies, and China among them. In the midst of the Napoleonic Wars and from Prussia, so severely dealt with by the Corsican, this school was providing missionaries for the fringes of much of Africa and Asia. It later decayed, but it left lasting results.

In 1815 a school was begun in Basel which was to have a much longer career and was to become the centre of a society which drew support and personnel from both Germany and Switzerland. Like Jänicke's enterprise, it came both from indigenous developments and from contacts with England. In 1780, from Pietist roots, a society arose for the purpose of effecting a revival in religious life. Several similar organizations sprang up in Germany and Switzerland. To these groups the new missionary societies in Great Britain brought an exciting stimulus. At Basel, through the parent society, in 1815 an institution was inaugurated for the training of missionaries. At first it provided recruits for the British missions, but beginning with 1822, it developed into an organ-

<hr>

[244] Warneck, *op. cit.*, p. 139.
[245] See *Johann Jänicke der evangelisch-lutherische Prediger an der böhmischen-oder Bethlehems-Kirche zu Berlin, nach seinen Leben und Wirken dargestellt von Karl Friedrich Ledderhose . . . und zum Besten der Mission für China herausgegeben von G. Knak* (Berlin, G. Knak, 1863, pp. xii, 246), pp. 19-30, 40, 41, 72, 73, 96ff.; Warneck, *op. cit.*, pp. 140, 141.

ization for sending and supporting its own graduates.[246] In Germany a number of regional and local societies came into existence to assist the Basel enterprise.[247] In the course of time several of these became independent with their own overseas missions. Thus in 1828 the Rhenish Missionary Society (Rheinische Missionsgesellschaft) was formed as a union of a society which had been brought into being by Basel with some other associations.[248] In 1836 an auxiliary of Basel at Dresden became the nucleus of an Evangelical Lutheran Mission, appealing to Lutherans rather than to those of more than one confession (or denomination) as did Basel.[249] Eventually its headquarters were moved to Leipzig and it took the name of that city (Evangelisch-lutherische Mission zu Leipzig). Its great leader was Karl Graul, who attempted, although with only partial success, to bring to its support the entire Lutheran Church.[250] In 1836 several local societies which had been affiliated with Basel united to form the North German Missionary Society (Norddeutsche Missionsgesellschaft).[251] To this a number of other societies later attached themselves.[252]

Before the middle of the nineteenth century several other missionary organizations came into being in Germany. Among those which undertook enterprises in other lands were the Berlin Missionary Society (Berliner Missionsgesellschaft), instituted in 1824,[253] the Hermannsburg Mission, centring around a training school founded by Louis Harms, a pastor in Hanover, in 1849,[254] and the Gossner Missionary Society (Gossnersche Missionsgesellschaft), begun by Gossner, who believed that missionaries should support themselves by working with their own hands and was opposed to the growing emphasis upon prolonged education of missionary candidates.[255] In 1842 a society of women was formed to assist in the Christian education of women in the East

---

[246] Schlatter, *Geschichte der Basler Mission,* Vol. I, pp. 3, 13ff.; Warneck, *op. cit.,* pp. 141, 142.

[247] Schlatter, *op. cit.,* Vol. I, pp. 13ff.

[248] L. von Rohden, *Geschichte der Rheinischen Missionsgesellschaft* (Barmen, J. F. Steinhaus, 1856, pp. 232), pp. 1ff.; Warneck, *op. cit.,* p. 145.

[249] Hermann Karsten, *Die Geschichte der evangelisch-lutherischen Mission in Leipzig* (Güstrow, Opitz & Co., 2 vols., 1893), Vol. I, pp. 9, 13, 15, 21ff.

[250] G. Hermann, *Dr. Karl Graul und seine Bedeutung für die lutherische Mission* (Halle, Buchhandlung des Waisenhauses, 1867, pp. vi, 234), *passim*; Warneck, *op. cit.,* pp. 147-149.

[251] Schlatter, *op. cit.,* Vol. I, p. 53.

[252] Warneck, *op. cit.,* pp. 146, 147.

[253] Julius Richter, *Geschichte der Berliner Missionsgesellschaft 1824-1924* (Berlin, Buchhandlung der Berliner ev. Missionsgesellschaft, 1924, pp. 740), pp. 8ff.

[254] Georg Haccius, *Hannoversche Missionsgeschichte* (Hermannsburg, Missionshandlung, 4 vols., 1909-1920), Vol. II, pp. 1ff. See also W. Wendebourg, *Louis Harms und Missionstaten des Begründers der Hermannsburger Mission* (Hermannsburg, Missionshandlung, 1910, pp. xiii, 431).

[255] Warneck, *op. cit.,* pp. 149, 150.

(Berliner Frauenverein für christliche Bildung des weiblichen Geschlechts im Morgenlande).[256] We must note, too, the labours of Gustav Warneck, in the second half of the nineteenth century. Through his books and his periodical, *Allgemeine Missionszeitschrift,* he exercised a profound influence upon the policies of missions, not only in Germany but also in other lands.[257]

In France the Protestant groups, although a small minority of the population, were given official recognition, and began to feel the new life which was stirring and to organize for a more active propagation of their faith. In 1792 a French Bible Society had been formed in London, but the disturbances in France and the Anglo-French conflict brought it a troubled existence.[258] In 1818, through the British and Foreign Bible Society, a Bible society was organized in Paris.[259] Contacts with Basel and with the missionary movement in Great Britain, and encouragement from an American missionary who was studying in Paris, joined with an awakening in the French churches of which Frédéric Monod was an outstanding figure to call into being, in 1882, the Paris Evangelical Missionary Society (Société des Missions Évangéliques de Paris).[260] This continued to be the chief organ of the French Protestant churches in aiding in the propagation of Christianity in other lands.

In Lutheran circles in Scandinavia the nineteenth century was marked by the creation and growth of societies whose aim was the spread of Christianity in other countries. In Denmark the organization through which in the course of the century the major part of the missionary interest of the kingdom found expression was the Danish Missionary Society (Danske Missionsselskab). It was founded in 1821 by Bone Falch Rønne and was led by him until his death (1833). It first concerned itself with providing clergy for Greenland, where missionaries had been labouring since the first half of the eighteenth century. Before its initial decade was past, in connexion with Basel it had sent missionaries to the Gold Coast in Africa.[261] In Norway the largest sending body, The Norwegian Missionary Society (Det Norske Missionsselskab) was organized in 1842. The interest which gave rise to it and supported it came in part from a fresh surge of life led by Hans Nilsen Hauge, and partly from contacts with the Moravians and with the Basel and Rhenish

---

[256] Warneck, *op. cit.,* p. 153.

[257] Martin Schlunk in *The International Review of Missions,* Vol. XXIII, pp. 395-404.

[258] Douen, *Histoire de la Société Biblique Protestante de Paris (1818 à 1868),* pp. 52ff.

[259] Douen, *op. cit.,* pp. 79ff.

[260] Jean Bianquis, *Les Origines de la Société des Missions Évangéliques de Paris 1822-1829* (Paris, Société des Missions Évangéliques, 2 vols., 1930, 1931), Vol. I, pp. 2ff.

[261] Niels Bundgaard, *Det Danske Missionsselskabs Historie* (Copenhagen, Det Danske Missionsselskab, 1935, pp. 398). pp. 7ff.

societies.[262] To Sweden came a variety of influences. Halle, the Moravians, Basel, the British foreign missionary movement, British Methodism, and contact with the revivalism of the United States, all made themselves felt.[263] Sweden, and, indeed, all Scandinavia, awakened to a more earnest religious life than it had ever known. In 1835 a Swedish Missionary Society (Svenska Missionssällskapet) was organized. It supported schools among the Lapps and assisted other foreign mission organizations. In 1855 it amalgamated with a society and training school at Lund which had been auxiliary to the Leipzig mission.[264] What was eventually the leading Swedish society, the Svenska Missionsförbundet, did not come into existence until 1878.[265] Gifts in money to foreign missionary undertakings were made from Finland, but not until 1859 did a distinct society of national scope, the Finnish Missionary Society (Suomen Lahetysseura), arise.[266] This remained the strongest of Finnish organizations for spreading the Protestant faith in other lands.

As in the case of Great Britain and the United States, it is beyond the scope of this work to give a complete catalogue of the organizations formed on the continent of Europe in the nineteenth century to assist the expansion of Christianity. Only the more prominent of the earliest associations have been mentioned.

Thus far in our sketch of the Protestant nineteenth century organizations for the spread of Christianity we have confined our attention to the origin of the oldest of the many societies which made the period so memorable and which were the instruments through which Protestantism led the other forms of Christianity in the expansion of the faith. Even then, the bodies were so numerous that we have had space only for some of the largest.

We must now trace the chief outlines of the development of this Protestant missionary movement during the remaining decades of the nineteenth century and in the first fourteen years of the twentieth century before the World War of 1914-1918 tragically and spectacularly ushered mankind into a new age. Here we must be even more adamant in resisting the temptation to give the story of all the organizations which were created to help spread Christianity.

[262] N. Landmark, *Det Norske Missionsselskab* (Christiania, Norske Missionsselskab, 1889, pp. viii, 320), pp. 3ff.

[263] Bengt Sundkler, *Svenska Missionssällskapet 1835-1876* (Stockholm, Svenska Kyrkans Diakonistyrelses Bokförlag, 1937, pp. xxxvi, 614; a careful, well documented study), pp. 7ff.

[264] Warneck, *op. cit.*, pp. 168-171.

[265] Axel Andersson, *Svenska Missionsförbundet Dess Uppkomst och Femtioåriga Verksamhet* (Stockholm, Svenska Missionsförbundet Forlag, 3 vols., 1928, 1929), gives a popular survey of the society and its work.

[266] Warneck, *op. cit.*, p. 171.

Nowhere, indeed, does any full list exist.[267] As the nineteenth century wore on, the numbers rapidly increased. The total of all the organizations, local, regional, and national, must have mounted into the thousands. What we can attempt is to indicate some of the main features of these years, and here and there, where it seems absolutely necessary, mention leading individuals and outstanding organizations.

First we must note that as Protestantism spread, in many additional countries societies for the propagation of Christianity came into being. The Protestantism of the period was strongly missionary. In land after land to which it was carried it was not passively accepted, but stirred its adherents to active efforts to extend it still more widely.

This was especially the case in the new nations founded by Protestant migration. In Canada, Australia, New Zealand, and South Africa organizations were formed to aid the expansion of the faith both inside and outside these lands.[268] As was to be expected, because of the cultural and religious ties with the United States, the foreign societies of Canada tended to send their missionaries to the regions in which those from their huge neighbour were the most numerous— the Far East, India, and Latin America. It is not strange, moreover, that from Australia and New Zealand most of the overseas missionaries went to the islands of the South Pacific and to India and the Far East, and that the fields of the South African churches were entirely within Africa.

In the second place, in the British Isles, the United States, and the continent of Europe societies multiplied. The latter half of the nineteenth century and especially the last quarter of the century and the opening years of the twentieth century, with their comparative peace and prosperity and their accumulated momentum of religious life and missionary interest, were particularly notable for the numbers of new missionary societies and the mounting incomes and staffs of the older organizations. In this was a second feature of these years.

A third feature of the latter part of the nineteenth century was the emerging prominence of the United States in the Protestant missionary enterprise. In this country occurred the largest numerical increase of Protestant Christianity.

---

[267] A list, chiefly of those nationally organized, is in Beach and Fahs, *World Missionary Atlas,* pp. 17-68. This does not, however, include the hundreds of local and regional organizations which, while usually auxiliaries to these others, had an existence of their own and in many cases had come into being without encouragement from any central office.

[268] See lists of these in Beach and Fahs, *op. cit.,* pp. 17, 18, 31-34, 53-56. For the development of organizations in Australasia in connexion with the Church Missionary Society, see S. M. Johnston, *A History of the Church Missionary Society in Australia and Tasmania.* (Sydney, The Church Missionary Society, 1925, pp. 415, vii), pp. 185ff.

That was partly by immigration, partly by further gains among the native white population, and in part through the conversion of a growing proportion of the Negroes and Indians. This domestic growth was in itself a major achievement, one of the most remarkable in all history. It was accomplished through a multiform and extensive home missionary enterprise which might have been supposed to engross all the resources of the churches. Yet simultaneously, as we have suggested, the Protestant churches of the United States extended their activities into all the continents, including the Europe from which they traced their descent. Even churches made up chiefly of nineteenth century immigrants and their children found energy not only to develop their own inner life but also to form societies to extend their faith to other lands.[269] This was both because of the growing wealth and the abounding vitality of the nation and because of the vigorous life within the churches.

The increasing share of the United States in the world-wide spread of Protestant Christianity is partly seen in the financial side of the enterprise. Whereas at the beginning of the century the British had led and the first large American societies for missions outside the borders of the country at the outset considered the possibility of becoming auxiliary to the older British organizations, and as late as 1900 more money was given and more missionaries went from the British Isles than from the United States,[270] by 1914 the Protestants of the United States were contributing more to foreign missions than were those of Great Britain and, indeed, provided almost half of what was given by Protestants the world around for that purpose.[271] In numbers of societies the United States had outstripped Great Britain.[272]

Moreover, it was in the United States that what became a fourth characteristic of the later part of the period, a notable outpouring of student life into Christian missions, had its inception. It took the form of the Student Volunteer Movement for Foreign Missions. Its origin is usually dated from a gathering of students held at Mt. Hermon, Massachusetts, under the leadership of Dwight

[269] Thus at the annual meeting of the Hauge Synod in 1890 the Norwegian Evangelical Lutheran China Mission Society was formed (Drach, *Our Church Abroad*, pp. 127-129). In 1894 the Synodical Conference (Lutheran) began work in India (Drach, *op. cit.*, pp. 232, 233). In 1880 the Augustana Synod (of the Swedish Lutherans) voted to aid work among the Telugus in India (Drach, *op. cit.*, pp. 157-187).

[270] Of the 13,607 Protestant foreign missionaries in 1900, 5,901 were from the British Isles and 4,110 from the United States. In that same year, of the $17,161,092 contributed to Protestant foreign missions, $8,225,645 was from the British Isles and $5,403,048 from the United States.—*Ecumenical Missionary Conference, New York, 1900*, Vol. II, p. 424.

[271] Harlan P. Beach and Burton St. John, *World Statistics of Christian Missions*, p. 54. Out of a total income of foreign mission societies of $38,922,822, $18,055,836 came from the United States and $13,819,000 from Great Britain and Ireland.

[272] *Ibid.* Of the societies listed, 128 were in the United States and 92 in Great Britain and Ireland.

L. Moody, during twenty-six days in the summer of 1886.[273] Although the gathering had not been called with that purpose, before it had ended, of the 251 present, the number who planned to become foreign missionaries rose from 21 to an even 100. Of the remainder, others later made that decision.[274] During the succeeding academic year one of the group, Robert P. Wilder, with a friend who had not been at Mt. Hermon, toured the colleges, theological seminaries, and universities of the United States and Canada and enrolled 2,106 "volunteers."[275] In 1888 a continuing organization was set up, the Student Volunteer Movement for Foreign Missions, with John R. Mott, one of the original Mt. Hermon hundred, as chairman.[276] In 1891 the first of the Quadrennial Conventions of the Movement was held.[277] These at once took their place as gatherings which drew more students from more institutions in the United States and Canada than any others, either secular or religious.

To the Student Volunteer Movement for Foreign Missions a number of streams contributed. Robert P. Wilder's father had been a missionary to India and in his student days at Andover had been one of the Brethren, of Williams College origin.[278] Young Men's Christian Associations had been organized in colleges and universities of the United States and Canada and had become both the main vehicle and the stimulus of religious life among students in these two countries.[279] It was through them that the Mt. Hermon conference was gathered.[280] In 1880 theological students had formed the Interseminary Missionary Alliance and that same year had given it continuing form at a convention which was the largest student religious gathering thus far assembled in the United States.[281] Through the contagion of the Moody movement, in 1883 seven students of Cambridge University had offered themselves for missions in China and in the academic year before the Mt. Hermon gathering one of their number, J. E. K. Studd, had visited the United States and had told in the colleges the story of their purpose.[282] It was on a rising tide that the Student Volunteer Movement swept into its remarkable career.

[273] On the origins of the Student Volunteer Movement, see John R. Mott, *History of the Student Volunteer Movement for Foreign Missions* (Chicago, Student Volunteer Movement for Foreign Missions, 1892, pp. 48), *passim;* Robert P. Wilder, *The Great Commission, passim;* Shedd, *Two Centuries of Student Christian Movements,* pp. 253ff.,; and Mott, *Five Decades and a Forward View,* pp. 2-5.
[274] Wilder, *op. cit.,* pp. 20-22; Mott, *Five Decades and a Forward View,* p. 5.
[275] Wilder, *op. cit.,* pp. 23-26. Mott, *op. cit.,* p. 6, gives the figure as 2,200.
[276] Wilder, *op. cit.,* p. 41; Mott, *op. cit.,* p. 7.
[277] Wilder, *op. cit.,* pp. 58-63.
[278] Wilder, *op. cit.,* pp. 15, 16.
[279] Shedd, *op. cit.,* pp. 122ff.
[280] Shedd, *op. cit.,* pp. 238ff.
[281] Shedd, *op. cit.,* pp. 214-219.
[282] Shedd, *op. cit.,* pp. 238, 239.

The Student Volunteer Movement sought to enlist all Protestants in the effort to bring the Christian message to all men. At the Mt. Hermon gathering the subject of one of the adresses was "All should go and go to all."[283] Leaders of the Movement rang the changes upon the challenge that because of the greater need in other lands and the smaller number of Christians there to tell of the Christian Gospel, every true Christian should ask himself not why he should go (for the command, "Go ye into all the world and preach the Gospel to every creature" was held to be binding on all Christians) but why he should not go.[284] By its "watchword," "the evangelization of the world in this generation," the Movement strove to inculcate the conviction that it was the duty of each generation of Christians to give to all their contemporaries a sufficient knowledge of the Christian message to permit of its intelligent acceptance or rejection.[285] Sometimes military and imperialistic slogans were used. Thus at the Mt. Hermon gathering one of the best remembered phrases was "the work of missions is not a wrecking expedition, but a war of conquest."[286] The chairman of the Movement published an account of a world-wide tour of colleges and universities under the title, *Strategic Points in the World's Conquest.*[287] Yet in this programme was none of the selfish desire for profit or power associated with economic and political imperialism. The challenge was to the unselfish dedication of life for the world's good.

From the United States the Student Volunteer Movement for Foreign Missions spread to other lands. Wilder carried the idea to Great Britain, and in 1892 the Student Volunteer Missionary Union came into being, larger in its scope than the Student Foreign Missionary Union which had been organized in 1889, and with the same declaration of purpose and later with the same watchword as the American movement.[288] Out of the Student Volunteer Missionary Union later came the Student Christian Movement of Great Britain and Ireland.[289] Partly through Wilder, the movement, too, stimulated mis-

[283] Wilder, *op. cit.,* p. 20.

[284] Wilder, *op. cit.,* pp. 15, 21. Two pamphlets printed by the Movement, used very widely, and reprinted again and again, carried this plea.—Robert E. Speer, *What Constitutes a Missionary Call,* and George Sherwood Eddy, *The Supreme Decision of the Christian Student.*

[285] See the official treatise of the watchword, John R. Mott, *The Evangelization of the World in This Generation* (New York, Student Volunteer Movement for Foreign Missions, 1900, pp. 245).

[286] Wilder, *op. cit.,* p. 20. See a slightly different form of the phrase in Mott, *Five Decades and a Forward View,* p. 4.

[287] John R. Mott, *Strategic Points in the World's Conquest. The Universities and Colleges as Related to the Progress of Christianity* (New York, Fleming H. Revell Co., 1897, pp. 218).

[288] Wilder, *op. cit.,* pp. 64ff.; Shedd, *op. cit.,* pp. 347ff.

[289] Shedd, *op. cit.,* pp. 351-353.

sionary interest among students in Scandinavia and Germany.[290] Contact with the British movement was a major factor in nourishing Volunteer Unions of students in Scandinavia, Germany, France, Switzerland, and Holland.[291] In 1896 Mott organized the Student Volunteer Movement among the universities of Australia and New Zealand.[292] He also helped to transplant the idea to the Near East, India, Ceylon, China, and Japan.[293]

It was through the Student Volunteer Movements in these various lands that a large proportion of the outstanding leaders in the world-wide spread of Protestant Christianity in the twentieth century were recruited.

A fifth feature of the latter part of the period was the prominence of women's organizations for the spread of the faith. These, too, had their largest development in the United States. We have seen that local missionary societies of women early came into being, particularly in the United States. Here, in 1860, the undenominational Woman's Union Missionary Society for Heathen Lands was formed.[294] In several of the major denominations the women's organizations for missions came together in nationally organized bodies. Some of them were auxiliary to the general societies of the denominations. Several were independent but worked in close co-operation with the general societies. They took the lead in developing a systematic study of missions among their constituencies.[295] In Great Britain and Ireland, while independent women's societies on a national scale were not so numerous as in the United States, a few appeared. Such was the Church of England Zenana Missionary Society, founded in 1880.[296] So, too, the rise of religious communities of women within the Church of England was followed by the extension of the labours of several of these among non-Christian peoples.[297] Young Women's Christian Associations, principally through their North American units, were planted in many lands, notably in India and the Far East.[298] The proportion of women in the missionary staffs of four of the leading American societies increased from 49 per cent. in 1830 to 57 per cent. in 1880 and to 67 per cent. in 1929.[299]

[290] Wilder, op. cit., pp. 91ff.
[291] Mott in Students and the Modern Missionary Crusade, p. 53.
[292] Ibid.
[293] Ibid.
[294] Reid, Missions and Missionary Society of the Methodist Episcopal Church, Vol. I, p. 48.
[295] Laymen's Foreign Missions Inquiry. Fact-Finders Reports, Vol. VII, pp. 80, 81.
[296] The Church of England Zenana Missionary Society. Jubilee Souvenir, 1880-1930 (London, 1930, pp. 40), pp. 9ff.
[297] Morgan, The Catholic Revival and Missions, pp. 66-81.
[298] International Survey of the Young Men's and Young Women's Christian Associations, pp. 49ff.
[299] W. G. Lennox, The Health and Turnover of Missionaries (New York, 1933, p. 217), pp. 28, 29.

A sixth development in the Protestant missionary enterprise in the decades immediately before 1914 was the increasing initiative of laymen. From the very beginning of Protestant efforts to propagate Christianity, even long before the nineteenth century, laymen had taken an active part. However, in the later years of the nineteenth century they had an even larger share.

This was particularly the case in the United States. Moody, the great evangelist of the second half of the century, was a layman. Robert E. Speer, a leader in the Student Volunteer Movement, in Presbyterian missions, and in interdenominational enterprises, was never ordained. It was from the United States that the major expansion of a predominantly lay organization, the Young Men's Christian Association, occurred. As we saw in the last chapter, the Young Men's Christian Association originated in Great Britain, developed on the continent of Europe, but had its most extensive growth in the United States. Before 1890 several Young Men's Christian Associations had sprung up in Christian colleges in Asia.[300] In 1889 the North American movement authorized the creation of a Foreign Division of its International Committee (which embraced the United States and Canada) for establishing Associations and placing secretaries "in the foreign mission field."[301] Beginning in 1888 the first college secretary of the International Committee, Luther D. Wishard, made a tour of the globe which occupied nearly four years, and did much to encourage student Associations.[302] It was under a layman, John R. Mott, that the North American Young Men's Christian Associations had their largest extension to other lands. Through prolonged journeys in 1895-1897 and 1901-1903 Mott increased and strengthened the student Associations.[303] As head of the foreign work of the North American Associations he did much to recruit secretaries and provide funds for the development in other lands, notably in the Far East, of city Associations of the North American type.[304] Many of the secretaries possessed marked ability, great latitude was allowed them in their programmes, and they and the Associations often exerted a profound influence.

In the United States, moreover, the Laymen's Missionary Movement had its origin and reached its largest dimensions. It began in 1906 as a direct result of the quadrennial convention of that year of the Student Volunteer Movement and of the centennial celebration of the "haystack meeting" at Williams College. Its purpose was to finance the enterprise to which young men and women

[300] *International Survey of the Young Men's and Young Women's Christian Associations*, p. 46.
[301] *International Survey of the Young Men's and Young Women's Christian Associations*, p. 47.
[302] Shedd, *Two Centuries of Student Christian Movements*, pp. 326-333.
[303] Shedd, *op. cit.*, pp. 359ff.; Mathews, *John R. Mott*, pp. 104ff., 122.
[304] Mathews, *op. cit.*, pp. 123, 402-406.

were devoting their lives. It was formed of denominational groups of laymen associated in an interdenominational fellowship. For a few years it enjoyed great prominence and its example led to the rise of similar movements in Great Britain, Germany, Scandinavia, Holland, South Africa, Australia, New Zealand, Egypt, and Ceylon. Partly as a result, a marked increase of giving to foreign missions followed.[305]

However, it was not the United States but Great Britain which produced Sidney James Wells Clark.[306] A layman, who by his industry had risen from poverty to wealth, in 1907, while still in his middle forties, he retired from business and gave his time and his fortune to foreign missions. He espoused principles of comprehensive planning and of encouraging self-reliance in the churches established by missionaries which, after his death, were continued by a trust endowed by him, and which was utilized to help make possible the World Dominion Movement.

A seventh characteristic of the Protestant missionary movement of the latter part of the nineteenth century was the rapid increase of undenominational societies for the spread of Christianity. Most of these expressly confined their efforts to particular countries, institutions, or needs. The largest was the China Inland Mission. It was founded in 1865 through the devotion and vision of James Hudson Taylor.[307] We are to hear much more of it in a subsequent volume, for, although its originator had no denomination back of him and was repeatedly ill, it eventually had a larger missionary body in China than any other single organization, either Roman Catholic or Protestant. Although beginning in England, it drew its support from a number of lands.[308] Associated with the China Inland Mission and sharing its general principles were several other bodies, also centring on China.[309] In part coming out of the China Inland Mission and related to it in purpose, but serving lands other than China, were a number of other enterprises. Thus Charles T. Studd, one of the Cambridge Seven who went out under the China Inland Mission, later became one of the promoters of the Worldwide Evangelization Crusade from which sprang projects for the interiors of Africa, Asia, and South America.[310] Of different origin was the Sudan United Mission, which arose in 1904 in response to an

[305] William T. Ellis, *Men and Missions* (Philadelphia, The Sunday School Times Co., 1909, pp. 313), pp. 71-80; Mott, *Five Decades and a Forward View*, pp. 30-47.

[306] Roland Allen, *Sidney James Wells Clark, A Vision of Foreign Missions* (London, The World Dominion Press, 1937, pp. xxii, 170), *passim*—by a close personal friend.

[307] Marshall Broomhall, *The Jubilee Story of the China Inland Mission*, pp. 23ff.

[308] Broomhall, *op. cit.*, pp. 183ff.

[309] Broomhall, *op. cit.*, pp. 357-365.

[310] Thomas B. Walters, *Charles T. Studd* (London, The Epworth Press, 1930, pp. 126), *passim*; Norman P. Grubb, *C. T. Studd* (London, The Religious Tract Society, 1933, pp. 256), *passim*.

appeal from leaders in several British denominations for an effort to stem the advance of Islam in Central Africa.[311] What was originally called the Mission for Lepers in India, then the Mission to Lepers in India and the East, and eventually, as its geographic scope broadened, merely the Mission to Lepers, was organized in 1874 in Dublin as an outgrowth of the service to lepers of Wellesley C. Bailey. Later its headquarters were moved to London and an affiliated organization was formed in the United States.[312] These are only a selection from the more prominent of the many undenominational societies which came into existence as the century progressed.

An eighth feature of the second half of the nineteenth century was the appearance of an increasing number of societies or missions bearing the names of universities and arising out of the enthusiasm of students and graduates of one or more of these institutions of higher learning. Of these the largest and the oldest was what eventually was named the Universities' Mission to Central Africa. This came into being as a result of addresses by David Livingstone at Cambridge and Oxford in 1857 when he charged his audiences: "Do you carry out the work which I have begun. I leave it with you." A committee was formed in Cambridge in 1858, another in Oxford in 1859, and a joint one in London. Later the Universities of Durham and Dublin co-operated. The appeal for support was not confined to members of these universities. The missionaries sent out were communicants of the Church of England and the original intention, although unfulfilled, was eventually to transfer the enterprise to the Society for the Propagation of the Gospel in Foreign Parts.[313] More of these university missions sprang from Oxford and Cambridge than from any other institutions of learning. In the United States the largest of the university undertakings was the Yale Foreign Missionary Society, later the Yale in China Association, which concentrated on education, including a medical school, in Central China.[314]

[311] *Sudan United Mission. Is It Time? Annual Report and Review, 1908* (London, Marshall Brothers, pp. 64), pp. 31-33.

[312] [Wellesley C. Bailey and others], *Fifty Years Work for Lepers 1874-1924* (London, The Mission to Lepers, 1924, pp. 86), *passim;* John Jackson, *Lepers. Thirty-One Years' Work Among Them. Being the History of the Mission to Lepers in India and the East 1874-1905* (London, Marshall Brothers, [1906], pp. xviii, 390), *passim.*

[313] A. E. M. Anderson-Morshead, *The History of the Universities' Mission to Central Africa 1859-1909* (London, Universities Mission to Central Africa, revised ed., 1909, pp. xxix, 448), *passim;* Henry Rawley, *The Story of the Universities Mission to Central Africa* (London, Saunders, Otley and Co., 1866, pp. xii, 493), *passim;* George Herbert Wilson, *The History of the Universities Mission to Central Africa* (Westminster, Universities Mission to Central Africa, 1936, pp. xvi, 278), *passim.*

[314] *The Yale Mission, Changsha, China. Annual Reports;* Henry B. Wright, *A Life with a Purpose. A Memorial of John Lawrence Thurston, First Missionary of the Yale Mission* (New York, Fleming H. Revell Co., 1908, pp. 317), *passim.*

A ninth development was the growth of Christian colleges and universities, chiefly in Asia, which in time sought support through boards of trustees partially or completely independent of any denominational missionary society. The majority of these were begun under the auspices of denominational bodies, but their tendency was to become undenominational and autonomous and each to cultivate a particular group of donors. Thus what was successively known as the Christian College in China, Canton Christian College, and Lingnan University, had its beginning in the efforts of two members of the American Presbyterian mission in Canton, in 1893 was incorporated in the United States with its own board of trustees, and became quite undenominational.[315]

A tenth and last feature of these years was an increase in co-operation. This became more and more marked as the century progressed. One of the characteristics of Protestantism was its endless proliferation. Its vitality was evidenced by the continuing emergence of new organizations. These multiplied as the nineteenth century wore on. In contrast with the Roman Catholic Church, no central administrative authority existed to co-ordinate the efforts of the hundreds of bodies which were seeking to spread the Protestant forms of the Christian message throughout the world. Yet such co-ordination was obviously desirable. Beginning at least as early as Carey, some of the leaders in the Protestant missionary enterprise had the whole world in their purview. The Student Volunteer Movement, with its watchword, "the evangelization of the world in this generation," had accentuated this emphasis. If the entire human race were to be reached, if the world were to be "won to Christ," an aspiration repeatedly voiced in prayer and song, some kind of co-ordination in planning and action was necessary. It is one of the striking facts of the decades which immediately preceded 1914 that this was accomplished. As we are to see in the final volume, the movement went on after 1914 with greatly enhanced power. Protestantism displayed the capacity to parallel its fissiparousness with inclusive co-operation.

In accordance with the genius of Protestantism, co-operation was not imposed from the top, for there was no top to enforce it. It arose spontaneously and from many quarters. Again in conformity with the nature of Protestantism, the dominant strain in the movement for co-ordination resisted efforts towards ecclesiastical uniformity but made for a unity in which diversity and individual conviction were preserved. Here was something new in Christian history. The union of all Christians was sought, not by the road of one ecclesiastical

---

[315] [Charles K. Edmunds], *Canton Christian College, Ling Naam Hok Hau. Its Growth and Outlook* (New York, Trustees of the Canton Christian College, 1919, pp. 66), p. 10.

structure with a central administration vested with absolute authority, but by that of the voluntary fellowship of autonomous bodies in worship and in the devising and execution of programmes.

The movement towards co-operation began very early. Such organizations as the London Missionary Society, the American Board of Commissioners for Foreign Missions, and the American Home Missionary Society in their plans, and for a time in their practice, included more than one denomination among their supporters and missionaries. Several of the denominational societies were ante-dated by local and regional societies and by their formation effected a denomination-wide co-ordination of missionary efforts which had previously been impossible.

The Young Men's and the Young Women's Christian Associations, the Young People's Societies of Christian Endeavour, the Sunday Schools, and the student Christian organizations were respectively gathered into world-wide fellowships—the World's Alliance of Young Men's Christian Associations, the World's Young Women's Christian Association, the World's Christian Endeavour Union, the World's Sunday School Association, and the World's Student Christian Federation.

Churches related to one another in doctrine and government began to seek fellowship through supra-national associations. Thus, in 1867, at the instance of the Provincial Synod of Canada, and at the call of the Archbishop of Canterbury, the bishops in communion with the Church of England met in what proved to be the first of a succession of Lambeth Conferences;[316] an Alliance of the Reformed Churches holding the Presbyterian System came into being; and out of a Baptist World Congress, held in London in 1905, the Baptist World Alliance was born.

Conferences were held and in time continuing interdenominational co-ordinating agencies were set up for particular regions and countries. Thus in 1848 the German Evangelical Church Diet (Deutscher Evangelischer Kirchentag) was founded in Germany to bring together the Evangelical churches of Germany.[317] In 1854 a visit of the great missionary to India, Alexander Duff, was made the occasion for a Union Missionary Convention in New York City, attended by members of several denominations.[318] The first ques-

[316] Randall T. Davidson (compiled under his direction), *The Five Lambeth Conferences* (London, Society for Promoting Christian Knowledge, 1920, pp. xii, 459), pp. 3ff.

[317] Schaff and Prime, editors, *History, Essays, Orations and Other Documents of the Sixth General Conference of the Evangelical Alliance . . . New York . . . 1873,* pp. 197ff.

[318] *Proceedings of the Union Missionary Convention Held in New York, May 4th and 5th, 1854* (New York, Taylor & Hogg, 1854, pp. 61), pp. 7-9, 14, 15.

tion discussed was, "To what extent are we authorized by the Word of God to expect the conversion of the world to Christ?"[319] In 1858 a conference was held of British, American, and continental European missionaries in South India,[320] and in 1879 a second and larger conference, embracing missionaries of South India and Ceylon, assembled.[321] In 1872-1873 the first of a series of decennial missionary conferences for all India met at Allahabad.[322] In 1877,[323] 1890,[324] and 1907,[325] on an ever-increasing scale, conferences of Protestant missionaries working in China were convened. In 1893 the Foreign Missions Conference of North America was begun.[326] Eventually it drew into its fellowship the large majority of the foreign missionary societies of the United States and Canada. In 1912 the similar Conference of Missionary Societies in Great Britain and Ireland was formed.[327] In the first decade of the twentieth century the missionary societies of Holland initiated a movement towards the common training of missionaries and associated action.[328] In 1908 two organizations were formed in the United States, the Home Missions Council, for the collaboration of the societies engaged in spreading Christianity in that country, and the Federal Council of Churches of Christ in America.[329] In 1900 a conference was held of Protestant missionaries working in Japan.[330] In 1913, as the result of a gathering under the auspices of the Foreign Missions Conference of North America, the Committee on Co-operation in Latin

[319] *Proceedings,* etc., pp. 14, 15.

[320] *Proceedings of the South India Missionary Conference Held at Ootacamund Apr. 19th-May 5th, 1858* (Madras, Society for Promoting Christian Knowledge, 1858, pp. vii, 342, xxxiii), *passim.*

[321] *The Missionary Conference South India and Ceylon, 1879* (Madras, Addison & Co., 2 vols., 1880), *passim.*

[322] *Report of the Second Decennial Missionary Conference held at Calcutta 1882-83* (Calcutta, Baptist Mission Press, 1883, pp. xxx, 462), p. ix.

[323] *Records of the General Conference of Protestant Missionaries of China Held at Shanghai, May 10-14, 1877* (Shanghai, 1878), *passim.*

[324] *Records of the General Conference of Protestant Missionaries of China Held at Shanghai, May 7-20, 1890* (Shanghai, American Presbyterian Mission Press, 1890, pp. lxviii, 744), *passim.*

[325] *China Centenary Missionary Conference Records* (New York, American Tract Society [no date], pp. xxxvii, 823), *passim.*

[326] Leslie B. Moss, *Adventures in Missionary Cooperation,* pp. 9, 10.

[327] Kenneth Maclennan, *Twenty Years of Missionary Co-operation* (London, Edinburgh House Press, 1927, pp. 96), pp. 15ff.

[328] Baron van Boetzelaer van Dubbledam in *The International Review of Missions,* Vol. XXII, pp. 233-239.

[329] Charles S. Macfarland, *Christian Unity in Practice and Prophecy* (New York, The Macmillan Co., 1933, pp. xvii, 396), pp. 56, 58.

[330] *Proceedings of the General Conference of Protestant Missionaries in Japan Held in Tokyo, October 24-31, 1900* (Tokyo, Methodist Publishing House, 1901, pp. xi, 1048), *passim.*

America was organized, to co-ordinate Protestant efforts for that region.[331] Through the avoidance of overlapping fields, through joint efforts in translating the Bible, in printing and circulating literature, and here and there through organic unions of churches, Protestants were working together.[332]

Gatherings assembled which drew together Protestants from several denominations and from more than one country. What was known as the Evangelical Alliance held a succession of meetings, beginning in London in 1846. Members came from many countries and communions and considered topics of common interest, including the spread of the faith in many parts of the world. However, they were not official delegates of their respective communions.[333] In 1884 what was known as the International Missionary Union was organized. It held annual meetings, but always in the United States.[334]

A series of gatherings which eventually issued in the most comprehensive organization of all, the International Missionary Council, dates back in part to the Union Missionary Convention, held in New York in 1854, but more directly to a Conference on Missions in Liverpool in 1860, at which 126 were present from various British societies and denominations.[335] Even earlier, William Carey had suggested decennial interdenominational and missionary conferences and had proposed that the first convene at the Cape of Good Hope in 1810.[336] However, the home authorities of his society vetoed the project and it was from the New York and Liverpool gatherings that the movement really started. The Liverpool meeting was followed, in 1878, by a larger conference on Protestant missions, in Mildmay Park, in London. The initiative came from Great Britain, but not only the British Isles, but also the United States, Canada, and the continent of Europe were represented.[337] In 1888 still another conference in the series assembled in Exeter Hall, London, under the chairmanship of the Earl of Shaftesbury. While predominantly British, it also drew from North America and the continent of Europe.[338]

[331] C. H. Fahs and Helen E. Davis, *Conspectus of Coöperative Missionary Enterprises* (New York, International Missionary Council, 1935, pp. v, 252), p. 15.

[332] See a summary of the situation as it was in 1910 in *World Missionary Conference, 1910,* Vol. VIII, *passim.*

[333] Schaff and Prime, editors, *op. cit.,* pp. 189ff.

[334] *International Missionary Index* (Clifton Springs, N. Y., 1898, pp. 76), p. 1.

[335] *Conference on Missions Held in 1860 at Liverpool* (London, James Nisbet & Co., 1860, pp. xi, 428), *passim.*

[336] S. Pearce Carey, *William Carey,* p. 253.

[337] *Proceedings of the General Conference on Foreign Missions Held at the Conference Hall, in Mildmay Park, London, in October 1878* (London, John F. Shaw & Co., 1879, pp. viii, 434), *passim.*

[338] James Johnston, editor, *Report of the Centenary Conference on the Protestant Missions of the World. Held in Exeter Hall (June 9th-19th) London, 1888* (London, James Nisbet & Co., 2 vols., 1888), *passim.*

Another in the series, what was known as the Ecumenical Missionary Conference (termed ecumenical not because it included all Christian churches but "because the plan of campaign which it proposes covers the whole area of the inhabited globe") met in 1900. It was symptomatic of the fashion in which the United States was assuming a larger proportion of the Protestant missionary load that the gathering originated in a suggestion of the Foreign Missions Conference of North America and that its place of meeting was New York City.[339] It was much larger than its predecessors and drew from a wider geographic area.[340] Even more fruitful was the World Missionary Conference which convened in Edinburgh in 1910. It was held, interestingly enough, just a century after the proposed date of the similar one suggested by Carey. The preparation was more extensive than that for its predecessors, the attendance was more carefully apportioned, and much more attention was given to comprehensive planning for the future. The preliminary committee was international, but the growing prominence of the United States was seen in the fact that the chairman was an American, John R. Mott.[341] Unlike its forerunners, the Edinburgh gathering formulated plans for consecutive co-operation. It appointed a Continuation Committee with Mott as chairman. Under the leadership of the chairman, Continuation Conferences were held in 1912-1913 in India, Burma, Singapore, China, Korea, and Japan.[342] There followed, after 1914, the International Missionary Council, the story of which we are to rehearse in our final volume. The fact that Protestant missions were so overwhelmingly from Great Britain, Canada, Australia, New Zealand, and the United States with a common language, English, and a similar cultural heritage, facilitated this world-wide co-operation. Progressively, through an increasing number of organizations, more and more co-ordinated through a central, comprehensive agency, Protestant Christians were learning to work together in plans which embraced the entire earth.

In their methods, Protestant missionaries approached peoples and cultures in a wide variety of ways.[343] This was especially the case in non-Occidental lands.

[339] *Ecumenical Missionary Conference, New York, 1900,* Vol. I, p. 10.

[340] *Ecumenical Missionary Conference, New York, 1900,* Vol. II, pp. 385ff.

[341] An account of the conference is to be found in *World Missionary Conference, 1910,* Vol. IX, pp. 1-138.

[342] *The Continuation Committee Conferences in Asia 1912-1913. A Brief Account of the Conferences Together with Their Findings and Lists of Members* (New York, Chairman of the Continuation Committee, 1913, pp. 488), *passim.*

[343] No single authoritative treatise exists on Protestant missionary methods. Methods have been discussed in the many missionary periodicals. Of these the most comprehensive is *The International Review of Missions.* They also have been given much attention in the many missionary conferences. For the latter part of the period the fullest treatment, representing a wider range of consultation than any other, is in the volumes, *World Mis-*

They sought to win individuals and groups to the Christian faith. They scattered their message broadcast through the printed page. They reduced scores of languages to writing. They translated part or all of the Bible into hundreds of tongues. In many lands they became the pioneers of modern Occidental medicine. They founded and conducted schools. They devised methods for teaching the blind to read. They helped relieve famine. They introduced new fruits and grains and improved methods of agriculture. In some islands and tribes they became advisers to the leaders in the reorganization of the entire life of the group. In an age when, under the impact of Western commercial and political imperialism, non-Occidental cultures were disintegrating, the Protestant missionary was seeking to mould the emerging new cultures in such fashion that they would be better than the old.

In the expansion of Christianity in the nineteenth century, the Russian Orthodox Church had a share. With a few exceptions, this was limited to the Russian Empire and to Russian emigrants to the United States. In influence and numerical strength Russian Orthodox missions did not even approach those of Roman Catholics and Protestants. For this reason, we need give them but very brief mention here, particularly since we are to recur to them in the appropriate places in our geographic pilgrimage.

More than either the Roman Catholic or Protestant missionary enterprises in the nineteenth century the spread of the Russian Orthodox form of Christianity was accomplished under the direction and through the financial support of the state. This was to be expected, for in Russia as in no other major country the established church was bound hand and foot to the government. The only missionary organizations of any prominence which corresponded to the hundreds which sprang up spontaneously in the Roman Catholic and Protestant folds were late in appearing and had official patronage. The most prominent, the Orthodox Missionary Society, was founded in 1870. Its purpose was not to send missionaries but to raise funds to support them. At first concerned only with missions within the Empire, within a few years it extended assistance also to those outside Russian domains. It followed an earlier, abortive effort, and arose out of the zeal of the head of the Altai mission, but it was

sionary Conference 1910, which contain reports of commissions appointed before the conference met. Two works which had a fairly wide circulation are Arthur Judson Brown, The Foreign Missionary (New York, Fleming H. Revell Co., 1907, pp. 412), giving an American programme, and Gustav Warneck, Evangelische Missionslehre. Ein Missionstheoretischer Versuch (Gotha, Friedrich Andreas Perthes, 5 vols., 1892-1903), which was especially influential in German missions.

organized by a Metropolitan of Moscow, partly at the request of the Empress. The Holy Synod, through which the state governed the Church, endorsed it and eventually made a mission Sunday, with a sermon and collection, obligatory upon all parishes. In 1904 branches existed in fifty-five dioceses.[344] In 1860 a Society for the Revival of Orthodoxy in the Caucasus came into being in Tiflis and assisted in the provision of churches, schools, priests, and teachers for the nominally Christian population of that region.[345] In 1894 the Emperor Alexander III created an institute to aid the founding of churches in Siberia, chiefly for Russian settlers. The support was mainly through official sources.[346] In 1867 a brotherhood was begun at Kazan to prepare Christian literature for the pagan peoples of Russia,[347] and in 1898 an institution was founded, also at Kazan, an outgrowth of earlier efforts there, to train missionaries for the Tartars and Mongols.[348] These, however, when compared with what was occurring in Roman Catholic and Protestant circles, were relatively slight undertakings.

In case this rather long chapter with its many details has proved bewildering, may we attempt to summarize in brief fashion the processes by which Christianity spread in the nineteenth century. It was chiefly through its Roman Catholic and Protestant forms that Christianity expanded. Of these two wings of the Christian movement, in contrast with the preceding three centuries, Protestantism displayed the greater vigour and enjoyed the larger proportional extension. While Roman Catholicism was active, the century was one in which Protestants led in the spread of the faith. This extension of Roman Catholic and Protestant Christianity was closely associated with the growth in power and wealth and with the expansion of Western peoples. It was also the result of an unprecedented upsurging of life within the Christian movement itself. Far from having lost its vigour with age and far from being nullified by the open and covert scepticism in what was known as Christendom, the Christian impulse had never before been so potent in inspiring the rank and file of those who professed the Christian name to propagate their faith. Now arose organization after organization for the dissemination of Christianity, more than in the entire preceding portions of the Christian era. They came into being spontaneously and in a wide variety of places. They owed their financial

[344] Raeder, in *Allgemeine Missionszeitschrift*, Vol. XXXII, pp. 507ff.
[345] Raeder, in *op. cit.*, Vol. XXXII, p. 514.
[346] Lübeck, *Die Christianisierung Russlands*, p. 92.
[347] Raeder, in *op. cit.*, Vol. XXXII, p. 514.
[348] Raeder, in *op. cit.*, Vol. XXXII, p. 513.

undergirding, not to the state or to a few princes or wealthy individuals, as had much of the previous expansion of the faith, but to the gifts of hundreds of thousands, largely in the humbler walks of life. It was by popular, voluntary movements and organizations that Christianity spread. Women and laymen had a larger share than ever before. Nothing at all equal to it had previously been seen in the history of Christianity or of any other religion. As the century passed, in both Roman Catholic and Protestant circles the missionary enterprise continued to grow. In organizations which implemented it, in numbers of missionaries, and in financial support it continued its upward swing. This was due in part to the peace and prosperity which were among the marked features of the Occident in the four decades before 1914. It was also due to the rising momentum in the missionary movement itself and in the convictions which inspired it.

Chapter V

EUROPE. JEWS: PAGANS: MOSLEMS: MISSIONS OF CHRISTIANS AMONG OTHER CHRISTIANS: HOLDING CHRISTIANS TO THEIR FAITH: THE EFFECT UPON THE ENVIRONMENT: THE EFFECT OF THE ENVIRONMENT

FROM the description of the general factors which conditioned the expansion of Christianity in the nineteenth century, and from the summary account of the reasons for the expansion and the processes of the spread, we turn, as in preceding volumes, to a narrative, region by region, of the extension of the faith. This will, as heretofore, require the major proportion of our space. For convenience, too, we will, at the end of each section devoted to a major area, attempt to say what effect Christianity had upon that particular environment and what effect the environment had upon Christianity.

In our geographic survey, we begin, as is fitting, with Europe. It was from Europe that Christianity had achieved most of its expansion since A.D. 500. Here, with the exception of the Near East, Egypt, and possibly Southern India, were the oldest existing Christian communities. Here, longer than in any other major area, Christianity had been the dominant religion.

Yet in Europe at the outset of the nineteenth century Christianity was not even the nominal faith of all the population. Hundreds of thousands of Jews held to their hereditary religion. Here and there were those who still adhered to cults which are usually regarded as primitive. In the South-east and East were many Moslems. Moreover, an ever-present problem, that of leading into the faith the children of professed Christians, became peculiarly acute in a transitional age such as was the nineteenth century, when so much of the old order with which Christianity had been identified was passing and when the traditional religion of the majority of Europeans was being so openly and so vigorously challenged by intellectual and social movements originating within Christendom itself.

The Jews presented a continuing challenge. Since the beginning of Christianity, efforts had been made to win the people among whom the faith had originated. Hundreds of thousands had come over to Christianity, some through persuasion, but many under the cruel pressure of crude force. Yet, at the dawn of the nineteenth century, millions remained true to their ancestral religion. It was to be expected that the heightened urge to propagate Christianity would lead, in Roman Catholic, Protestant, and Eastern Orthodox circles, to fresh efforts for the conversion of the Jews.

Throughout the nineteenth century, the vast majority of the Jews of the world were in Europe. On the eve of 1914, out of about 13,500,000 Jews, slightly more than 10,000,000 were in that continent.[1] Of these, a little more than 6,000,000, or more than half, were in Russia, including the Russian portions of Poland.[2] Nearly 1,000,000 were in Hungary,[3] and not far from 900,000 were in Galicia, which had once belonged to Poland.[4] Only a minority, therefore, dwelt in Western Europe. In Western Europe in the course of the nineteenth century the legal restrictions under which the Jew had laboured were largely relaxed,[5] but in Russia they remained in force and were even strengthened.[6] In Eastern Europe, therefore, the Jew remained apart and preserved his own life. In Western Europe he tended to neglect the religious observances of his ancestors and to become secularized.[7] In all of Europe he continued to be a city dweller and to prize education.

Of the three great branches of the Christian movement, the Roman Catholics seem to have had the smallest numerical success in the nineteenth century among the Jews of Europe. One estimate of the number of their Jewish converts places the total of baptisms at 55,300 as against approximately 61,000 in the Protestant groups and 74,500 in the Eastern Oxthodox churches.[8] Of these conversions to Roman Catholic Christianity, more than half were in Austria and Hungary.[9] However, the most notable individual accessions were not from Austria or Hungary but from Strasbourg. One of these was Libermann (as a Jew he bore as a given name Jacob, but as a Christian he took the baptismal name Franz Maria Paul). Born in 1802,

[1] Cohen, *Jewish Life in Modern Times*, p. 349. Gidney, *Missions to Jews*, p. 10, citing the *Jewish Year Book* for 1911, gives the total number of Jews in Europe as 8,850,083, and in the entire world as 11,861,386.
[2] Cohen, *op. cit.*, p. 346.
[3] *Ibid.*
[4] *Ibid.*
[5] Cohen, *op. cit.*, pp. 135ff.
[6] Cohen, *op. cit.*, pp. 145ff.
[7] Cohen, *op. cit.*, pp. 291ff.
[8] Cohen, *op. cit.*, p. 298, citing Joh. De le Roi, *Judentaufen im 19 Jahrhundert* (Leipzig, 1899).
[9] *Ibid.*

he was the son of a conservative rabbi and was prepared for his father's vocation. He came into the Christian faith through a brother, Simon, who, while a medical student, had found his traditional beliefs slipping from him, and through reading the New Testament had become a Christian. In attempting to bring this brother back to Judaism, Libermann's own misgivings were aroused. Through reading the New Testament and other Christian books and after great agony of soul, he in turn became a Christian and was baptized (1826). In time he became a priest and the founder of the Congregation of the Holy Heart of Mary. This organization took Negroes as its primary charge and before many years united with the Congregation of the Holy Ghost.[10] The joint body had an important part in missions to Africa in the nineteenth and twentieth centuries.[11] The other notable converts from Strasbourg were two brothers, Maria Theodore Ratisbonne (1802-1884) and Maria Alphonse Ratisbonne (1814-1884). The elder belonged to the circle in which the Libermanns moved and owed his conversion (1826) in part to the influence of Simon. The younger was late (1842) in following his brother, but, after a period when he had abandoned all religion, made a sudden *volte-face* when, on a chance visit to Rome, he had what he believed to be a vision of the Virgin Mary. Out of the efforts of Theodore came the Sisterhood of Our Lady of Sion for the Christian education of Jewish youth. Alphonse, after entering the priesthood and joining the Jesuits, left the latter to devote himself entirely to labours for the Jews and shared in the formation of the Fathers of Sion. These had as their object the conversion of Jews and Moslems.[12] The two organizations extended their activities to several centres in Europe, the Near East, and the Americas.[13]

Protestants were very active in efforts to convert the Jews. Near the close of the nineteenth century, forty different societies and 260 missionaries were said to be devoting themselves to this purpose.[14] A little later, in 1906, fifty-eight such societies were enumerated in Europe,[15] although among these

[10] Heinrich Döring, *Vom Juden zum Ordenstifter. Der ehrw. P. Libermann und die Gründung der afrikanischen Mission im 19 Jahrhundert* (Neuss, Missionshaus Knechtsteden, 2d ed., 1930, pp. xv, 343), *passim*.

[11] Schwager, *Die katholische Heidenmission der Gegenwart*, pp. 42, 43.

[12] *The Catholic Encyclopedia*, Vol. XII, p. 659; Marie, *Histoire des Institutes Religieux et Missionaires*, pp. 309-313.

[13] Marie, *op. cit.*, pp. 309-313.

[14] De le Roi, *Geschichte der evangelischen Juden-Mission seit Enstehung des neueren Judentums*, Vol. II, p. 368.

[15] Strack, *Jahrbuch der evangelischen Judenmission*, 1 Band, pp. 93ff. For another list naming 49 societies (28 in the British Isles and 21 on the Continent), see A. E. Thompson, *A Century of Jewish Missions* (New York, Fleming H. Revell Co., 1902, pp. 286), pp. 279-281. For an earlier summary of the Protestant enterprise, by comparison with which the growth in efforts to win the Jews can be seen, see Chr. H. Kalkar, *Missionen iblandt*

were included a few which directed most of their energies to others than Jews and at least two of which had their base in Europe but laboured outside of Europe.

Of the Protestant bodies, the most prominent was the London Society for Promoting Christianity amongst the Jews.[16] It was the outgrowth of the London Missionary Society, for it owed its inception to a Christian Jew who had come from Germany to seek service under that organization and who became impressed with the challenge of the Jewish population in London. The society was founded in 1808, under a somewhat different name from that which it was later given. At its inception it embraced in its membership both Nonconformists and members of the Church of England. In 1815, however, its rules were so reconstituted as to confine its membership to the Church of England. Its chief support was from the Evangelicals. Some of the most prominent of that school, among them several members of the "Clapham Sect," were members of its directing committee. The society early found a munificent benefactor in Lewis Way, a man of great charm and energy who devoted to the conversion of the Jews a very large fortune which he received through bequest.[17] Way travelled extensively in Europe to investigate the condition of the Jews. He formed a friendship with Alexander I of Russia and pled with that monarch, not without some success, to facilitate missions to the Jews. At the Congress of Aix-la-Chapelle, in 1818, he urged upon the assembled potentates kindlier treatment for the race and secured a protocol promising consideration of their condition. He obtained influential patrons for the society. The society conducted work in London and had

Jøderne (Copenhagen, 1868, pp. xi, 174), pp. 119-146, and Chr. H. Kalkar, *Israel og Kirken. Historisk Overblik over Gjensidige Forhold indtil de Nyeste Tider* (Copenhagen, C. A. Reitzels Vorlag, 1881, pp. xxi, 397), pp. 275ff.

[16] W. T. Gidney, *The History of the London Society for Promoting Christianity amongst the Jews from 1809 to 1908* (London, London Society for Promoting Christianity amongst the Jews, 1908, pp. xxx, 672; a centenary history, based on official records, by a secretary of the society), *passim*. A slightly older and briefer account is W. T. Gidney, *At Home and Abroad. A Description of the English and Continental Missions of the London Society for Promoting Christianity amongst the Jews* (London, Operative Jewish Converts' Institution, 1900, pp. x, 246). Unless otherwise indicated, the material for this paragraph is obtained from these two books. Brief earlier accounts of the separate missions of the society are in W. Ayerst, *The Jews of the Nineteenth Century* (London, 1848, pp. 431), pp. 389-426. A periodical (not the earliest one), an official organ of the society, is *Monthly Intelligence*, begun in 1830. In 1835 the title changed to *Jewish Intelligence*. The second series, under the latter title, was from 1861 to 1910, and a third series, under the title *Jewish Missionary Intelligence*, began in 1911.

[17] On Lewis Way, see Stirling, *The Ways of Yesterday. Being the Chronicles of the Way Family from 1307 to 1885*, pp. 83-288; Gidney, *The History of the London Society for Promoting Christianity amongst the Jews*, pp. 37, 41, 47, 54, 58-61, 65, 75, 76, 79, 82, 83, 95, 96, 118, 150.

there a centre for converts, for the training of missionaries, and for the education of Jewish children. It established missions in several other cities in the British Isles. It also extended its work widely on the continent, in North Africa, Abyssinia, India, and America. In Europe it was especially active in Holland, Germany, and Russia, including Poland. A convert, Joseph Wolff, ranged widely as a pioneer, making his way as far as India.[18] Another convert, a missionary of the society, the scholarly Michael Solomon Alexander, became the first incumbent of the Bishopric of Jerusalem established jointly by the Kings of Prussia and England.[19] The society prepared and distributed literature. In a number of cities it conducted schools for Jewish youth.[20]

More than half of the Protestant organizations in Europe which sought the conversion of the Jews were British.[21] Some limited their efforts to one city or to the British Isles. Some included other lands in their program.

In 1867, in London, as a result of a call sent out in 1865, the Hebrew-Christian Alliance was formed, of members of several different denominations, for fellowship and as witness to the faith of Jewish Christians.[22]

In Germany almost none of the organized effort to win the Jews which had flourished in the seventeenth and eighteenth centuries survived to the beginning of the nineteenth century. The *Institutum Judaicum* which Pietist zeal had founded at Halle came to an end in 1792.[23] A fund started by the zealous Esdras Edzard in the seventeenth century was still in existence and its income was used to assist needy Jewish converts and to aid publication.[24] Contact with missionaries of British organizations, especially of the London Society for Promoting Christianity amongst the Jews, contributed to the formation of several small organizations in Germany with similar objectives.[25] It was largely due to Lewis Way, of that same society, that there came into being (in 1822) the first important German body of the nineteenth century for the conversion of the Jews, the Berlin Society for the Promotion of

---

[18] Gidney, *op. cit.*, pp. 101-111, 115, 122; Stirling, *op. cit.*, pp. 198-214.

[19] J. F. A. De le Roi, *Michael Solomon Alexander, der erste evangelische Bischof in Jerusalem* (Gütersloh, C. Bertelsmann, 1897, p. 230), *passim;* Schonfield, *The History of Jewish Christianity from the First to the Twentieth Century* (London, Duckworth, 1936, pp. 256), pp. 216-218.

[20] Strack, *op. cit.*, pp..67ff.

[21] Strack, *op. cit.*, pp. 94-105. On one of these, issuing from the Mildmay centre in London, see Samuel Hinds Wilkinson, *The Life of John Wilkinson, the Jewish Missionary* (London, Morgan & Scott, 1908, pp. xi, 356), *passim.*

[22] Schonfield, *The History of Jewish Christianity,* pp. 220-223.

[23] De le Roi, *Geschichte der evangelischen Judenmission,* Vol. I, pp. 45, 46.

[24] Strack, *op. cit.*, p. 106.

[25] De le Roi, *op. cit.*, Vol. I, pp. 134-142.

Christianity among the Jews (*die Berliner Gesellschaft zur Beförderung des Christenthums unter der Juden*). Indeed, for a time it received financial aid from the London society.[26] In 1905 it employed seven missionaries.[27] In the course of the century several other projects were put on foot by German Protestants.[28] One of these, the *Institutum Judaicum Delitzschianum*, took its name and its purpose in part from the eighteenth century *Institutum Judaicum*. Its original founder, Franz Delitzsch (1813-1890), owed much of his education to the generosity of a Jew and became a distinguished scholar and teacher of the Old Testament. He gave much energy to missions to the Jews (he had, incidentally, the pleasure of seeing his benefactor baptized), sought to open to the Christian world some of the wealth of Hebrew literature, endeavoured to interest the entire Lutheran body in efforts to win the Jews, and at Leipzig, where he had a chair in the university, began an *Institutum Judaicum* which he hoped would be a centre for the Jewish missionary activity of the Lutheran bodies. For a time it was interrupted, but in 1880 it was revived by a pupil of Delitzsch.[29] Aided by subsidies from a number of societies for the Jews, it trained missionaries and prepared literature.[30]

In Switzerland, in France, in Holland, in Scandinavia, and in Baltic regions under Russian control, several societies were organized, most of them in the second half of the nineteenth century.[31]

As might be expected from the distribution of societies, the largest number of conversions of Jews to Protestant Christianity in the nineteenth century was in the British Isles, with Germany a close second. In these two countries were about three-fourths of the recorded baptisms.[32] The motives which led to the acceptance of Christianity varied. Many, notably in Germany, came into the Church in an attempt to become assimilated to the culture about them. This movement was heightened by the rise of German nationalism after the emancipation from Napoleon and by the accompanying belief that German culture was Christian and that to be a good German one must be baptized.[33] Somewhat akin to this seems to have been the purpose of Abraham, a son of the notable Jewish philosopher Moses Mendelssohn

[26] De le Roi, *op. cit.*, Vol. I, p. 142.
[27] Strack, *op. cit.*, p. 106.
[28] De le Roi, *op. cit.*, Vol. I, pp. 157ff.
[29] De le Roi, *op. cit.*, Vol. I, pp. 120-122, 132-135.
[30] Strack, *op. cit.*, p. 107.
[31] De le Roi, *op. cit.*, Vol. I, pp. 273ff.; Strack, *op. cit.*, pp. 108-110.
[32] Gidney, *Missions to Jews*, p. 143, citing De le Roi, *Judentaufen im 19 Jahrhundert*.
[33] De le Roi, *Geschichte der evangelischen Judenmission*, Vol. I, p. 182. As one example of this see Hensel, *The Mendelssohn Family*, Vol. I, p. 67.

(1729-1786) and father of the musician, Jakob Ludwig Felix Mendelssohn-Bartholdy. In an interesting letter Abraham declared that he himself, while not knowing whether God exists or what He is, and while not leaving his inherited Jewish faith, was having his children reared as Christians because that religion "is the creed of most civilized peoples" and because it "contains nothing that can lead . . . away from what is good and much that guides . . . to love, obedience, tolerance, and resignation."[34] Something like this may have lain back of the baptism as a child, through his father, of Karl Marx.[35] Personal ambition also had a part, and in Germany many became Christians to escape the disabilities imposed on Jews by law.[36] The sceptical father of Benjamin Disraeli, later Lord Beaconsfield, seems to have had his children baptized to assimilate them into English society and to free them from the social handicap of their Jewish faith. The step was precipitated by a quarrel with the officials of the synagogue.[37] Some converts were lured by the hope of an easy living through generous patrons of Jewish missions or by the prominence and flattery which conversion brought them in the churches.[38] Yet many made the break from Judaism out of profound conviction and not a few paid the cost of severe persecution and of complete ostracism from their families.[39] Among these was Isaac da Costa (1798-1860), a descendant of Marranos who had migrated to Holland and had there resumed their ancestral faith. He became an earnest Christian and spoke courageously for his faith.[40] Another was Friedrich Julius Stahl (1802-1861), who, reared as a strictly orthodox Jew, in his late teens became a Christian. He achieved distinction as an authority in law, held a chair in law and philosophy at Berlin, and became a leader of the conservatives in Prussia.[41] David Mendel (1789-1850), who on his baptism adopted the name of Neander, "new man," and is known as Johann August Wilhelm Neander, was a man of wide learning, became famous as a theologian and church historian, as a professor in the university attracted many students, and by his warm re-

---

[34] Hensel, op. cit., Vol. I, pp. 79-81.

[35] De le Roi, op. cit., Vol. I, p. 246.

[36] Cohen, Jewish Life in Modern Times, p. 294.

[37] Georg Brandes, Lord Beaconsfield, translated by Mrs. George Sturge (New York, Charles Scribner's Sons, 1880, pp. iv, 382), p. 20; J. A. Froude, Lord Beaconsfield (New York, Harper & Brothers, 1890, pp. x, 267), pp. 13, 14; D. L. Murray, in Encyclopædia Britannica, 14th ed., Vol. III, p. 246.

[38] Stirling, The Ways of Yesterday, pp. 136-138.

[39] See a number of biographies and autobiographies, most of them written for purposes of edification, in Dunlop, Memories of Gospel Triumphs among the Jews during the Victorian Era, passim.

[40] De le Roi, in Frank, Witnesses from Israel, pp. 1-15.

[41] De le Roi, in Frank, op. cit., pp. 31-38.

ligious faith and contagious friendship did much to bring new life into the Prussian Church.[42] Ridley Haim Herschell (1807-1864), the father of a Lord Chancellor of England, was reared an orthodox Jew, after a long inward conflict became a Christian, and for many years laboured in London as a clergyman and a missionary to his own race.[43] Chr. H. Kalkar (1803-1886), a native of Stockholm, spent most of his life in Denmark. He, too, after a severe struggle renounced orthodox Judaism for Christianity. He became a leader in stimulating missionary interest in the Lutheran Church of Denmark and was active through the Evangelical Alliance in promoting fellowship among Protestants the world around.[44] Alfred Edersheim (1825-1889), while a Jewish youth of great intellectual promise and a student in Budapest, was brought in touch with Scotch missionaries and through them became a Christian. First as a clergyman in the Free Church of Scotland and then in the Church of England, he won wide recognition as a preacher and scholar. His *Life of Jesus* had a large circulation.[45] The list might be greatly lengthened. Probably never since the first century in so short a space of time had so many able Jews voluntarily become Christians as in Western Europe between 1815 and 1914. By compulsory methods larger numbers had been baptized in a shorter space of time. Yet, particularly through the vigorous life in nineteenth century Protestantism, acting in an environment in which increasing civil and economic freedom was being accorded the Jews, possibly more individuals of that race were of their own choice and from the attraction of Jesus becoming Christians than at any time since the first hundred years of the Christian era.

Far otherwise was the situation in Russia. Here the older tradition persisted of conversion by coercion. More than half of the Jews of Europe lived in European Russia. The ancestors of most of these had entered Poland centuries before when the rulers of that state were tolerant. The annexation by Russia in the eighteenth century of a large part of Poland brought them under the Tsars. They were restricted to the western sections of Russia and were placed under disabilities. Alexander I, who reigned in the first quarter of the nineteenth century and who had been friendly to the missionaries from England, tended to take a liberal attitude towards them, but his successor, Nicholas I (1825-1855), instituted severe measures.[46] He accentuated

---

[42] K. Kunert, in Frank, *op. cit.*, pp. 39-47.
[43] A. Frank, in Frank, *op. cit.*, pp. 59-64; Dunlop, *op. cit.*, pp. 40-47.
[44] De le Roi, in Frank, *op. cit.*, pp. 65-70.
[45] De le Roi, in Frank, *op. cit.*, pp. 91-99.
[46] See S. M. Dubnow, *History of the Jews in Russia and Poland from the Earliest Times until the Present Day, passim.*

the pale and at the same time endeavoured to assimilate the Jews to the Russians and to constrain their young men to enter military service. He sought to compel all Jews in the service of the state, including those who had been forced into military service, to be baptized.[47] Between 1836 and 1872, 38,000 Jews are said to have been baptized into the Russian Orthodox Church.[48] Yet most of the Russian Jews held to their ancestral faith. Moreover, bad as was the lot of the Jews in Russia and severe as were the measures adopted against them, no such wholesale compulsory conversion was undertaken and no such extensive expulsions were carried out as had overtaken the Jews in Spain and Portugal at the close of the fifteenth century.

In spite of the earnest efforts of Roman Catholic and Protestant missionaries and of the endeavours of the Russian state, the vast majority of the Jews of Europe remained, as had their ancestors, outside the Church. The increasing tolerance which Christians of Western Europe had shown between A.D. 1500 and A.D. 1800 was growing, and legal disabilities against the Jews were being removed, but relatively few conversions followed. Most of the Jews who abandoned the faith of their fathers did so not to adopt Christianity but to become secularized and indifferent to all religion.

Of the open survival of pagan cults in the Europe of the nineteenth century there was relatively little. The conversions of the preceding centuries, superficial though many of them were and slow though the process had been, had eliminated the outward observance of the pre-Christian religions in all but the northern and eastern fringes of the continent. Nowhere were peoples predominantly Roman Catholic in direct touch with these remnants. At the outset of the nineteenth century, in the northern portions of Scandinavia some of the Lapps were still pagan or so superficially Christian as to be little better than pagan, and attracted missions from the prevailing Lutheranism. In Russia a number of tribes still clung to their inherited cults and were the object of the efforts of the Russian Orthodox Church.

Numerically the Lapps did not constitute a major problem. About the middle of the nineteenth century their total was said to be approximately 26,000, of whom not far from 16,000 were in Norway, 6,500 in Sweden,

---

[47] Dubnow, op. cit., Vol. II, pp. 44, 45; Cohen, Jewish Life in Modern Times, p. 295.
[48] De le Roi, Geschichte der evangelischen Judenmission, Vol. I, p. 330. On a Jew, Joseph Rabinowitz, who became a Christian from deep conviction and preached widely on his faith but did not join any existing Christian church, see Schonfield, The History of Jewish Christianity, pp. 223-226.

2,000 in Russia, and 1,000 in Finland.[49] As the result of efforts in preceding
centuries, Christianity had already made marked progress among them.
In the nineteenth century missions for them were continued, largely by
members of the state Lutheran churches of Scandinavia. Schools were conducted, the Christian scriptures, in translation, were circulated, the catechism
was taught, and prolonged itineration was undertaken. Now and then
a bishop interested himself in the Lapps.[50] In Sweden the mission of the
state church had a number of catechists among them.[51] In Norway Niels
Joakim Christian Vibe Stockfleth, a former army officer, volunteered for
religious service for the Lapps. After his ordination in the state church he
travelled extensively in their territories, shared their semi-nomadic life,
and prepared literature for them.[52] Private effort supplemented that of the
state church. For instance, a missionary society in Stockholm appointed as
an agent a Swede who had had preparation at the famous missionary training institution at Basel and had seen service in India and Smyrna.[53] Through
these and other measures the Protestant efforts which had been begun in
the sixteenth century and had been greatly augmented in the eighteenth
century were continued.

On the eastern borders of European Russia were numbers of non-Russian
tribes. Several of these had been pagan. We have seen[54] that, partly through
zealous missionaries and partly through attractive material inducements
offered by the state, many from among them had accepted baptism. Yet
even at the close of the nineteenth century thousands of pagans remained.
One set of figures declares that out of a population of 93,442,864 in European
Russia in 1897, 373,000 were pagans.[55] Some missions were conducted for
them, although not on the scale of earlier centuries. Early in the nineteenth
century, for instance, it was reported that the conversion had been completed
of the Ossetes, living in the Caucasus, descendants of the Alani, whose
ancestors had been Christian but had lapsed. The conversion had been begun
and nearly completed in the eighteenth century.[56] Efforts were made to win
the Kalmyks, Buddhists who lived not far from the north-western shores of
the Caspian, on the lower courses of the Volga and the Don and on the

[49] Vahl, *Lapperne og den lapske Mission*, Part I, p. 8.
[50] Vahl, *op. cit.*, Part II, pp. 49ff., 107ff.
[51] Vahl, *op. cit.*, Part II, pp. 119ff.
[52] Vahl, *op. cit.*, Part II, pp. 51ff.; Meylan, *Histoire de l'Evangélisation des Lapons*, pp. 90ff.
[53] Meylan, *op. cit.*, pp. 100ff.
[54] Vol. III, Chap. 2.
[55] Lübeck, *Die Christianisierung Russlands*, p. 93.
[56] Raeder in *Allgemeine Missions-Zeitschrift*, Vol. XXXII, p. 402.

borders of the Caucasus. Very few converts resulted, and of these few those who returned to the nomadic life led by the vast majority of their fellows resumed their ancestral faith.[57] Missions among the pagans in the valley of the Vyatka made little progress and were chiefly valuable as a bulwark against the further spread of Islam.[58] No such striking numerical advances against paganism were registered as in the eighteenth century.

As between Christianity and its long-standing rival, Islam, in the nineteenth century no very great gains or losses could be reported in Europe for either faith. Islam could record no such extensive accessions from Christianity as came to it in the wake of the conquests of the Ottoman Turks. Nor could Christianity show any victories over its ancient enemy comparable to those which it had won, largely by force, in the Iberian Peninsula in the middle ages and in the fourteenth, fifteenth, and sixteenth centuries. In Europe, as elsewhere, as against each other the two great religions had all but reached a stalemate.

In the Balkan Peninsula the recession of the Turkish wave was accompanied by the political independence of such traditionally Christian peoples as the Greeks, the Serbs, the Bulgars, and the Roumanians. However, no conversions of any consequence of Moslems to Christianity followed the change of political status. This was in sharp contrast with the earlier reemergence of Christian rule in the Iberian Peninsula, for there the political triumph of Christianity had been the precursor to the disappearance of Islam. The difference is probably partly to be accounted for by the fact that in the Balkans Turkey remained a formidable power which would have forcibly resented any restrictions on Moslems in recent Turkish territories. Probably fully as important was the failure of the Greek Orthodox to take any measures to win the Moslems. This was in contrast with the earlier vigorous missionary efforts from Roman Catholic circles in Spain and Portugal. Presumably, too, the secular tendencies in European political circles in Europe in the nineteenth century would have looked coolly upon proselyting endeavours, while in the former Spain and Portugal the leadership in effecting a change of faith sometimes, especially in the later stages of the elimination of Islam, came from the princes.

In European Russia some effort was expended on missions for the Moslems and towards checking the advance of Islam among pagans and nominal

[57] Raeder in *op. cit.*, Vol. XXXII, p. 543.
[58] Raeder in *op. cit.*, Vol. XXXII, pp. 541, 542.

Christians. The state-directed missions of the seventeenth and especially of the eighteenth century had led to thousands of baptisms among the Cheremis, the Mordvs, the Tartars (more accurately, Tatars), and other peoples in the eastern portions of European Russia.[59] A large proportion of the conversions had been superficial in the extreme and had not been followed by sufficient instruction to afford Christianity a firm rootage. In the first half of the nineteenth century, Islam began spreading from the Moslem Tartars among the neighbouring nominally Christian Tartars in the vicinity of Kazan and among the Cheremis, Chuvash, and Mordvs in the same general region, some of whom were supposedly Christian and some still pagan.[60] Among the Chuvash the adoption of Islam was facilitated by kinship in language with the Moslem Tartars. Steps were taken to check the further spread of Islam. Obviously this could partly be accomplished by raising the level of the Christianity of those who bore the Christian name. In 1803 a small catechism was published in the Cheremis tongue.[61] Beginning about 1817, Ambrose, Archbishop of Kazan, stimulated the preparation of translations into that language. In connexion with the Russian Bible Society, the New Testament was translated and printed. The liturgy, too, was put into Cheremis, but the translation failed of official approval. After the death of Ambrose these activities came to an end.[62] It is not clear that they had been called forth by the menace of Islam, but it is said that in 1829, 60,000 Cheremis returned to Christianity.[63]

In 1822 the Holy Synod decided to send missionaries to the Kirghis, a nominally but superficially Moslem people between the Urals and the Volga. Schools were ordered established for the children and about a thousand conversions were reported.[64]

With the alarming spread of Islam in the second quarter of the century, fresh efforts were called forth.

The leader in these new measures was Nicholai Ivanovitch Ilminski (1822-1891).[65] Ilminski was a man of unusual linguistic gifts and of great zeal. He began his labours in 1847 by attempts to put the Bible and the

[59] Vol. III, Chap. 2.
[60] Smirnoff, *A Short Account of the Historical Development and Present Position of Russian Orthodox Missions*, pp. 28ff.
[61] Smirnov, *Les Populations Finnoises des Bassins de la Volga et de la Kama*, pp. 1ff.
[62] *Ibid.*
[63] Lübeck, *op. cit.*, p. 53.
[64] Lübeck, *op. cit.*, pp. 62, 63.
[65] On Ilminski, see A. Yakovlev in *The East and the West*, Vol. XI, pp. 254-269; Smirnoff, *op cit.*, pp. 28-47; Lübeck, *op. cit.*, p. 91; Raeder in *Allgemeine Missions-Zeitschrift*, Vol. XXXII, pp. 545-547.

service books into the Tartar language. He travelled extensively among the Tartars, and by residence in the Near East acquired a knowledge of Arabic and Persian. For a time he taught in the ecclesiastical academy at Kazan, but the archbishop suspected him of being too friendly to Islam and he was dismissed from his post. Undiscouraged, he took a clerkship on the frontier, and used the opportunity to attain to a better mastery of the vernacular. In 1862 he returned to Kazan to a chair of Tartar in the university. Making his centre Kazan, Ilminski worked out plans for missionary activity which achieved marked success and were widely followed, not only in European Russia, but also in Siberia. He insisted that each people be approached through its own vernacular and not, as too often in the past, through Russian. To this end he encouraged preaching and the celebration of the liturgy in the vernacular and the translation of the Scriptures and the liturgy into that medium. He believed that each tribe should be reached by priests and teachers from their own number and helped to begin training schools for this purpose. He was convinced that Christian education should commence with the children and that schools should be established in which instruction should be given in the vernacular, with Russian added in the upper years. Normal schools for teachers were to be opened. As a means of promoting and assisting these measures the Brotherhood of St. Gurius was organized (1867), named, appropriately, after that first Archbishop of Kazan who in the sixteenth century had laboured indefatigably for the conversion of the diocese. Assistance came from the Orthodox Missionary Society. The use of the vernacular and the utilization of missionaries from the rank and file of the people achieved remarkable results. We hear of a Tartar, an assistant of Ilminski, who won a large following by the use of the vernacular and banded his hearers into choirs to sing Christian hymns.[66] Ilminski had the enthusiastic support of the energetic Pobiedonostsev, the Procurator of the Holy Synod, who presumably regarded him and his methods as convenient tools for the Russification of the unassimilated peoples.[67]

The movement survived the death of its originator and increased in popularity. By the end of the nineteenth century, in the diocese of Samara alone there were said to be 128 priests who knew the Chuvash language and in all of European Russia more than 300 mission schools with more than 11,000 pupils.[68] While the state gave encouragement, much of religious con-

[66] Yakovlev in *The East and the West*, Vol. XI, pp. 266-268.
[67] Smirnoff, *op. cit.*, pp. 28-39.
[68] Smirnoff, *op. cit.*, pp. 48-54.

viction and devotion entered into the enterprise and some progress seems
to have been registered in the deepening of what had been a very slight
tincture of Christianity among the non-Russian tribes. However, the advance
was chiefly among those who were already professedly Christian. In the
fifty years between 1840 and 1890 about 65,000 Moslems and about 155,000
pagans are said to have been converted,[69] but these totals may have been
exaggerated. Another account declares that in the thirty years beginning
with 1870 the number of baptisms in European Russia was only a few
thousand.[70] Even if the earlier figures are correct, in comparison with the
size of the population, Christianity made little fresh advance either at the
expense of Islam or of open paganism. In 1897 the number of Moslems in
European Russia was said to be more than 3,500,000.[71]

In the Europe of the nineteenth century the movement from Judaism and
paganism to Christianity was numerically not so great as between A.D. 1500
and A.D. 1800. Similarly, the shifts from Christianity to Islam and from Islam
to Christianity were not so marked as they had been in the preceding three
centuries.

In like manner the gains of the three great branches of Christianity, Roman
Catholicism, Greek Orthodoxy, and Protestantism, at the expense of one
another were not so extensive as in the three centuries that followed A.D. 1500.
Each made efforts to win adherents from the others. In these each had some
success. However, here, as in the relations between Christianity and non-
Christian religions, nineteenth century Europe did not see such extensive
movements of entire sections of the population as it had in preceding eras.
Striking alterations were not to come until after 1914, and then not because
of the older faiths but as the result of revolutionary movements which had
their inception in the nineteenth century but which did not arrive to their
full power until the age which began with the World War of 1914-1918.
In Europe the nineteenth century after 1815 was one of comparative peace
in the political struggles between nations. It was also one of relative calm
in the competition between rival religions and between the chief schools of
Christianity.

As in previous volumes, it is not the purpose of this work, dealing as it does
primarily with the expansion of Christianity rather than with its internal his-

[69] Milukow, *Skizzen russischer Kulturgeschichte,* Vol. II, p. 185.
[70] Smirnoff, *op. cit.,* pp. 54-74.
[71] Lübeck, *op. cit.,* p. 93.

tory, to enter in detail into the efforts of one branch of Christianity to win adherents from the others. We must content ourselves with bare and incomplete summaries.

The Roman Catholic Church made persistent attempts to regain the ground which it had lost to Protestantism. In practically all of the countries in Europe in which Protestantism was the prevailing form of Christianity, the nineteenth century witnessed the numerical increase and the strengthening of the organization of the Roman Catholic Church. The process was furthered by the political liberalism and growing religious tolerance of the age, for these brought the lightening or the complete removal of the civil disabilities under which Roman Catholics had been placed, and lessened, even when they did not remove, the chronic ill will against them.

In Great Britain the century saw a substantial growth of the Roman Catholic forces.[72] Roman Catholicism had never completely died out. It had had a continuous existence in parts of the Scottish highlands and here and there in England. In England some of the nobility and the landed gentry had remained true to the old church and in defiance of the laws had sheltered priests and encouraged the maintenance of Roman Catholic religious rites. At the outset of the century, the feeling against Roman Catholics was still strong, but relaxation of laws against them had begun. After several intermediate steps, in 1829 an act of Parliament removed practically all political and civil disabilities against Roman Catholics in Great Britain and Ireland. Beginning in the second quarter of the century came a great growth in numbers. On the one hand, some of the leaders in the Oxford or Anglo-Catholic movement, among them the brilliant and deeply spiritual John Henry Newman and the ascetic and able Henry Edward Manning, Archdeacon of Chichester and intimate friend of Gladstone, made their submission to Rome. In succeeding decades of the century came others, many of them from the Anglican clergy and the intellectuals and some from the Nonconformists. On the other hand, there was a vast influx of Irish Roman Catholics. For many years, poverty-stricken Irish had been taking refuge in England from the appalling economic conditions in the Emerald Isle. They came chiefly as unskilled labourers to the

---

[72] The best survey is Denis Gwynn, *A Hundred Years of Catholic Emancipation (1829-1929)* (London, Longmans, Green and Co., 1929, pp. xxxi, 292). Briefer on this period and less comprehensive is David Mayhew, *Catholicism in England 1535-1935. Portrait of a Minority: Its Culture and Tradition* (London, Longmans, Green and Co., 1936, pp. xii, 304). On a limited period an exhaustive work is Bernard Ward, *The Eve of Catholic Emancipation. Being the History of the English Catholics during the First Thirty Years of the Nineteenth Century* (London, Longmans, Green and Co., 3 vols., 1911, 1912). All three are by Roman Catholics and all three are limited geographically to England. The account of British Roman Catholicism is taken chiefly from these three books.

main cities and the growing factory towns. Then, beginning in 1845, a blight
brought failure to the Irish potato crop and threw a large part of the population
into destitution. Many died and millions sought relief in emigration. The large
majority of the refugees went to the United States, tens of thousands went to
Canada and Australia, but hundreds of thousands moved into England, Scotland, and Wales. The migration to England and Scotland continued through
the succeeding decades and into the twentieth century, although in not such
great numbers as in the famine years. It tended to be concentrated in the industrial and mining centres and in the urban areas. Its high birth rate brought
to the Roman Catholic community an increase larger than that of the population
as a whole. In 1850 the Pope removed Great Britain from the jurisdiction
of the Propaganda and gave it a hierarchy on the same status with that of
traditionally Roman Catholic countries. The Archbishops of Westminster
professed to continue the succession of Roman Catholic primates of Canterbury which had been interrupted by the separation of the Church of England
from Rome. The ardent expectations which the first of the Archbishops of
Westminster, Cardinal Wiseman, and some of his associates cherished for the
early return of most of England to the Roman communion failed of realization. So, too, the frantic fears of those who saw in the creation of a hierarchy
a fatal threat to Protestantism and to English liberties[73] proved to be without
foundation. Difficulties developed among the three main groups of Roman
Catholics—the descendants of the old Catholic communities, the converts, and
the Irish. The older Roman Catholic families were suspicious of recruits so
different from themselves and were opposed to the ultramontane tendencies
of the heads of the hierarchy. Eventually, however, the differences lessened.
Religious orders were re-introduced,[74] labours for the religiously and physically
destitute in the great cities multiplied, monastic houses became numerous, and
a clergy was trained. The Roman Catholic body rose in numbers from 90,000
in England and 30,000 in Scotland in 1800 ministered to by sixty-five priests,
to 500,000 in Great Britain in 1820, 900,000 in 1840, 1,300,000 in England and
320,000 in Scotland in 1880, and one and two-thirds millions in England and
nearly half a million in Scotland in 1907.[75]

In Holland and Luxemburg a phenomenal increase in Roman Catholics
took place, largely by natural growth through births, from 350,000 in 1800 to

[73] Carpenter, *Church and People, 1789-1889*, p. 208.
[74] See, for one of these, Francis Raphael Drane, *Life of Mother Margaret Mary Halla-
han, Foundress of the English Congregation of St. Catherine of Siena of the Third Order
of St. Dominic* (London, Longmans, Green and Co., 1929, pp. xviii, 540), *passim*.
[75] Baudrillart in Descamps, *Histoire Générale Comparée des Missions*, p. 533.

slightly more than 2,000,000 in 1907.[76] In Holland the hierarchy was restored in 1853.[77] In Switzerland the proportion of Roman Catholics slightly increased.[78] In Germany the bitter fight with Bismarck came to an end and during the three decades before 1914 the Roman Catholic Church flourished.[79] In Scandinavia Roman Catholics were emancipated—in Norway in 1845, in Denmark in 1847, and in Sweden in 1860. However, although they showed an increase—in Denmark from 300 in 1850 to about 12,000 in 1907, in Sweden from 200 in 1860 to about 2,500 in 1907, and in Norway from about 200 in 1869 to about 2,400 in 1907[80]—they remained inconsiderable minorities and were still under the jurisdiction of the Propaganda.

In all Europe, including even Great Britain and Holland, the gains of Roman Catholicism by conversions from Protestantism were slight and did not compare in extent with those achieved on the continent under the impetus of the counter-reformation in the sixteenth and seventeenth centuries. The fact that among the converts was a fairly large number of intellectuals[81] drew attention to the movement, but the main growth of Roman Catholicism in traditionally Protestant areas was through immigration and a high birth rate.

Against the various branches of the Eastern Orthodox Church the Roman Catholic Church made some advance. In Russia it first lost and then gained ground. In the latter part of the eighteenth century, through the partition of Poland, the majority of the Ruthenian Uniates came under Russian jurisdiction. The Ruthenian Uniates were largely Russians who had been Greek Orthodox in religion and in 1596 had united with Rome but had preserved their married clergy, their Byzantine rite, and Slavonic as their ecclesiastical language. In the nineteenth century the Russian Government forced the Uniates in its realm to renounce their connexion with Rome and to enter into fellowship with the Russian Orthodox Church. Many, however, declined to attend the Orthodox services. When, in 1906, the Tsar Nicholas II granted religious toleration, over three hundred thousand of the Ruthenians, former Roman Catholics and their descendants, left the Russian Orthodox Church. They were not allowed by the Russian authorities to resume their Uniate customs, but were required to conform fully to the Latin rite of Rome.[82] Only the Ruthenians under Austrian rule retained their Uniate status and practices.[83] Other acces-

---

[76] Baudrillart in Descamps, op. cit., p. 534.
[77] Schwager, Die katholische Heidenmission der Gegenwart, p. 50.
[78] Baudrillart in Descamps, op. cit., p. 534.
[79] Williams, The Catholic Church in Action, p. 54.
[80] Baudrillart in Descamps, op. cit., pp. 534, 535.
[81] Schmidlin, Katholische Missionsgeschichte, p. 444.
[82] Attwater. The Catholic Eastern Churches, pp. 78-80.
[83] Attwater, op. cit., p. 80.

sions came in Russia to the Roman Catholic Church. It is said that following the grant of religious freedom in 1905, about two hundred thousand Russians, apart from the Ruthenians mentioned above, made the change.[84] Among these were some from the higher social and intellectual strata of Russian society.[85] One of the greatest philosophers and thinkers produced by the Russian Orthodox Church in the nineteenth century, a man who achieved a European reputation, Vladimir Soloviev (1853-1900), in his later years was received into communion with Rome.[86] Some of the converts were from the Russian Orthodox Church and some from the Old Believers (those who in the seventeenth century separated from the official church because of innovations in the latter). Many preserved the Byzantine rite.[87] In the eighteen-eighties an archbishop in Moravia founded the Apostolate of Saints Cyril and Methodius under the Protection of the Blessed Virgin Mary, especially to win converts from the Slavs who were not in communion with Rome.[88] In Bulgaria several orders laboured for the conversion of the Orthodox.[89] In the nineteenth century the totals of Roman Catholics in the Balkan Peninsula are said to have risen from about a quarter of a million to nearly six hundred and forty thousand.[90] How much of this increase was due to conversions and how much to the excess of births over deaths is not clear. In areas in Europe in which the Greek Orthodox form of Christianity had traditionally been dominant, Roman Catholics were decidedly more numerous at the end than at the beginning of the century.

Among several of the Eastern churches which were not in communion with Rome, some important changes occurred. In the Balkan Peninsula the emancipation of the various nations—Greece, Serbia, Bulgaria, and Roumania—from the Turkish yoke was accompanied by the erection of autocephalous churches and freedom from the traditional control by the Œcumenical Patriarch.[91] Under the Christian Emperors, the Œcumenical Patriarchate had been the ecclesiastical wing of Byzantine imperialism. After their conquest of Constantinople, the Ottoman Turks utilized it to supervise the Orthodox Christians in their domains. In some areas this control was accompanied by the administration of

---

[84] E. A. Walsh in Guilday, *The Catholic Church in Contemporary Europe 1919-1931*, p. 263.
[85] Attwater, *The Dissident Eastern Churches*, p. 78.
[86] Attwater, *The Catholic Eastern Churches*, p. 126; Bevan, *Christianity*, p. 131.
[87] Attwater, *op. cit.*, p. 126.
[88] Georg Zischeck in *Priester und Mission, 1929*, p. 59.
[89] Louis Canisius, *Aux Avant-Postes du Monde Slave. Soixante Ans d'Apostolat Assomptionniste en Bulgarie* (Louvain, Xaveriana, 1931, pp. 30), p. 6.
[90] Baudrillart in Descamps, *op. cit.*, p. 539.
[91] Attwater, *The Dissident Eastern Churches*. p. 45.

the Church by Greek priests and bishops who did not understand the language of their parishioners and who frequently cared little or nothing for the welfare of their flocks but exploited them shamelessly. It was to be expected that the rising tide of nationalism would bring demands for independence from a Patriarchate which was dominated by the hated Turk and which in some regions was associated with the presence of an alien, greedy clergy. In Greece the Church was declared autocephalous in 1833, shortly after the achievement of political autonomy, but not until 1850 did the ecclesiastical authorities at Constantinople formally assent to the new status.[92] Bulgarian patriots were restive under the control of the Greek clergy, demanded bishops of their own race or at least familiar with their language, and about the middle of the century began to omit the name of the Patriarch from the public prayers in their churches. Negotiations with Rome led to the appointment of an archbishop for a Bulgarian Uniate Church which supposedly would have French protection. Partly under pressure from Russia, who, as a means of extending her influence in the Balkans, posed as a friend of the Orthodox and the Slavs in that region, in 1870 the Turkish authorities created an Exarchate for the Orthodox Church in Bulgaria. To this the Patriarch did not consent and riots and civil strife followed.[93] However, the autocephalous Bulgarian church had come into being. The Orthodox Church in Serbia became autocephalous in 1879.[94] After long-continued protest, in 1885 the Œcumenical Patriarch recognized the autonomy of the Orthodox Church of Roumania.[95] In Transylvania the Orthodox Church became independent in 1864.[96] Ecclesiastical freedom from the Œcumenical Patriarch did not mean departure from the accepted creeds. The autocephalous churches remained Orthodox in their doctrines.

Still on the defensive through most of the nineteenth century, none of the Orthodox churches of the Balkan Peninsula reached out to any extent to attract adherents from other Christian confessions or from the Moslems about them. Their share in the expansion of Christianity came almost entirely through migration of their members. This was chiefly to the United States. A little later in this volume we are to meet them there.

One member of the family of Eastern Orthodoxy, the Russian Church, made some gains at the expense of other Christian bodies. In their attempt to tie together an empire composed of many different races, the Tsars sought to encourage religious uniformity and to promote assimilation, or Russification,

[92] Miller, *The Ottoman Empire and Its Successors, 1801-1927*, p. 182.
[93] Miller, *op. cit.*, pp. 338ff.
[94] Attwater, *The Dissident Eastern Churches*, pp. 45, 105.
[95] Attwater, *op. cit.*, p. 112.
[96] Attwater, *op. cit.*, p. 113.

by bringing as many as possible of their subjects into membership in the state-dominated church. From this policy came official encouragement to missionary efforts among non-Christians in the empire. From it, too, issued attempts to bring at least some of the nonconforming Christians into the fellowship of the state church. These efforts were especially marked under the reactionary Tsars, but they were also seen under more liberal monarchs. It was in the reign of the supposedly progressive Alexander I that, after the annexation of Georgia, the church in that region was brought into submission to the Holy Synod (1811) and its autonomy cancelled.[97] In 1845 Russia expelled Roman Catholic missionaries from Georgia and a few years later it sought to weaken Roman Catholics of the Latin rite in the Caucasus.[98] Repeated efforts were made to win back those sects which had separated from the Russian Orthodox Church. In 1853 the Holy Synod ordered chairs to be established in the seminaries to train priests to confute the doctrines of these groups.[99] In 1886 confraternities of women were organized to combat the dissenters.[100] Under Alexander III, made ultra-conservative by the assassination of his formerly liberal father, Alexander II, and through the zealous head of the Holy Synod, Pobiedonostsev,[101] over four hundred missionaries were labouring to convert the Old Believers (Raskolniks). They were said to have won between eight and ten thousand a year, but after freedom of conscience was proclaimed early in the twentieth century, conversions are reported to have ceased and many converts fell away.[102] Efforts were made to gain Roman Catholics, especially those whose ancestors had belonged to the Russian Orthodox Church. In some periods force was employed. Between 1836 and 1839 more than one and two-thirds millions of Roman Catholics, largely from the Ruthenian Uniates, are said to have been brought back into the state church.[103] In 1875 about a quarter of a million more Uniates were constrained to take this step.[104] Official figures declared that between 1840 and 1890, 1,172,758 converts were made to the Russian Orthodox Church. Of these, 580,000 had been

[97] Tamarati, l'Église Géorgienne, pp. 384, 385.

[98] Tamarati, op. cit., pp. 658-668.

[99] Conybeare, Russian Dissenters, pp. 249, 250.

[100] Ibid.

[101] Pobiedonostsev put some of his ideals into writing in his book, K. P. Pobyedonostseff, Reflections of a Russian Statesman, translated from the Russian by Robert Crozier Long (London, Grant Richards, 1898, pp. xi, 271). Here, for example, he protested against the separation of Church and state and decried "a free church in a free state." Here, too, he revealed himself as a deeply religious man, but utterly opposed to the democracy and most of the liberalism of the nineteenth century.

[102] Conybeare, op. cit., p. 251.

[103] Milukow, Skizzen russischer Kulturgeschichte, Vol. II, p. 185.

[104] Ibid.

Roman Catholics, Protestants, and Uniates, 311,279 were from the Old Believers and the sects, about 65,000 were from the Moslems, and about 155,000 were former pagans.[105] About 100,000 of the Roman Catholic converts had come in the aftermath of the suppression of the Polish uprising of 1863. Approximately the same number of Protestants from the Esths and Letts had been forced to take a similar step after the same revolt.[106] It is said that in all these fifty years only 75,000 Roman Catholics and 35,000 Protestants had been brought over by preaching and the missionary efforts of priests, and that the remainder of the conversions from these two constituencies had been from political causes.[107] Obviously gains made in this fashion were superficial. The kind of careful teaching was lacking which, had it followed them, might have given them depth of root.

The phenomenal energy which characterized Protestantism in the nineteenth century was displayed in part in efforts to bring into that form of Christianity members of the Roman Catholic and Eastern Orthodox communions and to reach adherents from other branches of Protestantism. Seldom if ever were these activities undertaken primarily with the purpose of aggrandizing a denomination. They arose from a genuine conviction that the other forms of Christianity were false or inadequate or that those whom the missions were designed to reach had at best only a nominal Christian connexion and were spiritually destitute. Much of Protestant missions among traditionally Christian peoples deliberately eschewed any effort to alter denominational or confessional affiliations but endeavoured, rather, to inject new life into existing Christian bodies. Most of these Protestant missions in Europe were either from Great Britain or the United States. Particularly were they from the United States. It is interesting that while European and especially continental European Christians were assisting in holding to their hereditary faith the immigrants to the United States, missionaries from the United States were seeking to transform and deepen the religious life in Europe by efforts to make that life conform to American patterns. Influences were flowing across the Atlantic in both directions.

Some of the extension of British Protestantism on the continent of Europe had as its object the religious care of British subjects living or travelling abroad. This was particularly true of the Church of England. For many years, by annual Parliamentary grants made through the foreign office, chaplaincies were maintained in British embassies and legations and in consulates in the leading

[105] Ibid.
[106] Ibid.
[107] Ibid.

cities. Most of the Anglican churches and chaplains on the continent were under the patronage of societies in England.[108] In 1841 the Bishopric of Gibraltar was founded to care for the English congregations in Southern Europe.[109] Several churches were also established for Scotch Presbyterians and for American Protestants.

The growing and increasingly successful efforts of members of the Anglican communion to cultivate friendly relations with the Eastern churches did not arise from any desire to absorb these churches. Some were the outgrowth of the administration of the sacraments by the clergy of the Protestant Episcopal Church to scattered Orthodox immigrants in the United States and some, instituted largely by Anglo-Catholics, came from a longing for a union of all Christians which would not be the annexation of one church by another.[110] Similarly the attempts (which ended in an impasse) of Anglo-Catholics at *rapprochement* with the Roman Catholic Church sprang from an intense desire for the re-establishment of the ecclesiastical unity which had existed before Henry VIII[111]—although, had Rome acceded to them, it could only have been through acquiescence in much of the Anglican position.

British preachers visited the continent. Among these was Robert Haldane, a Scot of distinguished birth, prominent in an energetic spreading of a religious experience of the Evangelical type. Soon after the end of the Napoleonic wars he made an extended visit to France and Switzerland and did much to quicken the Protestants there, but the fruits of his labours were largely kept within the existing denominations.[112]

Most of the many American "evangelists" who itinerated in the British Isles did not seek to introduce new denominations but to contribute to the life of the old ones.[113]

The British and Foreign Bible Society distributed the Scriptures in the vernacular over much of Europe, from Russia and Scandinavia in the north to Greece and the Iberian Peninsula in the south.[114] It had translations prepared, saw to the printing of these and of existing versions, and employed colporteurs

---

[108] Pascoe, *Two Hundred Years of the S.P.G.*, pp. 738-742b.

[109] Pascoe, *op. cit.*, p. 736.

[110] J. A. Douglas, *The Relations of the Anglican Churches with Eastern-Orthodox, Especially in Regard to Anglican Orders* (London, Faith Press, 1921, pp. 198), *passim;* Slosser, *Christian Unity*, pp. 212ff.

[111] Slosser, *op. cit.*, pp. 196-200, 203-210.

[112] Haldane, *The Lives of Robert Haldane of Airthrey and of His Brother James Alexander Haldane*, pp. 413ff.

[113] On Scotland, see Fleming, *A History of the Church in Scotland, 1843-1874*, pp. 111, 234-237; Fleming, *A History of the Church in Scotland, 1875-1929*, p. 163.

[114] Canton, *History of the British and Foreign Bible Society*, Vol. I, pp. 143-264, 388-461, Vol. II, pp. 1-29, 191-258, Vol. III, pp. 79-211, 285-364, Vol. IV, pp. 233-403.

to distribute them. Much of this it did directly, but it also encouraged the formation of local and national Bible societies and in some places left the field entirely to them. The American Bible Society also extended its program to Europe, although chiefly in the form of occasional subsidies to a national society and of collaboration with American missionaries.[115] Its European work was not nearly so extensive as that of the British society. The larger part of this labour was primarily for the purpose of making available to Christians the Scriptures which all churches revered and through them to deepen and enrich the faith of nominal Christians. Wherever possible it was carried on with the approval of existing ecclesiastical authorities. However, the Bible societies were inevitably tinged with Protestantism, if in nothing more than in the endeavour to place the Bible in the hands of the laity and to encourage its reading, for this would logically be followed by the individual giving his own interpretation to what he read. Opposition, therefore, frequently developed from the Roman Catholic and Eastern Orthodox ecclesiastical authorities. Moreover, the Bible societies were by no means unhappy when conversions to Protestantism occurred. They were glad to record these, as, for instance, in Belgium,[116] in France,[117] and in the famine-stricken districts of Ireland,[118] and to note that the distribution of the Bible had contributed to them.

Methodists and Baptists from Great Britain and especially from the United States built up churches on the continent. Much of this effort was begun by sailors or emigrants from the continent who had come into a vigorous religious experience by contact with these denominations in America and had returned to spread their new-found faith in their home countries. The Disciples of Christ, Christian Science, Mormonism (the Church of Jesus Christ of Latter Day Saints), and the Seventh Day Adventists were groups of American origin which won footholds in Europe.

These denominations achieved their chief gains in predominantly Protestant lands. They made much less impression in Roman Catholic and Greek Orthodox countries. Of the latter, only in Russia did they have much effect and that was mainly in connexion with movements of indigenous origin.

A regional survey, necessarily brief and incomplete, may give something of an idea of the extent and nature of British and American missions which aided the growth of Protestantism on the continent.

In France an extensive Protestant enterprise was the McCall Mission. This

---

[115] Dwight, *Centennial History of the American Bible Society,* Vol. I, pp. 208-216, Vol. II, pp. 420-430.
[116] Canton, *op. cit.,* Vol. III, p. 291.
[117] Canton, *op. cit.,* Vol. IV, p. 258.
[118] Canton, *op. cit.,* Vol. II, p. 176.

was begun early in 1872 by R. W. McCall, an English pastor, who, while on a holiday the preceding year in France, was challenged by the religious destitution of the workingmen of Paris who had broken with the Roman Catholic Church. He opened a preaching hall in Paris. By the close of 1888 the Mission had spread until it numbered 126 stations, many of them in Paris, but some in other cities and even in Algeria and Tunis. It drew its support from both Great Britain and the United States and from members of several denominations and enjoyed the cordial support of French Protestants. It was primarily for the labourers who had drifted into irreligion.[119] Its methods and spirit had an influence upon much of native French Protestantism.[120] Before 1814 a number of societies on the plan of English Methodism had been begun by a Frenchman of noble birth who had come into a profound religious experience while on the island of Jersey. In 1818 a missionary of the English Wesleyans, Charles Cook, came to France. Thanks largely to his leadership, Methodism so multiplied that a national organization was formed with only a loose affiliation with the parent denomination.[121] Haldane had a marked effect on French Protestantism and helped to begin a revival out of which issued many of the later leaders of the churches.[122] J. M. Darby, of the Plymouth Brethren, gave an impulse which led to the formation of a number of congregations in sympathy with his views.[123] Not far from 1832 a Baptist congregation was founded by a Frenchman of some social standing. In 1868 American Baptists entered the country[124] and in 1913 reported thirty-five churches and 2,123 members.[125] French Protestants of the Reformed Churches also had their own societies for the propagation of their faith among Roman Catholics and the unchurched, and met with some success.[126]

In Germany British Methodism was introduced by a C. G. Müller, who had been converted in London, had returned home and gathered a congregation, and was appointed an agent of the English Wesleyans. Other missionaries followed and by about 1893 more than twenty-three hundred members were

[119] *A Cry from the Land of Calvin and Voltaire* (London, Hodder and Stoughton, 1887, pp. vii, 187, by several authors who had first-hand contact with the mission, among them R. W. McCall), *passim*.
[120] Houghton, *Handbook of French and Belgian Protestantism*, pp. 74-76.
[121] Finlay and Holdsworth, *The History of the Wesleyan Methodist Missionary Society*, Vol. IV, pp. 445ff.
[122] Houghton, *op. cit.*, pp. 36, 37.
[123] Houghton, *op. cit.*, pp. 69, 70.
[124] *American Baptist Missionary Union. Eighty-Third Annual Report . . . 1897*, p. 445.
[125] *Ninety-ninth Annual Report of the American Baptist Foreign Mission Society, 1913*, p. 130.
[126] Leonard W. Bacon, *God's Wonderful Work in France* (New York, The American Tract Society, no date, pp. 55), *passim;* Houghton, *op. cit.*, pp. 40-53, 61-108.

counted.[127] Methodism had spread among the German immigrants who were flooding into the United States. In 1849, following the increase in religious toleration brought by the political upheavals of 1848, the American Methodists sent as a missionary to the mother country a leading convert of this German-American movement.[128] Other missionaries followed, union was effected with the congregations which arose from English Methodism (1896), and in 1913 the membership was nearly twenty-eight thousand.[129] From Germany Methodism spread to Switzerland[130] and the Austrian Empire.[131] The United Brethren, who had arisen, at the outset in close friendship with Methodism, largely among the Germans in the United States, in 1881 appointed as a missionary to Germany a native of that country who had joined them while in America. Several other missionaries were sent and at one time a membership of about one thousand had been gathered. In 1905, however, the property and membership were transferred to the movement connected with the American Methodists.[132] American Baptists began a mission in Germany in 1834[133] and in 1913 counted over 200 churches and nearly 43,000 members.[134] The Baptist movement in Germany which became affiliated with that in the United States had its rise in J. G. Oncken, who had been in Scotland and had had contacts with both the Methodists and the Haldanes.[135] Partly through Oncken, the Baptist movement spread to Hungary and there found a slight footing among Magyars and Germans.[136] Seventh Day Adventists, a small American denomination noted for its energetic and worldwide missionary activity, in 1874 sent, as its first representatives to any foreign land, a family to Switzerland. In 1912 they had 138 churches and about 6,800 members in Germany, and 21 churches and over 1,000 members in Switzerland.[137]

In Sweden Methodism made its first great impression through George Scott, who came in 1830 as chaplain to a group of English workingmen employed

[127] Findlay and Holdsworth, *op. cit.*, Vol. IV, pp. 460ff.

[128] Reid, *Missions and Missionary Society of the Methodist Episcopal Church*, Vol. II, pp. 238ff.

[129] *Annual Report of the Board of Foreign Missions of the Methodist Episcopal Church for the Year 1913*, pp. 381, 382.

[130] *Annual Report of the Board of Foreign Missions of the Methodist Episcopal Church for the Year 1913*, pp. 381, 382, 384.

[131] *Annual Report of the Board of Foreign Missions of the Methodist Episcopal Church for the Year 1913*, p. 386.

[132] Drury, *History of the Church of the United Brethren in Christ*, p. 601.

[133] *American Baptist Missionary Union, Eighty-Third Annual Report . . . 1897*, p. 451.

[134] *Ninety-Ninth Annual Report of the American Baptist Foreign Mission Society*, p. 131.

[135] Vedder, *A Short History of Baptist Missions*, pp. 377ff.; Gammell, *A History of American Baptist Missions*, pp. 278ff.

[136] Gill, *Europe and the Gospel*, pp. 127-135.

[137] *1914 Year Book of the Seventh-Day Adventist Denominations*, pp. 254, 288ff

by a British manufacturer in Stockholm. He soon began preaching in Swedish and attracted large crowds. Within a few years persecution drove him out of the country, but he had introduced movements for temperance reform and for a warmer religious life which continued after he had gone.[138] American Methodism entered Sweden through a sailor who had become a sincere Christian through a mission for seamen in New York. He returned to Sweden in 1853 and in 1854 began receiving support from the Methodist Episcopal Church. Other missionaries followed, legal recognition was granted to Methodism in 1876, and in 1913 the membership was 17,637.[139] The currents set in motion by Scott joined with others which entered from the United States through Swedish sailors and emigrants who there had come into a fresh religious experience. In spite of initial persecution by the state and the banishment of an early leader, from them arose numerous Baptist churches. In 1913 these totalled 619 with a membership of 53,087.[140] In 1882 the Seventh Day Adventists recognized a Swedish conference, and in 1912 all Scandinavia, including Iceland, had ninety-three churches and 3,305 members of their denomination.[141] In 1850 came the first contingent of the Mormon missionaries, the following year the *Book of Mormon* was translated, and some converts were gathered. The latter were recruited chiefly from the poverty-stricken and ignorant. Many were induced to migrate to the Mormon centre in Utah, but in 1900 over two thousand were still in Sweden. Mormons also made their way to Denmark, Norway, and Iceland.[142] The number of Swedish converts to Mormonism between 1850 and 1909 is said to have been 17,259.[143] As in the rest of Scandinavia, by 1912 Christian Science had won only a slight foothold.[144]

To Norway came missionaries of a number of denominations. In 1850, from what was termed a "Bethel ship" in New York which ministered to seamen, arrived a Methodist who wished to give to his kindred what he had found in America. From this visit arose a Methodist movement. By 1893 more than forty-five hundred members had been gathered and many who remained in

[138] George Westin, *George Scott och hans Verksamhet i Sverige* (Stockholm, Svenska Kyrkans Diakonistyrelses Bokförlag, 2 vols., 1928, 1929), *passim;* Finlay and Holdsworth, *op. cit.,* Vol. IV, p. 424; Stephenson, *The Religious Aspects of Swedish Immigration,* pp. 8-16.

[139] *Annual Report of the Board of Foreign Missions of the Methodist Episcopal Church for the Year 1913,* p. 393; Reid, *op. cit.,* Vol. II, pp. 204ff.

[140] *Ninety-Ninth Annual Report of the American Baptist Foreign Mission Society, 1913,* p. 133; Stephenson, *op. cit.,* pp. 74-92; Janson, *The Background of Swedish Immigration,* pp. 196-198.

[141] *1914 Year Book of the Seventh-Day Adventist Denomination,* pp. 258, 288ff.

[142] Stephenson, *op. cit.,* pp. 93-102; Smith, *The Rise, Progress and Travels of the Church of Jesus Christ of Latter-Day Saints,* pp. 32, 33.

[143] Janson, *op. cit.,* p. 199.

[144] *Christian Science Journal,* Vol. XXX, p. vi.

the state church were profoundly affected by the message of the Methodist preachers.[145] About the middle of the century a religious awakening broke out from the preaching of Gustav Adolf Lammers, who owed his impulse to contact with the Moravians. Some of those touched by him became Baptists.[146] The movement was quickened by Baptist missionaries from America, notably by a Norwegian, F. L. Rymker, who was a convert of the Mariner's Bethel in New York City, by Baptist preachers from Sweden, by financial aid from English and American Baptists, and by Norwegian clergy trained in the United States. In 1877 Norway contained eighteen Baptist churches with 511 members, and in 1902 thirty-six churches with 2,766 members.[147] Beginning about 1865, Plymouth Brethren from England gathered a few hundred converts.[148] We hear, too, of an English mission to the fishermen along the coast of Norway and its adjacent islands.[149] Through Denmark came the Disciples of Christ. Assisted by annual financial grants from the parent body in the United States, the denomination enjoyed a slight growth.[150]

In Denmark Baptists from Germany, one of them Oncken, organized a small church of their denomination in 1839. In spite of persecution, by 1849 this had multiplied to six. The granting of religious liberty in 1849 led to further growth. Some pastors and financial assistance arrived from Baptists in the United States.[151] It was after 1849 and the more liberal attitude towards dissenters from the state church inaugurated in that year that American Methodism first actively entered the kingdom. The first missionary was a Dane. Copenhagen was the chief centre, but missions were inaugurated in a number of places. By Sunday Schools and other novel features of its programme, Methodism had an influence upon the majority church quite out of proportion to its own numbers.[152] It was through Denmark that the Disciples of Christ entered Scandinavia. In 1876 they sent as a missionary A. O. Holck, a native of the country who had lived in America. He later served in Parliament and was knighted.[153] The Church of the Brethren (Dunkers), although of Euro-

---

[145] Reid, *op. cit.*, Vol. II, pp. 193-204.

[146] Stiansen, *History of the Baptists in Norway*, pp. 59-70.

[147] Stiansen, *op. cit.*, pp. 140, 144.

[148] Stiansen, *op. cit.*, pp. 149-151.

[149] J. J. Armistead, *Ten Years Near the Arctic Circle* (London, Headley Brothers, 1913, pp. 252), *passim*.

[150] McLean, *The History of the Foreign Christian Missionary Society*, p. 131; *The Missionary Intelligencer*, Vol. XXVII, p. 509.

[151] Gammell, *op. cit.*, pp. 287ff.; Vedder, *A Short History of Baptist Missions*, pp. 399, 400.

[152] Reid, *op. cit.*, Vol. II, pp. 222ff.

[153] McLean, *op. cit.*, p. 55.

pean origin, was introduced from the United States by a convert who had been reared in Denmark. It won a small following.[154]

Although from 1808 throughout the nineteenth century all of Finland was in the possession of Russia, the Swedish cultural influence which had long been predominant remained powerful. It was from Sweden that Baptist preaching entered the country. It was reinforced by a sailor who had been baptized in the United States.[155] In 1913 fifty-four Baptist churches with 3,392 members were reported.[156] It was also from Sweden that Methodism first made its way into Finland. It was aided from the United States.[157] In 1913 Methodists recorded 1,281 members in the land.[158]

No such extensive migration to America took place from Holland as from Germany and Scandinavia. Possibly partly for this reason the influence of American denominations was not so marked in Holland as in these other lands. Largely because of geographical propinquity, British and German Protestantism made themselves felt. The latter was particularly powerful.

Belgium was overwhelmingly Roman Catholic. Before 1914 Protestantism from Great Britain and America had only a slight effect. The Reformed Church, which had been present since the Reformation, had an Evangelization Committee which supported several stations. The Evangelical Continental Society, a British organization, gave assistance to the Belgian Christian Missionary Church.[159] The latter movement arose in 1837 from Belgian Protestantism, specialized on labourers, particularly miners, and its members, numbering several thousands, came largely from Roman Catholicism or religious indifferentism.[160]

Between the Protestantism of the British Isles and that of the United States a constant interchange occurred. More than one movement, notably the Sunday Schools and the Young Men's Christian Associations, which originated in Great Britain spread to the United States and there had a phenomenal development. American "evangelists" toured the British Isles, some with striking results. As we saw in the preceding chapter, British example had much to do with the inauguration of foreign missions by the churches of the United States, and it was from the United States, in turn, that the impulse came which led to

[154] Moyer, *Missions in the Church of the Brethren*, pp. 149-159.
[155] Vedder, *op. cit.*, p. 402.
[156] *Ninety-Ninth Annual Report of the American Baptist Foreign Mission Society, 1913*, p. 134.
[157] Reid, *op. cit.*, Vol. II, pp. 218ff.
[158] *Annual Report of the Board of Foreign Missions of the Methodist Episcopal Church for the Year 1913*, p. 413.
[159] Ashton, *The Christian Travellers Continental Handbook*, p. 24.
[160] Houghton, *Handbook of French and Belgian Protestantism*, p. 72.

the Student Volunteer Movement and which was potent in the emergence of the Student Christian Movement in the British Isles. Most of this contact with American Protestantism served to strengthen existing denominations. It modified methods and introduced new ones, but it did not lead to the formation of new large bodies. However, some distinctly American denominations were planted in the British Isles or drew from them. Mormon missionaries arrived in 1837.[161] An emigration agency was established in Liverpool, and it is said that from 1840 to 1851 between thirteen and fourteen thousand left the British Isles for Utah. They were largely farmers and mechanics.[162] Presumably they were attracted fully as much by the economic opportunity offered by Utah as by the religious tenets of the Mormons. As the first agent of their Foreign Christian Missionary Society to go beyond North America, the Disciples of Christ sent a man to England in 1876. Other missionaries followed. Large financial assistance came from some of the English. In 1914 the British Isles contained thirteen missionaries, sixteen churches, and 1,673 members of that denomination.[163] In 1890 Mary Baker Eddy sent a Christian Science missionary to England, and in 1896 the first public meeting in Europe of that movement convened in London.[164] Not far from the same time groups began meeting in Ireland.[165] In Edinburgh, services, presumably at the outset not public, were held in 1895.[166] In 1912 England contained sixty-eight Christian Science societies and churches, Ireland two, Scotland three, and Wales one.[167]

In Southern Europe, in spite of efforts by missionaries from the British Isles and from the United States, Protestant groups made little headway. Most of those who were dissatisfied with the Roman Catholic Church, and they were very numerous, either preserved a nominal although tenuous connexion with it or sought fellowship in Freemasonry. In Latin countries the latter tended to be anti-religious and to engage in politics. Protestantism made little appeal. That may have been because the discontent arose from religious scepticism and not from religious hunger. It may also have been because Protestantism, coming chiefly from Anglo-Saxon lands, seemed incorrigibly alien. As we are to see in later chapters, in the nineteenth and twentieth centuries Protestantism

[161] Smith, *The Rise, Progress and Travels of the Church of Jesus Christ of Latter-Day Saints*, p. 30.

[162] [Henry Mayhew], *The Mormons or Latter-Day Saints. With Memoirs of the Life and Death of Joseph Smith* (London, Office of the National Illustrated Library, 1851, pp. x, 326), pp. v, vi.

[163] McLean, *The History of the Foreign Christian Missionary Society*, pp. 51-53; *The Missionary Intelligencer*, Vol. XXVII, p. 508.

[164] *The Christian Science Journal*, Vol. XXX, pp. 223, 224.

[165] *The Christian Science Journal*, Vol. XXX, p. 408.

[166] *The Christian Science Journal*, Vol. XXX, p. 285.

[167] *The Christian Science Journal*, Vol. XXX, pp. iii-v.

made far larger gains against Roman Catholicism in Latin America and the Philippines than in Europe. This may have been partly because of the larger number of missionaries sent to the former lands.

In Spain, in the first half of the nineteenth century Protestantism was almost non-existent. George Borrow, famous for the account which he wrote of his travels, distributed several thousand Bibles,[168] and a few other Protestants engaged in sporadic efforts. With the advent of religious liberty through the Revolution of 1868, Protestant communities sprang up in a number of places and were closely associated with political liberalism. Missionaries entered from the British Isles, the United States, and Germany. Among them were American Congregationalists, English Plymouth Brethren, Swedish Baptists, and American Baptists. Contacts with members of the Anglican communion from North America and the British Isles helped in the formation of a reformed church of the episcopal type. However, in the main, Spain resented Protestantism and the numbers of Protestants totalled only a few thousand.[169]

In spite of the historic friendship with England, Portugal afforded little rootage for Protestantism. Feeling against divergence from the Roman Catholic Church was intense, and vigorous persecution was long the fate of dissent. Some Protestant influence entered through chaplains in the British army during the Peninsular wars against Napoleon. In the second quarter of the century Scottish effort led to a Protestant movement in Madeira which was checked by the enforced emigration of the converts. Anglican contacts assisted in the formation and growth of a kindred body, the Lusitanian Church. The Bible societies, principally those of Great Britain, distributed the Scriptures very widely. In the second half of the century an increasing relaxation of the laws, due more to rising secularism and anti-clericalism than to Protestant effort, made the way of the Nonconformist easier. British and American missionaries— Anglicans, Presbyterians, Methodists, Congregationalists, Baptists of several groups, Brethren, Nazarenes, and Seventh Day Adventists—entered, and several hundred adherents were gathered. However, numbers were small, and most of the initiative was from abroad.[170]

In Italy a small Protestant minority, the Waldenses or Vaudois, with a history going back before the Reformation, had survived the rigours of re-

[168] Borrow, *The Bible in Spain, passim,* and especially pp. 172, 180.
[169] Gill, *Europe and the Gospel,* pp. 105-114; C. A. Garcia and K. G. Grubb, *Religion in the Republic of Spain* (London, World Dominion Press, 1933, pp. 109), pp. 54-92; Noyes, *Church Reform in Spain and Portugal. A Short History of the Reformed Episcopal Churches of Spain and Portugal,* pp. 1-116; Peers, *Spain, the Church and the Orders,* pp. 4, 5.
[170] Eduardo Moreira, *The Significance of Portugal. A Survey of the Religious Situation* (London, World Dominion Press, 1933, pp. 71), pp. 26ff.; Noyes, *op. cit.,* pp. 117ff.

peated and prolonged persecutions. In the nineteenth century, while the majority continued in the Alpine valleys above the Piedmont plain which had been their ancestral refuge, some moved to the cities. Periodically through their history they had been aided and moulded by Protestants of other lands. This was also true in the nineteenth century. Assistance partly in money and partly in leadership came from Great Britain and America. Under the growing religious liberty and the increasing relaxation of ancient restrictions which marked the century, they enjoyed a modest growth.[171] Taking advantage of the partial tolerance of the latter part of the century under the united Italy, missionaries from the United States and the British Isles planted several other branches of Protestantism in the country. They even penetrated to Rome itself and there built up congregations. Among these missionaries were Presbyterians from Scotland,[172] Baptists from the South of the United States (who were particularly active in Rome and in the part of the peninsula which lay south of Rome),[173] English Wesleyans,[174] Methodists from the United States,[175] Baptists from England,[176] and Seventh Day Adventists from the United States.[177] The Deaconess Institution of Kaiserswerth, Germany, was also represented.[178] However, none of these obtained a very large following. Protestants remained an almost infinitesimal proportion of the population.

In the Balkan Peninsula, Protestant efforts were not extensive. As we are to see in a later volume, Constantinople became the centre of several enterprises. Outside that city Protestant missions were not numerous. They devoted their energy chiefly to the members of the Eastern Orthodox churches. As a rule their purpose was not to weaken these bodies by winning adherents from them, but to help to quicken them to new vigour. Often, however, those influenced by the missionaries fell under suspicion of the hierarchy and were forced out of the parent body and had no option but to form fresh organizations. The latter inevitably took on something of the ecclesiastical complexion of the denominations which sent the missionaries. Most of the missionaries were from the United States, but some were from Great Britain.

---

[171] *Encyclopædia Britannica, 14th edition,* Vol. XXIII, pp. 288-290; W. F. Adeney in Hastings, *Encyclopædia of Religion and Ethics,* Vol. XII, pp. 663-673.

[172] Fleming, *A History of the Church in Scotland, 1843-1874,* pp. 66, 149.

[173] Gill, *Europe and the Gospel,* pp. 152-174; George Braxton Taylor, *Southern Baptists in Sunny Italy* (New York, Walter Neale, 1929, pp. 295), *passim.*

[174] Findlay and Holdsworth, *The History of the Wesleyan Methodist Missionary Society,* Vol. IV, pp. 477ff.

[175] *Annual Report of the Board of Foreign Missions of the Methodist Episcopal Church for the Year 1913,* p. 397.

[176] *120th Annual Report of the Baptist Missionary Society* (London, 1912, pp. 436), pp. 81-84, 152.

[177] *1914 Year Book of the Seventh-Day Adventist Denomination,* p. 288.

[178] *Annual Report of the Board of Foreign Missions of the Methodist Episcopal Church for the Year 1913,* p. 397.

The Greek struggle for independence was followed in the United States and Great Britain with marked sympathy. It is not surprising, therefore, that in 1829 the Church Missionary Society, the London Missionary Society, and the English Wesleyans had representatives on the Ionian Islands,[179] off the west coast of Greece, particularly since at that time the islands were a British protectorate. However, permanent British missions in Greece did not follow. In 1820, the American Board of Commissioners for Foreign Missions appointed its first missionaries to Greece. The Bible was circulated in a translation into modern Greek, and schools were opened. The ecclesiastical authorities of the Orthodox Church were aroused to hostility.[180] The Greek Evangelical Church, entirely independent of foreign control, was founded by a Greek who had been trained in his own country and the United States under the auspices of the American Board.[181] For a few years the American Baptists had a mission.[182] Through the efforts of the American Episcopalians a normal school for women was conducted, the first of its kind in the country, which made a substantial contribution to the intellectual awakening of the land.[183] Out of the labours of a missionary who first went to Greece under the American Board came an independent agricultural school for boys at Salonika.[184]

Bulgaria was the scene of a mission of the American Board of Commissioners for Foreign Missions which began in 1858. Through it the Bible was translated into the vernacular, other literature was prepared and circulated, schools were opened, and Evangelical churches were constituted independently of the Orthodox Church.[185] In 1857 the American Methodists, at the request of a Congregationalist, opened a mission in Bulgaria which gathered a membership only slightly smaller than that which arose out of the efforts of the American Board.[186] The Deutsche Orient Mission was represented, but with fewer results.[187]

[179] Anderson, *Observations upon the Peloponnesus and Greek Islands, made in 1829*, p. 314.
[180] Shaw, *American Contacts with the Eastern Churches, 1820-1870*, pp. 71ff.
[181] Shaw, *op cit.*, pp. 135-156.
[182] Shaw, *op. cit.*, pp. 120ff.
[183] Shaw, *op. cit.*, pp. 17-34.
[184] B. H. Hunnicutt and W. W. Reid, *The Story of Agricultural Missions* (New York, Missionary Education Movement, 1931, pp. ix, 180), pp. 98-101.
[185] William Webster Hall, Jr., *Puritans in the Balkans. The American Board Mission in Bulgaria, 1878-1918. A Study in Purpose and Procedure* (Sofia, Studia Historico-Philologica Serdicensia, Supplementi Vol. I, 1938, pp. xx, 280), *passim*.
[186] Reid, *Missions and Missionary Society of the Methodist Episcopal Church*, Vol. III, pp. 201-272; Dora Davis, *The Bulgaria Mission of the Methodist Episcopal Church* (New York, The Missionary Society of the Methodist Episcopal Church, 1906, pp. 37), *passim*.
[187] Dennis, Beach, and Fahs, *World Atlas of Christian Missions, 1911*, p. 93. By this table the American Board had 664 communicants, the Methodist 532, and the Deutsche Orient Mission 100 baptized Christians.

Within that vast domain in Eastern Europe which was included in the Russian Empire lived numbers of Protestants.[188] A large proportion of them were in the Baltic provinces and included many Germans and Finns. Some were in the German communities which were scattered in the Ukraine. Beginning in 1789, and continuing into the early part of the nineteenth century, occurred a migration of several thousand German Mennonites into Southern Russia.[189] The Russian dissenters from the state church seemed to offer a field for Protestant missions, especially since some of these Nonconformists appeared to hold beliefs which made them akin to one or another of the Protestant denominations. German Baptists entered the Empire in 1840. At first they confined their efforts to those who spoke German, but eventually their movement spread to non-Germans and several thousand members were reported.[190] In the Baltic provinces converts were made from Lutheranism, and in Poland from Roman Catholics and Uniates. In 1879 religious liberty was accorded German Baptists and in 1899 this was extended, with some restrictions, to other Baptists.[191] The Stundists arose not far from the middle of the century from contacts with German Protestants. They cherished views resembling those of the Baptists, and later came under Baptist influence. Efforts were made to bring them and the Baptist groups together.[192] Assistance came from American Baptists. Lord Radstock, an Englishman, helped to give rise to a movement not very different from that of the Baptists. He preached among the upper classes. Some of his converts carried his message to their retainers and thus it made its way to the common people.[193] Among the variants of the Baptists was a mystical sect, with ecstatic manifestations, the Maliovantsi.[194] The conservative reaction under Alexander III brought intensified persecution,[195] but the Stundist-Baptists continued to grow.[196] A striking figure of the period was Friedrich Wilhelm Baedeker (1823-1906), German by birth,

[188] Smirnoff, *A Short Account of the Historical Development and Present Position of Russian Orthodox Missions*, p. 73, says that the census of 1897 showed 6,213,237 Protestants, or 4.85% of the population.

[189] P. M. Friesen, *Die alt-evangelische mennonitische Brüderschaft in Russland (1789-1910) im Rahmender mennonitischen Gesamtgeschichte* (Halbstadt, Taurien, "Raduga," 1911, pp. xx, 776, 154), pp. 73ff.

[190] Vedder, *A Short History of Baptist Missions*, p. 408. In 1913, 178 churches with 28,900 members were reported.—*Ninety-ninth Annual Report of the American Baptist Foreign Mission Society, 1913*, p. 134.

[191] Latimer, *Liberty of Conscience under Three Tsars*, pp. 94ff.

[192] Milukow, *Skizzen russischer Kulturgeschichte*, Vol. II, p. 145; Latimer, *op. cit.*, pp. 58ff.; Curtiss, *Church and State in Russia*, pp. 164ff.

[193] Milukow, *op. cit.*, Vol. II, p. 145; Latimer, *op. cit.*, pp. 71-76.

[194] Latimer, *With Christ in Russia*, pp. 156ff.

[195] Latimer, *op. cit.*, pp. 198ff.

[196] Vernadsky, *A History of Russia*, pp. 206, 207; Latimer, *Dr. Baedeker in Russia*, pp. 189ff.

English by adoption, and a convert of Lord Radstock. For years he travelled through the Empire holding meetings, bringing encouragement to Stundists, Baptists, Mennonites, and other Protestant groups. He gave especial attention to prisoners and his tours of the convict camps carried him across Siberia.[197]

The partial toleration granted in 1899 was further extended in 1905, when a larger degree of religious liberty was granted. After 1905 restraint by officials and mob opposition were still common, but Protestant meetings could be held publicly for Russians as well as for those of non-Russian stock.[198]

In the course of the nineteenth century and the pre-1914 years of the twentieth century, a number of Protestant organizations from outside Russia extended their efforts to the Empire. Among these were the British and Foreign Bible Society, the Evangelical Alliance, which sought to bring the various Protestant groups into fellowship and to aid the persecuted Stundists, the Berlin Bible School, the Plymouth Brethren, the Evangelical Christians of Sweden, drawn from several denominations, the (British) Evangelical Continental Society, American Methodists, the London Missionary Society, the Continental Mission of the Sunday School Union, the Society of Friends,[199] the Young Men's Christian Association and the World's Student Christian Federation through John R. Mott,[200] and the Deutsche Orient Mission.[201] In Siberia colporteurs of the American Bible Society distributed hundreds of thousands of copies of the Scriptures.[202]

These preceding pages, so largely a condensed catalogue of missions and movements, some Roman Catholic, some Eastern, including Russian Orthodox, and some Protestant, seem to present a picture of intense and largely futile effort by each of the major divisions of organized Christianity to win adherents from the others. Scores of zealous missionaries laboured, and yet, except in a few rare cases where they took advantage of non-religious factors and in Russia, where the state gave determined support to Orthodox missions, only a relatively few thousands of converts were made. In general, apart from the large Irish Roman Catholic immigration into the British Isles, the shifts of allegiance of some of the Uniates, and the rapid growth of semi-Protestant sects in Russia, little change in ecclesiastical boundaries could be recorded.

[197] Latimer, Dr. Baedeker in Russia, passim.

[198] Latimer, With Christ in Russia, pp. 25ff.; Curtiss, op. cit, pp. 319ff.

[199] Latimer, Liberty of Conscience under Three Tsars, pp. 219ff. On an appointee of the London Missionary Society, see Charles M. Birrell, The Life of the Rev. Richard Knill of St. Petersburgh. Being Selections from His Reminiscences, Journals, and Correspondence (London, James Nisbet and Co., 1859, pp. viii, 268), passim.

[200] Mathews, John R. Mott, pp. 165, 170ff., 197ff.

[201] Richard Schäfer, Geschichte der Deutschen Orient-Mission (Potsdam, Lepsius, Fleischmann und Grauer, 1932, pp. 124), p. 60.

[202] Dwight, The Centennial History of the American Bible Society, Vol. II, p. 381.

No such extensive alterations in the ecclesiastical map occurred as were witnessed in Western Europe in the sixteenth and seventeenth centuries. However, it must be noted that these missions of one branch of Christians to another were manned by only a comparatively few active agents. In numbers the missionaries were only the merest fraction of those who during these years were carrying the Christian faith to non-Christian peoples or of those who were seeking to hold to the Christian faith the millions, by tradition and ancestry Christian, who were migrating to other continents or who were settling the frontiers of the United States and Canada. Had larger staffs been engaged, the results might have been more formidable.

In every period a persistent problem has been the perpetuation of the Christian faith among peoples of nominally Christian stock. In the nineteenth century this was peculiarly acute in Europe. Intellectual, political, and social currents set hundreds of thousands adrift from their inherited religion. Because of the Industrial Revolution, vast shifts of population moved millions from rural areas and older centres to the newer mining, manufacturing, and commercial districts. Cities expanded enormously. Separated from their accustomed environment and thrust into new living conditions, thousands tended to drop religious observances and beliefs along with other features of their old manner of life. To meet the challenge so rapidly and so rudely thrust upon them, Christians who took their faith seriously were faced with the necessity of erecting tens of thousands of new church buildings in urban areas and in mining and factory towns.[203] They had also to train thousands of clergy who would be adept at meeting the new conditions, devise new methods of religious effort, and make their Christianity effective in meeting the intellectual, economic, and social problems presented by an age in which science and the machine were apparently dominant.

The story of the remarkable accomplishments in dealing with this problem does not, strictly speaking, belong in these pages. We are here primarily concerned with the expansion of Christianity into new peoples, new lands, and along fresh geographical frontiers. Yet we must call attention to what was done, even though we somewhat grudgingly content ourselves with a painfully imperfect summary, made up of a hasty sampling of a myriad-fold enterprise.

---

[203] In 1824, in Manchester, with a population of 187,000, the buildings of the Church of England had a seating capacity for only 22,468, and in Birmingham, with a population of about one hundred thousand, there were church accommodations for only sixteen thousand.—Wearmouth, *Methodism and the Working-class Movements of England, 1800-1850*, p. 18.

Such a summary, however, may give some slight inkling of the exuberant life in the nineteenth century Christianity of Western Europe. As, in the succeeding chapters and volumes, we survey the prodigious and unprecedented territorial spread of the faith, carried on chiefly by individuals and ecclesiastical organizations with much less assistance from governments than had been accorded since the first three centuries, we ought also to recall that at the same time Christianity was fighting for its life in Europe. It was striving to preserve its hold upon a society in which old patterns were rapidly being supplanted by new, and in which powerful forces were at work which were either indifferent or, more frequently, hostile to the inner spirit of Christianity. Moreover, the challenge was greatest in those regions from which came the larger part of the support for the overseas expansion of Christianity. In Western Europe Christianity experienced losses. It did not fully rise to the situation. Yet to a remarkable extent it met the forces of the new age and retained and even strengthened its hold as a moulding element in European life.

In the preceding two chapters we have already seen some of the movements which perpetuated Christianity in Western Europe. In the Roman Catholic fold, the revival of religious devotion was marked. Many of the congregations, societies, and orders which sprang into being in larger numbers than in any preceding century were directed fully as much to the spread of the faith in Europe as to its propagation overseas. John Bosco, from whom issued three of these new organizations, came to the remarkable development of his latent powers through seeking to meet the challenge of neglected youth in Turin, one of the growing industrial cities of North Italy. Protestantism gave rise to the Young Men's and Young Women's Christian Associations, largely for city youth of the medium income levels, to the Salvation Army and the rescue missions for the submerged strata of the urban areas, and to the Sunday Schools. Moreover, we must remember that a large proportion of the schools through which most of the elementary and secondary education was given included religious instruction in their curricula.

These organizations and institutions by no means complete the picture. Many another means, evidence of the vitality of nineteenth century Christianity, was devised to bring the Christian message to the classes unreached by the traditional methods.

The Roman Catholic Church, although it suffered severe blows from the French Revolution and eighteenth and nineteenth century liberalism, and although in Germany Bismarck sought to curb it, developed many a new organization. We have already mentioned several of these. In Germany, as well, associations of the laity were formed for furthering the faith through banding youths together under religious auspices, through the circulation of books, through the assistance of charities, and through safeguarding Roman Catholic religious instruction in the schools.[204] To help students keep the faith, associations were instituted.[205] In 1913 a number of societies of university graduates joined in a federation. These had as their purpose the propagation by lectures and literature of the Roman Catholic viewpoint.[206] In Germany, in the course of the nineteenth century, many Roman Catholics, the majority of them from the lower income levels, attracted by opportunities for work, moved into traditionally Protestant regions. To provide for them church-buildings, priests, schools, orphanages, and hospitals, the Boniface Society was founded (1849) by Count Stolberg.[207] In 1845 a priest, Adolph Kolping, began the first of a series of societies of young artisans. Their purpose was the religious and secular instruction of their members.[208] In Belgium, beginning in 1890, the Boerenbond, or Peasants' League, was inaugurated. Its chaplains held annual religious conferences for its members.[209] In Belgium, too, large numbers of Roman Catholic societies of labourers in the industries for which the country was famous were formed to further the religious, moral, and material welfare of the working classes.[210] In France, Roman Catholic schools in which religious instruction was a normal part of the curriculum increased until in 1897 they contained nearly a million and a half pupils. The legislation of 1901 took these out of the hands of the teaching congregations and dissolved many of them. Yet Roman Catholics devised ways of carrying on schools in which they could continue to instruct their children and in 1910-1911 these enrolled nearly a million pupils.[211] One of the chief means used for perpetuating Roman Catholic Christianity was the schools conducted by brotherhoods and sisterhoods whose members had dedicated themselves to teaching. One list names twenty such brotherhoods which were inaugurated in the nineteenth century and ten, also begun in the nineteenth century, which incidentally engaged in teaching.[212] Fairly typical were the Christian Brothers of Ireland. They had as a founder Edmund Ignatius Rice. He had made a fortune in commerce, had thought of entering a monastery abroad to devote himself to good works, but had his attention directed to a group of neglected boys in

[204] Guilday, The Catholic Church in Contemporary Europe, 1919-1931, pp. 119ff.
[205] Guilday, op. cit., pp. 116, 117.
[206] Guilday, op. cit., p. 117.
[207] Guilday, op. cit., pp. 111, 112.
[208] Guilday, op. cit., p. 120.
[209] H. Anet in The International Review of Missions, Vol. XXI, pp. 265ff.
[210] Guilday, op. cit., pp. 12ff.
[211] Guilday, op. cit., pp. 73, 74.
[212] John J. Schuetz, The Origin of the Teaching Brotherhoods (Washington, The Catholic University of America, 1918, pp. 104), passim.

his own Ireland. In 1802 he opened a school for boys and from this humble beginning came a brotherhood which engaged in education not only in Ireland, but also in a number of other lands.[213] Within Roman Catholicism was a vitality which rose amazingly to meet the challenge of the age.

In the Balkan Peninsula, the chief ties which bound youth to the Eastern Orthodox churches were nationalism and group loyalty. In the Ottoman Empire the Christian groups had been treated as social and political entities. In the nineteenth century the contagion of nationalism reached them and accentuated the attachment to an institution that in each instance had been associated with the people's glorious past. Greeks could not forget that their church was an integral part of the Byzantine Empire. Serbs recalled Sava and his energy in creating a national church,[214] and Bulgars remembered the days when the ex-monk, Simeon, had headed what he deemed an empire, had had himself crowned Tsar, and had encouraged the bishops to declare their church independent and to place at its head a Patriarch.[215]

In Russia the state, particularly under the vigorous Procurator of the Holy Synod, Pobiedonostsev, made earnest efforts to strengthen the Orthodox Church. Yet ground was lost rather than gained. In 1890 the number of church buildings for each one hundred thousand of the population had declined nearly one half since 1840, and the number of secular clergy, from whom were drawn the parish priests, a little more than a third.[216] Most of the educated had scant respect for the Church and its faith.[217] The priesthood was largely an hereditary caste whose membership was from compulsion and not from religious conviction. Although near the end of the century a group of influential writers and scholars espoused its cause,[218] the Russian Church entered the twentieth century sadly handicapped, bound hand and foot to a decrepit despotism which was already being undermined, and a waning factor in national life.

In Protestantism, the rising tide of life gave birth to movement after movement to make more vital the hereditary faith. In Germany an Inner Mission was founded in 1849, the year after the revolutionary disturbances which had so shaken the land. Instituted by J. H. Wichern, who had been nourished in Pietism and who was led into its inauguration through his care for delinquent boys, it sought, partly through sisterhoods and lay brotherhoods, to

[213] *The Catholic Directory of South Africa, 1931*, pp. 29-33.
[214] Vol. II, p. 248.
[215] Vol. II, p. 246.
[216] Milukow, *Skizzen russischer Kulturgeschichte*, Vol. II, p. 184.
[217] Tolstoi, *My Confession*, pp. 1-4.
[218] Visser 't Hooft, *Anglo-Catholicism and Orthodoxy*, pp. 81-83.

reach the nominally Christian masses and to serve seamen, unemployed, prisoners, and underprivileged children. Its programme embraced Sunday Schools, city missions, colporteurs, and Christian lodging houses.[219] In 1833 Theodore Fliedner, a pastor at Kaiserswerth, inaugurated the use of deaconesses, and three years later organized the Rheinisch-Westfälische Diakonissen-Verein. In 1894 Protestant churches in Germany, as an outgrowth of this movement, employed nearly eight thousand deaconesses in hospitals, poor-houses, orphanages, and schools, and as parish helpers.[220] In England, in the latter half of the century, out of the purpose of Mrs. Ranyard, came the Female Bible and Domestic Mission which appointed Biblewomen to serve the poor and to help the latter help themselves. Eventually it supported Biblewomen not only in the British Isles, but also on the continent, in Egypt, and in Palestine.[221] While in London, studying medicine in preparation for service as a missionary in China, Thomas John Barnardo, of wealthy merchant stock, became interested in the child-waifs of the metropolis. Giving up his plans for China, he ran a mission for these neglected dregs of a *laissez-faire* industrialism. He adopted as a rule "no destitute child ever refused admission," opened homes for his wards, found useful occupations for them, and assisted many to go to the colonies.[222] In the second quarter of the century, out of the efforts of David Nasmith, city missions were founded in Glasgow, Dublin, London, Paris, and in a number of centres in North America.[223] Within two years of its inception, the London City Mission, an undenominational enterprise, had sixty-three full time missionaries.[224] Many missons were established in London and other great cities by various organizations to minister spiritually and physically to the flotsam and jetsam and to the very poor. For instance, in 1885 the East End Mission was begun.[225] From Mildmay as a centre, missions were established in a number of places in the poorer districts in London and deaconesses were trained and sent to them.[226] Through these and similar missions, hundreds of men and women were lifted from moral and physical degradation and made to live wholesome, triumphant

[219] Heuss, *Friedrich Naumann*, pp. 43, 45; Doggett, *History of the Young Men's Christian Association*, p. 148; McNeill, *Christian Hope for World Society*, p. 204; Uhlhorn, *Die christliche Liebesthätigkeit*, Vol. III, pp. 348-369.

[220] Uhlhorn, *op. cit.*, Vol. III, pp. 373-382; Doggett, *op. cit.*, p. 147.

[221] Elspeth Platt, *The Story of the Ranyard Mission, 1857-1937* (London, Hodder and Stoughton, 1937, pp. 128), *passim*.

[222] Bready, *Doctor Bernardo, passim*.

[223] Bready, *England: Before and After Wesley*, p. 408.

[224] Bready, *England: Before and After Wesley*, p. 409.

[225] R. G. Burnett, *Christ Down East*, pp. 20ff.

[226] Harriette J. Cooke, *Mildmay, or the Story of the First Deaconess Institution* (London, Elliot Stock, 2d ed., 1893, pp. ix, 214), *passim*.

lives.[227] The Wesleyans had the London Methodist Mission with branches in many parts of the city.[228] In the 1880's the Mission to Deep-Sea Fishermen was begun by a clergyman of the Church of England for the men of the fleet in the North Sea who supplied England with so much of its food. It fought drink, provided hospital ships, held religious services, and distributed Christian literature.[229] Through circles within the Church of England, increasing provision was made for the new centres of population. Church buildings were erected and clergy recruited and trained. The non-resident clergy, who had been one of the features of the lax eighteenth century, declined and the proportion of the incumbents of benefices who attended to their parishes rose. Voluntary organizations, such as the Church Building Society and the Additional Curates Society, came into being to enlarge church edifices and to provide additional clergy for populous parishes.[230] It is said that between 1801 and 1858 £11,000,000 were contributed towards the erection of 3,150 new edifices of the Church of England.[231] Parliamentary appropriations were voted towards the endowment and the strengthening of benefices in populous districts. Between 1809 and 1820 £100,000 was granted annually for this purpose.[232] The Oxford Movement was followed by the emergence of sisterhoods and of communities of men in the Church of England which gave themselves largely to the spiritual and material service of the poor.[233] In 1827 the Church Pastoral Aid Society was inaugurated.[234] Active interest of women and laymen in the parish activities mounted, and thousands of new parishes were created.[235]

In Scotland the rising level of religious life combined with the growing wealth of the country led to rapid expansion. Lay preachers, some from the upper social levels of society and some from the labouring classes, supplemented the work of the clergy.[236] The visits of Moody and other American evangelists reinforced the effects of the many Scotch preachers of similar

[227] See a few instances in Burnett, op. cit., pp. 29-31, and George F. Dempster, Finding Men for Christ (London, Hodder and Stoughton, 1935, pp. 128), passim.
[228] E. W. Walters, Ensor Walters and the London He Loves (London, The Epworth Press, 1937, pp. 166), passim.
[229] E. J. Mather, "Nor'ard of the Dogger" or Deep-Sea Trials and Gospel Triumphs (London, Simpkin, Marshall, Hamilton, Kent & Co., new edition, 1914, pp. xii, 321), passim; Grenfell, Forty Years for Labrador, pp. 63-74.
[230] Carpenter, Church and People, 1789-1889, pp. 74, 79, 98-103; Mathieson, English Church Reform, 1815-1840, pp. 127-175.
[231] Wagner, The Church of England and Social Reform since 1854, p. 12.
[232] Mathieson, op. cit., p. 18.
[233] Wagner, op. cit., p. 99.
[234] Binns, The Evangelical Movement in the English Church, p. 45.
[235] Carpenter, op. cit., p. 370.
[236] Fleming, A History of the Church in Scotland 1843-1874, pp. 111ff.

spirit and purpose.[237] Efforts, some of them strikingly successful, were made
to bring into active parish life the poor, the labourers, and the clerks in the
rapidly growing Glasgow and Edinburgh.[238] The Free Church of Scotland
displayed phenomenal activity in erecting new buildings, not only immediately after its separation from the Church of Scotland, but also in later decades.[239] The Church of Scotland, in spite of the severe blow dealt it by the
formation of the Free Church of Scotland, constructed many new buildings
and endowed new parishes.[240] It inaugurated Young Men's and Women's
Guilds and established an order of deaconesses.[241]

In Scandinavia, within the state churches a growing vitality effected something akin to a second Reformation. Unlike the one of the sixteenth century,
which was initiated by members of the upper classes and was largely doctrinal,
this welled up from below, spread out to the great mass of the common folk,
and stressed practical action and reform of life. Moreover, while the former had
come from Germany, the latter owed much to contact with Great Britain and
the United States.[242] From its beginning, Scandinavian Christianity had been
profoundly affected by both Anglo-Saxon and German Christianity. These influences continued, but those from Anglo-Saxon lands were now stronger than
they had been since the twelfth century. In Sweden, partly because of the contacts with British and American Christianity, about the middle of the century
lay preachers travelled from parish to parish, and some parish priests began
preaching in more popular style. Peter Fjellstedt (1802-1881), who had been
ordained in the established church of Sweden, founded at Lund an institute
for training colporteurs and lay preachers whose graduates were widely scattered at home and abroad.[243] In Norway the Hauge revival was followed, in
the 1850's, by an awakening in which Gisle Johnson, a professor of theology,
was the leading spirit. This later had as one of its fruits the Norwegian Lutheran Home Missionary Society. Other revivals followed.[244] In the Scandinavian
state churches, enrolling the overwhelming majority of the population, movements were afoot which for many were making nominal Christianity vital.

What effects did Christianity have upon nineteenth century Europe? From

[237] Fleming, *A History of the Church in Scotland 1875-1929*, pp. 162, 163.
[238] Fleming, *A History of the Church in Scotland 1843-1874*, pp. 141ff.; Fleming, *A History of the Church in Scotland 1875-1929*, pp. 159, 165ff.
[239] Fleming, *A History of the Church in Scotland 1843-1874*, p. 65; Fleming, *A History
of the Church in Scotland 1875-1929*, p. 165.
[240] Fleming, *A History of the Church in Scotland 1843-1874*, pp. 140, 141.
[241] Fleming, *A History of the Church in Scotland 1875-1929*, p. 164.
[242] Stephenson, *The Religious Aspects of Swedish Immigration*, p. 24.
[243] Stephenson, *op. cit.*, pp. 33, 36-38.
[244] E. Amdahl in *The International Review of Missions*, Vol. XXIX, pp. 358-360.

these summary accounts of the spread of Christianity among the avowedly non-Christians in Europe, the gains of various branches of Christianity at the expense of the others, and the efforts of the churches to hold the rising generation and the shifting population groups to the faith, we must turn to the influence of Christianity upon its environment. The majority of European peoples had now been professedly Christian for between seven hundred and a thousand years. Was that religion shaping their collective life less or more than formerly? In what fashion was it making itself felt? We have already noted two apparently contradictory movements. On the one hand, thousands were openly denouncing their inherited faith or preserved so tenuous a connexion with the churches that they were scarcely conscious of it and knew practically nothing of Christian tenets. On the other hand, the Roman Catholic Church was more closely knit than ever before, from within it were arising more new organizations than in any previous period of similar length, and Protestantism was more vigorous than at any other time in its history. Official Russian Christianity was probably declining in its influence on the life of the Empire, and it is debatable whether Russian dissenting sects, in spite of their growth, were more potent than in the preceding period. But what of Western Europe? In the impress made upon society as a whole, did the augmented life within the organized churches more than offset the negative results of the defections?

Precise measurements are not easily arrived at. In phase after phase of life they are, indeed, impossible. For instance, although some of the movements for social reform or revolution in which the century abounded were avowedly anti-Christian, yet in their origins and many of their basic purposes they were deeply indebted to Christianity. Many an institution whose founders were moved by passionate Christian conviction later passed into the control of leaders lukewarm or hostile to Christianity. It is clear that much of the temper of the century was anti-Christian. A *laissez-faire* capitalism, as yet imperfectly regulated, condemned thousands to unsanitary factories and mines and to squalid slums. An exuberant nationalism, equipped with mechanized weapons and supported by conscript armies, threatened more devastating wars than had yet been fought. An aggressive imperialism united with a still more aggressive commercialism to open to exploitation a large proportion of the non-European peoples of the earth. Education and the attendant intellectual life were restive under the control of the Church and tended to pass into the hands of a secular state which used them for nationalistic ends. In educated circles much scepticism existed. Many, both non-Christians and earnest Christians, believed Christianity and the findings of science to be incompatible. In other words, several of the outstanding features of the age were contradictory or openly hostile to Christianity. Under these circumstances, many believed that Christianity could probably not maintain its existing influence on European civilization and certainly could not increase it. Yet the Christian conscience instituted measure after measure either for the amelioration of the economic and social ills of the age or for their complete elimination. From it came movements to regulate or abolish war and to curb the heartless exploitation of subject races. In the realm of education and the intellect, Christianity continued potent. As we pursue our story to other continents, we are to see that, taken the world over, Christiantiy was unquestionably more of a factor in moulding the life of mankind as a whole than in any preceding age. It probably had fully as much to do with shaping the civilization of Europe as in any century. Indeed, in many respects it was more potent in European life than in any previous age.

Now, as in preceding centuries, Christianity had a profound effect upon the religious life of Europe. This seems so obvious as to be a banality, for the ostensible religion of the majority of the population was Christian. We must remind ourselves again, however, that, although the traditional tie between Church and state was being loosened and millions were drifting away from their inherited faith or openly repudiating it, probably more individuals, especially among the laity in Western Europe, were giving themselves fully to their faith than ever before. Thousands were experiencing a moral and religious remaking. Indeed, the tendency towards the separation of Church and state and the opposition or indifference of many probably helped to make Christianity more potent. More than at any other time since Constantine espoused the Christian cause, the line tended to be sharply drawn between Christians and non-Christians. This made for the decline of the nominal Christianity which had followed the mass conversions of earlier centuries and for the raising of the level of Christian living among those who held to the faith.

Largely as a result of the renewed Protestantism of the land, a marked improvement was registered in the morals of high society and of public life in Great Britain in the nineteenth century.

For generations, charitable institutions for the relief of poverty and sickness had been characteristic creations of Christianity. In the nineteenth century these continued to be prominent. Numerous older Roman Catholic orders continued this service and new ones came into being for that purpose.[245]

---

[245] Liese, *Geschichte der Caritas,* Vol. II, contains brief histories of various Roman Catholic orders and congregations which carried on charitable activities, including those of medieval and modern times.

Nineteenth century Protestantism gave rise to many societies and institutions for the relief of human suffering. A few paragraphs above we hinted at the extensive ministry to the sick and the poor in Germany given by Protestants through the Inner Mission and the deaconesses who had their inception at Kaiserswerth. From the Inner Mission came schools for infants and cripples, rescue homes, care for the poor, the sick, and the mentally subnormal, service for discharged prisoners and the families of prisoners, lodging houses, clubs for apprentices, and campaigns against beggary, drunkenness, and prostitution.[246] Theodore Fliedner, who for more than twenty-five years was pastor at Kaiserswerth, by his vision and devotion made that obscure village on the Rhine a training centre and an example for European philanthropy. In 1826 he founded the Prisoners' Society of Germany.[247] He and his wife inaugurated a home for discharged women convicts.[248] Florence Nightingale declared that it was one of his reports which made her vocation clear to her.[249] It was to Kaiserswerth that she went for her training in nursing,[250] so that through her from this Christian institution issued impulses which made major contributions to the care of the sick. It is one of the most familiar stories of the nineteenth century that largely from Florence Nightingale, beginning with her memorable service in the Crimean War, came schools which created the modern nursing profession.[251] Not only did Florence Nightingale obtain her training at an institution which was a fruit of Christianity. She also owed to Christianity the original purpose which made her desire to be of service to her fellows.[252] Moreover, on the model of Kaiserswerth, deaconess institutions were widely founded in Germany, Switzerland, Holland, England, and the United States.[253] Even apart from its influence on Florence Nightingale, Kaiserswerth became a chief pioneer centre for modern nursing.[254] From an idea which broke upon the deeply religious Daniel von der Heydt through the reading of the Bible was begun a plan for the organized care for the poor which was adopted in a number of German cities.[255] In England the communities of women arising out of the Oxford Movement—fourteen of them were founded between 1848 and 1858—taught school, nursed, visited women

---

[246] Stead, *The Story of Social Christianity*, Vol. II, p. 225.
[247] Winkworth, *Life of Pastor Fliedner of Kaiserswerth*, p. 46.
[248] Winkworth, *op. cit.*, pp. 53, 54.
[249] Winkworth, *op. cit.*, p. 128.
[250] Stead, *op. cit.*, Vol. II, pp. 205, 206.
[251] Nutting and Dock, *A History of Nursing*, Vol. II, pp. 101-311.
[252] Edward Cook, *The Life of Florence Nightingale* (London, Macmillan and Co., 2 vols., 1913), Vol. I, pp. 46ff., 101.
[253] Uhlhorn, *Die christliche Liebesthätigkeit*, Vol. III, pp. 373-382.
[254] Nutting and Dock, *op. cit.*, Vol. II, pp. 1ff.
[255] Stead, *op. cit.*, Vol. II, p. 227.

emigrants on shipboard, and gathered homeless girls into orphanages.[256] In Scotland the distinguished preacher, Thomas Chalmers (1780-1847), worked out in his Glasgow parish an improved system of poor relief to encourage the indigent to help themselves.[257] Toynbee Hall, the precursor of a large number of "settlements"—centres of opportunity and wholesome living in great cities—was named for one who made much of the "Imitation of Christ" and had as its real founder a clergyman.[258] We have already mentioned the gargantuan labours of Thomas John Barnardo in providing homes and finding opportunities for the underprivileged boys and girls of England.[259] Many prostitutes were saved from their unhappy lives—some by missions in the great cities,[260] and some by homes conducted especially for them.[261] George Müller (1805-1898), born in Germany but spending the greater part of a long life in England, through prayer and without directly soliciting funds, built orphanages which cared for oven ten thousand children.[262] These are simply a few examples of the fashion in which a vast flood of philanthropy, more extensive in the nineteenth century than in any preceding period of human history, had its inception largely in the Christian impulse. More than ever before the Christian conscience was stirring men and women to care for the maimed and the ill.

Men were not content with ministering to those wrecked by society and by the hereditary foes of mankind. They were seeking to remove the causes of disaster. At no previous time had so many efforts been put forth to eliminate the sources of man's ills. Some of these were aimed at reforms within the main outlines of the existing economic and political systems. Others strove for a complete erasure of the current social structure and for the achievement of a new, ideal society.

A large proportion of the reforms can be traced to Christianity as at least one of their sources. Many of the most active reformers clearly were such because of their Christian faith. For some measures a Christian origin cannot be demonstrated, but it is entirely possible and even probable that they came into being because of an atmosphere which was in part the product of Chris-

---

[256] Williams and Harris, *Northern Catholicism*, pp. 367-400.

[257] Stead, *op. cit.*, Vol. II, p. 226; Chadwick, *The Church, the State and the Poor*, pp. 171-173.

[258] Carpenter, *Church and People, 1789-1889*, pp. 330ff.; Stead, *op. cit.*, Vol. II, p. 215; Wagner, *The Church of England and Social Reform since 1854*, pp. 178-185.

[259] Bready, *Doctor Bernardo, passim*.

[260] As an example, see Burnett, *Christ Down East*, pp. 88ff.

[261] Carpenter, *op. cit.*, pp. 382-387, tells of a House of Mercy for prostitutes.

[262] George Müller, *Autobiography* (London, J. Nisbet and Co., 1905, pp. xiv, 735), *passim*.

tianity. The Christian call to perfection and the Christian confidence in God working in history were part of the inspiration of the struggle to bring in an ideal society.

Even to list the reformers and the reforms for which a Christian origin can be proved would extend this chapter to inordinate length. As in so much of our story, only a few examples can be given. One of the most famous reformers of the century was Anthony Ashley Cooper, the seventh Earl of Shaftesbury.[263] Born to a great name and in a conventionally aristocratic home in which the religious connexion was merely formal, he early came into a Christian faith of an earnestly Evangelical type. This he owed to a faithful servant who was his childhood nurse. For many years he sat in Parliament, first in the House of Commons and then in the House of Lords. He might have held high office, but he chose to remain unbound by party ties the better to advocate the causes in which he believed. Among the measures which owed their enactment largely to him were acts improving the treatment of the insane, legislation bringing better conditions for labourers in mills and factories and limiting the working day to ten hours, the barring of boys under thirteen and of women from the mines, protection for chimney sweeps, and an act which brought improved housing conditions. He himself built a model village on his estates. He was active in many a religious and missonary movement. Moved to the task by his Christian faith, Samuel Plimsoll (1824-1898) accomplished for the protection of those who toiled on the sea something equivalent to what Lord Shaftesbury did or labourers on the land.[264] The large majority of those who led in other legis .aon to improve the lot of the labourers had a deeply religious, usually an Evangelical, background.[265] Inspired by the examples of Pastor Oberlin and Lord Shaftesbury, Daniel Le Grand helped to institute a course of reform legislation in France.[266] Leading Evangelicals did yeoman's service in supporting the successful movement for bringing more mildness into the severely brutal criminal code.[267] Stephen Grellet (1773-1855), an emigré of the French nobility, who became a minister of the Friends, did much for the improvement of prisons in England and the continent. He was instrumental in leading Elizabeth Fry into a notable

[263] Edwin Hodder, *The Life and Work of the Seventh Earl of Shaftesbury* (London, Cassell & Co., 3 vols., 1886; based partly on the journals of Lord Shaftesbury), *passim*; J. Wesley Bready, *Lord Shaftesbury and Social-Industrial Progress* (London, George Allen & Unwin, 1926, pp. 446), *passim*; *Dictionary of National Biography*, Vol. XII, pp. 133-137; Carpenter, *Church and People, 1789-1859*, pp. 307-312.
[264] Stead, *The Story of Social Christianity*, Vol. II, p. 191.
[265] Bready, *England: Before and After Wesley*, p. 385, lists a number of these.
[266] McNeill, *Christian Hope for World Society*, p. 204.
[267] Bready, *op. cit.*, pp. 370-372.

career for the amelioration of prisons.[268] Elizabeth Fry (1780-1845), of Quaker ancestry, as a girl of seventeen had a religious experience which determined her later life. Although she married and became the mother of a large family, she found time to become a travelling Quaker preacher and to help to bring about more humane treatment of women prisoners.[269] Two other devout Quakers, George and Robert Cadbury, creators of a large cocoa business, moved their works into the country and built a model village for their employees.[270] Methodism was the means of marked improvement among the labouring classes. From men trained and stirred by Methodism came leaders in creating British trade unions, particularly among the miners.[271] It was Methodist local preachers who led in organizing the first unions of agricultural labourers.[272] Although the first important legislation in Great Britain was due to the Irishman, Richard Martin, who, apparently, was only conventionally religious, it was a clergyman, Arthur Broome, who founded (1824) the Royal Society for the Prevention of Cruelty to Animals, the precursor and inspirer of many similar organizations. William Wilberforce and T. F. Buxton, famous for their campaign against Negro slavery, were among the early committee members of the society.[273] The widespread National Society for the Prevention of Cruelty to Children had Lord Shaftesbury for its first president and a clergyman for its chief promoter and organizer.[274] Mrs. Josephine Butler, the wife of a clergyman, was led by the death of her daughter to devote herself to the care of wayward girls and to the fight against licensed prostitution and the white slave traffic.[275] In Scotland several leading churchmen, notably Thomas Chalmers, gave an impulse to social reform.[276]

In Germany, Bismarck, who, although frequently far more Machiavellian than Christian in his policies of state, had a serious religious strain, in his public addresses repeatedly insisted that Germany was a Christian state and must seek to realize the teachings of Jesus, and offered this as a reason for his social legislation for the benefit of the masses.[277]

[268] Stead, op. cit., Vol. II, p. 168.

[269] Janet Whitney, Elizabeth Fry, Quaker Heroine (Boston, Little, Brown & Co., 1936, pp. vii, 337; based upon careful research, well written), passim.

[270] Stead, op. cit., Vol. II, p. 229.

[271] Wearmouth, Methodism and the Working-Class Movements of England 1800-1850, pp. 225-227.

[272] Stead, op. cit., Vol. II, pp. 177-180.

[273] Edward G. Fairholme and Wellesley Pain, A Century of Work for Animals. A History of the R.S.P.C.A., 1824-1924 (London, John Murray, 1924, pp. xx, 298), pp. 49-54; Bready, op. cit., p. 407.

[274] Bready, op. cit., pp. 415, 416.

[275] Carpenter, Church and People, 1789-1889, pp. 382-387; Stead, op. cit., Vol. II, p. 208.

[276] Fleming, The Church in Scotland, 1843-1874, pp. 150ff.; McNeill, op. cit., p. 198.

[277] William Harbutt Dawson, Bismarck and State Socialism (London, Swan Sonnenschein & Co., 1891, pp. xii, 170), pp. 23, 24.

Pope Leo XIII in his encyclical *rerum novarum* (May 15, 1891) dealt so sympathetically with the problems of labour that he became known as the workingman's Pope.[278] Bearing his name was the Banco Popular de León XIII, organized in Madrid in 1904 to provide loans at moderate rate of interest to agricultural and industrial *sindicatos*.[279] In Belgium the Roman Catholic Boerenbond brought small farmers and farm labourers together for co-operative societies for buying, selling, insurance, and a number of other phases of social and economic life.[280]

In Denmark national regeneration in the nineteenth century after blows dealt by disastrous wars seems to have been due to Nicolai Frederick Severin Grundtvig (1783-1872) more than to any other one man. A clergyman, the son of a clergyman, and late in life a bishop, Grundtvig believed in an indissoluble connexion between the Christian life and national life, fought rationalism and dogmatic literalism in the Church, stressed baptism and the Lord's Supper as means to a living faith, wished a singing Church, struggled for liberalism in politics, in education emphasized practical subjects, and contributed greatly to the co-operative movement which became so characteristic of Danish economic organization.[281]

These examples, selected almost at random, may serve to give some indication of the extensive part that the Christian impulse had in promoting the reform movements which so characterized Europe, and especially Western Europe, in the nineteenth century.

Christianity was largely responsible for the widespread agitation for a more moderate use of alcoholic beverages. Hard drinking had marked the eighteenth and the early part of the nineteenth century, particularly in the British Isles and Scandinavia. Theobald Mathew, an Irish Capuchin, was a persuasive preacher of total abstinence who led thousands, notably in Ireland, but also in Great Britain and the United States, to pledge themselves to that stand.[282] The movement persisted, partly through the Pioneer Total Abstinence Association, founded in 1899.[283] In Great Britain "temperance" found large support in church circles. It was in an adult Sunday School that Joseph Livesay began a movement that soon grew into an agitation for total abstinence.[284] In Scot-

[278] Eckhardt, *The Papacy and World Affairs*, pp. 251-254; McNeill, *op. cit.*, p. 208.
[279] Guilday, *The Catholic Church in Contemporary Europe*, p. 343.
[280] Guilday, *op. cit.*, pp. 18, 19.
[281] Nöelle Davies, *Education for Life. A Danish Pioneer* (London, Williams and Norgate, 1931, pp. 207), *passim*; *Encyclopedia of the Social Sciences*, Vol. VII, pp. 189, 190, including a good bibliography; Frederic C. Howe, *Denmark, The Coöperative Way* (New York, Coward-McCann, 1936, pp. xvi, 277), pp. 50-60.
[282] Stead, *op. cit.*, Vol. II, p. 199; Krout, *The Origin of Prohibition*, pp. 178-181, 218ff.
[283] Guilday, *op. cit.*, p. 163.
[284] Henry Carter, *The English Temperance Movement. A Study in Objectives, Vol. I. The Formative Period, 1830-1899* (London, The Epworth Press, 1933, pp. 269), *passim*.

land several of the churches took positive action in favour of temperance and some of the clergy formed themselves into total abstinence associations.[285] In Sweden the first temperance society was organized by a pastor, Peter Wieselgren.[286]

Negro slavery is the most gigantic instance in human history of the selfish exploitation of one race by another. Before 1800 the Christian conscience had begun to be unquiet about it. In the course of the nineteenth century movements originating in Christianity brought it to an end. To emancipation in the United States we are to come in a later chapter. In the wide-flung British Empire the abolition of Negro slavery was primarily the work of British Protestantism. It was the charming scion of a wealthy family and a friend of the younger Pitt, William Wilberforce, who, transformed through contact with the Evangelical movement from a somewhat careless and pleasure-loving man to one of determined purpose, became the leader in the campaign. He was by no means the initiator of the movement. Many before him had condemned slavery, and in the eighteenth century the Quakers had taken measures against it. He had the support, therefore, of a rising tide. However, it was chiefly under his direction that the agitation obtained, in 1807, an act of Parliament abolishing the slave trade so far as the British were concerned. This was supplemented by additional legislation.[287] There followed, in 1833, an act which brought slavery to an end in the British Empire (1838). More than to any other one man, the responsibility for this latter measure must be attributed to Thomas Fowell Buxton, who succeeded Wilberforce as the head of the anti-slavery movement. Buxton had been reared by a Quaker mother in a hatred of slavery and declared that he owed his sustaining motive to the religious faith which had come to him in the chapel where he had worshipped.[288] In some countries actions curbing slavery ante-dated those taken by the British. In France the movement was due to the eighteenth century enthusiasm for the rights of man, and, while having its roots partly in Christianity, was not so obviously of Christian origin as was that in Great Britain.

---

especially pp. 21-53; Wagner, *The Church of England and Social Reform since 1854*, pp. 72-80.

[285] Fleming, *op. cit.*, pp. 77-80.

[286] Janson, *The Background of Swedish Immigration*, p. 172; Stephenson, *The Religious Aspects of Swedish Immigration*, p. 13.

[287] R. Coupland, *Wilberforce. A Narrative* (Oxford, The Clarendon Press, 1923, pp. vi, 528), *passim*; Harris, *A Century of Emancipation*, pp. 3-7, 10, 22; Stephen, *Essays in Ecclesiastical Biography*, Vol. II, pp. 133-186.

[288] Charles Buxton, editor, *Memoirs of Sir Thomas Fowell Buxton, with Selections from his Correspondence, edited by his son* (Philadelphia, Henry Longstreth, 1849, pp. 510), *passim;* Harris, *op. cit.*, pp. 14-24; Stead, *The Story of Social Christianity*, Vol. II, pp. 153, 154.

Even in France, in the second half of the century much leadership came from the Church in the person of Lavigerie, the chief figure in the re-establishment of Roman Catholicism in North Africa.[289] Action by Great Britain, the outstanding commercial and colonial power of the nineteenth century, followed as it was by determined agitation by English reformers to extinguish the slave trade throughout the world, contributed to a succession of steps in other lands which by the end of the century had all but erased what a hundred years before had seemed an almost ineradicable institution.

Closely associated with the campaign against slavery, and in part as an outgrowth of it, was the Aborigines Protection Society which, with the British and Foreign Anti-Slavery Society, laboured for the education and the political emancipation of subject races. We must note, too, that the rising currents of religious life in Great Britain in the nineteenth century were among the major sources of the new attitude of the officials of the British colonial administration which led them to look upon their posts as trusts to be discharged for the welfare of those whom they governed rather than as means for private gain.[290]

In the exuberant and hopeful nineteenth century, many were not content with reforms within the existing structure of society. They dreamed of a revolution which would be followed by a complete remaking of the social, economic, and political order. Some who agitated for this change were frankly anti-Christian. For instance, Karl Marx, whose philosophy was to have so powerful an effect after 1914, vigorously denounced Christian principles, declaring that they taught cowardice, self-contempt, abasement, subjection, and obsequiousness in contrast with the revolutionary proletariat which he advocated.[291] However, even Marx was probably under more obligation to the Jewish-Christian tradition than he quite realized. Of Jewish blood, on both his father's and his mother's side he was descended from a long line of rabbis. His father became a Protestant Christian while Karl was a child, probably to escape from the narrow bonds of Jewish intellectual life into the freedom offered by the liberal Protestantism with which he was acquainted.[292] Marx owed much to Hegel who, in turn, was deeply indebted to Christianity, even though in part from reaction against it. Hegel's semi-theological view of history left its impress upon the philosophy of history which Marx incorporated

---

[289] Harris, *op. cit.*, pp. 88-114.

[290] Harris, *op. cit.*, pp. 2, 88-114.

[291] Otto Rühle, *Karl Marx. His Life and Work* (New York, The Viking Press, 1929, pp. 419), pp. 121, 122.

[292] John Spargo, *Karl Marx: His Life and Work* (New York, B. W. Huebsch, 1910, pp. 359), pp. 19-27.

in his system. Marx, too, came in touch with a marked revival movement in Christianity. His wife's half sister was caught up actively in it.[293] Moreover, Marx, like nineteenth century socialists in general, assumed a view of history which had as its essence a millenarianism, a belief in the progress of society towards a golden age, which was almost certainly the result of the long impregnation of the thought of Europe with Jewish-Christian teaching.[294] It was primarily from Judaism and Christianity that the conviction of the perfectibility of human society was derived.

Leading individual Christians and the prevailing temper in the organized churches were often unsympathetic to some of the specific programmes which were offered for the early realization of a better age. William Wilberforce opposed trade unionism[295] and Lord Shaftesbury was against socialism and chartism.[296] The large majority of the Evangelicals in the Church of England long believed that the existing social order combined "the greatest measure of temporal comforts and spiritual privilege" and from their ranks came fierce opposition to the Christian Socialists.[297] Thomas Robert Malthus, a clergyman, although by no means callous to the sufferings of the poor, by propounding in his *Essay on the Principle of Population*, written in criticism of the feasibility of perfecting society, the theory that mankind tends to multiply beyond the limit of subsistence, gave ammunition for those who fought remedial legislation.[298] At the outset even Methodism, although drawing its membership largely from the middle and lower classes, and although reacting against the individualism of ultra-Protestantism, was sympathetic with benevolent Toryism.[299] It was only gradually that in the nineteenth century it became unofficially allied with the more progressive Liberalism.[300] The majority of professing Christians and the main weight of the ecclesiastical organizations were against movements which sought to hasten, through revolution, the arrival of a new and ideal society.

By no means all the social radicals were anti-Christian, nor were all Christians anti-radical. Several of the movements which sought the thorough remoulding of society owed their origin to men who believed that they were impelled by a

[293] Krummacher, *Gottfried Daniel Krummacher und die niederrheinische Erweckungs-bewegung zu Anfang des 19 Jahrhunderts*, pp. 222, 223.
[294] Dawson, *Progress and Religion*, p. 198.
[295] Peck, *The Social Implications of the Oxford Movement*, p. 11; Carpenter, *Church and People, 1789-1889*, pp. 44-47.
[296] Binyon, *The Christian Socialist Movement in England*, pp. 24-28.
[297] Raven, *Christian Socialism, 1848-1854*, pp. 13-15; Taylor, *Methodism and Politics, 1791-1851*, p. 96.
[298] Raven, *op. cit.*, p. 15.
[299] Taylor, *op. cit.*, p. 14.
[300] Taylor, *op. cit.*, p. 12.

Christian motive. Saint-Simon, who did much to create early French socialism, gave the title *Le Nouveau Christianisme* to his most important book and in it proposed a justly and happily ordered society.[301] Men influenced by Christian ideals were a source of the French Revolution of 1848[302] which, it was fondly hoped, would be more successful than that of 1789 in the permanent improvement of society. In Germany Christian Socialism was strong. To it the Protestant pastor, Rudolf Todt, contributed through his writings.[303] Friedrich Naumann, who in the twentieth century won a not unmixed fame by ardent advocacy of German nationalism and imperialism in his *Mitteleuropa*, was first active as a pastor in the Inner Mission, then broke with it because it was not radical enough to meet his views, and became a leader in Christian Socialism.[304] There were Evangelical labour unions.[305] The Roman Catholic Bishop Emanuel von Ketteler and his group taught that the rights of all take precedence over the rights of the few. In Austria there was a Christian Social movement. In Great Britain the Christian Socialist movement had as its chief figures John Malcolm Forbes Ludlow, a deeply religious layman, John Frederick Denison Maurice, a clergyman, and Charles Kingsley, also a clergyman. Maurice especially, vigorous, with profound convictions, with forthright expression, and drenched in Christianity, helped to turn the attention of English organized Christianity to the social problems of the age and left his impress on the writings of Tennyson and Browning. English Christian Socialism was largely non-political, but it furthered trade unions, it was of major service to the co-operative movement, and it was of great assistance to workingmen's education and to higher education for women.[306] In the spiritual succession of Christian Socialism was the Christian Social Union, with Brooke Foss Westcott, New Testament scholar, theologian, and, in his later years, Bishop of Durham, as its first president. Its influence on theory and action was great.[307] J. K. Hardie, socialist and a leading spirit in the formation of the Independent Labour Party, began his public career as a lay preacher in the Evangelical Union[308] and is said to have shocked an international conference of socialists by declaring that it was the business of labour parties to

[301] Stead, *The Story of Social Christianity*, Vol. II, p. 232; McNeill, *Christian Hope for World Society*, p. 200.

[302] Phillips, *The Church in France, 1848-1907*, p. 23.

[303] Heuss, *Friedrich Naumann*, p. 58; McNeill, *op. cit.*, p. 205.

[304] Heuss, *op. cit.*, *passim*.

[305] Heuss, *op. cit.*, p. 90.

[306] Raven, *op. cit.*, pp. 56-104, 182-301; Binyon, *op. cit.*, pp. 75-82, 91; Wagner, *The Church of England and Social Reform since 1854*, pp. 51-61.

[307] Binyon, *op. cit.*, pp. 97, 156, 160-164; Wagner, *op. cit.*, pp. 209-233; Peck, *The Social Implications of the Oxford Movement*, p. 6.

[308] Fleming, *The Church in Scotland, 1875-1929*, p. 163.

apply the principles of Jesus to politics.[309] Not only in their roots, often invisible, but also in some of their prominent expressions, the movements for the thorough reorganization of society were profoundly indebted to Christianity.

What effect did Christianity have upon the governmental organization of nineteenth century Europe? The two movements of the century which most modified the political structure were democracy and nationalism.

It is one of the commonplaces of history that through the hundred years the increasing tendency was towards more democracy in governmental institutions. As we saw in the preceding volume,[310] modern democracy was largely the result of Christianity and particularly of Protestant Christianity. The growth of democracy which marked the nineteenth century, therefore, represented an increase of the effect of Christianity upon government. One of the notable extensions of democracy, the movement to give the franchise to women, began partly from Christian sources. Quakers had long made a place for the voice of women in their meetings and it is no accident that the first society in Great Britain to demand votes for women was founded by a Quakeress.[311]

Could Christianity, having contributed to democracy, so mould it that it would overcome its inherent perils? Was Christianity strong enough to promote the unselfishness, the sense of responsibility, the poise, and the public spirit which would save democratic governments from desire for aggrandizement, demagogism, and financial corruption? It is not clear that the answer was affirmative. Many statesmen in whom the Christian motive was strong earnestly strove not only to promote democracy but also to save democracy from itself. Of these one of the most notable examples was William Ewart Gladstone.[312] Deeply religious throughout his long career, he endeavoured to govern his policies and actions by Christian principles and was upheld in his arduous life by his Christian faith. Yet many statesmen and government officials had either abandoned Christianity or had preserved only a nominal connexion with it.

Closely allied with democracy was nationalism. It has been called "a sour ferment of the new wine of democracy in the old bottles of tribalism."[313] To a certain extent nationalism, too, was a fruit of the Christian impulse. To be sure, some of the creators of eighteenth century humanitarian nationalism

---

[309] Reinhold Niebuhr in *The Christian Century,* Vol. LI, p. 493.

[310] Vol. II, Chap. 16.

[311] Stead, *The Story of Social Christianity,* Vol. II, p. 210.

[312] See the standard biography, John Morley, *The Life of William Ewart Gladstone* (New York, The Macmillan Co., 3 vols., 1903).

[313] Toynbee, *A Study of History,* Vol. I, p. 9.

were children of the rationalism of their age and had only a formal affiliation with their hereditary faith.[314] Yet Johann Gottfried von Herder (1744-1803), who did much to arouse the spirit of German nationalism, was a Lutheran clergyman, court preacher to the Grand Duke of Saxe-Weimar.[315] Indeed, one of the currents which contributed strongly to the German nationalism that played so prominent and at times so tragic a part in the nineteenth and twentieth centuries was Pietism.[316] By emphasizing feeling more than the intellect, Pietism prepared the way for romanticism and so for attachment to the nation. By stressing the education of the masses in the vernacular, and by contributing to enthusiasm for German art and literature, it reinforced an existing tendency. One of the creators of Italian nationalism, Mazzini, while eventually rejecting Christianity, was deeply religious and cherished a profound regard for the life and teachings of Jesus.[317] In the Balkan Peninsula the Orthodox churches, notably those of Greece and Bulgaria, were the bulwarks of nationalism in its early stages. Several of the French nationalists, while sceptical, showed the effects of their Roman Catholic rearing.[318] However, for many nationalism became a new religion, a substitute for an abandoned Christianity.[319] In its exaggerated forms, particularly after 1914, nationalism proved a major menace to civilization and to the human race.

Was Christianity sufficiently potent to control and overrule the excesses of nationalism? Through being a propelling factor in the creation of international law, it had done something to curb the absolute monarchies which were prominent in the preceding three centuries. Could it soften and regulate the impact of sovereign states upon one another, accentuated as that impact was by the intensified nationalism of the age? The growing use of the machine was drawing mankind physically ever more closely together. The world was becoming smaller. In that shrinking world, a mounting nationalism, equipped by science with weapons of unimaginable power of destruction, might so multiply conflicts that civilization would suffer irremediable damage. Was there in the Christian heritage that which could rise to the challenge? Could the Christian impulse achieve a unified world society?

For the hundred years between 1815 and 1914 success seemed appreciably near. International law continued and was strengthened. A great agency for

[314] Hayes, *The Historical Evolution of Modern Nationalism,* pp. 17ff.
[315] Hayes, *op. cit.,* pp. 27-33.
[316] Koppel S. Pinson, *Pietism as a Factor in the Rise of German Nationalism* (New York, Columbia University Press, 1934, pp. 227), *passim.*
[317] *Mazzini's Letters,* translated from the Italian by Alice de Rosen Jervis (London, J. M. Dent and Sons, 1930, pp. xvi, 211), p. x.
[318] Hayes, *op. cit.,* pp. 173-231.
[319] Hayes, *op. cit.,* p. 290.

alleviating the sufferings of war, the Red Cross, arose, and extended its ministrations of mercy to peacetime disasters. Its Christian rootage was shown by
its symbol. Emblematic of the growing power of Christianity in offsetting
man's brutality is the striking contrast between earlier times and the nineteenth century in the use of the cross in war. Constantine had placed the cross
on his banners to reinforce his arms against his enemies. In the Middle Ages,
Christian warriors "took the cross" as a badge and an incentive in wars against
pagans and Moslems. Under the stirring slogan of a crusade, the Popes sum-
moned Christians to battle. By the nineteenth century crusades had fallen into
desuetude. The cross was employed, not as a summons to war, but as a call
to heal the wounds of war. During the long agony of the wars evoked by the
French Revolution, the will to peace rose and, as never before, men dreamed
of a warless world and proposed plans to implement their dreams. Between
the end of those wars, in 1815, and the outbreak of the next general war, in
1914, projects multiplied for the regulation or the elimination of war and for
the peaceful settlement of international disputes. Peace congresses were held,
arbitration became an accepted feature of international procedure, the Hague
Conferences of 1899 and 1907 drew the majority of the nations together in an
attempt to place restrictions on the weapons of war, and a permanent court
of arbitration was set up.[320]

Indirectly or directly, most of this movement for peace had its origin in
Christianity. Much of it issued from the general humanitarianism of the
eighteenth century and the belief in the perfectibility of human society which
partly expressed themselves in the French Revolution. Eighteenth century
idealism, it will be recalled, however, even when antagonistic to the Church,
had its source in the Christian heritage of Europe.[321] Much of the peace movement can clearly be traced to individuals and groups whose inspiration was
from the Christian faith. By 1789 a number of Christian bodies, notably the
Quakers, were thoroughgoing pacifists.[322] In 1815 the Tsar Alexander I set on
foot what was termed the Holy Alliance, subscribed to by the majority of the
sovereigns of Europe, by which the signers undertook to base their reciprocal
relations "on the sublime truths which the Holy Religion of our Saviour
teaches" and avowed that "the precepts of Justice, Christian Charity and

[320] For an outline list of some of these, with bibliographies, see Edward Krehbiel,
Nationalism, War and Society (New York, The Macmillan Co., 1916, pp. xxxv, 276), pp.
157ff. See also Jacob ter Meulen, *Der Gedanke der Internationalen Organisation in seiner
Entwicklung* (Vol. II, Part 1, 1789-1870, the Hague, Martinus Nijhoff, 1929, pp. xii, 371).
[321] Carl L. Becker, *The Heavenly City of the Eighteenth-Century Philosophers* (Yale
University Press, 1932, pp. 168), pp. 29-31.
[322] Allen, *The Fight for Peace*, pp. 575-579.

Peace . . . must have an immediate influence on the councils of Princes and guide all their steps."[323] In initiating this remarkable document, the Tsar was moved by a profound religious experience which had come to him in mature life and had made him a devout, if not always a clear-thinking, Christian. Among the influences which played upon him were Madame de Krüdener, of aristocratic birth, who through contact with the Moravians had undergone a remarkable conversion, and Franz von Baader, a Roman Catholic theologian, who saw the salvation of Europe in a community ruled by a universal church.[324] Although a vaguely defined document, the Holy Alliance contributed to several moves on the international chessboard and was the inspiration of the rescript through which the Tsar Nicholas II brought about the international peace conference at the Hague in 1899.[325] Throughout his long career, Gladstone attempted to lead England to a Christian instead of a pagan conception of her duty to foreign peoples.[326] In the United States and in Great Britain[327] most of the many peace societies which were organized in the decades following the close of the Napoleonic wars had founders who were impelled by the New Testament. The unofficial international peace convention which assembled in London in 1843 opened its daily sittings with prayer and condemned even defensive war as un-Christian.[328] Elihu Burritt, the American who had much to do with bringing about a whole series of international peace conferences,[329] called his periodical The Christian Citizen and placed at its head the New Testament quotation "God hath made of one blood all the nations of men."[330] Pope Leo XIII or his representatives acted as arbiter in at least five international disputes and on several occasions the representatives of Pope Pius X were arbiters between South American states.[331] Never had so many active efforts been made to devise and utilize measures for international peace as in the century after 1815. Most of these were due very largely to Christianity. If they did not succeed in averting the wars which began in 1914, they provided

[323] W. A. Phillips in The Encyclopædia Britannica, 14th edition, Vol. XI, p. 683.
[324] Ernest John Knapton, The Lady of the Holy Alliance. The Life of Julie de Krüdener (New York, Columbia University Press, 1939, pp. ix, 262), pp. 4, 89, 147ff., 163; Sterling, The Ways of Yesterday, pp. 171ff.
[325] W. A. Phillips in The Encyclopædia Britannica, 14th edition, Vol. XI, p. 683.
[326] J. L. Hammond, Gladstone and the Irish Nation (London, Longmans, Green and Co., 1938, pp. xvii, 768), p. 727.
[327] Allen, op. cit., pp. 3, 4, 5, 7, 55, 375-384; Curti, The American Peace Crusade, 1815-1860, pp. 4-8, 34-39, 68-78, 136-140; Galpin, Pioneering for Peace, pp. 2-11, 67, 68.
[328] G. B. Henderson, in The Journal of Modern History, Vol. IX, pp. 315, 316; Curti, op. cit., pp. 136-140.
[329] Allen, op. cit., p. 403.
[330] Curti, op. cit., pp. 143ff.
[331] Eckhardt, The Papacy and World Affairs, p. 259.

the patterns for the only hopeful attempts after that year to achieve peace and justice between the nations.[332]

In music, painting, sculpture, and architecture, the influence of Christianity was probably not so great in the nineteenth as in some preceding centuries. That it was present, abundant examples give ample testimony. Even a casual knowledge of the aesthetic side of the century reveals them. However, perhaps because of the increase of wealth, artistic talent was diverted more than formerly to secular channels. Religious themes did not appear so prominently as in previous eras. Yet it may be that in intangible ways the Christian impulse made itself felt in many creations of the artistic spirit which outwardly seemed purely secular. The presumption is that in a cultural heritage so permeated with Christianity, nobility of conception, fidelity and perseverance in accomplishment, and honesty in craftsmanship had their roots at least partly in the Christian faith. So, too, some of the art galleries and public concerts existed because of a philanthropy which arose from Christian motives.

In the intellectual life of Europe, Christianity continued potent, and that in spite of an apparent antagonism between the two. Much of the greatest literature of the century was shot through and through with conceptions of Christian origin.[333] Many a distinguished writer, although later departing from conventional Christianity, in his youth had been affected by the hereditary faith of Europe in a fashion which contributed to his mature life. Tennyson was a son of the rectory.[334] Browning was reared in a devout home and in his boyhood was deeply religious. His poetry reflected his Christian background.[335] A transforming religious experience which came to him in middle life through Christianity moulded some of Tolstoi's greatest work.[336] Ibsen and Dostoievski each in his own way gave evidence of the strong impress of the inherited faith of his environment. In his youth Carlyle expected to enter the ministry and bore to the end the stamp given by his early Calvinism. The most persistently read story of Dickens was his *Christmas Carol*. One of the

---

[332] A number of these were proposed at the first international peace congress in London in 1843.—Curti, *op. cit.*, pp. 136-140.

[333] On the confidence in the existence of order in the universe voiced by the poets of the eighteenth and nineteenth centuries, with a personification of nature, sprung largely from Christianity, see Joseph Warren Beach, *The Concept of Nature in Nineteenth-Century English Poetry* (New York, The Macmillan Co., 1936, pp. xii, 618), *passim*, especially pp. 4ff.

[334] Hallam Tennyson, *Alfred Lord Tennyson. A Memoir. By His Son* (New York, The Macmillan Co., 2 vols., 1897), *passim*.

[335] Mrs. Sutherland Orr and Frederic G. Kenyon, *Life and Letters of Robert Browning* (Boston, Houghton Mifflin Co., preface 1908, pp. xvii, 431), *passim*, especially pp. 17, 25, 240.

[336] Tolstoi, *My Confession, passim*.

sources of the romanticism which was so strong in the nineteenth century was Protestantism, for the latter paved the way for the romantic doctrine of inspiration.[337] So great a journalist as C. P. Scott, who was the real creator of the *Manchester Guardian*, was reared in a Unitarian environment and felt that he must make the will of God the guiding principle of his life.[338] Examples might be multiplied almost endlessly.

As in previous periods, many of the fresh advances in education were made under the driving power of the Christian impulse. Between A.D. 500 and A.D. 1500 most of the universities of Western Europe sprang up under the aegis of the Church. Between A.D. 1500 and A.D. 1800, under the propulsion of Christian conviction, education had begun to penetrate to the masses. Most of the new ventures of that period, such as the academies in England, the charity schools, the Sunday Schools, the *realschulen* in Germany, the Lancastrian schools, and the schools of the Jesuits and the Jansenists, sprang out of Christian conviction. In the nineteenth century, the Christian impulse continued to be felt in all grades of education. From it arose new forms which became milestones in educational advance. In was Grundtvig who, in the day of Denmark's despair after crushing defeats in war, was moved by his Christian faith to inaugurate "folk schools,"[339] a type of institution which became widespread in Denmark as an agency of national regeneration and spread to the other Scandinavian countries. Kristen Kold, a Dane who did much to mould these schools, was an earnest Christian who in his youth had a religious awakening which made the guiding principle of his life love for God and man.[340] In Sweden, Church and school were long intimately related, and even after the partial secularization of education in the nineteenth century the pastor was often the head of the local school board.[341] Froebel, the founder of the kindergarten, was a son of the parsonage, was reared by a clergyman-uncle, was deeply religious, and claimed that his system of education was according to the spirit of Christ.[342] Maurice, one of the leaders in Christian Socialism, had an outstanding part in the founding of Queen's College for Women, the

---

[337] G. A. Borgese, in *Encyclopædia of the Social Sciences*, Vol. XIII, pp. 426-433.

[338] J. L. Hammond, C. P. Scott of the *Manchester Guardian* (London, G. Bell and Sons, 1934, pp. xv, 365).

[339] Davies, *Education for Life. A Danish Pioneer*, pp. 44, 69ff., 93.

[340] Davies, *op. cit.*, pp. 111ff.

[341] Christina Stael von Holstein Bogoslovsky, *The Educational Crisis in Sweden, in the Light of American Experience* (New York, Columbia University Press, 1932, pp. xiv, 301), pp. 14, 15.

[342] *Autobiography of Friedrich Froebel*, translated and annotated by Emilie Michaelis and H. Keatley Moore (Syracuse, N. Y., C. W. Bardeen, 1889, pp. xv, 167), pp. 3, 8, 9, 14, 19, 23, 63, 74, 119, 120.

first of a numerous succession of institutions of its kind.[343] He also helped to inaugurate better education for the labourers.[344] King's College in London and Durham University were begun by churchmen.[345] Early in the nineteenth century a number of Protestant societies were organized to aid popular education in backward and poverty-stricken Ireland.[346] Hannah More, noted for her literary achievements, in later life was one of the inner circle of Evangelicals and organized schools among neglected miners and colliers of the Mendip Hills.[347] In Scotland the distinguished preacher, Thomas Guthrie, had much to do with beginning the "Ragged Schools" for underprivileged children.[348] David Stow, moved by the great Christian, Thomas Chalmers, was the inaugurator of model schools and a training college for teachers which paved the way for the ultimate adoption in Scotland of a national system.[349] In the nineteenth century, societies, sprung out of the Christian impulse, planted elementary schools up and down Wales and gave education to a principality which until then had been largely illiterate.[350] In Wales, too, the Sunday School did much for the general education of the people.[351] We have already noticed the rise of a large number of teaching congregations in the Roman Catholic Church—more than in any other period of similar length—and the large part played by these in education on the continent and in Ireland. Many schools were becoming secularized, but Christianity was still the source of fresh and important contributions in education. As so often in its history, Christianity gave birth to institutions, only to have them eventually taken over by those who had little interest in it or were even antagonistic to it. Even though this happened, it continued to be the source of new movements and institutions.

What was the effect of Christianity upon the main intellectual currents of nineteenth century Europe? These were in part shaped by *belles-lettres* and by education, but they were not the product of either and modified them more than they were modified by them. In these currents were seen both the rationalism and the romanticism of the eighteenth century. In them the scien-

---

[343] Stead, *The Story of Social Christianity,* Vol. II, p. 207; Raven, *Jesus and the Gospel of Love,* pp. 409, 410.

[344] Raven, *op. cit.,* pp. 409, 410.

[345] Carpenter, *Church and People, 1789-1889,* p. 73.

[346] Dowling, *The Hedge Schools of Ireland,* pp. 39-42.

[347] Annette M. B. Meakin, *Hannah More. A Biographical Study* (London, Smith, Elder & Co., 1911, pp. xxxi, 415), *passim,* and pp. 284, 301, 302; William Roberts, *Memoirs of the Life and Correspondence of Hannah More* (New York, Harper & Brothers, 2 vols., 1835), *passim.*

[348] The inscription on the Edinburgh statue of Thomas Guthrie.

[349] Fleming, *A History of the Church in Scotland, 1843-1874,* p. 50.

[350] Jones, *The Story of Education in a Welsh Border Parish,* pp. 12, 14, 57.

[351] Oliver Thomas, in *The International Review of Missions,* Vol. XXVI, p. 386.

tific attitude and the interest in social and economic problems were outstanding. As was to be expected, the processes by which man achieved the amazing
knowledge and mastery of his physical environment were prominent. It was
natural, too, that the vast social and economic changes to which science and
the machine so powerfully contributed should engage the attention of men.
The nineteenth century was the age of science and of political, economic, and
social revolution. The intellectual life was, accordingly, largely concerned with
them. To the casual observer, these movements, and especially the swing to
the scientific temper, appeared to be antagonistic to Christianity. Science
seemed at war with theology.[352] Instead of being an outgrowth of the Christian impulse, science appeared to be antagonistic to it. A large proportion of
the leaders in scientific thought either had only a nominal connexion with the
churches or had abandoned faith in God.[353] Yet at least some men of science
not only remained devout Christians but also seemed to owe their achievements at least in part to their faith. Thus Michael Faraday, said to have been
the greatest physicist of the century, was an earnest member of a small
Christian sect, the Sandemanians, and the staunch individualism bred in that
group presumably made no small contribution to his attainments.[354] Pasteur,
notable for his contributions to the study and control of disease, was a devout
Roman Catholic of simple and sincere faith. Moreover, not only science itself
but also the conception of progress which accompanied the scientific advance
were greatly indebted to Christianity and may even have had it as their chief
source. The trust in the orderliness and dependability of the universe which
was basic in science was largely the result of the belief in God as the creator
and governor of the universe which had been implanted in the European mind
by Christianity. The Christian drama of salvation with its sense of history—a
series of divine acts in time—seems to have made possible the theory of
evolution which was so prominent in nineteenth century thought. This latter
could not possibly have arisen in Greece, with its cyclical theory of history,
or in Islam, with its fatalism, or in India, with its sense of the unreality of
the visible world. In its own way evolution was a plan of salvation enacted
in history. Even though the intellectual achievements of the age destroyed some
features of Christian theology and in several of their manifestations were

[352] See White, *A History of the Warfare of Science with Theology in Christendom,* a
book which arose out of this conviction and which gives many instances of the conflict.
[353] Crowther, *British Scientists of the Nineteenth Century,* describes three eminent men
of science and of these only one appears to have had more than a conventional religion.
Leuba, in *The Belief in God and Immortality,* reported the results of a *questionnaire* sent
to a large number of leading American scholars which seemed to disclose the waning of
a faith in God.
[354] Crowther, *op. cit.,* pp. 69-75.

antagonistic to the fundamental tenets of the faith, yet basically they seem to have been largely the fruit of Christianity.

From this last paragraph we turn, by only a slight transition, to the effect of nineteenth century Europe upon Christianity. In the second chapter of this volume we have noted some of the bearing of the environment upon the spread of Christianity. We must now say something of what the environment did to Christianity itself. The intellectual outlook of the nineteenth century made a marked impression. Its emphasis upon the scientific approach, the romanticism which ran like a thread through much of it, especially in its earlier course, its belief in evolution and in progress, and its freedom of thought, all left their imprint. So, too, did the outstanding tendencies in political theory and action —democracy, nationalism, and social reform. *Laissez faire* capitalism, individualism, the reaction towards collectivism, the growth of cities, the industrialization of economic life, and the expanding imperialism each helped to shape the Christianity of the century. To recount the ways in which these made themselves felt would require a volume. We must, however, essay the somewhat dubious task of a summary.

The fashion in which Roman Catholicism responded has been hinted at in a number of places. Freed in part from state control and suffering from the defection of millions who abandoned all but a nominal connexion with it, Roman Catholicism closed its ranks under the leadership of a Papacy which exercised an increasingly strict control over the entire church. This control was facilitated by the rapid communications which made it possible easily to keep in touch with a world-wide organization. It was no accident that the century saw the formal endorsement of the doctrine of Papal infallibility. With the Pope as spokesman, the Roman Catholic Church denounced any modification of its dogmas or of its attitude towards the Bible which might result through the application of the scientific methods. In their schools the clergy might teach science, and a few of the clergy and laymen made notable contributions to scientific advance. We have already mentioned Pasteur. The Roman Catholic Church, too, sought to adjust its methods in such manner that it could hold and serve the labourers in the new industries. Yet in the main outlines of its teaching the Roman Catholic Church adhered to what it believed was the deposit of faith entrusted to it by Christ and his Apostles. While making some concessions to the rising nationalism, it strove to be supra-national and centralized in Rome. Popular, democratic movements probably helped to encourage the appearance of new orders and societies, for many of these sprang from founders of humble birth, but obedience to authority was exacted of all.

Roman Catholicism availed itself of the opportunity given by imperialism, and especially by French imperialism, to expand on many new frontiers. Although suffering severe losses, it was more closely knit organizationally than ever before. It remained potent in Europe. Outside Europe, it achieved a greater extension than at any previous time.

In Russia, the Orthodox Church, dominated by the Government, largely set itself against the new currents. Especially did it do so under the convinced reactionary, Pobiedonostsev, to whom most of the modern temper was anathema. Unlike the Roman Catholic Church, it lost more ground than it gained. Yet liberalism had its effect and the intermittently mounting tolerance of the state permitted the rapid growth of dissenting bodies.[355]

By its very nature fissiparous, tending to individualism, and possessed of no central, authoritative administration, Protestantism was more adaptable and more nearly made its peace with the new movements than did Roman Catholicism. It produced no theologies comparable for potency with that of Calvin, but out of it came influential minds who departed from the traditional orthodoxy and helped to shape the Protestant interpretation of Christianity. Most of these were Germans. Schleiermacher, affected by Pietism and romanticism, Hegel, more philosopher than Christian theologian, and Ritschl were outstanding in their immediate influence.[356] Procedures inspired by the scientific attitude were applied to the study of the Bible. Especially as the nineteenth century wore on, the records of the life of Jesus were subjected to minute and fearless examination. The epoch-making works of Strauss and Renan, while not winning general acceptance, helped to provoke scholarship to fresh investigation of the New Testament. The results provoked controversy, but more and more Protestants were disposed to accept the principles on which this Biblical criticism was based and to take over some of the main conclusions which were reached. To many this proved bewildering, but before 1914 the adjustment was beginning to be made. To thousands of earnest souls, evolution appeared to be undermining Christian faith, but such a book as *Natural Law on the Spiritual World*, by Henry Drummond,[357] a friend and

[355] The Raskolniks are said to have increased from about a million in 1850 to about twenty millions in 1900 and twenty-five millions in 1917.—Conybeare, *Russian Dissenters,* p. 241. See also Curtiss, *Church and State in Russia,* p. 139. On the sad condition of the state church, tied hand and foot to the Government, see Curtiss, *op. cit., passim.*

[356] Hugh Ross Mackintosh, *Types of Modern Theology. Schleiermacher to Barth* (New York, Charles Scribner's Sons, 1937, pp. vii, 333), *passim;* Arthur Cushman McGiffert, *The Rise of Modern Religious Ideas* (New York, The Macmillan Co., 1915, pp. x, 315), *passim.*

[357] Henry Drummond, *Natural Law in the Spiritual World* (New York, James Pott & Co., 1884, pp. xxiv, 414), *passim;* George Adam Smith, *The Life of Henry Drummond* (New York, Doubleday & McClure Co., 1898, pp. xiii, 541), *passim.*

associate of Dwight L. Moody, helped numbers to the conviction that a belief in evolution could enrich their faith. We have already noted some of the multitudinous movements for social reform begun by Protestants to meet the changing social conditions of the age. Anglo-Saxon Protestantism especially became more activistic than ever. The popularity of democracy probably assisted the growth of Protestantism, for the two had much in common and democracy was in part the outgrowth of Protestantism. In Great Britain, and especially in England, Protestant denominations in which the democratic principle was strong experienced a rapid increase. In Great Britain, individualism had its effect in the emergence of religious leaders, some of them erratic, who attracted groups of followers.[358] In Germany, out of the intense nationalism of the century, some movements arose which sought to give to Christianity a more peculiarly German flavour.[359] In this volume we have repeatedly noted the numbers of organizations which Protestants created to enable Christianity to meet the challenge brought by the great cities. Partly because Great Britain was overwhelmingly Protestant, and also because it led in the application of machinery to production and became the wealthiest of the European nations, Protestantism, and especially British Protestantism, forged ahead and occupied a relatively more important position in European and world-wide Christianity than it had previously held. In this and ensuing volumes we are to record the expansion in which Protestantism, like Roman Catholicism, entered the doors opened by the Occidental imperialism of the century. More than any other branch of Christianity, Protestantism was conforming to the spirit of the age. By so doing, however, it seemed to have gained rather than lost.

This chapter can be rather quickly summarized. In Europe in the nineteenth century, Christianity registered gains at the expense of the few surviving pagan cults, of Judaism, and of Islam. Its progress against these rivals was not so marked as in the three preceding major divisions of our story. Each of the main branches of Christianity, Roman Catholicism, Eastern Orthodoxy, and Protestantism, won some converts from the others, and within Protestantism

[358] See some of these in Ronald Matthews, *English Messiahs. Studies of Six English Religious Pretenders 1656-1927* (London, Methuen and Co., 1936, pp. xvi, 230), *passim*. The writings of one of the most remarkable are in *The Collected Writings of Edward Irving*, edited by his nephew, G. Carlyle (London, Alexander Strahan, 5 vols., 1866). Also on Irving, see Andrew Landale Drummond, *Edward Irving and His Circle* (London, J. Clarke & Co. [no date—1937?], pp. xi, 13, 305), *passim*.

[359] J. Witte, *The German Faith Movement*, in *The International Review of Missions* (Vol. XXXIII, pp. 521-529).

several denominations grew at the expense of others. However, no one body of Christians took away any substantial percentage of the membership of another. No such violent alterations of ecclesiastical boundaries were witnessed as in the three centuries between A.D. 1500 and A.D. 1800.

The chief achievement of Christianity in Europe was in holding to the Christian faith those who were nominally attached to it and in shaping European culture. This had to be done in the face of enormous changes in the social, economic, political, and intellectual structure of Europe. The amazing fact is that, confronted by this challenge, in Western Europe Christianity displayed enough vitality to rise to it. It did not perfectly shape Europe to its pattern. It had never done so. Millions now either tacitly or openly repudiated Christianity or ignored it. Never, however, had Christianity won the whole-hearted and understanding allegiance of more than a minority. In the nineteenth century, out of the Christian impulse came movement after movement which organized religious instruction for the young, reached out to special groups, provided opportunities for worship in the new centres of population, and continued Christianity's age-old service to the sick, the orphans, and the poor. As never before, programmes were devised to bring society into conformity to Christian ideals. Some of these were for attack on special problems. Others aimed at the complete remaking of civilization. By no means all attained their objective. Yet several wrought striking changes and others met with partial success.

Christianity was least vigorous in Eastern Europe. In Russia the dominant church, while showing some vitality, lost ground. The growth of dissenting groups partially but not entirely offset the retreat of the state church.

The Roman Catholic Church was probably the source of fewer movements, especially those for the alteration of society, than was Protestantism. However, it was not without marked effects. It was reinforced by many new orders and congregations, and it achieved greater solidarity in morale and in organization than it had ever before known.

Protestantism, particularly that of the British Isles, gave rise to many a group and society, and stimulated many a man and woman to propagate the faith, to relieve distress, and to change social customs and institutions.

Although exact measurements are impossible, it is probable that never before had Christianity displayed in Western Europe such abounding vitality and been so potent in modifying and moulding the cultures in which it was set. In addition, as we have repeatedly said, and as we are to see more fully in subsequent chapters, Christianity was spreading throughout the world, and a very large proportion of the personnel and money which made this possible was from Western Europe. Far from being a waning factor in European life, Christianity, in spite of gigantic opposing forces, was at least retaining its influence and was probably growing in its effect.

As in preceding eras, Christianity was modified by its environment. In the Roman Catholic Church this partly took the form of resistance to prevailing currents and a closer integration of organization under the Pope and the affirmation and clarification of historic dogmas in such fashion that the Church was the better able to resist compromise. Russian Orthodoxy was so closely tied to a government which set itself against the trends of the times that it suffered severely. In Protestantism, by its nature more adjustable, a good deal of accommodation occurred. Both Protestantism and Roman Catholicism remained sufficiently apart from the existing order to be the source of continuing criticism of it and of attempts to bring it into conformity with Christian standards.

Chapter VI

THE UNITED STATES OF AMERICA. INTRODUCTORY. THE OLDER AMERICAN STOCK ON THE FRONTIER

IN NO other nation did the Christian movement of the nineteenth century face an opportunity which more severely tested it than in the United States.

Only Russia, and, possibly, India, surpassed the United States in its increase in population.[1] No country in Europe, not even Russia, had so large a proportional population growth.[2] A few other lands on the frontiers of European settlement, among them Canada and Australia, displayed a more rapid percentage of growth, but no other land which in 1914 had as many as fifty million people could show so striking a rate of increase in the preceding 125 years. Immigration and large families brought about an advance in numbers which had few parallels in the history of the race.

Only slightly less spectacular were the additions of territory. In 1783 the western boundary of the United States was the Mississippi River and the southern boundary was the northern line of Florida. In the course of the ensuing hundred years Florida was acquired, and by purchase, voluntary affiliation, and conquest the national domain was pushed westward to the Pacific, southward to the Rio Grande, and northward to Point Barrow.

Even more breath-taking were the growth in wealth, the changes in social and economic organization, and the alterations in the composition of its people. When in 1783 it achieved its independence, the United States was a comparatively poor country, predominantly rural and agricultural. Its white population was drawn chiefly from the British Isles, but had a strong admixture of blood from the Protestant populations of Germany, Holland, France, and, to a less extent, from Sweden. It possessed a large contingent of Negroes and thousands of Indians. In the thirteen decades which intervened between 1783 and 1914, the United States, while still counting agriculture as one of its major occupations, had become highly industrialized. The land had become

---

[1] See chart and figures in *The Encyclopædia Britannica*, 14th edition, Vol. XVIII, pp. 230, 231.
[2] *Ibid.*

sprinkled with cities, some of them huge. To the population had come addi‍tions from every land in Europe and, although in smaller numbers, from most of the countries of Asia. The Negroes had been emancipated. Rapid transporta‍tion, labour-saving machinery, and urban life had worked prodigious alterations in customs and institutions.

By heredity, the large majority of the population were Christian. However, in 1914 a very large proportion were either immigrants or first-generation Americans. The immigrants had been uprooted from their traditional environ‍ment, either from Europe or Asia. In their mother countries the majority had been members, as a matter of convention, of state churches. In the United States no church was established by law and the social pressure to induce church membership was at a minimum. Did Christianity have sufficient vitality to retain or strengthen its historic hold upon elements of the popula‍tion which by tradition were Christian? Could it win those who by ancestry were non-Christian—the Negroes, the Indians, the Jews, the Japanese, and the Chinese? Confronted with the rapidly shifting life of the nation, would it be left behind as a feature of the passing order, or was it strong enough to take advantage of the fluid state of the changing society and mould the nation more effectively than it had been able to shape the Europe from which the United States was sprung? The fate of Christianity might be at stake. The United States was the largest of the new nations which had arisen from the trans‍oceanic migration of European peoples. If Christianity failed to make progress there, its entire future might be jeopardized. If it could achieve a growing place in the new and rising country, it would be in a strong position to shape the life of the rest of mankind.

Fortunately for the future of Christianity, the test was met.

At the beginning of the period, conditions seemed by no means favourable to the spread of Christianity. To be sure, as we saw in the preceding volume, strong religious strains had entered into the early settlements, and churches had arisen which, in contrast to those in Latin America, were vigorously self-propagating. Yet in the last quarter of the eighteenth century religious life was at a low ebb.[3] The Great Awakening of the first half of the century seemed to have spent itself. The long struggle for independence had turned man's attention away from religion. War had brought a lowering of morals. Independence had weakened many of the old institutions. The chilling Deism of Europe made itself felt.[4] The French Revolution was popular in

[3] Weigle, *American Idealism*, pp. 138-140; W. W. Sweet, *Religion on the American Frontier, 1783-1850. Volume III, The Congregationalists*, pp. 5-10.

[4] Herbert M. Morais, *Deism in Eighteenth Century America* (New York, Columbia University Press, 1934, pp. 203), *passim;* Ludlum, *Social Ferment in Vermont, 1791-1850.*

many quarters and the religious scepticism associated with that movement found a ready hearing. The hold of Christianity appeared to be declining.[5]

But revival came. In no other land in the nineteenth century did the churches have so large a numerical increase. Indeed, in spite of the enormous growth in the population of the land, in 1914 the proportion of those who were members of some church was larger than it had been a century before. It had risen from about 5 per cent. in 1790 and 6.9 per cent. in 1800 to 15.5 per cent. in 1850, to 35.7 per cent. in 1900, and to 43.4 per cent. in 1910.[6] Great as was the growth in population, in attracting the allegiance of men and women the churches more than kept pace with it.[7] In every major group Christianity won ground—among the older American stock, on the frontier, among the traditionally Christian immigrants, among the confessedly non-Christian immigrants, among the Indians, among the Negroes, in the rural districts, and in the cities. More difficult of measurement was the effect upon the culture of the nation. It was obvious, however, that Christianity was making a profound impression, and in some important phases of life it clearly achieved momentous gains.

Christianity, in turn, responded to its environment. In the United States a Christianity was taking form which in some respects differed markedly from that of Europe. It was developing in directions already apparent in the colonial period. For richness of variety the Christianity of no other region or age, not even of the Græco-Roman world in the first five centuries, could equal it. At the outset the population of the United States was overwhelmingly Protestant by tradition. Even though only a small minority were sufficiently interested to effect a connexion with a church, most were of Protestant ancestry. Protestants continued to be in the large majority.[8] However, before 1914 practically every form of European and Asiatic Christianity was represented. To these historic communions were added others of American origin. All Christian bodies, whether imported or indigenous, showed to a greater or less extent the effect of the American setting. While having obvious kinship to the Christianity of other lands, and especially to Great Britain and the self-governing Dominions

---

pp. 26-28; G. Adolf Koch, *Republican Religion and the Cult of Reason* (New York, Henry Holt and Co., 1933, pp. xvi, 334), *passim*.

[5] Johnson, *Ante-Bellum North Carolina*, p. 331; Weigle, *op. cit.*, p. 139; Koch, *op. cit.*, *passim*.

[6] Dorchester, *Christianity in the United States*, p. 750; Weber, *1933 Edition Yearbook of American Churches*, p. 299.

[7] The amount invested in church edifices per capita of the adult population multiplied about three-fold between 1850 and 1906.—Fry, *The U. S. Looks at Its Churches*, p. 83.

[8] Douglass, *Church Unity Movements in the United States*, p. 4; C. L. Fry in Morse, *Home Missions Today and Tomorrow*, p. 35.

of the British Empire, this vigorous Christianity of the United States was distinct. The Christian impulse, transplanted to the United States, had sufficient vitality not only to augment its effect upon the new nation, but also to adapt itself to its environment without sacrificing its peculiar genius. The promise given by the hopeful beginnings in the colonial period was abundantly fulfilled.

For convenience, we will arrange the story of the expansion of Christianity in the United States topically. First we will tell of the spread among the older American stock on the frontier. Then we will summarize the steps by which Christianity dealt with the vast immigration of the century. We will pass on, in the third place, to the efforts to win the Indians. Then will come a chapter on the remarkable advance of Christianity among the Negroes. This will be followed by a short account of the fashion in which Christianity addressed itself to the problems presented by the changing social, intellectual, and economic conditions of the century. Finally there will be chapters on the familiar subjects, the effect of Christianity on its environment and the effect of the environment on Christianity. Although the treatment is topical, we must recall that in all of these areas developments were occurring simultaneously. Christianity was not allowed to meet and solve its problems one at a time. It was brought face to face with most of them at once.

We are postponing the consideration of certain areas under the American flag. Because of their problems, Hawaii, Samoa, Guam, and the Philippines fall more logically in those sections which deal with the peoples of the Pacific. Puerto Rico is better handled in connexion with Latin America. All of these must wait until the next volume.

In the United States our period begins slightly earlier than in some other parts of the world. It commences with the outbreak of the war which separated the Thirteen Colonies from the British Empire. That was in 1775. The war ended and independence was formally recognized through the Treaty of Paris, in 1783. However, the terminus is the same. As was true for the rest of the world, the outbreak of the World War of 1914-1918 may be said to have brought the period to an end.

We turn first of all to the frontier. For most of the nineteenth century the frontier was a constant and prominent factor in the development of the United States.[9] It had begun much earlier. From the very first English settle-

[9] Two of the best treatments of the frontier are Frederick Jackson Turner, *The Frontier in American History* (New York, Henry Holt and Co., 1931 [copyright 1920], pp. 375),

ments the westward movement of population had created it. Throughout the colonial period, the history and the institutions of the nascent country had been affected by it. Even after independence, in a large proportion of the territory of the original thirteen states east of the Appalachian Mountains frontier conditions persisted. That was particularly the case in Vermont, New Hampshire, Maine, Western New York, and the western portions of Pennsylvania and of the southern states. Almost simultaneously with the outbreak of the Revolutionary War settlers began to cross the Appalachians. In the closing decades of the eighteenth century and the opening decades of the nineteenth century, population poured into the valleys of the Ohio and the Mississippi. Before the middle of the nineteenth century pioneers had crossed the Mississippi and had settled the lands on its right bank. Before the middle of the century, moreover, they had flooded into Texas and had brought that vast state into the Union, and they had jumped the Rocky Mountains and had begun the settlement of Utah, Oregon, and California. In the second half of the century they occupied the Rocky Mountain region and the plains which flanked the Rockies on the east. By 1890 settlement had proceeded so far that the frontier was declared to have ceased to exist as an important part of the nation's life.[10]

Here was a vast colonial expansion, none the less significant because it was not usually regarded as such. While Great Britain and France were building their colonial empires by conquest and migration overseas, the United States was acquiring an empire most of which was continuous territorially and was not divided by vast oceans. By what proved an unusually wise and successful colonial policy, the newer areas were incorporated with the older on terms of equality. One by one the colonies were admitted as full members of the Union. By 1914 all of the continental possessions of the United States except Alaska had reached political maturity. Except for the District of Columbia in which was the national capital, all were now divided into forty-eight states. It was in 1912, on the very eve of the close of the period, that the last two had passed out of the colonial territorial status and had acquired statehood.

The white constituents of this population movement onto the frontier were partly from the older states and of the stock which had come to America before 1775. They were in part directly from Europe. The older American stock, as we remarked a few paragraphs back, was overwhelmingly Protestant

and Frederic L. Paxson, *History of the American Frontier 1763-1893* (Boston, Houghton Mifflin Co., 1924, pp. vi, 598).

[10] A quotation from a bulletin of the Superintendent of the Census for 1890, cited in Turner, *op. cit.*, p. 1.

by tradition. Even though, in 1775, only a small percentage were members of churches, the large majority were from an ancestry which in Europe had had a formal connexion with some one of the varieties of Protestantism. Of the newer immigration, many by tradition were Protestant and many Roman Catholic.

In the present chapter we are to confine our attention to those settlers on the frontier who were from the older American stock. In spite of a small sprinkling of adherents in the original thirteen states and enclaves in the Mississippi Valley, Texas, New Mexico, and California inherited from the French and Spanish occupations, Roman Catholicism was represented in it by only small minorities and made relatively few converts from it. We will, therefore, here confine ourselves entirely to Protestant efforts. In the next chapter, that on the nineteenth century immigrants, we will deal with those who came directly from abroad to the frontier as well as with those who settled in the older portions of the country. There our ecclesiastical picture will broaden, and we will have to do not only with Protestantism, but also with Roman Catholicism and with most of the Eastern churches.

Frontier conditions both opposed and favoured the spread of Christianity.

On the one hand, many, removed from the life of the older parts of the country and the control of accepted customs, tended to say farewell to all religious practices and morals inculcated by Christianity. Contemporary accounts speak of the use of Sunday for other purposes than worship, and tell of heavy drinking, gambling, sexual irregularities, quarrelling, fighting, and easy murder.[11] To these general conditions, common on most of the frontier in the earlier stages of settlement, was added, in the seventeen eighties and nineties, when the Mississippi and Ohio Valleys were first being occupied, the wave of scepticism which then swept across the country. In Kentucky at that time most of the outstanding political leaders were lukewarm to religion or openly defiant of it.[12] Only a small minority, most of them women, were firm advocates of the Christian faith.[13]

On the other hand, the very fluidity of manners and institutions and the general feeling that the frontier was a new country in which men could com-

---

[11] *Autobiography of Peter Cartwright*, pp. 25, 28, 30; *Correspondence of the Reverend Ezra Fisher*, pp. 163, 165; Gaddis in *Church History*, Vol. II, pp. 152ff.; Posey, *The Development of Methodism in the Old Southwest*, p. 12; Bishop, *An Outline of the History of the Church in the State of Kentucky*, p. 68; *The Biography of Eld. Barton Warren Stone*, p. 22.

[12] Arnold, *A History of Methodism in Kentucky*, Vol. I, p. 193. See also *The Biography of Eld. Barton Warren Stone*, p. 23.

[13] Bishop, *op. cit.*, p. 68.

mence afresh begot a receptiveness to the Christian message and gave opportunity for building churches into the emerging new order.

Moreover, the majority of the settlers on the frontier were partially prepared for Christianity. Even though only a small proportion were members of churches, almost all of the older American stock had been reared in a cultural atmosphere impregnated with the Protestant forms of Christianity. This Christianity, too, was of the vigorous kind which propagated itself with decreasing assistance from Europe. It speaks volumes for the vitality of Protestantism and for the depth of the impression which it had made on the white population in colonial days that, without any direct aid from Europe, the American-born settlers were followed on their westward migrations and that an increasing proportion of them were won to membership in the churches. It is also a striking evidence of vitality that Christianity was able to adapt itself to the frontier.

One element in the spread of Christianity in colonial days was not so prominent in the occupation of the frontier in the national period. Very little of the migration was for the purpose of obtaining religious liberty. Except for the Mormon settlements in Utah and the coming of a few groups directly from Europe, almost none was from this motive.

Much of the expansion of Christianity on the frontier was due to the initiative of the settlers and their children. True to the precedent set in the older sections of the land, the active Christians organized churches and propagated their faith among their fellows without awaiting help from the outside.

In some instances a group of settlers formed themselves into a church before leaving their old home and carried the organization with them. Thus what is said to have been one of the first Baptist churches in Kentucky was organized in Spotsylvania County, Virginia, and moved as a colony to Gilbert's Creek in the early seventeen-eighties.[14] We hear of another Baptist church organized in North Carolina and immediately afterward transplanted to Tennessee.[15] A company of settlers from Granville, Massachusetts, who had bought lands in Ohio in and near what, in appropriate reminiscence, they named Granville, before leaving their mother town organized a Congregational church and transplanted it, with themselves, to the West.[16]

In many instances the settlers voluntarily organized churches in their new homes, and with little or no direct encouragement from the outside. In the early days of the frontier, particularly in the regions south of the Ohio River

[14] Benedict, *A General History of the Baptist Denomination in America*, p. 811; Fortune, *The Disciples of Kentucky*, p. 16.
[15] Benedict, *op. cit.*, p. 799.
[16] Bushnell, *The History of Granville, Licking County, Ohio*, p. 37.

and in Missouri, the Baptists were prominent in forming churches in this fashion. Their democratic polity, their fervid and unconventional type of preaching, and their ministry, frequently self-supporting[17] and often scantily educated and therefore close to the masses of the people, were singularly adapted to the frontier. In the second half of the eighteenth century, partly from repercussions from the Great Awakening,[18] Baptists had had a phenomenal growth in Virginia, North Carolina, and South Carolina, largely among the humble classes.[19] It was to be expected that they would have a rapid extension in Kentucky, Tennessee, Missouri, and the South-west, where so large a proportion of the settlers were from the southern states of the eastern seaboard. Baptist churches gained strength, moreover, by their custom of voluntarily grouping themselves into associations and, later, state conventions.[20] In 1785 the Baptists organized three associations in Kentucky, and by 1790 these had forty-two churches and three thousand communicants.[21] By 1812 the Baptist numbers in Kentucky had grown to thirteen associations, 263 ministers, and over 17,000 communicants.[22] In 1788 in Tennessee, although outnumbered by the Presbyterians, the Baptists had ten churches.[23] Even before the Louisiana Purchase (1803) had carried the possessions of the United States across the Mississippi River, a few Baptist families from North Carolina, South Carolina, and Kentucky had migrated to what later became Missouri.[24] Immediately after the purchase the tide of migration rose, and in 1804 and 1805 at least two Baptist churches came into being in Missouri.[25] In 1808 a self-supporting farmer-preacher organized in a private house the first Baptist church in Alabama.[26] In 1814 a Baptist association was formed in Tennessee which included churches in Alabama[27] and two years later an association was organized on Alabama soil.[28] As another example of this initiative, in 1844 a group of Baptist settlers in Oregon, led by a layman, assembled themselves into the first church of their denomination west of the Rocky Mountains.[29]

[17] Riley, *History of the Baptists of Alabama*, p. 113.
[18] Benedict, *op. cit.*, pp. 688, 706, 723.
[19] Newman, *A History of the Baptist Churches in the United States*, pp. 296, 297; Sweet, *Religion on the American Frontier. The Baptists*, pp. 10ff.
[20] Douglass, *History of Missouri Baptists*, pp. 41-43.
[21] Benedict, *op. cit.*, p. 811.
[22] *Ibid.*
[23] Benedict, *op. cit.*, p. 791.
[24] Benedict, *op. cit.*, p. 833.
[25] Benedict, *op. cit.*, p. 834.
[26] Riley, *op. cit.*, p. 12.
[27] Riley, *op. cit.*, p. 23.
[28] Riley, *op. cit.*, p. 24.
[29] Mattoon, *Baptist Annals of Oregon, Vol. I*, pp. 1, 2, 39, 43.

Baptists were by no means the only denominations in which settlers, quite on their own impulse and with no assistance from the outside, grouped themselves into local churches. What is said to have been the first Protestant church in what later became the state of Mississippi was Congregational, organized soon after 1772 by a company of immigrants from New Jersey.[30] Quakers moved westward and inaugurated meeting after meeting in Tennessee.[31] Quakers migrated especially into what was known as the North-west Territory, north of the Ohio River. Here, according to the Ordinance of 1787, all were to be free, and the sensitive Quaker conscience, already beginning to be made decidedly unhappy by the spectacle of Negro slavery,[32] encouraged settlements in an area from which this institution was debarred. Quakers began moving into Iowa very soon after the Black Hawk Purchase (1832)[33] and in 1838 organized a monthly meeting.[34]

At the outset of the trans-Appalachian migrations, no denomination seemed in quite so good a position to spread the Christian faith on the new frontier as the Presbyterians. They were heavily represented among the Scotch-Irish, and the Scotch-Irish were numerous on the old frontier on the eastern side of the mountains.[35] It was natural that they should form a large proportion in the next wave of westward expansion. The Great Awakening had numbered Presbyterians among its outstanding leaders and had spread widely in Pennsylvania and the South, especially in the western regions from which came a large proportion of those who constituted the outward fringe of the frontier across the mountains.[36] A close association with the Congregational churches of New England, particularly with those in Connecticut, to which we are to revert in a moment, also reinforced Presbyterianism.[37] It is not surprising, therefore, that westward-moving pioneers, aided by clergymen, founded many Presbyterian churches in the new settlements. At the outset, Presbyterians were the leading denomination in Tennessee.[38] Not far from 1761 a Presbyterian school-master conducted religious services in Pittsburgh.[39] In 1783 David Rice, a Presbyterian clergyman, went from Virginia to Kentucky at the call of a

[30] Jones, *A Concise History of the Introduction of Protestant Missions into Mississippi and the Southwest*, p. 14.
[31] Jones, *The Quakers of Iowa*, p. 34.
[32] Jones, *The Quakers of Iowa*, pp. 34ff.
[33] Paxson, *History of the American Frontier*, pp. 289-291.
[34] Jones, *The Quakers of Iowa*, pp. 38ff.
[35] Sweet, *Religion on the American Frontier. The Presbyterians*, pp. 2, 3.
[36] Sweet, *op. cit.*, p. 6.
[37] Sweet, *op. cit.*, p. 3.
[38] Benedict, *op. cit.*, p. 791.
[39] McKinney, *Early Pittsburgh Presbyterianism*, pp. 29, 30.

congregation and served them.[40] Because of its type of organization, Presbyterianism did not spread so much by the unaided initiative of laymen and of unattached ministers as did some of the denominations in which the local church was the unit. The development of Presbyterianism on the frontier was usually in fairly close conjunction with supervision and assistance from bodies in the older sections. Moreover, the emphasis upon an educated ministry was something of a handicap in reaching the rough frontiersman. It was among the better educated and well-to-do minority that Presbyterianism was strongest.

Another method by which Christianity spread on the frontier was through the efforts of clergymen who came uncommissioned and unsupported by any agency. Many of these obtained their livelihood by farming and preached on Sundays. Some became salaried pastors of churches. Methodist local preachers early moved westward and began organizing classes.[41] In the old North-west north of the Ohio there were many unattached ministers.[42] We hear of one who was successively a Methodist, a Presbyterian, a Congregationalist, and a Presbyterian.[43] James Hervey Otey, who later became the first bishop of the Protestant Episcopal Church in Tennessee, when in the 1820's he first went as a clergyman to that region taught school as a means of support.[44] Much of the Baptist preaching in Missouri before 1850 was by men who travelled from place to place speaking wherever they could find audiences, baptizing converts, and organizing churches. Often they made their living by farming or by some other form of manual labour. Occasionally they were given clothing or a little money by those to whom they ministered.[45] Fairly typical was Joab Powell. Born in Tennessee in 1799, of Quaker stock, in his middle twenties he felt himself to be converted and to be called to preach as a Baptist minister. Like many of the pioneers, he became restless as the country around him was better settled and new horizons beckoned to the West. In 1830 he moved to the new frontier across the Mississippi. For more than twenty years he was in Missouri, farming and preaching. In 1852 he was caught in the great movement to Oregon, made the six months' arduous pilgrimage across the plains, and in that newly settled land won fame as an itinerant preacher of revivals. Huge of frame, stentorian of voice, with little formal education, but having a sense of humour, a sturdy conviction that Christian faith should be evidenced by righteous living, and a compelling fearlessness, he was widely known and

[40] Bishop, *An Outline of the History of the Church in the State of Kentucky*, pp. 65ff.
[41] Sweet, *The Rise of Methodism in the West*, p. 15.
[42] Bond, *The Civilization of the Old Northwest*, pp. 466-506.
[43] Bushnell, *The History of Granville, Licking County, Ohio*, p. 201.
[44] Goodwin, *The Colonial Church in Virginia*, pp. 233, 234.
[45] Douglass, *History of Missouri Baptists*, p. 31. See accounts of a few of these in Douglass, *op. cit.*, pp. 18, 109-116.

is said to have been the means of effecting three thousand conversions in his twenty-one years in Oregon.[46] The Church of the Brethren, a much smaller denomination than that of the Baptists, also owed much to its unpaid ministers, some of whom moved westward and made their homes on the frontier, and others of whom undertook long missionary journeys from the older portions of the country.[47] Timothy Dwight Hunter, a Presbyterian clergyman who was pastor of a church in Honolulu, came with some of his flock to San Francisco in 1848 at the time of the gold rush and, supported by the better elements, became chaplain at large of the town and eventually organized the First Congregational Church of the city.[48] To the efforts of these individual clergymen, without any central organization back of them, of several different denominations, and numbering many hundreds, was due much of the spread of Christianity on the frontier.

One of the religious bodies most active on the frontier was the Methodist Episcopal Church. In sharp contradistinction from the Baptists, who vied with it in numerical strength in the new regions, it possessed a nation-wide, closely knit organization. Through this it was able to bring to bear upon the frontier in co-ordinated effort both the resources of the older portions of the country and the devotion of those in the newer settlements who were won through it. Like the Baptists, through the enthusiasm of its preaching and its efforts to reach those outside the pale of the more staid churches, it appealed to the masses. In contrast with the Calvinism of the majority of Baptists, it was Arminian in theology. In its preaching it was not hampered by the doctrine of election by which God was said to have determined beforehand who should be saved. It held that Jesus had died for all men, and that every individual was able to choose whether he would avail himself of that sacrifice. Numbers who were repelled by the predestination preached by many of the Baptists welcomed the Methodists' message. By its system of classes with lay leaders and its local preachers and exhorters, Methodism made a place for laymen, a feature which commended it to the democratic frontier. Its circuit riders, a large proportion of them unmarried, gave an itinerant ministry suited to the sparse population of the new settlements.[49] In their devotion, their zeal, their poverty, their style of preaching, and their wide-ranging activity they had likenesses to the Franciscans and Dominicans who in the thirteenth cen-

[46] M. Leona Nichols, *Joab Powell: Homespun Missionary* (Portland, Oregon, Metropolitan Press, 1935, pp. 116), *passim*.

[47] Moyer, *Missions of the Church of the Brethren*, pp. 82ff.

[48] Wicher, *The Presbyterian Church in California, 1849-1927*, pp. 38, 39.

[49] Sweet, *The Rise of Methodism in the West*, p. 14; Goodykoontz, *Home Missions on the American Frontier*, p. 412.

tury did so much to bring the Christian message to the nominally Christian masses of Western Europe. Through their well integrated organization, with their bishops, conferences, and presiding elders,[50] the Methodists were singularly equipped to cover the country in a comprehensive plan systematically executed.

It is interesting that two denominations so diametrically opposite in organization and in theology should have been so prominent on the frontier. On the one hand were the Baptists, stressing the autonomy of a local church which in theory and largely in practice was a pure democracy, with a minimum of central organization, and prevailingly Calvinistic in doctrine. On the other were the Methodists, with a strong hierarchy, emphasizing a regionally and nationally closely co-ordinated ecclesiastical organism, and Arminian in theology. In general, Methodists were relatively stronger north of the Ohio River[51] and the Baptists were stronger in the South.[52] Yet both won so prominent a place in the West that, when it was no longer a frontier, they remained the largest of the Protestant groups. This was probably because by their zeal in carrying the Christian message to the unchurched and especially to the rank and file, they appealed to what was the nearest approach to a proletariat in the older American stock.

The story of the Methodist activity on the frontier would fill many volumes. We can here give only the barest outline of it and that merely in incomplete summary. Methodism had been introduced to the Thirteen Colonies in the 1760's, only a few years before the outbreak of the troubles which led to the independence of the United States. With its warm evangelism, its revivalism, and its popular hymns, it was congenial to much of the spirit of the new land and was spreading rapidly when the Revolutionary War broke. The war retarded its growth.[53] John Wesley was openly critical of the colonists' demand for independence. All of the missionaries whom he had sent were British by birth and all but one, Francis Asbury, left the country. When the war was over, Wesley, with his characteristic astuteness, saw clearly that if American Methodism were to be saved, it must have an ordained ministry to

[50] On Methodist organization, see James M. Buckley, *A Constitutional and Parliamentary History of the Methodist Episcopal Church, passim.*

[51] Bond, *op. cit.,* pp. 466-506.

[52] In 1915 the Northern Baptist churches had a membership of 1,252,633 and the Methodist Episcopal Church, which was overwhelmingly the largest of the Northern Methodist bodies, had a membership of 3,657,594. The Southern Baptist churches had a membership of 2,705,121 and the Methodist Episcopal Church South a membership of 2,072,035. In addition, the Coloured Baptist churches had a membership of 2,018,868 and the three leading Methodist Negro churches a total membership of 1,429,406.—Carroll, *Federal Council Year Book, 1915,* pp. 195, 199.

[53] Buckley, *A History of Methodism in the United States,* pp. 158ff.

administer the sacraments. He was unable to obtain ordination for his preachers from the Bishop of London, who was traditionally in charge of the Church of England in the colonies. American bishops of the Anglican communion had not yet been consecrated. Accordingly he appointed his warm friend, Thomas Coke, to be General Superintendent of the Methodist societies in the United States with power to ordain, and authorized him to consecrate Asbury to a similar position.[54] Asbury declined to assume the post unless he were unanimously chosen to it by the Methodist preachers of America.[55] A conference met (1784), formed the Methodist Episcopal Church, and voluntarily elected Coke and Asbury to the office[56] (soon to be given the title of bishop) to which Wesley had commissioned them. While respectful to Wesley and grateful for what he had meant in the Methodist movement, somewhat to his displeasure the new church did not admit that he had authority over it. It was fully independent.[57]

The real organizer of the Methodist Episcopal Church and its greatest creative spirit was Francis Asbury.[58] Coke was repeatedly out of the country on the extended journeys which made him a kind of foreign minister of Methodism. Most of the time Asbury was left in charge. Asbury was born in Staffordshire, England, August 20, 1745, of humble parentage. Reared in a devout home, from boyhood he was deeply religious. He was early caught up in the Methodist movement, became a lay preacher, and in 1771 offered himself for service in America and was accepted and sent by Wesley.[59] He had had, therefore, experience in his adopted home before he became the leader of the new church. As bishop, throughout the rest of his life Asbury was the acknowledged leader of the Methodist Episcopal Church. He remained unmarried that he might the more wholeheartedly give himself to his charge.[60] Although never very robust and often ill, he had no fixed home and travelled incessantly. Armed by his faith and spurred by his mission, he was undaunted by the hardships and perils of itineracy in the roughest sections of the new land. He ranged over the older states and through the crude settlements on the frontier. From Maine to Georgia and from the Atlantic seaboard to Kentucky,

[54] Buckley, op. cit., pp. 231ff.
[55] Asbury, Nov. 14, 1784, in The Heart of Asbury's Journal, p. 227.
[56] Asbury, Dec. 24, 1784, in op. cit., p. 230.
[57] Buckley, op. cit., pp. 255ff.
[58] In addition to Asbury's Journal, see, out of the large literature about him, Ezra Squier Tipple, Francis Asbury, the Prophet of the Long Road (Cincinnati, The Methodist Book Concern, 1916, pp. 333), and William Larkin Duren, Francis Asbury, Founder of American Methodism and Unofficial Minister of State (New York, The Macmillan Co., 1928, pp. 270).
[59] Asbury in The Heart of Asbury's Journal, p. 1.
[60] Asbury, Jan. 27, 1804, in op. cit., p. 542.

Ohio, and Tennessee he went, largely on horseback. He inspired and supervised circuit riders. He wished them, like himself, to remain unmarried. While they took no binding vows and many married, in effect in their early days the majority adhered to the three rules of the Roman Catholic monastic bodies—chastity, poverty, and obedience.[61] At the outset they were itinerant evangelists for the spread of Christianity rather than pastors. The pastoral function was performed by class leaders and local preachers.[62] They were a kind of Protestant order, fully Protestant in faith and spirit, admirably adapted to the new land with its rough life and scattered populations, and bound by their organization into a force which could be directed by its master mind to cover comprehensively and systematically the entire country. Like Wesley, Asbury went preaching. Preaching was a large part of his life. Also like Wesley, he was an able organizer and administrator. Well read, he did much to encourage education. Sensitive and serious, he had often to meet opposition which must have hurt him deeply. Shunning publicity for himself and distrusting personal popularity, he yet was the nearly autocratic head of his church. While he had associates in the episcopate, Asbury was the dominant spirit. When, in 1816, slightly past the scriptural term of seven decades, his frail body no longer able to serve him, death overtook him, he was still on his travels. He left behind him a well co-ordinated denomination numbering more than two hundred thousand.

Asbury's achievement would have been impossible but for the preachers whom he directly or indirectly supervised. The circuit system which Wesley had developed in England proved peculiarly fitted, with adaptations, to the United States, especially to the vast reaches of thinly settled new country. Preachers were assigned by presiding elders to circuits. Frequently these were so large that weeks of travel on horseback, on foot, or by canoe were needed to cover them.[63] One, for instance, was 475 miles in length and required four weeks to traverse.[64] Another was 500 miles in circumference and over much of the distance there were no roads.[65] The circuit rider gave his message wherever he could obtain a hearing. Sometimes he spoke in a log cabin, sometimes in a court house, sometimes in a tavern, and sometimes outdoors.[66] On

---

[61] Most of the early Methodist preachers in the West were unmarried and until 1816 all the bishops were also unmarried.—Sweet, *The Rise of Methodism in the West*, pp. 44, 45.

[62] Arnold, *A History of Methodism in Kentucky*, Vol. I, p. 266.

[63] Sweet, *op. cit.*, p. 41.

[64] *Autobiography of Rev. James B. Finley*, pp. 193, 194.

[65] Sweet, *Circuit-Rider Days Along the Ohio*, p. 51.

[66] Sweet, *The Rise of Methodism in the West*, pp. 14, 42, 43; Finley, *op. cit.*, pp. 196, 197.

one occasion a circuit rider turned a dance in an inn into a prayer meeting and organized the converts into a Methodist society with the landlord as leader.[67] Usually the circuit rider was a man of scanty formal education, but often he was a student and, like Wesley and Asbury, used his time on horseback for reading.[68] His was the language of the frontier. He adapted his words to his hearers and was ready at repartee. Again and again he faced ridicule and even violence.[69] His calling required courage as well as endurance. He sought, above all things, conversions.

One of the most famous of the circuit riders was Peter Cartwright.[70] He was born in Virginia in 1785 and in his childhood his parents migrated to Kentucky, taking him with them. There, on the frontier, he was reared. His mother was a Methodist and, to her joy, at the age of sixteen he was converted. He soon began to preach as an "exhorter." At eighteen he began riding a circuit. For years he served circuits in Tennessee and Kentucky. Then, in 1824, partly to move his family into a region where he could be away from slavery and where his children could be reared to work without being scorned by those who deemed manual labour degrading, partly because he could there procure land for them, and partly because he was lured by the frontier and its religious needs, he moved to Illinois. Muscular, fearless, prepared to subdue in physical encounter any who attacked him, quick of wit and 'with the frontiersman's rough humour, disdaining and distrusting an educated ministry, with a hot indignation against wickedness and a consuming passion to win those about him to his faith, he was a striking and famous figure. He lived on until 1872 and saw the frontier pass far to the West. He baptized about eight thousand children and about four thousand adults, saw eight of his nine children grow to maturity, and from his meagre income gave hundreds of dollars to charitable causes.[71] Cartwright was only one of the more prominent of scores of circuit riders.[72] Some were better educated than he, but in the pioneer days all were, perforce, as was he, inured to hardship.

Methodism had other methods of spreading. Its local preachers and exhorters provided a lay leadership.[73] Its quarterly meetings gathered its mem-

---

[67] *Autobiography of Peter Cartwright*, pp. 207, 208.
[68] Sweet, *The Rise of Methodism in the West*, p. 54; Finley, *op. cit.*, p. 196.
[69] Cartwright, *op. cit.*, pp. 141, 188, 287ff.; Finley, *op. cit.*, p. 196.
[70] Cartwright, *op. cit.*, *passim*.
[71] Cartwright, *op. cit.*, pp. 521, 522.
[72] See the biographies of a number of these in James B. Finley, *Sketches of Western Methodism: Biographical, Historical, and Miscellaneous, Illustrative of Pioneer Life*, edited by W. P. Strickland (Cincinnati, The Methodist Book Concern, 1854, pp. 551), *passim*.
[73] See an account of some of these in Arnold, *A History of Methodism in Kentucky*, Vol. I, pp. 69ff.

bers from farms and villages for fellowship, preaching, love-feasts, and the administration of baptism and the Lord's supper.[74] The camp-meetings of which we are to speak in a moment were widely used. The regional and national conferences which were part of the structure of the denomination promoted solidarity and permitted comprehensive planning.

The man who did most to organize and promote the Methodist Episcopal Church in the Mississippi Valley was William McKendree.[75] Born in Virginia in 1757 of planter parentage, a soldier in the Revolutionary War, McKendree was converted in a revival in 1787 and in 1788 entered the Methodist ministry. For years a circuit rider in various districts, in 1800 he was appointed by Asbury to be presiding elder over the Western Conference, which then embraced all of Methodism west of the Appalachians. Elected bishop in 1808, he continued to specialize on the West and made Tennessee his headquarters. He was single-hearted in purpose, an indefatigable traveller, a great preacher, and an even greater leader.

To trace the spread of Methodism would require a large volume. Here we can give only a few hints of its early course. On the frontier Methodism won most of its adherents from those who had had no previous church connexion.[76] It was an agency for expanding Christianity. Methodists were among the early migrants to Kentucky. Among them was a local preacher who organized a Methodist society in 1783.[77] In 1783 Jeremiah Lambert was appointed to a circuit which included South-western Virginia and Eastern Tennessee.[78] In 1786, only two years after the formation of the Methodist Episcopal Church, a circuit was mapped out for Kentucky and two men were assigned to it.[79] The following year a circuit was added in Tennessee[80] and in 1787 another was announced in Kentucky.[81] In 1798 a circuit was formed in Ohio.[82] In 1797 a missionary was selected for a circuit in the South-west. He went to his field and for four years did not see another Methodist preacher.[83] In 1800 a district was mapped out for all the Western circuits and a presiding elder

---

[74] Sweet, op. cit., pp. 42, 43.

[75] The official biography is based on the papers of McKendree and is by an old friend —Robert Paine, Life and Times of William McKendree (Nashville, Publishing House Methodist Episcopal Church, South, 1922, pp. 549. First published, 1869).

[76] Posey, The Development of Methodism in the Old South-west, pp. 13, 14.

[77] Arnold, op. cit., Vol. I, pp. 22, 23.

[78] Posey, op. cit., p. 6.

[79] Arnold, op. cit., Vol. I, p. 35.

[80] Arnold, op. cit., Vol. I, p. 47.

[81] Arnold, op. cit., Vol. I, p. 51.

[82] Sweet, The Rise of Methodism in the West, p. 17.

[83] Posey, op. cit., p. 9.

was placed at its head.[84] By 1802 the Western districts had increased to three and the circuits to seventeen.[85] In 1805 a call was issued for volunteers to go to Mississippi and Louisiana. Four men responded.[86] In 1806 a circuit was formed in Indiana.[87] In 1793 a local preacher visited Illinois and organized a class and in 1804 a missionary was appointed to that region.[88] In 1793 Jesse Lee, a man of giant physique, great endurance, and winning eloquence, was chosen by the New England Conference to go to Maine. There he preached what was believed to be the first Methodist sermon in that area.[89] In 1849 William Taylor, who had been a circuit rider and had in him much of the frontiersman, was appointed a missionary to California, then in the first throes of the gold rush. There he laid the foundations for Methodism. He then extended his labours to Asia, Australia, and Africa, where we are to meet him again in later volumes.[90] In a subsequent chapter we are to make the acquaintance of Jason Lee, who led a notable mission to Oregon, which had the Indians as its first objective but which soon spread to the white settlers. Expanding as it was simultaneously on the frontier in the West, South, and North, and proving singularly adapted to pioneer areas, it was not surprising that Methodism continued to make its rapid way westward and that it obtained a hold which was to render it numerically one of the two or three largest of the Protestant movements in the United States.

Another method by which Protestant Christianity spread on the frontier was the revival and a particular expression of the revival, the camp-meeting.

More than a generation before the Thirteen Colonies had become an independent nation, the Great Awakening had established a tradition which was to be a striking and persistent characteristic of Protestant Christianity in the United States. During the troubles preceding and accompanying the war for independence, the movement died down. However, it had not entirely disappeared, for we hear of conversions which repeated its convictions and experiences.[91] Notably in Virginia, beginning about 1785 a revival began which added thousands to the Baptist churches and many to other denominations.[92] Moreover, even during the dark days of the war, additional Congregational

[84] Sweet, *op. cit.,* p. 23.
[85] *Ibid.*
[86] Arnold, *op. cit.,* Vol. I, p. 288.
[87] Sweet, *op. cit.,* pp. 26, 27.
[88] Sweet, *op. cit.,* pp. 23, 24.
[89] Allen and Pilsbury, *History of Methodism in Maine,* pp. 7ff.
[90] William Taylor, *Story of My Life,* edited by John Clark Ridpath (New York, Hunt & Eaton, 1895, pp. 750), *passim.*
[91] Benedict, *A General History of the Baptist Denomination in America,* p. 509.
[92] Benedict, *op. cit.,* p. 657; Davidson, *History of the Presbyterian Church in the State of Kentucky,* p. 42.

churches had been formed in New England, and presumably this was in part an indication that the life shown in the Great Awakening was far from extinct.[93] Towards the close of the eighteenth century the movement reappeared. Beginning about 1797 New England witnessed what has sometimes been termed the Second Awakening.[94] Out of it came several of the missionary societies which were so marked a feature of the opening decades of the nineteenth century.

Not far from the same time, revivals began on the Western frontier which were to be of great assistance in the spread of Christianity in the new settlements in that area. About 1797, a religious awakening occurred in the south-central portion of Kentucky, south of the Green River.[95] It came in connexion with the preaching of a Presbyterian clergyman, James McGready, then in his later thirties. Although he was unprepossessing in appearance, his small, piercing eyes, his coarse, tremulous voice charged with gravity, his intense earnestness, and his stern denunciation of sin had several years before made a remarkable impression in North Carolina.[96] The opposition he aroused had forced him to move to the West.[97] In the summer of 1799 the awakening south of the Green River broke out afresh at a meeting in which several clergymen, Presbyterian and Methodist, were taking part. Extreme emotional manifestations electrified the congregation.[98] This was followed, in 1800, by what was sometimes regarded as the first of the camp-meetings.[99] Its purpose was "sacramental," for the celebration of the Lord's Supper.[100] In preparing participants for that rite and in certifying to those deemed fit to share in it, solemn exhortation and searching of conscience were to be expected. At the instance of McGready, who took pains to announce the gathering widely, people assembled from many miles around and came prepared to camp, either in wagons or in tents. Rude platforms had been erected and rough seats formed of

[93] In Massachusetts between 1770 and 1780 six churches had died and twenty-two had been organized. Between 1780 and 1790 twenty-four more were organized, and between 1790 and 1800 fifteen had been formed.—Clark, *A Historical Sketch of the Congregational Churches in Massachusetts*, pp. 200-202, 215-217, 224.

[94] *The New-York Missionary Magazine*, Vol. I (1800), pp. 192-194; Elsbree, *The Rise of the Missionary Spirit in America*, pp. 36, 37; Weigle, *American Idealism*, p. 142; Clark, *op. cit.*, p. 230.

[95] Davidson, *History of the Presbyteri... Church in the State of Kentucky*, p. 132.

[96] *Biography of Barton W. Stone*, pp. 7, 8.

[97] Cleveland, *The Great Revival in the West*, pp. 38, 39.

[98] Davidson, *op. cit.*, p. 33; John McGee (a participant) in *The Methodist Magazine*, Vol. IV, pp. 189-191.

[99] Something akin to it had been inaugurated by the Methodists as early as 1794.—Cleveland, *op. cit.*, p. 53.

[100] Davidson, *op. cit.*, p. 134. See also, on the Lord's Supper as the occasion for similar gatherings, Cleveland, *op. cit.*, pp. 63, 77.

hewn logs. A number of clergymen were present. Excitement mounted and forty-five converts were counted.[101] The movement spread like wildfire. Other meetings of a similar nature were held. Presbyterians, Baptists, and Methodists shared in them. Some were undenominational and some purely denominational.[102] In 1801 a number of camp-meetings assembled. One of them, at Cane Ridge, in Bourbon County in North-eastern Kentucky, lasted about a week, and at its height about twenty thousand were said to have been in attendance.[103] Religious services of praying, singing, exhorting, and preaching were kept up day and night. Physical expressions of the excitement were numerous and sometimes took bizarre forms. The groans and screams of those under conviction mingled with the shouts of those who had found release and joy. The fear of hell and damnation and the hopelessness of the lost would be succeeded by the bliss of assured salvation. The most common physical experience was "falling." About three thousand are said to have been prostrate at the Cane Ridge meeting.[104] Some of the "fallen" were insensible. Others were aware of what was happening about them but were powerless to move. Women and children[105] were especially suggestible and were the most affected. Yet men were also among "the slain." As consciousness returned, some would rejoice in a confidence in forgiveness and the love of God and others would still be in the gloom of despair.[106] A little later in the course of the revival, hundreds displayed convulsive physical contortions which were known as "the jerks."[107] Frequently those who came to remonstrate or to ridicule were themselves sudden victims.[108] Barking, running, jumping, and trances were common.[109] In Ohio somewhat similar scenes were witnessed.[110] Many of the more earnest and intelligent Christians were opposed to these exuberant extravagances and some of the meetings proceeded without them.[111]

As one result of the camp-meetings of the first few years of the century, many of the churches in the West experienced a phenomenal growth. Between 1800 and 1803 the Baptists in Kentucky are said to have gained about ten

---

[101] Davidson, op. cit., pp. 134, 135. See an account by a leader in The New-York Missionary Magazine, Vol. IV (1803), pp. 74, 75, 151-155, 192-199.

[102] Davidson, op. cit., p. 136; Cleveland, op. cit., p. 84.

[103] M'Nemar, The Kentucky Revival, p. 26.

[104] Ibid.

[105] M'Nemar, op. cit., p. 20; Cleveland, op. cit., pp. 90, 102, 103, 119.

[106] Cleveland, op. cit., p. 97.

[107] Cleveland, op. cit., pp. 98ff.; Autobiography of Rev. James B. Finley, p. 367.

[108] Autobiography of Peter Cartwright, pp. 49, 50.

[109] Cartwright, op. cit., p. 51; Cleveland, op. cit., p. 101; M'Nemar, op. cit., p. 64.

[110] Kennedy, The Plan of Union, pp. 25ff.

[111] Cartwright, op. cit., p. 51; Cleveland, op. cit., p. 111.

thousand members, the Methodists in the West more than six thousand in two years, and the Presbyterians several thousand.[112] Here was a kind of mass movement, in some respects similar to those by which Christianity had been accepted in much of Northern Europe. The emotional phases had parallels in other lands and ages among both Christians and the adherents of non-Christian faiths.[113]

The revival in Kentucky was paralleled by awakenings in the older parts of the country and in the frontier regions in New England. Indeed, they were nation-wide.[114] They continued until at least 1805.[115] In 1803 they began slightly to decline, but we hear of notable revivals in Vermont in 1806, 1809, 1810, and 1811.[116] The War of 1812 brought a slackening in religious interest, but after it revivals again broke out.[117] The majority of both clergy and laity seemed to prize, in the results of the movement, the moral and spiritual changes which were wrought.[118] While in some instances the aftermath was morally neutral or even deleterious, the trend appears to have been towards amendment of life, the correction of frontier and common human vices, and approximation to New Testament standards.[119]

While the revival died down, as all such emotional outbursts must, the camp-meeting long continued. At least in sections east of the Mississippi, it remained a normal part of life on the frontier. We hear of Methodists employing it for annual assemblies. Conversions were expected from among its attendants.[120] On the frontier, with its scattered settlements and isolated farmsteads, the camp-meeting afforded an occasion for bringing people together. As such it met a social need and was welcomed. As the frontier moved westward, towns increased, life became more varied, and, much of the reason for it having disappeared, the camp-meeting dwindled and died. Peter Cartwright lived long enough to bemoan its decease.[121] It had, however, played an important rôle in the spread of Christianity.

Camp-meetings passed into desuetude, but revivals continued and remained a major means of the spread of Christianity in both the older and the newer

[112] Cleveland, *op. cit.*, pp. 130, 131.
[113] Cleveland, *op. cit.*, pp. 104-109, mentions some of these instances.
[114] Cleveland, *op. cit.*, p. 85. For the revival in North Carolina, see Johnson, *Ante-Bellum North Carolina*, pp. 371-396. For the revival in Vermont, where it came in 1801, see Ludlum, *Social Ferment in Vermont, 1791-1850*, pp. 42ff.
[115] Cleveland, *op. cit.*, p. 86.
[116] Ludlum, *op cit.*, p. 47.
[117] Ludlum, *op. cit.*, pp. 50, 51.
[118] M'Nemar, *op. cit.*, p. 59; Cartwright, *op. cit.*, p. 238.
[119] Cleveland, *op. cit.*, pp. 132-134; Weigle, *American Idealism*, p. 153.
[120] *Autobiography of Rev. James B. Finley*, pp. 266, 398.
[121] Cartwright, *op. cit.*, p. 523.

sections of the country. The outstanding leader in the revivals in the first half of the nineteenth century was Charles G. Finney. Although born in Connecticut, he was reared in New York under pioneer conditions.[122] His preaching had in it much of the individualism, informality, and directness of the frontier. He deplored the belief which he found widely prevalent that men must remain under a conviction of sin until God should deign to give them salvation and taught that men should, by their own act, make an instant surrender to God.[123] This type of preaching powerfully aided the spread of Christianity.

Having an historic connexion with revivals and camp-meetings was another channel through which Christianity spread on the frontier, denominations of predominantly frontier origin. Outstanding among these were the Cumberland Presbyterians, the Christians, and the Disciples of Christ.

The revivals and the camp-meetings made a profound impression in the area covered by the Cumberland Presbytery of the Presbyterian Church, in Southwestern Kentucky and the adjoining portion of Tennessee. The Presbytery wished to admit to the ministry men who showed earnestness and skill in the type of preaching adapted to the frontier and who were committed to the revival but who lacked some of the education, especially in the ancient languages, normally required by the Presbyterian Church. Opposition arose, partly because of the proposed modification of the educational tests and partly out of distrust of some of the methods which less well trained men might employ. Appeal was taken to the General Assembly, but in vain. As a consequence, in 1810 three of the clergy formed themselves into the first presbytery of what became the Cumberland Presbyterian Church.[124] The new body spread rapidly. Its ministry was somewhat closer to the masses than the rank and file of the clergy of the parent body. Many of its preachers went on circuits somewhat after the fashion of the Methodists. It tended to be less strictly Calvinistic than the church from which it had separated. It encouraged revivals and throve on them.[125] It was, accordingly, well adapted to the frontier life of the Mississippi Valley. It spread to Western Pennsylvania, New York, Ohio, Illinois, Missouri, Alabama, Mississippi, Arkansas, and Texas.[126] By 1861 the Cumberland Pres-

[122] *Memoirs of Charles G. Finney, passim.*
[123] Finney, *op. cit.*, pp. 189, 190.
[124] Foster, *A Sketch of the History of the Cumberland Presbyterian Church*, pp. 259-289; Sweet, *Religion on the American Frontier, Vol. II. The Presbyterians*, pp. 90ff.; Davidson, *History of the Presbyterian Church in the State of Kentucky*, pp. 223ff.
[125] Foster, *op. cit.*, p. 293.
[126] Foster, *op. cit.*, pp. 228-291.

byterian Church numbered about one hundred thousand communicants,[127] and in 1893 about two hundred thousand.[128] Much of at least the earlier growth was by conversions from among those with no previous church connexion. Many thousands of those won through the preaching of its missionaries are said to have joined other denominations.[129]

The denominations called Christian (one of them also termed the Disciples of Christ) arose out of a number of movements, most of them originally independent of one another. The roots of some were in the British Isles, notably among the Sandemanians, a Scotch group of eighteenth century birth, and among the followers of the great Scotch evangelists, the Haldanes.[130] From these came a few congregations in the United States.[131] From Elias Smith and Abner Jones, reared and converted in pioneer conditions, in the opening decades of the nineteenth century a number of congregations terming themselves simply "Christian" came into being in New England.[132] A schism from the Methodist Episcopal Church led by James O'Kelly in protest against the extensive powers given to Asbury, and an expression of the democracy of the frontier, was called the Republican Methodist Church. In 1794 at a meeting of the Republican Methodists of Virginia, it was resolved that "henceforth the followers of Christ be known as Christians simply" and that the Bible be taken as the only creed.[133] In 1811, through a visit of Elias Smith, the New England and the Southern movement fused.[134] One of the Kentucky converts of a camp-meeting of 1802, William Kincaide, as he began preaching, rejected all creeds, held to the Bible alone as his standard, and declined to be called by any other name than Christian.[135]

Prominent in the beginning and the early development of the movement was Barton W. Stone.[136] Born in Maryland, in 1772, Stone was reared in what were then the backwoods of Virginia. He had some education, came under the influence of James McGready, and entered the Presbyterian ministry, although with many qualms about several of its doctrines. Before the close

---

[127] Vander Velde, *The Presbyterian Churches and the Federal Union, 1861-1869*, pp. 7-9.

[128] Foster, *op. cit.*, p. 293.

[129] Foster, *op. cit.*, pp. 291, 293.

[130] Garrison, *Religion Follows the Frontier*, pp. 35-38, 80-83; William H. Whitsitt, *Origin of the Disciples of Christ* (Louisville, Ky., Chas. T. Dearing, 4th ed., 1899, pp. 112. Controversial, anti-Disciple), *passim.*

[131] Garrison, *op. cit.*, p. 109.

[132] Garrison, *op. cit.*, pp. 59, 60.

[133] Garrison, *op. cit.*, p. 61.

[134] Garrison, *op. cit.*, p. 62.

[135] Garrison, *op. cit.*, pp. 62, 63.

[136] On Stone, see *The Biography of Eld. Barton Warren Stone. Written by Himself, passim;* Ware, *Barton Warren Stone, passim.*

of the century he had become a pastor in Kentucky. There he was caught up in the revivals and camp-meetings, and there the inward conflict which had long troubled him came to a head. He could no longer accept the Calvinism of his church with the doctrines of total depravity and of unconditional election and reprobation which he found in its Westminster Confession. It seemed to him futile to call on his audiences to repent and believe if God had already determined who were to be saved and who were not and if the sinner of himself were unable to take any step away from his condign doom.[137] It was a problem which vexed many another who had been reared in the Calvinist tradition when he strove to call his fellows to the Christian life. It was already an issue among the Congregationalists in New England who were in the stream of the Great Awakening and the Second Awakening. Stone and some others of the Presbyterian clergy who were active in the revival began proclaiming that God loved the whole world and sent his son to save all men on the condition that they believe in him, and that sinners were capable of fulfilling the condition. They urged their hearers to believe immediately.[138] The proclamation of this doctrine awakened controversy. The synod of which the men were members took action against them, and, withdrawing, they formed what they called the Springfield Presbytery.[139] However, in 1804, distressed by the dissensions produced by this action and pained by the contentions between denominations and parties, the Springfield Presbytery published what it termed its "last will and testament," voluntarily dissolved itself, desiring to "sink into union with the Body of Christ at large," contented itself with the simple name of Christian, forswore the right of ordination and passed that back to "the Church of Christ," asked that the Bible be taken "as the only sure guide to heaven," and pled "that preachers and people cultivate a spirit of mutual forbearance; pray more and dispute less."[140] Stone, meditating while he laboured on his farm, came to a view of the significance of the death of Jesus different from the one in which he had been reared.[141] He also found himself driven to the conviction that the baptism of infants was wrong, and he and his preachers baptized one another and by immersion.[142] The movement spread rapidly in the West, partly from accessions from other churches and partly from conversions from those outside any church. Stone travelled widely, preaching in the frontier settlements, and baptizing many.[143]

[137] Stone, *op. cit.*, pp. 30, 31.
[138] Stone, *op. cit.*, pp. 44, 45.
[139] Stone, *op. cit.*, pp. 46-48.
[140] Stone, *op. cit.*, pp. 50-55, giving the text of the document.
[141] Stone, *op. cit.*, pp. 56-60.
[142] Stone, *op. cit.*, pp. 60, 61.
[143] Stone, *op. cit.*, pp. 70-75.

Still another leader in the movement and, as it proved, the most influential, was Alexander Campbell. Alexander's father, Thomas, was of Scottish lineage and education and had been pastor of a Presbyterian congregation in Ireland. By temperament Thomas was grieved by the bitter divisions between Christian sects. He had contacts with one of the Haldanes. In 1807, in search of health, he came to the United States, to Western Pennsylvania. There his disregard of party divisions in the church and his liberalism in admitting Christians of various views to the Lord's Supper led to differences with the Presbyterian synod which he had joined, and he withdrew and became independent. In 1809 those attracted by his preaching formed themselves into "The Christian Association of Washington" (Pennsylvania) with the maxim, later to become famous as a slogan, "where the Scriptures speak, we speak; where the Scriptures are silent, we are silent." In a "Declaration and Address" composed by Thomas Campbell and adopted by the Christian Association (September 7, 1809) it was asserted as part of the ideal of the group, that "division among the Christians is a horrid evil. . . . It is anti-Christian."[144] That very year Thomas was joined by Alexander Campbell. Alexander had remained in the British Isles for two years after his father had come to America. There he had had a profound religious experience, precipitated by a shipwreck. In Glasgow, while studying theology, he had been brought into contact with the ideas of the Sandemanians and the Haldanes. On joining his father, he found himself in sympathy with the latter's views. Aggressive, genial, resourceful, powerful, an able and willing debater, Alexander Campbell quickly eclipsed his father and became the head of the movement. Through marriage, he came into possession of a farm at Bethany, in Western Virginia, the income from which made him independent of support from his followers.[145] A futile attempt of Thomas to effect fellowship with the Presbyterians soon followed (1810).[146] The baptism of infants was rejected as unscriptural and baptism of conscious believers, by immersion, was adopted (1812).[147] For a time the movement found union with some of the Baptists (1813), but conscientious differences developed over a number of points of doctrine and practice, tension became chronic, and separation, marked by acrimony, followed (1827-1830).[148] Many former Baptists cast in their fortunes with the Campbells.

So much similarity existed between the movement led by Stone and the

[144] Garrison, op. cit., pp. 71-78; Tyler, History of the Disciples of Christ, pp. 34-36; Moore, A Comprehensive History of the Disciples of Christ, pp. 97-120.

[145] Garrison, op. cit., pp. 79-86, 97, 98; Moore, op. cit., pp. 125-138.

[146] Garrison, op. cit., p. 98.

[147] Garrison, op. cit., p. 103.

[148] Garrison, op. cit., pp. 106-144.

one headed by Alexander Campbell that it was but natural that the two should in part coalesce. The two men first met in 1824, and Stone felt their views to be all but identical.[149] Such differences as existed were fairly easily adjusted.[150] In 1832 representatives of the Reformers or Disciples, as those who followed Campbell termed themselves, entered into conference with leaders of the Christians, as those affiliated with Stone preferred to be called. The conference agreed on union, but since both fellowships were made up of autonomous congregations, it could bring only moral pressure. Gradually about half of those associated with Stone became affiliated with those who followed Campbell.[151]

However, a large proportion of those who had looked to Stone as a leader remained aloof. Particularly was this true of those in Ohio and Indiana. Relatively few of those from the "Christian" movements of North Carolina, Virginia, and New England joined with the Disciples. Eventually these various elements drew together in what became known as the Christian Church (American Christian Convention).[152] In 1915 they numbered about 114,000 communicants.[153] While they carried on missionary effort as far west as Washington and as far north as Maine,[154] they remained strongest in what in the days of their beginning had been part of the frontier—Ohio, Indiana, and the western portions of North Carolina and Virginia.[155]

The Disciples, that is, those who had followed Campbell and Stone, continued to grow. Zealously evangelistic, they sought to win the unchurched to the Christian faith. With their emphasis upon the union of all Christians, their ardent preaching adapted to the average man, and their democratic form of government, they made a strong appeal to the frontier mind.[156] Their message of the

---

[149] Garrison, op. cit., p. 150; Stone, op. cit., pp. 75-78.

[150] On continuing differences in belief and temperament, but which the two tolerated in each other, see Ware, Barton Warren Stone, pp. 309ff.

[151] Garrison, op. cit., p. 154; Stone, op. cit., pp. 78, 79; Ware, op. cit., pp. 269-281.

[152] Ware, op. cit., pp. 269-281.

[153] Carroll, Federal Council Year Book, 1915, p. 196.

[154] The Christian Missionary (Nov., 1908), Vol. XV, p. 42. A most enlightening account of one of their early missionaries is Autobiography of Abraham Snethen. The Barefoot Preacher, Collected and Compiled by Mrs. N. E. Lamb, Corrected and Revised by J. F. Burnett (Dayton, Ohio, Christian Publishing Association, 1909, pp. 296). Born in Kentucky in 1794, the son of a frontiersman and hunter, Snethen did not hear a sermon until he was seventeen. He taught himself to read, was converted, and preached extensively in Ohio, Indiana, Illinois, Kansas, and North Dakota, bringing about conversions and organizing churches. Transparently sincere, fearless, peace-loving, winsome, he led many a rough frontiersman to the Christian faith.

[155] Ware, op. cit., p. 281.

[156] An organ of the movement, in its earlier years edited by Alexander Campbell was The Millennial Harbinger (Bethany, W. Va., 1830-1870). The title itself was evidence of much of the atmosphere and attitude of the movement.

erasure of ecclesiastical divisions under the simple name of Christian or Disciple attracted many from other religious bodies. By 1816 or 1817 they had spread to Missouri, then the Far West.[157] It was in the West that they remained strongest. In 1915 they counted a little over a million and a half members.[158]

Still another process by which Christianity spread on the frontier was through colonies bound together by a religious purpose.

Most of these were small. An example, picked almost at random, was a project to found a settlement after the pattern of Oberlin, Ohio, which would be a centre of active Christian influence. The initial group left Northern Ohio in 1848 and a centre was eventually established at Tabor, Iowa.[159] In 1853 a colony of the United Brethren left for Oregon with the object of undertaking missionary activity in that area, then on the forefront of the frontier.[160]

Some were groups which arose, several of them on the frontier, out of the ecstasy of revival movements and which sought asylum from their opponents.[161]

The largest enterprise of the kind was the Mormon colony in Utah. The Mormons, or the Church of Jesus Christ of Latter Day Saints, originated on the frontier. The movement was among the strangest of those which claimed for themselves a Christian origin and was so far removed from the principles and teachings of the majority of the churches that it was considered by most of the latter to be outside the Christian pale.

The Church of Jesus Christ of Latter Day Saints had its inception among the underprivileged.[162] Its founder was Joseph Smith (1805-1844). Smith was

[157] George L. Peters, *The Disciples of Christ in Missouri* (The Centennial Commission, 1937, pp. 244), p. 29.

[158] Carroll, *Federal Council Year Book, 1915*, p. 197.

[159] John Todd, *Early Settlement and Growth of Western Iowa or Reminiscences* (Des Moines, The Historical Department of Iowa, 1906, pp. 203), *passim*. See another somewhat similar instance in Ohio in Julian M. Sturtevant, *An Autobiography*, pp. 55, 56.

[160] Drury, *History of the Church of the United Brethren in Christ*, p. 437.

[161] On a few of these, see Ludlum, *Social Ferment in Vermont 1791-1850*, pp. 239ff.

[162] On Mormonism, see an official history, B. H. Roberts, *A Comprehensive History of the Church of Jesus Christ of Latter-day Saints* (Salt Lake City, Desert News Press, 6 vols., 1930) ; William Alexander Linn, *The Story of the Mormons from the Date of their Origin to the Year 1901* (New York, The Macmillan Co., 1902, pp. xxv, 637), based on extensive research, and antagonistic to the Mormons; M. R. Werner, *Brigham Young* (New York, Harcourt, Brace and Co., 1925, pp. xvi, 478), scholarly, but somewhat critical of Young; John Henry Evans, *Joseph Smith, An American Prophet* (New York, The Macmillan Co., 1933, pp. xi, 447), friendly to Smith. See also the following biographical sketches with their accompanying bibliographies in *Dictionary of American Biography*: Heber Chase Kimball, Vol. X, pp. 377, 378; Sidney Rigdon, Vol. XV, pp. 600, 601; Joseph Smith, Vol. XVII, pp. 310-312; Joseph Fielding Smith, Vol. XVII, pp. 313, 314; Brigham Young, Vol. XX, pp. 620-623. On one of the leaders see Reva Stanley, *The Biography of Parley P. Pratt, The Archer of Paradise* (Caldwell, Idaho, The Caxton Printers, 1937, pp. 349). On organization for economic co-operation, see Edward J. Allen, *The Second Order among the Mormons* (New York, Columbia University

of old New England stock, and his family were of the floating, semi-illiterate, poverty-stricken type which frequently formed an element on the frontier or in communities not far removed from frontier conditions. He was born in Vermont, but as a boy he went with his family to Western New York, then only just beginning to emerge from the period of initial settlement. The region had been swept with revivals which had spread a certain acquaintance with inherited Christian beliefs as interpreted by itinerant or semi-itinerant Baptist and Methodist preachers. Joseph Smith's family had been touched with the emotional experiences of the revival and Smith himself had been affected by them. In his adolescence he said that visions began coming to him. These told him, he averred, that no existing church represented the will of God, and that God had chosen him to restore the true church. He declared that in obedience to them he had dug in a hill and had found plates of gold on which was writing in strange characters. These, he said, he had translated through miraculous assistance. The resulting *Book of Mormon* was published in 1830. The sources became a subject of violent and chronic controversy, but the work reflected many of the ideas of the popular revivalistic Protestantism then current on the frontier, including the impatience with existing churches and the ambition to build something new and better, and contained stories and views which may have issued from the mind of Smith. A few years later a second work, a *Book of Commandments,* soon called *Doctrine and Covenants*, came out of the sermons and revelations of Smith and with the *Book of Mormon* constituted the basis of the new cult. In its teachings Mormonism contained elements derived from historic Christianity. It also prized features which were so alien to the faith of the large majority of Christians and so repugnant to the other bodies which claimed the Christian name that it was usually regarded by non-Mormons as non-Christian and even anti-Christian.

The Church of Jesus Christ of Latter Day Saints was founded in 1830, at Fayette, Seneca County, New York. Into it was early drawn Sidney Rigdon (1793 1876), who had been a preacher, first for the Baptists and then for the Disciples, and who contributed to its doctrines convictions which he had adopted in the course of his religious pilgrimage. Into it, too, in 1832, came Brigham Young, who, like Smith, was New England born and an early migrant to Western New York. Smith proved a forceful if somewhat erratic leader. He was self-confident, egoistic, witty, virile, athletic, tall, and of distinguished appearance, and although a poor business manager, he attracted

Press, 1936, pp. 148). On   phase of Mormon doctrine, see Arbaugh in *Church History*, Vol. IX, pp. 157-169.
  It is on this bibliography that the material in this paragraph is based.

and dominated followers. His adherents first formed a colony at Kirtland, Ohio, next in Missouri, and then at Nauvoo in Illinois. They met persecution and in Illinois Smith was killed. The majority were then, in 1846 and 1847, led by Brigham Young to Utah, to an area unpeopled by white men. Young proved to be an extraordinarily able organizer and administrator. Practical, discouraging the prophecies, the miracles, and the speaking with tongues which were marked in the early days of the movement, he built the church into a co-operative society under an ecclesiastical oligarchy which furthered the material prosperity of its members and sought to erect an ideal commonwealth. Organizations were developed for mutual economic assistance. Remarkable energy was shown and machinery was skilfully developed for propagating the Mormon faith. Missionaries were sent out to many sections and countries. They even, as we saw in the preceding chapter, quickly made their way to Great Britain and the continent of Europe. They appealed especially to the poor—the tenant farmers and the unemployed—and offered them the new Eden in Utah. Because of some of their teachings, notably polygamy, the Mormons aroused widespread opposition, but before the end of the century polygamy had been all but abandoned and the church had become somewhat more nearly conformed to many of the outward features of American Protestantism. It remained, however, a closely knit economic-social-ecclesiastical organization and continued to send out missionaries.

Not all the Mormons followed Brigham Young to Utah. After Joseph Smith's death, contentions arose for the prophet's mantle and divisions ensued. Some were attracted by James Jesse Strang (1813-1856). He founded a communistic Mormon colony on the Beaver Islands, in Lake Michigan, but it eventually died out.[163] The great majority of the Mormons who remained in the Middle West eventually acknowledged the leadership of Joseph Smith (1832-1914), a son of the founder. He moved to Iowa and then to Missouri. He opposed polygamy and declared that his father had never practised it. He also placed under taboo the use of alcohol, tobacco, tea, and coffee. After the frontier fashion, he was active in farming. Large of frame and in his old age patriarchal in appearance, he made an imposing head of his group. Under his leadership it grew to number seventy thousand.[164]

In all of the movements thus far mentioned, the spread of Christianity on the frontier was chiefly by the pioneers themselves, although at times with some assistance from the older sections.

[163] O. W. Riegel, *Crown of Glory, The Life of James J. Strang, Moses of the Mormons* (Yale University Press, 1935, pp. 281), *passim; Dictionary of American Biography*, Vol. XVIII, pp. 123, 124.

[164] *Dictionary of American Biography*, Vol. XVII, pp. 312, 313.

Much of the expansion of Christianity on the frontier, however, was through societies organized in the older states of the Union and drawing most of their support from these regions. These societies sent missionaries and in other ways aided in planting and nourishing the churches in the West.

In this home missionary effort to win the West, the Congregational churches were in the forefront.[165]

Through them many of the first societies were formed. It was from the Congregational stock of Connecticut (although his parents were not confessed Christians) that the most influential leader of revivals in the first half of the nineteenth century, Charles G. Finney, was born, and after some years as a Presbyterian, during which he never fitted fully or happily into the theology of that denomination, it was in the Congregational fellowship that he spent most of the mature years of his life.[166] From Congregationalism issued several of the outstanding colleges which, as we are to see in a moment, had a large part in undergirding with trained leadership the Christianity of the new territories. From it, either directly or indirectly, came the initiative and support for many of the organized efforts for spreading the Christian faith throughout the nation and for many of the movements which fought the collective evils of the land and strove to make the country's institutions conform more nearly to Christian principles.

The prominence of Congregationalism was due to a number of factors. To a large degree it was because Congregationalism was the prevailing form of Christianity in New England. Since the earliest settlements in New England had been from a religious motive and constituted the spiritual ancestry of Congregationalism, and since in New England the Congregational churches, as the Standing Order, were dominant in the religious life, Congregationalism was more intimately associated with New England than was any other denomination with any other section of the country.[167] At the outset of the century, New England Congregationalism presented the largest fairly compact body of churches in the United States. It was not bound together by a national or even a sectional organization, and it was far from united in doctrine, but, except for the Unitarian wing, soon to detach itself from the majority, it enjoyed a community of feeling which gave it a certain degree of coherence and which facilitated joint undertakings. This New England heritage proved a weakness, for it tended to identify Congregationalism with a particular section of the population and to keep it from becoming as national in scope as were

[165] Foster, *A Genetic History of New England Theology*, pp. 3, 4.
[166] *Memoirs of Charles G. Finney, passim.*
[167] See a description of this by a contemporary in Julian M. Sturtevant, *An Autobiography*, p. 23.

some of the other large denominations. On the other hand, it gave Congregationalism solidarity and the strength that comes from a certain degree of homogeneity. Since New England was long prominent in the life of the nation and since from it came a large proportion of the settlers of that part of the frontier which lay directly west of it, especially in Western New York, Northern Pennsylvania, Northern and South-eastern Ohio, Northern Indiana, Southern Michigan, Northern Illinois, Southern Wisconsin, Iowa, and Kansas,[168] it is not surprising that from Congregationalism sprang much of the missionary activity for the frontier. To a large extent, the spread of Congregationalism was the religious phase of the westward expansion of New England.

New England Congregationalism was reinvigorated by the revivals of the eighteenth and nineteenth centuries. It was from the Great Awakening which in the eighteenth century so greatly stirred New England, from the Second Awakening which swept up and down New England in the closing years of the eighteenth and the opening years of the nineteenth century,[169] and from the revivals which continued to visit New England during the first half of the nineteenth century that most of the agents and supporters of the Congregational missionary movements came. It is significant that from the Unitarian wing of New England Congregationalism, which was but little touched by the revivals except to react against them, issued very little missionary effort.

This revivalism in New England Congregationalism was closely associated with what came to be known as New England Theology. New England Theology progressively made more room for freedom of the will than did the traditional Calvinism of New England. It began with Jonathan Edwards, who had been the outstanding preacher in the Great Awakening. It was further developed by Bellamy and Hopkins. It was long closely associated with Yale. Edwards was a graduate of Yale. A grandson of Edwards, Timothy Dwight, while President of Yale was one of the outstanding leaders of the Second Awakening and continued, with modifications, his grandfather's theology.[170] It was a teacher at Yale, a pupil and younger contemporary of Dwight, and himself a persuasive preacher, Nathaniel W. Taylor, who gave New England Theology a further trend towards freedom of the will.[171] Finney adopted most of Taylor's positions and in some respects was the latter's suc-

---

[168] For a map showing the westward migration of people from New England, see frontispiece of W. W. Street, *Religion on the American Frontier, 1783-1850. Vol. III, The Congregationalists.*

[169] Elsbree, *The rise of Missionary Spirit in America,* pp. 36ff.

[170] Foster, *op. cit.,* p. 279.

[171] Foster, *op. cit.,* pp. 247, 381. For the effect of Taylor on a student, see Sturtevant, *op. cit.,* pp. 121ff.

cessor.[172] New England Theology, then, was in part the outgrowth of revivalism. Moreover, by keeping some of the features of Calvinism—its emphasis on the sovereignty of God, the awfulness of sin, and the lost condition of the sinner—but at the same time making more room for the freedom of the individual to accept the salvation offered through Christ, it gave added incentive to revivalism.[173] While still stressing the necessity of repentance, it encouraged men to believe that they could repent and need not await, helplessly, the course of the inscrutable predetermination of God. It was the New England Theology rather than the older Calvinism or the intellectual liberalism of Unitarianism which spread on the frontier.[174]

As early as 1774 the General Association, the organization of the Congregational churches in Connecticut, appointed missionaries to the new settlements "north-westward of this colony." However, because of the Revolutionary War the project was not carried out.[175] In 1780, even before peace was declared, the project was being revived,[176] and in the last two decades of the century a number of missionaries were sent by local associations or the General Association of Connecticut to the new settlements in Vermont and New York.[177]

Late in the eighteenth and early in the nineteenth century, several state and local missionary societies sprang up among the Congregational churches of New England, having as their chief objects the Indians and the white colonists on the frontier. In 1798 the General Association of the State of Connecticut adopted a constitution for the Missionary Society of Connecticut, which was to be the Association itself functioning through twelve trustees. The purpose was "to Christianize the Heathen in North America, and to support and promote Christian knowledge in the new settlements within the United States."[178] In 1809 the society had twenty-four missionaries, and their labours extended to "the new settlements" in Vermont, in the Western Reserve in Ohio, in the vicinity of Granville in Central Ohio, in Pennsylvania, and in the state of New York.[179] In 1799 the Massachusetts Missionary Society was organ-

---

[172] Foster, op. cit., pp. 252, 453.

[173] Bacon, Leonard Bacon, pp. 44-55.

[174] Thus the Congregationalism of Vermont looked to New Haven rather than to Boston for its inspiration.—Ludlum, Social Ferment in Vermont, 1791-1850, p. 42.

[175] Parker, Historical Discourse In Commemoration of the One Hundredth Anniversary of the Missionary Society of Connecticut, p. 7.

[176] Parker, op. cit., p. 8.

[177] Parker, op. cit., pp. 8-12.

[178] Parker, op. cit., pp. 12, 13.

[179] The Connecticut Evangelical Magazine and Religious Intelligencer, Vol. III, p. 19. On the biography of one who served for a time in the West under the Missionary Society of Connecticut, see John Ervin Kirkpatrick, Timothy Flint, Pioneer, Missionary, Author, Editor, 1780-1840 (Cleveland, The Arthur H. Clark Co., 1911, pp. 331), passim.

ized with substantially the same objectives.[180] In 1800 it appointed four missionaries, two to Maine and two to "the western frontiers."[181] A similar body was formed in New Hampshire in 1801.[182] In the following two years it sent missionaries to Northern New Hampshire and Northern New York.[183] In 1807 the Maine Missionary Society was organized "to send the glorious Gospel to those that are destitute of the public and stated means of religious instruction."[184] While not originally limited in its scope, in practice the society confined its efforts chiefly to Maine.[185] This was natural, for Maine was largely frontier territory and was filling up with settlers. Some of its missionaries were itinerant, and others temporary or resident pastors.[186] In 1807 the General Convention of Congregational and Presbyterian ministers of Vermont constituted itself a missionary society.[187] Somewhat similar bodies were formed in New England in districts of more restricted size.[188] Women's societies were also organized to give assistance to the state bodies.[189] In 1812 and 1813 and again in 1814 and 1815, Samuel J. Mills, with his comprehensive, wide-ranging vision, travelled extensively in the Mississippi Valley to survey the needs of the region and, where he could, to start local Bible societies to help make good the dearth of religious literature. The first journey was subsidized by the Connecticut and Massachusetts Missionary Societies, the second by the latter and some others in the Middle States.[190] New England Congregationalism was organizing to follow members of its traditional constituency as they moved westward and northward and was seeking to learn the scope of its task.

Presbyterians of the older sections also began taking active steps to care for the frontier. In 1789, the year that the United States began its course under its Constitution, the Synod of Philadelphia issued a plea to all its churches "to take collections for the supporting of missionaries on the frontier."[191] In 1789 the Presbyterians of the new nation formed as their countrywide organ their General Assembly.[192] The following year that body sent

---

[180] *The New-York Missionary Magazine*, Vol. I (1800), pp. 434, 435.
[181] *Ibid.*
[182] Elsbree, *The Rise of the Missionary Spirit in America*, p. 67.
[183] *Ibid.*
[184] Clark, *History of the Congregational Churches in Maine. Vol. I, History of the Maine Missionary Society 1807-1925*, pp. 19ff., 117.
[185] Clark, *op. cit.*, Vol. I, p. 118.
[186] Clark, *op. cit.*, Vol. I, pp. 153-159.
[187] Elsbree, *op. cit.*, p. 70.
[188] Elsbree, *op. cit.*, pp. 60, 67, 69.
[189] Elsbree, *op. cit.*, pp. 58, 63.
[190] Richards, *Samuel J. Mills*, pp. 103-165; Spring, *Memoirs of the Rev. Samuel J. Mills*, pp. 59ff.; Dwight, *The Centennial History of the American Bible Society*, Vol. I, pp. 11-13.
[191] Hanzsche, *The Presbyterians*, pp. 127-130.
[192] Hanzsche, *op. cit.*, p. 90.

two missionaries to Kentucky.[193] From 1791 to 1800 the Synod of Virginia dispatched eight missionaries beyond the mountains.[194] The Synod of Pittsburgh occasionally sent missionaries to the West on limited tours.[195] In 1802 the Synod of Pittsburgh became in effect the Western Missionary Society[196] and in subsequent years commissioned many clergymen to the West. In 1802 the General Assembly appointed a standing committee on home missions and in 1816, as a result of the report of Mills, it transferred the functions of this body to a newly created Board of Home Missions.[197] In 1803 the Presbyterian Synod of the Carolinas had eight missionaries.[198]

In their efforts in the West, for many years the Congregationalists and Presbyterians co-operated through what was known as the Plan of Union, especially in those regions into which New Englanders moved. Since the migration from New England tended to follow the parallels of latitude, the Plan of Union was particularly influential in Western New York, Ohio, Indiana, Michigan, and Wisconsin. The project was furthered by the similarity in doctrine and polity of many of the Congregational and Presbyterian churches. This was notably true of the Congregational churches of Connecticut. The latter were semi-Presbyterian in organization. They were grouped in *consociations* to which cases of discipline could be referred and through which ordinations, installations, and dismissions of clergy were effected.[199] In doctrine the views associated with the name of Jonathan Edwards had a wide following among the Presbyterians of the Middle States, and the New England Theology was influential in Presbyterian as well as in Congregational circles.[200] Many ministers from New England were active in the Presbyterian churches in New York, New Jersey, and Pennsylvania.[201] Timothy Dwight led in endeavouring to effect a closer union, and beginning in the seventeen nineties, the Presbyterian General Assembly and the Connecticut General Association sent delegates to each other's annual meetings. Within the next few years a programme for a similar exchange of delegates was instituted between the state Congregational organizations of Massachusetts, Vermont, and New Hampshire on the one hand, and

[193] Sweet, *Religion on the American Frontier. Vol. II, The Presbyterians*, p. 32.
[194] *Ibid.*
[195] Kennedy, *The Plan of Union*, p. 35.
[196] Zorbaugh in *Church History*, Vol. VI, p. 147.
[197] Thompson, *A History of the Presbyterian Churches in the United States*, p. 81; Goodykoontz, *Home Missions on the American Frontier*, pp. 146-148.
[198] Johnson, *Ante-Bellum North Carolina*, p. 411.
[199] Walker, *A History of the Congregational Churches in the United States*, pp. 203, 206-208.
[200] Walker, *op. cit.*, p. 314.
[201] R. H. Nichols in *Church History*, Vol. V, p. 32.

the Presbyterian General Assembly on the other.[202] This led quite naturally to co-operation between Presbyterians and Congregationalists in societies of many kinds, including those for the aid of the frontier. It also prepared the way for the Plan of Union. This was adopted in 1801 by the Presbyterian General Assembly and the Congregational General Association of Connecticut.[203] Later it was also approved by other General Associations in New England.[204] It enjoined upon the missionaries of both denominations in the new settlements reciprocal forbearance and accommodation, provided for the introduction of certain features of Presbyterian government in Congregational churches served by Presbyterian ministers, for some Congregational features for Presbyterian churches with Congregational pastors, and prescribed the procedure when Presbyterians and Congregationalists were in the same congregation. Each denomination made concessions to the other. In New York State the Plan was supplemented in 1808 by a further "Accomodation Plan" whereby a consociation of Congregational churches could enter a synod in the same relation as that of a presbytery.[205] It paved the way for co-operation in such interdenominational bodies as the American Board of Commissioners for Foreign Missions, the American Education Society, the American Home Missionary Society, the American Tract Society, the American Bible Society, and the American Sunday School Union.[206]

In practice, the Plan of Union worked to the advantage of the Presbyterians. For a variety of reasons, many of the Congregational churches on the frontier which were conducted under it became Presbyterian.[207] A very large proportion of New England Congregationalists who moved into Northern New York, Ohio, Michigan, and Illinois entered the Presbyterian fold.[208] It was said that Congregationalism was a stream which rose in New England, flowed west, and emptied into Presbyterianism.[209]

The Plan of Union did not prove permanent. Many Presbyterians, particularly those of Scotch and Scotch-Irish antecedents, were fearful of the departure from strict Calvinism which they saw in the New England Theology, and especially in the variety of it which was developed by Na-

[202] Walker, op. cit., pp. 315, 316.
[203] Kennedy, The Plan of Union, p. 149. See the text of the Plan in Kennedy, op. cit., pp. 150, 151. See also R. H. Nichols in Church History, Vol. V, pp. 34-37.
[204] Walker, op. cit., p. 317.
[205] R. H. Nichols in Church History, Vol. V, pp. 39-42.
[206] R. H. Nichols in Church History, Vol. V, p. 48.
[207] Walker, op. cit., p. 318; Julian M. Sturtevant, An Autobiography, pp. 65-67.
[208] R. H. Nichols, The Plan of Union in New York, in Church History, Vol. V, pp. 29-51; Charles L. Zorbaugh, The Plan of Union in Ohio, in Church History, Vol. VI, pp. 145-164.
[209] Bacon, Leonard Bacon, p. 299.

thaniel W. Taylor and which bore, from the seat of Yale, where Taylor taught, the name of New Haven. In 1826 this element reorganized the Board of Missions for more effective work in the West.[210] In 1837 the conservatives, or "Old School" men, obtained control of the Presbyterian General Assembly, repudiated the Plan of Union, severed the ties which bound them with the adherents of the distrusted theology in interdenominational societies, and cut off from their fellowship four synods which had been formed under the Plan and which were, accordingly, infected with the obnoxious views.[211] The latter, dubbed New School Presbyterians, formed their own General Assembly and continued their co-operation with the Congregationalists.[212] Some of the Congregationalists, borne along by a rising tide of denominational consciousness, were unhappy under the Plan and began organizing against it.[213] In 1852 a national convention of Congregationalists, the first general synod or gathering of that fellowship which had been held since the seventeenth century, abrogated it.[214] Locally, too, the Plan had long been encountering rough weather. For instance, in the Western Reserve, in Northern Ohio, a number of Congregational ministers and churches had long been restive. They had been reinforced by the influences emanating from Oberlin and John G. Finney, with their accentuated departure from the Calvinism of Presbyterianism, and in 1836 the Congregational churches of the Western Reserve had formed a General Association.[215] In Wisconsin the Presbyterians had withdrawn (beginning about 1851) from the state organization in which they and the Congregationalists co-operated.[216] Yet the Plan of Union had contributed markedly to the growth of the New School Presbyterians.

While the Plan of Union was still in full force there was formed, in 1826, the American Home Missionary Society. Into this merged the United Domestic Missionary Society of New York, a body which had been in existence for a few years and was chiefly Presbyterian and Reformed in its membership.[217] The American Home Missionary Society was designed to be an agency for uniting Christians of several denominations in comprehen-

[210] R. D. Leonard in *Church History*, Vol. VII, p. 347.
[211] Weigle, *American Idealism*, p. 161; Hanzsche, *The Presbyterians*, p. 99.
[212] Walker, *op. cit.*, p. 317.
[213] R. D. Leonard in *Church History*, Vol. VII, p. 348.
[214] Walker, *op. cit.*, p. 317; Bacon, *Leonard Bacon*, pp. 360-363.
[215] Kennedy, *op. cit.*, pp. 186ff.
[216] R. D. Leonard in *Church History*, Vol. VII, pp. 261, 362. On a part of the history of the Plan of Union in Wisconsin by one of its chief participants, see Peet, *History of the Presbyterian and Congregational Churches and Ministers in Wisconsin*, pp. 22ff.
[217] Goodykoontz, *Home Missions on the American Frontier*, pp. 173-179; Clark, *Leavening the Nation*, pp. 59-62.

sive planning and action on a nation-wide scale. In bringing together the Congregationalists and the Presbyterians and, for a time, the Reformed and the Associate Reformed, it enlisted a very large proportion of the financial and intellectual resources of American Protestantism in spreading Christianity throughout the United States. It is not surprising that during the ensuing decades it had a leading part in establishing Christianity as an integral part of the life of the new communities which arose on the frontier. It did little in the South and South-west, but its agents followed the moving frontier to the Pacific Coast and at one time or another were active in most of the West which lay north of the Ohio River, in the regions between that old North-west and the Rockies, and along most of the Pacific Coast.[218] Eventually all but the Congregationalists withdrew to support their own denominational societies. The last to depart, the New School Presbyterians, left in 1861. In 1893, to meet the altered circumstances, the name was somewhat tardily altered to the Congregational Home Missionary Society.[219]

One can only regret that limitations of space preclude a comprehensive summary of the achievements of the American Home Missionary Society. We must, however, take the space to cull out a few scattered examples of its work.

Prominent in the history of the society were "bands," groups of missionaries who went out together to a particular section to build the Church. The earliest of these to attract wide attention was the Illinois Band. A number of students at the Yale Divinity School bound themselves to go together to Illinois, there to establish a "seminary of learning," as the terminology of the time called it, some to teach and others to be pastors in the surrounding country.[220] They were accepted by the American Home Missionary Society and in 1829 the first two went to their new post. The others followed. Fifteen in all were numbered in the band and of these, twelve gave the major part and most of them the whole of the rest of their lives to Illinois. Illinois College was founded and some of the band became missionaries in the state, travelling, and organizing churches and Sunday schools.[221] One of the Illinois Band, Asa Turner, after several years as pastor in Quincy, Illinois, in 1838 went on to Iowa and there became pastor of a new Con-

---

[218] Clark, *op. cit.*, pp. 59ff.

[219] Walker, *op. cit.*, pp. 328, 329.

[220] The story of the origin of the Band, together with the document which they framed and signed, is in Julian M. Sturtevant, *An Autobiography*, pp. 134-139. See also Magoun, *Asa Turner and His Times*, pp. 60, 61, and Clark, *op. cit.*, pp. 69, 70.

[221] Sturtevant, *op. cit.*, pp. 143ff.; Magoun, *op. cit.*, pp. 98ff.; Clark, *op. cit.*, pp. 70-72.

gregational church.[222] In Iowa he assisted in steps which led to Iowa College, later Grinnell College.[223] In 1843 there came to Iowa a band of men, also under the American Home Missionary Society, who had graduated at Andover Theological Seminary in that year. They were ordained in the church of which Turner was pastor and scattered to various parts of the territory. They organized Congregational churches and contributed to the founding of Iowa College.[224] Four of the class of 1857 of Andover Theological Seminary went to Kansas, then frontier country, as a band, and became pastors of Congregational churches. One of them brought into being over one hundred churches.[225] In 1880 a band of eleven came from Yale to the Dakotas.[226] A group of six from the class of 1890 of the Yale Divinity School went to Washington, which had been admitted as a state in 1889. One became President of Whitman College and others pastors of churches.[227] Most of these bands did not continue as self-conscious groups. They were not like the religious orders which had so large a part in the spread of the Roman Catholic form of Christianity. All of them, however, went out to at least initial poverty, and their members had a large share in planting and developing churches on the frontier.

The American Home Missionary Society did not do its work entirely or even chiefly through these bands. They were the exception. Most of its agents and collaborators went out one by one. Among those who were especially remembered were Samuel H. Willey, who organized a Presbyterian church in San Francisco in 1850 and was one of the founders of the University of California;[228] Stephen Peet, a native of Vermont, a graduate of Yale, who went to Wisconsin under the society in 1837, from 1841 to 1848 was the agent of the society in Wisconsin, was a great traveller in his vast field and responsible for the founding of churches and the appointment of pastors, was the prime mover in the founding of Beloit College, and was then the chief promoter of the Chicago Theological Seminary for the training of clergy in the West;[229] George H. Atkinson (1819-1889), who did much

[222] Magoun, op. cit., p. 190.
[223] Magoun, op. cit., pp. 241ff.
[224] Ephraim Adams, The Iowa Band (Boston, The Pilgrim Press, revised edition, no date, pp. xx, 240), by one of the band; Clark, op. cit., pp. 97-102; Truman O. Douglass, The Pilgrims of Iowa (Boston, The Pilgrim Press, pp. xiv, 422), pp. 51-73.
[225] Clark, op. cit., pp. 109, 110.
[226] Clark, op. cit., pp. 134-136.
[227] Clark, op. cit., pp. 209-211.
[228] Weigle, American Idealism, p. 252; Pond, Gospel Pioneering, pp. 26, 27.
[229] R. D. Leonard in Church History, Vol. III, pp. 346-363; Sweet, Religion on the American Frontier, 1783-1850, Vol. III. The Congregationalists, pp. 38, 39; Clark, op. cit.,

to establish Congregational churches in Oregon and Washington, had a large part in the founding of the public school system of Oregon and with the inception of Pacific University, and was to some degree responsible for the initiation of the vast development of wheat-growing in Eastern Oregon and Eastern Washington;[230] Joseph Ward (1838-1889), sometimes called the father of Congregationalism in the Dakotas, for years the most influential citizen in the territory, the main force behind the enactment of the education law of South Dakota, and the founder of Yankton College;[231] Stewart Sheldon, the brother-in-law of Ward, for nearly ten years general missionary and the superintendent of the Congregational churches in the Dakotas;[232] and Reuben Gaylord (1812-1880), a graduate of Yale who taught in Illinois College, then was a colleague of Asa Turner in Iowa, in middle life, in the face of great hardship became a pioneer in Nebraska, and for years toured Nebraska and Western Iowa as superintendent for his society.[233]

After the Presbyterians withdrew their support from the American Home Missionary Society, they continued to send representatives to the frontier, but under their own organizations. Of these one of the most famous was Sheldon Jackson (1834-1909).[234] Born in New York, looking back upon grandfathers who had both been prominent in the political life of the state, and dedicated from childhood by his parents to the Christian ministry, after graduating from Union College and Princeton Theological Seminary he became a missionary to the Choctaws in Indian Territory. Ill health and the prospect of the disruption of missions by the approaching Civil War led him to resign from that task and to seek service under the Presbyterian Board of Domestic Missions. He was appointed (1859) to Minnesota, then a frontier region. He travelled extensively, and helped to found a church

pp. 82-84. Peet, *History of the Presbyterian and Congregational Churches and Ministers in Wisconsin,* pp. 93ff., tells of several churches which Peet helped to found.

[230] *Diary of Reverend G. H. Atkinson 1847-1858,* edited by E. R. Rockwood, in *Oregon Historical Quarterly,* March, 1939ff; Nancy Bates Atkinson, *Biography of Rev. G. H. Atkinson. D.D.* (Portland, Oregon, F. W. Baltes and Co., 1893, pp. 508, containing numbers of addresses and papers by Atkinson), *passim;* Weigle, *op. cit.,* p. 251; *Dictionary of American Biography,* Vol. I, pp. 408, 409; Clark, *op. cit.,* pp. 200-206.

[231] *Dictionary of American Biography,* Vol. XIX, pp. 429, 430; Clark, *op. cit.,* pp. 129-134.

[232] Clark, *op cit.,* p. 134.

[233] *Life and Labors of Rev. Reuben Gaylord, by His Wife* (Omaha, Rees Printing Co., 1889, pp. x. 437).

[234] The standard life of Jackson, based chiefly upon records and information supplied by Jackson and members of his family and by former associates, is Robert Laird Stewart, *Sheldon Jackson* (New York, Fleming H. Revell Co., 2d ed., 1908, pp. 488). A more popular book, utilizing Stewart's account and diaries and other records of Jackson, is John T. Faris, *The Alaskan Pathfinder. The Story of Sheldon Jackson for Boys* (New York, Fleming H. Revell Co., 1913, pp. 221).

at Northfield and became its pastor. Following the Civil War, the vast area between Iowa and the West Coast became a new frontier. Transcontinental railways were built and towns and mining camps sprang up. The new situation was a challenge to the churches, and to meet it, through the vision and initiative of the Presbyterians of Iowa, Jackson was appointed "superintendent of missions for Western Iowa, Nebraska, Dakota, Montana, Wyoming, and Utah."[235] Through this huge region Jackson travelled by train, stagecoach, burro, and horse-back, and on foot and on snow-shoes. He planted churches, often ahead of settlement, seeking to place them in strategic centres. In twelve months in 1869 and 1870, he covered twenty-nine thousand miles and organized twenty-three churches. This was only a sample of his achievements. He recruited and assigned missionaries. He procured funds. He was aided by a Board of Church Erection which the Presbyterians had founded for purposes obvious in its title and the headquarters of which had been placed, significantly, at St. Louis, a chief entrêpot for the West.[236] He extended his labours to Colorado, and even to New Mexico, Arizona, and Nevada. He cared not only for the settlers, but also for Indians, made restless, bewildered, and often angry by the irruption of the white man. He preached wherever he could obtain a hearing, in hotels, and in halls over beer parlors, often being the first Christian minister to be heard in a community. Sometimes he helped with his own hands to build a church. He founded schools. In this he was assisted by a Woman's Home Missionary Association, authorized in 1875, which had been preceded by a Union Missionary Society which had sought to found schools in Arizona and New Mexico, and by the Ladies' Board of Missions.[237] He began a religious periodical, *The Rocky Mountain Presbyterian*. Touched by an appeal for a missionary to the Indians of Alaska, which had been bought by the United States only a scant decade before, in 1877 he visited that territory. Indefatigable pioneer that he was, his imagination was gripped by this new frontier. He sought to induce Congress to provide it with schools and a government. He undertook trip after trip to the territory, introduced missionaries to it, and eventually made it his home. He became the General Agent of Education in Alaska for the Government of the United States, and in that capacity travelled widely through the North, starting schools for the natives. Distressed by the suffering brought to the Eskimos by the dwindling of the animals upon which they had depended for their food

---

[235] Stewart, *op. cit.*, p. 101.
[236] Stewart, *op. cit.*, pp. 121, 122.
[237] Stewart, *op. cit.*, pp. 256ff.

through the advent of white whalers and sealers, he brought about the introduction (1893) of domesticated reindeer from Siberia. The experiment proved eminently successful. He continued his active connexion with religious work and became Moderator of the General Assembly of his church. Few individuals in all the history of the Christian movement have accomplished so much in planting the faith over so wide an area.

Presbyterians and Congregationalists were by no means the only denominations to organize societies for the spread of Christianity on the frontier. In one form or another practically every denomination did likewise.

The Baptists of the eastern states early took steps to meet the needs of the frontier. In 1802, possibly stimulated by what the New England Congregationalists were doing, Baptists in Boston founded the Massachusetts Baptist Missionary Society "to promote the knowledge of evangelic truth in the new settlements within these United States."[238] The following year one of their agents reported having visited in the State of New York forty-one towns which had no resident minister of any denomination and in thirteen of which no missionary had ever before been.[239] In 1807 the Lake Baptist Missionary Society, later the Hamilton Missionary Society, was organized at Pompey, New York. In 1825 it united with the Baptist Domestic Missionary Convention of the State of New York to form the Baptist Missionary Convention of the State of New York. Missionaries were sent to New Jersey, Pennsylvania, Ohio, Michigan, Wisconsin, and Canada.[240] At least as early as 1817 what was called the General Missionary Convention of the Baptist Denomination in the United States (also, more popularly, termed the Triennial Convention), although it had been brought into existence to support Judson and his associates and was primarily for foreign missions, began commissioning men for the settlements in the West.[241]

The chief creator of nationally organized Baptist effort for the frontier and the Indians was John Mason Peck (1789-1838).[242] Born in Litchfield County, Connecticut, that centre which fathered many a leader in American Christianity, he was reared a Congregationalist, but became a Baptist. As

---

[238] See the text of the society's constitution in *The Massachusetts Baptist Missionary Magazine*, Vol. I, pp. 5-7.
[239] *The Massachusetts Baptist Missionary Magazine*, Vol. I, pp. 10-17.
[240] White, *A Century of Faith*, pp. 28, 29.
[241] White, *op. cit.*, p. 30.
[242] On Peck, see Rufus Babcock, *Memoir of John Mason Peck D.D. Edited from His Journals and Correspondence* (Philadelphia, American Baptist Publication Society, 1864, pp. 360), *passim*; Coe Hayne, *Vanguard of the Caravans. The Life-Story of John Mason Peck* (Philadelphia, The Judson Press, 1931, pp. 157); *Dictionary of American Biography*, Vol. XIV, p. 381; Goodykoontz, *Home Missions on the American Frontier*, pp. 202, 203.

a young Baptist minister in the State of New York he met Luther Rice, who had returned from Asia to stir the Baptists to the support of Judson, and through him became deeply committed to missions. He chose as his field the region west of the Mississippi. Sent by the Triennial Convention, he reached St. Louis in 1817,[243] in 1818 formed a church there, very early proposed a plan for "the United Society for the Spread of the Gospel," and soon made it an actuality. When, in 1820, the Triennial Convention withdrew from the mission to the West, he was thrown on his own resources. For a time after 1822 he was given some assistance by the Massachusetts Baptist Missionary Society. He cultivated a farm to pay expenses, traversed Illinois, Indiana, and Missouri, establishing Bible societies and Sunday Schools and placing teachers. He was the founder of what became Shurtleff College, in Illinois, and edited a religious periodical. He aroused in Jonathan Going, an influential and able pastor in Worcester, Massachusetts,[244] an interest in the West, and together they agreed upon the plan for the American Baptist Home Mission Society. With the hearty encouragement of the Massachusetts and New York societies, that body came into existence (1832) and adopted all of North America as its field.[245] Jonathan Going was its first corresponding secretary, and then resigned to become president of a new college in Ohio which was later to be Denison University. A national organization of Baptists for comprehensive effort for the continent had been brought into existence. At the outset concentrating chiefly on the older American white population of the Mississippi Valley, in time the society extended its activities to various immigrant groups, to Indians, to Negroes, and to Canada, Mexico, Central America, and the Caribbean.[246]

In its first year, fifty missionaries served under the society.[247] More than half of these were in New York, Ohio, Michigan, Indiana, and Illinois. One of the number appointed at that time, Ezra Fisher, had a career which in some ways epitomized the society's labours on the frontier.[248] Born on a farm in Massachusetts in 1800, he graduated from Amherst College, studied at Newton Theological Institution, and became a pastor in Vermont. Appointed by the American Baptist Home Mission Society, he went to Indiana, was pastor of the Baptist church in Indianapolis, and assisted in founding

[243] Douglass, *History of Missouri Baptists,* p. 36.
[244] On Going see *Dictionary of American Biography,* Vol. VII, p. 362.
[245] White, *op. cit.,* pp. 34, 40-45.
[246] *Sixtieth Annual Report of the American Baptist Home Mission Society* (New York, 1892), pp. 36-43; White, *op. cit.,* pp. 173ff.
[247] White, *op. cit.,* p. 49.
[248] *Correspondence of the Reverend Ezra Fisher, passim.*

what became Franklin College. He then went on to Illinois, supplementing his income by teaching while pastor of a struggling church at Quincy. After three and a half years, he passed on to Iowa, and for a time was the only Baptist minister in an area along the Mississippi from twenty to fifty miles wide. There he helped to organize churches. Still drawn by the lure of the far frontier and believing that men could be found more easily for the Middle than the Far West, he was first attracted by Texas, then the goal of many who sought a new country, but, instead, in 1845 went with his family by wagon on the seven and a half months' journey to the even more remote Oregon. There he explored the land, reporting the centres at which he believed churches should be organized, and gave much energy to inaugurating what he hopefully named a college. In 1855 he severed his connexion with the society, but continued as pastor of small churches, making his living chiefly by farming and, latterly, as county school superintendent, until his death (November 1, 1874).

Sharing in the Baptist efforts for the frontier was the Baptist General Tract Society, formed in 1824 and in 1840 altered to become the American Baptist Publication Society.[249] Through its colporteurs for the distribution of literature and the organizing of Sunday Schools, and through chapel-cars designed to utilize the railways to reach unchurched communities, it joined in the task of spreading Christianity in the new settlements.

As Baptist churches associated themselves in regional and state conventions, these latter took over an increasing proportion of the responsibility for missions within their own bounds.[250]

The Church of England had suffered severely through the American Revolution. At the outset of the war, the Society for the Propagation of the Gospel in Foreign Parts, from which had been coming most of the aid in the spread of that church in the Colonies, was helping to support seventy-seven missionaries in what became the United States. As the war progressed, nearly all of these were forced to retire from their fields.[251] During the war, many of the clergy, especially in New England, were loyal to the King and were compelled to leave their parishes. Disestablishment followed independence in such of the states as had had it as colonies, notably in Virginia. Since they were now outside the bounds of the British Empire, the churches of the Anglican communion were without bishops.[252]

---

[249] Newman, *A History of the Baptist Churches in the United States*, pp. 426, 427.
[250] As an example see Mattoon, *Baptist Annals of Oregon*, Vol. II, p. 193ff.
[251] Pascoe, *Two Hundred Years of the S. P. G.*, pp. 79ff.
[252] Manross, *A History of the American Episcopal Church*, pp. 172ff; Weigle, *American Idealism*, pp. 122, 123.

Following independence, recovery was achieved. Bishops were elected and received consecration in the British Isles. In 1789 a national organization was effected of what became the Protestant Episcopal Church.[253] The Diocese of Maryland sent missionaries to Kentucky, and in Virginia parochial missionary societies were formed to aid in the extension of the church, the education of young men for the ministry, and the circulation of religious literature.[254] Individual clergymen began moving to the West and there found their own support as they carried on their religious work. One of these, Philander Chase, after becoming the first bishop in Ohio, went to England and collected funds for a college and theological seminary which he established at Gambier, in his diocese.[255] Another was James Harvey Otey, the organizer and first Bishop of his church in Tennessee.[256] In 1821 what became the Domestic and Foreign Missionary Society of the Protestant Episcopal Church was organized. In 1835 its base was so broadened that all members of the church were declared to be members of the society.[257] In that year the custom was inaugurated of having the General Convention elect missionary bishops for territories not yet fully organized ecclesiastically. These actions were revolutionary. They prepared the way for the nation-wide extension of the church and for national planning. The church ceased to be a federation of churches and became a national church organized in dioceses.[258] In 1838 missionaries went to Texas and there began the Episcopal Church.[259] In 1841 the impact of the Oxford movement sent a group of young men from the General Seminary in New York City to Wisconsin, where, although they took no vows, they established something akin to a monastic community, served a wide area about them, and began training a few theological students.[260] In the course of time the Domestic and Foreign Missionary Society gave assistance to a large number of dioceses and states and, thanks in part to its aid, an ecclesiastical structure arose as comprehensive as the nation itself. Sometimes a diocese was created and a bishop

[253] Weigle, op. cit., pp. 155, 156.
[254] Goodwin, The Colonial Church in Virginia, pp. 228-230.
[255] Manross, op. cit., p. 250; McConnell, History of the American Episcopal Church, pp. 301-306.
[256] McConnell, op. cit., pp. 307-309.
[257] Proceedings of the Board of Missions of the Protestant Episcopal Church in the United States of America at their forty-first annual meeting . . . October, 1876, appendix, p. 3.
[258] Ibid.; Manross, op. cit., p. 257; McConnell, op. cit., pp. 309, 310.
[259] Du Bose Murphy, A Short History of the Protestant Episcopal Church in Texas, pp. 1, 2, 4.
[260] Manross, op. cit., pp. 259ff.

appointed before many local congregations had come into being. The bishop himself became a missionary and led in planting the church.[261]

The bodies which we have mentioned in the past several pages are only a few of the many which were organized in the older sections of the country to assist in the spread of Christianity on the frontier. In the course of time practically every denomination had one. In most of them the winning of the frontier was merely part of the objective. Almost all denominations, however, strove to share in the planting of Christianity on the rapidly advancing western borders of the nation.[262]

It was only slowly that the various Protestant denominations learned to co-operate and to plan together in any comprehensive fashion to reach the entire nation. Vigorous and sometimes bitter debates between spokesmen of rival religious bodies helped to give zest to life on the frontier.[263] Even in small villages several denominations would be represented by struggling congregations, and each major denomination sought a foothold in every town of any size. In the days of frontier optimism, when in the eyes of the pioneer every cross-roads and every village seemed a possible metropolis, this duplication appeared warranted. By the end of the century, however, the swing towards co-operation was marked. In 1908 three organizations significant of the tendency came into being, the Federal Council of the Churches of Christ in America, the Home Missions Council, and the Council of Women for Home Missions.[264] By 1912 the Home Missions Council comprised twenty-six societies representing sixteen denominations.[265]

Long before these co-operative bodies were born, Christians of many denominations were joining in the support of societies which endeavoured to perform certain specialized functions over the entire country. Several of

[261] *Proceedings of the Board of Missions of the Protestant Episcopal Church in the United States of America at their forty-first annual meeting . . : October, 1876,* appendix, p. 5. For an autobiographical account of one of these missionary bishops see Ethelbert Talbot, *My People of the Plains* (New York, Harper & Brothers, 1906, pp. xi, 265), *passim.*

[262] As instances gathered almost at random, see Johnson, *Ante-Bellum North Carolina,* p. 361, in which the appointment of travelling missionaries by the Lutheran Synod to serve congregations without pastors is mentioned; C. A. Hawley in *Church History,* Vol. VI, pp. 211-222, in which the spread of Swedenborgianism, largely through Francis Bailey, is recorded and the statement is made that by 1850 every state east of the Mississippi had reading groups of Swedenborgian literature; Drury, *History of the Church of the United Brethren in Christ,* pp. 611ff., in which an account is given of the home missions of that denomination.

[263] As a few examples of this, see Magoun, *Asa Turner,* p. 126; *Autobiography of Rev. James B. Finley,* pp. 233, 287, 288, 369, 370; *Autobiography of Peter Cartwright,* pp. 114, 115, 123, 124, 150, 151, 386, 449-451.

[264] King, *History of the Home Missions Council,* pp. 11, 14.

[265] King, *op. cit.,* p. 15.

these came into existence in the halcyon years between the close of the Napoleonic Wars in 1815 and the economic depression of the eighteen thirties. Optimism ran high. National spirit was strong. Expansion was in the air. In Great Britain and America those of what was called the Evangelical tradition were inclined to work together in partial disregard of denominational barriers. The recrudescence of denominational feeling of the second and third quarters of the century was yet to appear. Of the undenominational agencies formed in this expansive era of good feeling, one of the most prominent was the American Bible Society. This had come into being in 1816 to unite the efforts of numerous local and state Bible societies.[266] Gradually, and not without difficulties, many of the older societies became auxiliaries of the national body.[267] In 1829 the society entered upon the ambitious project of attempting to supply with a Bible every family in the nation which did not have one.[268] While at the end of two years it reported that it had not quite reached its goal,[269] it believed that most families in the United States had been provided with the Scriptures.[270] Since the effort was one which, in the nature of the case, needed to be repeated to meet increases and shifts in population, it was undertaken a number of times. In the fourth of these campaigns, made in the eight years from 1882 to 1890, colporteurs were sent into sparsely settled regions, more than six million families were visited, nearly half a million families without a Bible were supplied, and more than eight million copies of the Bible were distributed by sale or gift.[271] However, even then more than a quarter of a million families were left without the Bible, either because they refused it or could not read.[272]

Another undenominational national organization was the American Sunday School Union, formed in 1824.[273] In 1828 it determined to take steps to establish a Sunday School in every place in the United States and its territories where there was a sufficient population.[274] In 1830 it framed a

[266] Dwight, *The Centennial History of the American Bible Society*, Vol. I, pp. 7-9.
[267] Dwight, *op. cit.*, Vol. I, pp. 36-47.
[268] *Thirteenth Annual Report of the American Bible Society* (1829), in *Annual Reports of the American Bible Society*, Vol. I, p. 442.
[269] *Fifteenth Annual Report of the American Bible Society*, in *Annual Reports of the American Bible Society*, Vol. I, p. 550; Dwight, *op. cit.*, Vol. I, pp. 85-91; J. O. Oliphant in *Church History*, Vol. VII, p. 130.
[270] *Sixteenth Annual Report of the American Bible Society*, in *Annual Reports of the American Bible Society*, Vol. I, p. 608.
[271] *Sixty-Sixth Annual Report of the American Bible Society* (1882), p. 38; *Seventy-Fourth Annual Report of the American Bible Society* (1890), pp. 44-47.
[272] *Seventy-Fourth Annual Report of the American Bible Society* (1890), pp. 44, 45.
[273] Brown, *A History of Religious Education in Recent Times*, pp. 166, 167; Fergusson, *Historic Chapters in Christian Education in America*, pp. 18-24.
[274] J. O. Oliphant in *Church History*, Vol. VII, p. 133.

programme for placing within two years a Sunday School in every community beyond the Alleghenies where one was needed. Within that decade it launched a similar enterprise for the southern states.[275] National Sunday School Conventions were held, beginning in 1832. Out of these came the International Sunday School Conventions (the first assembled in 1875) and the International Sunday School Association. Auxiliary to the latter were state Sunday School Associations. Denominational Sunday School organizations eventually co-operated through the Sunday School Council of Evangelical Denominations. In 1903 came the formation of the Religious Education Association.[276] All of these agencies aided directly or indirectly in education in the Christian faith in newer as well as older sections of the land.

Still another of the undenominational bodies formed in the two decades after 1815, the American Tract Society, was founded in 1825. It early gave special attention to the Mississippi Valley and in 1832 adopted a plan to provide with some of its literature every religiously destitute person or family in the United States.[277] In 1847 it had 267 colporteurs, the majority of them in the Mississippi Valley. These were the chief distributing agents of its literature. The appointees of the American Home Missionary Society also used large quantities of its publications.[278]

Educational institutions constituted one of the most important and characteristic means for the propagation of Protestant Christianity on the frontier. Schools, and especially higher schools, were necessary if the churches were to have a trained clerical and lay leadership. Schools, moreover, if under warmly Christian auspices, could be communities of earnest and vigorous Christian experience. In compact and fairly homogeneous student bodies led by teachers with strong religious convictions, revivals again and again broke out.[279] Such campuses were centres in which youths spent the impressionable years of adolescence, when conversions most frequently occur, and many went out from them transformed, to be the backbone of the churches. Little attempt was made to create a comprehensive system of primary schools under church auspices.[280] Indeed, more than one missionary

---

[275] Ibid.; Fergusson, op. cit., p. 25; J. O. Oliphant in Church History, Vol. VII, p. 133.
[276] Brown, op. cit., pp. 165-188.
[277] J. O. Oliphant in Church History, Vol. VII, pp. 125-137.
[278] Twenty-Second Annual Report of the American Tract Society (1847), pp. 25-27.
[279] Tewksbury, The Founding of American Colleges and Universities before the Civil War, pp. 65-68.
[280] A strong group of the Old School Presbyterians advocated a system of church schools, with a primary school in each parish, an academy in each presbytery, and a college in each synod. By 1861 the plan had largely broken down.—Lewis Joseph Sherrill, Presbyterian Parochial Schools, 1846-1870, passim.

had much to do with inaugurating a system of state schools.[281] It was for the erection of colleges and universities that the Protestant forces were more concerned. Back of them was the conviction, partly Protestant in origin and partly sprung from frontier democracy, that higher education should not be an aristocratic privilege but was the right of all.[282] Instead of being undenominational, most of them were founded by individual denominations.[283] Many of them, with the optimism of the frontier, were dubbed universities, but at the outset most of them were compelled by the backwardness of the state schools to include secondary and many of them even the primary stages of instruction. Only a very few ever achieved true university status. As a rule each denomination endeavoured to have at least one college in each state. A large proportion of the colleges were inaugurated in pioneer days while frontier conditions still maintained. Many were begun by graduates of Yale and Princeton. Repeatedly in the first half of the nineteenth century each of these two institutions, the one Congregational and the other Presbyterian, was visited by revivals, and from them ardently religious graduates went westward to seek to reproduce the kind of education permeated by warm religious purpose which they had known as students.[284] In 1910 the country had 403 educational institutions of college grade under Protestant auspices,[285] fully half of them dating from the frontier or near frontier days of their constituencies.[286] Of the 180 denominational colleges in existence in 1860 which achieved enduring life, four-fifths were Baptist, Methodist, Presbyterian, or Congregational in affiliation. Presbyterians led with forty-nine, Methodists were next with thirty-four, Baptists were third with twenty-five, and Congregationalists fourth with twenty-one. Of these four denominations, in proportion to their numerical strength, Congregationalists led, Presbyterians were second, Baptists third, and Methodists last.[287] The funds for equipping the colleges came chiefly from the Eastern states. Several societies were founded to raise funds for this purpose. Of them the chief was the Society for Promoting Collegiate and Theological Education at the West. It was predominantly Congregational and Presbyterian and had Theron Baldwin, a member of the Illinois Band, as its first secretary.[288]

[281] Dictionary of American Biography, Vol. I, pp. 408, 409, Vol. XIX, pp. 429, 430.
[282] Tewksbury, op. cit., pp. 1-5.
[283] Tewksbury, op. cit., pp. 55-62.
[284] Tewksbury, op. cit., p. 14.
[285] F. W. Padelford in Christian Education, Vol. XIX, pp. 210ff.
[286] Tewksbury, op. cit., p. 16, gives partial figures.
[287] Tewksbury, op. cit., p. 69; Goodykoontz, Home Missions on the American Frontier, pp. 377ff.
[288] Tewksbury, op. cit., pp. 7-12; Julian M. Sturtevant, An Autobiography, p. 249.

Societies, too, were instituted to aid in their education youths who were preparing for the ministry.[289] Theological seminaries were begun.[290] The churches led in inaugurating higher education on the frontier and in doing so prepared a trained leadership against the day of the maturity of the West.

Even this brief survey of the efforts of Protestant Christianity to hold or win to the faith the older American stock as it moved westward gives some inkling of the enormous expenditure of energy and devotion and of the abounding life and conviction from which it arose. A complete picture would show it to have been even richer and more bewildering in the multiplicity of the organizations and individuals engaged in it. We must remember, too, that in the very years of this prodigious effort to win the West, American Protestant Christianity was seeking to reach the immigrants who were pouring into the United States and to win the Indians and the Negroes, and was sending missionaries to all the other continents and to many of the islands of the sea. The Christianity which had been planted in colonial days had taken root and flourished in a fashion never surpassed and but seldom equalled in the entire history of Christianity, or, indeed, of any other religion.

So well and firmly had Protestant Christianity been established on the westward moving frontier, that, in the main, it was nearly as strong in the older American stock in the newer as in the older states. That strength varied somewhat from section to section. In the twentieth century the proportion of the population having church membership was higher in the East and South than in the Middle West and considerably higher than in the Far West, showing that the frontier had not been fully won.[291] Yet even the lowest percentage of the adult population who had membership in churches, which was less than thirty out of a hundred in Washington, Nevada, and Montana, was several times that of the country as a whole at the dawn of the nineteenth century. How many of these were late immigrants and how many were of older American stock, the figures do not show. However, it is clear that the progress had been amazing.

Denominationally the complexion of Protestantism was far from uniform

---

[289] Magoun, *Asa Turner and His Times*, p. 205; Sturtevant, *op. cit.*, p. 81; Ludlum, *Social Ferment in Vermont 1791-1850*, p. 53.

[290] On one of these, see Pond, *Gospel Pioneering*, pp. 104ff.

[291] C. L. Fry in *Data Book Volume I For the Use of Delegates to the North American Home Missions Congress . . . Washington, D. C., December 1 to 5, 1930* (pp. x, 299), p. 292; Fry, *The U. S. Looks at Its Churches*, pp. 11, 12, and Chart III.

in all regions.[292] In general, the differences between the hold of Protestantism upon urban and rural areas, regardless of sections, was fairly marked.[293] In the main Protestantism was strongest in the rural districts and smaller towns and weakest in the cities. To this phenomenon and its attendant problems we must revert in a later chapter.

So well did Protestantism rise to the challenge presented by the frontier that as the newer states passed out of the pioneer stage into maturity, their churches were fully as effective in moulding the life of their communities and became as much a source of movements for the further expansion of the faith as the churches in the older states. In both East and West the proportion of those professing adherence to Protestant Christianity continued to rise. Protestant Christianity was a growing and important factor in the life of the states formed on what had been the frontier.

[292] Fry, *The U. S. Looks at Its Churches*, pp. 32-39.
[293] Fry, *op. cit.*, p. 30.

Chapter VII

THE UNITED STATES OF AMERICA. WINNING THE IMMI-GRANTS: ROMAN CATHOLICS: EASTERN CHURCHES: PROT-ESTANTS

WHILE the older American stock was pushing the frontier westward and adding more states to the Union, the stream of immigration was mounting. Not until 1820 did more than twenty thousand arrive in any one year.[1] Between 1820 and 1860 about five millions entered the United States.[2] In the latter year slightly over four millions of the somewhat more than thirty millions who then constituted the total population of the country were foreign-born.[3] During the Civil War the number coming each year subsided, but with the end of hostilities it quickly revived. In the decade from 1870 through 1879 it was about what it had been in the decade before the Civil War.[4] In the decade from 1880 through 1889 the immigration to-talled more than five millions. Because of depressed economic conditions, it subsided again in the eighteen-nineties, but in the decade 1900-1909 it was more than eight millions.[5] The largest influx in any one year was in 1907, when 1,433,469 arrived.[6] With the outbreak of the World War in 1914 immigration rapidly fell to almost negligible proportions, and after the war the sharp restrictions which were applied kept it down to much smaller dimensions than in the preceding century. The census of 1920 revealed the fact that 47,491,000, or slightly more than half of the white population, was foreign-born, of foreign parentage, or chiefly descended from those who had entered the country since independence had been achieved.[7] Since 1870 the proportion of the white population who were of native parentage had never been more than 60 per cent.[8] Here was a movement of peoples which

[1] Carpenter, *Immigrants and Their Children*, p. 63.
[2] Carpenter, *op. cit.*, p. 45.
[3] Bassett, *A Short History of the United States*, pp. 461, 518.
[4] Carpenter, *op. cit.*, p. 45.
[5] *Ibid.*
[6] Steiner, *The Immigrant Tide*, p. 363.
[7] Carpenter, *op. cit.*, pp. 4, 5.
[8] Carpenter, *op. cit.*, p. 5.

for magnitude was unapproached in the nineteenth century. It has seldom if ever been equalled in the entire history of mankind.

The causes of this vast migration were to be found partly in the United States and partly in Europe. In the United States the apparently limitless natural resources called for labour to develop them.[9] While at times the prodigious influx aroused misgivings and even opposition, in general the prevailing opinion in the United States declared the country to be the land of opportunity to which all who wished to come were welcome. The first restrictions placed by the national government were directed against the Chinese and were not effective until after 1880. Only slowly was legislation adopted to keep out even such undesirable elements as convicts and prostitutes (1875), persons likely to become public charges (1882), contract labourers (1885), and anarchists (1903).[10] Not until after 1900 were serious efforts made to prevent Japanese from coming. The overwhelming majority of the immigrants were from Europe. To most of them the appeal was economic. To a few it was political liberty. To still fewer it was religious freedom. Here and there, as we are to see, came religious colonies. These, however, were much less prominent than in the seventeenth century. Adverse economic conditions, such as existed in Ireland through the first part of the nineteenth century and were aggravated by the famine brought by the failure of the potato crop in 1847, were responsible for the larger part of the immigration. Untoward political conditions and compulsory military service impelled many to seek refuge in the New World. The increased ease of crossing the Atlantic brought by the steamship augmented the influx. Transportation companies and American employers encouraged a movement which meant their own profit. Often, although not always, the governments of the lands from which the migrants came were not averse to their leaving.[11] A series of favouring factors combined to bring about the great migration.

The "new Americans" came from many lands. Down to the 1880's the majority were from Western and Northern Europe.[12] From 1820 to 1865 1,880,943 Irish, 1,545,508 Germans, and 744,285 from England entered the United States.[13] Of those who arrived in 1882, 27.7 per cent. were from Great Britain and Ireland, 38.7 per cent. were from Germany, and 16.3 per

[9] Warne, The Immigrant Invasion, pp. 25ff.

[10] Encyclopaedia of the Social Sciences, Vol. VII, p. 592.

[11] On the causes of immigration, see Abbott, Historical Aspects of the Immigration Problem, pp. 11-198; Warne, op. cit., pp. 25ff.; Commons, Races and Immigrants in America, pp. 64ff.

[12] For a chart showing the provenance of foreign-born by decades, see Warne, op. cit., opposite p. 86.

[13] Bassett, op. cit., p. 461.

cent. were from Denmark, Norway, and Sweden.[14] In 1902, however, of those who were admitted, only 7.4 per cent. were from Great Britain and Ireland, only 4.2 per cent. were from Germany, and only 8.7 per cent. were from the three Scandinavian kingdoms, while 28.6 per cent. were from Italy, 27.6 per cent. were from the Austrian-Hungarian Empire, and 17.2 per cent. were from Russia.[15] Of those from the Russian Empire, by far the largest number were Jews, with Poles next, and with Lithuanians, Finns, and Germans constituting considerable minorities.[16] From Austria-Hungary Czechs, Slovaks, Magyars, and Roumanians were the chief racial groups.[17] Early in the nineteenth century most of the Jews were from Germany,[18] but later they came mainly from Austria-Hungary, Roumania, and Russia, with Russia leading.[19] Many French Canadians moved to the United States, largely to New England. Of the approximately 2,400,000 French Canadians in existence in 1901, one-third are said to have been in the United States.[20] A few thousand Syrians and Armenians came.[21] Into the South-west moved Mexicans, a large proportion of them as transient labourers. In 1900 they numbered 103,393, and in 1910 221,915.[22] A few thousand came from the Far East, mostly Chinese and Japanese. In 1900 the Chinese residing in continental United States totalled 89,863, but in 1910, because of the restriction on their entrance, numbered only 71,531. In 1900 the Japanese were 24,326 and in 1910, 72,157.[23] Hawaii contained large Chinese and Japanese contingents, but of these we are not to speak until the next volume. It was predominantly from Europe that the newer Americans were derived.

When these waves of immigration reached the United States, they distributed themselves somewhat unevenly over the country. Only a small proportion went to the section which lay south of the Potomac and the Ohio and east of the Mississippi. Most of it was unskilled labour and it would there have been driven into competition with the Negroes.[24] Whether as slaves or as freedman, the Negroes, as cheap labour, would have proved dis-

---

[14] Commons, *op. cit.*, p. 71.
[15] *Ibid.*
[16] Commons, *op. cit.*, p. 87.
[17] Commons, *op. cit.*, p. 83.
[18] Commons, *op. cit.*, p. 89.
[19] Joseph, *Jewish Immigration to the United States from 1881 to 1910*, p. 94.
[20] Commons, *op. cit.*, p. 97. Another authority declares that in 1901, on the basis of returns from ecclesiastical authorities of each diocese, the number of French Canadians in the United States was 921,989. Bracq, *The Evolution of French Canada*, p. 214.
[21] Commons, *op. cit.*, p. 100.
[22] Bamio, *Mexican Immigration to the United States*, p. 2.
[23] Mears, *Resident Orientals on the American Pacific Coast*, p. 412.
[24] Warne, *op. cit.*, pp. 90ff.

couraging rivals. Much of the older immigration, namely that which arrived before 1882, sought the inexpensive or free virgin lands which were found west of the Alleghenies. This was notably true of the Germans and Scandinavians.[25] The Irish tended to congregate as unskilled labourers in the cities in New England and the Middle Atlantic states or helped to construct the roads, canals, and railways which were being rapidly built.[26] After 1882 the immigrants settled chiefly on the North-eastern portions of the Atlantic seaboard, but many of them went to the Middle West, to the Pacific Coast, and to the Rocky Mountain regions.[27] Some moved onto the land, buying farms in New England from which the older American stock had moved in their cityward or westward migration.[28] The large majority of the immigrants were resident in the cities. They tended to be concentrated especially in the chief metropolitan centres.[29] In Europe the larger proportion of them had been peasants. In the United States most of them were suddenly thrown not only into a nation with a quite different cultural heritage, but also found themselves in an urban environment.

For Christianity the immigrant constituted a major problem. Here were millions whose inherited faith was Christianity but who were now uprooted from their accustomed surroundings and transplanted to a strange land. Most of them, especially the young, tended to drop their old culture and to adopt that of their new habitat. The second generation especially were averse to being thought of as foreigners and wished to be known as Americans. They were inclined to be ashamed of the language, the dress, and the manners of the "old country." Would the immigrants and their children abandon, along with the other customs peculiar to their ancestral past, the faith which had come to them from their fathers? The vast majority had been members of state or community churches in which membership was a normal accompaniment of citizenship or of association with a particular group. In the United States, no one church was espoused by the state, and churches were supported by the voluntary gifts of their constituencies.

For those of Protestant background, and especially for Protestants from the British Isles, the transition was comparatively easy. Most of them found in the United States denominations akin to those which they had known across the water. For Roman Catholics the situation was much more difficult, for at the outset the United States had very few of their form of the

[25] Carpenter, *Immigrants and Their Children*, pp. 50, 51; Warne, *op. cit.*, pp. 77-89.
[26] Warne, *op. cit.*, pp. 77, 78.
[27] Carpenter, *op. cit.*, pp. 12, 50.
[28] Carpenter, *op. cit.*, p. 55.
[29] Carpenter, *op. cit.*, pp. 21-24.

faith and the general atmosphere, so far as it was religious, was permeated by Protestantism. Members of the Eastern churches were even less at home, for the United States of 1783 had none, or practically none, of their communions.

Where, as was often the case, large numbers of one nation or race lived together in one community, they tended to build churches of their inherited form of Christianity and to rally about them as the chief social institution which connected them with their past. Where they were scattered as individuals or families among older Americans, the tie to their religious past was more tenuous.

A substantial minority of the immigrants were non-Christian in background. The Jews particularly were numerous. The Chinese and Japanese were not Christian. Presumably, removed from their traditional setting to a land where religious toleration was the rule, they would be more susceptible to Christian influence. However, in the absence of compulsion, would more than a small proportion of them become Christians?

In summarizing the attempts to meet this situation, we will first speak of the Roman Catholic Church, second of the Eastern churches, and third of Protestantism. We must then tell of what was done to reach the Jews, the Chinese, and the Japanese. The record, we shall discover, is amazing. All three major branches of Christianity, especially Roman Catholicism and Protestantism, displayed remarkable vitality in meeting or following the immigrant and in adapting themselves to the American scene.

A marked difference existed between the problems presented to Christianity by the westward spread of the older American stock and the influx of this newer immigration. To be sure, there were similarities. Both were vast colonizing movements of peoples. In both, old environments were left behind and the customs and institutions of the migrants were in a state of flux. In both this constituted a threat and an opportunity to Christianity—a threat that whatever of Christianity the migrants possessed might be left behind, and an opportunity to deepen the hold of the faith upon peoples which had long been subjected to Christian influence. Moreover, both older and newer stocks often lived side by side on the frontier and were subjected to the same frontier conditions. However, the older stock had been shaped by the traditions accumulated through the centuries of development which had made the United States. It was consciously American. Its Old World heritage was remote and was that of the Europe of the seventeenth and eighteenth centuries. The newer immigration was directly from Europe and brought with it attitudes of mind which characterized the Old World—and the Old World of the nineteenth century. The older stock, so far as it had a religious connexion, was overwhelmingly Protestant and its Protestantism was largely that of churches which in Europe were in the minority and represented the radical wing of Christianity. At the outset of the nineteenth century, fully nine-tenths of these older Americans were not members of any church. Because of the cultural heritage and atmosphere, they had a tincture of Christianity, but they had not even been baptized. Until reached by the vast spread of Christianity among them which characterized the nineteenth century, they seemed to be drifting away from that faith. The newer stock was chiefly from state churches and the large majority had been baptized in infancy and thus had a formal church connexion. Yet they were not so much accustomed to taking the initiative in the government and financial support of their churches as were church members of the older stock. In the newer immigration, the Roman Catholic and Eastern forms of Christianity were much more prominent than in the older. Here, then, were contrasts which complicated the problem presented to Christianity in the United States. We must, accordingly, deal with the spread of Christianity through the newer immigration as a set of movements somewhat distinct from the expansion of Christianity among the older stock on the frontier.

For the Roman Catholic Church especially the task was gigantic. A very large proportion of the immigration were Roman Catholic by tradition. Of the thirteen and a half millions of foreign-born in the United States in 1910, probably at least seven and a half millions, or nearly 60 per cent., were baptized as Roman Catholics.[30] On their arrival, the overwhelming majority of these were desperately poor. They could provide only scanty support for the clergy and could spare little money for the erection of churches and schools. These Roman Catholics were from several different countries. Each group was inclined to be loyal to its own traditions and to wish to perpetuate them. The task of welding the various nationalities together into one church was not easy. Moreover, left without direct episcopal supervision, they were in danger of breaking apart and of failing to achieve cohesion. This peril was augmented by the tendency of various congregations to seek to govern their own affairs and to be restive under the authority of their

[30] Reckoned on the basis of the table in Shaughnessy, *Has the Immigrant Kept the Faith?*, p. 175.

ecclesiastical superiors.[31] Moreover, at the time when the United States became independent the country had only a very few Roman Catholics and these were with a hierarchy. Just how numerous they were we do not know.[32] In 1789 they may have totalled thirty-five thousand.[33] Fully half of these were in Maryland and about a fourth were in Pennsylvania.[34] By 1820, when immigration began to mount, the total seems to have been not far from two hundred thousand, of whom about 40 per cent. had come through immigration and about 15 per cent. through the annexation of Louisiana and Florida.[35] This was not a large body to care for the flood which was soon to break upon the land.

The Roman Catholics found their task made more difficult by a strong feeling against them. In colonial days hostility was pronounced. In Protestant Christendom in general the bitterness engendered by the religious struggles which followed the separation from Rome was still strong. In the Thirteen Colonies antagonism and suspicion were accentuated by the repeated wars with Roman Catholic France and the fear of Roman Catholic French Canada.[36] In the Revolutionary War this anti-Roman Catholic feeling was somewhat allayed by the alliance with Roman Catholic France and by the entrance of Roman Catholic Spain into the war against Great Britain. Roman Catholic colonials were on both sides of the struggle, but the majority seem to have been against the British[37] and four of them, including Daniel and Charles Carroll, affixed their signatures to the Declaration of Independence.[38] Moreover, the constitution adopted by the new nation, by forbidding religious tests for office in the federal government and, in its first amendment, proscribing restrictions on religious liberty, gave to Roman Catholics equal legal status with Protestants.[39] However, while liberty of worship and of

[31] Dignan, *A History of the Legal Incorporation of Catholic Church Property in the United States (1784-1932)*, pp. 67ff.; Guilday, *The Life and Times of John Carroll*, pp. 262ff.

[32] See various estimates in Shaughnessy, *op. cit.*, p. 36. n. 1.

[33] Shaughnessy, *op. cit.*, p. 38.

[34] Shaughnessy, *op. cit.*, p. 37.

[35] Based upon figures in Shaughnessy, *op. cit.*, p. 73. A. Baudrillart, in Descamps, *Histoire Générale Comparée des Missions*, p. 379, places the number of Roman Catholics in 1820 at 400,000.

[36] Mary Augustina Ray, *American Opinion of Roman Catholicism in the Eighteenth Century*, *passim*.

[37] Mary Augustina Ray, *op. cit.*, pp. 310-349. On the part that Roman Catholics had in achieving independence, see Ives, *The Ark and the Dove*, pp. 314-345.

[38] O'Gorman, *A History of the Roman Catholic Church in the United States*, p. 257.

[39] *Constitution of the United States of America*, Article VI and First Amendment. On the share of Roman Catholics in framing the Constitution and in writing religious liberty into that document, see Ives, *op. cit.*, pp. 365-413.

religious instruction prevailed, several of the state constitutions for a time debarred Roman Catholics from some or all offices.[40] By many, Roman Catholics were despised or distrusted, and more than once in the nineteenth and twentieth centuries this antipathy assumed pronounced and even violent form.[41] Roman Catholics were a minority, although a growing minority, in a land whose traditions had been largely shaped by Protestantism. This proved both a handicap and an incentive.

Although at the outset of the century Roman Catholics were not very numerous, they rapidly developed an organization. The favouring atmosphere of legal toleration combined with their own initiative to create, with assistance from Rome and from Europe, a growing ecclesiastical structure which was not unfitted to cope with the gigantic task that was thrust upon it.

In colonial days, Roman Catholics had been under the ecclesiastical jurisdiction of the Vicar Apostolic of London and had been served by Jesuits.[42] The suppression of the Society of Jesus in 1773, on the eve of the Revolutionary War, had been a severe blow, but all of the Jesuits in the colonies remained at their posts, becoming automatically seculars instead of regulars.[43]

The war cut off correspondence with the Vicar Apostolic of London and peace did not remove the breach.[44] It became necessary for Rome to provide episcopal supervision for the new nation. For a time there was talk, because of the French-American alliance, of appointing a French priest to the post and training an American clergy in France.[45] However, the American priests had met and had asked of the Pope one of their own number as head. Franklin, the American minister to France, was known to be favourable to John Carroll.[46] In 1784 the latter was made Prefect Apostolic[47] and in 1789, at the request of the American clergy, was appointed the first Bishop of the newly created see of Baltimore.[48]

John Carroll was from the prominent Maryland Roman Catholic family which had supplied two signers of the Declaration of Independence. Born

[40] Mary Augustina Ray, op. cit., pp. 350ff.

[41] For brief accounts of the most energetic of these movements, see O'Gorman, op. cit., pp. 356-360, 374, 375, 380-384, 450. A fuller account of the movements down to 1860 is the scholarly Ray Allen Billington, The Protestant Crusade of 1800-1860. A Study of the Origins of American Nativism (New York, The Macmillan Co., 1938, pp. viii, 514), passim.

[42] O'Donnell, The Catholic Hierarchy of the United States, 1790-1922, p. xiii.

[43] O'Gorman, op. cit., p. 254.

[44] O'Gorman, op. cit., p. 259.

[45] O'Gorman, op. cit., p. 261. Shearer, Pontificia Americana, pp. 27ff., gives some of the documents.

[46] O'Gorman, op. cit., pp. 260, 261; Shearer, op. cit., pp. 48-52.

[47] Shearer, op. cit., pp. 52-59.

[48] Shearer, op. cit., pp. 75-80.

in 1735, he had been educated in France, had joined the Jesuits, and, after the suppression of that Society, had returned to Maryland and, until his elevation to the leadership of the Roman Catholic Church in the United States, had spent most of his time as a missionary among those of his branch of the faith in Maryland and Virginia.[49] Carroll proved an excellent choice and gave to the young church able leadership. He travelled extensively through his enormous diocese. He contended for the authority of his office against what was known as trusteeism, the effort of local congregations represented by trustees who were the legal owners of the property of a parish to choose and dismiss pastors without reference to ecclesiastical superiors. He strove to annul the rivalries of various national groups which would perpetuate in the United States divisions brought in from abroad. He founded a college at Georgetown which soon (1815) received the title of university,[50] that American Roman Catholic youth might not need, as he had done, to go to Europe if they wished to study under the auspices of their own church. He furthered missions in various parts of his vast diocese. He encouraged the coming of missionaries from across the Atlantic. He obtained the creation of additional bishoprics, and in 1808 was himself raised to the archiepiscopate. In other words, he endeavoured to build a national church, united under the direction of a hierarchy subject only to the control of Rome. Before his death (1815) he saw important steps achieved towards the consummation of this ideal.

The four suffragan sees of the Archdiocese of Baltimore created in 1808 illustrate somewhat the expansion of Rome Catholicism during the opening years of the new nation and the elements which went into the initial stages of the church. It was to be expected that Philadelphia would be the centre of a see, for in Pennsylvania, because of the religious toleration inaugurated by its Quaker founder, had been a large proportion of the Roman Catholics at the time of independence. Both Germans and Irish had entered,[51] and a number of German Jesuits had served their fellow-countrymen.[52] However, it was not a German but an Irishman, Michael Egan, who was chosen to be the first bishop. Egan seems to have been born in Ireland. He came to America in 1802. Able to preach in German as well as in English, he

[49] For a bibliography of Carroll, see O'Donnell, op. cit., pp. 2, 3. A standard biography is Peter Guilday, The Life and Times of John Carroll Archbishop of Baltimore (1735-1815) (New York, The Encyclopedia Press, 1922, pp. xiv, 864). For a brief summary of his life, see Walsh, American Jesuits, pp. 119-133. See also Ives, op. cit., pp. 346-364.

[50] Guilday, op. cit., p. 559.

[51] Schrott, Pioneer German Catholics in the American Colonies (1734-1784), pp. 94, 95.

[52] Schrott, op. cit., pp. 35-88.

appeared in some ways peculiarly fitted for his mixed constituency. However, struggles with trusteeism and with some of his clergy brought him to an early grave.[53] In New York City, which from colonial days had given indication of its future cosmopolitan character, the first two bishops, Luke Concanen and John Connolly, were Irish, appointed, so it is said, through the influence of Irish bishops and not on nomination of Carroll.[54] In Boston a French priest, Jean-Louis Lefebvre Cheverus, a refugee from the French Revolution, was made bishop, although all New England held very few Roman Catholics. Scholarly, and a gentleman by rearing and character, he seems to have won personal respect in a community traditionally unfriendly to his church. In late middle life he returned to France, and became in time Archbishop of Bordeaux and Cardinal.[55] The fourth of the suffragan sees was at Bardstown, in Kentucky. Several Roman Catholics had been among the early settlers in Kentucky. Beginning in 1785 colonies of Roman Catholics, chiefly from Maryland, had collected there.[56] These were served by various priests, the majority of them French, most of whom were in the uncouth wilderness for only relatively short periods.[57] To the diocese was appointed a Frenchman, a Sulpician, Benedict J. Flaget.[58] In the diocese was at first included what eventually became the states of Tennessee, Kentucky, Ohio, Indiana, Illinois, Michigan, Wisconsin, and part of Minnesota.[59]

Before many years, other sees were added—Richmond in 1820,[60] Charleston in 1820,[61] Cincinnati in 1821,[62] St. Louis in 1826,[63] and New Orleans in 1826.[64] With the passing years they were augmented by still others and new

[53] *Dictionary of American Biography*, Vol. VI, p. 50.

[54] O'Gorman, *A History of the Roman Catholic Church in the United States*, pp. 291, 297. For a different account of the appointment, see Guilday, *op. cit.*, pp. 632-641.

[55] Guilday, *op. cit.*, pp. 613-625.

[56] Webb, *The Centenary of Catholicity in Kentucky*, pp. 24ff.; O'Daniel, *The Right Rev. Edward Dominic Fenwick*, pp. 66-70; Mattingly, *The Catholic Church on the Kentucky Frontier (1785-1812)*, pp. 14-36; Spalding, *Sketches of the Early Roman Catholic Missions of Kentucky*, pp. 22ff.

[57] Webb, *op. cit.*, pp. 156ff.; O'Daniel, *op. cit.*, pp. 71ff.; Guilday, *op. cit.*, pp. 688-690; Mattingly, *op. cit.*, pp. 37-69; Spalding, *op. cit.*, pp. 41ff.

[58] M. J. Spalding, *Sketches of the Life, Times, and Character of the Rt. Rev. Benedict Joseph Flaget, First Bishop of Nashville* (Louisville, Ky., Webb & Levering, 1852, pp. 405. By a successor in the see), *passim;* Spalding, *Sketches of the Early Roman Catholic Missions of Kentucky*, pp. 178ff. Webb, *op. cit.*, pp. 213ff.; Guilday, *op. cit.*, pp. 690ff.

[59] Guilday, *op. cit.*, p. 688.

[60] O'Donnell, *The Catholic Hierarchy of the United States 1790-1922*, p. 10.

[61] O'Donnell, *op. cit.*, p. 13.

[62] O'Daniel, *op. cit.*, p. 242.

[63] O'Donnell, *op. cit.*, p. 39.

[64] O'Donnell, *op. cit.*, p. 50.

archiepiscopal sees were marked out. Rome was endeavouring to keep pace with the growing nation and with the mounting Roman Catholic population by creating bishoprics as they were needed.

To the Roman Catholic Church in the United States came extensive assistance from Europe. Some of it was in men and some in money. This was needed, for the few thousands who composed the Roman Catholic body in that country in colonial days and their descendants could scarcely supply enough of either to meet the demands of the expanding population and the vast influx of immigrants. That older stock was, to be sure, the source of several notable leaders. We have noted that from it came the first bishop, John Carroll. From it also sprang the second Bishop of Boston, Benedict Joseph Fenwick;[65] the first Bishop of Cincinnati and the founder of the Dominicans in the United States, Edward Dominic Fenwick, a cousin of the second Bishop of Boston;[66] Richard Pius Miles, Dominican, early missionary in Ohio and Tennessee, and the first Bishop of Nashville;[67] and Leonard Neale, the coadjutor and successor of Carroll as Archbishop of Baltimore.[68] Yet these were too few for the huge task.

A large part of this aid from Europe was in personnel—in priests, lay brothers, and nuns. Some of the priests who arrived soon after the American Revolution are said to have been unable to work amicably with their religious superiors in Europe and to have run true to form in their new habitat, causing trouble for their bishops.[69]

Many of the foreign personnel were French. The French Revolution, especially in the anti-Christian stage which came early in its course, and with its cavalier treatment of the Church and at times its anti-clericalism, drove numbers of the clergy into exile. Some of the refugees sought shelter in the United States. The first Roman Catholic priest ordained in the United States, Stephen Theodore Badin, came in 1792 and served for many years in poverty on the Kentucky frontier.[70] In 1791 and 1792 a number of French priests arrived who were to have a large part in ecclesiastical leadership and in training an American clergy.[71] Two of the first five bishops of the young hierarchy, Cheverus of Boston and Flaget of Bardstown, were French

---

[65] O'Donnell, *op. cit.*, p. 135.

[66] O'Daniel, *op. cit., passim.*

[67] O'Daniel, *The Father of the Church in Tennessee, passim;* Minogue, *Pages from a Hundred Years of Dominican History*, p. 251.

[68] Guilday, *The Catholic Church in Virginia (1815-1822)*, pp. 1ff.

[69] Walsh, *American Jesuits*, pp. 129, 130.

[70] Spalding, *Sketches of the Early Catholic Missions of Kentucky*, pp. 55-72, 111-129; *Dictionary of American Biography*, Vol. I, pp. 488, 489.

[71] Guilday, *The Life and Times of John Carroll*, pp. 755, 756.

émigrés. Louis William Valentine DuBourg, second (or possibly third) Bishop of Louisiana and the Floridas, and the first incumbent of that see after the acquisition of its territory by the United States, was born in San Domingo, but was educated in France and was serving in that country when the storm of the French Revolution broke.[72] The third Archbishop of Baltimore, Ambrose Marechal;[73] the third Bishop of New York, John Dubois;[74] and the second Bishop of Bardstown, John Baptist Mary David,[75] were also among the *émigrés*. Of the thirty-four bishops in the American hierarchy between 1820 and 1842, thirteen were French, as against nine who were born in Ireland, six who were natives of the United States, two Belgians, one Englishman, one German, one Spaniard, and one Italian.[76] In 1791 there arrived in Baltimore a group of the Society of St. Sulpice. This body, founded in the seventeenth century, had given its chief attention to the preparation of young men for the priesthood. The contingent came to the United States through the invitation of Bishop Carroll, but the project of finding a foreign centre in which to continue the work of the organization had already been formed by the Superior of the Society.[77] Two more groups followed in 1792. The Sulpicians founded in Baltimore St. Mary's Seminary, the first of its kind in the United States, for the training of priests in the new country. In the first ten years much difficulty was encountered in obtaining students, and several of the Sulpicians were assigned to parish or missionary effort. Discouraged and annoyed, the Superior recalled some of the staff to France. But for the advice of Pope Pius VII the project would possibly have been suspended. However, it was continued, students increased, and other institutions, among them St. Mary's University, arose in connexion with the enterprise.[78] To the United States there also came, early in the century, a contingent of Trappists. Within the next few years some others of the order arrived. A monastery was founded in Kentucky, but the rigorous life imposed by the community's rule proved ill-adapted to conditions on the frontier and cost the lives of several of the members. Moved in part by

[72] Garraghan, *The Jesuits of the Middle United States*, Vol. I, pp. 36ff.; O'Donnell, *op. cit.*, p. 50.
[73] O'Donnell, *op. cit.*, p. 4.
[74] O'Donnell, *op. cit.*, p. 75.
[75] Fox, *The Life of the Right Reverend John Baptist Mary David*, pp. 1-13.
[76] Guilday, *The Life and Times of John England*, Vol. I, p. 475, n.1.
[77] Ruane, *The Beginnings of the Society of St. Sulpice in the United States (1791-1829)*, pp. 16ff.; Dilhet, *État de l'Église Catholique ou Diocèse des États-Unis de l'Amérique Septentrionale*, pp. 14-19.
[78] Ruane, *op. cit.*, pp. 37ff.; Guilday, *The Life and Times of John Carroll*, pp. 469ff.; Dionne, *Gabriel Richard*, pp. vii-xv.

these losses and by the desire for greater solitude, the monks moved to Missouri, but here again met with deaths and with almost insuperable obstacles. In 1814 and 1815 the survivors returned to France.[79] In 1848 French Trappists renewed the effort in Kentucky and with greater success. Later, too, Irish Trappists from an offshoot of a French Trappist monastery went to Iowa.[80] A few other priests of French origin were also in the country.[81] In New Orleans French Ursulines had had a convent since about 1727 and had been conducting a day-school and academy. When Louisiana passed into the hands of the United States, they remained.[82] From 1792 to 1805 a few of the Second Order of St. Francis, or Poor Clares, were in the United States and for a time had an academy for girls.[83]

With the end of the rule of Napoleon I and the re-establishment of the Bourbons in France, assistance in personnel continued to come from France. Part of this was in response to requests from French bishops who headed sees in the United States and part from the prominent rôle that the French were having in the world-wide missions of the Roman Catholic Church in the nineteenth century. Many of the American bishops were natives of France.[84] Among the French missionaries who came because of episcopal appeal were sisters of the Society of the Sacred Heart. The initial contingent arrived in 1818 on the invitation of Bishop DuBourg of New Orleans. The society spread widely and was in charge of many schools and orphanages.[85] However, very few immigrants were directly from France. Most of the French stock in the United States was either of Huguenot descent or was Canadian in its immediate provenance. Without a constituency of their own cultural background, such as furnished the natural field for priests of several other nationalities, the French clergy found difficulty in adjusting themselves to the American scene. It is not surprising, therefore, that the stream dwindled.

To serve the French Canadians in the United States, by tradition clannish and loyally Roman Catholic, many French Canadian priests came to the country. Hundreds of French Canadian sisters of several congregations conducted schools and hospitals.[86]

---

[79] Guilday, op. cit., pp. 513-516; Fox, op. cit., p. 42; Spalding, Sketches of the Early Roman Catholic Missions of Kentucky, pp. 162ff. Guilday gives 1802 as the date of arrival. Spalding says 1804.

[80] Hoffman, The Church Founders of the Northwest, pp. 259ff.

[81] For the names of some, see Dilhet, op. cit., pp. 51-55.

[82] Guilday, op. cit., pp. 479-486.

[83] Guilday, op. cit., pp. 492, 493.

[84] O'Donnell, op. cit., pp. 53, 62, 64, 66, 100, 105, 106, 141, 180, 195.

[85] Callan, The Society of the Sacred Heart in North America, passim.

[86] Bracq, The Evolution of French Canada, pp. 217-237.

Both before and after its appearance as a separate kingdom, the territory embraced in what in 1830 became Belgium was the source of important contributions to the personnel of the Roman Catholic Church in the United States. In colonial days, a number of Belgians had served as missionaries.[87] From Belgium in 1790 came Carmelite nuns, some of them American by birth, who founded a convent where they pursued the contemplative life prescribed by their rule.[88] From Belgium, too, came a priest, Charles Nerinckx, who in 1805 went to Kentucky and there long had a prominent part in caring for the Roman Catholic community.[89] In response to an appeal from Nerinckx, a number of Belgians cast in their lot with the United States. Some of these were Jesuits or came as young men to enter the Jesuit novitiate. One important contingent arrived in 1817 and another, out of the second trip of Nerinckx, in 1821.[90] It was a Belgian, Charles Felix Van Quickenborne, who became superior of a party of Jesuits who founded a centre for his Society at Florissant, not far from St. Louis.[91] For a number of years this western mission, which had a large part in efforts for the Indians and in the care of the white settlers on the Missouri and Illinois frontier, was predominantly Belgian.[92] From Belgium, too, came Dominicans to share in the pioneer missions west of the Alleghenies.[93] It was at the college of the English Dominicans at Bornheim, in Belgium, that the American-born Edward Dominic Fenwick, the first Bishop of Cincinnati, had been educated, and it was there that he had been admitted to the Order of Preachers.[94] Fenwick introduced the Dominicans to the United States, and while at least two of the three others of the original contingent were English, they had been trained in Belgium.[95] It was with this group that the great development of the Order of Preachers in the United States began. From a party of six which arrived in the United States in 1832 the American province of the Congregation of the Most Holy Redeemer, or the Redemptorists, arose.[96] From Belgium came nuns who belonged to the

[87] Griffin, *The Contribution of Belgium to the Catholic Church in America (1523-1857)*, pp. 51-62.

[88] Griffin, *op. cit.*, pp. 72-75; Guilday, *op. cit.*, pp. 486-492.

[89] Maes, *The Life of Rev. Charles Nerinckx, passim;* Spalding, *Sketches of the Early Catholic Missions of Kentucky*, pp. 130-148, 196-214; *Dictionary of American Biography*, Vol. XIII, pp. 428, 429; Griffin, *op. cit.*, pp. 97ff.

[90] Garraghan, *The Jesuits of the Middle United States*, Vol. I, pp. 13, 15-22; Griffin, *op. cit.*, pp. 84ff.

[91] Garraghan, *op. cit.*, Vol. I, pp. 22-28, 79ff.

[92] Garraghan, *op. cit.*, Vol. I, pp. 147ff.

[93] Maes, *op. cit.*, p. 147; Griffin, *op. cit.*, p. 122.

[94] O'Daniel, *The Right Rev. Edward Dominic Fenwick*, pp. 33-40.

[95] O'Daniel, *op. cit.*, pp. 99ff.; Griffin, *op. cit.*, pp. 122ff.; Minogue, *Pages from a Hundred Years of Dominican History*, pp. 31, 32.

[96] Griffin, *op. cit.*, pp. 92, 93.

Poor Clares and the Beguines.[97] In 1840, on invitation of Bishop Purcell of Cincinnati, a contingent of Sisters of Notre Dame de Namur reached the United States and began a development which was to scatter convents of that congregation and schools conducted by them from the Atlantic to the Pacific.[98] In 1854 the Xaverian Brothers, a teaching congregation, were introduced into the United States from Belgium. They spread to a number of dioceses.[99] In 1857 there was founded at Louvain what was officially known as the American College of the Immaculate Conception of the Blessed Virgin Mary. It was for the purpose of training American-born students for the priesthood in their own country and of recruiting and preparing Europeans for the dioceses of the United States. In the course of its first seventy-five years it educated over a thousand men. From among these came many missionaries and bishops.[100] Only a small percentage of the immigration to the United States was from Belgium. The Roman Catholic Church of Belgium provided a far larger proportion of the missionaries to the great republic than would have been necessary had these confined their efforts to the care of their fellow-countrymen.

It is not surprising that Ireland was the source of much of the personnel of the growing Roman Catholic Church in the United States. The majority of the Irish were ardent adherents of that branch of organized Christianity. For them that church was a symbol of their nationalism. It was the one comprehensive institution which was theirs and which their English masters, who were predominantly Protestants, did not control. From Ireland came more immigrants to the United States than from any other one country between 1820 and 1855. The overwhelming majority of these were Roman Catholics. Roman Catholic Irish had begun to arrive in colonial times and in the first few decades of the nineteenth century.[101] Clergy, brothers, and nuns of their own race were needed to keep these Irish from being lost to the Roman Catholic form of the faith. Moreover, since Ireland used the English language, in the early part of the century, Rome looked to it for priests to appoint to bishoprics

[97] Griffin, op. cit., pp. 142, 165.

[98] Helen Louise Nugent, Sister Louise (Josephine van der Schrieck (1813-1886) American Foundress of the Sisters of Notre Dame de Namur (Washington, D. C., The Catholic University of America Studies in American Church History, Vol. X, 1931, pp. ix, 352), passim; F. de Chantal, Julie Billiart and Her Institute (London, Longmans, Green and Co., 1938, pp. x, 280), pp. 206ff.; Griffin op. cit., pp. 181-186.

[99] Griffin, op. cit., pp. 187, 188.

[100] J. Van der Heyden, The Louvain American College, 1857-1907 (Louvain, F. and R. Ceuterick, 1909, pp. x, 412), passim; Griffin, op. cit., pp. 219ff. On some former students at Louvain who became bishops in the United States, see O'Donnell, The Catholic Hierarchy in the United States, 1790-1922, pp. 33, 34, 114.

[101] See, for instance, a letter of W. V. Harold in Guilday, The Life and Times of John England, Vol. I, pp. 16-21.

in the United States, especially since the Roman Catholic Church in England and Scotland was too weak to spare many and since relations between England and the United States were strained.[102] Early in the nineteenth century some of the Irish in the United States displayed a vigorous animosity against the French clergy who were then prominent in the Roman Catholic Church in that country. For a time this feeling, mixed with trusteeism, threatened to carry off many communicants in the South into a separate church which would obtain its episcopal succession through the Archbishop of Utrecht of a church in Holland which had separated from Rome in the eighteenth century.[103] Here was a further incentive to find Irish clergy and bishops. It led, in 1820, to the creation of the sees of Richmond and Charleston and to the appointment of Irish priests to fill them.[104] From Ireland arrived Richard Baker, who became the leading spirit in the seminary which the first Bishop of Charleston, John England, established for the training of clergy for his diocese.[105] A number of the priests who first came from Ireland were restive and insubordinate under ecclesiastical authority and proved most annoying to their bishops.[106] Others became capable leaders and contributed to the growth of the episcopate.[107] Some of these arrived with their preparation for the priesthood begun and completed it in the United States, thus becoming better fitted for their duties in their adopted land. However, a very large proportion of the American hierarchy who were of Irish descent either were born in the United States or arrived in infancy or boyhood with their parents. They were not missionaries from Ireland. One of the most prominent of these was John Joseph Hughes (1797-1864), the first Archbishop of New York. Forceful, a fighter, and an able administrator, he promoted the building of churches, institutions, and parochial schools, brought clergy and nuns from Europe, and became a national figure, especially in his espousal of the North in the Civil War.[108] From Ireland came nuns. For instance, Irish Ursulines arrived in 1834 for work in Charleston.[109]

It was to be expected that numbers of German missionaries would labour in the United States. In colonial days Germans, some of them Roman Catholics,

---

[102] O'Brien, John England, pp. 6, 7.
[103] Guilday, The Catholic Church in Virginia (1815-1822), passim, especially pp. 9, 91, 103; Guilday, The Life and Times of John England, Vol. I, pp. 154-156, 164ff.
[104] Guilday, The Life and Times of John England, Vol. I, pp. 283ff.
[105] Guilday, The Life and Times of John England, Vol. I, p. 498.
[106] Guilday, The Life and Times of John Carroll, pp. 757-759.
[107] For some of these see O'Donnell, The Catholic Hierarchy in the United States, 1790-1922, pp. 6, 13, 19, 23, 40, 42, 47, 59, 84, 130, 131, 132, 146, 152, 154, 156, 157.
[108] Dictionary of American Biography, Vol. IX, pp. 352-355. See this sketch for a bibliography.
[109] Guilday, The Life and Times of John England, Vol. II, pp. 143ff.

had formed a considerable proportion of the population, notably in Pennsylvania. In the nineteenth and twentieth centuries more than five millions of Germans,[110] many of them Roman Catholics, were among the immigrants to the United States. Obviously, German priests, brothers, and nuns were attracted to care for their fellow-countrymen. Some of the first of these to arrive after the independence of the United States, like some of the earliest of the Irish, gave the American bishops much trouble. To the great annoyance of Bishop Carroll, they wished separate churches for the Germans, insisted upon preaching and giving religious instruction in German, and were insubordinate when the bishop sought to amalgamate them into an inclusive American church. There was even a demand for a separate diocese for German Roman Catholics instead of the territorial episcopate such as prevailed in Europe.[111] While eventually separate churches were provided in many places for Germans,[112] for decades numbers of German immigrants proved restive under episcopal supervision and gave trouble to their priests.[113] Difficulties, too, were encountered in finding enough German priests for the German Roman Catholic settlers who lived outside the cities in rural communities.[114] In spite of the fact that German immigrants were even more numerous than the Irish and many times more so than the French, and in spite of the command of the Propaganda that the American hierarchy nominate for the episcopate in sections where Germans predominated priests of that race or who knew the German language and customs,[115] a larger proportion of the nineteenth and twentieth century episcopate were of Irish and of French than of German birth and training.[116]

Yet numbers of missionaries came from Germany and had an important part in holding the immigrant to the faith and in building the Roman Catholic Church. Some Germans were early in the Jesuit mission which had headquarters near St. Louis. Redemptorists from Vienna landed in New York in 1832 and before many years houses and parishes of that group were found in cities from New York to Buffalo and Pittsburgh. Some of them specialized on public retreats.[117] Among other German regulars who arrived were Premonstratensians; German Swiss of the Society of the Precious Blood, led by Franz Sales

---

[110] Commons, *Races and Immigrants in America,* p. 67.
[111] Guilday, *The Life and Times of John Carroll,* pp. 291-295, 723-728.
[112] Garraghan, *The Jesuits of the Middle United States,* Vol. II, pp. 25, 28, 35.
[113] Garraghan, *op. cit.,* Vol. II, pp. 46, 47.
[114] Garraghan, *op. cit.,* Vol. II, pp. 65, 66.
[115] Guilday, *A History of the Councils of Baltimore,* pp. 151, 152.
[116] O'Donnell, *op. cit., passim.* For those of German blood and European training, see O'Donnell, *op. cit.,* pp. 31, 59, 102, 153, 166, 168, 170, 171, 173.
[117] Elliott, *The Life of Father Hecker,* p. 241.

Brunner, the founder of the Swiss branch of his order; Franciscans from the Tyrol; and Boniface Wimmer, a Benedictine from Bavaria who reached America in 1846 and founded a monastery at St. Mary's between Beatty and Latrobe, Pennsylvania, which later became an arch-abbey with eleven other abbeys associated with it. There were also Bavarian Sisters of Our Lady, and German Ursulines.[118] For a time a college was maintained at Münster for training German clergy for the United States and many Germans went to the American College in Louvain to prepare for service across the Atlantic.[119] The Kulturkampf in the eighteen-seventies drove a number of German regulars to seek refuge in America.[120] In 1852 German Swiss Benedictines from Einsiedeln founded an abbey in Indiana. Benedictines from Engelberg, in Switzerland, established an abbey at Mt. Angel, Oregon.[121] In 1870 the abbeys springing from Einsiedeln and Engelberg were created an independent congregation.[122] Franciscans from Fulda formed houses at Paterson, New Jersey, and in Columbus, Ohio.[123] Franciscans of the Saxon Province arrived in 1858. In 1882 German Carmelites came to the United States, established themselves in Texas, and extended their activities to Louisiana and New Mexico.[124] In 1852, at the instance of Wimmer, who initiated the enterprise of the Bavarian Benedictines in the United States, Benedictine sisters from St. Walburg's Convent, Eichstätt, a foundation dating back to the ninth century and named for an English missionary nun, a niece of Boniface, came to the United States and made a home at St. Mary's in Pennsylvania. Here was a colony of German Roman Catholics who had fled from the persecutions of the Know Nothing movement in the cities of the Eastern seaboard and had hewn themselves homes out of the wilderness. From St. Mary's as a beginning, houses were established in several parts of the country, largely out of recruits from the United States, and were later organized into the Congregation of Saint Scholastica. Its members were chiefly engaged in teaching.[125] Thus the impulse which had come from the great English missionary to the Germans more

---

[118] For brief sketches of these various enterprises, see Engelbert Krebs, *Um die Erde*, pp. 217-238. On Wimmer and the Benedictines, see also A. Hoffmann in Timpe, *Katholisches Deutschtum in den Vereinigten Staaten von Amerika*, pp. 85-90.

[119] Roemer, *The Ludwig-Missionsverein and the Church in the United States (1838-1918)*, p. 50.

[120] Callahan, *Medieval Francis in Modern America*, pp. 168-184.

[121] Roemer, *op. cit.*, pp. 73-79.

[122] Marie, *Histoire des Institutes Religieux et Missionaires*, p. 37.

[123] Callahan, *op. cit.*, pp. 168-184, 287ff.

[124] Roemer, *op. cit.*, pp. 78-84.

[125] Mary Regina Baska, *The Benedictine Congregation of Saint Scholastica: Its Foundation and Development (1852-1930)* (Washington, D. C., The Catholic University of America Studies in American Church History, Vol. XX, 1935, pp. viii, 154), *passim*.

than a thousand years later made itself felt in a continent of which Boniface had never heard. A few of the Gesellenvereine, or Societies of Young Journeymen, begun by Kolping in the nineteenth century for the religious, moral, and intellectual improvement of young men, and which enjoyed a great vogue in Germany, were founded in America, but they did not flourish in the conditions peculiar to the New World.[126]

The groups of German regulars and nuns became centres for extension of their orders and congregations and thus for the recruiting and training of leadership. They drew from the immigrants and the children of immigrants and multiplied their houses and their numbers through accessions in the United States. They did much to strengthen the Roman Catholic Church in the United States.

The major part of the personnel from abroad which aided in holding Roman Catholic immigrants and their children to the Roman Catholic form of the Christian faith were from France, Belgium, Ireland, and Germany. However, some assistance came from several other lands. Thus Whitefield, the fourth Archbishop of Baltimore, was of English birth and education.[127] Among the hierarchy was at least one bishop who had been born and educated in Holland.[128] Another was a Pole.[129] The fourth Bishop of Savannah was Ignatius Persico, who was Italian born and trained, was transferred to the United States from India, and after about two years in America returned to his native land and died a cardinal.[130] The Lazarist provinces of Barcelona and Poland extended their activities to the United States to care respectively for the immigrants from Spain and Poland.[131] In 1867 Jesuits of the province of Naples were assigned fields in New Mexico and Colorado. There they not only were missionaries to the Indians, but also laboured among the European stock and built schools and churches.[132] In 1887 Bishop Scalabrini of Piacenza founded the Pious Society of the Missionaries of St. Charles Borromeo to train missionaries for the Italians in the United States. The following year this movement acquired a church in New York City. It soon entered several dioceses.[133] The first of the Pallotine Sisters arrived in 1889 and devoted themselves to

[126] Dexl in Timpe, op. cit., pp. 156ff.
[127] O'Donnell, The Catholic Hierarchy in the United States, 1790-1922, p. 5.
[128] O'Donnell, op. cit., p. 65.
[129] O'Donnell, op. cit., p. 169.
[130] O'Donnell, op. cit., p. 20.
[131] Coste, La Congregation de la Mission, pp. 226-228.
[132] La Missioné di Galle nell' isola di Ceylan (India) affidata ai Padri della Provincia di Napoli della Compagnia di Gesù (Naples, Procura delle Missioni, 1925, pp. 36), p. 4.
[133] Cullen, The Catholic Church in Rhode Island, pp. 362-364.

the Italians on the east side of New York.[134] They later spread widely. Italian Franciscans also served in the United States.[135]

These examples by no means exhaust the list of the contributions in personnel which the Roman Catholic Church in the United States owed to Europe. They may suffice, however, to give some hint of the large number of priests who served as missionaries, and of the many orders and congregations of monks and nuns which were introduced by devoted contingents from the Old World who braved the discomforts and difficulties of an alien environment to help build their church into the life of the new nation.

From Europe, too, came financial assistance. It was to be expected that the Society for the Propagation of the Faith would contribute largely to extending the Roman Catholic Church in the United States, for the organization owed its inception in part to the appeal of Bishop DuBourg of New Orleans for aid for his diocese.[136] In the very first year of the society, $2,757.20 were sent to the United States. From then until 1914 a total of more than six million dollars was given to various dioceses. The largest sum apportioned in any one year was $173,623.80, in 1859. However, even though in time the Roman Catholics of the United States became substantial and eventually the largest contributors to the society, and although beginning with 1891 each year gave more than they received, subventions from the society continued down to 1914 and even beyond that date.[137] The Ludwig-Missionsverein had been founded in Bavaria in part at the instance of Bishop Rese of Detroit, who was soliciting funds in Austria and Bavaria for his diocese. In its earliest years it made the United States its chief beneficiary.[138] From 1844 to 1916 it gave a total of nearly one million dollars. However, the proportion of the society's income devoted to the United States declined from 60 per cent. in 1846 to about 2 per cent. in 1913.[139] Much of this subvention went to the assistance of German Roman Catholic enterprises, for the complaint was made that the Society for the Propagation of the Faith, by making its appropriations through the bishops, worked to the disadvantage of German immigrants. The bishops, so it was said, withheld aid from some Germans, seeking to compel them to join English-speaking parishes and thus to hasten the erasure of racial and national lines in the Ameri-

[134] Cullen, op. cit., p. 407.
[135] Callahan, Medieval Francis in Modern America, pp. 61-70; O'Connell, Recollections of Seventy Years, pp. 306-309.
[136] Hickey, The Society for the Propagation of the Faith, pp. 18ff.
[137] Hickey, op. cit., p. 153; Freri, The Society for the Propagation of the Faith and the Catholic Missions, pp. 27-29.
[138] Roemer, The Ludwig-Missionsverein and the Church in the United States (1838-1918), p. 13.
[139] Roemer, op. cit., pp. 138, 139.

can church. On the other hand, the countercharge was raised that by giving directly to priests rather than through the bishops, the Ludwig-Missionsverein was encouraging the clergy to be independent of the episcopate.[140]

These financial subsidies from Europe aroused much apprehension in the United States outside Roman Catholic circles. It was asserted that although ostensibly for religious purposes they were in fact tools used by designing European monarchs to undermine republican institutions in the United States.[141] With the decline of the appropriations and the decrease of anti-Roman Catholic sentiment, the suspicions faded.

An interesting development from one phase of this financial assistance brought irritating perplexity to the American hierarchy. In 1871, under the leadership of a merchant, Cahensly, and at the instance of Franziska Schervier, the foundress of the Sisters of St. Francis of Aachen, the Raphaelsverein (the Archangel Raphael Society) was organized to aid German immigrants. It sought primarily their religious welfare.[142] In the course of time, the society, with Cahensly as its outstanding figure, vigorously advocated a method of affording spiritual care to the immigrants which would take account of their hereditary languages and national loyalties. For this the society found backing in several nations of Europe, including notably Italy and France. In 1890 and 1891 petitions were presented to Rome declaring that by ignoring these national differences millions of immigrants were being lost to the Roman Catholic Church and advocating, as a remedy, that parishes and missions be set up for the several nationalities, that each of these be entrusted to priests of the appropriate race, that in the parochial schools instruction be entirely in the language of the parents, that church societies be grouped according to nationality, and that in each diocese the bishop be appointed from whichever group was in the majority. This programme would have tended to make the church an agent for perpetuating Old World loyalties and divisions. It was viewed with apprehension by non-Roman Catholics and was hailed by the enemies of the church as confirmation of their reiterated charge that Roman Catholicism was hostile to the basic institutions of the United States. The hierarchy, led by Cardinal Gibbons, Archbishop of Baltimore, opposed it, and Rome decided against it.[143]

---

[140] Roemer, *op. cit.*, pp. 17-28.

[141] Theodore Roemer, *The Leopoldine Foundation and the Church in the United States (1829-1839)* (New York, United States Catholic Historical Society Monograph Series XIII, 1933, pp. 143-211), p. 204; Goodykoontz, *Home Missions on the American Frontier* pp. 224ff.

[142] Krebs, *Um die Erde*, pp. 210-216.

[143] Will, *Life of Cardinal Gibbons*, Vol. I, pp. 498ff.

Although the American hierarchy, supported by Rome, set its face against the perpetuation of Old World groupings in the United States, these could not quickly be eliminated. Immigrants tended to settle by nationalities in the same sections of cities or rural districts. At least for the first generation, until assimilation could be completed, many parishes were made up predominantly of communicants of a particular race and language. Thus in 1917 320 parishes were said to be primarily of Czechs, although a few of these included other nationalities.[144] In Texas, which had the largest number of these Czech parishes, a Bohemian Catholic Alliance and a Catholic Union of Bohemian Men were reported.[145] In 1856, the Salesianum was founded near Milwaukee to train German-speaking priests for the service of German immigrants.[146] These are only a few scattered examples of what was for long and almost inevitably a feature of the Roman Catholic Church in the United States.

This brings us to another series of means by which the Roman Catholic immigrants were held to their faith—the part which immigrants and their descendants played in making provision for their own care. Large as was the aid received from Europe, leadership and financial means for the expansion of the Roman Catholic Church in the United States came increasingly and predominantly from that country itself. We have noted the fact that from the small Roman Catholic community which emerged from colonial days were derived several of the early bishops, including the first two heads of the hierarchy. Early in the life of the new nation, steps were taken to train a native clergy. Although St. Mary's Seminary, manned by the Sulpicians, at first attracted disappointingly few students, the institution survived the disheartened recall of some of its first staff and prepared, among others, the future Cardinal Gibbons, the American-born son of Irish immigrants.[147] By 1822 at least eight colleges had been established in the United States in which the philosophical and theological education necessary for ordination to the priesthood could be obtained.[148] Some Americans, mostly of Irish descent, were trained in the Urban College of the Propaganda at Rome.[149] Dissatisfied with the French temper of the education given at St. Mary's Seminary, Bishop England of Charleston developed his own diocesan institution.[150] With the aid of Franciscans from Rome, the first Bishop of Buffalo began a diocesan seminary.[151]

[144] Čapek, *The Čechs (Bohemians) in America*, pp. 246, 247.
[145] Hudson, *Czech Pioneers of the Southwest*, pp. 198-210; Čapek, *op. cit.*, p. 247.
[146] Roemer, *The Ludwig-Missionsverein and the Church in the United States*, p. 49.
[147] Will, *op. cit.*, Vol. I, pp. 37, 38.
[148] Guilday, *The Life and Times of John England*, Vol. I, p. 483.
[149] Guilday, *op. cit.*, Vol. I, p. 477; Bell, *Rebel, Priest and Prophet*, pp. 7, 8.
[150] Guilday, *op. cit.*, Vol. I, pp. 476ff.
[151] Callahan, *Medieval Francis in Modern America*, pp. 30-39.

In 1884 Archbishop Williams of Boston opened a seminary and, in default of competent help from his own diocese, entrusted it to the Sulpicians.[152] In 1859, with the cordial endorsement and substantial assistance of Pope Pius IX, the American College was opened at Rome for the preparation of priests for the United States. It had the backing of the American hierarchy and funds for it came from many dioceses.[153] By 1900 the number of major seminaries in the United States, namely those giving young men direct preparation for the priesthood, had risen to thirty-seven and by 1924 to seventy-nine.[154] Of preparatory seminaries, those fitting students for the major seminaries, in 1915 the United States contained thirty-four, eleven of them diocesan and twenty-three maintained by sixteen different religious orders.[155] Increasingly priests were emerging from among American-born Roman Catholics and were receiving their education in the United States. Many theological students went to Rome, to various institutions in that city, but in that they were simply following the practice of their fellows from other nations. The Roman Catholic Church in the United States was more and more producing its own leadership.

American Roman Catholics were entering religious orders. Many orders and congregations which had been founded in Europe established houses in the United States. The original contingents were foreign but later growth was chiefly by accessions from the United States. In several instances this was very rapid.

In the United States, moreover, new orders and congregations came into being. As early as 1805 Charles Nerinckx, a pioneer priest in Kentucky, began planning for a religious community of women.[156] This took form under the name of the Friends of Mary at the Foot of the Cross.[157] The sisters found part of their occupation in teaching. Headquarters were established at Loretto, Kentucky, and it was by the name of Loretto that the society was usually known. Approval was obtained at Rome in 1916.[158] It was also early in the nineteenth century that a convert to Roman Catholicism, a widow, Elizabeth Ann Bayley Seton, founded the Sisters of Charity at Emmitsburg, Maryland. They also gave themselves to teaching.[159] In Kentucky, in 1812, partly on the

[152] O'Connell, *Recollections of Seventy Years*, pp. 285-287.

[153] Callahan, *op. cit.*, p. 45; *The Catholic Encyclopedia*, Vol. I, pp. 423, 424.

[154] *Catholic Colleges and Schools in the United States. Major Seminaries. Preparatory Seminaries*, p. 5.

[155] *Catholic Colleges and Schools in the United States. Major Seminaries. Preparatory Seminaries*, p. 15.

[156] Maes, *The Life of Rev. Charles Nerinckx*, pp. 135, 136.

[157] Maes, *op. cit.*, pp. 238-251.

[158] Maes, *op. cit.*, p. 304.

[159] Mary Agnes McCann, *The History of Mother Seton's Daughters. The Sisters of Charity of Cincinnati, Ohio, 1809-1917* (New York, Longmans, Green and Co., 2 vols., 1917), *passim*; Fox, *The Life of Bishop David*, pp. 26ff.

initiative of Bishop David of Bardstown, the Society of the Sisters of Nazareth was inaugurated. Its first members were of pre-Revolutionary American stock.[160] In 1822, at the instance of the head of the American province of Dominicans, the Congregation of St. Mary Magdalen, after 1851 renamed the Society of St. Catherine of Siena, was founded. Its first mother superior was of an old Maryland family. Its chief functions were teaching. Until 1888 it was confined to Kentucky and adjoining states.[161] Thus, in the early days of the republic, religious organizations were arising spontaneously out of native Roman Catholic stock which took their place in the spread of the faith in the United States.

By far the larger part of the money required for the building and the maintenance of the Roman Catholic Church and its many institutions in the United States was contributed not from Europe but from the United States itself. The immigrants and their children were the chief source of the financial undergirding of their church. This was in spite of the penury of the great majority of the immigrants upon their arrival. The newcomers were overwhelmingly from the lower economic strata of their various countries. Many of the Irish were fleeing from actual famine. It was the dream of bettering their lot in the material goods of life which drew them to the New World. Once in the United States, most of them became unskilled labourers who hired themselves to factory and mine owners and to those who built canals and railways. A substantial minority settled on the soil, but at the outset had to hew their farms out of the frontier wilderness. Here and there a few early acquired wealth and gave generously of it to their church.[162] The majority contributed out of their poverty. It is striking evidence of their religious conviction and of the fashion in which their faith had become an integral part of their lives that, coming as most of them did from lands in which the Roman Catholic Church had state support, was well equipped with buildings, and was maintained by endowments or public taxation, they voluntarily gave out of their small incomes to construct churches, monasteries, orphanages, and schools, and to maintain their clergy.

One of the striking phases of this willingness of the immigrants to pay for the perpetuation of their faith was the system of schools which the Roman Catholic Church developed. Unlike Protestants, who in building educational

[160] Fox, op. cit., pp. 67-75, 128-134; Spalding, Sketches of the Early Catholic Missions of Kentucky, pp. 229-241; Webb, The Centenary of Catholicity in Kentucky, pp. 245ff.
[161] Minogue, Pages from a Hundred Years of Dominican History, passim.
[162] See, as one instance of this, Nicholas Devereux, Irish immigrant, who became a wealthy banker in Utica, New York, and gave so generously of time and money that he was called "the father of Catholicity in Western New York."—Callahan, Medieval Francis in Modern America, pp. 16-27.

institutions under church auspices stressed secondary and higher schools and as time passed left primary education to the state, the Roman Catholics, while not omitting secondary schools, colleges, and theological seminaries, emphasized parochial schools. They feared the state schools, for in a land where many different religious groups were present and where no one church was established by law, these were perforce religiously neutral and more and more omitted religious exercises and instruction in religion. Roman Catholics believed that the Christian religion should be an integral part of education and that unless adequate provision was made for it in the curriculum their children would be lost to the faith. They therefore were willing to pay for schools under the control of their church. Usually this involved a double burden, for part of the taxes which they paid to the state went towards the support of the state ("public") schools, and in addition they contributed to their own schools. In a few instances, in communities which were overwhelmingly Roman Catholic, the public school was in effect the parochial school, but this was the exception.

The Roman Catholic school system expanded to meet the rising tide of immigration. Even in colonial days the Roman Catholics had had schools, not only in areas then under the control of governments friendly to the church, but also in the Thirteen Colonies.[163] After independence, Roman Catholic schools began to show a growth. Notable was the contribution of Gabriel Richard, a French Sulpician, who in 1798 was placed in charge of an area which included Detroit. At that time the scanty white population was overwhelmingly French and Roman Catholic and he developed a system of education from primary through secondary grades and had teachers trained for it.[164] Congregations which early came into existence or were introduced from Europe and which we have noted in earlier paragraphs inaugurated or were placed in charge of schools. Between 1812 and 1818 nineteen elementary schools, ten of which were conducted by Sisters of Charity, were established in the Archdiocese of Baltimore.[165] It is said that by 1840 there were at least two hundred parish schools, over half of them west of the Allegheny Mountains.[166] Much of the conduct of these was in the hands of religious communities of women, of which there were then thirteen.[167] After 1840 numbers of other

[163] Burns, *The Principles, Origin and Establishment of the Catholic School System in the United States*, pp. 39-165.

[164] Burns, *op. cit.*, pp. 179-198.

[165] Burns, *op. cit.*, p. 258.

[166] Burns, *The Growth and Development of the Catholic School System in the United States*, p. 19.

[167] Burns, *op. cit.*, p. 22.

teaching congregations of men and women were introduced from Europe.[168] Before the systems of free non-sectarian state schools were developed in the various states, Roman Catholic schools, along with those maintained by other religious bodies, often shared in the public funds. This was true for a time in Lowell, Massachusetts,[169] in some of the states of the Middle West,[170] and in New York City.[171] As free public schools increased, however, these grants were usually withdrawn. In New York City, in the early part of the 1840's, Bishop Hughes led in what proved to be a futile fight for state subsidies for denominational schools.[172] In 1884 the Third Plenary Council, following the spirit of instructions from Rome,[173] commanded that a parochial school be erected near each church, and that with certain authorized exceptions Roman Catholic parents send their children to these schools.[174] The Third Plenary Council also ordered that diocesan school boards be organized and that normal schools be erected.[175] Partly as a consequence, in 1910 parish schools were reported to have an enrollment of 1,237,251 pupils under about 31,000 teachers.[176] Yet by no means all parishes possessed schools. For instance, in Connecticut in 1890 only 27 per cent. had them and in 1910 only 44 per cent.[177] Secondary schools also multiplied.[178] In 1915 these had an enrollment of nearly seventy-five thousand.[179] Colleges and universities were founded. The Third Plenary Council decided to establish the Catholic University of America, but higher education had been begun earlier and higher educational institutions continued to be founded later. In 1838 15 colleges for men were listed and in 1921 130 universities and colleges.[180] It was to this system of schools, making religious

[168] Burns, op. cit., pp. 35-122.
[169] Burns, The Principles, Origin and Establishment of the Catholic School System in the United States, pp. 285-290.
[170] Burns, op. cit., p. 360.
[171] Burns, op. cit., pp. 360, 361.
[172] Burns, op. cit., pp. 362-374.
[173] Burns, The Growth and Development of the Catholic School System of the United States, pp. 183-189.
[174] Burns, op. cit., pp. 189, 190; Guilday, A History of the Councils of Baltimore, p. 238.
[175] Burns, op. cit., pp. 191-196; Guilday, op. cit., p. 238.
[176] Burns, op. cit., p. 216.
[177] Arthur J. Hefferman, A History of Catholic Education in Connecticut (Washington, D. C., The Catholic Education Press, 1937, pp. 186), p. 137.
[178] On secondary schools, see Edmund J. Goebel, A Study of Catholic Secondary Education during the Colonial Period Up to the First Plenary Council of Baltimore, 1852 (New York, Benziger Brothers, 1937, pp. xii, 269), passim; William E. North, Catholic Education in Southern California (Washington, D. C., The Catholic University of America, 1936, pp. viii, 227), passim.
[179] Catholic Colleges and Schools in the United States. High Schools and Academies. Elementary Schools. National Summary (Washington, D. C., National Catholic Welfare Conference, 1936, pp. 21), p. 6.
[180] Catholic Colleges and Schools in the United States. Universities and Colleges. Normal Schools (Washington, D. C., National Catholic Welfare Conference, 1936, pp. 26), p. 7; O'Connell, Recollections of Seventy Years, p. 157.

instruction an integral part of the educational programme and developed through the sacrifices of clergy, teachers, and laity, that much of the growth and life of the church must be ascribed. .

Another method by which the immigrant was held to the Roman Catholic faith, but one by no means so extensive as the schools, was colonies of Roman Catholics. These were fairly numerous and were found in several of the Northern states. They were made up of groups who bought lands in the same vicinity and for the most part were farmers. Here and there were colonies which migrated together from Europe with priests as leaders.[181] More seem to have been made up of those who came from the cities and from longer settled Eastern states. Numbers had priests as organizers or heads.[182] Many of the settlers were seeking to escape the strong anti-Roman Catholic feeling which at times rendered life disagreeable in several of the larger cities.[183] Sometimes the colony did not have a religious purpose. It was formed by those of the same nationality who were brought together by their common background. Being traditionally Roman Catholics, the settlers would be sought out by the church and the fact that they constituted an incipient community facilitated developing them into a parish.[184] Being in groups, they were more readily reached and held for the church than if they had been isolated individuals.

Several of the Uniate churches of the Roman Catholic communion were represented in the United States. These required specialized methods and their own clergy.

Prominent among them were the Ruthenians, chiefly from what in the nineteenth century was the Austro-Hungarian Empire. They were from both north and south of the Carpathians and were divided into a number of groups. With Slavonic as the language of their church services, with a married parish clergy, and with such customs as the administration of confirmation by the priest immediately after baptism and the giving of the communion in both kinds to the laity, they differed markedly from Roman Catholics of the Latin rite. They began coming to the United States in large numbers about 1879 and 1880 and at first went chiefly to Pennsylvania as labourers in the coal mines. In the years 1905 to 1908 inclusive, more than two hundred thousand of them arrived. By 1908 those of the Greek Catholic, or Ruthenian rite in the United States totalled not far from four hundred thousand. Over half were in Penn-

---

[181] Kelly, *Catholic Immigrant Colonization Projects in the United States, 1815-1860*, pp. 116, 190, describes one of these.

[182] Kelly, *op. cit.*, pp. 108-115; Martin, *The Catholic Church on the Nebraska Frontier (1854-1885)*, pp. 28-31.

[183] Kelly, *op. cit.*, pp. 119ff.

[184] Kelly, *op. cit.*, p. 65.

sylvania. With their peculiar ecclesiastical traditions, they were out of place in the usual Roman Catholic parish in the United States, with its Latin rite. In 1885, at the request of some of them, a married priest of their own rite, Ivan Volanski, was sent them by the head of the Ukrainian church in Galicia. In spite of opposition from the celibate Roman Catholic clergy, in his three years in the United States he travelled extensively, organizing churches and co-operative stores. Other priests followed. Many of these were unworthy, seeking to make money off their flocks. In 1907 a bishop, Stephan Ortinsky, was appointed. Energetic and hard-working, he brought many of the churches under his control and gave forceful leadership. By 1909 140 churches had come into being, served by a bishop and 118 priests. Divided into a number of groups, the Ruthenians were by no means united in spirit. Rome required that no married men be ordained in the United States and that confirmation be administered by a bishop. These innovations and the efforts of Bishop Ortinsky to establish his authority aroused resentment and from time to time groups of the Ruthenians went over to the Russian Orthodox Church.[185]

About 1900 Roumanian Uniates began arriving in the United States in fairly large numbers. In 1904 a priest of their own number was sent them from Europe.[186] Eventually additional priests came who were trained in Blaj, in Transylvania, and in Rome, and churches, schools, publications, and social organizations were developed.[187]

With the South Italian immigration came several thousand whose traditional ecclesiastical language was Greek. Most of them settled in New York and Philadelphia and were being rapidly lost to the church. In 1904 a priest of their own rite was sent them. He established for them a number of mission stations.[188]

Before the close of the nineteenth century Melchites, whose religious services were in Arabic, were arriving from Syria. In 1891 the Patriarch of Antioch sent them a priest and by 1909 there were twelve churches for them.[189]

We hear, too, of Maronites, subject to their own chorepiskopoi,[190] of a few Chaldeans (Nestorian Uniates),[191] and of Syrians (drawn from the Jacobites).[192]

[185] The Catholic Encyclopedia, Vol. VI, pp. 744-750; Attwater, The Catholic Eastern Churches, pp. 86, 94; Halich, Ukrainians in the United States, pp. 98ff.
[186] The Catholic Encyclopedia, Vol. VI, p. 750; Attwater, op. cit., p. 105.
[187] Galitzi, A Study of Assimilation among the Roumanians in the United States, pp. 99, 100.
[188] The Catholic Encyclopedia, Vol. VI, p. 752; Attwater, op. cit., p. 74.
[189] The Catholic Encyclopedia, Vol. VI, p. 751; Attwater, op. cit., p. 115.
[190] Attwater, op. cit., p. 188.
[191] Attwater, op. cit., p. 232.
[192] Attwater, op. cit., p. 168.

In the United States the Roman Catholic Church was not only more diversified racially than in any one country in Europe. It also contained more different rites than any one European land or city except Rome. Into it flowed streams from almost every branch of the Roman Catholic Church. It was more inclusive than any national church had ever been.

The Roman Catholic Church effected gains from those who did not traditionally belong to it. Converts were made, both from the older American stock and from the newer immigration. Thus William Tyler, the first Bishop of Hartford, was from an old New England Protestant family.[193] As we have seen, the foundress of the Sisters of Charity, Mrs. Seton, was a convert. James Kent Stone, a clergyman of the Protestant Episcopal Church and successively president of Kenyon and Hobart Colleges, became a priest and joined the Passionist order.[194] Orestes A. Brownson (1803-1876), whose pilgrimage of faith had led him from Presbyterianism into the Universalist and then into the Unitarian ministry, and whose vigorous pen had made him known as a pronounced social and intellectual liberal, in his early forties became a Roman Catholic and was noted as a trenchant advocate of that form of the Christian faith.[195] Partly through the influence of Brownson, Isaac Thomas Hecker, a scion of German immigrant stock, who had been connected with a radical workingman's party and had participated in that famous adventure in utopian living, Brook Farm, became a Roman Catholic. After study abroad he was ordained priest. He returned to the United States as a Redemptorist missionary. He later had differences with his superiors which led to his exclusion from the order, but with a small group of like-minded friends he then formed the Missionary Priests of St. Paul the Apostle, usually better known as the Paulists. Through this new community Hecker endeavoured to adapt Roman Catholicism to the American environment. To this end the Paulists were at first made up largely of American converts separated from the control of European superiors, and he assisted in introducing congregational singing. The Paulists were active as missionaries, and Hecker himself became one of the foremost advocates of Roman Catholicism through the public platform and the press.[196] Numbers of children from Protestant families studied in Roman Catholic schools.[197] One estimate, by a Roman Catholic, declares that in the ninety years ending in 1910 not far from six hundred thousand converts

[193] O'Donnell, The Catholic Hierarchy in the United States, 1790-1922, p. 138.
[194] Graves, Annals of the Osage Mission, p. 24.
[195] Arthur M. Schlesinger, Jr., Orestes A. Brownson. A Pilgrim's Progress (Boston, Little, Brown and Co., 1939, pp. 320. Very well done), passim.
[196] Walter Elliott, The Life of Father Hecker, passim.
[197] Goodykoontz, Home Missions on the American Frontier, p. 362.

were made by his church in the United States.[198] Presumably many of these had come through marriages of Roman Catholics with non-Roman Catholics and through the insistence of the church (not always successfully enforced) that such marriages were not permissible unless the non-Roman Catholic became a Roman Catholic. Even if this estimate is accepted as accurate—and being made by a Roman Catholic it probably leans to the side of optimism—probably not much more than two per cent. of the total number of Roman Catholics in 1910 were converts. Compared with the total population of the country and with the membership of Protestant churches, relatively few were made. The Roman Catholic Church in the United States had its phenomenal growth primarily through its success in retaining its hold on immigrants already of its faith and through the high birth rate among its adherents.

Much of the achievement of the Roman Catholic Church in meeting the problems presented by immigration must be ascribed to the comprehensive organization effected through the episcopate. The territorial episcopate, developed in the Roman Empire and characteristic of the Roman Catholic Church, was extended to the United States. As soon as conditions warranted and usually ahead of the flood tide of settlement, an episcopal see was created for a frontier region or a rising city. Although here and there concessions were made to the nationality of the immigrants and in some regions bishops tended to be of the same tongue and blood as the major immigrant stock,[199] in general the objective was a national church within the great Roman Catholic family. Programmes which would have continued in perpetuity the national and racial divisions of Europe were frowned upon. Out of the bewildering diversity and the sharply conflicting traditions brought by an immigration from every Roman Catholic group in Europe and from several of those of Asia and Africa, a unified church was progressively developed and, when the obstacles are considered, with amazing rapidity. This achievement was in part due to the solvent American atmosphere which rapidly assimilated alien elements and placed on them a uniform, if at the outset a superficial stamp. It was also facilitated by the comprehensive hierarchy.

Much, too, of the success of the Roman Catholic Church must be ascribed to the supervision and control exercised by Rome. Through the Papacy and the organs through which it functioned, plans could be made for an inclusive

[198] Shaughnessy, *Has the Immigrant Kept the Faith?*, p. 189. For some of the converts made by Nerinckx, see Spalding, *Sketches of the Early Catholic Missions of Kentucky*, p. 199.

[199] In Milwaukee, Wisconsin, for example, the centre of a large German population, archbishops were mostly of Bavarian, Austrian, or German Swiss stock.—O'Donnell, *op. cit.*, pp. 166, 167.

effort to build a church from the vast and inchoate hordes of immigrants. Rome was a court to which conflicts between strong leaders and the recurring clashes between nationalities could and, if they were not otherwise composed, must be referred. Rome was a unifying agency without which coherence would probably not have been attained. Up to 1908 Rome exercised this control chiefly through the Congregation for the Propagation of the Faith.[200] Until then the United States was regarded as a mission field. When, in 1908, only six years before the outbreak of the great war which marked the subsidence of the immigrant flood, the United States was removed from the jurisdiction of the Propaganda, the act was a symbol that the missionary stage had passed and that the Roman Catholic Church in the land was approaching maturity. No longer was the major problem the newly arriving immigrant.

In the main, the Roman Catholic Church had successfully met the challenge presented to it by the nineteenth century immigration to the United States. That it had not retained the allegiance of all those traditionally of its fold was indisputable. Some took advantage of freedom from Old World traditions and restrictions to break with the church. Some wandered off into indifference, absorbed in making a living in a new land or lured by the rush for wealth. As one instance picked at random, in a town in Nebraska in which about a third were of Czech and presumably for the most part of Roman Catholic ancestry, more than two-thirds reported that they had no church connexion.[201] It is said that a larger proportion of the Czechs abandoned Roman Catholicism than of any other traditionally Roman Catholic national group.[202] As we are to see in a few moments, many Roman Catholics became Protestants. Surprisingly few lasting schisms took members away from the church. Of these one of the most important numerically was the Polish National Catholic Church of America which came into being in 1904 through discontent with the power exercised by the priesthood over laymen.[203] Yet its size was inconsiderable. In 1916 it had only 28,245 and in 1926 only 61,574 members.[204] Several thousand of the Ruthenian Uniates went over to the Orthodox Church.[205] The Old Catholic movements of Europe, eighteenth and nineteenth century secessions from the Roman Catholic Church, spread to the

[200] Shaughnessy, op. cit., p. 177.

[201] Kutak, The Story of a Bohemian-American Village, p. 41.

[202] Morse, Home Missions Today and Tomorrow, p. 126.

[203] U. S. Department of Commerce, Bureau of the Census, Religious Bodies: 1926, Vol. II, pp. 1108, 1109.

[204] U. S. Department of Commerce, Bureau of the Census, Religious Bodies: 1926, Vol. II, p. 1106.

[205] Theophilus, A Short History of the Christian Church and the Ritual of the Eastern Orthodox Church, pp. 31, 32.

United States, partly by immigration, partly through missionaries. It was not until the twentieth century that they took definite form, with their own episcopate. They were divided into several churches, none of them with more than ten thousand members in 1916.[206] In the main, however, the Roman Catholic Church, while winning comparatively few who were not traditionally of its flock, seems to have retained the allegiance of the large majority of the immigrants who in Europe had been in its fold.[207]

In 1900 the Roman Catholic Church in the United States claimed about twelve millions and in 1910 over sixteen millions.[208] From being one of the smaller denominations in 1783, it had become the largest. It had equipped itself with churches, clergy, and schools. Most of the funds for this spectacular growth had been obtained not from Europe but from the immigrants and their children. Increasingly the clergy were of American birth and training. Here was a religious body, strongly entrenched in the affections of millions of Americans, supported by the voluntary gifts of its members, and manned by its own clergy drawn chiefly from its own ranks. It was largely a spontaneous movement arising out of religious conviction. It is not surprising that when, in 1914, the subsidence of the flood of immigration gave it leisure for other tasks it rapidly rose to an important rôle in spreading the Roman Catholic form of the faith in other lands.

To the United States came immigrants who traditionally were members of one or another of the Eastern churches. Many of them remained true to their faith. Through them still other forms of historic Christianity were added to the varieties of Protestantism and to Roman Catholicism. Through them the Christianity of the United States eventually included not only the types which prevailed in Western Europe, but also most of those of the East.

Of the Eastern communions, the one most numerously represented in the United States was the Orthodox Church, that which originally had had as its ranking ecclesiastic the Œcumenical Patriarch of Constantinople. Within this communion national churches had developed, especially after the subjugation of the Byzantine Empire in the fifteenth century and after the emergence in the nineteenth century of various nationalities in the Balkans from under

---

[206] U. S. Department of Commerce, Bureau of the Census, *Religious Bodies: 1926*, Vol. II, pp. 688-693, 1069ff.

[207] Shaughnessy, *op. cit., passim.* See chart based upon Shaughnessy in Weigle, *American Idealism*, p. 168.

[208] Shaughnessy, *op. cit.*, p. 251. The Bureau of the Census of the United States Government gave the number of baptized members in 1906 as 14,210,755 and in 1916 as 15,721,815.—U. S. Department of Commerce, Bureau of the Census, *Religious Bodies: 1926*, Vol. II, p. 1257.

the Turkish yoke and, accordingly, from the control of the Turkish-dominated Greek clergy. Adherents of several of these national churches migrated to the United States and in time organized congregations of their own.

It was to be expected that the Russian would be the first of the Orthodox churches to be represented in the United States. Beginning with the second half of the eighteenth century, Russians had penetrated to Alaska. With them had come missionaries.[209] In 1840, by order of the Holy Synod, the four churches and eight chapels then existing in Russian America were organized into a huge diocese which included Okhotsk and Kamchatka, and at its head was placed John Veniaminoff who sixteen years before had come to Unalaska and had been a zealous missionary to the Aleuts and the Kaloshs. So able was he that he was later called to Siberia and then recalled to Russia, and died as Metropolitan of Moscow.[210] During the American Civil War a Russian fleet was on the Pacific Coast and its chaplains served Russians, Serbs, and Greeks in San Francisco.[211] When in 1867 Alaska was sold to the United States, the Russian Government withdrew its support of the church in that territory, but in 1870 a diocese for Alaska and the Aleutian Islands was organized and the Holy Synod appointed for it a bishop who was to have jurisdiction over all of North America.[212] In 1872 the bishop transferred his residence from Sitka to San Francisco.[213] Until after 1914 this Russian Orthodox bishopric had ecclesiastical jurisdiction over all the Orthodox of all nationalities in North America.[214] From 1891 to 1898 there was at the head of this diocese a man of marked vigour, Bishop Nicholas. Under him parishes were inaugurated in several states. During these years many of the Ruthenian Uniates, whose ancestors had been Orthodox, irked by uncongenial conditions in the Roman Catholic Church in the United States, returned to the Orthodox fold.[215] The Holy Synod is said to have sent several thousand dollars a year for the support of the Russian mission, and financial aid is also said to have been given by a Russian missionary society.[216]

Roumanians came to the United States, and where they settled in groups they organized societies for social purposes and mutual aid. Through these

[209] Vol. III, p. 370.

[210] Bancroft, *History of Alaska*, pp. 699-710; Theophilus, *op. cit.*, p. 30.

[211] Theophilus, *op. cit.*, p. 31.

[212] *Ibid.*

[213] *Ibid.*

[214] Theophilus, *op. cit.*, p. 34.

[215] Theophilus, *op. cit.*, pp. 31, 32; Smirnoff, *A Short Account of the Historical Development and Present Position of Russian Orthodox Missions in North America*, pp. 77-79.

[216] Jerome Davis, *The Russian Immigrant* (New York, The Macmillan Co., 1922, pp. xv, 219), p. 91.

societies requests were sent to Transylvania for priests and parishes were initiated. The first priest is said to have arrived in 1902 and the first Roumanian parish is reported to have been organized in 1904.[217] Conflicts developed between clergy and laity, for the former sought to exercise over the communities the kind of control which they had wielded in Europe and the latter believed that since they paid the priests' salaries the clergy should be at their command. It was not until after 1918 that a better type of clergy arrived and that conditions improved.[218]

Beginning about 1890 Greek immigration became important and up to 1914 increased rapidly.[219] In the early part of the 1890's Greek societies were organized in New York and Chicago which sent to Greece for priests. Parishes were formed and with funds raised by the immigrants, church buildings were bought or erected. The church was usually the centre of Greek community life. Several of the priests were of inferior quality and had come to the United States to make money. Each congregation managed its own affairs.[220] Priests were sent by the Holy Synod of Greece and by the Œcumenical Patriarch of Constantinople, but in 1908 the latter resigned to the former his ecclesiastical relations to the Greeks in America and until 1922 did not seek to resume them. It was only after 1914 that a Greek bishop was sent to the United States.[221]

Late in the nineteenth and early in the twentieth century, several thousand Syrians, many of whom were of the Orthodox faith, came to the United States. To minister to them there arrived a priest, Raphael Hawawiny, who had been educated in a Russian school in Damascus and in the clerical academy at Kiev. He founded parishes in a number of cities and built a cathedral in Brooklyn which was dedicated in 1902. He put himself under the Russian bishop and in 1904 the Holy Synod of Russia made him a vicar-bishop for Orthodox Syrians and Arabs.[222]

After the drastic and bloody suppression by the Turks of the Macedonian insurrection of 1903, several thousand Bulgars sought refuge in the United States. It was only slowly that steps were taken for their ecclesiastical care.[223]

[217] Galitzi, A Study of Assimilation among the Roumanians in the United States, p. 94.
[218] Galitzi, op. cit., pp. 95, 96.
[219] U. S. Department of Commerce, Bureau of the Census, Religious Bodies: 1926, Vol. II, p. 497.
[220] Thomas Burgess, Greeks in America (Boston, Sherman French & Co., 1913, pp. xiv, 256), pp. 53-58, 143, 145.
[221] U. S. Department of Commerce, Bureau of the Census, Religious Bodies: 1926, Vol. II, pp. 497, 498.
[222] Lübeck, Die russischen Missionen, pp. 52, 53.
[223] U. S. Department of Commerce, Bureau of the Census, Religious Bodies: 1926, Vol. II, p. 492.

Before 1914 a few Albanians who traditionally were members of the Orthodox Church had come to the United States. In 1916 they had two churches with 410 members.[224] Their founder and head was Fan Stylian Noli who had been consecrated bishop in 1908 at the age of nineteen and in 1912 had graduated at Harvard with distinction as scholar and athlete and in 1924 for a brief time was to be the Premier of Albania.[225]

Serbs of the Orthodox faith were also part of the immigrant flood. Since they were Slavic and could understand the service of the Russian churches, and since there were not many of them in any one place, separate parishes were not organized for them, but they were under the Russian bishop and were supervised directly by a Serbian priest or archimandrite. In 1906 the Orthodox churches were reported to have as members 15,742 Serbs.[226]

As we have said, until after 1914 episcopal supervision over most of these Eastern Orthodox churches, so far as any was given, was through the Russian episcopate. From 1898 to 1907 the occupant of this see was Tikon. It was during his incumbency, in 1904, that the see was raised to an archiepiscopate and (1905) that the headquarters were transferred from San Francisco to New York. Tikon was succeeded as archbishop by Platon, formerly the rector of the theological academy of Kiev. Most of the priests were foreign, but in time a theological seminary was established, first at Minneapolis and then transferred to New Jersey.[227] In 1906 the various Orthodox churches were reported as having a membership of 129,606, and in 1916 of 249,840.[228]

Armenians came to the United States. Their influx was greatly accentuated by the outbreaks and massacres in the 1890's. Their church, dating back to Gregory the Illuminator, in the early Christian centuries,[229] was distinct from the Eastern Orthodox churches. In 1889 a priest, Hovsep Sarajian, was sent from Constantinople to minister to them and a building erected in 1891 at Worcester, Massachusetts, was long the centre of the Armenian Church in the United States. In time, with the rapid addition of Armenian immigrants, the Catholicos made Sarajian bishop. In 1902 the Catholicos granted the church a special constitution and in 1903 raised the bishopric to an archbishopric. The mission was then divided into pastorates. Frequently rectors of Protestant

[224] U. S. Department of Commerce, Bureau of the Census, *Religious Bodies: 1926,* Vol. II, p. 488.

[225] *Time,* March 28, 1938, p. 41.

[226] U. S. Department of Commerce, Bureau of the Census, *Religious Bodies: 1926,* Vol. II, pp. 516-518.

[227] Theophilus, *op. cit.,* pp. 33, 34; Lübeck, *op. cit.,* pp. 53-56.

[228] U. S. Department of Commerce, Bureau of the Census, *Religious Bodies: 1926,* Vol. II, p. 486.

[229] Vol. I, pp. 105, 106.

Episcopal churches offered Armenian priests and congregations the hospitality of their buildings for services. In 1906 the Armenian Church was said to have 19,889 members in the United States and in 1916, 27,450 members.[230]

Assyrian Christians, from remnants of the churches which once flourished in the Persian Empire and under the Abbasid Caliphs, also sought refuge in the United States from Turkish massacres and modern Turkish rule. Some of these were Uniates, some Protestants, others Nestorians, and still others Jacobites. Uniates were cared for by the Roman Catholics and Protestants were looked after by their respective denominations, but Nestorians seem not to have developed a church organization. Most of the Assyrians appear to have been Jacobites. In 1907 they sent a deacon from Paterson, New Jersey, to Jerusalem for ordination. Soon after his return he assembled his flock for worship in a Protestant Episcopal Church. Congregations were also organized in New England. In 1916 a membership of 748 was reported.[231]

Of the immigration into the United States of the nineteenth and twentieth centuries, a considerable proportion was Protestant by heritage. Of this, the very large part which came from the British Isles tended to affiliate itself naturally and almost imperceptibly with existing denominations. Except for some of the Welsh and a few of the Scotch, language offered no barrier and practically all the religious bodies of the British Isles had their counterparts in the United States. For instance, in the 1870's and 1880's a number of Englishmen bought large holdings of land in Iowa and brought out a number of labourers from their home land. Their chief centre was at Le Mar and here their church and its English-trained rector became affiliated with the Protestant Episcopal Church.[232]

Sometimes the ecclesiastical amalgamation of those of British stock was not quickly accomplished. Thus, Welsh immigrants organized an American branch of the Calvinistic Methodist Church of Wales. This denomination had arisen in the eighteenth century out of the Wesleyan revival. George Whitefield had had great influence upon it, and, like Whitefield, it was Calvinistic in theology rather than Arminian.[233] In the last decade of the eighteenth cen-

[230] U. S. Department of Commerce, Bureau of the Census, *Religious Bodies: 1926*, Vol. II, pp. 335-343; Malcolm, *The Armenians in America*, pp. 62-79, 99-103.

[231] U. S. Department of Commerce, Bureau of the Census, *Religious Bodies: 1926*, Vol. II, pp. 67-69.

[232] Jacob Van der Zee, *The British in Iowa* (Iowa City, Iowa, The State Historical Society of Iowa, 1922, pp. 340), *passim*, but see especially pp. 237-244.

[233] Williams, *One Hundred Years of Welsh Calvinistic Methodism in America*, pp. 1-4.

tury a large Welsh migration began arriving in the United States. Its constituents tended to move to the cheap lands on the frontier in Northern New
York and in the Middle West and to cluster in communities which preserved
the Welsh speech.[234] Often those of more than one denomination formed
congregations for worship. Most of these in time became Congregational
churches.[235] Before many years local organizations of Welsh Calvinistic
Methodists began to appear. At first they were particularly strong in Oneida
County, New York, New York City, and Pennsylvania.[236] In the second quarter of the nineteenth century they were also formed in Ohio. Between 1832 and
1840 one of the clergy, Edward Jones, travelled thousands of miles on foot in
Ohio founding and strengthening churches.[237] As the frontier moved westward, Welsh settlers took advantage of the new lands and Welsh Calvinistic
Methodist churches were organized—notably in Wisconsin, Illinois, Minnesota,
Iowa, Nebraska, and Missouri, and even as far west as Colorado and California.[238] Most of them were rural churches. Many of them were in mining
regions. Their origin and growth seem to have been due primarily to the
initiative and leadership of the immigrants themselves and not to aid from
the older American denominations or from Wales—although many visiting
preachers came from Wales.[239] The congregations grouped themselves into
gymanvas and presbyteries. In 1841 a national organization was effected which
lasted until 1853.[240] In 1869 a national General Assembly was formed.[241]
Home missionary societies were instituted and in time a national society
for home and foreign missions was organized.[242] The tie which kept the denomination apart from other Presbyterian bodies was the Welsh language
and blood. As time passed, English gradually supplanted Welsh as the tongue
of the younger generation and of the church services. The reason for a separate
existence passed. In 1920 union was consummated with the Presbyterian
Church in the United States of America.[243] The separate Welsh body, numbering about fourteen thousand communicants,[244] merged with the Northern
Presbyterians.

A movement introduced to the United States through immigration was

[234] Williams, *op. cit.,* pp. 35ff.
[235] Williams, *op. cit.,* pp. 37-39.
[236] Williams, *op. cit.,* pp. 43-125.
[237] Williams, *op. cit.,* pp. 126ff.
[238] Williams, *op. cit.,* pp. 167ff.
[239] Williams, *op. cit.,* pp. 283, 284.
[240] Williams, *op. cit.,* pp. 257-265.
[241] Williams, *op. cit.,* pp. 266ff.
[242] Williams, *op. cit.,* pp. 343ff.
[243] Williams, *op. cit.,* pp. 395ff.
[244] Williams, *op. cit.,* p. 411.

that of the Plymouth Brethren. The Plymouth Brethren rose in England and Ireland early in the nineteenth century. They began partly in protest against the formalism of the Anglican Church and partly from dissatisfaction with sectarian divisions. Spiritually they had kinship with the Christians and Disciples of Christ in the United States. About the middle of the nineteenth century some of the Brethren came to the United States. John Nelson Darby, a godson of Admiral Lord Nelson and outstanding in the British movement, made several visits to the United States. Other leaders also visited America. Congregations arose. The Brethren seem to have spread even more by conversions than by immigration. They divided into a number of groups which in 1906 together had a membership of slightly over ten thousand.[245]

Although most of the Protestants from the British Isles merged with denominations already existing in the United States, the majority of those from the continent of Europe tended to group themselves by nationalities into churches which perpetuated their Old World religious customs and traditions. To be sure, thousands of individuals affiliated themselves with the denominations of the older American stock. However, when groups came over to these denominations, they often formed themselves into congregations and associated themselves into regional or national bodies which preserved the national name and, at the outset, the tongue of the fatherland. Because of the fissiparous genius of Protestantism, no central authority co-ordinated all the diverse national elements into a national church within an inclusive world fellowship as did the Papacy the Roman Catholics. However, gradually, although more slowly than the Roman Catholics, more and more of the Protestant bodies drew together into a national fellowship which allowed that variety and autonomy which was part of the Protestant tradition. Partly because of this experience, American Protestantism had a leading part in calling into existence organizations which knit Protestantism into a worldwide fellowship. This development, however, was not well under way until the twentieth century and its most striking expressions were to wait until after 1914.

Prominent among the immigrant Protestants were the Germans. The German influx had begun in colonial days and had contributed important elements to the older American stock. It mounted rapidly after 1830. Because of political troubles in Germany it was especially pronounced between 1846 and 1854. It rose again after the American Civil War and in 1882 reached a peak of a

[245] Napoleon Noel, *The History of the Brethren,* edited by William F. Knapp (Denver Colorado, W. F. Knapp, 2 vols., 1936), Vol. I, pp. 29, 42, 57, 114, 120, 287, 325, Vol. II, p. 603; U. S. Department of Commerce, Bureau of the Census, *Religious Bodies: 1926,* Vol. II, pp. 255-258.

quarter of a million in one year. In the last decade of the century, with the growing prosperity of Germany and an economic depression in the United States, it rapidly dwindled.[246] Many of the German immigrants, especially in the first half of the nineteenth century, settled on the inviting cheap lands of the frontier in the Mississippi Valley and beyond. Others, particularly of the later arrivals, made their homes in the cities.[247] It is estimated that in 1900 over eight millions in the United States were of German parentage, that in addition over three millions were descended from German immigrants of the nineteenth century, and that over six millions were sprung from those of German stock who had arrived before 1790. This meant that about a fourth of the population of 1900 were predominantly of German ancestry.[248]

In the large German immigration of the nineteenth century, relatively few came from predominantly religious motives. Many, notably among the intellectuals and liberals who sought refuge in the United States from uncongenial political conditions in Europe, recalling contemptuously the state-controlled clergy in Germany, were inclined to be opposed to the Church. Rationalists were in rebellion against the formalistic orthodoxy of many Lutherans and the obscurantism of some Pietists. The new communities of German immigrants tended to be religiously destitute. Some were served by free-lance preachers who were liberal theologically and, all too frequently, of easy morals.[249]

However, some of the German immigrants were impelled primarily by religious idealism. Thus the Rappists, following their leader, the vigorous and able Johann Georg Rapp (1757-1847), who left Würtemberg in 1803, in 1805 established a colony, Harmony, in Butler County, Pennsylvania. In 1815, they went to New Harmony, Indiana. In 1824 they sold their lands there to Robert Owen for his famous experiment in community living and removed to Economy, Pennsylvania. The membership of the society never numbered much more than four hundred at any one time. Celibacy was enforced, no efforts were made to gain recruits, and, accordingly, the group died out. The tenets of the Rappists were a mixture of Lutheranism, Pietism, millenarianism, and influences derived from Swedenborg and various other mystics.[250]

[246] Faust, *The German Element in the United States*, Vol. I, pp. 583-587.

[247] Faust, *op. cit.*, Vol. I, pp. 587-591.

[248] Faust, *op. cit.*, Vol. II, pp. 5-24.

[249] C. E. Schneider in *Church History*, Vol. IV, pp. 268-270, 274.

[250] John A. Bole, *The Harmony Society: a Chapter in German-American Culture History*, in *German American Annals*, Vol. II (Philadelphia, The German American Historical Society, 1904), pp. 274-308, 339-366, 403-434, 467-491, 571-581, 597-628, 665-677; Faust, *op. cit.*, Vol. I, pp. 455, 456; *Dictionary of American Biography*, Vol. XV, pp. 383, 384.

Another colony centred about William Keil (1812-1877), a native of Prussia. who came to New York in his youth and reached the conviction that the New Testament was against all sects, that the command "love one another" was the cornerstone of all Christianity, and that this meant community of goods. He attracted followers from among the Germans, chiefly from those already in the United States, and established colonies first in Missouri and then at Aurora in Oregon. After Keil's death the communities broke up and their properties were divided.[251]

Still another small group were the Zoarites, from Swabia, who settled in Tuscarawas County, Ohio, in 1817.[252]

In 1851 German Swedenborgians moved to Iowa and founded the Jasper colony. From this as a centre, missionary efforts were made. However, by 1900 the younger generation were ceasing to speak German or to read Swedenborg's works. The church waned and after 1910 ceased to have a resident pastor.[253]

Somewhat more numerous were the Mennonites. Sprung from the Anabaptist movement, they took their name from Menno Simons (1492-1559). They were largely of Swiss, German, and Dutch stock and had been subject to repeated and severe persecutions. Attracted by the religious liberty offered by William Penn, a number had settled in Pennsylvania in colonial days.[254] Very few entered the country between 1760 and 1820,[255] but beginning about the latter year more began to arrive. Largely farming folk, tending to cluster together and usually not especially active in seeking converts, they were never one of the larger denominations. They broke up into several groups (among them the Amish and the Hutterian Brethren), some of them of European and some of American origin.[256] In 1906, in spite of multiplication by natural increase the total membership of all the branches was only 54,789.[257] Many of the older American Mennonite stock moved westward to take advantage of the cheap lands. Of the Mennonites who came directly from Europe, some

[251] Hendricks, *Bethel and Aurora*, *passim*.

[252] Faust, *op. cit.*, Vol. I, p. 421.

[253] C. A. Hawley in *Church History*, Vol. VI, pp. 212-222.

[254] Smith, *The Mennonites of America*, pp. 81ff.; John C. Wenger, *History of the Mennonites of the Franconia Conference* (Telford, Pennsylvania, Franconia Mennonite Historical Society, 1937, pp. xvi, 523), pp. 7-25.

[255] Smith, *op. cit.*, p. 225.

[256] Smith, *op. cit.*, pp. 291-323, 343-352, gives some of these. What seems to be a complete list, with a brief description of each division, is in U. S. Department of Commerce, Bureau of the Census, *Religious Bodies: 1926*, Vol. II, p. 842-913. See also Gingerich, *The Mennonites in Iowa*, pp. 124ff.

[257] U. S. Department of Commerce, Bureau of the Census, *Religious Bodies: 1926*, Vol. II, p. 846.

were from Switzerland, France, Germany,[258] and Holland.[259] Quite a number were from Russia. Late in the eighteenth century Catherine the Great invited the Mennonites to her domains to help develop Southern Russia. Lured by the offer of free land, religious liberty, and exemption from military service, many from Prussia accepted. In 1800 the Tsar Paul I renewed these guarantees and added to them other privileges. Still others therefore entered Russia.[260] About 1870, however, the Russian government resolved to assimilate the Mennonites and withdrew the exemption from military service. Dismayed by the threat to their strict pacifism, in the 1870's hundreds migrated to America. In their exodus they received financial assistance from their brethren in the United States.[261]

A colony which in influence upon the German immigration proved numerically far more important than any of these other groups arrived in St. Louis in 1839. Its members were followers of Martin Stephan, a Saxon Lutheran, who was dissatisfied with the easy-going liberalism which marked the state church. They totalled about seven hundred. Among them were six clergymen and several candidates for the ministry. Some found homes in St. Louis and others settled on a tract of land in Perry County, Missouri. Before long Stephan was found to be a libertine and a rascal and was deposed. Stunned by this disheartening experience, the group might have lost coherence and vigour. However, one of their number, Carl Ferdinand Wilhelm Walther, came forward and proved to be a leader of rare ability. Walther had studied theology at the University of Leipzig and while there had consorted with a pietistically minded group and had read deeply in Luther. In Missouri he was pastor of a church, edited a paper, was a leading spirit in the organization of Concordia Theological Seminary which in time is said to have had the largest enrolment of any Protestant theological school in the United States, and became the first president of the German Evangelical Lutheran Synod of Missouri, Ohio, and Other States (usually known as the Missouri Synod, formed in 1847). The Missouri Synod was conservative, staunchly loyal to strict Lutheranism, and under Walther was organized with striking efficiency and closely integrated coherence. It attempted to hold its youth through a system of parochial schools.[262] Thanks largely to Walther's leadership, the

[258] Smith, *op. cit.*, pp. 277, 284, 285; Gingerich, *op. cit.*, pp. 47, 48, 50, 51, 54, 67, 72, 76, 77, 93, 94, 139, 147.

[259] Smith, *op. cit.*, p. 282.

[260] Smith, *op. cit.*, pp. 324, 325; Horsch, *The Hutterian Brethren*, p. 113; Friesen, *Alt-Evangelische Brüderschaft in Russland (1789-1910)*, pp. 73ff.

[261] Smith, *op. cit.*, pp. 327ff.; Horsch, *op. cit.*, pp. 115, 116; Faust, *op. cit.*, Vol. I, p. 501; Friesen, *op. cit.*, Teil II, *passim*.

[262] *Dictionary of American Biography*, Vol. XIX, pp. 402, 403 (with an excellent bibliography); Wentz, *The Lutheran Church in American History*, pp. 181-186.

little band of Saxons became the nucleus around which arose, through attracting other German immigrants, what by 1906 was the largest of the many Lutheran bodies in the United States.[263]

The Missouri Synod spread to many different parts of the country. In 1872, moreover, it entered into a loose confederation with several other smaller Lutheran synods of similar doctrine in the Middle West which was termed the Evangelical Lutheran Conference of America.[264]

Still another German colony which migrated from religious motives and which became the centre of a sturdy religious community—although very much smaller than the Missouri Synod—was one which numbered nearly a thousand and was led by a pastor, Grabau. They were Lutherans who held out against that union of their own church with the Reformed which was being enforced by the King of Prussia. Persecuted for their recalcitrancy, they emigrated to the United States and settled in and near Buffalo. Negotiations for union with the followers of Walther broke down. They organized their own synod (1845) and began to train their own pastors. They were very rigid in doctrine and discipline and did not attract many adherents.[265]

In holding the German Protestant immigrant to the Christian faith missionaries had an active and important part.

Numbers of these were from the Lutheran bodies which had taken root in colonial days. As scions of the older German stock joined in the westward migration, missionaries were sent to follow them to their new homes[266] and new synods were organized.[267] Between 1775 and 1800 the Lutheran Church membership is said to have risen from about fifteen thousand to about twenty-five thousand, and between 1800 and 1825 to about forty-five thousand.[268] Most of this increase must have been from the pre-Revolutionary German immigration. In 1820 the majority of the Lutherans formed a national organization, the General Synod of the Evangelical Church in the United States, which was usually called, for brief, the General Synod.[269] Theological schools for the training of clergy were begun, in 1815, in Otsego County, New York, through a bequest from J. C. Hartwick,[270] and, more important, at Gettysburg

[263] U. S. Department of Commerce, Bureau of the Census, *Religious Bodies: 1926*, Vol. II, pp. 705, 706.
[264] Wentz, *op. cit.*, p. 189.
[265] Wentz, *op. cit.*, pp. 186, 187.
[266] Schneider, *The German Church on the American Frontier*, pp. 42-47.
[267] Wentz, *op. cit.*, pp. 107-112.
[268] Wentz, *op. cit.*, p. 106.
[269] *The Lutheran World Almanac, 1921*, p. 71. See chart summarizing the history of the General Synod and of the bodies which separated from it, in *The Lutheran World Almanac, 1921*, p. 84.
[270] Wentz, *op. cit.*, p. 140.

in 1826 under the dominant influence of Samuel Simon Schmucker (1799-1873).[271] From these schools trained clergy went out, some of whom became missionaries to the frontier.[272] In 1835 the Central Missionary Society of the Evangelical Lutheran Church in the United States was organized and met in connexion with the General Synod. It sent missionaries to the West. In 1845 the Home Missionary Society of the General Synod was formed. In 1866 it transferred its funds and its interests to the General Synod. Thus home missions became officially the charge of the entire church.[273] The Reformed Church, which also had arisen in Pennsylvania in colonial times, likewise sent missionaries to the West. As a natural sequel to political independence and to obtain freedom to ordain its own ministry and so to provide for its growing needs, in 1791 the Coetus of Pennsylvania severed its dependence on Holland[274] and in 1793 the Synod of the German Reformed Church in the United States was organized.[275] In 1812 the Synod ordered that ministers be sent to the West to care for its members there.[276] The Western Synod (the Reformed Synod of Ohio), formed in 1824, largely from the older American stock which had moved to the frontier, undertook missions for the newer arrivals from Germany.[277] The General Synod, which was organized in 1863 to effect a national union of the churches of the German Reformed tradition, was active in seeking to reach the German immigrants, especially those who in Europe had been members of Reformed congregations. Among the outstanding missionaries were Max Stern and H. A. Muehlmeier, men who had been born in Europe but had been trained in the United States.[278] In 1859 the Classis of Sheboygan, Wisconsin, decided to found a mission house in which German ministers could be trained for service in the United States. In it hundreds of young men were prepared.[279] Periodicals and publishing houses were founded to educate the constituency.[280] It is not surprising that, partly as a result of this activity, several synods came into being in the West, to a large extent from among the nineteenth century immigration.[281]

German missionaries arrived from Europe. Most of these, it is important

---

[271] *Dictionary of American Biography*, Vol. XVI, pp. 443, 444; Wentz, *op. cit.*, pp. 142-145.
[272] Schneider, *op. cit.*, p. 46; Wentz, *op. cit.*, p. 167.
[273] Wentz, *op. cit.*, pp. 165-169.
[274] Dubbs, *History of the Reformed Church, German*, pp. 322, 323.
[275] Schneider, *op. cit.*, p. 69.
[276] Dubbs, *op. cit.*, p. 382.
[277] Dubbs, *op. cit.*, p. 387.
[278] Dubbs, *op. cit.*, pp. 401-404.
[279] Dubbs, *op. cit.*, p. 405.
[280] Dubbs, *op. cit.*, p. 406.
[281] *Ibid.*

to note, were from circles which had been profoundly influenced by the Pietist tradition and were theologically conservative. Quite a number were prepared in Basel. In 1833, at the request of German colonists at Ann Arbor, Michigan, one of the graduates of Basel came as pastor.[282] He began preaching in several different places, and in 1834 a contingent of two arrived to assist him.[283] Between 1833 and 1881, 189 from Basel served in the United States and Canada.[284] Some of these were attracted by the invitation of a semi-secret organization, the L. U. P. O. Society, which sought through them to counteract the influence of the Roman Catholic Church among the immigrants.[285] A very few missionaries were from the Rhenish missionary societies of Barmen and Langenberg.[286] Konrad Wilhelm Loehe, a pastor in the village of Neuendettelsau in Germany and a leader in the Inner Mission, became interested in the religious needs of the German immigrants in the United States. He began to educate missionaries and to send them to America. This led to the formation of the Mission Institute of Neuendettelsau. Some of his men joined in the formation of the Missouri Synod. They served in Michigan and in Ohio. They laid the foundations, too, for the Evangelical Synod of Iowa and Other States.[287] Through Loehe a theological seminary was formed at Fort Wayne, Indiana. It later moved to Iowa.[288] Aided by funds from the Neuendettelsau Mission, the Synod of Iowa extended its missionary activities very widely in the West. Eventually it had congregations in every state west of the Mississippi except Arizona and New Mexico.[289] In inaugurating the Lutheran Evangelical Synod of Texas, in 1851, missionaries sent by C. F. Spittler, the founder of the Pilgrim Mission of St. Chrischona, played an important part. Later this synod joined with the Synod of Iowa and Other States.[290] Johannes Evangelista Gossner, a remarkable pastor in Berlin who had come into Protestantism from the Roman Catholic priesthood, and who initiated important institutions in Germany and a foreign missionary society, became interested in the religious welfare of the Germans in the United States. Thirty of the men whom he trained went to America. They served in a number of sections and had a share in several synods.[291]

---

[282] Schlatter, *Geschichte der Basler Mission 1815-1915*, Vol. I, p. 91.
[283] Schneider, *op. cit.*, p. 49.
[284] Schlatter, *op. cit.*, Vol. I, p. 91.
[285] Schneider, *op. cit.*, pp. 84ff.
[286] Schneider, *op. cit.*, pp. 53-58.
[287] Zeilinger, *A Missionary Synod with a Mission, 1854-1929*, pp. 7-26.
[288] *Ibid.*
[289] Zeilinger, *op. cit.*, pp. 27, 55-59.
[290] Zeilinger, *op. cit.*, pp. 53-55.
[291] G. B. Arbaugh in *Church History*, Vol. VIII, pp. 222-230.

An interesting and important phase of the development of Lutheran churches among nineteenth century German immigrants was the division between the newer bodies and those in which the seventeenth and eighteenth century German immigration predominated. The latter failed to assimilate the former. No such imperceptible melting into the existing Lutheran organizations occurred as marked the merging of the Protestant immigrants from the British Isles into the American counterparts of the denominations with which they were familiar in the mother country. The obstacle was partly linguistic and partly doctrinal. The Lutheranism of the older German-American stock showed the effect of its environment. It was in process of substituting English for German as the language of its services (although not without severe struggles). The outstanding figure in its General Synod, Samuel Simon Schmucker, had received his theological training at Princeton Theological Seminary, a Presbyterian institution, and was an active co-operator with other denominations. The synods formed by the newer immigration clung tenaciously to the tongue of the fatherland. They were led by clergy who were not accustomed to the tolerance sprung from the interplay of the many denominations so characteristic of the United States but had as a background the dominance of Lutheranism as a state religion. Moreover, the European missionaries who laid the foundations of most of the Western synods (in spite of the liberalism of an occasional congregation gathered by a free-lance clergyman) were theologically very conservative. In opposition to the easygoing rationalism of much of contemporary German Lutheranism and to the merger of Reformed and Lutherans in Prussia, they were staunchly Lutheran. It was this loyal conservatism which sent them to brave the discomforts and uncertainties of missionary life in the New World. No central authority existed, as for the Roman Catholics, to compel them to compose their differences with the older Lutheran churches of the United States. Union, therefore, was not achieved.[292] The General Synod could not even hold all of the churches in which the older German-American stock was strong. In 1867 a secession from it formed the General Council of the Evangelical Lutheran Church in North America which in the use of English and in its strict Lutheranism occupied a median position between the General Synod and the synods of the more recent immigration.[293]

[292] For brief accounts of this development, see *Dictionary of American Biography*, Vol. XVI, pp. 443, 444; Weigle, *American Idealism*, pp. 157, 166, 167; Wentz, *The Lutheran Church in American History*, pp. 178-191, 198-210. See a longer account in Virgilius Ferm, *The Crisis in American Lutheran Theology. A Study of the Issue Between American Lutheranism and Old Lutheranism* (New York, The Century Co., 1927, pp. xiii, 409), *passim*.

[293] Wentz, *op. cit.*, pp. 219-233; *Lutheran World Almanac, 1921*, pp. 73, 74.

The majority of the nineteenth century German immigration of Protestant background, if they formed a church connexion, did so with Lutheran bodies. However, some, as we have seen, joined the German Reformed churches. Moreover, thousands of them entered into a fusion of the Lutherans and the Reformed, the Evangelical Synod of North America. Congregations in which Reformed and Lutherans combined in what were known as German Evangelical churches early came into existence in the West. Some of their members had been accustomed to similar mergers in Europe. Others were brought together by the exigencies of frontier conditions. In 1840, in Gravois Settlement, Missouri, the *Kirchenverein des Westens* was organized by six missionaries from Germany, two of them being from the Rhenish Missionary Society, two from Basel, one from Bremen, and one from Strasbourg. They instanced as a cause for their action the opposition on the one hand of the English-using Lutheran synods and on the other of the "ultra-Lutherans."[294] In the first twenty-five years the congregations of the new movement continued to be served by a foreign-born ministry, of whom nearly one-third were from pietistic Württemberg.[295] In the course of that quarter of a century the *Kirchenverein* spread widely, largely in Missouri, Indiana, Illinois, Ohio, Iowa, and Wisconsin. It later took the name of the Evangelical Synod of the West.[296] In 1877 this combined with several others of a similar type to form the Evangelical Synod of North America.[297]

Of major importance as a source of a traditionally Protestant immigration was Scandinavia. Some migration from that region had occurred before 1850, but early in the second half of the nineteenth century an extensive movement took place. In 1910 about a million and a quarter of the population of the United States had been born in Scandinavia. Of these slightly more than half were Swedes, about a third Norwegians, and a little less than a sixth Danes.[298] Much smaller contingents were from Iceland and Finland. If all those of Scandinavian descent were included, the total would be even more impressive.[299] In contrast with the larger German immigration, of which

---

[294] Schneider, *The German Church on the American Frontier*, pp. 98-113; U. S. Department of Commerce, Bureau of the Census, *Religious Bodies: 1926*, Vol. II, p. 541; Schneider in *Church History*, Vol. IV, pp. 274-281.
[295] Schneider, *The German Church on the American Frontier*, p. 441.
[296] Schneider, *op. cit.*, p. 462.
[297] U. S. Department of Commerce, Bureau of the Census, *Religious Bodies: 1926*, Vol. II, p. 541.
[298] Warne, *The Immigrant Invasion*, pp. 18, 19.
[299] One estimate gives those of Norwegian descent in 1925 as about two and a half millions.—Norlie, *History of the Norwegian People in America*, p. 313. In 1930 those born in Sweden or with one or both parents Swedish-born were approximately one and a half millions.—Ekblaw in Benson and Hedin, *Swedes in America 1638-1939*, p. 111.

an important proportion were Roman Catholics, the overwhelming majority of the Scandinavians were by tradition Protestants. In Scandinavia all but a few had been members of state churches which were part of the great Lutheran family. The majority of this Scandinavian immigration settled in the Northwest, in Northern Illinois, Wisconsin, Iowa, and Minnesota, although large contingents were in the cities of the North Atlantic coast and sprinklings were found elsewhere, even on the West coast.[300] In the North-west the Scandinavian settlement was overwhelmingly rural, for it had been attracted by the virgin lands of that area.

As with most of the immigration of the nineteenth and twentieth centuries, and, indeed, of the colonial era, the prevailing motive was economic—the lure of the new country for the landless and the poor.[301]

For some, however, the quest for religious liberty was also an incentive. Thus the initial group of Norwegians, numbering about half a hundred, from Stavanger, with Cleng Peerson as its pathfinder, who arrived in 1825 and most of whom settled in Northern New York, were in part Quakers and were in search of freedom from the galling restrictions placed on them by the Norwegian government and the state church.[302] Some of the movement of Norwegians, too, arose out of the labours of Hans Nielson Hauge (1771-1824). Hauge was the leading spirit in a Pietistic revival in Norway. He travelled up and down the land, largely on foot, preaching from two to four times a day, and writing hundreds of pamphlets and devotional books. He had a profound influence upon the religious life of Norway, especially upon that of the common people. Although he was imprisoned for his faith, he and most of those touched by him remained within the state church.[303] For some of Hauge's followers, unhappy over restrictions at home, the religious toleration of the United States seems to have been a motive for emigration.[304] In the 1840's Eric Janson, a farmer who, after a striking conversion, had preached zealously and had fallen out with the state church, to escape persecution came to the United States. He was followed by about fifteen hundred of his disciples. With him as their head, they established, in Illinois, at Bishop Hill, a communistic society. The experiment had a stormy course. In 1850 Janson was

---

[300] See charts in Norlie, *op. cit.,* pp. 83, 227, 314. See also Ekblaw in Benson and Hedin, *op. cit.,* pp. 111-121.

[301] Janson, *The Background of Swedish Immigration,* p. 116; Norlie, *op. cit.,* p. 77.

[302] Blegen, *Norwegian Migration to America 1825-1860,* pp. 24-56; Norlie, *op. cit.,* pp. 112-135; Henry J. Cadbury, *The Norwegian Quakers of 1825,* in *The Norwegian-American Historical Association Studies and Records,* Vol. I, pp. 60-94.

[303] A. Chr. Bang, *Hans Nielsen Hauge og hans Samtid* (Christiania, Jacob Dybwad, 1874, pp. 552), *passim;* Blegen, *op. cit.,* pp. 30, 31, 161.

[304] Blegen, *op. cit.,* pp. 126, 162.

assassinated. Under subsequent leadership dissensions arose. The community broke up, and extensive litigation marked its end.[305] In and near Ephraim, in Door County, Wisconsin, Moravians from Norway grouped themselves in a settlement—although the project of the wealthy Nils Otto Tank to establish a communistic Moravian settlement at Green Bay, Wisconsin, failed of realization.[306] In 1869 Olof Olsson led a group of about two hundred and fifty to America with the purpose of founding a Christian colony. After a few years, however, the congregation was disrupted.[307]

While the religious imperative did not have a leading place in the motives of emigration, religious leaders early began coming from Scandinavia to minister to the settlers and to hold them to the Christian faith.

A very large proportion of these were men who believed the state churches in Scandinavia to be too lax and who sought to implant among the immigrants a more earnest religious life. They gave to the Lutheranism of Scandinavians in the United States a temper quite different from that of the mother countries. Thus Elling Eielsen, originally a blacksmith and carpenter, and who as a lay preacher in the Haugean tradition, but outspoken in his denunciations of the clergy, had traversed much of Norway, came to the United States in 1839, established congregations, was eventually ordained, founded schools, published books, and organized the first Norwegian synod in the country, a synod which perpetuated his memory by bearing his name.[308] In 1875 this synod was reorganized, taking the title Hauge's Norwegian Evangelical Lutheran Synod, but Eielsen continued to lead a minority under the old organization and constitution.[309] The founders of the Swedish Lutheran churches in America were largely puritans in morals, were influenced by the revival movement, and distrusted the state church which they had left behind in the Old World.[310] Småland, the province of Sweden from which came a large proportion of the early religious leaders among the Swedish-Americans, had been swept by religious awakenings, especially marked in 1841 and 1842, which had resemblances to the camp-meeting revivals of the American frontier.[311] Men from such a background had little use for the stately formalism of the official Church of Sweden.

On the other hand, some of the missionary pastors from the Old World,

[305] Stephenson, *The Religious Aspects of Swedish Immigration*, pp. 49-73.
[306] Blegen, *op. cit.*, pp. 335, 336.
[307] Stephenson, *op. cit.*, pp. 285, 286.
[308] Norlie, *op. cit.*, pp. 193-195, 259; Rohne, *Norwegian American Lutheranism*, pp. 38-41, 89-111.
[309] *The Lutheran World Almanac, 1921*, p. 101.
[310] Stephenson, *op. cit.*, pp. 10, 20.
[311] Stephenson, *op. cit.*, pp. 28-32.

notably among the Norwegians, desired to perpetuate so far as possible the type of church which existed in the mother countries. Thus J. W. C. Dietrichson, who was of a prominent family of Norway, felt called, soon after he had finished his theological studies, especially since a dyer of Christiania offered to bear his expenses, to go to the United States to help found a permanent church order among the immigrants. Touched by the movement stemming from Grundtvig of Denmark, masterful, an aristocrat, he represented a endency very different from that of those influenced by Hauge, and had a strong inclination to the churchmanship of the old country.[312] He had an important part in the steps leading to the formation of the Norwegian Evangelical Lutheran Church of America, usually called the Norwegian Synod. He himself returned permanently to Norway (1850) before the formal organization of the synod (1853),[313] but this body had as its first president Dietrichson's brother-in-law, A. C. Preus, who in his twelve years (1850-1862) in America organized twenty congregations.[314] Here was a high church position which proved very influential. Several of its outstanding leaders were university graduates who had come to the United States as missionaries and who represented the tradition of the state church.[315]

No Scandinavian Lutheran churches existed to greet the first contingents of nineteenth century Scandinavian immigrants. Those that had been founded by the Swedes in the colonial period had lost their Lutheran identity, usually by joining the Church of England or its successor, the Episcopal Church.[316] In contradistinction from German Lutheranism, fairly extensively represented in the older American stock, Scandinavian Lutheranism in the United States was forced to begin *de novo*. The contrast was not so great as might at first sight be expected, for, as we have seen, between the Lutheranism of the older German-Americans and that of the nineteenth century immigrants a gulf existed and the latter owed its initial development chiefly to missionaries from the fatherland and to the energy and conviction of the immigrants themselves. Yet a difference existed. Moreover, although some attempts were made to bring the Scandinavian Lutherans into the same synods and churches with the German Lutherans, cleavages of language, of traditions, and, to a certain extent, of doctrine proved obstacles which for the majority were not bridged.[317]

[312] Rhone, *op. cit.*, pp. 65, 66, 88, 91, 92, 112-114, 118; Norlie, *op. cit.*, pp. 198, 199.
[313] Rhone, *op. cit.*, pp. 114-135; Norlie, *op. cit.*, p. 205.
[314] Rhone, *op. cit.*, p. 114.
[315] Norlie, *op. cit.*, p. 197; Rhone, *op. cit.*, pp. 116, 128.
[316] Vol. III, p. 197.
[317] For instances of this, see Rhone, *op. cit.*, pp. 123, 126, 127; Norlie, *op. cit.*, p. 202.

Partly for these reasons, the nineteenth century Scandinavian immigration developed its own organizations. We have already noted two of those developed by the Norwegians. A third, the Norwegian Augustana Synod, came into being in 1879 as a separation from the Scandinavian Augustana Synod, of which we are to speak in a moment. Also in 1870, the Norwegian-Danish Conference arose, as a secession from the Norwegian Augustana Synod which combined with a group led by Claus L. Clausen from the Norwegian Synod.[318] The first head of the Conference was Clausen. Clausen had come to America in 1843 and had become a pastor in Wisconsin and one of the initial leaders in the formation of the Norwegian Evangelical Lutheran Church. He had an important part in the early stages of Norwegian migration to Minnesota and as farmer, missionary, teacher, army chaplain, justice of the peace, and member of the state legislature of Iowa was an outstanding figure among Norwegian-Americans.[319] In 1886 some who were opposed to views held by the Missouri Synod and favoured by the majority in the Norwegian Synod withdrew from the latter body and formed the Anti-Missouri Brotherhood.[320] In 1890, however, a union was achieved of the Norwegian Augustana Synod, the Norwegian-Danish Conference, and the Anti-Missouri Brotherhood, into the United Norwegian Lutheran Church.[321] In 1917, as a consummation of negotiations and movements which had been under way for several years, this last body coalesced with the Hauge Synod and the Norwegian Synod to form the Norwegian Lutheran Church of America.[322] However, not quite all the Norwegian Lutherans joined the new body. Minorities held aloof. The largest of these was the Lutheran Free Church, formed in 1897.[323] Smaller was the church of the Lutheran Brethren of America.[324] There was also at least one other still smaller group.[325]

These various synods took over the task of caring religiously for their fellow Norwegian-Americans which had been begun by clergy and lay preachers from the fatherland. It is said that of about seventy-five hundred Norwegian Lutheran congregations in the United States, at least seven thousand were established under the direction of home mission boards and com-

---

[318] Norlie, *op. cit.*, p. 259; Rhone, *op. cit.*, pp. 234-236.

[319] C. C. Qualey, *Claus L. Clausen, Pioneer Pastor and Settlement Promoter, Illustrative Documents,* in the *Norwegian-American Historical Association Studies and Records,* Vol. VI, pp. 12-29.

[320] Norlie, *op. cit.*, pp. 262, 263.

[321] Norlie, *op. cit.*, p. 263.

[322] Norlie, *op. cit.*, p. 364.

[323] *The Lutheran World Almanac, 1921,* p. 103.

[324] *The Lutheran World Almanac, 1921,* p. 105.

[325] U. S. Department of Commerce, Bureau of the Census, *Religious Bodies: 1926,* Vol. II, pp. 832, 833.

mittees of the various synods.[326] Most of this was accomplished by the efforts of individual pastors and not by specially appointed missionaries.[327]

The chief Swedish-American Lutheran body was the Augustana Synod. One of the founders was Lars Paul Esbjörn. Esbjörn was a clergyman of the Church of Sweden who had in him a strong strain of Pietism, had been influenced by the Methodist, George Scott, and by the religious awakenings in Sweden, and was a strong advocate of temperance. In 1849 he came to the United States, partly to minister to his fellow-countrymen and, it has been suggested, partly because promotion in Sweden seemed closed to him. He went to Andover, Illinois, and there gathered (1850) a Lutheran congregation. He organized other congregations, toured several states to raise funds to assist the movement, and farmed to help with his own support. He joined in the formation of the Evangelical Lutheran Synod of Northern Illinois (1851), a movement which had as its leading spirit Paul Anderson, a Norwegian who had been educated at Beloit College under Congregational-Presbyterian influences and was sympathetic with much of non-Lutheran American Protestantism.[328] Another important leader was Tuve Nilsson Hasselquist. Hasselquist was a clergyman of the Church of Sweden who had become noted for his zeal as a preacher, his pietistic convictions, and his earnestness as a reformer of morals. Under him a revival had broken out in his parish.[329] It was partly through Esbjörn that, in 1852, he came to America.[330] It is significant as showing the influences which played upon the nascent Swedish Lutheranism of the United States that Hasselquist decided to throw in his lot with the New World also in part through contact with Peter Fjellstedt, a clergyman of the state church who had been a missionary and itinerant preacher in Asia and Europe and who established a school in which a number of men were trained who were later pastors in the United States.[331] Hasselquist proved forceful and able and became an outstanding figure in Swedish-American Lutheranism. At first, affected by the freedom of the American atmosphere, he was often extremely unconventional in his conduct of church services. While in time he became somewhat more formal, he remained low-churchly, an earnest Pietist, and strict in the moral standards he exacted of his flock.[332] From Sweden also came Erland Carlsson, a clergyman of the state church

---

[326] Norlie, op. cit., p. 422.
[327] Norlie, op. cit., p. 426.
[328] Stephenson, The Religious Aspects of Swedish Immigration, pp. 147-166; Ander, T. N. Hasselquist, pp. 10, 19-21, 40.
[329] Ander, op. cit., pp. 5-10.
[330] Ander, op. cit., p. 10.
[331] Stephenson, op. cit., pp. 36-38, 167, 168.
[332] Stephenson, op. cit., p. 169.

who was sympathetic with the revivals of the period.[333] Scanty assistance in men and money was given from the mother country. Most of the help was in the form of young men who completed in America their preparation for the pastorate.[334] Among these was Eric Norelius, who reached America in 1850 and became important as pastor, teacher, editor, and president of the Synod.[335]

In 1860 the Scandinavians separated from the Evangelical Synod of Northern Illinois and formed the Scandinavian Evangelical Lutheran Augustana Synod, with Hasselquist as its first president.[336] To train their own ministry, they organized Augustana College and Theological Seminary.[337] In 1870 those Norwegians who had joined in the Synod withdrew, leaving it exclusively Swedish.[338] The Augustana Synod was far from being a reproduction of the Church of Sweden. In polity and practice it bore more resemblance to Congregationalism and Presbyterianism than to what was supposedly its parent body.[339] For years the Church of Sweden looked at it askance and did not grant it formal recognition until 1903.[340] Yet, in spite of its adaptation to the American atmosphere, the Augustana Synod did not succeed in holding the Swedish immigrants, especially those who flooded in after the Civil War. In 1870, out of a total of two hundred thousand Swedes, it had a membership of only thirty thousand.[341] Although the immigration from Sweden was more numerous than that from Norway, in 1906 the membership of the Augustana Synod was less than 60 per cent. of the sum of that of the various Norwegian Lutheran bodies.[342]

Part of the failure of the Augustana Synod to attract a larger proportion of the immigrants from Sweden was due to the existence of other bodies, even less resembling the Church of Sweden, which had their origin in impulses stemming from Sweden and which in turn had been inspired or modified by movements in Great Britain and the United States. One of the great religious leaders in Sweden in the nineteenth century was Carl Olaf Rosenius

[333] Stephenson, *op. cit.*, p. 171.

[334] Ander, *op. cit.*, pp. 211-216.

[335] *Early Life of Eric Norelius (1838-1862). Journal of a Swedish Immigrant in the Middle West,* rendered into English by E. Johnson (Rock Island, Illinois, Augustana Book Concern, 1934, pp. 319), *passim;* Stephenson, *op. cit.*, pp. 175, 176.

[336] Ander, *op. cit.*, p. 52; Stephenson, *op. cit.*, p. 193.

[337] Ander, *op. cit.*, pp. 53ff.

[338] Ander, *op. cit.*, pp. 106, 107; Stephenson, *op. cit.*, pp. 310, 311.

[339] Stephenson, *op. cit.*, p. 177.

[340] Ander, *op. cit.*, p. 223.

[341] Stephenson, *op. cit.*, pp. 225, 226.

[342] U. S. Department of Commerce, Bureau of the Census, *Religious Bodies: 1926,* Vol. II, pp. 721, 757. Also, on chapters in the history of the Augustana Synod, see *Augustana Historical Society Publications,* No. 2, pp. 1-26, No. 3, pp. 81ff.

(1816-1868). He had been moulded in part by the Methodist, George Scott, and was in touch with the revivals in the United States, especially those of 1857-1858. He was reinforced by the songs of Lina Sandell and Oscar Ahnfelt. He emphasized a religious experience through the atonement and justification by faith and declared that it must lead to moral transformation and to altered relations with one's neighbours. Distrusting much in the state church, he yet chose to remain within it and thus to seek to transform it.[343] Those among the immigrants who while in Sweden had been committed to the Rosenian movement, in the United States found even the low-church Augustana Synod uncongenial. Later they were strengthened by repercussions from revivals in Sweden in 1876-1877 and by one of the great preachers of that awakening, A. August Skogsbergh, who came to America in 1876 and was known as the "Swedish Moody." This Mission Friend Movement, partly under the guidance of Paul Anderson, who had already had a part in the formation of the Evangelical Lutheran Synod of Northern Illinois, constituted the Swedish Evangelical Lutheran Mission Synod (1873) and (less far removed in sympathy from the Augustana position) the Swedish Evangelical Lutheran Ansgarius Synod (1874).[344] In 1885 these two synods, together with some independent congregations, united in the Swedish Evangelical Mission Covenant.[345]

Related to the Mission Covenant but organized in reciprocally independent congregations were the Free Churches, each of which ordained its own ministers. In 1908 some of them joined in a fellowship which they called the Swedish Evangelical Free Church.[346] A prominent figure associated with this movement was Frederick Franson.[347] Born in Sweden (1852), in his teens he came with his parents to America. During a prolonged illness he had a profound religious experience. He first joined a Baptist Church, then the Moody Church in Chicago, and later was ordained by a Free Mission Church in Nebraska. He travelled over much of the world as a missionary, first in Utah, then in Scandinavia and Germany, and later in Asia, South Africa, South America, and the West Indies, preaching the imminent second coming of Christ and repentance. He was the means of sending scores of missionaries to various parts of the world, notably to China.

The Danes also formed themselves into Lutheran bodies. Danes did not

---

[343] Stephenson, *op. cit.*, pp. 38ff.

[344] Stephenson, *op. cit.*, pp. 264ff.

[345] Stephenson, *op. cit.*, pp. 278ff.

[346] Stephenson, *op. cit.*, p. 288.

[347] Josephine Princell, *Frederick Franson, World Missionary* (Chicago, Chicago-Bladet Publishing Co., no date, pp. 156), *passim;* Stephenson, *op. cit.*, pp. 126-128.

come in numbers to the United States until after the defeat of their country by Austria and Prussia in 1864. Pastors from the state church arrived in 1871 and 1872 to care for the immigrants, and in 1872, with a few laymen, organized what later became known as the Danish Evangelical Lutheran Church in America. This body embraced those adhering to three tendencies imported from Denmark—the high church wing, those in the Grundtvig tradition, and those of the Inner Mission, with kinship to Pietism and to the revivalistic movements in nineteenth century Protestantism.[348] In 1883 the Danes, who since its formation had co-operated with the Norwegian-Danish Conference, withdrew and organized the Danish Evangelical Lutheran Church in North America. In 1896 this body united with a group which had separated from the other Danish Lutheran body to constitute the United Danish Evangelical Lutheran Church in America.[349] In 1906 the two chief Danish Lutheran bodies together had not far from twenty-nine thousand members.[350]

Icelandic immigration to the United States began about 1870. Through pastors trained in Iceland congregations were organized which in 1885 associated themselves, together with other congregations in Canada, in the Icelandic Evangelical Lutheran Synod in North America.[351] In 1906 this synod had in the United States fourteen congregations and 2,101 members.[352]

Out of the Finnish immigration, decidedly larger than that from Iceland, came Lutheran churches. These constituted themselves into three distinct synods, each keenly conscious of its separateness from the others. The Finnish Evangelical Lutheran Church of America (the Suomi Synod) was organized in Michigan in 1890.[353] The Finnish Evangelical Lutheran National Church had its nucleus in dissatisfaction with the Suomi Synod and was formed, also in Michigan, in 1900.[354] The Apostolic Lutheran Synod (Finnish) grew out of a congregation which was organized in 1872 and which later associated itself with other bodies of the same convictions. This Synod continued the tradition of Lars Levi Laestadius.[355] Laestadius (1800-1861) was a pastor of the Church of Sweden who, reared in abject poverty, became a distinguished botanist, through his colloquial address won a hearing among the common

[348] *The Lutheran World Almanac, 1921*, p. 106.
[349] *The Lutheran World Almanac, 1921*, p. 105.
[350] U. S. Department of Commerce, Bureau of the Census, *Religious Bodies: 1926*, Vol. II, p. 707.
[351] *The Lutheran World Almanac, 1921*, p. 107.
[352] U. S. Department of Commerce, Bureau of the Census, *Religious Bodies: 1926*, Vol. II, p. 707.
[353] *The Lutheran World Almanac, 1921*, p. 107.
[354] *The Lutheran World Almanac, 1921*, p. 108.
[355] *Ibid.*

people, and transformed his parish from habits of drunkenness to sober temperance.[356] In 1906 the three bodies enrolled a total of slightly over thirty
thousand members.[357]

Lutheran Slovaks were among the later immigrants to the United States
and did not become numerous until the 1880's and 1890's. Missions were
begun among them. As early as 1885 a congregation was organized. In 1901
what was denominated the Slovak Lutheran Synod of Pennsylvania and
Other States was formed. In 1905 the name was altered to the Slovak Evangelical Synod of America.[358] In the latter year it had fifty-nine congregations
and 12,141 members.[359]

The Dutch who settled in the United States were largely Protestant, the
majority of them of the Reformed tradition. Beginning in 1846, a marked increase in immigration occurred. A large proportion of the newcomers established their homes in the Middle West. Many of them had come because of
religious persecution in Holland. At times whole congregations arrived together, led by their pastors. They represented a protest against what they
deemed the doctrinal laxity and lack of conviction of the state churches and
stood for a strict adherence to historic Calvinism. Among them were lay
preachers and revivalistic movements. At the outset, the overwhelming majority of these immigrant churches affiliated themselves with the Dutch Reformed churches which dated back to colonial days and which in the course
of the last third of the eighteenth century had come together and, along with
some which were of German and some of French provenance, had formed
themselves into a national body, which eventually (1867) had as its official
title the Reformed Church in America.[360] The centre of the newer Dutch
churches was the Classis of Holland, Michigan. In 1850 this applied for admission to the older national body. The process of growth and affiliation was
aided by missionaries sent under the Board of Domestic Missions (organized
in 1831).[361]

A portion of the immigrants found themselves in disagreement with the
majority and withdrew (1857) to form what later (1904) came to be known

[356] Stephenson, *The Religious Aspects of Swedish Immigration*, p. 28.

[357] U. S. Department of Commerce, Bureau of the Census, *Religious Bodies: 1926*,
Vol. II, p. 707.

[358] *The Lutheran World Almanac, 1921*, p. 115.

[359] U. S. Department of Commerce, Bureau of the Census, *Religious Bodies: 1926*,
Vol. II, p. 707.

[360] Corwin, *A History of the Reformed Church, Dutch*, pp. 159ff., 195; U. S. Department of Commerce, Bureau of the Census, *Religious Bodies: 1926*, Vol. II, pp. 1221, 1222.

[361] Corwin, *op. cit.*, p. 194; Corwin, *A Manual of the Reformed Church in America
1628-1902*, pp. 136-140.

as the Christian Reformed Church. This movement was augmented by the desire to retain the Dutch language and by opposition to secret societies. With it united (1889) some of the older congregations in New York and New Jersey who were more conservative Calvinists than the majority and who in 1824 had associated themselves in a General Synod. The Christian Reformed Church adhered more closely to Calvinism than did the Reformed Church in America.[362] The Middle Western congregations of the Christian Reformed Church were slow to yield the Dutch language. In 1906 more than half their membership of 26,669 was in Michigan and considerably more than half was of the newer immigration.[363]

By 1914 about half a million Hungarians were in the United States.[364] Of these a good many had in Europe been members of the Reformed Church, for in Hungary that church was largely of Magyar stock and embraced a substantial proportion of the population. Congregations were organized which received ministers and financial assistance from the Reformed Church in Hungary. Some of these joined, in 1904, in constituting the Hungarian Reformed Church in America under the general care and supervision of the mother body in the fatherland.[365] Beginning about 1891 the (German) Reformed Church in the United States engaged in efforts to minister to the Hungarians and under its auspices a number of congregations arose. The World War of 1914-1918 made difficult the maintenance of relations with the Reformed Church in Hungary, and in 1921 twenty-eight congregations in America formerly connected with that body joined the Reformed Church in the United States.[366] A few of the congregations, however, were not satisfied with merging in that union and organized the Free Magyar Reformed Church in America.[367]

Here and there, beginning about 1892, Waldensians, of the indigenous Italian Protestantism, began coming in small bands. Groups of them settled

[362] Corwin, *A History of the Reformed Church, Dutch,* pp. 211, 212; Corwin, *A Manual of the Reformed Church in America, 1628-1902,* pp. 140, 141; U. S. Department of Commerce, Bureau of the Census, *Religious Bodies: 1926,* Vol. II, pp. 1241, 1242.

[363] U. S. Department of Commerce, Bureau of the Census, *Religious Bodies: 1926,* Vol. II, p. 1239.

[364] Warne, *The Immigrant Invasion,* p. 19.

[365] U. S. Department of Commerce, Bureau of the Census, *Religious Bodies: 1926,* Vol. II, p. 1246.

[366] *The Twentieth Triennial Report of the Board of Home Missions of the Reformed Church in the United States. Presented to the General Synod at Hickory, N. C.,* May, 1923 (Philadelphia, 1923, pp. 69), pp. 10, 11.

[367] U. S. Department of Commerce, Bureau of the Census, *Religious Bodies: 1926,* Vol. II, p. 1247.

in several states and in at least one instance formed a congregation which affiliated itself with the Presbyterians.[368]

Thus far in narrating the efforts to hold to their ancestral faith the immigrants of Protestant stock we have dealt chiefly with the movements which arose out of the immigrants themselves. We have seen that these newcomers, usually poor and with their way to make in the new land, had sufficient religious conviction to found and maintain congregations and to gather them into national and regional bodies, some of them eventually of impressive numerical strength. Their achievement was chiefly by their own resources and with little financial assistance from the mother churches of Europe or from the older churches of the United States. This was in spite of the fact that in Europe they had been members of state churches which were supported by public taxation and, in contrast, in the New World had to maintain their churches by voluntary contributions. Rather less financial help was contributed from the Old World to the Protestant than to the Roman Catholic immigrant religious bodies. Most of the initial leadership in these Protestant immigrant churches was given by clergy who had come from Europe on their own resources to take their chances with their fellow-countrymen. A large proportion of these clergymen represented minority strains in the state churches. They were conservative in theology, were opposed to the liberal rationalism in the mother bodies, were deeply touched with the traditions of Pietism, and were affected by the movements, some of them indigenous and some of them from Great Britain and the United States, which were making for revivals. Most of them tended to exact adherence to high moral standards and were opposed to laxity in amusements and to intemperance. Language separated them from the older American bodies, especially during the first generation, for generally they maintained services in the tongues of the fatherlands. Their doctrinal conservatism also bred aloofness. In contrast with the older American stock, in which Lutherans were in the decided minority, most of them were Lutherans from Germany and Scandinavia. However, basically they represented the same strains which were dominant in the Protestantism of colonial days—dissatisfaction with conditions in the majority churches in Europe, a demand for a personal religious experience and commitment leading to high moral conduct, a tendency to revivalism, and a protest against the tradition arising out of the mass conversions of Europe which made church membership coterminous with citizenship and not contingent upon individual decision. It was to be expected that when, after 1914, immigration suddenly dwindled almost to the vanishing

[368] Fred S. Goodman, *Glimpses of the Story of the Waldensians* (New York, The American Waldensian Society, 1928, pp. 20), p. 16.

point, this community of tradition, combined with the general American environment, would work for the gradual assimilation of these groups and the emergence of an American Protestantism, having the same general characteristics and more and more federated organizationally.

This immigrant Protestantism, like the Protestantism of the older American stock, was predominantly of what was called Evangelical Christianity. It had arisen out of Pietism, the Methodist movement, and the other similar religious awakenings of the eighteenth and nineteenth centuries. Even before they were fully established in the United States, several of the immigrant churches began foreign missions. It is not surprising that they fitted into those strains of Protestantism which were spreading the globe around and were giving rise to a world-wide Protestantism which was somewhat different in temper and even in form from the state churches of Europe.

In this immigrant Protestantism political factors and motives were less marked than in the original Protestant movement. Church and state were more nearly separated than in Europe and the state did not use the Church, as it had so often done in the Old World, as a tool for its own purposes. Partly for this reason, the immigrant Protestantism was less aristocratic than were the state churches from which it was largely sprung. It was more nearly a spontaneous movement from the masses. It gave evidence that Christianity, so often introduced to Western Europe through the ruling classes, had so gripped the affections and loyalties of the rank and file that the latter, removed to a new environment, on their own initiative took steps to perpetuate it.

The Protestant bodies of the older American stock were by no means oblivious to the newer immigration. In addition to the efforts which the Lutheran and Reformed churches made to reach those of the newcomers who were of their communions, most of the other denominations also endeavoured to serve religiously this vast immigrant flood. Here were millions pouring into the country. Most of them were nominally Christian. As a rule their connexion had been with state churches. For many that membership was purely formal. Although thousands voluntarily organized congregations of their hereditary communions and millions joined and supported them, others felt resentment against the churches of their rearing and were glad to break with them. Still more were indifferent and were inclined to abandon them along with the other features of the social pattern of which they had been a part in the Old World.[369] Here was both an opportunity and a challenge. Some felt that if

[369] As one instance, see Kutak, *The Story of a Bohemian-American Village*, p. 41.

the immigrants were not reached they would become a menace to American institutions. It was held that the best American citizen was one who was thoroughly imbued with the ideals of Protestant Christianity.[370] One Protestant leader declared: "If we do not permeate them with the spirit of our Christianity, they will permeate us with the spirit of anarchism. This country cannot exist half-Christian, half-pagan."[371] Another insisted that the issue was: Shall they "turn materialistic in America, or shall they find a new religious life springing out of their new experience and relations?"[372]

Presumably, the immigrants, now in different surroundings, would be more readily reached by other forms of Christianity than they would have been in the lands of their birth. In seeking to fit into the fresh environment and to lose the opprobrious status of alien, they were not unfavourable to affiliating themselves with churches which seemed to them part of the life to which they wished to be assimilated.

We cannot give a complete picture or even a full summary of these efforts for the immigrant by the Protestant churches of the older American stock. That is partly because they were so multitudinous. It is also because, being largely attempts to win adherents from one form of Christianity to another, they are, by our announced purpose, only on the periphery of the major theme of our story. We must content ourselves with generalizations and a few concrete examples.

First, it must be said that in the main the immigrant was slower to abandon his ancestral church than any other of his Old World loyalties.[373] For the first generation, he tended to hold to the church of his fathers as the centre of his group life and as the one tie with the past. At least in immigrant farming communities, the English-using congregations of indigenous denominations were much weaker than the imported, foreign ones.[374] Some from the second and third generations might drift away, but by the time they were old enough to make a choice for themselves the denominations of their parents had become sufficiently well established and acclimatized to hold a very large proportion of them.

In the second place, we must note the fact that the older American Protestant denominations seem not to have made such substantial gains from immigrants who were nominally Roman Catholic as from those whose traditional allegiance was Protestant. On this generalization it is unwise to be dogmatic.

---

[370] Abel, *Protestant Home Missions to Catholic Immigrants*, p. 3.
[371] Padelford, *The Commonwealths and the Kingdom*, pp. 148, 149.
[372] Douglass, *The New Home Missions*, p. 114.
[373] Brunner, *Immigrant Farmers and Their Children*, p. 116.
[374] Brunner, *op. cit.*, p. 124.

Accurate statistics are not to be had. Yet it seems clear that in spite of the expenditure by Protestant churches of millions of dollars in religious and social efforts for immigrants, largely of the Roman Catholic form of the faith, no large movements of Roman Catholics to Protestantism occurred, the size of most Protestant congregations gathered from Roman Catholic immigrants was small, the growth of such congregations was unimpressive, and many of the converts who were made were unstable in their faith.[375] The relative failure of this direct and conscious endeavour to win Roman Catholics was said to be due to such factors as loyalty to the ancestral church, preoccupation with achieving economic independence and a consequent lack of concern for religion, the feeling that a change of religion involved treason to the group, the inability of the Protestant mission to become an integral part of the immigrant community, and the difference in cultural backgrounds.[376] One suspects that the last cause was of large importance, for through it the kinship seems to be accounted for between the meagre results of Protestant missions among Roman Catholics in the United States and those in Europe. This conclusion will be both confirmed and contradicted by what we are to discover in subsequent volumes of the course of Protestant missions in the overwhelmingly Roman Catholic Latin America and Philippine Islands. It must also be said that much of the activity of the older Protestant denominations among Roman Catholic immigrants was not for the purpose of gaining converts from another church, but from the desire to be helpful to strangers, and to assist them in making a successful adjustment to their new surroundings. Such service did not result in many proselytes.

A few examples, chosen somewhat at random, of these Protestant attempts to win Roman Catholic immigrants may make these generalizations slightly more concrete. In 1849 the American and Foreign Christian Union was constituted from a fusion of the American Protestant Society, the Foreign Evangelical Society, and the Christian Alliance.[377] Its purpose was "the diffusion of evangelical truth wherever a corrupt Christianity exists, at home and abroad."[378] By this was meant especially missions among Roman Catholics.[379] These were conducted in Europe, South America, and the United States. The first annual report of the society, in 1850, announced missions in the United States among Roman Catholic French, Germans, Italians, Irish, Spaniards, and Portuguese, and in places scattered from Texas and New Orleans to New

[375] Abel, *op. cit.,* pp. 36-42, 58, 104.
[376] Abel, *op. cit.,* p. 104.
[377] *The American and Foreign Christian Union,* Vol. I, p. 254.
[378] *The American and Foreign Christian Union,* Vol. I, p. 252.
[379] *The American and Foreign Christian Union,* Vol. I, p. 1.

England. It spoke of a number of "Free German Catholic Churches," served by clergymen of several Protestant denominations. At least some of these German churches seem to have arisen as schisms from the Roman Catholic Church out of the struggle over trusteeism.[380] Annual reports indicate a progressive decline in the Union's efforts in the United States and a greater emphasis upon those in Europe and Latin America.[381] The Presbyterians had fairly extensive efforts, some of them through local congregations, presbyteries, and synods, and some through their national home missionary societies. We hear of enterprises for French, Poles, Bohemians, Portuguese,[382] and Mexicans.[383] In 1883 the American Home Mission Society organized a Slavic department,[384] but this was not necessarily exclusively for Roman Catholics. In 1906 the Methodist Episcopal Church, after more than thirty-five years of missions among the Spanish-speaking population in New Mexico, had twenty-three ordained preachers and 2,063 members.[385] The Northern Baptists maintained missions for several of the Roman Catholic race groups, notably the Italians, the French Canadians,[386] and the Poles.[387] A convention of Slavic Baptist churches, embracing Poles, Czechs, and Slovaks, was held in 1909.[388] As late as 1933, however, totals of membership for all the major and several of the minor Protestant denominations in congregations using a foreign language showed only 28,084 Mexicans, 27,099 Italians, and 109,207 Slavs to be in these churches.[389] Incomplete figures for about 1906, a quarter of a century earlier, show only seven thousand former Roman Catholics in special Protestant mission churches for these groups.[390] Apparently the twentieth century witnessed a rapid growth. Yet even with this growth, the numbers of Roman Catholics in Protestant congregations organized especially for them was small when compared with the total size of the respective national contingents. To be sure, these figures do not tell all the story. Many former Roman Catholics

[380] *The American and Foreign Christian Union,* Vol. I, pp. 257, 263-273.

[381] *The Christian World,* Vol. XVII, pp. 169ff., Vol. XXXIII, pp. 162-165.

[382] Doyle, *Presbyterian Home Missions,* pp. 233-240.

[383] *One Hundred Twelfth Annual Report Board of Home Missions of the Presbyterian Church in the United States of America,* p. 23.

[384] Clark, *Leavening the Nation,* pp. 268-270.

[385] *The Methodist Forward Movement in the United States. Annual of the Board of Home Missions and Church Extension of the Methodist Episcopal Church for the year 1907-1908,* pp. 73-75.

[386] Padelford, *The Commonwealth and the Kingdom,* pp. 156-161.

[387] J. Rzepecki in *The Chronicle,* Vol. II, pp. 139, 140.

[388] V. P. Stupka in *The Chronicle,* Vol. II, p. 122.

[389] Morse, *Home Missions Today and Tomorrow,* p. 142. On Protestant missions among Italians, see Mangano, *Sons of Italy. A Social and Religious Study of the Italians in America,* pp. 165-194.

[390] Grose, *Aliens or Americans,* pp. 314-318.

came one by one or by families into English-using congregations of the older American stock. In the nature of the case, these could not be all recorded in comprehensive statistics. For instance, Frank Kiefer, who led in organizing the first German Baptist church in Texas, was reared a Roman Catholic, came from Germany in 1850 at the age of seventeen, and in the United States became a Baptist and a missionary of that denomination.[391] One of the early Methodist preachers in Kentucky was James O'Cull, who was born and educated a Roman Catholic.[392] Hundreds of French Canadian Roman Catholics became Baptists but instead of being formed into separate congregations were taken into English-speaking churches.[393] From time to time a Roman Catholic priest became a Protestant and did faithful service as a Protestant pastor.[394] Many a Protestant pastor could tell of former Roman Catholics joining his flock.[395] Figures do not exist which make it possible to determine whether the number of Roman Catholics who became Protestant was larger than that of Protestants who became Roman Catholics. There was movement in both directions.

Here and there some from the Eastern churches became Protestants. For instance, a few hundred Roumanians became Baptists, and churches were organized, the first of them, in Cincinnati, in 1910. In 1913 the Roumanian Baptist Association of North America was founded.[396] Some Armenian Protestants, the fruits of American missions in the Near East, migrated to the United States.[397] Not many of these Easterners, however, were added to the Protestant ranks.

Although Protestant accessions from Roman Catholic and Eastern church immigrants were not spectacular, gains of the older American denominations from those whose European background was Protestant were more numerous. The Methodists and Baptists especially won followings of considerable size from Germans and Scandinavians. With their zeal and with a type of preaching congenial to the masses, they were particularly successful among immigrants who came, as the majority did, from the lower income levels and the relatively uneducated and unsophisticated. If the older American stock can

[391] Held, *European Missions in Texas*, pp. 49ff.

[392] Arnold, *A History of Methodism in Kentucky*, Vol. I, p. 88.

[393] Padelford, *op. cit.*, p. 152.

[394] From the author's personal knowledge. Yet converted priests were held not always to make good Protestant pastors—Mangano, *op. cit.*, pp. 185, 186.

[395] From the author's personal knowledge. See, too, as an instance, *Autobiography of Rev. James B. Finley*, pp. 195, 196.

[396] Galitzi, *A Study of Assimilation among the Roumanians in the United States*, p. 101; V. W. Jones in *The Chronicle*, Vol. II, pp. 131, 132.

[397] U. S. Department of Commerce, Bureau of the Census, *Religious Bodies: 1926*, Vol. II, p. 339; Malcolm, *The Armenians in America*, pp. 76-78, 99.

be said to have had class distinctions, it was to the proletariat among it that the Methodists and Baptists made their greatest appeal. It is not surprising that, since most of the Protestant immigrants were from the corresponding social strata of Europe, they responded to the approach of these denominations.

The Methodists were early very active among the German-speaking portions of the population. Indeed, the first Methodist meeting in what later became the United States was held in 1765 in New York City in the home of a German immigrant by a little group from a German colony in Ireland who had become Methodists before crossing the Atlantic.[398] Contact with the Methodists contributed to the growth of two independent religious bodies, the United Brethren in Christ and the Evangelical Association, and in the Methodist Episcopal Church a number of German Conferences were built up.

In their origin the United Brethren in Christ were largely distinct from the Methodists but were parallel with them. The leaders of the two movements had close and cordial relations.[399] The outstanding figure in the founding and early growth of the United Brethren was Philip William Otterbein (1726-1813).[400] Otterbein was born in Germany of a family of clergymen. He himself became a minister in the Reformed Church and was noted for his strictness and his zeal. In 1753 he journeyed to America as one of the six young men whom Michael Schlatter recruited to assist in those labours among the German immigrants which had so much to do with the founding and early growth of the German Reformed churches in the Colonies.[401] While a pastor at Lancaster, Pennsylvania, Otterbein came into a profound religious experience which sent him out as an earnest and compelling preacher of a new life. For years he was pastor of a congregation in Baltimore which was Reformed by background but was independent of the denominational organization. He became a warm friend of Asbury and joined in the latter's ordination as Superintendent, or Bishop, of the Methodist Episcopal Church.[402] With Otterbein was associated Martin Boehm (1725-1812),[403] of Pennsylvania German Mennonite stock who, after a marked conversion, began to preach in a heart-stirring manner and eventually was expelled by the Mennonites because of his departure from their

---

[398] Faust, *The German Element in the United States,* Vol. II, pp. 420, 421.

[399] On the United Brethren, see Drury, *History of the Church of the United Brethren in Christ, passim;* Berger, *History of the Church of the United Brethren in Christ, passim;* Lawrence, *The History of the Church of the United Brethren in Christ, passim.*

[400] See his life in Drury, *op. cit.,* Part I; *Dictionary of American Biography,* Vol. XIV, pp. 107, 108.

[401] Vol. III, p. 202.

[402] Asbury, June 19, 1776, Aug. 19, 1804, March 22, 1813, March 24, 1814, in *The Heart of Asbury's Journal,* pp. 99, 550, 655, 671-673; Drury, *op. cit.,* p. 181.

[403] On Boehm, see Drury, *op. cit.,* pp. 95ff.; Lawrence, *op. cit.,* Vol. I, pp. 152ff.; *Dictionary of American Biography,* Vol. II, pp. 405, 406.

traditions. He was affiliated with the Methodists. Out of the labours of Otterbein and Boehm and of lay itinerant preachers of their fellowship arose, by gradual steps which began with the framing of a constitution in 1789 and the holding of the first annual conference in 1800, a new denomination, the United Brethren in Christ. It resembled the Methodists in its evangelistic fervour and in its revivalistic preaching to the masses. It imitated the Methodist procedures.[404] Consciously following the Methodist pattern, it had bishops.[405] Between many in the two movements marked friendliness existed.[406] For years the United Brethren preached only in German.[407] Their itinerant preachers followed the Germans as the latter began to move beyond the Alleghenies.[408] The United Brethren fitted into the atmosphere of the frontier and into the frontier type of Protestantism. Their ministry was chiefly to Germans of the pre-Revolutionary immigration rather than to those who came in the nineteenth century. However, some converts were made among the latter.[409] Gradually non-Germans began to enter the fellowship and in time English supplanted German as the language of the denomination.[410]

The Evangelical Association was smaller numerically than the United Brethren, but like the latter it owed much to Methodism and had its rise and initial growth chiefly among Germans of the older immigration.[411] Its founder was Jacob Albright (1759-1808).[412] Albright was born in Pennsylvania, the child of German immigrants. He was baptized and confirmed a Lutheran, but it was not until 1790, when he was past thirty years of age, that the death of several of his children started him upon a spiritual experience which led him through deep anguish to a joyous Christian faith. Not long after this transformation he joined the Methodists. Within a few years the conviction came to him that he must preach to his fellow German-Americans.[413] He travelled among them, his faith proved contagious, and in the Methodist fashion he formed his converts into classes. Although he had little formal

[404] Drury, op. cit., p. 144.
[405] Berger, op. cit., pp. 363, 364.
[406] Ibid.; Drury, op. cit., pp. 202, 203; Lawrence, op. cit., Vol. I, pp. 340ff.
[407] Berger, op. cit., p. 355.
[408] Drury, op. cit., pp. 289ff.
[409] Drury, op. cit., p. 601.
[410] Drury, op. cit., pp. 373ff.; Lawrence, op. cit., Vol. II, pp. 117ff.
[411] Spreng, History of the Evangelical Association, passim.
[412] R. Yeakel, Jacob Albright and His Co-Laborers. Translated from the German (Cleveland, Publishing House of the Evangelical Association, 1883, pp. 329. Based partly on the personal reminiscences of a close friend), passim; Dictionary of American Biography, Vol. I, pp. 136, 137; Spreng, op. cit., pp. 392-407.
[413] Spreng, op. cit., pp. 394-396.

education and no theological training, in 1803 a council of his followers ordained him. In 1807 they held an Annual Conference and elected him bishop. After his death his movement continued. It is said that Asbury proposed union with the Methodists, but declined to meet the condition which Albright's followers laid down that there should be separate German circuits, districts, and conferences. He believed that the German language was doomed in the United States.[414] Like the United Brethren, the Evangelical Association followed the German migration on the frontier. Relatively it gained about as much in the Middle West as did the former.[415]

Although Asbury had opposed the formation of special German units within the Methodist Episcopal Church, he encouraged preaching to the Germans. Henry Boehm (1775-1875), son of Martin Boehm, became a Methodist preacher, for a time travelled with Asbury, used both English and German in his public addresses, translated the Methodist discipline into German, itinerated widely among Germans, and lived to pass the century mark.[416] As the newer German immigration began flooding the country, a change of policy was adopted and German congregations and conferences were gathered. The chief leader in this new movement was William Nast (1807-1899). Born and educated in Germany, after a spiritual and physical pilgrimage which took him to various parts of the United States, while a teacher at Kenyon College, in Ohio, he at last found the answer to his doubts. He thereupon became a Methodist minister and was appointed a missionary to the growing German communities in Ohio. Together with one of his converts, John Swahlen, he founded German Methodism. Additional missionaries were engaged. German churches followed, then (1844) German districts, and eventually (1864) German conferences. In 1907 there were ten such conferences with nearly sixty-four thousand members.[417] This, however, was only about a sixth as large as the total of the United Brethren and the Evangelical Association.[418]

Through converts among the immigrants the Methodists also assembled a

[414] Spreng, op. cit., p. 409.

[415] See comparative figures in U. S. Department of Commerce, Bureau of the Census, *Religious Bodies: 1926*, Vol. II, pp. 525, 1360, 1361. In 1906 the membership of the United Brethren was 274,649, and of the Evangelical Association 104,898.

[416] *Dictionary of American Biography*, Vol. II, pp. 403, 404; Faust, *The German Element in the United States*, Vol. I, pp. 430, 431, Vol. II, p. 421.

[417] Paul F. Douglass, *The Story of German Methodism. Biography of an Immigrant Soul* (Cincinnati, The Methodist Book Concern, 1939, pp. xviii, 297, 64), *passim; Dictionary of American Biography*, Vol. XIII, p. 393; *The Methodist Forward Movement in the United States. Annual of the Board of Home Missions and Church Extension of the Methodist Episcopal Church for the Year 1907-1908*, pp. 17-19.

[418] See figures under note 415.

Danish-Norwegian Conference, in 1907 about five thousand strong,[419] and Swedish churches, in 1907 having a total membership of not far from eighteen thousand.[420]

Baptist churches arose among the newer immigration partly from independent movements among the newcomers themselves and partly through the assistance and active missionary effort of the Baptists of older American stock.

Among the Germans were those who had entered into an earnest religious experience, sometimes after prolonged inward struggle, and had come to believe that baptism must be not for infants but only for those who were consciously Christian and that church membership and the Lord's Supper should be open only to those who had been really converted. A few had arrived at these convictions in Europe. Others reached them through contacts with Baptists in the United States. In 1838 Conrad Anton Fleischmann crossed the Atlantic and began preaching this doctrine, at first in New Jersey, and later in Philadelphia. A group of German and Dutch Pietists in St. Louis were immersed by John Mason Peck. Assistance was accorded by the American Baptist Home Mission Society. Baptist State Conventions gave aid. German Baptist churches sprang up. A seminary for the training of clergy for these churches was conducted in Rochester, New York, with August Rauschenbusch, who had come by a devious and stormy road to Baptist convictions, as its initial central figure. The churches were gathered into conferences, and eventually had a total membership of more than thirty thousand.[421]

Baptists made large gains among the Scandinavians. Some of the first of these came from converts of the Baptist Seaman's Bethel, opened in New York City in 1843.[422] In 1848 a Norwegian Baptist church was organized in La Salle County, Illinois.[423] The first Swedish Baptist church was assembled in Rock Island, Illinois, in 1852.[424] The first Danish Baptist church in the United States was begun in 1855 in Patten County, Illinois.[425] Assistance was given by the American Baptist Home Mission Society and the state conventions.[426] These churches were formed into associations and conferences, some-

[419] The Methodist Forward Movement in the United States . . . 1907-1908, pp. 27, 28.
[420] The Methodist Forward Movement in the United States . . . 1907-1908, pp. 29, 30. See also on the Swedish Methodists, Stephenson, The Religious Aspects of Swedish Immigration, pp. 256ff.
[421] O. E. Krueger in The Chronicle, Vol. II, pp. 98-110; Held, European Missions in Texas, pp. 49ff.
[422] R. A. Arländer in The Chronicle, Vol. II, pp. 116, 117; Stiansen, History of the Norwegian Baptists in America, p. 23.
[423] R. A. Arlander in op. cit., Vol. II, p. 113.
[424] Stephenson, op. cit., p. 246.
[425] R. A. Arlander in The Chronicle, Vol. II, p. 115.
[426] Stephenson, op. cit., pp. 253, 254; Padelford, The Commonwealths and the Kingdom, p. 154.

times including all Scandinavians, but most of them separately for the Danish, the Norwegian, and the Swedish churches.[427] Provisions were made for theological training of candidates for the ministry.[428] Some of the Finns also became Baptists.[429] Of the Scandinavian Baptist groups, the Swedish was the largest. In 1913 it had about twenty-eight thousand members, or only slightly less than the German Baptist movement.[430]

The Congregationalists were active in seeking to reach the newer immigration. Among the Germans and the Scandinavians were those to whom the Congregational tradition was congenial. Many of those touched by Pietism and the revivals of the nineteenth century and who believed that conscious conversion was essential to church membership found in the Congregationalism of the period a sympathetic home. The American Home Missionary Society, as early as the days when it represented both Congregationalists and New School Presbyterians, was active in supporting missionaries among both Germans and Scandinavians. In 1846 it appointed Peter Flury. Born in Switzerland in 1804, as a youth in England and on the continent Flury had contact with those stressing personal religious experience and in his thirties became a pastor in Switzerland. In 1846 he came to America intending to be a missionary to the Indians. Instead, for about two and a half years he laboured among the Germans in Iowa and founded several churches.[431] Still other missionaries were appointed. In the 1870's and 1880's the Congregationalists found that the Germans who were then beginning to arrive in substantial numbers from Russia welcomed the type of religious experience and church government represented by that denomination.[432] Churches multiplied and were found over a wide area, largely in the northern states between the Mississippi and the Rocky Mountains. In 1883 they formed a conference.[433] Provision was made for training clergy, first at Crete, Nebraska, then in Chicago in connexion with the Chicago Theological Seminary, and, beginning in 1916, in conjunction with Redfield College, in South Dakota.[434] By 1911, the total membership of the German Congregational churches was over thir-

[427] R. A. Arlander in The Chronicle, Vol. II, pp. 113-118; Eighty-First Annual Report of the American Baptist Home Mission Society, 1913, p. 34.

[428] Stephenson, op. cit., pp. 249ff.; R. A. Arlander in The Chronicle, Vol. II, pp. 114, 118; Stiansen, op. cit., pp. 98ff.

[429] Padelford, op. cit., p. 156.

[430] Eighty-First Annual Report of the American Baptist Home Mission Society, 1913, p. 34.

[431] Eisenach, A History of the German Congregational Churches in the United States, pp. 3-9.

[432] Eisenach, op. cit., pp. 36ff.

[433] Eisenach, op. cit., p. 48.

[434] Eisenach, op. cit., pp. 163ff.

teen thousand. The later accessions were chiefly from the Germans from Russia.[435]

The religious awakenings in Scandinavia prepared many of those touched by them to welcome Congregationalism. This was especially true of those who had departed most widely from Lutheranism, members of the Free Churches or Free Mission churches which were springing up. In 1883 the American Home Missionary Society organized a department to care for the Scandinavians. Provision was made, notably at the Chicago Theological Seminary, for training Scandinavians for home and foreign missions.[436]

Presbyterians were active among the Bohemians, Slovaks, and Hungarians.[437] They also made gains among the Germans.

The Protestant Episcopal Church made friendly advances to the Swedes. This was natural. The Church of Sweden was episcopally governed, and the Swedish-American Lutheran congregations of colonial days had become affiliated with the Anglicans. In 1849 a Swedish Episcopal congregation was organized in Chicago. Beginning in 1856 the Protestant Episcopal Church had a committee on friendly relations with the Church of Sweden. It wished the latter body to consecrate a bishop for the Swedes in the United States and offered to receive him into its own House of Bishops. By this step and by suggesting that before leaving Sweden communicant members of the Church of Sweden be given letters of dismission recommending them to its congregations in places where no Lutheran ones existed, the Protestant Episcopal Church hoped that the leakage of Swedes away from any church connexion might be lessened. No bishop was appointed, but by 1900 the Protestant Episcopal body had about a dozen Swedish congregations with approximately two thousand communicant members.[438]

From 1881 to 1893 the American Unitarian Association had as a missionary in Minnesota and Wisconsin, forming among Scandinavians societies of their branch of the faith, a Norwegian, Kristofer Nagel Janson, who had become a Unitarian while still in Norway.[439]

The Mormons drew heavily from Scandinavia. The missionaries who began coming in 1850 attracted many to the United States. The double lure of the new faith and the new, far lands, with what seemed both religious and economic opportunity, proved compelling. Numbers joined after they reached

[435] Eisenach, op. cit., p. 124.
[436] Clark, Leavening the Nation, pp. 268, 270-275.
[437] One Hundred Twelfth Annual Report of the Board of Home Missions of the Presbyterian Church in the U. S. A., 1914, pp. 15, 16.
[438] Stephenson, The Religious Aspects of Swedish Immigration, pp. 210ff.
[439] Dictionary of American Biography, Vol. IX, p. 612.

America. It is said that in 1900 not far from sixty thousand of the Scandinavians in the United States belonged to the Church of Jesus Christ of Latter Day Saints. Perhaps half of these were Danes, a third Swedes (of whom 35 per cent. were born in Sweden), and a sixth Norwegians.[440] Of the Swedes who came to America as Mormons, it is said that as many as 50 per cent., disillusioned, abandoned that church after reaching Utah.[441]

The comparatively small proportion of Germans and Scandinavians who were gathered into Methodist, Baptist, and Congregational churches which preserved the mother tongue and a distinct national complexion is not an accurate indication of the numbers who joined the older American denominations. A great many came singly or by families into English-speaking congregations of these bodies.[442] That was to be expected. It was part of the process of assimilation to American culture. As a rule the children of immigrants and at times even the immigrants themselves wished to merge as quickly as possible into the life about them and to be thought of as Americans, without the prefix of a hyphenated label. It was natural that when they had a religious interest they should seek to satisfy it in an English-speaking church which appeared to them to be American. Non-English using congregations preserving the racial and national divisions of Europe were foredoomed. They might endure for a generation or two. They might even permanently transmit the denominational character of their Old World heritage. Inevitably, however, English would become the language of all, and all would show in their methods, their services, and even their doctrines the effect of the new environment.

Jews formed a substantial proportion of the nineteenth century immigration to the United States.[443] As the century wore on, the number increased. One estimate declares that from 1881 to 1910 inclusive, over a million and a half entered the country. Of these more than two-thirds were from Russia and between a fifth and a sixth were from Austria-Hungary.[444] The number of Jews in the country rose from about three thousand in 1818 to nearly three million in 1914.[445]

[440] Stephenson, *op. cit.,* p. 97.
[441] Stephenson, *op. cit.,* p. 99.
[442] *The Chronicle,* Vol. II, p. 107, tells of a phase of this tendency.
[443] For a semi-popular account, containing much useful information, see Peter Wiernik, *History of the Jews in America. From the Period of the Discovery of the New World to the Present Time* (New York, The Jewish Press Publishing Co., 1912, pp. xxiv, 449), *passim.*
[444] Joseph, *Jewish Immigration to the United States from 1881 to 1910,* p. 93.
[445] *Christians and Jews. A Report of the Conference on the Christian Approach to the Jews, Atlantic City, New Jersey, May 12-15, 1931* (New York, International Missionary Council, 1931, pp. 155), Appendix I.

It was to be expected that the Christian churches would see in this Jewish influx an opportunity of the first magnitude. Here was an immense body of non-Christians. Removed from the ghettos of Europe and, freed from all legal disabilities, thrown into the American stream, the majority of Jews tended to drop their old customs and to lose their connexion with the synagogue. They wished to become assimilated to American life. Increasingly the churches were a normal and prominent part of that life. Would not the churches find here the most favourable situation which they had ever faced to bring the Jews to the Christian faith?

Somewhat surprisingly, relatively little effort was made by either Roman Catholics or Protestants to win this vast body of non-Christians. Although the churches were developing multiform and widely spread enterprises for following the frontier, reaching other immigrants, converting the Indian and the Negro, and giving the Christian message to other lands, they paid singularly little attention to the Jew. Indeed, much less energy was being directed towards reaching of the Jew than in contemporary Western Europe. In the bulky reports of the great Protestant home mission societies with their wide range of activities almost no mention is made of attempts to approach the Jews.

Some Jews became Roman Catholics. This was apparently brought about through no organizations directed especially towards them. In some cases it was through attendance at a Roman Catholic school, through personal acquaintance with Roman Catholics, and, less frequently, through being a patient in a Roman Catholic hospital. Some came by way of Protestantism. Chance contacts seem to have been the chief sources of conversion.[446]

A few Protestants organized to reach the Jews. In 1820 the American Society for Meliorating the Condition of the Jews was begun.[447] It raised money for missions to Jews in other lands and had missionaries in some of the larger cities of the United States.[448] In 1878, after an earlier organization, in the Protestant Episcopal Church the Church Society for Promoting Christianity among the Jews was formed.[449] From time to time it employed missionaries. Its income was never large, but in 1901 it reported an institution, Emmanuel House, in Philadelphia, a school and a missionary in New York City, and a

---

[446] See a number of specified examples in Rosalie Marie Levy, *Why Jews Become Catholics. Authentic Narratives* (New York, published by the author, 1924, pp. v, 203), *passim*.

[447] De le Roi, *Geschichte der evangelischen Judenmission seit Entstehung des neueren Judentums*, Part II, p. 372; Thompson, *A Century of Jewish Missions*, p. 228.

[448] *The Jewish Chronicle. Published under the Direction of the American Society for Meliorating the Condition of the Jews* (New York, 1845ff.), *passim*, especially Vol. IV, pp. 208-212, 249, Vol. XI, pp. 34, 35.

[449] De le Roi, *op. cit.*, Part II, p. 377; Thompson, *op. cit.*, pp. 229, 230.

farm school.[450] In 1845 we hear of a Baptist Society for the Evangelization of the Jews.[451] Some of the Lutheran bodies were actively interested in missions to the Jews.[452] In 1888 the Chicago Hebrew Mission was founded and persisted for many years.[453] We hear of one convert of this mission who became a Christian clergyman but who eventually, disillusioned, returned to Judaism.[454] Here and there in other cities there were somewhat similar missions or individual missionaries, usually converted Jews.[455] Now and again a pastor of a church would interest himself in the Jews.[456] As with Roman Catholics, so with Protestantism, some Jews became Christians through contacts made in the fluid American life. For instance, one Jew was converted through his Gentile wife and later became an officer of the Salvation Army.[457] Most of such Jews as affiliated themselves with a Christian body in the United States were reported to have joined the Church of Christ, Scientist.[458]

The great masses of Jews were comparatively untouched by either the Roman Catholic Church or by what were usually deemed the standard Protestant denominations.

Much more extensive efforts were made, especially by Protestants, for two other groups of non-Christian peoples, far less numerous than the Jews, the Chinese and Japanese immigrants.

The numbers of Far Easterners in the United States were not large. This was because of the barriers raised by the Government of the United States under the pressure of American public opinion. Most of those who came were on the West Coast. The Chinese were the first to arrive. After a few scattering ones on the East Coast, a fairly large movement began in the days of the Gold Rush in California. At first the Chinese were welcomed as inexpensive labourers, but antipathy soon developed, partly because of their competition

---

[450] See the thirty-third annual report in *The Domestic and Foreign Missionary Society of the Protestant Episcopal Church in the United States of America . . . for the year ending August 31st, 1901* (New York, 1901, pp. 430), pp. 346-351.

[451] Thompson, *op. cit.*, pp. 230, 231.

[452] Zeilinger, *A Missionary Synod with a Mission*, p. 69; Norlie, *History of the Norwegian People in America*, p. 421; De le Roi, *op. cit.*, Part II, pp. 382-384.

[453] See annual reports in *The Jewish Era. A Christian Quarterly in Behalf of Israel* (Chicago, The Chicago Hebrew Mission, 1892ff.).

[454] See his autobiography, Samuel Freuder, *A Missionary's Return to Judaism* (New York, The Sinai Publishing Co., 1915, pp. 203), *passim*.

[455] De le Roi, *op. cit.*, Part II, pp. 382, 385-389.

[456] *The Jewish Era*, Vol. XXI, pp. 18, 19; De le Roi, *op. cit.*, Part II, pp. 384, 385.

[457] See his autobiography, Julius H. Abrams, *Out of the House of Judah. A Story of Conversion to Christianity* (New York, Fleming H. Revell Co., 1923, pp. 215), *passim*.

[458] Ruppin, *The Jews in the Modern World*, p. 333.

with the whites. Anti-Chinese feeling mounted, marked by violence, and in the eighteen-eighties restrictions began to be placed on further immigration which eventually culminated in a policy of prohibition, or exclusion, as it was called.[459] The Chinese in the country rose from 34,933 in 1860 to 107,488 in 1890, and then declined to 89,963 in 1900.[460] They long tended to live apart in special sections of the cities and towns. Only slowly did assimilation begin.[461]

Until 1891 Japanese immigration did not rise above a thousand a year.[462] In 1900 it suddenly jumped to more than ten thousand and in 1903 was about twenty thousand.[463] In 1910 the official census showed the Japanese population to be 72,157, but the true figure may have been nearer 90,000.[464] Feeling against the Japanese also developed, especially in the state in which the Japanese were most numerous, California, and the Japanese Government undertook, by the Gentlemen's Agreement (1907-1908) not to issue passports to the United States to manual labourers.[465] This did not end the difficulty, for discriminatory legislation by California ensued, directed especially against Japanese ownership of land.[466] In the second generation of American-born Japanese, assimilation began, but by 1914 was only in its initial stages.[467]

Koreans were not so important numerically as Chinese and Japanese, and until after 1910 Filipinos did not enter in marked numbers.

For these Far Easterners, the overwhelming majority of them non-Christians upon their arrival, many American Christians, especially Protestants, felt a strong responsibility. In 1852 William Speer, who had been a missionary in Canton, in the region from which most of the Chinese came, was assigned to California by the Presbyterian Board of Foreign Missions and began a mission in San Francisco.[468] Baptists followed, in Sacramento, in 1854, Methodists, in San Francisco, in 1868, and Congregationalists in 1870.[469] In 1870 a Chinese Young Men's Christian Association was formed.[470] Missions were opened in a number of cities by various denominations, notably the four which were first in the field. Sunday Schools and schools for teaching English were promi-

---

[459] Coolidge, *Chinese Immigration*, pp. 15-336.
[460] Coolidge, *op. cit.*, p. 501.
[461] Tow, *The Real Chinese in America*, *passim*.
[462] Ichihashi, *Japanese in the United States*, p. 52.
[463] Ichihashi, *op. cit.*, pp. 55, 57.
[464] Millis, *The Japanese Problem in the United States*, p. 1.
[465] Ichihashi, *op. cit.*, pp. 243ff.
[466] Ichihashi, *op. cit.*, pp. 261ff.; Millis, *op. cit.*, pp. 197ff.
[467] Ichihashi, *op. cit.*, pp. 319ff.; Millis, *op. cit.*, pp. 251ff.
[468] Condit, *The Chinaman as We See Him*, p. 91.
[469] Condit, *op. cit.*, p. 101.
[470] Condit, *op. cit.*, p. 116.

nent.[471] It was estimated that in 1900 about sixteen hundred of the Chinese, or not quite 2 per cent. of the total Chinese population, were professing Christians.[472]

As early as 1877 a Protestant mission for Japanese was begun in San Francisco.[473] Eventually several denominations were active, especially the four which were most prominent among the Chinese—the Methodists, the Presbyterians, the Baptists, and the Congregationalists.[474] In 1913 California contained forty-three Japanese Churches with a membership of 2,430.[475] Some Japanese were to be found in English-speaking white churches.[476]

For both Chinese and Japanese the desire to conform to American ways and to learn English proved a strong incentive which aided the Christian missionary.

Special efforts, particularly by the Young Men's and Young Women's Christian Associations, were made to reach the students from the Far East who were coming in large and increasing numbers to American universities. In them were seen potential leaders and it was felt to be of strategic importance in aiding the growth of Christianity in their homelands that as many as possible be reached by the Christian message during their student days.[477]

In this vast immigration which poured into the United States in the nineteenth and twentieth centuries, the religious impetus was not so prominent as in colonial times. While the majority who settled the Thirteen Colonies came from economic and not from religious motives, and although when independence arrived only about one in twenty of the population were members of churches, in nearly half of the Thirteen Colonies the initial settlements had been made chiefly because of the Christian impulse and through them Christianity had exercised a profound influence upon the nascent nation. While in the later immigration groups tied together by a common Christian purpose were by no means absent and some came to escape religious persecution, the economic factor was even more prominent than in colonial days.

[471] Condit, op. cit., pp. 156ff. See a list of missions in Tow, op. cit., p. 167. On the Methodists see The Methodist Forward Movement in the United States, pp. 44ff.
[472] Condit, op. cit., p. 233.
[473] Ichihashi, op. cit., p. 220.
[474] See figures in Grose, Aliens or Americans, pp. 314ff. On the Methodists, see The Methodist Forward Movement in the United States, pp. 5-9. On the work of the Disciples of Christ, see popularly written sketches in Maude Whitmore Madden, When the East is in the West (New York, Fleming H. Revell Co., 1923, pp. 153), passim.
[475] Millis, op. cit., p. 267.
[476] Ichihashi, op. cit., p. 222.
[477] See W. R. Wheeler, H. H. King, and A. B. Davison, editors, The Foreign Student in America, pp. 189ff., 228ff.

In spite of the secular drive behind it, the newer immigration was composed overwhelmingly of nominally Christian peoples. Only the Jews, the Far Easterners, and a few Europeans who had discarded their hereditary faith were avowedly non-Christian.

Through this immigration almost all the kinds of Christianity of Europe and Asia were represented in the United States. Because of it, and by the addition of American-born denominations, American Christianity became more variegated than the Christianity of any other nation which the world had thus far seen.

This Christianity was transplanted and perpetuated, not by the aid of governments, and not even chiefly by funds and personnel from the churches of Europe, but by the voluntary efforts and gifts of the immigrants and of the older American churches and by leadership, lay and clerical, which arose from the immigrants themselves. In contrast with the state-subsidized and controlled spread of Spanish and Portuguese Christianity to the Americas in the three centuries before 1800 A.D., through which the larger part of pre-nineteenth century American Christianity had been planted and nourished, this achievement was primarily the product of the spontaneous efforts of the immigrants with some slight aid from Europe, secondarily the fruit of the efforts of older American churches, and almost entirely without state subsidies. The record becomes all the more significant when it is recalled that in Europe most of the immigrants had been members of state churches which were supported by taxation or endowments and had been unaccustomed to voluntary contributions for the maintenance of the clergy and of public worship. Yet through these freely willed efforts the proportion of the population of the United States who were members of churches increased fairly constantly. It is an amazing story.

The achievement must be ascribed partly to the fact that the church was often the centre of the community life of the immigrants. In the strange new world in which the immigrant found himself, the church was usually the one institution which reminded him of the familiar home which he had left. Here at least the sermon was in the vernacular of his fatherland and the ritual was as he had known it from childhood. For those who joined the older American English-using churches the attraction was often in part the natural desire to become assimilated to American life and to lose the inner reproach and the outward opprobrium of being alien. Yet as strong as any of these motives and, in many instances, much more compelling, was religious conviction. It was this which dominated most of the leaders in the newly forming churches.

In the Protestant churches of the newer immigration those who took the initiative were usually the elements who represented the more earnest and theologically conservative minorities in the corresponding European bodies. Among them Pietism and the revival movements of the eighteenth and nineteenth centuries were prominent. In this, although sometimes more conservative and fighting a losing, rear-guard battle for the Old Country speech, they had kinship to the major strains in the older American Christianity. In spite of the fact that it seemed a Joseph's coat of many colours, this American Protestant Christianity bore increasingly a common complexion.

Moreover, thrown into a common melting pot in which the separation of church and state and religious freedom prevented any one variety from having the prestige of governmental support, all forms of Christianity were compelled to rub shoulders with one another. In doing so they gradually, although slowly and only after spasms of resentment, lost some of their reciprocal intolerance and, at least in methods and often in ritual even when not in creeds, began to influence one another. After 1914, when the subsidence of immigration gave more opportunity for assimilation to take its course, the process was accelerated. In the United States a Christianity was coming into being which, although by no means completely divorced from its historic roots in Europe and Asia, was beginning to show the effects of its new environment.

Could this Christianity which persisted and developed among the immigrants overcome and transmute the materialistic, economic motive which had brought the majority to the New World? Was it to be a dwindling even though hardy survival of the old life in Europe? Or was it to grow, more and more constraining men to listen as it spoke of man's call to an endless life with God, and of man's sin in his exclusive absorption with bread, clothing, shelter, and the amusements which gratified his flesh? That is a question to which we must recur in a later chapter. Here we can merely pause to remark that in holding the avowed allegiance of so many of the newcomers, Christianity was strikingly successful. This cannot be fully accounted for merely on the ground that in the church the nostalgic immigrant found something which reminded him of his old home. Basically it was because he was stirred by what he believed was Christianity's message to the eternal longings of man.

Chapter VIII

THE UNITED STATES OF AMERICA. EFFORTS TO WIN THE INDIANS: ROMAN CATHOLIC; RUSSIAN ORTHODOX; PROTESTANT

IN THE Indians of the United States Christianity faced an extraordinarily difficult problem. Compared with the western migration of the whites, or with the immigration from Europe, or even with the Negroes, the numbers involved were not great. In 1837 the Indians in the United States were officially estimated to total 332,498[1]—although this semblance of an exact figure must not be allowed to give the impression of accuracy. In 1870 they were reported at 278,000,[2] apparently a marked decline, and that in spite of the fact that the United States now embraced a much larger area than in 1837. In 1890 the national census declared that they were 248,253 and that, in addition, Alaska held 25,354 of them.[3] In 1910 the census showed 265,683, a substantial increase, and in Alaska disclosed 25,331.[4] The figures for 1890 and 1910 were believed to be approximately correct.[5] In spite of these relatively small numbers, the Indians presented conundrums which neither Church nor state succeeded in solving. In 1914 the Indian was still as baffling to the conscientious white man, although not always in the same ways, as he had been a century and a half before.

The reasons for the chronic perplexity were several. The Indians were widely scattered and often in relatively small units. In 1910 there were Indians in every state in the Union.[6] Although Oklahoma then contained over a fourth of them, and approximately half were in Oklahoma, Arizona, New Mexico, and South Dakota,[7] even in these areas they were divided into many tribes. No mass movements, such as had been so frequent in the earlier ex-

[1] Paxson, *History of the American Frontier*, p. 284.
[2] Department of Commerce, Bureau of the Census, *Indian Population in the United States and Alaska 1910*, p. 10.
[3] *Ibid.*
[4] *Ibid.*
[5] *Ibid.*
[6] Department of Commerce, Bureau of the Census, *Indian Population in the United States and Alaska 1910*, p. 12.
[7] *Ibid.*

pansion of Christianity, were possible among them on any large scale. They represented a great variety of languages as well as tribes, and no one mission could hope to reach a large number. Many missions and missionaries were needed if all were to be won. Then, too, in culture the Indians were utterly different from the whites from whom the missionaries came. Theirs was a "primitive," hunting, semi-agricultural life in contrast with the settled, "advanced" civilization of the whites. Unlike the Negroes, they did not make docile labourers on white plantations and they did not easily adjust themselves to the farming economy of the whites or to the industries of the older white communities. In contrast to the Negroes, whose tribal organization had been lost in America and who were distributed widely among the whites and so were fairly readily assimilated in religion as in other phases of culture, most of the Indians long kept something of their tribal structure under their own rulers and their autonomous economic organization. In this respect, too, the Indians of the United States differed from those of Mexico and Peru, where white masters had supplanted Indian masters and the docile masses had tended to accept, rather passively, the faith of their new rulers. Moreover, the Indian proved unusually susceptible to the white man's diseases and to the white man's "fire water." He had not, as had the white, through long contact developed a partial immunity against them. He was demoralized by both. This demoralization was accentuated by lawless adventurers of the kind all too frequently in the vanguard of the white contacts with non-white peoples who exploited the Indian and introduced him to their vices. Added to these circumstances was the sad fact that, as the frontier of white settlement advanced westward, the Indians of the United States were again and again uprooted by the aggressive "pale face." In many a tribe a mission was initiated and progress was made in gathering congregations and conducting schools, only to have the enterprise disrupted by the forcible removal of the tribe to another habitat. The wars which frequently punctuated these removals temporarily made the work of the missionary all but impossible. In later years, moreover, vast sums of money, often administered by officials who obtained their appointments as political plums and had neither interest nor competence in their task, were poured out by the Federal Government in a paternalistic fashion which discouraged Indian initiative. It is not surprising that Christian missionaries often found their task discouraging.

Yet in the face of these obstacles, hundreds of Christian missionaries, both Roman Catholic and Protestant, laboured for the Indian, often with high unselfishness and marked heroism, and sometimes with outstanding ability. In the course of the nineteenth century, thousands of lives and millions of dollars were devoted to bringing the Christian message to the Indian and assisting him to make a wholesome adjustment to the white man's world so rudely thrust upon him by the advancing wave of an expanding Europe. The entire story, even if narrated only in condensed fashion, would extend this chapter into a large volume. If it is to be kept within limits proportionate to the numerical strength of the Indians, we must exercise rigid self-restraint and content ourselves, however grudgingly, with the briefest of summaries and with notices of a few outstanding missionaries and projects.

We must first attempt a condensed outline of the pattern of white and Indian relations into which Christian missions were constrained to fit. From its inception the Government of the United States acted on the theory that the Indians had the right of occupancy of the land on which they lived, but that full title was subject to the superior right of the National Government. Until 1871, relations with Indians were based upon treaties between the tribes and the Government of the United States.[8] Often the Indians ceded their lands and in return received annuities. In 1819 Congress passed an act "for the purpose of providing against the further decline and final extinction of the Indian tribes . . . and for introducing among them the habits and arts of civilization." To implement this ideal, Congress provided an annual appropriation of $10,000 for the education of Indians in agriculture and in reading, writing, and arithmetic.[9] Since the Federal Government had no machinery of its own for administering this fund, it apportioned it among missionaries to enable them to establish and maintain schools. As additional sums for education became available through treaties with the tribes, these, too, were largely entrusted to Christian missionary organizations.[10] In other words, while making these appropriations for secular education and not ostensibly encouraging the conversion of the Indians to Christianity, the Federal Government was effectively subsidizing the efforts of the churches to win the Indians to the Christian faith. By these subventions the Federal Government, quite unintentionally, placed a damper on any movements to render the Indians self-supporting, either in their schools or in their churches. Christianity tended to be accepted passively, along with other phases of the white man's culture. The prospect was not bright for the vitality of the Christianity or of the culture thus implanted.

[8] Schmeckebier, *The Office of Indian Affairs*, pp. 2-11.
[9] Schmeckebier, *op. cit.*, p. 39.
[10] Schmeckebier, *op. cit.*, p. 40. In 1886, although by this time only twenty-one per cent. of the government appropriations for the education of Indians were going to such insitutions, $228,259 was expended by the Federal Government through mission schools, and in 1892 27 per cent., or $611, 570.—Schmeckebier, *op. cit.*, p. 212.

In the first half of the nineteenth century, chiefly after 1825, a large proportion of the Indians east of the Mississippi were removed to lands west of that river. This was to satisfy the demands of the advancing land-hungry whites.[11] For a time it was widely assumed that white settlement would not proceed beyond the first tier of states west of the Mississippi. Indeed, an attempt was made to mark out in the Far West an Indian country where the tribes could be secure in permanent possession of assigned lands and to which white men, with their corrupting manners, would not be allowed to penetrate.[12] Notably, what were known as the Five Civilized Tribes, the Cherokees, Creeks, Seminoles, Chickasaws, and Choctaws, by measures memorable for the accompanying agitations, wars, and hardships, were removed from the Southeast to what was known as the Indian Territory and which roughly corresponded to the later State of Oklahoma.[13]

The western frontier of white settlement, aided by the unforeseen transcontinental railways, defied legislation and treaties, and in the third quarter of the century the white man was invading even these supposedly inviolable preserves. A fresh series of wars between whites and Indians followed. More and more the Indians who kept their tribal organization were confined to sections of lands termed reservations. Often the Federal Government paid them for the relinquished soil. In many areas lands which had belonged to the tribe as a whole were divided up, after the white man's manner of private ownership, among the individuals, "in severalty."[14] In spite of legislative and administrative efforts to protect them, numbers of Indians lost the land thus assigned them. Many lapsed into wretched, shiftless poverty. The process of the adjustment of the Indians to the white man's world at best was painful and at worst was tragically unsuccessful.[15]

The state support of Christian undertakings for the Indian progressively declined. To be sure, beginning in 1869 President Grant delegated the nomination of governmental Indian agents to the various religious bodies engaged in missions. Apparently this was an effort to lift the Indian Service from the morass of incompetence and corruption into which it had fallen through political appointments.[16] The practice was progressively abandoned,[17] but, fortunately, some of the abuses which it was designed to obviate were even-

---

[11] Schmeckebier, *op. cit.,* pp. 28ff.; Kinney, *A Continent Lost—A Civilization Won,* pp. 27ff.
[12] Paxson, *op. cit.,* pp. 275-285.
[13] Schmeckebier, *op. cit.,* pp. 90ff.
[14] Kinney, *op. cit.,* pp. 81ff.
[15] Schmeckebier, *op. cit.,* pp. 42ff.; Paxson, *op. cit.,* pp. 502-512.
[16] Schmeckebier, *op cit.,* pp. 54, 55.
[17] Schmeckebier, *op. cit.,* pp. 77, 78.

tually met by the application of civil service rules.[18] Gradually schools were placed directly under the Indian Service of the Federal Government rather than under missions. By 1887 this was the status of more than two-thirds of them.[19] After 1900 all governmental financial aid to mission schools ceased.[20] However, Indian children attending schools were still allowed to receive from the Government the rations of food and clothing provided for in the treaties.[21] Moreover, beginning in 1905 contracts were again made between the Federal Government and mission schools, the appropriate subsidies being taken from the tribal funds at the request of the Indians.[22] Government buildings were made available[23] for religious services and the Government gave to missions title to the Indian lands used for religious or educational purposes.[24]

As we saw in the preceding volume, Roman Catholic missionaries had long been at work among the Indians in territories which were eventually occupied by the United States.[25] This was notably true in areas occupied by Spain and France in Texas, New Mexico, Florida, Georgia, Arizona, California, along the Great Lakes, in the Mississippi Valley, and south of the French border in Maine. In Maryland the Jesuits were active among the Indians.[26]

The wars and other upheavals of the eighteenth and the first part of the nineteenth century brought some of these missions to an end and sadly reduced the others. Georgia came into the possession of the English, then strongly anti-Roman Catholic. For a time Florida was in English hands: the Franciscans left and their converts died or lapsed into paganism.[27] Canada passed to the British crown and the left bank of the Mississippi became British and then American. On the eve of that event the suppression of the Society of Jesus had dealt a severe blow to missions in the French possessions. Mexico was disturbed through the repercussions of the Napoleonic wars and eventually broke away from Spanish rule, and missions in California (which

[18] Schmeckebier, *op. cit.*, p. 81.
[19] Schmeckebier, *op. cit.*, p. 71.
[20] Schmeckebier, *op. cit.*, p. 85. See extract from statue of 1897 in Schmeckebier, *op. cit.*, p. 484.
[21] Text of statute in Schmeckebier, *op. cit.*, p. 483.
[22] Schmeckebier, *op. cit.*, p. 212.
[23] Schmeckebier, *op. cit.*, p. 269.
[24] Text of statute in Schmeckebier, *op. cit.*, p. 438.
[25] Vol. III, pp. 125ff., 177ff.
[26] O'Gorman, *A History of the Roman Catholic Church in the United States*, p. 222; Shea, *History of the Catholic Missions among the Indian Tribes of the United States, 1529-1854*, pp. 483ff.
[27] Shea, *op. cit.*, p. 75.

was then governed from Mexico) suffered. In the first decade of the nineteenth century the Franciscan enterprise in what later was the State of California was in its heyday.[28] However, in 1810 revolt against Spain broke out in Mexico and the ensuing disturbances contributed to the decline in the funds and personnel sent to California.[29] The disintegration in California was slow. In 1820 the number of Indian Christians attached to the missions was about twenty thousand, which had been approximately the total in 1805.[30] In 1830, although the number of missionaries, twenty-six, was a third less than in 1810, the missions had actually increased.[31] As late as 1833 ten Franciscans arrived as reinforcements.[32] However, the Mexican law of 1833 decreed the long threatened secularization. By this was meant the completion of what had normally been the Spanish colonial policy, the removal of the Christianized Indians from the control of the regulars and arranging for them a parish administration under secular priests.[33] Before 1836 nearly four-fifths of the missions had been secularized and in most instances the lands had been distributed in severalty among the Christian Indians.[34] In 1836 Santa Anna, then dominant in Mexico, confiscated the Pious Fund which had long been a source of financial support for the California missions.[35] Although in 1843 an attempt was made to restore the friars to their management of the missions, by 1848 only seven of the Brothers Minor were left.[36] In 1845 several of the missions were sold at auction.[37] The old system was practically dead. As early as 1810 the majority of the Franciscans who ministered to the Roman Catholics in New Mexico were living in the centres of Spanish rather than of Indian population.[38] In Texas a few priests remained in the country, but the missions had dwindled sharply before the end of the eighteenth century.[39]

In spite of the passing of the old colonial order and the ruin of the missions connected with it, the Roman Catholic enterprise for Indians was renewed,

[28] Englehardt, *The Missions and Missionaries of California,* Vol. II, Part I, pp. 667ff.
[29] *Ibid.*
[30] Bancroft, *History of California,* Vol. II, p. 395.
[31] Bancroft, *op. cit.,* Vol. II, pp. 393, 654.
[32] Bancroft, *op. cit.,* Vol. III, p. 318.
[33] Bancroft, *op. cit.,* Vol. III, pp. 336ff.
[34] Bancroft, *op. cit.,* Vol. IV, pp. 42, 43.
[35] Engelhardt, *op. cit.,* Vol. IV, pp. 241ff.
[36] Bancroft, *op. cit.,* Vol. IV, p. 369, Vol. V, p. 565.
[37] Engelhardt, *op. cit.,* Vol. IV, pp. 459, 460.
[38] Pedro Bautista Pino, *Noticias de Nuevo Mexico,* p. 31, cited in R. E. Twitchell, *The Leading Facts of New Mexican History* (Cedar Rapids, Iowa, The Torch Press, 5 vols., 1911-1917), Vol. I, pp. 478, 479.
[39] H. E. Bolton, *Texas in the Middle Eighteenth Century* (Berkeley, University Press, 1915, pp. x, 501), pp. 102ff., 377-379; D. G. Wooten, *A Complete History of Texas* (Dallas, The Texas History Co., 1899, pp. xxii, 498), p. 76; Shea, *op. cit.,* p. 87.

although in other forms, and attained greater dimensions than before 1800. In addition to their stupendous task of caring for the mounting flood of Roman Catholic immigrants, numbers of the bishops and clergy found time to give attention to the Indians. Thus Carroll, the first Roman Catholic bishop in the United States, and Cheverus, the first Bishop of Boston, interested themselves in seeing that clerical care was provided for the Indians of Maine who during colonial days had been reached by French missionaries.[40] Flaget, the first Bishop of Bardstown, and, a little later, Fenwick, the first Bishop of Cincinnati, with dioceses which covered a vast area in the Middle West, endeavoured, and with some success, to amend the loss sustained through the lapse of the French missions. Many of the Indians who had been won by the Jesuits had dropped back into paganism, but some retained vestiges of their Christian faith.[41] In 1821, at the request of Flaget, a priest made an extensive tour through Michigan.[42] A French priest, Stephen T. Badin, one of the Kentucky pioneers, in 1819 had returned to France, but after a time yielded to the lure of America and for some years served among the scattered Roman Catholic groups in Michigan and Northern Indiana.[43] Bishop Fenwick sent other priests to the Indians in Michigan and Wisconsin, obtained government funds for schools, and himself made exhausting journeys to visit the scattered red members of his flock.[44] He had the joy of seeing some progress and of knowing that two of his Indians had been admitted to the College of the Propaganda, in Rome.[45] Frederic Baraga, the only son of wealthy Slavonic parents of Carniola, a highly sensitive spirit, well educated, came to America to be a missionary to the aborigines. He first served under Fenwick among the Indians of Michigan. He extended his labours into Wisconsin. He travelled extensively in a pioneer country, founding and ministering to missions. Later he became vicar apostolic in that area, then the first Bishop of Sault Ste. Marie-Marquette, and worked among both whites and Indians. He brought in personnel and funds from Europe.[46] Cretin, the first Bishop of

[40] Mary Celeste Leger, *The Catholic Indian Missions in Maine (1611-1820)* (Washington, Catholic University of America, 1929, pp. x, 184), pp. 132ff.; Guilday, *The Life and Times of John Carroll*, pp. 605-613; letter of Bishop Fenwick, April 6, 1832, in *Annales de l'Association de la Propagation de la Foi*, Vol. V, pp. 447ff.

[41] McNamara, *The Catholic Church on the Northern Indiana Frontier, 1789-1844*, p. 15.

[42] McNamara, *op. cit.*, p. 14.

[43] McNamara, *op. cit.*, pp. 24ff.; O'Daniel, *The Right Rev. Edward Dominic Fenwick, O. P.*, pp. 350, 375.

[44] O'Daniel, *op. cit.*, pp. 327-332, 388-391, 403, 404; *Annales de l'Association de la Propagation de la Foi*, Vol. VI, pp. 154ff., 178ff.

[45] O'Daniel, *op. cit.*, pp. 412, 429.

[46] Chrysostomus Verwyst, *Life and Labors of Rt. Rev. Frederic Baraga, First Bishop of Marquette, Mich.* (Milwaukee, Wis., M. H. Wiltzius & Co., 1900, pp. xv, 476),

St. Paul, and Loras, first Bishop of Dubuque, were active in promoting missions to Indians in their jurisdictions.[47]

It was to Bishop Du Bourg of Louisiana and the Floridas, who contributed so notably to the formation of the Society for the Propagation of the Faith, that the inception of some of the most extensive enterprises for the Indians, those of the revived Society of Jesus west of the Mississippi River, was due. At the urgent request of Bishop Du Bourg, in 1823 the Jesuits agreed to undertake missions in this area.[48] Bishop Du Bourg had already obtained the promise of a subvention from the Federal Government for this purpose.[49] He promised to confide to the Jesuits the spiritual care of the Indians on the Missouri River and its tributaries and to cede to them a tract of land at Florissant, on the outskirts of St. Louis, as headquarters.[50] To Florissant went a party of Belgians and Jesuits, largely novices, under the direction of the Belgian, Charles Felix Van Quickenborne.[51] In pursuance of the design of Bishop Du Bourg, in 1825 a school for Indian boys was begun at Florissant, but it did not prosper and in 1831 came to an end.[52] Van Quickenborne elaborated a plan for missions to the Indians, but it was not adopted.[53] Through the Belgian Jesuits a mission was established for the Osage Indians, in the later Kansas.[54] To this mission came also Sisters of Loretto, of the congregation initiated in Kentucky through the vision of Nerinckx.[55] From 1836 to 1841 what proved to be an unsuccessful mission was conducted for the Kickapoo Indians.[56] Short-lived, too, was a mission among the Potawatomis at Council Bluffs, Iowa. The havoc wrought by liquor seems to have been partly responsible for the failure.[57] Longer-lived was an undertaking among the Potawatomis in Kansas. These Potawatomis had been moved from their ancient homes in Indiana, near the Michigan border, where some of them had become Roman Catholics. From 1838 to 1877 the Jesuits laboured among them. By the latter year the disintegration of the tribe through the distribution

---

passim; O'Donnell, The Catholic Hierarchy in the United States, 1790-1922, p. 168; Schmidlin and Braun, Catholic Mission History, p. 689.

[47] Schmidlin and Braun, op. cit., p. 688. See Schmidlin and Braun, op. cit., pp. 688, 689, for brief mention of a number of missionaries to the Indians, with the appropriate citations to sources.

[48] Garraghan, The Jesuits of the Middle United States, Vol. I, pp. 40-64.

[49] Garraghan, op. cit., Vol. I, pp. 45-55; Graves, Annals of the Osage Mission, p. 14.

[50] Garraghan, op. cit., Vol. I, pp. 61-64.

[51] Garraghan, op. cit., Vol. I, pp. 79ff.

[52] Garraghan, op. cit., Vol. I, pp. 147ff.

[53] Garraghan, op. cit., Vol. I, pp. 173ff.

[54] Garraghan, op. cit., Vol. I, pp. 176ff.; Graves, op. cit., pp. 4, 11, 17, 24, 30.

[55] Graves, op. cit., p. 29.

[56] Garraghan, op. cit., Vol. I, pp. 376ff.

[57] Garraghan, op. cit., Vol. I, pp. 422ff.

of the communal lands in severalty and through strong drink had all but dissipated the constituency.[58] Some missionary efforts, too, were made among the Miamis,[59] the Ottawas, and the Chippewas. The Chippewas and the Ottawas were close of kin to the Potawatomis, and therefore welcomed Roman Catholic missionaries.[60] For many years Jesuits conducted a mission among the Osages.[61] One of the Jesuits, Paul Ponziglione, was an Italian, born to wealth and to the title of count, but devoted himself to this alien people in a strange country.[62]

The most famous of all the Belgian Jesuit missionaries to the Indians was Pierre-Jean De Smet (1801-1873).[63] One of the original group of novices who formed the first contingent of Florissant, he had been ordained in 1827. Active, strong, handsome, genial, and friendly, he proved ideally fitted for his pioneer labours. In 1838 he was one of the group who inaugurated the mission among the Potawatomis at Council Bluffs, and had brief experience among the Sioux, seeking to make peace between them and the Potawatomis. A prolonged Odyssey began in 1840 as the outgrowth of an incident which was also to be famous in the annals of Protestant missions. In the autumn of 1831 there came to St. Louis, then the main western outpost of the white man's advance, a group of four Indians from beyond the Rocky Mountains, probably from the Nez Perce and Flathead tribes, asking for information concerning the pale face's religion. Some knowledge of Christianity had seeped through to them, probably from a variety of sources.[64] Two of the four died in St. Louis and while ill were baptized by two priests.[65] However, no

[58] Garraghan, op. cit., Vol. II, pp. 175-235, 594-699, Vol. III, pp. 1-65.
[59] Garraghan, op. cit., Vol. II, pp. 229ff.
[60] Garraghan, op. cit., Vol. II, pp. 220, 221.
[61] Graves, op. cit., passim; W. W. Graves, Life and Letters of Rev. Father John Schoenmakers, S. J., Apostle to the Osages (Parsons, Kansas, The Commercial Publishers, 1928, pp. 144), passim.
[62] W. W. Graves, Life and Letters of Fathers Paul Ponziglione, Schoenmakers and Other Early Jesuits at Osage Mission. Sketch of St. Francis' Church. Life of Mother Bridget (St. Paul, Kansas, W. W. Graves, 1916, pp. 287), passim.
[63] On De Smet, see Garraghan, op. cit., Vol. II, pp. 248ff., Vol. III, pp. 66ff.; Hiram Martin Chittenden and Alfred Talbot Richardson, Life, Letters and Travels of Father Pierre-Jean De Smet, S. J., 1801-1873 (New York, Francis P. Harper, 4 vols., 1905), passim; P. J. De Smet, Oregon Missions and Travels over the Rocky Mountains in 1845-46 (New York, Edward Dunigan, 1847, pp. 408), passim; P. J. De Smet, Western Missions and Missionaries (New York, James B. Kirker, 1863, pp. 532), passim; Dictionary of American Biography, Vol. V, p. 255.
[64] A good critical account of this incident and of the various versions of it is in Drury, Henry Harmon Spalding, pp. 72-90. Another good summary of the accounts of the mission is in Brosnan, Jason Lee, Prophet of the New Oregon, pp. 2-10.
[65] See letter of Bishop Rosati, Dec. 31, 1831, which gives the earliest first-hand account of the incident, in Annales de l'Association de la Propagation de la Foi, Vol. V, pp. 599, 600.

other attempt was made immediately to follow up the opportunity given by the startling quest. It was not until after 1839 that the challenge was accepted. In that year there came to St. Louis two Roman Catholic Iroquois who were living in the region of the Columbia River with Flatheads and other tribes. They made their confessions, were confirmed, were given the Holy Communion, and were promised two missionaries.[66] Only one could be sent. De Smet volunteered for the distant expedition and set out in March, 1840. He reached the Flatheads in the Oregon Country. In the succeeding years he founded missions among the Flatheads, Kalispels, and Cœur d'Alenes, made trips to Europe for assistance, and again and again accomplished the arduous passage across the plains and mountains west of the Mississippi River. He came to know some of the tribes, especially the Blackfeet and the Sioux, who lived between the Mississippi and the distant Indians on the Columbia who had first drawn him. More than once he helped to make peace, notably in 1868 between the whites and Sitting Bull's warriors. His was a full and adventurous life. However, he was not permitted to give his entire life to the Indians he loved. Rome distrusted his judgment: he appeared to be planning on too large a scale. His ardour sometimes led him to projects beyond the bounds of the possible. For a time the mission he had begun among the Flatheads declined, seemingly because the Indians believed him to have made promises of animals, ploughs, and other material aid which he had not kept.[67] He had marked ability in raising and disbursing money, and it was, accordingly, to the post of procurator, or business agent, of his province of the Society of Jesus that he was required to devote most of his time. Yet in the trail of De Smet came missions not only to the Flatheads, but also to the Blackfeet and the Gros Ventres.[68]

Shortly before De Smet began his first journey to the Pacific North-west, that region was entered from Canada by two priests, François Norbert Blanchet (1795-1883) and Modeste Demers. The area then known as the Oregon Country, embracing roughly the later Oregon, Washington, Idaho, Western Montana, and British Columbia, was at that time the joint possession of Great Britain and the United States. The leading white authority in the vast region was the Hudson Bay Company, with John McLoughlin, a Roman Catholic, as its resident ranking official. Serving the Hudson Bay Company were a number of Roman Catholics, largely French Canadians,

[66] Garraghan, op. cit., Vol. II, pp. 248-250.

[67] Garraghan, op. cit., Vol. II, pp. 376-380.

[68] L. B. Palladius, Indian and White in the Northwest, or, A History of Catholicity in Montana (Baltimore, John Murphy & Co., 1894, pp. xxv, 411), Part I, passim.

and in the region were a few other Roman Catholics, mostly former employees of the Company. McLoughlin requested the ecclesiastical authorities of Canada to send priests. In response Blanchet was commissioned and was joined by Demers. Blanchet arrived at Fort Vancouver, on the Columbia, in 1838, and before long was dreaming in large terms of missions to the Indians of the region and of care for the white population whose influx he foresaw. He was made the first head of the Vicariate Apostolic of Oregon, created late in 1843. He convinced Rome of the future importance of the country, insisted that to occupy it properly for the Church an episcopate must be created in advance of population rather than after it, outlined a comprehensive ecclesiastical structure, and in 1846 was appointed the first Archbishop of Oregon City, with a vast territory. Interestingly enough, his was the second archiepiscopal see in the United States. With the aid of various priests, some of whom, together with several nuns, Blanchet obtained directly from Europe, and others of whom came through De Smet, a number of missions were inaugurated for the Indians of the Oregon Country. Blanchet lived to see the influx of white settlers force the Indian missions into the background, but he did not forget them.[69]

To enumerate all the Roman Catholic missionary efforts for the Indians would unduly prolong these pages. Memorable were the efforts of the Benedictines in Minnesota, the Dakotas, and what later became Oklahoma.[70] Missions were extended to Alaska.[71] We hear of a mission among the Choctaws of Louisiana.[72] Katharine Drexel, from a wealthy family noted for its philanthropics, contributed hundreds of thousands of dollars to Indian missions and founded (1889) the Sisters of the Blessed Sacrament for Indians and Negroes.[73] In 1901 the Society for the Preservation of the Faith among Indian Children was inaugurated, to collect funds for missions.[74] Auxiliary to it, in 1904 the Marquette League was formed.[75] In the 1880's Cataldo, a Jesuit, began a mission among the Eskimos of Alaska.[76] Franciscans of the St.

[69] Garraghan, op. cit., Vol. II, pp. 271ff.; Dictionary of American Biography, Vol. II, pp. 352-354.

[70] Schwager, Die katholische Heidenmission der Gegenwart, p. 70.

[71] For the biography of one of the Jesuits in Alaska, made up largely of the subject's letters and containing vivid pictures of the mission, see Charles J. Judge, An American Missionary. A Record of the Work of Rev. William H. Judge, S. J. (Maryknoll, N. Y., Catholic Foreign Mission Society of America, 1907, pp. xix, 304), passim.

[72] Mrs. S. B. Elder, Life of the Abbe Adrien Roquette "Chahta-Ima" (New Orleans, Bienville Assembly, Knights of Columbus, 1913, pp. 187), pp. 127ff.

[73] The Catholic Encyclopedia, Vol. II, p. 599.

[74] The Catholic Encyclopedia, Vol. VII, p. 747.

[75] Ibid.

[76] Walsh, American Jesuits, pp. 255-264.

Louis Province of their order filled the gap left in California by the decay of the Spanish Franciscan efforts, and the Franciscans of Cincinnati opened (1898) a mission for the Navajos in Arizona and took over (1900-1903) a few of the old missions in New Mexico.[77] The Brothers Minor also laboured among the Chippewas and the Ottawas.[78]

To co-ordinate Roman Catholic efforts for the Red Man and to be an agency for dealing with the United States Government, in 1874 the Bureau of Catholic Indian Missions was organized at Washington, D. C. It arose largely out of a feeling among Roman Catholics that their missions, as compared with those of Protestants, were being discriminated against in the appointment of government Indian agents, but it became not only a means for obtaining more generous treatment by the state, but also an instrument for soliciting government funds and private gifts and exercised a limited jurisdiction over Indian missions.[79]

The results of Roman Catholic missions to Indians are not easily summarized. In numbers, about 1921 the total of Roman Catholic Indians was said to be 61,456, and this was declared to be a marked increase during the past decade.[80] Roman Catholic missions contributed enormously to the education of Indians in an attempt to help the Red Man fit himself for life in the white man's world. In the last decade of the nineteenth century, because of their enterprise, the Roman Catholic schools were reported to be receiving seventy per cent. of all the government contracts for mission schools.[81] More than once, missionaries helped to prevent Indian outbreaks or, when war broke out, aided in negotiating peace.[82] On at least one occasion a missionary assisted in winning Indians to favour individual rather than tribal ownership of land.[83] Missionaries fought drink. Upon some of the religious life of the Pueblo Indians, even when predominantly non-Christian, the influence of Roman Catholic Christianity was apparent.[84] How far they modified home and family life is debatable.[85] In producing a native clergy there was a signal failure. Up to at least 1908, only one full-blooded Indian seems to have been

[77] Schwager, op. cit., p. 70; Lemmens, Geschichte der Franziskanermissionen, pp. 267, 268.
[78] Lemmens, op. cit., pp. 267, 268.
[79] The Catholic Encyclopedia, Vol. VII, pp. 745-747.
[80] Lindquist, The Red Man in the United States, p. 430.
[81] Meriam, The Problem of Indian Administration, pp. 823-825; Eastman, Pratt, The Red Man's Moses, p. 113.
[82] Berg, Die katholische Heidenmission als Kulturträger, Vol. III, pp. 297ff.
[83] Berg, op. cit., Vol. III, pp. 272, 274-279.
[84] Elsie Clews Parsons, Pueblo Indian Religion (University of Chicago Press, 2 vols., 1939), passim, and especially pp. viii, 548, 549, 1068-1070.
[85] Meriam, op. cit., p. 825.

ordained to the priesthood.[86] The Christian communities were still dependent financially and for leadership upon the whites.

The missions of the Russian Orthodox Church to the aborigines of what eventually was included within the United States arose in connexion with the Russian commercial and political occupation of Alaska. It was not a long period. The Russian discovery of Alaska is commonly dated from 1741. Effective settlement and administration did not begin until nearly the close of the eighteenth century, and in 1867, before the nineteenth century was three-quarters gone, the vast area had been sold to the United States. The aborigines were made up of various tribes and groups of Eskimos and Indians. It was among these that Russian Orthodox missionaries laboured.

The first contingent of missionaries, from two monasteries near Lake Ladoga, in Western Russia, reached Kodiak Island, off the Alaska Peninsula, in 1794.[87] The docile natives easily assented to the wishes of the strangers, coming as they did with the prestige of the white man. Within a few months several thousand on Kodiak Island were baptized, and before the end of 1796 the inhabitants of the neighbouring peninsula became nominally Christian.[88] In the same brief period, 1795-1796, the entire population of several of the Aleutian Islands were baptized.[89] For a time the agents of the Russian American Company, which had a monopoly of the region, bent upon obtaining as many pelts as possible, treated the inhabitants with shameful cruelty and were hostile to the missionaries.[90] It may have been that this feeling had caused a leading spirit of the Russian American Company to view the missions with jaundiced eye when he declared that baptism had not affected the converts' morals or customs and that the Russian priests lived in idleness, seldom learned the native tongues, and fomented trouble for the company.[91] However, a few additional priests arrived. Among these was the extraordinarily able and zealous John Veniaminoff. A native of Siberia, he had been trained in the seminary in Irkutsk. Athletic, of towering stature, forceful and impressive, in 1824, when not quite twenty-seven years old, he arrived in Unalaska, one of the Aleutian Islands. Here he set himself to raise the moral and religious tone of the debased, nominally Christian native population. He

[86] Anton Huonder, *Der einheimische Klerus in den Heidenländern*, pp. 39-47.
[87] Lübeck, *Die russischen Missionen*, p. 47.
[88] *Ibid.*
[89] *Ibid.*
[90] Lübeck, *op. cit.*, p. 48.
[91] Bancroft, *History of Alaska*, p. 459.

became expert in the language, manners, and institutions of the Aleuts. He prepared a catechism and a Bible history in the native tongue and translated portions of the New Testament. He conducted schools to such good effect that in time in some localities most of the Aleuts were literate. Later he moved to Sitka, the capital, and still later was made bishop of a new see which embraced Kamchatka, the Kurile Islands, and the Aleutians. He was zealous in encouraging his clergy to master the local idioms and to prepare literature in them. Between 1841 and 1860, 4,700 Indians are said to have been baptized. Veniaminoff removed his residence from Sitka to Yakutsk, in Siberia, for this had been added to his see, but later he named a vicar-bishop for Alaska.[92] In 1900 the Orthodox Missionary Society entered Alaska. Although in the meantime the territory had been sold to the United States, in 1872 the Holy Synod created an independent bishopric which included it.[93] Most of the priests in the mission were of mixed white and indigenous blood. In 1903 the membership was said to be 10,225, of whom 320 were Russians and 2,110 were of mixed blood. Losses were being suffered to Roman Catholics and Protestants and the complaint was heard that the American Government was restricting the few schools on the ground that they were seeking to make Russians of their pupils.[94]

As was to be expected, Protestant efforts for the Indians were extensive. In colonial days they had been numerous. At its outset, much of the rising missionary spirit of the new era was directed to the Indians, as the most obvious pagans immediately at hand. In the course of the years, when other appealing projects moved to the fore, relatively less attention was devoted to them. However, they remained a concern of the churches. Denomination after denomination and society after society conducted missions among them. Some assistance, although relatively little, and not so much as in the case of the Roman Catholics, came from Europe. The story of all these efforts has never been fully told. To do so would require a shelf of generous volumes. Here, as in so much else of our narrative, we can take the space to notice only a few of the outstanding incidents, individuals, organizations, and movements.

By 1800, with the dwindling of the Indian communities in New England, the centre of missionary interest had moved westward, partly to Northern and Western New York. Indeed, at the initiative of some of their leaders, about

[92] Lübeck, op. cit., pp. 49-51; Bancroft, op. cit., pp. 699-710.
[93] Lübeck, op. cit., p. 52.
[94] Raeder in Allgemeine Missions-Zeitschrift, Vol. XXXII, p. 554.

1795 a number of destitute Indians, remnants of six tribes, moved from Connecticut, Rhode Island, Massachusetts, and Long Island to North-western New York and, thence, about 1817, to Wisconsin.[95]

A number of the early Protestant missionary organizations of the United States gave much attention to the Indians. Thus in 1800 the Northern Missionary Society of the State of New York was supporting emissaries among the Oneidas.[96] In 1811 the Massachusetts Missionary Society made an appropriation for an enterprise among the Wyandottes.[97] The Missionary Society of Connecticut sent emissaries to the Indians, at least one of them going to Northern Michigan, to the Ojibways, in an area that had earlier been touched by Roman Catholics.[98] About 1807 the Baptist Missionary Society in Massachusetts cooperated with the New York Baptist Missionary Society in supporting a representative among the Tuscaroras in North-western New York.[99]

The Quakers were long active among the Indians, but did not have many converts. They had also endeavoured to deal with the Indians on the basis of peace and fairness. The first attempts to win converts were in colonial days, by individuals under the inner promptings which were so characteristic of the Friends.[100] In the last decade of the eighteenth century, partly as the result of a concern quickened by the Indian wars of the period, individual efforts were enhanced and organized activities were begun for the tribes which were being pressed by the white man. Various yearly meetings conducted missions and schools among tribes in regions ranging at one time or another from New York to Alaska. Quakers, too, repeatedly exerted themselves to right wrongs from which the Indians suffered.[101] Beginning in 1869, President Grant, remembering the traditional friendship of the Quakers for the Indians, entrusted to them the responsibility of nominating Indian agents, officials supervising the Indians, for vast areas, and a number of Friends undertook these difficult posts.[102]

[95] Coe Hayne, *The Long Trail of the Brothertowns* (mimeographed ms., c. 1935), *passim.*

[96] *The New-York Missionary Magazine,* Vol. I, pp. 401-405.

[97] *The Connecticut Evangelical Magazine,* Vol. IV, p. 353.

[98] Bacon, *Leonard Bacon,* pp. 4-20.

[99] *The Massachusetts Baptist Missionary Magazine,* Vol. II, p. 314.

[100] Kelsey, *Friends and the Indians,* pp. 19-37.

[101] Kelsey, *op. cit.,* pp. 89ff.; *Some Account of the Conduct of the Religious Society of Friends towards the Indian Tribes in the Settlement of the Colonies of East and West Jersey and Pennsylvania: with a Brief Narrative of Their Labours for the Civilization and Christian Instruction of the Indians from the Time of Their Settlement in America, to the year 1843* (London, Edward Marsh, 1844, pp. 247), pp. 115ff.; Jones, *The Quakers of Iowa,* pp. 215ff.

[102] Kelsey, *op. cit.,* pp. 162ff.; Jones, *op. cit.,* pp. 205-214.

In colonial days the Moravians had devoted much effort to the Indians. Although later outstripped by denominations with much larger memberships, they continued enterprises for them. Notable and tragic was the mission to the Delawares. Under pressure from white settlers, some from this tribe, on whom the Moravians, with David Zeisberger as the most prominent of their personnel, were concentrating, moved westward to Ohio. There, in the valleys of the Muskingum and Tuscawaras Rivers, the Christians built model settlements—peaceable, farming communities. Zeisberger had dreamed of having Ohio kept an Indian preserve, away from the contaminating influence of the whites. But his hopes were dashed. White men began to come in. In the course of the Revolutionary War, the Christian Indians, wishing to remain neutral, were suspected by both sides. Zeisberger and some of his colleagues, with several of the Indians, were carried off by the British to Detroit. Scores of the remaining Indians were massacred in cold blood by whites who espoused the cause of the Colonies. The villages were laid waste. After the war attempts were made to resume the project on tracts given by the British and the Americans, but contacts with the white man, especially with his liquor, proved deleterious. After Zeisberger's death (1808) rapid deterioration set in.[103] A brave but brief attempt in the first decade of the nineteenth century to found a mission among the Delawares in the White River region, in Indiana, came to nought, partly because of the deluge of firewater from white traders.[104] In the eighteenth century the Moravians essayed missions among the Indians in the South, especially the Creeks, but without lasting success. In 1801, from the Moravian centre at Salem, North Carolina, a mission was sent to Georgia to the Cherokees. In 1810 it had the only school in the Cherokee nation. For a time it seemed to flourish, but the forcible removal of the Cherokees to the West interrupted it. In spite of the agony of the migration, several of the Christians remained true to their faith. The mission was resumed in the new home of the tribe in the Indian Territory and continued until the time when, late in the nineteenth century, the Indian churches were deemed ready for full

[103] George Henry Loskiel, History of the Missions of the United Brethren among the Indians in North America, translated from the German by C. I. La Trobe (London, The Brethren's Society for the Furtherance of the Gospel, 3 Parts, 1794), Part III, passim; John Heckwelder, A Narrative of the Mission of the United Brethren among the Delaware and Mohegan Indians, from Its Commencement, in the Year 1740, to the Close of the Year 1808 (Philadelphia, McCarty & Davis, 1820, pp. 429. By a participant), passim; J. E. Hutton, A History of Moravian Missions (London, Moravian Publication Office, 1923, pp. 550), pp. 102-116, 246, 247.

[104] Lawrence Henry Gipson, The Moravian Indian Mission on the White River. Diaries and Letters, May 5, 1799 to November 12, 1806 (Indianapolis, Indiana Historical Bureau, 1938, pp. xv, 674), passim.

independence.[105] Among other missions of the Moravians were ones in Alaska, in which John Kilbuck, of Delaware stock, was a pioneer,[106] and in California, where the Roman Catholics offered opposition.[107]

The Cherokees were the field of a mission manned from New England. This also had a prosperous period followed by one of intense hardships. In the eighteenth century the Cherokees claimed a country of about forty thousand square miles in the piedmont and mountains in a section which was later included in parts of Alabama, Georgia, Tennessee, South Carolina, North Carolina, and Virginia.[108] In 1810 they were said to number about twelve thousand.[109] They suffered severely from the wars of the eighteenth century and from the white man's diseases, and the encroaching tide of white settlement took from them an increasing proportion of their lands.[110] Yet by the early part of the nineteenth century they had made considerable advance towards an agricultural economy[111] and one of their number had invented for them a syllabary.[112] In addition to what the Moravians were doing to introduce Christianity among the Cherokees, in 1804 the Presbyterians opened a school for them.[113] In 1817 the Baptist Triennial Convention appointed a missionary to the Cherokees of Georgia.[114] In 1817 Cyrus Kingsbury (1786-1870), a native of Vermont and a graduate of Brown, began a mission under the American Board of Commissioners for Foreign Missions.[115] A school was opened, more missionaries arrived from New England, literature was prepared in the vernacular, temperance societies were organized to help the Indian guard himself against one of his most dangerous temptations, converts were made, and some of the more promising boys were sent for further education to a school at Cornwall, Connecticut, which the American Board had inaugurated for the youths of several of the tribes and peoples among whom it conducted missions.[116] How-

[105] Edmund Schwarze, *History of the Moravian Missions Among Southern Indian Tribes of the United States* (Transactions of the Moravian Historical Society, Special Series, Vol. I, Bethlehem, Pa., Times Publishing Co., 1923, pp. xvii, 331), *passim;* Walker, *Torchlights to the Cherokees*, pp. 25-40.
[106] Schulze, *200 Jahre Brudermission,* Vol. II, pp. 90ff.
[107] Schulze, *op. cit.,* Vol. II, pp. 118ff.
[108] Walker, *op. cit.,* p. 1.
[109] Tracy, *History of the American Board of Commissioners for Foreign Missions,* p. 69.
[110] Walker, *op. cit.,* pp. 3-14.
[111] Tracy, *op. cit.,* p. 69.
[112] Walker, *op. cit.,* pp. 227ff.
[113] Tracy, *op. cit.,* p. 68.
[114] Hamilton, *The Gospel among the Red Men,* pp. 47ff.
[115] Walker, *op. cit.,* pp. 16ff., 41, 42; Tracy, *op. cit.,* p. 69.
[116] Walker, *op. cit.,* pp. 41-255; Bass, *Cherokee Messenger,* pp. 34, 76. See also Ralph H. Gabriel, *Elias Boudinot, Cherokee, and His America* (Norman, Okla., University of Oklahoma Press, 1940 or 1941). The school at Cornwall (1817-1826) was a most in-

ever, interruption came from the increasing determination of the whites to possess themselves of the Indians' lands. In its resolution to oust the Indians, the State of Georgia attempted to shut out the missionaries. In a test case two of the latter, Samuel A. Worcester and Elizur Butler, underwent imprisonment at the hands of Georgia. In spite of a decision in their favour by the Supreme Court of the United States (1832) and their release, the measures against the Cherokees were carried out.[117] The American Board and its friends made efforts to prevent the deportation,[118] but the majority of the Cherokees were moved beyond the Mississippi. The American Board had already begun a mission (1819-1821) in Arkansas among the Cherokees who had earlier crossed the river.[119] Some of the missionaries followed the later migrants to their new homes. It was not until 1860, when it had decided that the Cherokees were so far civilized and Christianized as to be no longer a foreign mission field, that the American Board finally discontinued its efforts among them.[120]

The American Board also had missions among three of the other four of the so-called civilized tribes who were removed from the east to the west of the Mississippi—the Creeks, the Choctaws, and the Chickasaws. It extended its labours to some other tribes, among them the Osages, the Pawnees, the Abernaquis, the New York Indians, the Stockbridge Indians after their removal to the West, and the Ojibwas.[121]

Both the Methodists and the American Board responded to the appeal which was implied in the dramatic embassy of the Flatheads and Nez Perces to St. Louis in 1831.

At least as early as 1807 the Methodists numbered an Indian among their converts,[122] and in 1821, with the appointment by Bishop McKendree of William Capers, from a prominent South Carolinian family, as a missionary

---

teresting project. At first it was welcomed by the Cornwall Community but in time local opposition became bitter. For this and other reasons, especially because experience seemed to prove that the youths suffered from being educated in an environment so alien to the ones in which they had been reared and to which they must return, the school was discontinued (1826). *Report of the American Board of Commissioners for Foreign Missions, 1826*, pp. 103ff.

[117] Walker, *op. cit.*, pp. 256-307; Tracy, *op. cit.*, pp. 249-254; Bass, *op. cit.*, pp. 137-160.

[118] Jeremiah Evarts to Leonard Bacon, Dec. 30, 1829, and Jan. 23, 1830 (Mss. in Day Missions Library).

[119] Cephas Washburn, *Reminiscences of the Indians* (Richmond, Presbyterian Committee of Publication, 1869, pp. 236), *passim*.

[120] *Report of the American Board of Commissioners for Foreign Missions, 1839*, pp. 135ff., *1840*, pp. 169ff.; Strong, *The Story of the American Board*, pp. 46-186.

[121] Tracy, *op. cit.*, pp. 220, 221, 254, 331, 400; Strong, *op. cit.*, 38, 41, 42, 45, 46; Bass, *op. cit.*, pp. 178-196; *Report of the American Board of Commissioners for Foreign Missions, 1836*, pp. 85ff.

[122] Paine, *Life and Times of William McKendree*, p. 127.

to the Indians, the denomination became active and within a few years had inaugurated missions among the Creeks and Cherokees.[123] In 1816 John Stewart, part white, part Negro, and possibly part Indian, who from a life of degradation had been converted and had become a Methodist, on his own initiative began a mission to the Wyandottes, on the borders of Ohio, Indiana, and Michigan. Many of the tribe were nominally Roman Catholic, but liquor and defeat in war had worked demoralization. Stewart made some converts. The Ohio conference of the Methodists sent preachers to assist him, a school was started, aid came from Methodist missionary societies, and marked improvement was noted in the economic and moral condition of those who became Christians.[124] The Methodists, therefore, were not unprepared to undertake a mission to Indians on the West Coast. Somewhat tardily, in 1833, more than a year after the event, the news of the Indians' search for the white man's religion was given publicity in the Methodist press. It created a profound sensation and money poured in to meet the challenge. To head the mission, the Methodists appointed Jason Lee (1803-1845), of New England ancestry and education, athletic and of towering physique. In 1834 Lee made the difficult overland trip to Oregon and chose a site for a mission in the fertile Willamette Valley. Extensive reinforcements arrived, and missions were opened in a number of centres in the Pacific North-west. Some converts were won, but the tribes were dying, and the Methodists found their chief task in caring religiously for the white settlers who before long began pouring into the country. Through them what was said to be the first Protestant church building west of the Rocky Mountains was erected, schools were opened, and the foundations of their denomination in the Oregon Country were laid.[125]

The project of a mission to the Pacific North-west was not new to the American Board of Commissioners for Foreign Missions. Since 1788 American

[123] Paine, op. cit., pp. 278-282; Posey, The Development of Methodism in the Old Southwest, pp. 81-90.

[124] James B. Finley, Life among the Indians; or, Personal Reminiscences and Historical Incidents Illustrative of Indian Life and Character (Cincinnati, Cranston and Curts, no date, pp. 548), pp. 233ff.; James B. Finley, History of the Wyandott Mission, at Upper Sandusky, Ohio, under the Direction of the Methodist Episcopal Church (Cincinnati, J. F. Wright and L. Swormstedt, 1840, pp. 432), passim.

[125] The story of this mission has evoked a large literature. Among the more important books are H. K. Hines, Missionary History of the Pacific Northwest (Portland, Oregon, H. K. Hines, 1899, pp. 510); C. J. Brosnan, Jason Lee, Prophet of the New Oregon (New York, The Macmillan Co., 1932, pp. x, 348); D. Lee and J. H. Frost, Ten Years in Oregon (New York, J. Collord, 1844, pp. 344); James W. Bashford, The Oregon Missions (New York, The Abingdon Press, 1918, pp. 311); Theressa Gay, Life and Letters of Mrs. Jason Lee (Portland, Oregon, Metropolitan Press, 1936, pp. 224); A. B. and D. P. Hulbert, editors, The Oregon Crusade (The Stewart Commission of Colorado College and the Denver Public Library, 1935, pp. xvi, 301), chiefly selected documents.

vessels had been coming to the North-west Coast to trade for furs and it was natural that the American Board should think of following them with missionaries. This was especially true since in 1819 the Board had sent a first contingent of missionaries to the Hawaiian Islands, where ships from the Northwest Coast frequently touched. The subject had been broached as early as 1821.[126] In 1827 a formal resolution was passed expressing the desirability of undertaking such a mission.[127] In 1829 a missionary to the Hawaiian Islands was sent on an exploratory tour of the Coast.[128] However, it was a report of the request of the 1831 delegation of Nez Perces and Flatheads which brought the decisive action. A Congregational clergyman, Samuel Parker (1779-1855), was stirred by the same account which had led to the sending of Jason Lee. Although he was then in his middle fifties, he dreamed of going himself to respond to the plea. He raised funds and found recruits, among them a physician, Marcus Whitman, and the future Mrs. Whitman, Narcissa Prentiss. In 1835 Parker and Whitman started across the plains to the Far West on a reconnoitring expedition. Whitman did not then complete the journey, but Parker went on to the West Coast, returning by boat. In 1836 Whitman and his bride moved to the Oregon Country together with Mr. and Mrs. Henry H. Spalding and W. H. Gray. The Spaldings settled among the Nez Perces at Lapwai, not far from the later Lewiston, Idaho, and the Whitmans among the Cayuses at Waiilatpu, in what was eventually South-eastern Washington. Reinforcements came. Converts were made. In 1847 the Whitmans were massacred by the Indians, but the missions continued and spread and enduring churches (largely Presbyterian) were established.[129]

The American Board of Commissioners for Foreign Missions also inaugurated what proved to be a long-lived enterprise among one of the largest and

[126] See the urgent suggestion of the Hawaiian mission in *The Missionary Herald,* Vol. XVII (Sept., 1821), p. 280.

[127] *Report of the American Board of Commissioners for Foreign Missions . . . 1827,* p. 153.

[128] *Report of the American Board of Commissioners for Foreign Missions . . . 1830,* pp. 99-103.

[129] Of the extensive bibliography on this Oregon mission of the American Board the following are among the most important books: Clifford Merrill Drury, *Marcus Whitman, M.D., Pioneer and Martyr* (Caldwell, Idaho, The Caxton Printers, 1937, pp. 473); Clifford Merrill Drury, *Henry Harmon Spalding* (Caldwell, Idaho, The Caxton Printers, 1936, pp. 438); A. B. and D. P. Hulbert, *op. cit.*; Myron Eells, *Father Eells* (Boston, Congregational Sunday-School and Publishing Society, 1894, pp. 342); M. Eells, *Ten Years of Missionary Work Among the Indians at Skokomish, Washington Territory, 1874-1884* (Boston, Congregational Sunday-School and Publishing Society, 1886, pp. 271); Myron Eells, *History of Indian Missions on the Pacific Coast, Oregon, Washington and Idaho* (Philadelphia, The American Sunday-School Union, 1882, pp. 270); Miles Cannon, *Waiilatpu, Its Rise and Fall 1836-1847* (Boise, Idaho, Capital News Job Rooms, 1915, pp. ix, 171).

most warlike of the Indian tribes, the Sioux, or Dakotas. In the middle of the nineteenth century these occupied much of the later states of Minnesota and North and South Dakota. In 1834, the year before Parker and Whitman started for Oregon, the American Board sent among them Thomas S. Williamson, a physician, to explore the possibility of founding a mission. The following year, in 1835, a party of missionaries, led by Williamson, came to the Sioux and opened stations among them, one being near the site of the later Minneapolis. They were assisted by two brothers, Samuel W. and Gideon H. Pond, from that Litchfield County, in Connecticut, from which Samuel J. Mills had come. Stirred by a revival, they had determined to give their lives to the West and in 1834 had reached the Sioux and there, at first quite without any support by a society, were beginning missionary effort. In 1837 Stephen R. Riggs and his wife, Mary, came. There was co-operation with missionaries sent by a society of Lausanne, Switzerland. Converts were won, some of them of worthy life and others unstable, and churches were organized. The removal of numbers of the Indians to a reservation and the dislocation brought by the new life and by the idleness nourished by government annuities brought altered conditions and made necessary fresh beginnings. Yet the enterprise continued, and a son and a grandson of Riggs helped to carry on the undertaking.[130]

It was among the Sioux that the Protestant Episcopal Church maintained one of its strongest missions. This arose in part from a chain of events which had its beginnings in colonial days. Before the Thirteen Colonies had broken away from the British Empire, missionaries belonging to the Church of England had engaged in efforts to win the Iroquois. With the Revolutionary War these enterprises tended to lapse. However, in 1816, after the Protestant Episcopal Church had been organized and after Henry Hobart had been consecrated Bishop of New York (1811), Eleazer Williams, one of the many upon whom the romantic surmise was attached of being the lost Dauphin of France, resumed the mission among the Oneidas, one of the Iroquois tribes. In 1823, to make way for the on-rolling wave of white settlement, many of the Oneidas were removed to Wisconsin. Eleazer Williams accompanied them.[131] Among the group of young men whom the enthusiasm of the Oxford Movement sent

[130] Stephen R. Riggs, *Tah'-koo Wah-kan'; or the Gospel among the Dakotas* (Boston, Congregational Sabbath-School and Publishing Society, 1869, pp. xxxvi, 491), *passim;* Stephen R. Riggs, *Mary and I: Forty Years with the Sioux* (Boston, Congregational Sunday-School and Publishing Society, 1887, pp. 437), *passim;* S. W. Pond, Jr., *Two Volunteer Missionaries among the Dakotas or the Story of the Labors of Samuel W. and Gideon H. Pond* (Boston, Congregational Sunday-School and Publishing Society, pp. xii, 278), *passim;* F. B. Riggs in *Facing Facts* [Annual Report of the American Missionary Association, 1935], pp. 1-5.
[131] Robbins, *A Handbook of the Church's Missions to the Indians*, pp. 85-88.

to the Wisconsin frontier was James Lloyd Breck. For a time he was head of the establishment founded at Nashotah, Wisconsin. Later he moved to Minnesota and there became the chief spirit in a mission among the Indians—the Chippewas first and late the Sioux.[132] In 1859 Henry Benjamin Whipple was elected the first Bishop of Minnesota. He immediately became deeply interested and active in missions among the Indians and was a champion of Indian rights.[133] In 1872, upon nomination by Bishop Whipple, William Hobart Hare was chosen to be bishop of a large area with Indians as his particular care. He specialized on the Sioux, and although later his territorial jurisdiction was more narrowly delimited and was made to include whites as well as Indians, he was pre-eminently an apostle to the Red Men.[134] By the time of his death (1909) about ten thousand of the Sioux had been baptized.[135] In contrast with the Roman Catholic Church, the Protestant Episcopal Church ordained a number of Indians.[136]

It is embarrassing to be compelled to give only the barest mention of a few other Protestant enterprises for the Indians and to realize that because of limitations of space many others are having to be passed by in silence. There were the notable and comprehensive labours of Sheldon Jackson for the Indians and Eskimos of Alaska, begun after he had already accomplished more than the equivalent of a full lifetime's work in the Rocky Mountain area.[137] There was Hall Young, the Presbyterian, whose health seemed to forbid the tropics as a mission field, but who spent the major part of a long life in Alaska, often amid great hardships.[138] Hampton Institute, which we are to meet in the next chapter, at first cared for Indians as well as Negroes. James Bradley, whose father had come from England, joined the Chickahominy tribe in Virginia and in 1793 married an Indian wife. Through him the tribe became Baptists.[139] Bacone College, in Oklahoma, was the outgrowth of Baptist efforts.[140] A graduate of Bacone, a Cherokee Baptist clergyman, George W. Hicks, was

---

[132] Theodore T. Holcombe, *An Apostle of the Wilderness, James Lloyd Breck, D.D. His Missions and His Schools* (New York, Thomas Whittaker, 1903, pp. xiii, 195), *passim.*

[133] Henry Benjamin Whipple, *Lights and Shadows of a Long Episcopate. Being Reminiscences and Recollections* (New York, The Macmillan Co., 1912, pp. vi, 576), *passim.*

[134] M. A. DeWolfe Howe, *The Life and Labors of Bishop Hare, Apostle to the Sioux* (New York, Sturgis & Walton, 1911, pp. 417), *passim.*

[135] Eastman, *Pratt, The Red Man's Friend*, p. 116. See also Addison, *Our Expanding Church*, p. 82.

[136] For a list of Indian clergymen see Robbins, *op. cit.,* pp. 322-324.

[137] Stewart, *Sheldon Jackson*, pp. 308ff.; Faris, *The Alaskan Pathfinder*, pp. 83ff.

[138] S. Hall Young, *Hall Young of Alaska "The Mushing Parson"* (New York, Fleming H. Revell Co., pp. 448; an autobiography), *passim.*

[139] Hamilton, *The Gospel Among the Red Men*, p. 40.

[140] Hamilton, *op. cit.,* pp. 228ff.

partly responsible for inaugurating a mission among the Kiowas.[141] To the
Kiowas went a Baptist, Isabel Crawford, of unusual sprightliness and charm.[142]
Much earlier, in 1817, Isaac McCoy (1784-1846), a Baptist clergyman who had
been reared in Kentucky, began labours for the Indians which took him to
several tribes. He was a leader in planning and organizing Baptist missions
to the Indians. He became convinced that the Red Men would be infinitely
better off if they could be separated from the contaminating influence of the
white man and urged their removal to the West and the reservation for them
of an Indian Territory. This became the policy of the United States, although
not necessarily through his advocacy. For a time he served under the Federal
Government to help facilitate this programme.[143] In the 1890's the (Dutch)
Reformed Church in America inaugurated a mission among the Indians
which had as its outstanding pioneer Walter C. Roe. In the face of chronic
and debilitating ill health, Roe touched several tribes.[144] A mission of the
(German) Reformed Church in the United States among the Winnebagos in
Wisconsin arose out of the efforts of German immigrants.[145] William Duncan,
of English birth and rearing, came as a missionary first to Canada under the
Church Missionary Society, and in 1887, after unfortunate difficulties, moved
with many of his converts into Alaska under the American flag and at Metlakahtla conducted an independent undenominational mission.[146] Several of the
Lutheran synods, formed by nineteenth century immigrants, German and
Scandinavian, in spite of the burden of providing for the influx from Europe,
carried on missions among the Indians.[147] The National Indian Association,
organized in 1881 by Christian women, assisted in securing the legal rights
of the Indian and promoted medical, educational, and religious enterprises
among a number of tribes. Its policy was to turn over its missions when well

[141] Hamilton, op. cit., pp. 203-211.
[142] Isabel Crawford, Kiowa. The History of the Blanket Indian Mission (New York,
Fleming H. Revell Co., 1915, pp. 242. Largely the journal of the author), passim.
[143] Isaac McCoy, History of Baptist Indian Missions (Washington, W. M. Morrison,
1840, pp. 611. Largely autobiographical), passim; Dictionary of American Biography,
Vol. XI, pp. 617, 618.
[144] Elizabeth M. Page, In Camp and Tepee. An Indian Mission Story (New York,
Fleming H. Revell Co., 1915, pp. 245), passim.
[145] A. V. Casselman, The Winnebago Finds a Friend (Philadelphia, Heidelberg Press,
1932, pp. xii, 177), passim; Theodore P. Bolliger, The Wisconsin Winnebago Indians and
the Mission of the Reformed Church (Cleveland, Central Publishing House, 1922, pp.
43), passim.
[146] John W. Arctander, The Apostle of Alaska. The Story of William Duncan of Metlakahtla (New York, Fleming H. Revell Co., 2d ed., 1909, pp. 395), passim.
[147] Albert Keiser, Lutheran Mission Work among the American Indians (Minneapolis,
Augsburg Publishing House, 1922, pp. 189), passim; Drach, Our Church Abroad, pp. 157-
187; Zeilinger, A Missionary Synod with a Mission, pp. 31-38.

started to some denominational agency.[148] In numerical strength, the denominations which led in efforts for the Indians were the Baptists, Northern and Southern, the Methodists, Northern and Southern, the Presbyterians, Northern and Southern, the Protestant Episcopalians, and the Congregationalists.[149] With the drawing together of home mission agencies after 1908 through the creation of the Home Missions Council, co-operation in counsel and planning was provided through a committee on the Indians.[150]

Some of the effects of Protestant efforts for the Indians can be stated in summary fashion. In 1913 communicants were said to total 31,815 and other adherents about 35,000.[151] Protestants were, therefore, of about the same numerical strength as Roman Catholics. That for many of these converts only a slight modification of life was involved appears clear. For instance, in one tribe which was nominally Protestant, the new faith was adopted much as American citizenship was accepted, as part of the new order brought by the white man: not much alteration in morals followed and older concepts were assimilated to those which came with Christianity.[152] On the other hand, for many Christianity made for striking spiritual and moral change and numbers were felt to be worthy representatives of the Christian name.[153] Even though many Indian Christians seemed to depart from their faith and affiliated themselves with the peyote cults, a strange religious movement which arose out of the use of a drug which induced stupor and visions, they made those cults progressively emphasize the elements in which they professed resemblances to Christianity.[154] Clergy were trained and ordained and self-supporting congregations came into being. The Bible was translated in whole or in part into several of the Indian vernaculars.[155] Much was done to protect the Indian against exploitation and to further his adjustment to the new life about him. Many a missionary laboured to this end. Under the impulse of the Christian

[148] *The National Indian Association. Report of Missions* (annual), and *Annual Reports, passim;* Lindquist, *The Red Man in the United States,* p. 433.
[149] Moffett, *The American Indian on the New Trail,* p. 289.
[150] Lindquist, *op. cit.,* p. 433.
[151] Moffett, *op. cit.,* p. 289.
[152] Mead, *The Changing Culture of an Indian Tribe,* pp. 102, 103.
[153] As instances of this, see Coe Hayne in *Missions* (June, 1937), Vol. XXVIII, pp. 346-349; Moore, *The Challenge of Change,* p. 76.
[154] Weston La Barre, *The Peyote Cult* (Yale University Press, 1938, pp. 188), *passim;* Mead, *op. cit.,* pp. 106ff. On the peyote cults see also Meriam, *The Problem of Indian Administration,* pp. 222, 629. On another indigenous Indian cult which was strong among the Iroquois and grew out of the visions of Handsome Lake (1735-1815) and which, while anti-Christian, seems to show some slight Christian influence, see Arthur C. Parker, *The Code of Handsome Lake, the Seneca Prophet* (New York State Museum Bulletin 163, Albany, N. Y., 1912, pp. 148).
[155] F. M. Sims, *The Bible in America* (New York, Wilson-Erickson, 1936, pp. xxiv, 394), pp. 195-199.

conscience, organizations for this purpose were developed. Thus for many years beginning in 1883 the Quaker, Albert Keith Smiley (1828-1912), held annually at Lake Mohonk a conference of the Friends of the Indians in which various measures in behalf of the Red Man were discussed by those in a position to take action.[156] The Indian Rights Association, although non-sectarian, had in its membership many with strong Christian convictions.[157] Protestant missions, too, through schools, medical aid, and other means contributed to the solution of the difficult problem presented to the Indian by the overwhelming wave of white culture.

When one surveys the course of the spread of Christianity among the Indians of the United States from the time of national independence to 1914 he finds himself pressed to a number of generalizations.

He again becomes aware of the extraordinary agony through which the Indian was passing and the challenge and the dismaying difficulties faced by those who would make Christianity effective among the Red Men. Here was a race in process of being engulfed in an irresistible flood of peoples of an utterly different culture. Dislocated from their accustomed seats, transplanted again and again, treated by whites as hostile encumbrances of the fertile earth to be brushed aside or destroyed, bewildered by a type of economy for which they were unprepared, decimated by diseases and vices to which they had built up no resistance, repeatedly seeing solemn treaties violated, subject to shifting governmental policies, preyed upon by incompetent and greedy officials, and at times demoralized by an excess of well intentioned but ill directed paternalistic kindness, it is a wonder that the Indians survived.

That the race endured and that thousands of individuals rose through their distresses to a richer life than their forefathers knew was due in no small degree to the missionary. In numbers, by 1914 between a third and a half of the Indians were at least nominally Christian or were under Christian influences. For many of these the new faith was a compound of the old and the new, and was neither fully the one nor the other. Others bore the unmistakable marks of growth towards the New Testament ideal. As in the case of the extensive Spanish American missions of earlier centuries, the state used Christian missionaries as a means towards solving the problem of the Indian and of protecting and assimilating him. More rapidly than in the case of these

[156] *Proceedings of the Annual Meetings of the Lake Mohonk Conference of Friends of the Indians,* 1883ff.; *Dictionary of American Biography,* Vol. XVII, pp. 230, 231.

[157] *Annual Reports of the Executive Committee of the Indian Rights Association* (Philadelphia, 1884ff.).

Spanish missions, the utilization by the state progressively declined. In contrast to most of the Spanish missions, moreover, the missionaries seldom gathered the Indians apart into separate communities which they could completely mould and control, but sought them as they were in their accustomed tribal organizations or in the new communities which they formed when the tribe dissolved. As a rule the Indians were won individually or in families rather than by entire communities or tribes. Missionaries assisted in education and for a time bore the major load. They and other Christians among the whites struggled to protect the Indian and to secure for him justice and opportunity. By 1914 the Indians were beginning, even though far from perfectly, to make their adjustment to the new day. That they did so was due in large part to the Christian missionary and to those in private and government circles who were led by their Christian faith to espouse the Red Man's cause.

Chapter IX

THE UNITED STATES OF AMERICA. THE NEGROES

THE Negroes constituted a major problem for Christianity in the United States. Here was a large body of non-Christians of another race and culture forming a substantial proportion of the population. They were many times more numerous than the Indians. In contrast with the latter, of whom there seem never to have been more than half a million and probably not much more than a third of a million in the United States at any one time, in 1790 the Negroes are said to have totalled 757,208, or 19.3 per cent. of the population, and in 1910, 9,827,763, or 10.7 per cent. of the population.[1] In a certain sense the Negroes of the United States gradually became a new race. They were formed by a mixture derived from several different parts of Africa and of many tribes. Most of them were from the region around the Gulf of Guinea, but some were Hottentots from the South and a few had Arab and Moorish blood. The large majority were from animistic faiths, but some were Moslems. Presumably they were of sturdy stock, for only the more hardy could survive the rigours of the forced journey to the African coast and of the trans-Atlantic passage.[2] In them was an increasing proportion of white blood.[3] The Negroes were not distributed evenly through the United States, but were largely concentrated in one section, the South. In 1790 nearly nine-tenths were in the South Atlantic states. In 1910 over 40 per cent. were in the South Atlantic states and 89 per cent. were in the South as a whole.[4] In some areas in the South Negroes comprised more than half of the population.[5] This massing of the Negroes in a particular section made the task of assimilation more difficult and with it such spread of Christianity as would come from contact with the whites. Moreover, until past the middle of the nineteenth century, the majority of the Negroes were slaves. It was only after the act of President Lincoln on January 1, 1863,

---

[1] Department of Commerce, Bureau of the Census, *Negro Population 1790-1915*, p. 25.
[2] Embree, *Brown America*, pp. 3-14.
[3] Department of Commerce, Bureau of the Census, *Negro Population 1790-1915*, p. 208, says that the percentage of Negroes obviously showing white blood rose from 11.2 per cent. in 1850 to 20.9 per cent. in 1910.
[4] *Op. cit.*, p. 33.
[5] *Op. cit.*, p. 16.

that all were emancipated. In some respects slavery presented an obstacle to conversion. For a time the resistance against the agitation for the abolition of slavery and the fear of slave insurrections slowed down the efforts for winning the Negro to the Christian faith. Slavery, too, constituted a major concern of the Christian conscience. Sudden emancipation brought with it the problem of adjustment to the new status. This proved a challenge to Christians, both white and black. Could this large body of non-Christians be won to the Christian faith? Could Christianity aid in solving the problems presented by the Negro? Could it transmute the cruelties, the sufferings, and the tears of the traffic which had brought the Negro to America and the agony of the ensuing slavery into a life for the Negro which would be better than that of his African ancestors?

Several aspects of the situation facilitated the spread of Christianity among the Negroes. In their compulsory migration to the New World and their dispersion among their white masters, with rare exceptions the Negroes had lost their tribal solidarity and their communal customs and traditions. Their older cults, associated as they were with tribal life, largely dropped away. Only certain attitudes persisted—notably a belief in magic and in spirits. Deprived of their hereditary manners and institutions, the Negroes were ready to accept new ones. They were placed under the absolute rule of white owners, sometimes in large groups on great plantations but often singly or in comparatively small units. Inevitably they adopted much of the *mores* of their masters. English quickly became the language of the great majority. With English they tended to absorb the ideas carried by that tongue. Generally docile, they were inclined to imitate the dominant race. The process of assimilation was facilitated by the slowing down of the influx from Africa. Beginning with 1808 the importation of slaves became illegal. While, in spite of the law, down to the Civil War many continued to be brought in, especially in the decade between 1850 and 1860, and some were imported as late as 1862,[6] after 1808 the trade became more difficult. An increasing proportion of the Negroes were American-born. With emancipation immigration practically ceased and the adoption of white culture could go on all but unhampered by fresh arrivals from non-American cultures. Christianity was a growing force among the Negroes' masters. Revivals were sweeping the white population and the proportion of church members was increasing. Impelled by the rising

<hr>

[6] W. E. Burghardt DuBois, *The Suppression of the African Slave-Trade to the United States of America* (New York, Longmans, Green and Co., 1896, pp. xi, 335), *passim*, especially pp. 158ff.; Bassett, *A Short History of the United States*, p. 352; Washington, *The Story of the Negro*, Vol. I, pp. 101-105.

tide of religious life, it is not surprising that many whites sought to spread their faith among the Negroes or that Negroes became preachers to their own people. In the North, where emancipation early prevailed, the Negroes were mainly in the cities. Here they tended to conform to the dominant white civilization and to respond to the religious movements in progress among the whites. In the South abrupt emancipation wrought revolutionary changes. In general these hastened the assimilation of the Negro. White philanthropy, impelled largely by Christian purpose, sought to equip the freedman for his new status. The fact that these efforts were made in no small degree through missionary channels furthered the spread of Christianity among the Negroes. For many years after emancipation the Negro churches were the chief institutions under the full control of the coloured people. This also hastened the spread of the faith. So favouring were many of the circumstances that the rapid adherence of the Negroes to Christianity need not surprise us.

Among no other body of peoples of non-European stock did nineteenth century Christianity make such large numerical gains. By 1914 Protestant churches had approximately as large a total of members among the Negroes of the United States as they had among all the peoples of Asia and Africa. In others words, all the extensive Protestant missionary effort of Europeans and Americans in Asia and Africa in the century between 1815 and 1914 had resulted in no greater numerical gains than had been achieved among the Negroes of the United States in the same period. Indeed, in 1914 the membership of Negro churches in the United States was not far from two-thirds as large as the total number of Roman Catholics in all Asia and Africa, and that in spite of the fact that the latter was the product of several centuries of effort.

Moreover, Christianity had a profound effect upon Negro life. It was partly responsible for emancipation. It also had a major share in the education of the Negro and in the formation of his social institutions and of his ethical and spiritual ideals.

To this story we now turn. In narrating it we must seek to answer the familiar questions: What was it that spread? Why did it spread? By what processes did it spread? What effect did it have upon the Negroes? What effect did the Negroes have upon Christianity?

Roman Catholicism had only a small part in the propagation of the faith among the Negroes. It was strongest in the North, and the vast majority of Negroes were in the South. Geographically its efforts in behalf of the Negro were widely extended, but its gains were particularly marked in Maryland, Louisiana, and Kentucky. Here it enjoyed the favourable combination of being fairly influential and of contact with a numerous Negro population.

In Maryland, with its background of Roman Catholic settlement and effort, it was to be expected that many converts would be made from among the Negroes. In 1785 John Carroll, soon to be Bishop of Baltimore, estimated that about three thousand of the nearly sixteen thousand Roman Catholics in the state were coloured.[7] In Maryland and the adjoining District of Columbia Roman Catholic clergy and sisters ministered to the Negroes. The Sulpicians were especially attentive.[8] Education was provided, particularly for coloured women. In 1829, through a Sulpician, James Hector Nicholas Joubert de la Muraille, usually known as Nicholas Joubert, a refugee from the revolution which drove the French out of San Domingo, a school was opened in Baltimore to train coloured girls as homemakers and servants.[9] It was Joubert who in 1828 organized a society of Negro women to assist him in efforts for their race. The following year this became officially established as the Oblate Sisters of Providence.[10] In Georgetown schools were early begun for the Negroes.[11] Roman Catholics were noted for admitting Negroes to their churches in Washington on equal footing with the whites when most of the Protestant churches in the city had erected the colour bar,[12] but it was in Baltimore that one of the first Roman Catholic church buildings for the exclusive use of Negroes was set aside.[13]

In Louisiana in the days of French control many Negroes had been won to the Roman Catholic form of the faith. Their numbers had been augmented by several hundreds who fled from the revolt in San Domingo.[14] In New Orleans, in 1842, a community of coloured women, the Sisters of the Holy Family, was founded for service among the Negroes.[15] There, too, the Sisters of Our Lady of Mount Carmel were educating coloured girls.[16]

[7] Letter of Carroll to Cardinal Antonelli, March 1, 1785; text in Guilday, *The Life and Times of John Carroll*, p. 223.
[8] Gillard, *The Catholic Church and the American Negro*, pp. 15, 16.
[9] Woodson, *The Education of the Negro Prior to 1861*, p. 139.
[10] Rouse, *A Study of the Development of Negro Education under Catholic Auspices in Maryland and the District of Columbia*, p. 11; Gillard, *op. cit.*, p. 16.
[11] Woodson, *op. cit.*, p. 108; Gillard, *op. cit.*, pp. 137, 138.
[12] Woodson, *op. cit.*, p. 135.
[13] Gillard, *op. cit.*, pp. 29, 30. Gillard seems to be in error in saying that this was the first of its kind in the United States. Some years before, in 1832, a church in St. Louis had been set aside for the use of Negroes.—Garraghan, *The Jesuits of the Middle United States*, Vol. I, p. 273n.
[14] Gillard, *op. cit.*, pp. 16-19.
[15] Gillard, *op. cit.*, pp. 30, 31, 140.
[16] *Annales de la Propagation de la Foi*, Vol. XXXIII (1851), p. 413.

Here and there in other places before the Civil War Roman Catholics were seeking to win and to serve the Negro. In Kentucky Nerinckx dreamed of inaugurating an institute of Negro sisters and was happy when, in 1824, three coloured children whom he had had reared at Loretto took the veil with the Friends of Mary at the Foot of the Cross. He planned for them a habit and employment different from the others.[17] Very shortly, however, his successor as the ecclesiastical superior of the community, believing the time not ripe for such an undertaking, released the Negro novices from their vows.[18] In 1832 a church building in St. Louis was designated for Negroes.[19] Before 1860 the Jesuits and the Sisters of Mercy had begun work for the Negroes of that city.[20] Bishop England, of Charleston, was active in seeking the spiritual welfare of the Negroes. For a time, until the rising fear of Negro education stopped the enterprise, he had schools for them.[21] We hear of a free school for Negroes maintained by Roman Catholics in the Diocese of Nashville, Tennessee, and of Roman Catholic Negroes in Boston, New York, and Philadelphia.[22]

One of the first results of emancipation was a marked defection of Roman Catholic Negroes from their former allegiance. It is said that in one section of Louisiana alone, in the years immediately subsequent to the Civil War, about sixty-five thousand fell away from the Roman Catholic Church. This loss was ascribed to restiveness under authority, a dearth of clergy, and the appeal of Protestant denominations with their emotional revivalism.[23]

However, in the half century between the Civil War and 1914 the Roman Catholic Church achieved some progress among the Negroes. In 1866, the second Plenary Council of the American hierarchy urged bishops in diocesan synods and provincial councils to give attention to the spiritual care of Negroes.[24] In 1871 the Society of St. Joseph, from its headquarters at Mill Hill, not far from London, was assigned the Negroes of the United States as its first field. Its initial contingent arrived in 1871.[25] In 1887 it opened in Baltimore a seminary for the training of missionaries.[26] In 1893, largely at the

[17] Maes, *The Life of Rev. Charles Nerinckx*, p. 510.
[18] Gillard, *op. cit.*, p. 136.
[19] Garraghan, *op. cit.*, Vol. I, p. 273n.
[20] Garraghan, *op. cit.*, Vol. III, pp. 560, 561.
[21] Gillard, *op. cit.*, pp. 24-27.
[22] Gillard, *op. cit.*, p. 31.
[23] Gillard, *op. cit.*, pp. 258-261.
[24] Guilday, *A History of the Councils of Baltimore*, p. 213.
[25] Gillard, *op. cit.*, pp. 39, 40.
[26] Gillard, *op. cit.*, p. 41.

instance of Vaughan, the American branch became independent, as St. Joseph's Society of the Sacred Heart, usually known as St. Joseph's Society for Coloured Missions, and subsequently had a healthy growth.[27] In 1872, the Society of the Holy Ghost, which was specializing on missions to Africans, sent a group to the United States. This was followed by others.[28] In several places Benedictines undertook missions for Negroes.[29] The Sisters of the Blessed Sacrament, founded in 1889 by Katharine Drexel, had for their object missions to Negroes as well as Indians.[30] In 1910 the Franciscans began an enterprise for Negroes in Kansas City.[31] In 1877 the Catherine of Siena Congregation of Dominican Sisters opened a school in Kentucky for coloured children.[32] Taking a leaf out of the experience of Protestants with Hampton Institute with its industrial training designed to fit the Negro for occupations open to him in American society, beginning in 1895, Roman Catholics opened industrial schools, one in Rock Castle, Virginia, and one in Wilmington, Delaware.[33] The Society of the Divine Word undertook missions for Negroes.[34] In 1909 the Knights of Peter Claver were organized as a fraternal organization for Roman Catholic Negroes.[35] As an outgrowth of the Third Plenary Council, held in 1884, the Commission for Catholic Missions Among the Coloured People and Indians was set up by the hierarchy.[36] In 1907 the Catholic Board for Mission Work Among the Coloured People was launched.[37] Cardinal Gibbons, long the ranking member of the American hierarchy, was known as an ardent advocate of better treatment of the Negroes and was hailed by Booker T. Washington, a great spokesman of the race, as one of their champions.[38] In 1888 the total number of Negro Roman Catholics was said by official figures of the church to be 138,312, in 1892 152,692, and in 1928 204,000.[39] While this indicated a growth, the increase proportionately was not as rapid as that of the Negro population as a whole. One set of figures declares Roman Catholics to have had in 1914 less than 1 per cent. of the Negro Christian

[27] Gillard, *op. cit.*, p. 44.
[28] Gillard, *op. cit.*, p. 41.
[29] Gillard, *op. cit.*, pp. 41, 42.
[30] *The Catholic Encyclopedia*, Vol. II, p. 599; Schwager, *Die katholische Heidenmission der Gegenwart*, p. 71.
[31] Lemmens, *Geschichte der Franziskanermissionen*, p. 278.
[32] Minogue, *Pages from a Hundred Years of Dominican History*, p. 149.
[33] Gillard, *op. cit.*, pp. 184, 185.
[34] Work, *Negro Year Book . . . 1914-1915*, p. 185.
[35] *Ibid.*
[36] Gillard, *op. cit.*, p. 43.
[37] Gillard, *op. cit.*, p. 45.
[38] Will, *Life of Cardinal Gibbons*, Vol. II, pp. 794-796.
[39] Gillard, *op. cit.*, p. 1.

communicants of the United States,[40] and the government census of 1906 showed them to have only 1¼ per cent. of the Negro church membership.[41]

The reasons for this relative lack of success of Roman Catholics among Negroes is not entirely clear.[42] It was not due to the Negro temperament: in Africa in the nineteenth and twentieth centuries the Roman Catholic Church was making fully as great strides among the Negroes as were the Protestants. It may have been in part because of a lack of coloured clergy, for until 1888 no Negro priest was ordained for his fellows in the United States and by 1914 only four had been ordained.[43] However, this, if a cause, was a minor one, for in Africa, where large gains were registered, very few Negroes were ordained until after a large body of Roman Catholics had been gathered. A more probable reason seems to have been the fact that the majority of Negroes were in sections of the country in which the whites regarded Protestantism as the normal type of Christianity and looked upon Roman Catholicism with aversion. Surrounded by this atmosphere, Negroes, when they became Christian, joined Protestant churches: Roman Catholicism would presumably seem to them alien. What appears to have been another factor was the desire of the Negroes to control their own churches. Particularly after the Civil War and Reconstruction, the Protestant churches were the chief centres of Negro community life. Protestant denominations that were fully under Negro administration grew much more rapidly than the coloured branches of predominantly white bodies. Since in the Roman Catholic Church they would be under white bishops and clergy, the Negroes were not strongly attracted. It may be, moreover, that a major reason was to be found in the paucity of financial support and of personnel for Roman Catholic missions to Negroes. Roman Catholics were so absorbed in looking after the immigrant and such surplus energy as existed for non-Christians was so directed to a traditional field, the Indians, that relatively little attention was paid to the Negroes. Certainly those engaged in missions for the Negroes seem to have been much fewer than those devoting themselves to the Indians. Whatever the cause, comparatively few of the Negroes of the United States became Roman Catholics.

It was to be expected that the Eastern churches would be represented among

[40] Work, op. cit., pp. 177, 178.
[41] U. S. Department of Commerce, Bureau of the Census, Religious Bodies: 1926, Vol. I, p. 760.
[42] See a number of reasons suggested in Gillard, op. cit., pp. 212-272, and Moore, Will America Become Catholic, pp. 200-215.
[43] Gillard, op. cit., pp. 85, 86.

the Negroes slightly if at all. They played so small a part in the American religious scene, and so few of such congregations as they had were in areas in which there were many Negroes, that conversions from among the coloured population were not to be anticipated. However, we hear of one Negro priest of the Anglican communion who sought ordination from the Greek Church in Constantinople and was made a missionary to members of his race in the United States.[44]

The Christianity which spread among the Negroes was chiefly Protestant. Protestant efforts for Negroes were begun in colonial days, as we have seen, by members of several denominations.[45] These continued and were augmented after the independence of the country. They were by whites and by Negroes. As in colonial days, several denominations were represented in them. However, the overwhelming proportion of those Negroes who became Christians joined Methodist or Baptist churches. These were the two denominational families which spread most rapidly and widely on the frontier in the South. They were not confined to the less well educated portions of the white population, but they appealed most largely to them. It is not surprising that these forms of the faith, with their fervour and their adaptation to the less well educated and to those of the lower income levels, should make more rapid gains among the Negroes than those denominations, notably the Presbyterians and the Episcopalians, whose strength lay among the better educated and more prosperous members of the white communities. Several others of the larger denominations were too closely associated with special strains in the white population which were scantily represented in the South to have much contact with the Negroes. This was notably true of the Congregationalists, who were chiefly identified with those of New England ancestry, and with the Lutherans, who were mainly of German and Scandinavian blood. Another large denomination, the Disciples of Christ, which drew in general from the same social strata as the Baptists and Methodists, and might have been expected, therefore, to have won a Negro following, did not have as wide a constituency in the South as did these other two. It is said that in 1859 of the 468,000 Negro church members in the South 215,000 were Methodists and 175,000 Baptists.[46] In other words 83 1/3 per cent. of the Negro Christians of that year were in these two denominational groups. Approximately 95 per cent. of all Negro members

[44] Work, op. cit., p. 184.
[45] Volume III, pp. 225, 226.
[46] Du Bois, The Negro Church, p. 29.

in 1906 were either Baptists or Methodists. Baptists were about twice as numerous as Methodists.[47]

In the years between the independence of the United States and emancipation, numbers of Christians among the whites sought to win the Negroes to their faith. Many a master and a mistress gave instruction to their slaves.[48] Local pastors concerned themselves with the spiritual welfare of the coloured people about them. Frequently presbyteries or missionary societies appointed an agent to labour among the blacks. From time to time Negroes were present at camp-meetings which were primarily for their masters and were caught by the emotional contagion. In many church-buildings, galleries were set aside for Negroes.[49]

A detailed account of these many activities is beyond the compass of this book. As usual, we must content ourselves with singling out, almost at random, a few instances to give concreteness to the generalizations which we have ventured. From these something of the whole picture may be dimly discerned.

The Baptists with their enthusiasm and their methods of reaching the masses early touched the Negroes. It is said that in the 1770's a Baptist church composed wholly of Negroes was constituted in South Carolina,[50] and that in 1795 there were 17,664 Negro Baptists south and east of Maryland.[51] In numbers of Baptist churches in the South the membership was both white and coloured. In some the Negroes were in the majority.[52] Negro Baptists were especially numerous in Virginia. Here, in 1860, out of about sixty thousand Negro church members, about fifty-four thousand were said to be Baptists. This was in contrast with South Carolina and North Carolina, where the proportion of Methodists was higher.[53]

Methodists early sought to spread the Christian message to Negroes. In 1785 William Elliott, a Methodist, made provision for a Sunday School in which his slaves were taught to read the Bible and the catechism.[54] In 1787 the Methodist General Conference urged preachers to labour among the slaves

[47] U. S. Department of Commerce, Bureau of the Census, *Religious Bodies: 1926,* Vol. I, pp. 758, 760.
[48] See instances in Earnest, *The Religious Development of the Negro in Virginia,* p. 60.
[49] Bassett, *Slavery in the State of North Carolina,* p. 52.
[50] Townsend, *South Carolina Baptists,* p. 259. This was at Silver Bluff, on the South Carolina side of the Savannah River, twelve miles from Augusta, Georgia.—W. H. Brooks in *The Journal of Negro History,* Vol. VII, pp. 172-196.
[51] Sweet, *Religion on the American Frontier, The Baptists, 1783-1830,* p. 78, citing Asplund, *Universal Annual Register, 1796,* p. 82.
[52] Woodson, *The History of the Negro Church,* pp. 112-119.
[53] L. J. Jackson in *The Journal of Negro History,* Vol. XVI, p. 234.
[54] Ferguson, *Historic Chapters in Christian Education in America,* p. 15.

and to receive the worthy into church membership.[55] In that year 21,949 white members and 3,893 coloured members were reported.[56] Ten years later, in 1797, the totals were said to be 48,445 white and 12,218 coloured. Of the latter, 5,106 were in Maryland, 2,490 in Virginia, and 2,071 in North Carolina.[57] In 1828 the corresponding figures were 361,562 whites and 59,056 Negroes.[58] In 1800 the bishops were allowed under certain conditions to ordain Negro deacons.[59] About 1829 William Capers, later a bishop of the Methodist Episcopal Church, South, became the leading spirit in an effort to reach the slaves. By the time of his death (1855) the Methodists of South Carolina had twenty-six missions and thirty-two preachers caring for 11,546 coloured communicants.[60] In 1851 in the entire Southern Methodist Church ninety-nine missionaries were giving their full time to the plantation Negroes.[61] It is asserted that in 1860 the Methodist Episcopal Church, South, had not far from two hundred thousand Negroes in its membership.[62]

In the early part of the nineteenth century Bishop Meade, of the Protestant Episcopal Church, preached to Negroes on a number of plantations in Virginia.[63] In 1860 the Protestant Episcopal Church had two missionaries in South Carolina giving full time to the slaves.[64] In North Carolina in 1853 out of 2,686 communicants of the Protestant Episcopal Church, 345 were coloured, and out of 1,593 catechumens, 488 were coloured.[65] Special churches for Negroes were early founded by Episcopalians in Philadelphia, New York, and Baltimore.[66] Alexander Crummell, a coloured clergyman of the Protestant Episcopal Church, in spite of prejudice against his race, acquired an excellent education, graduated from Cambridge University in England in 1853, long served in Liberia and Sierra Leone, and in later years was pastor of a church in Washington, D. C.[67]

The Presbyterians were also active among the Negroes. In many areas in the South it was customary for Presbyterian pastors to devote a large part

[55] Bassett, op. cit., p. 55.
[56] Minutes of the Annual Conferences of the Methodist Episcopal Church, Vol. I, p. 28.
[57] Minutes of the Annual Conferences of the Methodist Episcopal Church, Vol. I, p. 74.
[58] Minutes of the Annual Conferences of the Methodist Episcopal Church, Vol. I, p. 572.
[59] Journals of the General Conference of the Methodist Episcopal Church, Vol. I, p. 44.
[60] Woodson, The Education of the Negro Prior to 1861, pp. 189-191.
[61] J. M. Batten in Church History, Vol. VII, p. 234.
[62] U. S. Department of Commerce, Bureau of the Census, Religious Bodies: 1926, Vol. II, p. 1030, says "over 200,000." The African Repository, Vol. XL, p. 209, says 188,000.
[63] Woodson, op. cit., p. 187.
[64] L. J. Jackson in The Journal of Negro History, Vol. XV, p. 97.
[65] Bassett, Slavery in the State of North Carolina, p. 76.
[66] Woodson, The History of the Negro Church, pp. 94-97.
[67] Cromwell, The Negro in American History, pp. 130-138.

of their time to giving Negroes religious instruction. Places were often provided for Negroes in church buildings so that white and black might worship together.[68] Charles Colcock Jones, a Presbyterian, in 1832 organized the interdenominational Association for the Religious Instruction of Negroes and himself spent much of his life as a missionary among the slaves in Liberty County, Georgia.[69]

Negroes were not numerous in areas in which Congregationalism was strong, but as early as 1829 a Negro Congregational Church was organized in New Haven, Connecticut.[70]

Between 1845 and the outbreak of the Civil War the white churches of the South redoubled their efforts for the slaves. In this they had the co-operation of many of the planters. They continued their labours even after the outbreak of the war.[71]

Christians among the whites did much for the education of Negroes. Thus in 1789 Quakers in Philadelphia founded The Society for the Free Instruction of Orderly Blacks and People of Colour. This set up evening schools.[72] In New Haven, Connecticut, a clergyman planned an academy for Negroes, but was thwarted by popular feeling against the abolition movement.[73] A clergyman, Charles Avery, of Pennsylvania, left an estate of about $300,000 for the education and Christianization of Negroes, and in 1849, with this as a backing, Avery College was incorporated.[74] In 1856 Presbyterians in Pennsylvania founded for Negroes Asmun Institute (incorporated in 1854, opened in 1856), later renamed Lincoln University.[75] John G. Fee, of Kentucky, was the son of a slave-holder. After a severe inward struggle he came to the conviction that slavery was contrary to the New Testament. For his stand he was disowned by his father. He became a clergyman, organized an anti-slavery church, and, with the assistance of others of like mind, among them John A. R. Rogers, founded Berea College (opened 1859) for the co-education of Negro and white students. Although meeting with physical violence from pro-slavery elements, he was a pacifist by conviction, never carried arms, and prayed for his enemies, while they were mobbing him.[76] In 1856, through the Methodists, Wilberforce

[68] Woodson, op. cit., pp. 155-158.
[69] L. J. Jackson in The Journal of Negro History, Vol. XV, p. 89.
[70] Woodson, op. cit., p. 99.
[71] Bruner, An Abstract of the Religious Instruction of the Slaves in the Antebellum South, p. 5.
[72] Embree, Brown America, p. 61.
[73] Bacon, Leonard Bacon, pp. 197-202.
[74] Woodson, op. cit., p. 270.
[75] Woodson, op. cit., p. 271.
[76] Embree, op. cit., pp. 69-88; Beard, A Crusade of Brotherhood, pp. 97-104.

University was incorporated, for Negroes, in Ohio.[77] In the South, legislation, especially in the last few decades before emancipation, sought to prevent the education of the Negro, partly out of fear that literacy might lead to revolt.[78] This led to the decline of education of Negroes by the southern churches and tended to the limitation of instruction in religion to verbal methods.[79] Negro education made greatest headway in the free states in the North.

Negro Christians were active in spreading their faith among members of their own race. Indeed, a very large proportion of the conversions before emancipation and the large majority of those after emancipation arose from contacts with Negro believers. Increasingly Christianity expanded spontaneously from Negro to Negro. More and more the participation of white Christians was confined to inaugurating and assisting schools for the training of leadership for the Negro churches. Before emancipation, slave codes in the South were intended to suppress Negro preachers, but in any state it was usually possible for a Negro clergyman to engage in religious work if some white person of standing would vouch for him. In the *ante bellum* South the Christian ministry afforded almost the only opportunity for a Negro to rise to effective group leadership.[80] This circumstance facilitated the extension of Christianity.

Most of the Negro preachers who served as voluntary missionaries among their own people were obscure and quickly forgotten. Some, however, were long remembered. In Fayetteville, North Carolina, Henry Evans (died 1810), a full-blooded free Negro shoemaker, a Methodist licensed preacher, worked at his trade during the week and preached on Sundays until a large congregation came into being.[81] In North Carolina, too, was John Clavis, a Presbyterian, who studied for a time at Princeton and who by 1801 was an itinerant missionary under the General Assembly. He preached to both whites and blacks, until, in 1831, the state legislature forbade Negroes that function.[82] Famous in his day was Jack of Virginia. He was African-born, was a slave in a region in Virginia in which little religious instruction was given, but through hearing occasional sermons by white Presbyterian preachers came to a Christian faith. He became a preacher in the Baptist church, was listened to gladly by black and white, and, freed through a subscription gift by whites, gathered a large Negro Baptist church, and was noted for the high standard of conduct which

[77] Woodson, *op. cit.*, p. 272.
[78] *The African Repository*, Vol. VI, p. 343.
[79] Woodson, *op. cit.*, pp. 180, 182, 186.
[80] J. M. Batten in *Church History*, Vol. VII, p. 234.
[81] Bassett, *op. cit.*, pp. 57, 58.
[82] Bassett, *op. cit.*, pp. 73-76.

he demanded of its members.[83] In 1830, so we read, two Negro preachers came to Rochester, New York, and were responsible for a number of conversions among members of their race which were accompanied by marked moral improvement.[84]

Congregations and denominations exclusively Negro in membership and control arose late in the eighteenth and early in the nineteenth century. This was partly from the desire of the Negroes to be masters of their own organizations. At times, too, when congregations had been made up of both whites and Negroes, the whites withdrew or encouraged the Negroes to withdraw, and a distinctly Negro group came into being.[85] Thousands of Negroes were members of white congregations and denominations, but other thousands formed themselves into distinct ecclesiastical groups. One reason for the rapid spread of Christianity among the Negroes is probably to be found in the fact that in these churches the Negro was more nearly free from white supervision than in any other phase of his organized activity.[86] In some states it was usual to place severe legal restrictions, even prohibition, on the assembling of Negroes,[87] but these measures by no means always prevented the formation of coloured churches or the holding of religious services for Negroes. As a rule in the South each Negro congregation was sponsored by a white congregation or denomination which kept a general oversight over it,[88] but usually the Negro congregation seems to have had a large degree of freedom in its internal life. A white man might have to be present if a Negro were preaching, but that precaution was often only formal and the Negro clergymen appear to have enjoyed a good deal of liberty of expression.[89]

Precisely which was the earliest Negro church is not certain. What is said to have been the first was Baptist and was the one which was organized, probably between 1773 and 1775, in South Carolina, not far from Augusta, Georgia.[90] Another Negro Baptist church is reported to have come into being at Petersburg, Virginia, in 1776, and still another in Richmond, Virginia, in 1780.[91] Before 1800 several other Negro Baptist churches were formed in the

[83] Du Bois, The Negro Church, pp. 36, 37.
[84] The African Repository, Vol. VII, p. 61.
[85] Mays and Nicholson, The Negro's Church, pp. 22-27.
[86] Mays and Nicholson, op. cit., p. 279.
[87] Goodell, The American Slave Code, pp. 326ff.
[88] Mays and Nicholson, op. cit., pp. 22-27.
[89] Olmstead, A Journey in the Seaboard Slave States, pp. 106, 107.
[90] Work, Negro Year Book . . . 1931-1932, p. 259; U. S. Department of Commerce, Bureau of the Census, Religious Bodies: 1926, Vol. II, p. 136; Cromwell, The Negro in American History, p. 63; W. H. Brooks in The Journal of Negro History, Vol. VII, pp. 172-196.
[91] Work, op. cit., p. 259.

South.[92] In the first decade of the nineteenth century Negro Baptist churches sprang up in Boston, New York, and Philadelphia.[93] What appear to have been the earliest bodies to draw Negro Baptist churches together were the Providence Association, in Ohio, in 1836, the Wood River Association, in Illinois, in 1838, and an association in Louisiana, also in 1838.[94] In 1853 the Western Coloured Baptist Convention was organized.[95]

In the closing years of the eighteenth century two Negro Methodist movements had their inception which in the first quarter of the following century became denominations and in the latter half of the century grew to large proportions. These were the African Methodist Episcopal Church and the African Methodist Episcopal Zion Church.

The moving spirit in the formation of the African Methodist Episcopal Church was Richard Allen (1760-1831).[96] Allen was born a slave, was converted in 1777 at the age of seventeen and in that same year purchased his freedom. He joined the Methodists and preached widely, often travelling on foot. Thrifty, hard-working, noted for scrupulous adherence to his word, he was a leader of enterprise and integrity. In 1787 he and Absalom Jones, another free Negro and Methodist, organized in Philadelphia the Free African Society. In 1791 this group decided to adopt a form of church government. The majority favoured that of the Protestant Episcopal Church and in 1796 incorporated themselves as the African Episcopal Church of St. Thomas. Absalom Jones served as their pastor and in due course was ordained.[97] Allen, however, held to his Methodism and with those of similar mind organized (1792) the Bethel African Methodist Episcopal Church. Bishop Asbury of the Methodist Episcopal Church preached the dedicatory sermon, the congregation recognized his authority, and Allen was ordained by him. In spite of their denominational differences, Allen and Jones continued to co-operate in behalf of their race and were officers of the first Negro Masonic lodge in Philadelphia. In time the Bethel African Methodist Episcopal Church established its legal right to freedom of control by the white church. Similar Negro Methodist churches arose in several other cities, including Baltimore. Connected with them were

[92] Ibid.
[93] U. S. Department of Commerce, Bureau of the Census, Religious Bodies: 1926, Vol. II, p. 136.
[94] Ibid.; Benedict, A General History of the Baptist Denomination in America, p. 890, speaks of a Union Association of coloured Baptist churches in Ohio becoming fully independent in 1840 after having a connexion with white churches since its formation in 1836. Another date given for the formation of the Providence Association is 1833.— W. H. Brooks in The Journal of Negro History, Vol. VII, p. 19.
[95] Work, Negro Year Book . . . 1914-1915, p. 169.
[96] Wesley, Richard Allen Apostle of Freedom, passim.
[97] Du Bois, The Philadelphia Negro, p. 198.

at least five who had been ordained by Asbury. One of these was Daniel Coker, who was born a slave, the son of a Negro slave and of an indentured English woman. He had been active in Baltimore.[98] In 1816 representatives of several of these congregations came together in Philadelphia and organized the African Methodist Church of the United States of America (later the African Methodist Episcopal Church). The greater part of the discipline of the Methodist Episcopal Church was adopted. Coker was elected bishop, but declined, and Allen was chosen in his stead.[99] Coker later went to Liberia as a missionary and died there.[100] Allen proved a capable leader. He continued as pastor of the original Bethel Church in Philadelphia, and also, as bishop, travelled, founded churches, planned new circuits, and held conferences. The movement expanded chiefly among the free Negroes in the North and in Maryland. In 1860 the membership of the denomination was estimated as being about twenty thousand.[101]

Prominent in the denomination was Daniel Alexander Payne (1811-1893).[102] He was born of free parents, Methodists, and was a mixture of white, Negro, and Indian. He studied at Gettysburg under Schmucker and for a time was a Lutheran pastor. In 1840 he joined the African Methodist Episcopal Church and eventually was chosen bishop. In 1863 he engineered the purchase for his church of Wilberforce University, which had been begun for Negroes by the Methodist Episcopal Church but had encountered serious financial difficulties. He became its head, and was thus the first Negro to be president of a university in the United States.

The African Methodist Episcopal Zion Church had its origin in a congregation in New York City. In 1796, in what seems to have been an entirely friendly fashion, some of the Negroes who had been members of the historic John Street Methodist Episcopal Church withdrew and with a few others of their race formed a congregation in which they might have more freedom than seemed possible in one of mixed white and black membership. In 1800 a building was erected which was denominated the African Methodist Episcopal Zion Church. For a time supervision and financial assistance were given by the whites, but eventually autonomy and full self-support were achieved. Ne-

[98] Wesley, *op. cit.,* p. 130.
[99] Wesley, *op. cit.,* pp. 150-157.
[100] Wesley, *op. cit.,* p. 154.
[101] *The African Repository,* Vol. XL, p. 209.
[102] Daniel Alexander Payne, *Recollections of Seventy Years,* compiled and arranged by Sarah C. Bierce Scarborough, edited by C. S. Smith (Nashville, Pubishing House of the A.M.E. Sunday School Union, 1888, pp. 335), *passim;* Josephus Roosevelt Coan, *Daniel Alexander Payne, Christian Educator* (Philadelphia, The A.M.E. Book Concern, 1935, pp. viii, 139), *passim.*

gotiations with the denomin⊕tion led by Richard Allen failed to bring the adhesion of the New York body. Zion Church sent missionaries to various towns and cities and encouraged the formation of Negro congregations. In 1821 leaders in the movement organized the African Methodist Episcopal Church in America. To this national body the name Zion, from the parent congregation, was later added. In 1822 James Varick was elected the first bishop.[103] In doctrine the denomination did not differ in any revolutionary fashion from the Methodist Episcopal Church. However, provision was made for lay representation in its conferences and for the ordination of women, and for many years its bishops were chosen only for a quadrennium instead of for life.[104] In 1860 the denomination is said to have had a membership of about six thousand.[105]

Not far from the time of the formation of the African Methodist Episcopal and the African Methodist Episcopal Zion Church, another Negro Methodist body came into being. This had its origin in Wilmington, Delaware. There, in 1805, the Negro members withdrew from an existing Methodist congregation and erected their own building. In 1812, restive under the control of the white presiding elder, they revolted against it, were expelled, and in 1813 incorporated the Union Church of Africans. The movement grew. and by 1850 had forty-one congregations in Delaware, Pennsylvania, New Jersey, and New York. In that year it divided into the African Union Church and the Union American Methodist Episcopal Church.[106] Neither body was nearly so large as either of the two older Negro Methodist denominations. The former eventually united with the First Coloured Methodist Protestant Church to form what was generally known as the African Union Methodist Protestant Church.[107] A still smaller group, the Coloured Methodist Protestant Church, had its inception about 1840. Like the similar white denomination, it emphasized the equal rights of members, both lay and clerical.[108]

Although no independent Negro Presbyterian church seems to have come into existence before the Civil War, here and there we hear of churches especially for Negroes within the Presbyterian fellowship. Thus in 1807 two

[103] Woodson, *The History of the Negro Church,* pp. 78-85; Wesley, *op. cit.,* pp. 131-133.
[104] Du Bois, *The Negro Church,* p. 45.
[105] *The African Repository,* Vol. XL, p. 209.
[106] U. S. Department of Commerce, Bureau of the Census, *Religious Bodies:1926,* Vol. II, pp. 1020, 1021; Wesley, *op. cit.,* pp. 133, 134.
[107] U. S. Department of Commerce, Bureau of the Census, *Religious Bodies: 1926,* Vol. II, pp. 1024, 1025.
[108] U. S. Department of Commerce, Bureau of the Census, *Religious Bodies: 1926,* Vol. II, p. 1016.

Negro missionaries were responsible for inaugurating a Negro Presbyterian church in Philadelphia, and in 1838 that city contained two such churches.[109]

Precisely how rapid the spread of Protestant Christianity was among Negroes before the Civil War we do not know. Comprehensive statistics which can claim even approximate accuracy are lacking. That substantial growth occurred in the number of Negro church members there can be no doubt. Of this the rise of Negroes in the Methodist Episcopal Church from 3,893 in 1787 to 58,056 in 1828[110] is simply one indication. Although exactitude is impossible, certain conjectures can be hazarded which are probably in rough accord with the facts. If in 1795 there were 17,664 Negro Baptists "south and east of Maryland"[111] (although this total is unquestionably far less accurate than its seemingly meticulous precision would indicate), and if in 1797 the Methodist Episcopal Church had 12,218 coloured members,[112] and if, as appears likely in consideration of the fact that in 1906 nineteen-twentieths of the Negro church members were affiliated with those two groups of denominations, in 1797 four-fifths of the Negro church members were either Baptists or Methodists, and if, as also seems probable, at least one-half of the Negro Baptists were "south and east of Maryland," then in 1797 the Negro Protestant church membership was not in excess of sixty thousand. If we add five thousand as the total of Negro Roman Catholics in that year, which, in view of Bishop Carroll's figures for 1785[113] is presumably above rather than below the fact, we had an outside figure for church membership in 1797 of sixty-five thousand. In 1800 the number of Negroes in the United States was given as 1,002,037.[114] Since in 1790 it was 757,208,[115] in 1797 it was probably about 925,000. This would mean that in 1797 slightly more than 7 per cent. of the Negroes were church members. That, interestingly enough, was almost the same as among the whites, 6.9 per cent.[116] One figure for 1859 gives the number of Negro church members in the South as 468,000, of whom 215,000 were said to be Methodists and 175,000 Baptists.[117] This is probably

[109] Du Bois, *The Philadelphia Negro*, pp. 199, 200.
[110] *Minutes of the Annual Conferences of the Methodist Episcopal Church*, Vol. I, pp. 28, 572.
[111] Sweet, *Religion of the American Frontier, The Baptists, 1783-1830*, p. 78, citing Asplund, *Universal Annual Register, 1796*, p. 82.
[112] *Minutes of the Annual Conferences of the Methodist Episcopal Church*, Vol. I, p. 74.
[113] Letter of Carroll to Antonelli, March 1, 1785, in Guilday, *The Life and Times of John Carroll*, p. 223.
[114] Department of Commerce, Bureau of the Census, *Negro Population, 1790-1915*, p. 29.
[115] *Ibid.*
[116] Dorchester, *Christianity in the United States*, p. 750; Weber, *1933 Yearbook of the American Churches*, p. 299.
[117] Du Bois, *The Negro Church*, p. 29.

not far from correct. Presumably it is under rather than over the precise figure, for another estimate declares the Negro membership of the Methodist Episcopal Church, South, in 1860 to have been 188,000,[118] and, in addition, the Methodist Episcopal Church is said to have had 30,516 Negro members in 1846, of whom about 20,000 were slaves in the South,[119] and Virginia alone is reported to have had 54,000 Negro Baptists in 1860.[120] If to the total of 468,000 in the South in 1859 there be added the estimated membership of the two leading independent Negro Methodist bodies in 1860, 26,000,[121] and an equal number, which is probably far below the true figure, for the Negro membership of other churches in the North, one arrives at a figure of about 520,000 for the entire country in 1860, or six times that of 1797. This was 11.7 per cent. of the Negro population of 1860 (4,441,830),[122] or about one and a half times the proportion of 1797. It was, however, only about half of the corresponding proportion of church members in the population of the country as a whole in 1860, 22.7 per cent.[123] It seems clear that, although these estimates are at best only rough approximations to the facts, since the figure for Negro membership in 1797 is probably above rather than below the true one and since that of 1860 may be slightly below the correct one, in the first six decades of the century Christianity had numerically made striking gains among the Negroes.

The numerical increase is only part of the story. In some ways it is the least significant part. It is far more important to know what this affiliation with the churches meant to the individual members. The precise degree to which it made for moral change we cannot know. Some records indicate that this was often marked.[124] Some observers believed that church membership was usually entered upon with a minimum of knowledge of Christianity[125] and worked

---

[118] *The African Repository,* Vol. XL, p. 209.
[119] J. C. Hartzell in *The Journal of Negro History,* Vol. VIII, p. 307.
[120] L. J. Jackson in *The Journal of Negro History,* Vol. XVI, p. 234.
[121] *The African Repository,* Vol. XL, p. 209.
[122] Department of Commerce, Bureau of the Census, *Negro Population 1790-1915,* p. 29. This percentage is slightly below that for Philadelphia. In 1864 that city was said to have 4,000 Negro communicants, or 15.2 per cent., out of a Negro population of 23,000.—*The African Repository,* Vol. XL, p. 147. Since the proportion of church members in Philadelphia, a northern city in which Negro churches had been active for years, was probably higher than for the country as a whole, the 11.7 per cent. for the latter may not be far from correct. The figure for Philadelphia can be checked with that in Du Bois, *The Philadelphia Negro,* p. 200, in which seventeen of the nearly twenty Negro churches of the city are said to have had in 1867 a membership of 4,931—which is not far from the 4,000 given for 1860 if allowance be made for normal growth. Bruner, *An Abstract of the Religious Instruction of Slaves in the Antebellum South,* p. 5, says that in 1860 one-fourth of the slaves over eighteen years of age were church members.
[123] Weber, *op. cit.,* p. 299.
[124] Bassett, *Slavery in the State of North Carolina,* p. 71.
[125] Olmstead, *A Journey in the Back Country in the Winter of 1853-4,* Vol. I, pp. 116-122.

very little if any moral improvement among the majority.[126] However, it is clear that to the slave Christianity gave an institution in which in a land of bondage he could express himself and in which he could find fellowship. It opened to him a door of hope. It offered him a God whom he could trust. Frederick Douglass, later famous as a leader in the abolition movement and as one of the most honoured men of his race, tells how as a lad in his teens, and while still a slave, he first came into conscious contact with Christianity and how a Negro Christian whom he consulted told him to cast all his care upon God, how after weeks of doubt and struggle he found his heart lightened, how he loved all mankind, including the slave-owner, and how he had his passion to acquire an education accentuated.[127] Christian conversion gave to the Negro a degree of dignity. It disclosed to him a vista of a far future of happy and glorious immortality. Much of the preaching dwelt upon the bliss of the Christian's life beyond the grave.[128] Usually (although to this there were exceptions) the Negro pastor or preacher had only a smattering of education, but even if he were a slave he had a certain position of authority and leadership among his fellows.[129] By some, it is true, Negro preachers were said to be of poorer character than their fellows,[130] but this appears to have been a darker picture than a full knowledge of the facts would warrant. Certainly numbers of Negro clergymen were held in high respect by both white and black.[131] Marriage was frequently solemnized by Christian ceremonies[132] and although families of slaves might be separated by sale,[133] yet by being given the stamp of religion the institution was accorded somewhat greater sanctity than it would otherwise have had.[134] However, even among church members sexual laxity and children born out of wedlock seem to have been fairly common.[135] While among Negro Christians a great deal of what many Christians would call superstition existed, and although for many, possibly a majority, church membership was entered upon lightly and with little moral alteration, that was not very different from the first stages of the acceptance of Christianity

[126] Olmstead, *A Journey in the Seaboard Slave States,* pp. 113-125. See also Du Bois, *The Negro Church,* pp. 49 56.

[127] *Life and Times of Frederick Douglass Written by Himself* (Hartford, Park Publishing Co., 1882, pp. 564), pp. 102-104.

[128] Olmstead, *A Journey in the Seaboard Slave States,* pp. 118, 124.

[129] Olmstead, *op. cit.,* p. 450.

[130] Olmstead, *A Journey in the Back Country in the Winter of 1853-4,* Vol. I, p. 96.

[131] Bassett, *op. cit.,* pp. 73-76; Woodson, *The History of the Negro Church,* pp. 40ff.

[132] Olmstead, *A Journey in the Seaboard Slave States,* pp. 448, 449; Olmstead, *A Journey in the Back Country in the Winter of 1853-4,* Vol. I, p. 169.

[133] Goodell, *The American Slave Code,* pp. 113ff.

[134] Du Bois, *op. cit.,* p. 56.

[135] Olmstead, *A Journey in the Back Country in the Winter of 1853-4,* Vol. I, pp. 121, 122.

in Western Europe a thousand years before. It was characteristic of mass movements to Christianity, and such a mass movement was in progress among the Negroes. For some and probably many Negroes, acceptance of the Christian faith was accompanied or followed by marked steps towards an approximation to Christian ethical standards.

Many white Christians were constrained by their faith to labour for better conditions in this life for the Negro.

As may be gathered from what we have already recorded, a large proportion of such formal education as was given to the Negro before emancipation was initiated and conducted by those who were impelled by motives of Christian origin.[136]

Christians, too, were active in one of the most ambitious of the projects for solving the problem presented by the Negro, the American Colonization Society. This organization, inaugurated late in 1816, declared its object to be "colonizing (with their consent) the Free People of Colour residing in our country, in Africa, or such other place as Congress shall deem most expedient."[137] The free Negro presented a problem to himself and to society, and it was felt that both he and the United States would be the better for his removal to the continent from which his ancestors had come. In Africa, so it was held, these Negroes from the United States could become the centre of a civilized, Christian state which would contribute to the advance of the indigenous population of that continent. Many slave-holders who sincerely deplored slavery were deterred from manumitting their blacks by the feeling that bad as servitude was, the Negroes were better off under it than if they were free and that free Negroes were a menace to white society. If, then, a home could be found for freedmen in Africa where they could be happy, emancipation would be furthered.[138] Even if only the equivalent of the annual increase, about thirty-five thousand, could be sent each year to Africa,[139] this would be a gain. The idea was partly suggested by the earlier British project of Sierra Leone, inaugurated for a somewhat similar purpose and in which Evangelicals had been prominent. The leading spirit in the organization of the American Colonization Society was a clergyman, Robert Finley.[140] Samuel J. Mills, who had so outstanding a place in the early stages of foreign missions from the United States, was a member of the party sent to Africa

[136] For some instances, see Woodson, *The Education of the Negro. Prior to 1861*, pp. 96, 100, 102, 104, 109, 111, 140, 141, 145.
[137] Constitution of the American Colonization Society, cited in Fox, *The American Colonization Society, 1817-1840*, p. 47.
[138] Fox, *op. cit.*, pp. 13-40.
[139] Bacon, *Leonard Bacon*, p. 180.
[140] Fox, *op. cit.*, p. 43.

to discover whether, in the vicinity of Sierra Leone, land could be purchased for the foundation of a colony. Mills died on the homeward voyage.[141] A clergyman, William Meade, who was later Bishop of Virginia, was the first agent of the society.[142] When the colony, Liberia, was in its initial stages and in desperate straits, it was a clergyman, Jehudi Ashmun, who, staying heroically by it, helped to save it.[143] Another clergyman, Ralph Randolph Gurley, long had more effect upon the society's life and policies than any other one man.[144] A large proportion of the society's funds came from clergymen and churches.[145] Annual collections for the benefit of the society were taken in the churches of the country.[146] Several ecclesiastical bodies officially endorsed the society.[147] To Liberia went Negro missionaries. Thus Lott Cary, who after a youth of profligacy had been converted and had become an exemplary leader of Christian Negroes in Virginia, was the moving spirit in the formation, in 1815, of the Richmond African Baptist Missionary Society, whose purpose it was to send the Christian message to Africa, in 1821 himself went to Liberia and there until his early death (1828) was a prominent figure in the infant colony.[148] In the pioneer days of Liberia another Negro, Harrison Ellis, was sent by the Presbyterians of Alabama.[149] Although the American Colonization Society devoted itself to a programme which proved impracticable, and although for a time its management was more visionary than efficient,[150] it was an honest attempt, sponsored by some of the outstanding men of the nation, to solve the Negro problem by another method than the sudden abolition of slavery. If it could have been carried out it might have prevented the tragedy of the Civil War.

The Christian conscience early sought the elimination of Negro slavery and was a powerful factor in the movements which finally led to emancipation. The abolition of slavery arose from a variety of movements. In some of these the Christian rootage was obvious. In others Christianity was clearly demonstrable as one of the sources. In still others, if present at all, it was only as an

---

[141] Spring, *Memoirs of the Rev. Samuel J. Mills*, pp. 135ff.

[142] Fox, *op. cit.*, pp. 48, 49.

[143] Ralph Randolph Gurley, *Life of Jehudi Ashmun* (Washington, James C. Dunn, 1835, pp. 396, 160), *passim*.

[144] Fox, *op. cit.*, p. 73.

[145] See sample lists in *The African Repository*, Vol. V, pp. 254ff., 319, 320, Vol. VIII, pp. 348-352.

[146] Fox, *op. cit.*, pp. 63, 64.

[147] Fox, *op. cit.*, pp. 70, 78, 79.

[148] Miles Mark Fisher in *The Journal of Negro History*, Vol. VII, pp. 380-418; Woodson, *The History of the Negro Church*, pp. 137-140.

[149] Woodson, *op. cit.*, pp. 140-142.

[150] Bacon, *op. cit.*, pp. 187, 188.

underlying cause of the belief in the dignity of man which was outraged by the spectacle of servitude. We are here chiefly concerned with the influences which were fairly clearly Christian in origin.

It is highly significant that fresh religious awakenings with their renewed emphasis upon putting into practice the ideals of the New Testament usually gave rise to attempts to free the slaves. In the eighteenth century the Quakers were already taking action against slavery. John Woolman, one of the most highly sensitive, courageous, and deeply religious souls of the Society of Friends, was profoundly concerned about slavery and gave telling witness against it.[151] Even before his day, in 1693, the Philadelphia Yearly Meeting determined that Friends should set their slaves at liberty "after a reasonable time of service . . . and during the time they have them, to teach them to read and to give them a Christian education."[152] In 1776 it decided that those who declined to emancipate their slaves should be excluded from membership. It is said that by 1787 no slave remained in the hands of an acknowledged Quaker.[153] Again and again in the last quarter of the eighteenth century the Quakers of North Carolina sought to induce the state Assembly to remove the legal restrictions upon emancipation.[154] In 1776 Samuel Hopkins, an important figure in the New England Theology in the succession of Jonathan Edwards and of the Great Awakening, issued an address to the Continental Congress asking for the total abolition of slavery.[155] In the early stages of their development in the United States, the Methodists were outspoken in their denunciation of the institution. Asbury was grieved by slavery.[156] Some Methodists defended it,[157] but as early as 1780 the Virginia Conference declared slavery to be "contrary to the laws of God, man, and nature, and hurtful to society."[158] In 1794 about thirty of the Methodist preachers almost unanimously agreed not to hold slaves in any state where the law would permit manumission.[159] In 1796 the General Conference ordered that no slave-holder be received into the Society until he had been spoken to on the subject, that those who sold their slaves were to be expelled, and that those holding office with the Methodists were to free their

[151] *The Journal and Essays of John Woolman Edited from the Original Manuscripts with a Biographical Introduction by Amelia Mott Gummere* (New York, The Macmillan Co., 1922, pp. xxii, 643), pp. 58-75, 334-402.
[152] Weigle, *American Idealism*, p. 161.
[153] *Ibid.*
[154] Bassett, *Slavery in the State of North Carolina*, pp. 65, 66.
[155] *The Works of Samuel Hopkins*, Vol. II, pp. 549ff.
[156] Asbury, June 10, 1778, June 4, 1780, July 3, 1780, Dec. 19, 1796, in *The Heart of Asbury's Journal*, pp. 130, 172, 175, 421.
[157] Asbury, Jan. 9, 1798, in *The Heart of Asbury's Journal*, p. 439.
[158] *Minutes of the Annual Conference*, Vol. II, p. 12.
[159] Asbury, Nov. 25, 1794, in *The Heart of Asbury's Journal*, p. 389.

slaves where it was legal to do so.[160] The Baptist movement which was growing through the revivals of the eighteenth and the early part of the nineteenth century also gave rise to efforts for emancipation. Several prominent Virginia Baptists manumitted their slaves as soon as the statute of 1782 made that action possible.[161] Again and again, beginning at least as far back as 1789, various Baptist bodies, local and regional, condemned slavery.[162] David Rice, an indefatigable evangelist and missionary trained at Princeton with its memories of the Great Awakening, and one of the earliest Presbyterian ministers in Kentucky, sought to induce that state from its very inception to adopt gradual emancipation and to prohibit the importation of slaves.[163] At one time the majority of the slave-holding members of the Cane Ridge Church in Kentucky, memorable for its connexion with the camp-meetings, freed their Negroes.[164] Barton W. Stone, the leader of the Christian movement which arose from the Kentucky revivals, out of religious conviction manumitted his slaves.[165] From the revivals of which Charles G. Finney was the outstanding leader issued fresh anti-slavery impulses which greatly strengthened the movement for emancipation.[166] When Finney went to the newly organized Christian colony and college at Oberlin, Ohio, to become professor of theology, he did so on the explicit condition that Negroes were to be received on the same condition as whites.[167] Theodore Dwight Weld, descended from a long line of clergymen of New England stock, a convert of Finney, was conspicuous in the anti-slavery movement. It was through him that James G. Birney, later presidential candidate of the Liberty Party, freed his slaves and became an advocate of abolition.[168] A leader in the first student body of Lane Theological Seminary, Weld arranged for a debate on slavery which brought abolition sentiment to a white heat and was followed by the expulsion of the abolitionists. With these students as a nucleus he organized anti-slavery agitation, and he and his emissaries went out, often at great personal risk, with the passionate zeal of evangelists. He engineered an anti-slavery lobby in Congress and had much to do with enlisting the powerful John Quincy Adams in the support

---

[160] *Journals of the General Conference*, Vol. I, pp. 22, 23.
[161] Sweet, *Religion on the American Frontier, The Baptists, 1783-1830*, p. 79.
[162] Sweet, *op. cit.*, pp. 79ff.
[163] Sweet, *op. cit.*, p. 80; Asbury, Apr. 10, 1792, in *The Heart of Asbury's Journal*, p. 334; *Dictionary of American Biography*, Vol. XV, pp. 537, 538.
[164] Fortune, *The Disciples of Kentucky*, p. 24.
[165] Fortune, *op. cit.*, p. 44.
[166] Barnes, *The Anti-Slavery Impulse 1830-1844, passim*, but see especially pp. 10-12; Niebuhr, *The Kingdom of God in America*, pp. 158, 159.
[167] *Memoirs of Rev. Charles G. Finney*, pp. 332, 333.
[168] Barnes, *op. cit.*, pp. 39, 69.

of the cause.[169] It was no accident that the successive new tides of life in Protestantism issued in part in anti-slavery convictions. With their emphasis upon the infinite value of every human being with his immortal soul and with their efforts to bring the Christian message to all, a system by which some human beings were slaves of others was repugnant to them. The "universal disinterested benevolence" of Hopkins which came out of the Great Awakening and the insistence of Finney that true conversion must be accompanied by repentance and restitution and must lead to a life of beneficence could not but give rise to attacks upon a social institution by which men exploited their fellows.

Anti-slavery convictions were not exclusively the fruit of the sporadic revivals. They were also found in some of the constant currents of the Christian movement which in part sprang from revivals and from time to time were reinforced by them. William E. Channing, who had been reared under the preaching of Samuel Hopkins but had become one of the leaders of Unitarianism with a theology quite divergent from that of his early mentor, was an outspoken opponent of slavery.[170] So was another Unitarian, Henry Ware, of the teaching staff of the Harvard Divinity School.[171] From the orthodox wing of New England Congregationalism and in the spiritual stream of Jonathan Edwards, Timothy Dwight, and the New Haven Theology were the Beechers. Lyman Beecher, a pupil of Dwight, and one of the famous preachers of his day, favoured abolition, although not by violence.[172] His son, Henry Ward Beecher, an even more distinguished preacher than his father, was opposed to slavery, but had too profound a respect for the duty of each man to do what he believed right without interference from others to contend that abolitionists should impose their will upon the South.[173] *Uncle Tom's Cabin*, written by a daughter of Lyman Beecher, the earnestly Christian Harriet Beecher Stowe, did more to arouse feeling in the North against slavery than

[169] Barnes, *op. cit.*, pp. 12, 14, 15, 33, 79-87, 104, 105. See especially *Letters of Theodore Dwight Weld, Angelina Grimké and Sarah Grimké 1822-1844*, edited by Gilbert H. Barnes and Dwight L. Dumond (New York, D. Appleton-Century Co., 2 vols., 1934), *passim*. These volumes contain a biography of Weld and through his letters reveal the Christian conviction which inspired him.

[170] *The Works of William Ellery Channing, D.D. With an Introduction* (Boston, American Unitarian Association, 1891); on slavery, see pp. 688-752; on the influence of Hopkins on him see pp. 423-428.

[171] Commager, *Theodore Parker*, p. 28.

[172] *Autobiography, Correspondence, etc., of Lyman Beecher, D.D.*, edited by Charles Beecher (New York, Harper & Brothers, 2 vols., 1864, 1865), Vol. II, p. 323.

[173] Paxton Hibben, *Henry Ward Beecher: An American Portrait* (New York, George H. Doran Co., 1927, pp. x, 390), pp. 78, 92, 147-151.

any other book of the time. Its author had been profoundly influenced by Weld and drew her inspiration in large part from his *Slavery As It Is*.[174]

Some of the other most celebrated figures in the organized anti-slavery movement seem to have espoused the unpopular enterprise because of their Christian faith. Benjamin Lundy (1789-1839), a pioneer in the organizing of anti-slavery societies, was a Friend of old Quaker stock.[175] Elijah Parish Lovejoy (1802-1837), whose courageous, persistent, and forthright attacks on slavery led to the violent death at the hands of a mob which made him one of the two or three most revered martyrs of the cause, was the son of a clergyman, was trained for the ministry, and was licensed by the Philadelphia Presbytery.[176] The most famous of the advocates of immediate and unconditional abolition, William Lloyd Garrison, although he eventually broke with orthodox Christianity, was for a time a regular attendant at Lyman Beecher's church and was enlisted for anti-slavery by the Quaker, Lundy.[177]

Indeed, at the outset, to a large degree the drive against slavery was a part of what may be called the Christian movement. By that term is meant organizations and trends, non-ecclesiastical as well as ecclesiastical, whose controlling purpose can be traced to Jesus. Not only were most of the initial outstanding leaders men whose Christian faith had brought them to oppose slavery, but several of the subordinate figures were also those whose dominating motive was the desire to act in a Christian fashion. It was on the call of a clergyman, Joshua Leavitt, that the New York City Anti-slavery Society was begun.[178] Of the group of twelve who founded the New England Anti-slavery Society one was a pastor and two were theological students.[179] Leonard Bacon, pastor of Centre Church, New Haven, early organized an anti-slavery association.[180]

As time passed, three developments, possibly interrelated, took place in the anti-slavery movement. First, those in whom the Christian motive was uppermost tended to be pushed into the background by those who were either not professedly Christian or were not so pronouncedly Christian as the earlier leaders. For instance, in Vermont the anti-slavery agitation was late in getting under way and was not so clearly connected with religion as were the anti-

[174] Barnes, *op. cit.*, pp. 73, 231.
[175] *Dictionary of American Biography*, Vol. XI, pp. 506, 507.
[176] *Dictionary of American Biography*, Vol. XI, p. 434.
[177] Dorchester, *Christianity in the United States*, pp. 449, 456; Stead, *The Story of Social Christianity*, Vol. II, pp. 160-163.
[178] Dorchester, *op. cit.*, p. 457.
[179] Dorchester, *op. cit.*, p. 455.
[180] Bacon, *Leonard Bacon*, pp. 77-84.

masonry and temperance movements.[181] Second, as the actively Christian element declined, the abolitionists became more violent in their denunciations of those who disagreed with them. The hope that slave-owners, won by reason and the appeal to conscience, would repent and of their own volition become emancipators dwindled. Fierce diatribes against the sinner as well as his sin became more common.[182] Finney had been alarmed at the drift from love to hatred.[183] Third, as anger increased, it was met by anger, and the rift between the free North and the slave-holding South widened. In the struggle between the champions of slavery and anti-slavery agitators for the control of Kansas, one of the stormy episodes which preceded open civil war, many pastors and churches in the North gave support to measures designed to restrict the spread of slavery. In 1854 more than three thousand New England clergymen memorialized Congress against the repeal of the Missouri Compromise which precipitated the Kansas contest. The Emigrant Aid Company, which was designed to send anti-slavery settlers into Kansas, at the outset had its chief support from clergymen and churches.[184] As passions mounted, they even divided some of the churches. In the Congregational fellowship some felt that the American Board of Commissioners for Foreign Missions took too compromising a view towards slavery and founded (1846) the unequivocally anti-slavery American Missionary Association.[185] In the South some of the clergy came forward in defense of slavery and declared it to be wise, benevolent, and based upon the Bible.[186] A few of the larger denominations with a nation-wide organization separated regionally, chiefly over the issue of slavery. In 1845 the Southern Baptist Convention and the Methodist Episcopal Church, South, were formed, the incentive in each case being Southern dissent from the anti-slavery attitude of the national bodies.[187] In 1858 several Southern synods and presbyteries withdrew from the New School Presbyterian Assembly, in which the Northern, anti-slavery elements were dominant.[188] In 1861, after the outbreak of the Civil War, forty-seven presbyteries of the Old School General Assembly constituted the General Assembly in the Confederate

---

[181] Ludlum, *Social Ferment in Vermont 1791-1850,* pp. 134ff.

[182] Barnes, *op. cit.,* p. 161.

[183] Barnes, *op. cit.,* p. 162; *Memoirs of Rev. Charles G. Finney,* p. 328.

[184] Eli Thayer, *A History of the Kansas Crusade* (New York, Harper & Brothers, 1889, pp. xxii, 294. By a leader in the enterprise), pp. 123-136.

[185] Strong, *The Story of the American Board,* pp. 52, 53; Beard, *A Crusade of Brotherhood,* pp. 29-31.

[186] Weigle, *American Idealism,* p. 165.

[187] U. S. Department of Commerce, Bureau of the Census, *Religious Bodies: 1926,* Vol. II, pp. 125, 126, 964-967.

[188] U. S. Department of Commerce, Bureau of the Census, *Religious Bodies: 1926,* Vol. II, pp. 1166, 1167.

States of America.[189] The bond of love had proved too weak to stand the strain brought by the indignation which had first been aroused by a love outraged by the spectacle of black folk in bondage. Christianity had proved powerless to control the forces which it had evoked.

Then came the horror of the Civil War. That fratricidal struggle had been brought on by a variety of causes. Sectional differences, conflicting theories concerning the nature of the constitutional tie which bound the states together, economic rivalries, the insistence of the North that the Union be preserved clashing with the Southern conception of state sovereignty, the conviction in the North that the very existence of democracy was at stake, and the counter-conviction that the North was trying to impose its will on the South, combined to bring about the holocaust. Yet the issue of slavery was the exciting cause.

In the course of the struggle slavery was swept away. President Lincoln's emancipation proclamation of January 1, 1863, was followed, in 1864 and 1865, by abolition measures in several of the states, in 1865 by the Thirteenth Amendment which wrote emancipation into the Constitution of the United States, in 1868 by the Fourteenth Amendment which was designed to give the Negro citizenship, and in 1870 by the Fifteenth Amendment which was intended to secure to him the franchise. What programmes initiated by Christians had failed to achieve peaceably, war had suddenly accomplished. The dream of the American Colonization Society, with its design of solving the race problem by geographic separation of the white and black, had from the first been fantastic. Those who sought abolition by gradual processes executed with the consent and co-operation of the majority of the slave-owners had proved impotent to stay the tide of anger evoked by the extremists on both sides. The Negro problem now abruptly entered a new stage for whose solution the passions engendered by battle were a poor preparation.

The revolution in the legal status of the Negro was accompanied and followed by the stormy days of Reconstruction. For a time, under the stress of the feelings born of the war, the extremists in the victorious North disfranchised many of the Southern whites and inaugurated a programme of reconstruction by which Negroes led by whites from the North and a minority of Southern whites controlled several of the Southern states. The Southern whites eventually regained power, partly through methods of terror symbolized by the Ku Klux Klan, the majority of the Negroes were debarred from voting, and an intensified bitterness entered into the relations between the races.

---

[189] *Ibid.* On the relations of the Presbyterians to slavery, see I. S. Kull, *Presbyterian Attitudes Toward Slavery*, in *Church History*, Vol. VII, pp. 101-114.

These startling sudden changes had hurried the Negroes into a world for which neither they nor their former owners were prepared. The Negroes, now legally free, must in ·theory fend for themselves without the paternalistic direction and protection of white masters. In many instances freedom made them heady. The whites, impoverished by the war and by the loss of their slaves, had neither the resources nor the will to be of much assistance. To be sure, many of the whites felt a responsibility for their former slaves, but they themselves were facing a difficult problem of readjustment and could not do much.

Under these altered circumstances would Christianity continue the rapid spread which it had begun under the former conditions? Could it assist Negroes and whites to meet the new age and go forward together in reciprocally helpful relations?

One of the signal achievements of Christian history follows. Under these new and difficult circumstances the faith maintained and even accelerated its expansion among the Negroes, it contributed notably to the moral, economic, and intellectual as well as the spiritual development of the blacks, and eventually it helped to ease the tension between the races.

No similarly large body of relatively primitive peoples has ever made such gains in civilization in so brief a time as did the Negroes in the first six decades after emancipation.[190] That they did so was due in part to the fact that they were surrounded by white society and in part to their own native ability. Their progress must also be largely ascribed to Christianity. It was the Negro churches which arose out of Protestant Christianity that proved to be the chief institutions through which the Negro helped himself. It was through the missionary societies and other agencies organized by white Christians, at first mainly those of the North, that a large proportion of the substantial aid which came from the whites was administered. In the six decades which elapsed between emancipation and 1914, Protestant Christianity made amazing gains and even more amazing contributions to the freedmen. If in giving rise to the anti-slavery movement it had contributed to the onset of the Civil War, it assisted mightily in making the outcome to the war of benefit to the Negro.

We must recount, first of all, the achievements of the Negro churches. Much more than in *ante bellum* days, it was through Negroes rather than through whites that Christianity was propagated among the people of colour. In their churches the Negroes long had almost the only institutions which were clearly

---

[190] As an example of this, the proportion of the Negro population which could read and write is said to have risen from about 5 per cent. in 1860 to about 69.6 per cent. in 1910.—Johnson, *The Negro in American Civilization*, p. 227.

their own. Their brief entrance into politics was followed by their effective exclusion from active participation in government. In their churches, however, they were independent of the white man. In them the Negroes possessed the first community organization which they completely controlled.[191] In their segregated life, shut off by white antipathy from the main stream of the life of the nation, the Negroes found in their churches intellectual development and emotional outlet.[192] Often connected with the churches were insurance and burial societies by which the Negroes sought economic security.[193] Frequently a Negro bank was closely associated with a church.[194] The Negro churches were the centres of movements for social betterment. From them sprang schools and educational agencies and in them were held lectures and lyceums.[195] Better than churches of mixed white and coloured membership, they ministered to the peculiar religious needs and temperament of the Negroes.

The clergyman held a unique position of leadership. The ministry and teaching were long almost the only professions which were open to the Negro. When compared with their white brothers, the Negro clergymen on the average were poorly educated, but usually they had a better training than their parishioners. They were idealists, orators, and politicians. They were as much executives and organizers as preachers and pastors. Often they were employment agents. For years no other profession or occupation was so prominent in the Negro communities.[196] Often the clergyman took the initiative in forming fraternal organizations with their sick benefits and life insurance.[197] Some Negro clergymen were guilty of sexual irregularity, some were dishonest, and some used alcoholic beverages intemperately, but the majority seem not to have been guilty of any of these infringements of the moral code, and as time passed the level of both conduct and education appears to have been raised.[198]

As two examples among many of notable leadership by Negro clergymen, one may cite Henry M. Turner and William B. Derrick. Turner was descended from an African chief and was born in 1833 in South Carolina of free Negro parents. In 1851 he was converted at a camp-meeting through plantation mis-

[191] Mays and Nicholson, *The Negro's Church*, pp. 279ff.
[192] Mays and Nicholson, *op. cit.*, pp. 284ff.
[193] Harris, *The Negro as Capitalist*, p. 47.
[194] *Ibid.*
[195] Du Bois, *The Philadelphia Negro*, p. 207.
[196] Mays and Nicholson, *op. cit.*, pp. 38-57; Kelly Miller, *Out of the House of Bondage* (New York, The Neale Publishing Co., 1914, pp. 242), pp. 202ff.; Du Bois, *op. cit.*, pp. 205, 206. Also on the Negro clergy, see W. A. Daniel, *The Education of Negro Ministers* (New York, George H. Doran Co., 1925, pp. vii, 187), *passim*.
[197] Harris, *op. cit.*, p. 62.
[198] Washington, *Up from Slavery*, pp. 81, 82; Du Bois, *The Negro Church*, pp. 64, 72, 73, 155-158, 170-175.

sionaries and for several years was himself a missionary of the Methodist Episcopal Church, South, among the slaves. In 1858 he joined the African Methodist Episcopal Church. During the Civil War he served as a pastor in Washington, D. C., and then as a chaplain in the Federal army. After the war he went to Georgia. For ten years he was the leading Negro politician of that state and for a time sat in the legislature. He endeavoured both to promote inter-racial goodwill and to champion the rights of his own people. He organized the African Methodist Episcopal Church in Georgia and from 1880 to 1915 was a bishop. He was influential in establishing twelve schools and colleges, strove to obtain state aid for Negro education, and helped to create a Christian literature for Negroes. He dreamed of missions to Africa and even after the Civil War he advocated the removal of the Negroes to Africa as a solution of the race problem.[199] Derrick was born in the British West Indies in 1843 and came to the United States during the Civil War. He served the African Methodist Episcopal Church successively as pastor, presiding elder, and bishop. In Virginia he won the confidence of both blacks and whites and for a time entered politics. He made himself temporarily unpopular with many of his race by opposing a project which sought to avoid the payment in full of the state debt.[200]

With the coming of emancipation, the Negroes tended to withdraw from the predominantly white churches in the South into denominations of which they had complete control. Even while the Civil War was in progress, both the African Methodist Episcopal Church and the African Methodist Episcopal Zion Church began to expand southward. In 1863 the former entered Virginia.[201] In the same year the latter sent representatives to Louisiana and North Carolina.[202] After the war, both bodies grew very rapidly in the South, partly from accessions from the Methodist Episcopal Church, South. Within a few years the latter body lost more than half its Negro members.[203] To make provision for greater autonomy for such Negroes as remained in its fellowship, in 1866 the Methodist Episcopal Church, South, adopted a plan for the organization of separate Negro congregations and conferences. In 1870, with the hearty concurrence of the parent body, the Negroes formed their own general conference as an independent denomination under the name, the Coloured Metho-

[199] J. M. Batten in *Church History*, Vol. VII, pp. 231-246.
[200] A. A. Taylor in *The Journal of Negro History*, Vol. XI, p. 432.
[201] A. A. Taylor in *op. cit.*, Vol. XI, p. 430.
[202] U. S. Department of Commerce, Bureau of the Census, *Religious Bodies: 1926*, Vol. II, p. 1013.
[203] U. S. Department of Commerce, Bureau of the Census, *Religious Bodies: 1926*, Vol. II, p. 1030.

dist Episcopal Church.[204] The Northern body, the Methodist Episcopal Church, retained Negroes within its membership. In 1856 it had authorized separate coloured conferences, and in 1860 these were raised to full powers. In 1868 Negroes sat as delegates in the General Conference. The church expanded its work in the South and ordained numbers of Negroes to its ministry.[205] In 1869 Negro Methodists in South-eastern Virginia, formerly members of the Methodist Episcopal Church, formed the Zion Union Apostolic Church, but dissensions and disorganization followed, and in 1881 the denomination was reconstituted as the Reformed Zion Union Apostolic Church.[206] The Negro members of the Cumberland Presbyterian Church, of whom there were about twenty thousand in 1860, organized separate congregations, and in 1869 the General Assembly of the denomination authorized their formation into presbyteries. In 1874 the first General Assembly of the Coloured Cumberland Presbyterian Church was convened.[207]

The Negro Christians tended especially to associate themselves in Baptist churches. In Virginia, where coloured Baptists had been particularly numerous before the Civil War, those who held membership in white churches, encouraged by the latter, withdrew and set up their own bodies. In 1867 the Negro churches of the state organized the Virginia Baptist State Convention. The state was divided into districts, each with a secretary who was also a missionary. Itinerants were employed who organized churches and Sunday Schools. By 1880 churches or missions had been established in nearly every community in the state.[208] Eventually conventions of Negro Baptist churches were formed in each state in the South.[209] National and regional associations and conventions were constituted—the North-western and Southern Baptist Convention in 1864, the Consolidated American Baptist Missionary Convention in 1866, the Baptist Association of the Western States and Territories in 1873, the New England Missionary Convention in 1875, the Baptist Foreign Mission Convention of the United States in 1880, the American National Baptist Convention in 1886, and the National Educational Convention in 1893. In 1893 the large

---

[204] U. S. Department of Commerce, Bureau of the Census, *Religious Bodies: 1926*, Vol. II, pp. 1031-1033. On the policies and attitudes of the Methodist Episcopal Church, South, towards the Negro, see Hunter Dickinson Farish, *The Circuit Rider Dismounts. A Social History of Southern Methodist 1865-1900* (Richmond, The Dietz Press, 1938, pp. 400), pp. 163-233.

[205] Du Bois, *The Negro Church*, pp. 137, 138.

[206] U. S. Department of Commerce, Bureau of the Census, *Religious Bodies: 1926*, Vol. II, p. 1038.

[207] U. S. Department of Commerce, Bureau of the Census, *Religious Bodies: 1926*, Vol. II, pp. 1153, 1154.

[208] A. A. Taylor in *The Journal of Negro History*, Vol. XI, pp. 434-437.

[209] Woodson, *The History of the Negro Church*, p. 200.

majority of Negro Baptists became associated in the National Baptist Convention.[210]

In 1916 almost nine-tenths of the Negroes who were church members were comprised in the five bodies, the National Baptist Convention, the Coloured Methodist Episcopal Church, the African Methodist Episcopal Church, the African Methodist Episcopal Zion Church, and the Methodist Episcopal Church. Eighty-seven per cent. were in the first four bodies, which were completely autonomous. Sixty-three and a half per cent., or almost two-thirds of the Negro church members, were associated with the National Baptist Convention.[211]

It was in connexion with the Baptist movement that the National Baptist Publishing Board developed. This was largely the creation of a former slave, Richard Henry Boyd, who felt the need of his race for religious literature and began to issue it on a modest scale. Eventually it had a staff of one hundred and fifty in a block of seven buildings. It specialized on Sunday School materials and sent them not only throughout the United States but also to all five continents.[212]

It was chiefly through the initiative of Negroes that after emancipation Christianity continued its rapid numerical expansion among the race. In 1916 the number of Negroes who were members of churches was reported as being 4,602,805.[213] This was about seven times the total of approximately 520,000 in 1860. It was also a striking increase in the proportion of the Negro population of the country, for whereas in 1860 the percentage of Negroes who were church members was about 11.7, in 1916 it was about 44.2.[214] This was not far from the percentage of church members, 43.4 in 1910,[215] in the population of the country as a whole. In other words, Christianity had so rapidly advanced among the Negroes that relatively it was about as strong at the close of our period, 1914, as it was among the whites.

In the spread of Christianity among the Negroes the chief contributions of

[210] U. S. Department of Commerce, Bureau of the Census, *Religious Bodies: 1926*, Vol. II, p. 137; Woodson, *op. cit.*, pp. 200, 201.

[211] U. S. Department of Commerce, Bureau of the Census, *Religious Bodies: 1916*, Vol. I, p. 554.

[212] Shepherd, *Literature for the South African Bantu*, p. 34; Washington, *The Story of the Negro*, Vol. II, p. 340; Frederick G. Detweiler, *The Negro Press in the United States* (University of Chicago Press, 1922, pp. x, 274), pp. 48-50.

[213] Department of Commerce, Bureau of the Census, *Religious Bodies: 1916*, Vol. I, p. 554.

[214] The Negro population in 1910 was 9,827,763 (Department of Commerce, Bureau of the Census, *Negro Population 1790-1915*, p. 29) and, allowing for the probable increase, in 1916 was probably not far from 10,400,000.

[215] Weber, *1933 Yearbook of the American Churches*, p. 299.

white Christians was in education. This does not mean that the white churches left the propagation of the faith entirely to the Negro denominations. Several of the denominations whose membership was overwhelmingly white had contingents of Negroes. In 1916 those having the largest numbers of Negroes, in addition to the Methodist Episcopal Church, were the Protestant Episcopal Church, with 51,502 the (Northern) Presbyterian Church in the United States of America, with 37,090, the Disciples of Christ, with 37,325, and the Congregationalists, with 16,000.[216] When compared with the largest of the Negro denominations, however, these figures are insignificant. It was on founding and sustaining schools that white Christians expended most of such energy as they devoted to the welfare of the Negro. Much of this educational effort was through missionary societies. Much was through foundations and endowments which were not always avowedly Christian, but which arose from the Christian faith of the donors. Moreover, many schools supported by public funds owed their existence in no small degree to whites whose motive seems to have been of Christian origin.

To detail all of these educational activities of white Christians is beyond the compass of these pages. Even if space permitted, a complete account would not be feasible. To disentangle the impelling forces of unquestionably Christian sources from those of other provenance would in many teachers, organizers, and movements be quite impossible. However, even a brief selection from the schools of unmistakably Christian rootage should reveal the extraordinary contribution which Christianity made to the education of the Negro. Most of the outstanding pioneer institutions are traceable to the Christian impulse. From these schools came much of the leadership not only of the Negro churches but also of many of the non-ecclesiastical movements which contributed to the progress of the race.

A large outpouring of life for the freedmen issued from the churches of the North. It was from them that the initiative first came which culminated in the abolition of slavery. Christian folk who had advocated the termination of slavery felt a responsibility for the Negroes whom they had helped to free. Hundreds believed themselves called by their Christian faith to labour as teachers among the Negroes in the South. Many of them were supported by Northern missionary societies. Usually they faced ostracism and obloquy by the Southern whites.[217] It was only a sense of Christian duty which kept them at their task. To them the Negroes owed an incalculable debt.

[216] Department of Commerce, Bureau of the Census, *Religious Bodies: 1916*, Vol. I, p. 554.
[217] *Nineteenth Annual Report of the American Missionary Association* (1865), p. 12; Beard, *A Crusade of Brotherhood*, p. 169.

While the Civil War was still being fought, several Freedmen's Aid Societies began schools for Negroes in areas occupied by the Union armies and behind the Union lines. Clergy were prominent in several of these societies. In at least one the purpose was declared to be the moral and religious as well as the industrial, social, and intellectual improvement of the freed blacks, and more than one of them later merged with the American Missionary Association.[218]

The organization which contributed to the founding of some of the most important of the schools for Negroes was the American Missionary Association. The American Missionary Association was the outgrowth of several smaller organizations. By its constitution its membership was open to all "of evangelical sentiments who profess faith in our Lord Jesus Christ, who is not a slaveholder, or in the practice of other immoralities," and who had made a financial contribution to it.[219] It was, then, emphatically anti-slavery and it was meant to be undenominational. Before the Civil War it had had missions in Africa, Siam, Jamaica, and among the American Indians. With the coming of the war, and especially after emancipation, while continuing most of its other missions, it concentrated the major part of its attention upon the freedmen. It stressed schools. It appointed teachers from several denominations. Although its support came mainly from the Congregationalists, for a time some other denominations made it their agency for aiding the Negro.[220] It conducted schools from primary grade through institutions of college and university standing. It also maintained theological schools for the training of the Negro ministry. Under its auspices a number of institutions were begun which became outstanding in the preparation of Negro leaders. From them went thousands of teachers. Notable among the institutions inaugurated were Hampton Institute, in Virginia, Fisk University, in Tennessee, Atlanta University, in Georgia, Talladega College, in Alabama, Tougaloo University, in Mississippi, Straight University, in Louisiana, and Tillotson College, in Georgia.[221] Berea College, which the American Missionary Association assisted, although later exclusively for whites, for a time was for Negroes as well. It will be noticed that these institutions were so distributed that they covered much of the South. By 1872 the governments of the Southern states had made such strides in providing elementary education for the Negro that the American Missionary Association began directing most of its resources

---

[218] J. H. Parmelee in Jones, *Negro Education*, Vol. I, pp. 268-275.
[219] See constitution in *Nineteenth Annual Report of the American Missionary Association.*
[220] *Nineteenth Annual Report of the American Missionary Association*, p. 14.
[221] *Twenty-Ninth Report of the American Missionary Association* (1875), p. 76; *Fifty-Sixth Annual Report of the American Missionary Association* (1902), p. 15.

to secondary and higher education.[222] To it came large funds, among them a gift of over a million dollars by Daniel Hand who, Connecticut-born, had made his fortune in the South and who specified that the income from his endowment should be used for Negro education in that region.[223] In 1875 the society was assisting thirty-two schools in the South with an enrollment of over seven thousand, and it estimated that former pupils in its schools were teaching about sixty-four thousand.[224] In 1913 it was aiding sixty-five schools which had an enrollment of over twelve thousand students.[225]

The American Missionary Association did not build up a large church membership. However, in 1913 it had connexions with 181 churches, chiefly Negro, with 10,746 members.[226] Many of these churches were associated with the schools of the society.[227]

The first day-school opened for the freedmen by the American Missionary Association became independent of the society and grew into one of the most famous of the institutions for Negroes, the Hampton Normal and Agricultural Institute.[228] After a few years it contained Indians as well as Negroes, but the former were in the minority and it was through the latter that its main contribution was made. Its chief creator and its director for many years was Samuel Chapman Armstrong.[229] Born in Hawaii in 1839, the son of missionaries, after graduating from Williams College Armstrong had been in the Union army, and had risen rapidly to the rank of brevet brigadier-general. He had been in command of Negroes and after the war served them as an appointee of the government Freedmen's Bureau. In 1867 he became the head of the school which the American Missionary Association had begun at Hampton. Inspired partly by a mission project which he had seen in his Hawaiian boyhood, he adopted as an essential part of his programme the training of Negroes in handicrafts and industries through which they could make a living. The school opened in 1868. It enrolled members of both sexes. Armstrong raised money, organized, procured and inspired teachers, and in addition to his own duties found time to advocate national aid for Negro education. Long before his death, in 1893, Hampton had become recognized as the out-

[222] Beard, op. cit., p. 197.
[223] Beard, op. cit., pp. 256-259.
[224] Twenty-Ninth Report of the American Missionary Association (1875), pp. 76, 77.
[225] Sixty-Seventh Annual Report of the American Missionary Association (1913), p. 9.
[226] Sixty-Seventh Annual Report of the American Missionary Association (1913), p. 11.
[227] Twenty-Ninth Annual Report of the American Missionary Association (1875), p. 19.
[228] Beard, op. cit., pp. 121-128. On Hampton Institute, see Francis Greenwood Peabody, Education for Life. The Story of Hampton Institute (Garden City, Doubleday, Page & Co., 1918, pp. xxiv, 393), passim.
[229] Edith Armstrong Talbot, Samuel Chapman Armstrong, A Biographical Study (New York, Doubleday, Page & Co., 1904, pp. vi, 301. By a daughter), passim.

standing successful example of a type of education peculiarly fitted for the Negroes' needs.

True to their concern for the Negroes, Friends were active in founding and maintaining schools for the freedmen.[230] Famous among these was Penn School on St. Helena Island off the coast of South Carolina.[231] It was founded in 1862 by Laura M. Towne and Ellen Murray soon after the capture of the island by the Union forces. In addition to the school itself, Sunday Schools were begun and a temperance society was organized. Graduates from Hampton came, bringing with them its methods and ideals. The entire life of the island felt the effects.

The Protestant Episcopal Church conducted several institutions, among them Bishop Payne Divinity School, in which were trained about two-thirds of the clergy for the Negroes of the denomination.[232]

The American Baptist Home Mission Society opened a number of schools, among them colleges. What became the most noted higher school for Negro women, Spelman College, was founded by Baptists and was aided by both the American Baptist Home Mission Society and the Woman's American Baptist Home Mission Society.[233] In 1885 the Home Mission Board of the Southern Baptist Convention reported the holding of institutes in Georgia for the instruction of the coloured ministry.[234]

From their past history it was to be expected that the Methodists would be active among the Negroes. The (Northern) Methodist Episcopal Church through its Freedmen's Aid Society built up and supported twenty-six schools, and, in addition, its women conducted sixteen homes for the training of girls in domestic science and other appropriate arts and occupations. They sent out missionaries and assisted in the erection of about three thousand church buildings.[235] The Methodist Episcopal Church, South, aided a number of colleges for Negroes, notably Paine College, in Augusta, Georgia, a joint enterprise of that church and of the Coloured Methodist Episcopal Church.[236]

The Northern Presbyterians (the Presbyterian Church in the United States

[230] G. S. Dickerman in Jones, Negro Education, Vol. I, p. 253.

[231] Cooley, School Acres, passim.

[232] Addison, Our Expanding Church, p. 83.

[233] White, A Century of Faith, pp. 102-119; Phila M. Whipple, Negro Neighbors Bond and Free (Boston, Woman's American Baptist Home Mission Society, 1907, p. 143), pp. 122ff.

[234] Proceedings of the Southern Baptist Convention, 1885, Annual Report of the Home Mission Board, p. vii.

[235] The Methodist Forward Movement in the United States. Annual of the Board of Home Missions and Church Extension of the Methodist Episcopal Church for the Year 1907-1908, p. 11.

[236] Missionary Yearbook of the Methodist Episcopal Church South, 1936, p. 24.

of America) had a Board of Missions for Freedmen which assisted a number of schools—in 1914, 136 of them.[237] In 1890 the Northern Presbyterians began appointing Negro missionaries to organize Sunday Schools in the South. In the next quarter of a century over three thousand such schools had been formed and from them over two hundred churches had sprung.[238]

The Lutheran Board for Coloured Missions and the Board of Freedmen's Missions of the United Presbyterian Church also maintained schools.[239]

The denominations we have mentioned were the ones which had the largest share in conducting schools for Negroes, but several others had a less extensive part.[240]

An institution which had an important place in the education of Negroes was Howard University, in the nation's capital. It began in 1866 in a prayer meeting in the First Congregational Church of the city and was chartered the following year. A normal school was its initial department. It received aid from the national government through the Freedmen's Bureau. When the end of the Freedmen's Bureau and the panic of 1873 brought it into dire straits, a clergyman, W. W. Patton, reorganized it. Much of the money for its maintenance came from Congregationalists.[241]

Several private foundations contributed to the education of the Negro. Most, although not all, owed their inception at least in part to the Christian impulse. The Peabody Education Fund, established in 1867 for education of both white and black in the South and South-west, was the gift of George Peabody, who declared that he was moved by gratitude to God for His blessings.[242] The John F. Slater Fund, begun in 1882, was for the avowed purpose of conferring on the Negroes of the South "the blessings of Christian education."[243] The Jeanes Fund, for the aid of rural schools for Negroes, was given by Anna T. Jeanes, of a Quaker family.[244] The first directing head of that fund, James Hardy Dillard, came from a prominent white Virginia family, was active in the Protestant Episcopal Church, and, in a time of bitter race feeling, led in

[237] Work, *Negro Year Book 1914-1915*, p. 215.
[238] Work, *op. cit.*, p. 197.
[239] Jones, *Negro Education*, Vol. I, pp. 303, 304.
[240] See lists in Jones, *op. cit.*, Vol. I, pp. 254, 303, 304.
[241] Embree, *Brown America*, pp. 103-107; D. O. W. Holmes in *The Journal of Negro History*, Vol. III, pp. 131ff.
[242] J. L. M. Curry, *Peabody Education Fund. A Brief Sketch of George Peabody and a History of the Peabody Education Fund through Thirty Years* (Cambridge University Press, 1898, pp. x, 161), pp. 18-20.
[243] Brawley, *Doctor Dillard of the Jeanes Fund*, pp. 67-76.
[244] Brawley, *op. cit.*, pp. 55-106; Bond, *The Education of the Negro in the American Social Order*, p. 135.

promoting a friendlier attitude of Southern whites towards the Negroes, and, among other duties, became a trustee of four colleges for Negroes.[245] The Phelps-Stokes Fund, in part for the education of Negroes in the United States and Africa, was endowed by the bequest of Caroline Phelps Stokes, who wished through it to continue some of the philanthropies to which she had been drawn by a controlling Christian faith.[246] John D. Rockefeller, who seems to have been impelled to his gigantic philanthropies largely by his Christian faith, contributed to the education of the Negro through the Baptist home mission societies, especially to Morehouse College and Spelman College. In 1903 the General Education Board was incorporated as a channel for his contributions to education. It was in part an outgrowth of the Baptist Education Society, but was undenominational. It gave millions for the education of the Negro.[247]

Negro Christians were not content to leave permanently with their white brethren the burden of educating their people. The Negro churches early began, out of their poverty, to establish schools. In this they often received some assistance from white churches, but the initiative was theirs. By 1917 Negro church boards owned 153 schools, of which 60 were said to have sufficient equipment and income to render valuable service.[248]

The outstanding Negro educator of the first half century after emancipation and the best known leader of his race in his generation was Booker T. Washington.[249] He received most of his training at Hampton Institute and thus was a contribution of white Christian philanthropy to the coloured people. He was born a slave in Virginia shortly before the Civil War, of an unknown white father and a Negro mother. He early displayed a hunger for learning and in 1872 made his way to Hampton. There he conceived the intense admiration for Armstrong which he never lost. After graduating from Hampton and teaching elsewhere he returned to the faculty of his *alma mater*. From there he went to be head of a normal school at Tuskegee, Alabama. At Tuskegee, taking his inspiration from Hampton, and with the aid of gifts from many sources, he built up an institution which became famous as one of the best for

[245] Brawley, *op. cit., passim.*

[246] Bond, *op. cit.,* p. 143; *Dictionary of American Biography,* Vol. XVIII, p. 68.

[247] Bond, *op. cit.,* p. 137; *The General Education Board,* pp. 6, 7, 190ff.

[248] Jones, *op. cit.,* Vol. I, pp. 149-152, 254. On some of these and the gifts for their support, see Washington, *The Story of the Negro,* Vol. II, pp. 339ff. On an undenominational but avowedly Christian school, see Laurence C. Jones, *Piney Woods and Its Story* (New York, Fleming H. Revell Co., 1922, pp. 154), *passim.*

[249] *Booker T. Washington's Own Story of His Life and Work* (Naperville, Ill., J. L. Nichols & Co., 1916, pp. 510), *passim;* Booker T. Washington, *Up From Slavery. An Autobiography* (New York, Doubleday, Page & Co., 1901, pp. ix, 330), *passim.*

his race and one of the most progressive in fitting the Negro to share and improve the life of the community.

The Protestant Christianity of the Negro developed characteristics which marked it as somewhat distinct from that of the whites.

This was not true of its organization, of most of its methods, or of much of its spirit. The Negroes created no major new denominational types. They were content to reproduce those which had come to them from the whites. The vast majority of them were Baptists or Methodists, and most of the rest were Episcopalians, Presbyterians, or Congregationalists. This was in striking contrast with the Negroes of South Africa, for these broke up into hundreds of separate churches. Indeed, the Negroes of the United States tended to concentrate into rather fewer denominations than did white Protestants. They accepted the Young Men's Christian Association[250] and made no revolutionary changes in it. Moreover, in their church services, while inaugurating some innovations, the Negroes followed in general what they had seen in the white churches in the order of service, in preaching, in the holding of prayer-meetings, in Sunday Schools, and in societies and auxiliary organizations.[251] The sermons preached treated of much the same themes as those heard in white churches.[252] The "revivals" and "protracted meetings" of the whites were reproduced, although with an intensification of their emotional features. As time passed, indeed, Negro churches tended, if anything, to conform rather more than less closely to the patterns of the white churches. Although some attitudes from his African past persisted, notably his emotionalism and belief in magic, few customs of pre-American origin carried over into the Negro's Christianity. Even the emotionalism, the confidence in magic, and the acceptance of spirits were possibly not so much African as primitive. Nor did the Negroes reach out much beyond their own country and race in an attempt to spread their faith. In spite of the fact that by 1914 the proportion of Negroes possessing a church affiliation was about as high as that among the whites, practically the only organized efforts which the Negro churches made to propagate their religion beyond the members of their own race in the United States were missions to coloured peoples in the West Indies, Guiana, and Africa.[253] Even these enterprises were small. The total financial contributions

---

[250] For a brief sketch of the history of the Young Men's Christian Association among the Negroes, see J. E. Moorland in *The Journal of Negro History*, Vol. IX, pp. 127-138.

[251] Mays and Nicholson, *The Negro's Church*, p. 119.

[252] Mays and Nicholson, *op. cit.*, pp. 58-93, reports that of one hundred sermons studied, twenty-six touched concrete life situations, fifty-four were predominantly on the after life rather than on daily living, and twenty were highly doctrinal.

[253] Beach and Fahs, *World Missionary Atlas* (1925), pp. 19, 23, 24. See also Washington, *The Story of the Negro*, Vol. II, pp. 332ff.

for their support were insignificant. In proportion to their income, the Negro churches contributed only about one-fifteenth as much to foreign missions as did the white churches.[254] Part of this absorption with the problems of their own people can be ascribed to poverty, part of it to the challenge of winning the Negroes to the Christian faith and educating them, and even more to the attitudes of the whites which placed the Negroes emotionally on the defensive and centred their energies upon achieving social and economic emancipation. As yet this Negro Christianity was not looking much beyond its own borders.

When all of these qualifications are made, it is clear that Negro Protestant Christianity in the United States was much less passive and was more creative than was the Christianity which had been planted among the Indians and Negroes of Latin America in the preceding period. Even though its foreign missions were not so extensive as those of the white churches, it initiated and maintained them, and by the gifts of a constituency from the lower income levels of the nation. This was more than was done by the Indians and Negroes of Latin America. In general it supported and controlled its own churches and did much for the education of the race. The Negro Protestant Christianity of the United States developed, especially before emancipation, a religious dance, or, more accurately, dances.[255] It contributed some unique personalities who were a blend of Christianity with Negro characteristics. Among these was an amazing woman, best known by her chosen name, Sojourner Truth, who had a strange spiritual pilgrimage, and, especially before emancipation, travelled widely, was a combination of prophet, preacher, and mystic, and exerted a remarkable influence.[256] In some areas were what were known as "praise houses," in which meetings were held several evenings in the week.[257] The most widely influential of all of the creations of Negro Protestant Christianity was the Negro "spiritual." These songs appeared in great number, spontaneous utterances of the Negro's Christian faith. Both in music and words many of these had as a basis "spirituals" which were current among the whites of the South in *ante bellum* times. However, they were not exact reproductions of their white prototypes but bore indelibly the stamp of the peculiar Negro genius. Some of them gained wide currency among whites as well as blacks and enriched the

[254] This is arrived at from figures in U. S. Department of Commerce, Bureau of the Census, *Religious Bodies: 1926*, Vol. I, pp. 107, 714, and Beach and Fahs, *op. cit.*, p. 69.

[255] Puckett, *Folk Beliefs of the Southern Negro*, p. 531; G. R. Wilson in *The Journal of Negro History*, Vol. VIII, pp. 56-58.

[256] Arthur Huff Fauset, *Sojourner Truth, God's Faithful Pilgrim* (Chapel Hill, The University of North Carolina Press, 1938, pp. viii, 187), *passim*.

[257] Puckett, *op. cit.*, p. 531; Cooley, *School Acres*, pp. 135ff. Puckett, *op. cit.*, pp. 520ff., describes ways in which superstition mingled with Christianity in Negro life.

emotional life of millions.[258] Their Christian faith stimulated the Negroes to creation, especially in song, which reflected their racial genius.

We can best summarize this account of the expansion of Christianity among the Negroes of the United States between the Revolutionary War and 1914 by employing the facts which we have assembled in our narrative to answer our recurring five questions. The Christianity which spread was overwhelmingly Protestant, and, of the Protestant denominations, those of the proletarian elements of the older white stock, the Baptists and the Methodists, were most largely represented. Christianity spread partly because of the zeal of white Christians and the missions of white churches, partly through the devotion of Negro Christians and the activities of Negro churches, partly by reason of the complete disappearance of the tribal life and customs which had shaped the Negro in Africa and the desire of the Negro to conform to the culture in which he found himself, and partly because his churches were long the only social institutions in which the Negro had complete control and which he could use as centres for his community life. Christianity spread through the instruction and example of white masters and mistresses, through individual clergymen, white and black, through organized missions of white and black churches and societies, and through the activities of individual denominations. Christianity profoundly affected the Negro. By 1914 nearly half of the Negroes were members of churches. While large numbers of these professing Christians were notoriously lax in their observance of Christian ethics, increasingly Christian moral standards made themselves felt among clergy and laity. The churches, organized expressions of Christianity, long afforded the Negro greater freedom for development and for ordering his own social life than did any other set of institutions. Christianity made for the sanctity of the marriage tie and the stability of the family. Through the churches and through Christian folk acting apart from the churches there came to the Negro most of his initial opportunities for education, both before and after emancipation. Only later did secular agencies enter. Even down to 1914 most of the best educational institutions of higher learning owed their origin to the Christian impulse. It was from the Christian conscience stirred by religious awakenings

[258] E. A. McIlhenny, *Befo' de War Spirituals Words and Melodies* (Boston, The Christopher Publishing House, no date, pp. 255), *passim;* W. E. DuBois, *The Gift of Black Folk. The Negroes in the Making of America* (Boston, The Stratford Co., 1924, pp. iv, 349), pp. 274ff.; Jackson, *White Spirituals in the Southern Uplands,* pp. 242ff. Jackson is the best discussion of the relation of the Negro "spirituals" to white music. Less thorough is Henry Edward Krehbiel, *Afro-American Folksongs. A Study in Racial and Social Music* (New York, 1914, pp. xii, 176), pp. 11-41.

that the movement for emancipation began and had its early growth. When once emancipation was accomplished, it was men and women impelled by a Christian purpose who had a major share in helping the freedmen to adjust themselves to their new status. While the Negro environment did not revolutionize the Christianity received from the whites and although few practices and beliefs of unquestionably African provenance persisted in the Negro's new faith, the Negro was stimulated by Christianity to make original contributions to the religious life of the nation. This he did notably in song. In the conversion, the shaping, and the stimulation of the Negro, nineteenth century Christianity registered one of its outstanding achievements.

Chapter X

THE UNITED STATES OF AMERICA. SHIFTING POPULATIONS AND CHANGING SOCIAL CONDITIONS

TO THE problems which confronted Christianity in the United States there were added the ones brought by population movements from country to city and to new occupations and by changing social and economic conditions. In this lusty young country Christianity was faced not only with the westward shifting frontier and the flood of peoples from other lands, with the widely scattered Indians, and with the Negroes, although these would have seemingly taxed to the utmost the energies and resources of the Christian minority with which the century began. It was also compelled to meet vast alterations wrought by the fresh knowledge and the machines of the age. The Industrial Revolution affected the United States fully as much as it did Europe. The factory, the railway, the steamship, the telegraph, the telephone, and all the myriad appliances of the century with the scientific approach and the new learning were especially prominent in the United States. Some of them were the creations of Americans. By 1914 they had brought into existence a society which in many respects was utterly different from that of 1776. In 1776 the Thirteen Colonies were predominantly rural and agricultural with an extensive frontier and had no large cities. A century and a half later the United States contained several of the largest urban centres of the globe, the frontier had all but disappeared, a prodigious exodus was taking place from country to city, and the land was increasingly one of factories. Huge mining enterprises had developed, and the forests were being stripped by a gigantic lumber industry. Families were becoming smaller and less stable. Rural life itself was being metamorphosed. The intellectual outlook was in process of revolution. Education had been altered almost beyond recognition and was being secularized.

These movements were mounting rather than declining and Christianity was only beginning to meet the challenge with which they confronted it. The problems to which the churches, and especially the Protestant churches, had directed most of their energies were disappearing or were on the way to solution. By 1914 the frontier had vanished, but so energetically had the churches dealt with it that Christianity had been firmly planted in every region across

367

which it had moved. Immigration had continued, to be brought abruptly to all but a complete halt by the outbreak of the World War of 1914-1918, but in general the churches had kept pace with it and had held to their traditional faith a large proportion of the newcomers and their children and had won some of the non-Christian Orientals. So widely had Christianity spread among the Indians and the Negroes that almost as large a proportion of these peoples as of those of European ancestry bore the Christian name. In 1914, however, the other trends seemed to be only in their beginning, and as yet Christianity had by no means dealt successfully with the problems which they presented. Cities were continuing to grow and church programmes designed to meet populations living on farms and in small towns could not adequately cope with them. Constituencies of once well-established congregations were scattering to the suburbs. Industrial and mining centres were multiplying and the churches had not caught up with them and their peculiar needs. Some agricultural communities were being drained of their most energetic leadership and, left in the backwash of civilization, were becoming rural slums. Once flourishing country churches were languishing or disappearing. In the intellectual life, science seemed to be erasing religion, colleges and universities founded as Christian institutions were becoming indifferent or hostile to the faith to which they owed their existence, and in the public school system through which the overwhelming majority of the younger generation were reared the teaching of religion was increasingly tabooed. The daily prayers and Bible reading once a feature of the family routine of church members were disappearing under the pressure of a complex, mechanized life. The rapidly growing divorce rate made for family instability and further jeopardized the religious instruction of children. At first sight it seemed that the churches, engrossed in meeting the conditions which were outstanding in the first three-quarters of the century, were yielding ground to these fresh attacks. It appeared that Christianity was being undermined in the hour of some of its greatest successes. It was in danger of losing the children of the parents whom it had won.

However, this pessimistic appraisal gives by no means a complete picture. Many Christians were aware of the new challenges to their faith and were devising measures to meet them. As had so frequently been the case in preceding centuries, a lag occurred between the emergence of the problems and the attempts to solve them. Yet by 1914 many efforts were being put forth and some progress had been registered.

These endeavours must not long detain us. Strictly speaking, they belong only incidentally in an account of the expansion of Christianity. However, since by their success or failure they were certain to affect the future of that expansion, we must take account of them. Moreover, some of them have directly to do with the geographic extension of the faith and must be included. Confronted by the cities Christians were by no means inactive. Because a large proportion of the later immigration, largely Roman Catholic and Eastern Orthodox in background, came to the cities, especially to industrial and mining centres, as unskilled labourers, it was here that the Roman Catholic and Eastern Orthodox bodies concentrated much of their effort. Shortly after the close of this period, approximately four-fifths of the Roman Catholic membership was in cities of twenty-five hundred or more and only one-fifth in what were technically denominated rural areas.[1] For members of the Greek Orthodox[2] and Russian Orthodox Churches[3] the percentage which was classified as urban was even higher. Obviously these bodies had had a fairly high degree of success in holding in their fellowship those in the cities who by heredity were affiliated with them.

Since the older American stock was by tradition overwhelmingly Protestant, since the Protestant denominations had devoted so much energy to winning this stock when it was advancing westward on the frontier, and because much of the nineteenth century Protestant immigration went West to take up the then inexpensive farming lands, Protestant churches had a somewhat harder time in focussing their attention on the cities and in adjusting their programmes to large urban communities. Then, too, Protestant Christianity, by its very nature divided, and having its tendency to individualism heightened by long contact with the frontier, experienced much more difficulty in planning comprehensively for a given urban area than did the Roman Catholics, organized as they were by territorial dioceses and under episcopal direction. At least in some instances, Roman Catholics were more successful in formulating and executing an inclusive programme for reaching the cities than were Protestants.[4] Moreover, the older American stock, predominantly Protestant, tended to disappear from the more congested parts of the cities and to leave them to the newer, prevailingly Roman Catholic elements. This was partly because Protestants were in general more prosperous and could afford to live in the pleasanter but more expensive marginal and suburban sections. Thus Boston, once the stronghold of Puritanism, became one of the most Roman

---

[1] U. S. Department of Commerce, Bureau of the Census, *Religious Bodies: 1926*, Vol. II, p. 1254.
[2] *Op. cit.*, Vol. II, p. 494.
[3] *Op. cit.*, Vol. II, p. 506.
[4] Douglass, *The Springfield Church Survey*, pp. 43, 44, 73; Douglass, *The St. Louis Church Survey*, pp. 51, 52.

Catholic of cities,[5] and in Springfield, Massachusetts, the declining proportion of older American stock tended to concentrate in the socially more desirable areas.[6]

Yet Protestant Christianity did not totally fail in its attack on the urban problem. In meeting it, it displayed to no small degree initiative, imagination, and intelligence. Adaptability varied from congregation to congregation. Yet it was by no means absent. Thus, when their accustomed constituencies shifted to the periphery, some congregations chose to follow them, to put up new buildings, and to adjust their plans to the fresh environment. Others elected to remain on their downtown sites, and, with a nucleus of their older membership, to seek through altered programmes and modifications in their edifices to serve the new population about them.[7] Moreover, Protestants organized city mission societies. In the first third of the nineteenth century these were usually without marked denominational emphasis and were for the religious education of the poor and underprivileged. Those formed in the latter part of the century were as a rule particularistic, and were the means by which each denomination sought fellowship and comprehensive planning for the entire city.[8] They were generally of the larger, older American denominations.[9] In the opening years of the twentieth century these urban organizations expanded and diversified their plans.[10] At least as early as the 1850's interdenominational associations of the Protestant clergy began to spring up city by city for joint action. City-wide federations and councils of Protestant churches for still more inclusive programmes began to appear.[11] After 1914 they became much more numerous.

The Protestant revivals of the nineteenth century increasingly centred in the cities. The Great Awakening of the eighteenth century and the revivals of the first decade of the nineteenth century were primarily on the frontier. They were mass movements through which those on the fringes of settlement were reached and Christianity was firmly planted in new areas. As time passed, revivals first of all affected the older American stock in the cities and spread from them to the towns and the rural districts. Finney, the outstanding evangelist of the middle of the century, was largely a product of the frontier

[5] Douglass, *The St. Louis Church Survey*, pp. 51, 52.
[6] Douglass, *The Springfield Church Survey*, pp. 42, 64.
[7] See examples in Douglas, *The Church in the Changing City, passim,* and Strong, *The Challenge of the City*, pp. 209ff.
[8] Hallenbeck, *Urban Organization of Protestantism*, pp. 13-19.
[9] Hallenbeck, *op. cit.*, pp. 3-6.
[10] Hallenbeck, *op. cit.*, pp. 19-24.
[11] On a Federation of Churches and an interdenominational City Missions Committee in New York City, see Brown, *A Teacher and His Times*, pp. 118-120.

and began his preaching in the smaller towns, but for years he made his residence in the largest city, New York, and there built up a congregation.[12] The so-called "prayer-meeting revival" of 1857 and 1858 began among business men in New York City.[13] The outstanding evangelist of the latter part of the century, Dwight L. Moody, although reared in a rural village, entered upon his transforming religious experience in Boston, first rose to prominence as a religious leader in Chicago, and concentrated most of his efforts on the cities.[14]

It was no accident that the Young Men's and Young Women's Christian Associations, although they began in Great Britain, had their greatest development in the United States. They were Protestant agencies through which laymen and women of varied denominational affiliations joined in serving the youth of the cities. They sought to mould all phases of the life of youth, especially of urban youth.[15]

For the underprivileged members of urban society, especially for those broken morally, the Salvation Army, also of British origin, entered and enjoyed a nation-wide growth. In 1916 it had 749 organizations, and its membership of 35,954[16] was only a small fraction of those served by it. An offshoot of the Salvation Army, the Volunteers of America, in 1916 had ninety-seven organizations and 10,204 members.[17]

Many rescue missions sought to save the moral dregs of the cities. Unlike the Salvation Army and the Volunteers of America, they were not knit together in a closely integrated national or even regional organization. Each was autonomous. Yet they bore a striking family likeness. In them was preached a personal new birth through faith in God's love as seen in Jesus and the Cross.[18] Usually each drew its support from members of several Protestant denominations.

Social settlements, neighbourhood houses, and institutional churches were

---

[12] *Memoirs of Rev. Charles G. Finney, passim.*
[13] Weigle, *American Idealism*, pp. 182, 183; Beardsley, *A History of American Revivals*, pp. 213ff.
[14] Moody, *D. L. Moody, passim.*
[15] On the development of the Young Men's Christian Association, see Richard C. Morse, *History of the North American Young Men's Christian Associations* (New York, Association Press, 1922, pp. xiv, 290), *passim; Year Book of the Young Men's Christian Associations of North America* (New York, Association Press, 1914, pp. 400), *passim.*
[16] Department of Commerce, Bureau of the Census, *Religious Bodies: 1916*, Vol. II, p. 661.
[17] Department of Commerce, Bureau of the Census, *Religious Bodies: 1916*, Vol. II, p. 716.
[18] As examples of these, see the autobiographical *Jerry McAuley His Life and Work*, edited by R. M. Offord (New York, The New York Observer, 2d ed., 1885, pp. xi, 227), *passim,* and *Mother Whittemore's Records of Modern Miracles* (Toronto, Missions of Biblical Education, 1931, pp. 304), *passim.*

brought into being. Not all in the first two categories were avowedly religious, but most of them went back to founders impelled by a Christian purpose. Through clubs, classes, kindergartens, nurseries, clinics, and entertainments they gave opportunity for wholesome recreation, education, and physical and moral health to the poorer urban districts.[19]

Protestantism was, then, displaying amazing resourcefulness in addressing itself to the new problems presented to it by the city. As a counterpart of the city was the changing rural life. Some rural areas were slowly drained of their energetic elements. Inadequate methods of cultivation, the competition of virgin, more fertile regions, and the drift of youth to urban centres led in many areas to a decrease in cultivated lands and a decay of morale. Better roads and more rapid communication, especially towards the close of the period, brought the decline of some rural villages and the growth of others. In several regions, especially in those longest settled, the decades immediately before 1914 witnessed a dwindling attendance at churches, the demise of numbers of congregations, and a falling off in the purchasing power of financial contributions.[20] Since these communities were mainly of the older American stock, Protestant Christianity was the chief sufferer.

By 1914 efforts were being made to meet these conditions. In several educational institutions specialized preparation was introduced for clergy who were to serve in rural parishes.[21] Here and there two or more denominations joined forces in what were called federated churches, thus to remedy the evils brought by the multiplication of small, weak congregations.[22] The Federal Council of the Churches of Christ in America created a Commission on Church and Country Life.[23] Increasingly, in the twentieth century organized

---

[19] Strong, *op. cit.*, pp. 209ff. In 1906, 163 settlements were reported.—Strong, *op. cit.*, p. 227. On the beginnings of one of these see Brown, *op. cit.*, pp. 158-164. On the history of a combination of church, rescue mission, and settlement, see E. C. E. Dorion, *The Redemption of the South End* (New York, The Abingdon Press, 1915, pp. 124), *passim*. On an autobiographical account of a famous settlement which united those of widely varying religious beliefs, see Jane Addams, *Forty Years at Hull-House* (New York, The Macmillan Co., 1935, pp. 462, 459), *passim*. On something of the religious faith and purpose of Miss Addams, see *op. cit.*, Part I (*Twenty Years at Hull-House*), pp. 51-53, 77-79, 83. On South End House in Boston, which was an outgrowth of Andover House, founded by a graduate of Andover Theological Seminary, see Eleanor H. Woods, *Robert W. Woods, Champion of Democracy* (Boston, Houghton Mifflin Co., 1929, pp. x, 376), *passim*.

[20] Charles Otis Gill and Gifford Pinchot, *The Country Church. The Decline of Its Influence and the Remedy* (New York, The Macmillan Co., 1913, pp. xii, 222), *passim;* Gill and Pinchot, *Six Thousand Country Churches, passim*.

[21] Douglass, *The New Home Missions*, pp. 67, 68.

[22] Gill and Pinchot, *Six Thousand Country Churches*, pp. 63, 67.

[23] Gill and Pinchot, *op. cit.*, p. xiii.

denominational forces gave attention to the problem.[24] In addition to these newer measures, for many years state denominational organizations had been according financial aid to feeble rural churches.[25] Here, as in the changing city, Protestant Christianity was displaying a vitality which expressed itself in adaptability.

A special phase of the rural problem was what was called the "mountain white." In the Cumberlands and Appalachians in the South and, to a somewhat less extent, in the Ozarks in the South-west, were enclaves of older American stock, largely of English and Scotch-Irish descent, traditionally Protestant, which had been partly isolated by poor communications and had suffered from adverse economic and intellectual conditions. In methods and attitudes their religious life was a degenerate survival of that of the early Western frontier.[26] In 1884 the American Missionary Association asked for a special fund for "educational and evangelistic work in the mountain regions of Kentucky, Tennessee, and the adjacent states."[27] Other denominations entered through home mission societies, largely from the North. Thus the (Northern) Methodist Episcopal Church conducted schools in which clergymen, teachers, and other leaders were trained and assisted with the building of churches and the payment of pastors' salaries.[28] In 1879 the Northern Presbyterians began establishing schools and organizing churches.[29] Towards the end of the century the Southern Baptists initiated schools, at first through their North Carolina state convention and later through their Home Mission Board.[30] In the course of the years, increasing help came from Christians in more prosperous parts of the land for the religious, educational, economic, and social life of the mountain areas.

Some occupational groups called for specialized attention. In the earlier part of the period, shipping loomed large in the economic life of the nation. Many young Americans "went to sea." Many were employed on the boats on the inland rivers, the Great Lakes, and the canals. For these, Christians made special provision. About 1818 a Mariner's Church was organized in New York City, assisted by what was called the New York Port Society.[31]

---

[24] Padelford, *The Commonwealths and the Kingdom*, pp. 40ff.; Masters, *The Home Mission Task*, pp. 309ff.; Brown, *op. cit.*, p. 123.

[25] Bacon, *Leonard Bacon*, pp. 146, 147.

[26] Douglass, *op. cit.*, pp. 78-82; *The Methodist Forward Movement in the United States*, pp. 13ff.; Morse, *Home Missions Today and Tomorrow*, pp. 176-194.

[27] Beard, *A Crusade of Brotherhood*, p. 238.

[28] *The Methodist Forward Movement in the United States*, pp. 13ff.

[29] Doyle, *Presbyterian Home Missions*, p. 182. On one of these Presbyterian missionaries, see *The Missionary Review of the World*, Vol. LX, pp. 343-345.

[30] Masters, *op. cit.*, pp. 232-238.

[31] *Thirty-Third Annual Report of the Seamen's Friend Society*, p. 49.

About 1828 the American Seamen's Friend Society was organized, with the purpose of improving the social and moral conditions of seamen by promoting boarding-houses of good character, savings banks, register offices, libraries, reading rooms, and schools, and by providing religious services.[32] The society was undenominational, but, like so many of its kind, its support came chiefly from Congregationalists, with some assistance from Presbyterians, Dutch Reformed, and a little from Baptists, Episcopalians, and Methodists.[33] In 1830 it could report eight churches, seventeen boarding houses, two banks, three register offices, eight stated preachers, and a chaplain for seamen in Canton, the one open port in China. It could say that many ships had given up the use of alcoholic beverages, that many had daily services, and that naval chaplaincies had been "rescued from the degradation of being filled with men of debauched lives."[34] In 1836 the American Bethel Society was organized in affiliation with the American Seamen's Friend Society to serve sailors and boatmen on inland waters. In 1848 it employed six clergymen in ports on the Great Lakes and twelve lay missionaries on canals.[35] A Western Seamen's Friend Society was organized in 1848.[36] In 1861, when the American merchant marine was not far from a peak, we read of "bethels" for seamen in a number of American ports, some of them supported by the American Seamen's Friend Society, some by local societies, some by the Episcopal Mission to Seamen (founded in 1834), and some by Methodist and Baptist organizations. Chaplains for seamen were maintained in several ports in Europe, Asia Minor, China, South America, and the Pacific Islands.[37] Even in 1914, when shipping was no longer relatively as prominent as it had been in the first half of the nineteenth century, the American Seamen's Friend Society reported chaplains in several ports abroad and in the United States, and a number of lodging houses and lending libraries.[38]

Thousands of men were employed in the lumber industry, especially in the latter part of the period. Many were unmarried and were transients or semi-transients. Towns and villages sprang up around sawmills, flourished for a

[32] See the constitution of the society in the *Second Annual Report of the American Seamen's Friend Society*, p. 19.

[33] *Thirty-Third Annual Report of the Seamen's Friend Society*, pp. 8off.

[34] *Second Annual Report of the American Seamen's Friend Society, passim.*

[35] *Twentieth Annual Report of the American Seamen's Friend Society*, p. 13.

[36] *Thirty-Third Annual Report of the American Seamen's Friend Society*, pp. 58-63.

[37] *Thirty-Third Annual Report of the American Seamen's Friend Society, passim.*

[38] *The American Seamen's Friend Society, Eighty-Sixth Annual Report, passim.* For a biography of one who served the seamen, see Gilbert Haven and Thomas Russell, *Father Taylor, The Sailor Preacher. Incidents and Anecdotes of Rev. Edward T. Taylor for Over Forty Years Pastor of the Seamen's Bethel, Boston* (Boston, B. B. Russell, 1872, pp. 445), *passim.*

time, and then, as the timber was cut off, dwindled to a ghostlike existence or disappeared. Some of the grosser vices battened off the lumbermen. The problem was serious, for, with the shifting population, permanent church organizations were difficult to maintain. Some of the home mission societies took account of the situation. In 1914 the Board of Home Missions of the (Northern) Presbyterian Church in the United States of America supported twenty men in the lumber camps.[39] Miners and mining camps also constituted a problem of much the same character. For them, too, special provision was often made.[40]

Christians rose to meet the problem brought by the decline of religious teaching in the homes and in the public schools. Roman Catholics constructed, at great expense, growing systems of parochial schools served chiefly by congregations of women. They also founded secondary schools, colleges, and universities. Protestants did not institute any large number of primary schools under ecclesiastical auspices. Many of their leaders encouraged the growth of state education. It was to building and maintaining secondary schools and especially to higher education that the Protestant churches gave more of their attention. In the Sunday School the Protestants developed their chief agency for religious education. As a result, it was in the United States that the Sunday School had its most extensive growth. It became an accepted part of the programme of the large majority of Protestant churches.

Religious instruction did not suddenly disappear from the public schools nor did the Sunday School quickly achieve its full growth. For years the reading of the Bible and prayer at the beginning and close of the day was a part of the routine in many public schools.[41] In some of the early free schools provision was made for teaching the pupils the catechisms of their respective denominations.[42] However, even this marked a striking decline from the practice in colonial times, and early in the nineteenth century it, too, began to lapse.[43] For about a quarter of a century between 1844 and 1870 the Old School Presbyterians attempted to meet the problem with parochial schools, but the

[39] One Hundred Twelfth Annual Report Board of Home Missions of the Presbyterian Church in the United States of America (1914), p. 11.

[40] One Hundred Twelfth Annual Report Board of Home Missions of the Presbyterian Church in the United States of America (1914), p. 18.

[41] Stewart, A History of Religious Education in Connecticut, pp. 251, 365; Lankard, A History of the American Sunday School Curriculum, pp. 42, 43. On the status of religious instruction in the public schools, see the very careful study, Alvin W. Johnson, The Legal Status of Church-State Relationships in the United States with Special Reference to the Public Schools (The University of Minnesota Press, 1934, pp. ix, 332).

[42] Lankard, op. cit., p. 42.

[43] Lankard, op. cit., pp. 27ff.; Stewart, op. cit., p. 251.

experiment did not achieve what had been hoped.[44] Some Lutherans maintained parochial schools. Many pastors, especially among the Lutherans, had catechetical classes to prepare children for confirmation and their first communion. Methods akin to the Sunday School had existed in colonial days,[45] but it was the movement dating from Robert Raikes and originating in Great Britain through which the main growth occurred. At the outset the Sunday School was for the children of the poor and gave general as well as religious education.[46] At first it was frowned upon by many of the churches.[47] Eventually most of the Protestant churches adopted it and confined its curriculum to religious instruction. By the middle of the nineteenth century it had won general acceptance.[48] Denominational organizations arose to promote and direct it.[49] In general, however, it was an interdenominational movement with an undenominational organization formed comprehensively to fit the geographic framework of counties, states, and nation. After several local Sunday School unions had been instituted, in 1817 a national body, the Sunday and Adult School Union came into being. In 1824 this became the American Sunday School Union. Then came the National Sunday School Conventions (beginning in 1832), the International Sunday School Conventions (the first assembled in 1875), the International Sunday School Association, the International Primary Union, county and state Sunday School conventions, the World's Sunday School Conventions (the first in 1889), the World's Sunday School Association (1907), and the Religious Education Association (1903).[50] As the result of a gradual evolution, uniform lessons were developed, centring each week upon a particular passage in the Bible. In 1872 the *International Uniform Lesson System* was inaugurated, with a programme drawn up and supervised by the International Lesson Committee. Eventually graded lessons were introduced.[51] In an effort to include all untouched elements, geographic surveys were carried out by the American Sunday School Union and agents were employed to organize schools.[52]

[44] Sherrill, *Presbyterian Parochial Schools 1846-1870, passim.*
[45] Rice, *The Sunday-School Movement 1780-1917 and the American Sunday-School Union 1817-1917,* pp. 42, 43.
[46] Rice, *op. cit.,* pp. 44ff.; Fergusson, *Historic Chapters in Christian Education in America,* pp. 14ff.
[47] Rice, *op. cit.,* pp. 45, 49.
[48] Stewart, *op. cit.,* p. 332.
[49] A. D. Wardle, *History of the Sunday School Movement in the Methodist Episcopal Church* (New York, The Methodist Book Concern, 1918, pp. 232), pp. 61ff.; C. H. Brewer, *A History of Religious Education in the Episcopal Church to 1835* (Yale University Press, 1924, pp. xi, 362), pp. 183ff.
[50] Rice, *op. cit.,* pp. 59ff.; Fergusson, *op. cit.,* pp. 30ff.; Brown, *A History of Religious Education in Recent Times,* pp. 168-179.
[51] Rice, *op. cit.,* pp. 102ff., 294ff.; Brown, *op. cit.,* pp. 95ff.
[52] Rice, *op. cit.,* pp. 219ff.

Added impetus was given to the Sunday School by the growing conviction that individuals should come into the Christian faith more through the processes of education than through the cataclysmic methods of the revival. Indeed, the latter, unless prepared for and followed by such education might, so it was held, lead to a religious life which was an alternation of high emotional excitement and moral and spiritual lethargy.

An outstanding leader in the emphasis upon "Christian nurture" was Horace Bushnell (1802-1876).[53] Of New England background and rearing, and long pastor of a Congregational church in Hartford, Connecticut, he marked a further stage in the departure of New England Theology from strict Calvinism. While still maintaining that at the outset human beings have sinful tendencies, he hopefully believed that they could struggle against them and need not wait to become Christians until some act of divine grace had accomplished the new birth which God had designed for the elect. The child, Bushnell held, should grow up as a Christian and never know himself as being otherwise.

Bushnell's attitude was important because it developed in a region which had been accustomed to revivals as the normal method of the transmission of Christianity to the rising generation and which had cherished the associated belief that entrance into the Christian life should be preceded by a period of deep gloom and intense inward struggle. It was also significant as a symptom of the change which was taking place not only in New England, but also through much of the length and breadth of the United States. Revivals as a means of propagating the Christian faith did not die out, but relatively less emphasis was placed upon them and more upon education.

Bushnell stressed the home as the natural place for religious and moral education, but the home increasingly abdicated that function and the convictions which he represented in large part made the Sunday School the medium of their expression.

By 1914 the Sunday Schools of the United States had an enrollment of about fifteen and a half million pupils and over a million and a half officers and teachers.[54] Here was a vast popular religious movement. It was predominantly lay rather than clerical. Hundreds of thousands of men and

[53] For a life of Bushnell, see *Life and Letters of Horace Bushnell* (New York, Charles Scribner's Sons, 1903, pp x, 601). For his famous treatise, see Horace Bushnell, *Christian Nurture Biographical Sketch by Williston Walker—Revision by Luther A. Weigle* (New York, Charles Scribner's Sons, 1916, pp. xxx, 351). For an interpretation of his place in American religious thought, see Theodore T. Munger, *Horace Bushnell, Preacher and Theologian* (Boston, Houghton Mifflin Co., 1899, pp. xiv, 425), *passim*.

[54] *Organized Sunday School Work in America 1911-1914. Official Report of the Fourteenth International Sunday School Convention* (Chicago, Executive Committee of the International Sunday School Association, 1914, pp. 550), pp. 514, 515.

women were giving freely of their time and energy to the religious instruction of youth. The faults of the Sunday School were obvious and numerous. Much of the teaching was crude, the brief hour or half hour a week was inadequate, and curriculum, literature, and physical equipment left much to be desired. Yet here was a great enterprise, the expression of the Christian faith and the product of the devotion of the rank and file of American Protestantism. With its supra-denominational curriculum and methods, it was inculcating a type of Christianity which was more inclusive than any one religious group. It tended to increase the family likeness of Protestant churches.

In addition to the Sunday School, other agencies were devised for educating youth in the Christian faith. The Young People's Societies of Christian Endeavour had what were known as junior societies for children as well as senior societies for youths in their late teens and twenties. Similar bodies, denominational, came into existence, such as the Luther League, the Baptist Young People's Union, and the (Methodist) Epworth League. By 1914, summer conferences, later to enjoy a large growth, had begun to be held. What were known as Daily Vacation Bible Schools came into being. It was to be expected that among the churches would be those with the imagination to see in the long summer recess of the public schools an opportunity and a need. Not far from the middle of the nineteenth century something akin to the Daily Vacation Bible Schools began to be held.[55] About the end of the century similar schools sprang up spontaneously in several parts of the country.[56] However, what proved to be the most widely extended organization had its rise in New York City. There, in 1899, in one of the Baptist churches Mrs. W. A. Hawes began teaching the Bible in summer vacations to children. R. G. Boville, the secretary of the New York City Baptist Mission Society, saw the possibilities in the plan and promoted similar schools. In 1907 the National Vacation Bible School Committee was formed and in 1916 this was merged into the International Association of Daily Vacation Bible Schools.[57] In 1910 the Presbyterians inaugurated a similar movement within their denomination.[58] By 1923 it was said that at least five thousand Daily Vacation Bible Schools with approximately half a million children were being conducted.[59] Programmes of recreation, worship, and religious instruction were devised to fill some of the leisure hours of the child's summer.

In the colleges and universities Protestants developed methods of religious

[55] Ikenberry, *The Daily Vacation Bible School,* p. 25.
[56] Ikenberry, *op. cit.,* p. 29; Stout, *The Daily Vacation Church School,* p. 11.
[57] Stout, *op. cit.,* p. 11; Ikenberry, *op. cit.,* p. 26.
[58] Ikenberry, *op cit.,* p. 32.
[59] Stout, *op. cit.,* p. 12.

instruction and facilities for worship, fellowship, and service. Various student organizations early arose, and in the last quarter of the nineteenth century the Young Men's and Young Women's Christian Associations became widely extended in institutions of higher learning as channels for voluntary student religious activities.[60] In the first decade of the twentieth century, several denominations began planning comprehensively for such of their students as were enrolled in state colleges and universities. By 1914 clergy giving their major time to students—"student pastors" as they were called—were being placed on university campuses.[61] The secularization of colleges and universities which had been founded as avowedly Christian institutions was not halted. In academic life, among teachers as well as students, the trend towards religious indifference and overt scepticism and agnosticism continued. It was, indeed, a striking feature of the intellectual world. However, partly because of these new devices, substantial minorities made an adjustment between the new knowledge and their inherited faith and were convinced Christians, seeking to carry the Christian message to all the world and to make it effective in the various phases of the life of their own and other lands.

A number of nation-wide organizations existed which sought to reach all classes of the population through Christian literature. Notable were the American Bible Society and its auxiliaries and the American Tract Society. To their programmes and achievements we have already referred.[62] To these, drawing their support from members of more than one denomination, were added denominational bodies with a similar purpose, such as the American Baptist Publication Society.

Even from the brief survey of these pages, manifestly an incomplete account which only hints at some extensive movements and passes over many others in silence, it must be clear that in the United States Christianity was displaying a phenomenal vitality in meeting the kaleidoscopic changes in society and culture which marked the period. The problems presented had by no means been fully solved. In the great cities hundreds of thousands had little or no formal connexion with the churches. In many a rural section, especially in the older portions of the country, the latter part of the period witnessed a decay in religious life. Industrial workers, miners, and loggers tended to lose touch with the churches. The secularizing of education and the decline of religious instruction in the home brought superficiality in the religious faith of the rising generation. Among many, particularly as the twentieth century

[60] Shedd, *Two Centuries of Student Christian Movements, passim.*
[61] Clarence Prouty Shedd, *The Church Follows Its Students* (Yale University Press, 1938, pp. xvii, 32), pp. 12ff.
[62] Chapter VI.

got under way, religious illiteracy increased. Much of higher education was tacitly ignoring religion and many of the intellectuals were more or less openly discarding the faith of their fathers. Yet it is doubtful whether, even in these new circumstances, when the picture is seen as a whole, Christianity could be said to be losing ground. Certainly the proportion of church membership in the total population was increasing. Christians were devising and putting into effect new methods. Through one or another organization millions of Christians, the vast majority of them without financial recompense, were labouring for the perpetuation of their faith. They had voluntarily committed themselves to the religion of their forebears and had found it sufficiently compelling to move them to original and persistent efforts to transmit it to their contemporaries and to the oncoming generation.

Chapter XI

THE UNITED STATES OF AMERICA. THE EFFECT OF CHRISTIANITY UPON ITS ENVIRONMENT

TO UNDERSTAND the influence of Christianity upon the United States, we must remind ourselves of several of the distinctive characteristics of the Christianity which was present in that country. To this subject we are to recur in the next chapter. However, the peculiar nature of the Christianity which spread in the United States had so much to do with the effects that we must endeavour to summarize some pertinent features of the former before attempting to ascertain and describe the latter.

First of all we must note the fact that, so far as its results were concerned, the Christianity of the United States was predominantly Protestant. Although in 1842 Roman Catholics were said to have about a third of the church members of the country, those in attendance at Protestant churches or in some way counted as part of the constituency of those churches were said to be more than ten times as numerous as those then primarily within the circle of the Roman Catholic Church.[1] As late as 1890, after the large flood of Roman Catholic immigration in the preceding fifty years, Roman Catholics were reported as being only 33.8 per cent. of the church membership of the land,[2] and in 1916 37.5 per cent.[3] The Eastern churches were relatively much less significant numerically. Roman Catholics were for the most part of the newer American stock, and from the lower income levels of the population. They did not provide a corresponding proportion of the leadership of the nation. Even as late as 1932, when Roman Catholics were at least 15 per cent. of the population, and when they had risen in wealth and in education, they had only slightly less than 3 per cent. of the names in the standard list of living Americans who led in the various phases of the country's activities.[4] While in that list a slightly larger proportion recorded some kind of connexion

---

[1] Baird, *Religion in the United States of America*, pp. 601, 615.
[2] Department of Commerce, Bureau of the Census, *Religious Bodies, 1916*, Part I, p. 31.
[3] *Ibid.*
[4] This was in the 1932-1933 edition of *Who's Who in America*. The compilations are in Weber, *1933 Yearbook of the American Churches*, pp. 314-316.

with a religious body than was true of the population as a whole, Roman Catholics had less than a fifth as many as their numbers in the country at large would have given reason to anticipate.[5] If leaders shape the ideals and institutions of a people, then Roman Catholic Christianity had but a slight share in moulding American culture.

In the second place, the Protestantism which was most influential was of denominations which drew chiefly from the older American stock and were of British provenance. Thus in that same standard list to which we have referred of outstanding Americans living in 1932, the largest numbers were from the Episcopalians, Presbyterians, Methodists, Congregationalists, and Baptists, in the order named. In it Unitarians were more than forty times, Episcopalians between eight and nine times, Congregationalists and Quakers six times, and Presbyterians four times more numerous than their proportionate numerical strength in the total population. Even the Methodists, who drew so largely from the humbler walks of life and from the Negroes, were slightly better represented than their percentage of the gross population would have led one to expect, and the Baptists, also from the lower social levels and with a still larger proportion of Negroes than the Methodists, had only slightly less than their proportionate share. On the other hand, the Lutherans, in spite of their fairly strong pre-nineteenth century elements, but with large additions from the nineteenth century immigration, and overwhelmingly of non-British background, had less than half as many in the list as their numbers in the country as a whole would have warranted.[6]

Not only was the Christianity which counted most in influencing the United States Protestant and of British background, but, in the third place, it was also particular strains of British Protestantism which tended to stand out. The Protestant Episcopal Church was much less prominent in the United States than was its parent, the Church of England, in England, and the Presbyterian churches, especially those of Scotch antecedents, were far from being dominant, as was the Church of Scotland in Scotland. Proportionately more potent than in Great Britain were those denominations which arose out of the radical wing of Protestantism and which had been inaugurated by those who in colonial times had sought refuge in the New World. New England Puritanism, which issued partly in Congregationalism, partly in the New School wing of Presbyterianism, and partly in Unitarianism and Uni-

---

[5] Weber, *op. cit.*, pp. 314-316. But see a somewhat different set of ratios, on the whole smaller, based upon a study by C. L. Fry of the 1930-1931 edition of *Who's Who in America*, in Douglass, *Church Unity Movements in the United States*, pp. 7, 8.
[6] *Ibid.*

versalism, which contributed to the Baptists, and which shared in shaping the background out of which came Seventh Day Adventism, Mormonism, and Christian Science, was especially important. Although never more than a small fraction of the population, the Quakers were to be reckoned with. In colonial days the vast majority of the immigrants had come from other than religious motives, but the ideals and the purposes of those in whom the religious factor had been controlling played a major role in moulding the nation.

In the presence of this religious radicalism which sought haven and opportunity in the New World, the Christianity and even the Protestantism of the United States differed somewhat from that of the other nations formed in the eighteenth and nineteenth centuries out of British colonial enterprise. In Canada, Australia, New Zealand, and South Africa the religious complexion lacked the tinge that was given to the Christianity of the United States by these refugee idealists. In these other new countries the standard Protestant denominations were also of British background, but Anglicanism and Presbyterianism, with the tradition of conservatism derived from their position as state churches, were somewhat more prominent, Methodism had less competition from the Baptists, and Congregationalism was not nearly so outstanding and was of a somewhat different temper.

The question inevitably arises as to why this radical Protestantism of the older American stock continued so potent throughout the nineteenth and into the twentieth century. In colonial days those with an active commitment to it were only a small minority of the population. In spite of the growth in the nineteenth century of denominations that represented it, in 1906 it comprised only about 40 per cent. of the church membership[7] and only about a sixth of the total population of the land. Yet it was this minority which led in the influence which Christianity exerted and which largely formed the idealism of the nation. Why should it have done so? The answer must be in part conjectural. It may have been the advantage of time: these radical phases of Protestantism had much to do with the planting of several of the early settlements and so acquired the prestige of priority. It may have been that biologically the elements represented by this type of Protestantism were superior: the courage required to stand out for religious convictions unpopular in the Old World and to break away from Europe and pioneer in the New World may have given rise to a natural selection of individuals possessing more imagination, initiative, courage, and stamina than others. It may have been because of something in this particular type of Christianity: possibly here was

[7] Department of Commerce and Labor, Bureau of the Census, *Religious Bodies: 1906,* Part I, pp. 148-153.

more activism and greater incentive to social vision and change. Probably all three factors entered into the result.

In this American Protestantism, as ·a fourth important feature of the Christianity of the United States, two strong trends must be remarked.

One was towards a personal religious experience and the conversion and transformation of the individual. This is sometimes thought to be the product of a frontier environment. That environment may have contributed to it, for a certain kinship existed between the self reliance bred of lone combat with the wilderness and the individualism of this kind of Protestantism. It is significant, however, that it did not emerge on the frontier in Roman Catholic Latin America or on the advancing border of Roman Catholic French Canada. It seems to have been due not to the frontier but to strains most prominent in some types of Protestantism. In the United States the emphasis upon a personal new birth was reinforced by the elements which were largely active in the creation of Lutheran bodies out of the nineteenth century immigration from Germany and Scandinavia. These, as we saw a few chapters above, had more of Pietism and of the revivalism which had come to the continent of Europe from Great Britain and the United States than did continental Lutheranism as a whole.

The other trend was the impulse to social reform, to a struggle against the collective ills of mankind, to the achievement of an ideal society. This was not new in Christianity. American Protestantism came by it legitimately. It had been marked in the Christianity of Western as contrasted with that of Eastern Europe. Probably it had there been strengthened by the Roman spirit of practical administration and the collapse of the imperial government after the fifth century which left the Church the chief bulwark of civilization. It had been accentuated in some forms of Protestantism, notably in the radical elements in Protestantism of Great Britain which gave rise to the Cromwellian Commonwealth and which contributed to the reform movements of the eighteenth and nineteenth centuries. Since these elements were particularly strong in the Protestantism of the United States, it is not strange that they took advantage of the fluid society and the relative freedom from the dead hand of the past presented by the new nation to come to even more vigorous life. In this, American Protestantism differed so decidedly from the Protestantism and especially from the Lutheranism of much of the continent of Europe, as to bewilder and scandalize many of the latter's adherents.

A fifth characteristic of the Christianity of the United States which bore upon the effect upon the environment was the separation of Church and state. In this the United States was not unique. It was a nineteenth century tendency throughout much of the world. Yet it was achieved earlier in the United States than in any other major country. In the United States one consequence seems to have been the intensification both of the vigour of the churches and of the activity of the Christian spirit in reconstructing society. The absence of subsidies from the state impelled Christians not only to support their churches but also to give of their means for the spread of their faith in the land as a whole and to other peoples. The fact that the churches were not bound to the civil government or supervised by it and the consequent partial emancipation from commitment to the existing order seem to have reinforced the efforts to make over the society in which the churches were set.

A sixth quality of the Christianity of the United States was its unprecedented diversity. Never before in any one land had Christianity been so multiform. Every main kind of existing Christianity and many a minor one found its way to the United States. To these imported varieties were added many of indigenous creation. The diversity had a profound effect upon religious life which we are to note in the next chapter. Although it is not easy always to determine the precise fashion in which it did so, this complexity was also reflected in the effect of Christianity upon non-religious phases of the environment. In some of the states, for instance, it hastened the cutting of the tie between government and Church.

With those features of the Christianity of the country as a background, we must now attempt to discover the impress of that faith upon the various aspects of the culture of the nation.

Obviously the religious life of the country was profoundly affected. From the beginning, because of its Western European heritage, the religious side of the people's culture had been indebted to Christianity more than to any other religion. At the outset, only a small fraction of the population had a formal church membership. As the decades passed that minority substantially increased. In 1800 the percentage was said to be 6.9, in 1850 15.5, in 1900 35.7, and in 1910 43.5.[8] As we have seen, by 1910 not far from the same proportion of Indians and Negroes were members of churches. These figures do not give by any means a full picture of the numbers who possessed some kind of connexion with the churches. In several denominations local congregations had the practice of dropping from their rolls those who ceased to show an interest in the church. In some congregations the numbers of those so eliminated were almost as large if not larger than those who retained an active membership. Many attended the services of the churches without ever becom-

[8] Weber, *1933 Yearbook of the American Churches*, p. 299; Dorchester, *Christianity in the United States*, p. 750. Baird, *Religion in the United States of America*, pp. 600-603, gives somewhat higher figures for 1842 than those of Weber and Dorchester for 1850.

ing members. Several denominations counted as members only full communicants and not baptized non-communicants. By 1914, therefore, the proportion of the population who either then possessed or at one time had possessed some form of active connexion with a church must have been considerably more than 50 per cent.

More important than the numerical strength of the churches was the influence of Christianity upon the conduct and the attitudes of those who bore the Christian name. That effect cannot be determined in any satisfactory statistical fashion. Through the confessional and its other methods of education and discipline, the Roman Catholic Church was able to exert a degree of control over its members. In the early part of the century, when the percentage of church members in the population was smaller, many Protestant congregations took positive measures against those of their fold who transgressed what was deemed the Christian code. Thus the Baptist churches on the frontier examined charges against their members of drunkenness, fighting, lying, stealing, irregular sexual relations, malicious gossip, failure to pay just debts, gambling, and horse racing.[9] If found guilty, the offender, especially if obdurate, might be excluded from fellowship. As time passed and the proportion of church members to the total population increased, discipline in Protestant churches became more lax. Members were seldom brought before the bar of the church. They might be dealt with privately and then, if unrepentant, be unobtrusively dropped from the church roll. As the century wore on, church-membership became a more normal part of a citizen's life. Although church-membership never became coterminous with citizenship, as it had in many European countries except for the Jews, the trend was in that direction. This tended to lower the significance of a church connexion. In contrast with the Europe of the nineteenth century, where the movement was away from universal church-membership and in the direction of setting the Church and its *milieu* against each other, in the United States that opposition, although by no means eliminated, was inclined to be less sharp as the period moved to its close. Somewhat paralleling this drift and possibly associated with it was the trend in Protestant circles away from an experience of sudden conversion preceded by gloom and intense inward struggle as the normal process of becoming a Christian to the less painful and more gradual procedure of religious education advocated by Bushnell's *Christian Nurture*.[10] Yet Chris-

[9] Sweet, *Religion on the American Frontier. The Baptists, 1783-1830*, pp. 48, 49; Douglass, *History of Missouri Baptists*, p. 24. On the practice of Protestant churches about 1842, see Baird, *op. cit.*, pp. 426-428.

[10] See on this Sandford Fleming, *Children & Puritanism. The Place of Children in the Life and Thought of the New England Churches 1620-1847* (Yale University Press, 1933, pp. xii, 236), *passim*.

tianity had striking effects upon individual lives. A prisoner known to the police as a hardened criminal is touched by the reports of Moody's meetings, is transformed, remains true during the difficult period after discharge from jail, and eventually so wins the confidence of those about him that he becomes deputy sheriff and then treasurer in the sheriff's office.[11] A pioneer home missionary on the Pacific Coast in the latter half of the nineteenth century espouses an unpopular cause, condemns from his pulpit mob action against the Chinese, and in face of turbulent elements starts a fight for law and order. Insulted by a saloon-keeper, he yet goes to the house where the man's child is ill, remains, doing what he can to help, until death comes, conducts the funeral, and wins the friendship of the one who had wronged him.[12] One of the half-dozen outstanding university presidents of the century early determined that his ruling motive should be to do all to the glory of God and governed his choice of a profession accordingly.[13] Robert E. Lee, the leading general of the Confederate States of America, dedicated himself to what he believed to be God's purpose and accepted defeat in the Civil War as part of that will.[14] These examples, chosen at random, are only four out of thousands which show the fashion in which men were moulded by their Christian faith. Intimate acquaintance with any one of hundreds of communities would enable one to tell of scores whose Christian profession was accompanied by self-control, fortitude in the face of adversity, unselfish neighbourliness, honesty when honesty was costly, courage, hope, and a conviction that life was ennobled by trust in the forgiveness and fellowship of a living and loving God. In these results, impossible of accurate measurement, were some of the most notable fruits of Christianity. Never did those who called themselves Christians fully embody the ideals of their faith. Again and again much in the lives of church-members and of the churches themselves contradicted the standards of the Gospels. Yet in the Christian impulse was that which made for efforts, not always unsuccessful, to approximate to these standards.

The clergy as the presumptive leaders and exemplars of Christianity often were prominent in their communities. Some of them were national figures. William Ellery Channing, Henry Ward Beecher, and Phillips Brooks, to mention only a few out of many, had the ear of the thoughtful of much of the nation. Ralph Waldo Emerson, while eventually giving up the pastorate and departing in many ways from traditional Christianity, bore indelibly the

[11] Moody, *D. L. Moody*, pp. 293, 294.
[12] Robert N. McLean, *God and the Census* (New York, Council of Women for Home Missions and Missionary Education Movement, 1931, pp. xii, 164), pp. 14-23.
[13] James, *Charles W. Eliot*, pp. 60ff.
[14] Hendrick, *The Lees of Virginia*, pp. 419ff.

marks of his long clerical lineage and as itinerant lecturer was preacher extraordinary to the American people. Not all of the clergy were assets. Many, especially of the uneducated on the Western frontier, were said to have done positive harm to the cause of religion.[15] Yet for a time the Christian ministry was the chief learned profession, ranking ahead of law and medicine in the preparation required.[16] However, the proportion of college graduates entering the ministry dwindled.[17] With the rising level of education of the population as a whole, the relative intellectual leadership of the clergy declined.[18] Whether this meant a decrease in their moral and spiritual influence is not certain. Moreover, since in the Christianity, and particularly in the Protestant Christianity of the United States, lay initiative was prominent, the effect of Christianity upon the religion and ethics of the country could not be gauged fully by the position of the clergy.

Christianity, and notably Protestant Christianity, was a major factor in shaping the ideals of the United States. In that idealism was a belief in a moral order in a universe which is the creation of God and upon which society and its laws must rest. This came in large part through Christianity. Upon confidence in this order rested much of the belief in constitutional democracy.[19] In colonial times the New England clergy had taught a political philosophy based, they believed, on the Bible, which emphasized the natural rights of man, freedom of conscience in civil affairs, freedom of the press and of speech, and the sanctity of contracts.[20] It is no accident that "America," the song which by general adoption and without the need of legislative action was used more than any other to voice at all kinds of gatherings the aspirations of the people of the United States and their vision of freedom and liberty, was written by Samuel Francis Smith, a New England Baptist, while a student in Andover Theological Seminary, and was shot through with a Christian faith which looked upon liberty as the gift of God.[21] The more martial "Star Spangled Banner" with its dream of "the land of the free" had for author the devout Francis Scott Key, long a lay reader in an Episcopal church and later a vice-president of the American Bible Society.[22] How far Key's Christian

---

[15] Goodykoontz, *Home Missions on the American Frontier*, p. 33.
[16] May, *The Education of American Ministers*, Vol. III, p. 69.
[17] May, *op. cit.*, Vol. II, pp. 23ff.
[18] May, *op. cit.*, Vol. II, p. 33.
[19] Gabriel, *The Course of American Democratic Thought*, pp. 14ff.
[20] Baldwin, *The New England Clergy and the American Revolution*, p. 82.
[21] *Dictionary of American Biography*, Vol. XVII, pp. 342, 343.
[22] Dwight, *The Centennial History of the American Bible Society*, Vol. I, p. 73; *Dictionary of American Biography*, Vol. X, p. 363.

faith entered into that national anthem and so helped to shape the ideals of the nation it would be impossible to determine.

In the United States, moreover, the optimism which was so characteristic of the nineteenth century Occident was peculiarly marked and had in part a Christian rootage and was believed to be supported by Christian sanctions.[23] The author of "America" also composed a widely sung hymn, "The Morning Light is Breaking," expressing a glad confidence that all over the earth men were turning with "penitential tears" to the Christian faith.[24] The United States was believed to afford a unique opportunity to realize the ideal society ordained of God and to have a divine mission to assist in bringing in for all mankind a civilization from which the age-long ills which beset the human race would be banished. Some exuberant spirits proclaimed the imminence of the millennium, the thousand years in which the Devil was to be bound and Christ and the martyrs were to reign.[25] Some groups, notably the Millerites, the followers of a New Englander, William Miller, and denominations which sprang from that movement, the most prominent of which was the Seventh Day Adventists, announced the speedy second coming of Christ.[26] Even among the soberer spirits were those who believed that the time was at hand when "the Christian religion shall be acknowledged through the world, errors be exploded . . . and the world be filled with peace."[27] It is significant that Alexander Campbell, who contributed so powerfully to the formation and growth of the frontier denomination, the Disciples of Christ, announced in the initial number of his periodical, named confidently, *The Millennial Harbinger,* that the journal had "as its object the development and introduction of that political and social order of society called the Millennium which will be the consummation of that ultimate amelioration of society proposed in the Christian Scriptures."[28] Theodore Parker, radical Unitarian clergyman, believed that "a Christian church should be the means of reforming the world."[29] In his inaugural address (1869) President Eliot of Harvard spoke of the spirit of that institution as being the quintessence of that New England character which, so he declared, had produced a free and enlightened people and

---

[23] Niebuhr, *The Kingdom of God in America,* p. 150.
[24] *Dictionary of American Biography,* Vol. XVII, p. 343.
[25] Rev. XX, 1-6.
[26] Weigle, *American Idealism,* pp. 170, 171; U. S. Department of Commerce, Bureau of the Census, *Religious Bodies: 1926,* Vol. II, pp. 3ff.
[27] *The Connecticut Evangelical Magazine and Religious Intelligencer* (Jan., 1809), Vol. II, pp. 21-26. See also, for examples of the millenarian hope, Gabriel, *op. cit.,* pp. 34ff.
[28] *The Millennial Harbinger,* Vol. I, p. 1.
[29] Commager, *Theodore Parker,* p. 165.

which, under God, was still to make for the uplift of humanity.[30] Although a great moulder of Southern Presbyterian thought, James H. Thornwell, insisted that education and humanitarian projects were not proper functions of the organized churches, he saw a place for Christians as individuals to work for changes in society.[31] It was a scion of a Southern Presbyterian parsonage, Woodrow Wilson, who, impelled by his Christian faith, at the close of the period, believing that the United States had been founded upon the ideals of democracy and the well-being of men, that Christianity had come into the world to save it, that individual responsibility before God was the basis of liberty, and that the earth was governed by a righteous God, set out first, as President, to seek to realize these ideals more fully in the life of the nation and then, at the beginning of the next period, endeavoured to make them effective the world around.[32] This attitude of hope, of belief in the divinely given mission to realize in the United States, free from the trammels of the Old World, a society which would attain to Christian ideals, was reflected in utterance after utterance of those who shaped the thought and policies of the nation. It was due partly to the temper of Europe, partly to the opportunity afforded by the boundless virgin natural resources of the land, but in no small degree also to the strain of Protestant Christianity which had been so potent in the original settlements of colonial days reinforced by subsequent contacts with the Christianity, and especially the British Protestant Christianity, of the Old World. In view of the spirit of this Protestantism, it is not surprising that the movement to spread the Christian message throughout the world should have as its counterpart the purpose to make the society of the United States conform to Christian principles.

This idealism sprung from Christian sources expressed itself in experiment after experiment in founding communities which would embody here and now Christian principles. Their number was legion. The huge colony in Utah created by Mormons, the Church of Jesus Christ of Latter Day Saints, was one of the most notable. Tallmadge, Ohio, was founded by David Bacon, a New England clergyman, as an idealistic Christian town.[33] The better known Oberlin, Ohio, was begun with a somewhat similar objective by two home missionaries and took its name from the Alsatian pastor who had done so much to make over a mountain rural district in Europe. One of the founders of Oberlin, in writing of his purpose, declared that it was to assist in convert-

---

[30] James, *Charles W. Eliot*, p. 233.
[31] H. Shelton Smith in *Church History*, Vol. VII, pp. 115-124.
[32] Harley Notter, *The Origins of the Foreign Policy of Woodrow Wilson* (Baltimore, The Johns Hopkins Press, 1937, pp. vi, 695), pp. 7-10, 643, 651.
[33] Bacon, *Leonard Bacon*, pp. 22ff.

ing the world and bringing in the millennium by the contribution of a colony whose chief aim it would be to glorify God and do good to men.[34] The Quakers sometimes settled in groups on the frontier in which they maintained their way of life.[35] The Shakers founded several centres built on religious principles.[36] John Humphrey Noyes established a communistic fellowship at Oneida, New York.[37] William Keil gathered a Christian communistic society, first at Bethel, Missouri, and then at Aurora, Oregon.[38] The Amana Community, in Iowa, of German provenance, was another such.[39] A fellowship of German Christian pacifists had its centre at Zoar, Ohio.[40] The Universalist clergyman, Ballou, founded at Hopedale, Massachusetts, a group which he termed a Church of Christ and intended as a centre for universal reform and the conversion of the world.[41] The famous Brook Farm, while departing far from orthodox Christianity, grew out of a Transcendental Club composed largely of Unitarian clergymen. Some of the latter, distressed at the seeming futility of preaching Christian ethics in a competitive society, wished to build a community on what they deemed Christian principles.[42] In 1896 Ralph Albertson, a Congregational clergyman and a graduate of Oberlin, founded in Georgia the Christian Commonwealth Colony, a project which had only a short life.[43] Several of the communities named in this paragraph acquired a certain amount of notoriety for features which made for publicity. The vast majority escaped much general attention. These idealistic societies were Protestant parallels to the monasteries within the Roman Catholic and Eastern churches. They arose from somewhat similar although by no means identical motives. While they were emerging, Roman Catholics were founding in the United States monastic centres, usually extensions of orders which had

[34] James H. Fairchild, *Oberlin: The Colony and the College, 1833-1883* (Oberlin, E. J. Goodrich, 1883, pp. 377), pp. 9ff.

[35] For one example, see Jones, *The Quakers of Iowa*, pp. 38ff.

[36] Hendricks, *Bethel and Aurora*, p. 43; Weigle, *op. cit.*, p. 243; Nordhoff, *The Communistic Societies of the United States*, pp. 117ff.; Bates, *American Faith*, pp. 359ff.

[37] George Wallingford Noyes, compiler and editor, *Religious Experience of John Humphrey Noyes, Founder of the Oneida Community* (New York, The Macmillan Co., 1923, pp. xiii, 416), *passim;* Robert Allerton Parker, *A Yankee Saint. John Humphrey Noyes and the Oneida Community* (New York, G. P. Putnam's Sons, 1935, pp. 322), *passim;* Bates, *op. cit.*, pp. 390-399.

[38] Hendricks, *Bethel and Aurora, passim;* Nordhoff, *op. cit.*, pp. 305ff.

[39] Hendricks, *op. cit.*, pp. 253ff.; Nordhoff, *op. cit.*, pp. 25ff.

[40] Nordhoff, *op. cit.*, pp. 99ff.

[41] Bliss, *The Encyclopedia for Social Reform*, p. 694; Bates, *op. cit.*, pp. 374-378.

[42] Georgiana Bruce Kirby, *Years of Experience. An Autobiographical Narrative* (New York, G. P. Putnam's Sons, 1887, pp. iii, 315), p. 91; Lindsay Swift, *Brook Farm. Its Members, Scholars, and Visitors* (New York, The Macmillan Co., 1900, pp. x, 303), pp. 6ff.; Hendricks, *op. cit.*, pp. 44, 45; Commager, *Theodore Parker, passim,* especially p. 51; Bates, *op. cit.,* pp. 378-381.

[43] Gabriel, *The Course of American Democratic Thought*, pp. 322-324.

originated in the Old World. However, Roman Catholicism, partly perhaps because in the United States it was so largely urban and partly because it had become more stereotyped, did not give rise to as many exuberant fresh experiments at communal living as did Protestantism.

From the dream of making actual in the society of the United States the principles of the Christian faith came a large number of reform movements which attacked specific ills and fought for new and supposedly improved customs. Some of these spread by contagion from Europe, and especially from Great Britain. Others were of local origin. Most of them flourished even more luxuriantly than in the British Isles. They were largely from the radical wings of Protestantism.

Some of these movements we have already noticed. We must not, therefore, here take the room to elaborate upon them. We must content ourselves with the simple mention of the struggle to protect the Indian, to educate him, and to better his lot, and of the campaign against Negro slavery, the education of the freedmen, and the attempts at more just and amicable relations between white and coloured elements in the population.

Added to these were others. Among the more prominent were the fight against alcoholic beverages, the efforts for international peace, campaigns against secret societies and especially the Masonic Order, the advocacy of greater opportunities for women, including higher education and the suffrage, prison reform, better treatment of the insane, education for the blind, the deaf, and the dumb, attempts to eliminate gambling and prostitution, and the endeavour to obtain a more just economic order.

These reforms, like the one which attacked slavery, were given a great impetus by the revivals, especially those led by Finney.[44] Many of those touched by the awakenings advocated a number of them at once. The reforms were thought of as phases of a comprehensive programme for the remaking of society and the elimination of the chronic evils of civilization. Thus Gerrit Smith, one of the outstanding philanthropists of the first half of the nineteenth century, began his activities with participation in the American Tract and Bible Societies and the Sunday School Union and from there proceeded to support home and foreign missions, temperance, the anti-slavery movement, education, international peace, women's rights, vegetarianism, dress reform, the abolition of capital punishment, the anti-tobacco campaign, the anti-Masonic agitation, and the cause of Ireland.[45] Regarding himself as "the

---

[44] Barnes, *The Anti-Slavery Impulse*, pp. 10-12; R. H. Nichols in *Church History*, Vol. V, p. 49; Ludlum, *Social Ferment in Vermont, 1791-1853*, p. 14.

[45] Harlow, *Gerrit Smith*, p. 46; *Dictionary of American Biography*, Vol. XVII, pp. 270, 271.

steward of the Lord," the wealthy Arthur Tappan, a friend of Finney, and his brother Lewis gave liberally to several of the national religious organizations and to some of the reform projects, notably the anti-slavery societies.[46] Finney himself joined temperance, moral reform, and anti-slavery societies.[47] In the 1830's benevolent nationally organized societies for home and foreign missions, for the distribution of Bibles and tracts, for aiding Sunday Schools, for temperance, and for serving sailors held their anniversaries in the same month, May, had interlocking directorates, and were associated with societies for peace, prison reform, and other humanitarian objects.[48] All stemmed chiefly from Christianity, and particularly from the radical wing of Protestantism which was so prominent in the United States.

One of the most persistent of the reform movements was the one directed against the use of alcohol. In the early decades of the period strong liquors were prominent as beverages. Whiskey was almost universally made and drunk on the frontier. Rum entered through the extensive trade with the West Indies. Even in the eighteenth century a number of earnest Christians had come out for restraint in the use of liquor.[49] Before 1800 all the religious denominations in North Carolina are said to have placed a ban upon drunkenness.[50] Asbury, the great promoter and organizer of Methodism, believed drink the prime curse of the United States.[51] In 1796 the Methodist General Conference commanded the discipline of any member of the society who sold or gave away "spiritous liquors."[52] As early as 1811, as one result of the revivals of the first part of the century, the General Convention of the Congregational Churches of Vermont had formally condemned the use of spirits.[53] In 1826 the American Society for the Promotion of Temperance, usually called the American Temperance Society, was organized, largely by clergymen.[54] Before the first half of the century had passed, a number of organizations had arisen, chiefly from impulses which had come from the churches.[55] Among these were the Wash-

---

[46] *Dictionary of American Biography*, Vol. XVIII, pp. 298-300, 303, 304.

[47] Weld to Lewis Tappan, Nov. 17, 1835, in Barnes and Dumond, *Letters of Theodore Dwight Weld, Angelina Grimké Weld and Sarah Grimké*, Vol. I, p. 243.

[48] Barnes and Dumond, *op. cit.*, Vol. I, p. v; Barnes, *The Anti-Slavery Impulse*, p. 17.

[49] Krout, *The Origins of Prohibition*, pp. 51ff.

[50] Johnson, *Ante-Bellum North Carolina*, p. 454.

[51] Asbury, Aug. 5, 1812, in *The Heart of Asbury's Journal*, p. 649.

[52] *Journals of the General Conference of the Methodist Episcopal Church*, Vol. I, pp. 28, 29. After the Civil War, drinking became prevalent among Methodists in the South, but increasingly the conferences of the church denounced it.—Farish, *The Circuit Rider Dismounts*, pp. 305ff.

[53] Ludlum, *op. cit.*, p. 65.

[54] Cherrington, *Standard Encyclopedia of the Alcohol Problem*, Vol. I, pp. 157ff.

[55] For a map of the temperance societies about 1830, showing the tendency to a close connexion with New England and New England settlements in the West, see Krout, *op. cit.* p. 120.

ingtonians,[56] and the Independent Order of Good Templars.[57] Controversy developed as to whether the campaign should be directed against all alcoholic beverages, or only the distilled, exempting light wines and malt liquors.[58] In general, the trend was towards the more drastic stand. Before 1840 here and there, under pressure from the temperance advocates, states had begun to enact legislation to restrict the sale of intoxicants.[59]

The temperance movement was reinforced by Theobald Mathew (1790-1856), an Irish Roman Catholic priest. Mathew, a devoted Capuchin, had been won to the support of temperance by a Quaker, had spoken with great effectiveness in Ireland and Scotland, and had led thousands to sign a pledge for total abstinence. In 1840-1851 he extended his mission to the United States and won national recognition.[60] Other priests, seculars and regulars, took up the cause, and in 1872 the Catholic Total Abstinence Union was constituted.[61] John Ireland, Roman Catholic Bishop of St. Paul, fought the liquor interests and organized total abstinence societies. He was sometimes called "the Father Mathew of the West."[62]

In the 1850's temperance sentiment continued to rise. In 1851, partly at the instance of Neal Dow,[63] who derived his convictions on the subject from his Quaker rearing, and who as reform mayor of the state's chief city, Portland, was attacking the lawless elements, Maine passed a law which prohibited the manufacture or sale of intoxicating liquors except for medicinal and mechanical purposes. This was in spite of the fact that Maine was noted for its hard drinking and that Portland was a centre of distilleries and breweries.[64] By the close of 1855 the Maine example had been followed by twelve other states, all of them except Texas in the North.[65] A reaction ensued. This was accelerated by the Civil War. By 1875 only Maine, Vermont, and New Hampshire retained their prohibition laws.[66]

However, the tide again swung towards greater restrictions on liquor. By 1914 greater progress had been registered than before the Civil War. In 1856 the American Temperance Society joined with state societies to form the

[56] Cherrington, op. cit., Vol. VI, pp. 2807ff.; Krout, op. cit., pp. 182ff.
[57] Cherrington, op. cit., Vol. III, pp. 1332ff.
[58] Krout, op. cit., pp. 153ff.
[59] Krout, op. cit., pp. 262ff.
[60] Cherrington, op. cit., Vol. IV, pp. 1727-1730; Krout, op. cit., pp. 178-181, 218ff.
[61] Weigle, American Idealism, p. 180.
[62] Dictionary of American Biography, Vol. IX, pp. 494-497.
[63] Dictionary of American Biography, Vol. V, pp. 411, 412; Cherrington, op. cit., Vol. II, pp. 842-844.
[64] Cherrington, op. cit., Vol. IV, pp. 1659ff.
[65] Weigle, op. cit., p. 175.
[66] Weigle, op. cit., p. 181.

THE UNITED STATES. EFFECT OF CHRISTIANITY

United States Temperance Union, later the American Temperance Union. In 1865, at the fifth National Temperance Convention, the American Temperance Union merged with a new body, the National Temperance Society and Publication House. This had as its first president William E. Dodge, famous as a philanthropist and as a lay leader in the Protestant forces. Most of its succeeding presidents were clergymen.[67] In 1869 a National Prohibition party was formed, with a clergyman as the first chairman of the executive committee. Its purpose was political action and at successive national elections it put candidates in the field. However, only a minority were attracted. Never did it poll more than 260,000 votes.[68] Women became active. In 1873, after beginnings going back at least as far as 1830, the Woman's Temperance Crusade was launched, a religious movement which sought to induce saloon-keepers to abandon their businesses.[69] Partly out of this Crusade arose, also in 1873, the Woman's Christian Temperance Union. It quickly became national in scope and eventually international.[70] Its most famous leader was Frances E. Willard (1839-1898).[71] What proved to be the most effective organization for obtaining legislation for curbing the liquor traffic was the Anti-Saloon League. It had as its chief pioneer a Congregational clergyman, Howard Hyde Russell, who was mainly responsible for a state-wide campaign in Ohio (beginning in 1893) which enlisted support from members of all churches and parties. In 1895 the National Anti-Saloon League was formed. It drew its financial undergirding largely from the Protestant churches, chiefly those of the traditional radical wing represented in the old American stock. It was, in effect, an interdenominational Christian agency for obtaining local, state, and national prohibition.[72]

Through the efforts of these various agencies the sale of liquor was gradually outlawed, until by 1900 about thirty-seven states had allowed the voters in a given area to decide by "local option" whether they would or would not permit it. By 1916 nineteen states had entirely forbidden the sale of liquor,

[67] Cherrington, op. cit., Vol. IV, pp. 1863, 1864.
[68] Cherrington, op. cit., Vol. V, pp. 2217-2220.
[69] Cherrington, op. cit., Vol. VI, p. 2902.
[70] Cherrington, op. cit., Vol. VI, pp. 2891ff.
[71] Frances E. Willard, Glimpses of Fifty Years. An Autobiography of An American Woman (Woman's Christian Temperance Union, 1889, pp. xvi, 698); Dictionary of American Biography, Vol. XX, pp. 233, 234; Lydia Trowbridge, Frances Willard of Evanston (Chicago, Willett, Clark & Co., 1938, pp. xii, 209).
[72] Cherrington, op. cit., Vol. I, pp. 176ff.; Peter H. Odegard, Pressure Politics. The Story of the Anti-Saloon League (New York, Columbia University Press, 1928, pp. x, 299), passim. The Protestant nature of the enterprise is seen, among other ways, in the fact that in 1908 the president of the Anti-Saloon League and all but one of the vice-presidents were clergymen, and that of thirty-nine state superintendents, thirty-one were clergymen. —Ernest Hurst Cherrington, The Anti-Saloon League Year Book (Columbus, The Anti-Saloon League of America, 1908, pp. 256), pp. 7ff.

twenty-six others had local option, and in the remaining three the trade was excluded from certain limited districts.[73] In 1919 an amendment was ratified which wrote prohibition into the Constitution of the United States.[74] It was primarily the Christian, and especially the Protestant forces of the country which had brought about this consummation. The implementing of the laws, moreover, depended mainly upon sentiment created through the churches. Whether local, state, or national, prohibition was by no means fully enforced. The achievement, for such it was, even though by no means perfect, must be attributed primarily to the Christian conscience. Not all professing Christians favoured prohibition. Some vigorously opposed it. However, enough felt called upon by their faith to fight alcoholic beverages to make an appreciable difference in the laws and in the practices of the nation.

Part of the energy which issued from the Christian impulse in the nineteenth century was directed against war. The churches and Christian leaders did not always make for peace. From them came reinforcement to all of the wars (except perhaps some of those fought against the Indians) in which the United States engaged. Yet also from those impelled by Christian conviction sprang multiform movements against war and for the achievement of peace. Agitation and organization for peace went by waves, with occasional recessions. The source was primarily Christianity, and, as with most of the other campaigns for the reform of society, chiefly radical Protestant Christianity.

The Revolutionary War was in part the outcome of generations of teaching by many of the clergy. When it broke out, numbers of the clergy, in the name of the Christian faith, urged their parishioners to armed resistance to Great Britain. In New England especially, but also in some other parts of the country, the public had long heard from the pulpit the doctrine that government was a compact between rulers and people and that if the former were guilty of violating that compact the latter might consider it void and could rebel. Fear that the Anglican episcopacy would be introduced into the Colonies and bring with it curtailment of the religious liberty of dissenters also contributed to the unrest. When war came, at least some sermons declared those who were contending against the King to be fighting in a righteous cause.[75]

---

[73] Cherrington, *Standard Encyclopedia of the Alcohol Problem,* Vol. IV, p. 1586.

[74] Cherrington, *op. cit.,* Vol. V, p. 2211.

[75] For a brief summary of this contribution of Christianity to the Revolution, see Claude H. Van Tyne, *The Causes of the War of Independence* (Boston, Houghton Mifflin Co., 1922, pp. 346-368). For a selection of New England sermons of the period, see John Wingate Thornton, *The Pulpit of the American Revolution: or, the Political Sermons of the Period of 1776* (Boston, D. Lothrop & Co., 2d ed., 1876, pp. 537), *passim.* See also the carefully documented monograph, Alice M. Baldwin, *The New England Clergy and the American Revolution, passim,* and W. P. Breed, *Presbyterians and the Revolution* (Philadelphia, Presbyterian Board of Publication and Sabbath-School Work, 1906, pp. 205), pp. 58-179, which deals especially with the Middle Colonies and the South.

Numbers of church-members and clergy, especially in the Church of England, were loyal to the Crown, but even they believed armed participation on their side to be righteous. In general, the Quakers, true to their pacifist convictions, endeavoured to hold aloof from the struggle. Their tendency was to expel from their fellowship those of their number who participated in military service. That stand brought fines and, for some, exile.[76] The majority of Mennonites took no part in the war, and while a few were temporarily imprisoned for their refusal of army service, most government officials respected their scruples.[77]

In the War of 1812 the Shakers obtained exemption from military service[78] and the Quakers, although declining to share in it, did not suffer greatly.[79]

Following 1815 and the cessation of the wars which had wracked Europe for nearly a quarter of a century, a strong peace movement began. We have noted its presence in Europe.[80] It was particularly vigorous in the United States. That need not surprise us. The abounding hopefulness which marked the Europe of these years was accentuated in the United States, where both the sense of opportunity for a fresh beginning in a new country and the expectation, born of the radical Protestant wing of the Christian faith, of the early coming of a better order were outstanding features of national life. Indeed, during the course of the Napoleonic struggle, there was a mounting protest against wars as contrary to Christian principles.[81] As was to be expected, Quakers were active in pioneer peace movements.[82] In 1809 David Low Dodge, of New England birth and ancestry, a merchant and the progenitor of a line whose members became noted for their leadership in religious and philanthropic activities, put forth a pamphlet in which he boldly declared that it was wrong for Christians to engage in war. His father-in-law, Aaron Cleveland, a clergyman who had been strongly influenced by Whitefield, became a convert to this view and its uncompromising advocate. In 1815 Dodge and some like-minded friends inaugurated the New York Peace Society, which is said to have been the earliest of the many similar organizations which were constituted in that century in Europe and America. He based his convictions upon what he believed he found in the Bible.[83] Others joined in the condemnation of war on Christian grounds. Notable was the New England

[76] Wright, *Conscientious Objectors in the Civil War*, pp. 11ff.
[77] Wright, *op. cit.*, p. 18.
[78] Wright, *op. cit.*, p. 26.
[79] Wright, *op. cit.*, pp. 14, 15.
[80] Vol. IV, Chap. 5.
[81] Galpin, *Pioneering for Peace*, pp. 2-11.
[82] Allen, *The Fight for Peace*, pp. 5, 6.
[83] Allen, *op. cit.*, pp. 7, 8; Curti, *The American Peace Crusade, 1815-1860*, pp. 6-8; Galpin, *op. cit.*, pp. 12-15; E. M. Mead in *World Unity*, Vol. XI, pp. 365-372, Vol. XII, pp. 29ff.; *Dictionary of American Biography*, Vol. V, pp. 344, 345.

clergyman, Noah Worcester, who in 1814 issued a tract which had wide repercussions. It suggested that Christians form peace societies and that eventually a confederation of nations and a high court of equity for the settlement of international disputes be set up. Largely through Worcester's initiative the Massachusetts Peace Society was formed—in 1815, in the study of another pastor, William Ellery Channing.[84] In the succeeding years numbers of local and state peace societies were organized. Several ecclesiastical bodies came out with resolutions against war.[85] In the early days of the movement, the leaders believed that prayer was one of the most "promising instrumentalities" which could be employed for peace.[86] Many New England churches, both Congregational and Unitarian, really became branches of peace societies and formed reading circles for peace literature.[87]

Christian influences brought strong leaders to the peace movement. The devout Thomas Smith Grimké, who had once planned to be an Episcopalian clergymen, of a wealthy aristocratic South Carolina family, lawyer, judge, and state senator in South Carolina, was won to a pacifist position by the writings of a British Quaker.[88] William Ladd, New England Congregationalist and eventually licensed as a Congregational minister, robust, florid, at one time a ship's commander, through the study of the Bible came to the conviction that all war, defensive as well as offensive, was wrong. For about a decade, until his death, in 1841, he devoted his abounding energy to travel in behalf of peace, promoting peace societies and establishing contacts with men of like purpose in Great Britain. Joyously sanguine, he advocated an international organization with a legislative body to frame laws and a court to adjudicate them. He wore himself out in his labours for the cause.[89] In 1828, largely through Ladd's leadership, the American Peace Society came into being.[90] Thus for peace, as for the fight against slavery, the campaign for temperance, the promotion of Sunday Schools, the distribution of religious literature, and the support of home missions, and not far from the same time, a national organization was effected. All appealed to much the same constituency. Ladd's mantle fell on Elihu Burritt, "the learned blacksmith," also

[84] [N. Worcester], *The Friend of Peace. To Which is Prefixed a Solemn Review of the Custom of War; Showing that War is the Effect of Popular Delusion and Proposing a Remedy* (Greenfield, Mass., Ansel Phelps, 1817, pp. 281), *passim;* Galpin, *op. cit.,* pp. 21, 22; Curti, *op. cit.,* pp. 9-12.

[85] Allen, *op. cit.,* pp. 55, 56.

[86] Galpin, *op. cit.,* p. 82.

[87] Galpin, *op. cit.,* p. 68.

[88] Allen, *op. cit.,* pp. 375ff.; Curti, *op. cit.,* pp. 68ff.; *Dictionary of American Biography,* Vol. VII, pp. 635, 636.

[89] Curti, *op. cit.,* pp. 34-37, 42-50, 68ff.; Allen, *op. cit.,* pp. 370-375; *Dictionary of American Biography,* Vol. X, pp. 527, 528.

[90] Curti, *op. cit.,* pp. 34-37.

a New England Congregationalist. Believing that the Bible condemned all war, by 1844 he became actively identified with the peace cause. He went to England and Europe, in 1846 founded the League of Universal Brotherhood, and in 1848 organized a peace congress which met at Brussels and which was the first of a series of such gatherings.[91]

To this rising peace sentiment the Mexican War (1846-1848) brought something of a shock. The American Peace Society condemned the conflict.[92] The youthful James Russell Lowell, son of a clergyman, denounced the war in caustic verse in the homely vernacular of his native New England, and on Scriptural grounds. However, the churches were not so unanimous. Some flatly opposed the war, some were non-committal, and others favoured it.[93]

The Civil War dealt a more severe blow to the peace movement. This was not only because it was on a much more extensive scale than the war with Mexico. It was also because, to churches on both sides of the conflict, the combatants seemed to be fighting in a holy cause. To be sure, Elihu Burritt remained true to his convictions and opposed the war.[94] William E. Dodge, a son of David Low Dodge, was a member of a conference which sought at the last moment, in vain as it proved, to avert hostilities, and at their close bravely pointed out what he believed to be the evils and ultimate futility of war.[95] Here and there a clergyman either came out against the struggle on pacifist grounds or declared that he would continue to hold in affection those on the other side.[96] In general, members of the Christian denominations and groups which were committed to non-participation in war, such as the Quakers, Mennonites, the Church of the Brethren, Shakers, Schwenkfelders, Christadelphians, and Rogerines, declined to serve in the armies. These conscientious objectors met with more lenience in the North than in the South,[97] possibly because the dearth of men was less acute in the former section. However, a number of ecclesiastical bodies officially declared their support of the war.[98] Even the American Peace Society denounced the pacifists.[99]

[91] Curti, op. cit., pp. 88, 143-188; Dictionary of American Biography, Vol. III, pp. 328-330.
[92] Curti, op. cit., pp. 122-126.
[93] C. S. Ellsworth in The American Historical Review, Vol. XLV, pp. 301-326. After the war broke out, the Roman Catholic press supported the Government in it.—Blanche Marie McEniry, American Catholics in the War with Mexico (Washington, D. C., The Catholic University of America, 1937, pp. xi, 178), pp. 13-32.
[94] Dictionary of American Biography, Vol. III, p. 329.
[95] Dictionary of American Biography, Vol. V, pp. 352, 353.
[96] Allen, op. cit., p. 37.
[97] Wright, Conscientious Objectors in the Civil War, passim, especially pp. 6-9, 32, 33, 42-70, 75, 82, 91-179, 182.
[98] Wright, op. cit., pp. 35-38.
[99] Allen, op. cit., p. 38.

Yet Christianity was not without a mollifying influence upon the asperities of the Civil War. Robert E. Lee encouraged religious meetings among his soldiers.[100] In the North, the United States Christian Commission ministered to the "spiritual good, intellectual improvement, and social and physical comfort" of the troops.[101] In both armies, the Christian forces strove to offset the moral disintegration wrought among soldiers by war. Moreover, President Lincoln's memorable Second Inaugural Address, with its frank recognition that both sides had prayed to the same God and that the prayers of neither had been answered fully, and with its plea for "malice toward none" and "charity for all," did what one man could do, although that proved to be little enough, to allay the bitterness engendered by the struggle.

In the second half of the century the peace movement began to recover. Commencing in 1895 the Quaker Albert K. Smiley instituted at the hotel at Lake Mohonk of which he was part owner annual conferences on international arbitration and peace.[102] To be sure, in the Spanish-American War (1898) most of the church periodicals, except those of the Quakers and the Unitarians, justified the part of the United States in it and favoured retaining the Philippines and other Spanish islands which had yielded to American arms.[103] However, this conflict was only an interlude. In 1905 in California, churches were standing out against the anti-Japanese agitation which was then violent in the state.[104] In 1909 over two hundred clergymen of Massachusetts wrote to Congress in opposition to an increase in the navy or to any step which looked like a preparation for war.[105] In 1914 American Protestant clergymen formed the Church Peace Union. In August of that year, just as the World War of 1914-1918 was breaking out, a conference was scheduled in Switzerland at the call of this body. Out of the Church Peace Union came the World Alliance for the Promotion of International Friendship through the Churches, an organization subsidized by a grant from Andrew Carnegie.[106] As time passed, peace bodies were increasingly in the hands of those whose Christian purpose was not so obvious as had been that of the pioneers. This, however, was simply repeating the experience of many another humanitarian enter-

[100] J. William Jones, *Christ in the Camp or Religion in Lee's Army* (Richmond, Va., B. F. Johnson & Co., 1887, pp. 528), *passim;* Douglass Soothill Freeman, *R. E. Lee. A Biography* (New York, Charles Scribner's Sons, Vol. III, 1936), pp. 241, 244; Hendrick, *The Lees of Virginia,* pp. 413ff.

[101] Weigle, *American Idealism,* p. 188.

[102] Allen, *op. cit.,* p. 482; *Dictionary of American Biography,* Vol. XVII, p. 231.

[103] Julius W. Pratt, *Expansionists of 1898. The Acquisition of Hawaii and the Spanish Islands* (Baltimore, The Johns Hopkins Press, 1936, pp. viii, 393), pp. 286, 314.

[104] Tupper and McReynolds, *Japan in American Public Opinion,* p. 23.

[105] Tupper and McReynolds, *op. cit.,* p. 90.

[106] Francis Miller and Helen Hill, *The Giant of the Western World* (New York, William Morrow and Co., 1930, pp. x, 308), pp. 95, 96.

prise. The origin had been predominantly from the Christian impulse, even though in later developments this was not always apparent.

A campaign which had much of its strength in some of the churches was that against secret societies. A strong feeling existed in many religious groups, notably among Baptists, that membership in secret societies was inconsistent with church-membership. It was widely believed, moreover, that secret societies were in principle in opposition to the equality of full democracy. Beginning about 1826, a vigorous anti-Masonic agitation swept across the country. It had the support of thousands who believed that they were acting from Christian motives.[107] As late as 1868 a National Christian Convention opposed to Secret Societies assembled at Pittsburgh. It is not surprising that the President of Oberlin was one of its leaders.[108]

A more persistent movement and one which grew in force was that which strove to obtain for women an equality with men in legal status and in social, intellectual, and economic opportunity. Although at the outset the majority of church bodies and even of members of such reform organizations as anti-slavery and temperance societies looked askance at these efforts for women and at times opposed them, the pioneers were largely from church circles and seem to have been actuated by motives derived from their Christian background. Long before the nineteenth century the Quakers had made a place for women and had opened the floor of their meetings and their ministry to them as well as to men. As a random illustration from another religious group, we hear of Orson S. Murray, the publisher of a Baptist periodical in Vermont, who joined to his advocacy of temperance and anti-Masonry that of "women's rights."[109] A frontier denomination, the Christians, in contra-distinction from the closely related body, the Disciples of Christ, permitted women to preach and ordained them.[110] One of their pioneer clergy, Abraham Snethen, stood for women's rights when that position was unpopular.[111] An early leader in the movement was the New England-born Quaker preacher, Lucretia Coffin Mott. She was kept from taking her place as a delegate at the World's Anti-Slavery Convention in London in 1840 because of her sex, but that rebuff stirred up so much criticism that it gave an impetus to the struggle for equal rights.[112] At least partly through contacts with the Quakers (they both left the Protestant Episcopal Church of their birth to join the Friends), the gently

[107] Ludlum, *Social Ferment in Vermont, 1791-1850*, pp. 86ff.
[108] Harlow, *Gerrit Smith*, p. 472.
[109] Ludlum, *op. cit.*, pp. 57-59.
[110] *Autobiography of Abraham Snethen*, p. 186.
[111] *Autobiography of Abraham Snethen*, p. 269.
[112] Lloyd C. Hare, *The Great American Woman, Lucretia Mott* (New York, The American Historical Society, 1937, pp. 307), *passim; Dictionary of American Biography*, Vol. XIII, pp. 288-290.

reared Sarah Moore Grimké and Angelina Emily Grimké, sisters of Thomas Smith Grimké, linked championship of greater privileges for women to their opposition to slavery.[113] The close affiliation of the two movements is seen in the marriage of Angelina Grimké to Theodore Dwight Weld, the anti-slavery leader. One of the outstanding figures in the organized fight for better conditions for her sex, Susan B. Anthony, was born a Quaker and, while her family later broke from that group, she bore indelibly the marks of her early environment.[114] Lucy Stone (1818-1893), although not certainly owing her first rebellion against woman's subordinate status to a Christian faith, and while deeply resenting the seeming insurance by the Bible of the rule of men over women, found her opportunity for college education at Oberlin and made her first public address on woman's rights from her brother's pulpit.[115] Another of the strongest leaders, Elizabeth Cady Stanton, had been reared under strong Presbyterian influence, had been profoundly affected by Finney, although she was later critical of his methods, and married a convert of Finney. She was active in the anti-slavery cause and taught a Sunday School class of coloured children in a day when race lines were drawn even in the Northern churches.[116] Julia Ward Howe (1819-1910), from a distinguished family, cradled in a deeply religious home, from time to time preaching from Unitarian pulpits, and active in the anti-slavery movement, became famous as the author of "The Battle Hymn of the Republic" which saw God in the Civil War and which culminated in its appeal to the example of Jesus. She was even better known to her contemporaries as a leader in whatever made for greater opportunities for women.[117] The earnestly Christian anti-slavery Oberlin was a pioneer in the co-education of men and women.[118] Henry Ward Beecher was president of the American Woman Suffrage Association.[119] It was not a far step from emancipation for Negroes to emancipation for women, and it was not strange that in the eyes of many advanced members of the Christian reform movements the two should be joined. Gerrit Smith

---

[113] *Dictionary of American Biography,* Vol. VII, pp. 634, 635. Some of the letters of the sisters are in Barnes and Dumond, *Letters of Theodore Dwight Weld, Angelina Grimké Weld and Sarah Grimké 1822-1844.* These letters reveal the deeply religious spirit of the sisters.

[114] Ida Husted Harper, *The Life and Work of Susan B. Anthony* (Indianapolis, 3 vols., 1899-1908), *passim.*

[115] *Dictionary of American Biography,* Vol. XVIII, pp. 80, 81.

[116] Theodore Stanton and Harriet Stanton Blatch, editors, *Elizabeth Cady Stanton as Revealed in Her Letters, Diary and Reminiscences* (New York, Harper & Brothers, 2 vols., 1922), *passim; Dictionary of American Biography,* Vol. XVII, pp. 521, 525.

[117] *Dictionary of American Biography,* Vol. IX, pp. 291-293, Vol. XIX, p. 438.

[118] Hosford, *Father Shipherd's Magna Charta. A Century of Coeducation in Oberlin College, passim.*

[119] Harlow, *Gerrit Smith,* p. 471.

supported both.[120] It was natural that when once abolition of Negro servitude had 'triumphed, the agitation for larger opportunities for women moved forward with increasing momentum. As in so many others of these reform projects, a growing proportion of the advocates of greater privileges for women were not conscious of acting from Christian motives. The movement was largely secularized. Yet its inception and its early progress had been due chiefly to those who were earnest in what they believed to be the Christian faith.

One of the greatest reformers of the nineteenth century was a woman, Dorothea Lynde Dix (1802-1887). Deeply sensitive, her infancy spent in a New England home made unhappy by the vagaries of a fanatically religious father, and her girlhood under the strict discipline of a stern grandmother, and long fighting ill health, Miss Dix nevertheless was the outstanding leader in providing better care for the insane of the United States. Through personal investigation she disclosed the ill-treatment of insane and idiots and put on foot measures which led to the founding of hospital after hospital for the unfortunates. She extended her labours to Great Britain and the continent of Europe. She found time to advocate prison reform. She was the superintendent of women nurses for the United States Government during the Civil War. If one seeks the driving force which kept this frail, soft-voiced woman at her herculean labours, the clue is at least in part to be found in the fact that it was through a clergyman that her attention was first drawn to the prisons and the state of the insane, and that she had been profoundly influenced by another clergyman, William Ellery Channing, whose insistence upon the inherent possibilities for development of every human soul was fundamental in her religious belief. She was primarily a product of Christianity.[121]

As an instance of the contribution of Christianity in initiating efforts for the amelioration of penal institutions it is worth recording that at the outset clergy were prominent in the Prison Discipline Society, whose purpose was "the improvement of public prisons." The first annual meeting was held in the vestry of a church and the project was believed to be "approved by the Saviour of the World."[122]

[120] Harlow, op. cit., pp. 106, 107, 471, 472.

[121] Francis Tiffany, Life of Dorothea Lynde Dix (Boston, Houghton Mifflin Co., 1890, pp. xiii, 392), passim; Dictionary of American Biography, Vol. V, pp. 323, 324. For one of her writings, see D. L. Dix, Remarks on Prisons and Prison Discipline in the United States (2d ed., Philadelphia, Joseph Kite & Co., 1845, pp. 108). On the part of Quakers in pioneering in the humane care of the insane, see Schneider, The History of Public Welfare in New York State 1609-1866, p. 200.

[122] First Annual Report of the Board of Managers of the Prison Discipline Society, Boston, June 2, 1826 (Boston, T. R. Marwin, 1827, pp. 88), passim.

An interesting example of the social and religious radicalism which the New England strain, nurtured in Puritanism, sometimes produced, was Elizur Wright.[123] Wright was born in Connecticut in 1804. When he was still a child his parents took him with them to the idealistic Christian community which David Bacon founded at Tallmadge, Ohio. Graduating from Yale, for a time he prepared for the ministry. Instead he went into teaching. He was early caught up in the anti-slavery enterprise. He tilted at war, the liquor traffic, and the tariff. He advocated cheap postage. He became an ardent proponent of life insurance as a benefit to widows, the poor, and orphans. However, he found that as operated it had many shortcomings. These he set himself to remedy. He had much to do with the computation of actuarial tables which put life insurance on a sound basis. In Massachusetts he obtained state supervision of life insurance companies, helped to drive out dishonest concerns, prevented the companies from appropriating reserves on lapsed policies, and in other ways obtained greater protection for the policy-holder. Even in adolescence he had begun to move away from the orthodoxy about him. By successive steps he broke with the churches and abandoned many of the beliefs of his inherited Christianity. It was, however, radical Protestant Christianity from which had come the impulse that started him upon his career and from which his ethical ideals had been derived.

Another leader who illustrated the fashion in which an early Christian faith shaped a later career of philanthropy was Benjamin Rush (1745-1813) of Philadelphia.[124] Reared under strong Christian influences and swayed as a youth by the preaching of Whitefield, he became ecclesiastically broad in his sympathies, but remained deeply religious. He was chiefly distinguished as a physician, but he was also a pioneer in the temperance movement, advocated prison reform and the abolition of public and capital punishments, championed education for girls, and proposed a theory of education which gave greater freedom to children.

An instance of the fashion in which Christianity made for the refinement of manners and the curbing of cruelty to animals was the decline of cockfighting. In North Carolina, as camp-meetings spread, opposition to cockfighting grew, and, since the sport had fallen under the ban of the churches, after 1815 the public press no longer carried advertisements of it.[125]

As the nineteenth century wore on and the industrialization of the United States increased by leaps and bounds, it was natural that many, their con-

[123] Philip Green Wright and Elizabeth Q. Wright, *Elizur Wright, The Father of Life Insurance* (The University of Chicago Press, 1937, pp. xi, 380), *passim.*
[124] *Dictionary of American Biography*, Vol. XVI, pp. 227-230.
[125] Johnson, *Ante-Bellum North Carolina*, p. 181.

sciences made sensitive and their courage reinforced by the Christian faith, should grapple with the human problems which the machine was bringing. The reforming spirit, so strong in the older American Protestantism, which had long impelled men and women to attack the ills of the community and had led them to dream of an ideal society, broke out in fresh ways to wrestle with the issues precipitated by the contrasts between wealth and poverty in the growing cities, the accumulation of huge fortunes under the ruthless competition of *laissez faire* individualism, the exploitation of labour in the factories, mines, and transportation systems of the land, and the emerging conflicts between employers and employed.[126] It was to be expected that those from ecclesiastical fellowships which had contributed powerfully to the anti-slavery movement should now embark upon crusades against the evils of the new industrial society. Nor was it strange that part of this phase of the reform movement should arise from contagion from Europe and especially from Great Britain. The earlier large development of industrialization on the other side of the Atlantic had, as we have seen, already called forth efforts by Christians to devise better social and economic systems.

In the United States the plans proposed and the measures adopted were often grouped under what was termed the social gospel movement.[127] This was not an organization. It did not have any one programme. It was, rather, an attitude and a conviction. It arose from the belief that Christian ethics should be operative in all phases of human society and incorporated the hope that Christianity could be applied successfully to all forms of the collective life of mankind. In a sense it was not novel. It was akin to what many American Protestants had long believed. Indeed, in general its optimism was not so exuberant as that of some writers and preachers of the eighteenth and the early part of the nineteenth century. It had a spiritual ancestry which carried it back to the European side of the Atlantic and to much earlier centuries. Its distinctive feature was chiefly its attention to the social and economic problems of the latter part of the nineteenth and the opening decades of the twentieth century.

It would be hard to give a precise date for the beginning of the movement. As early as 1849 the brilliant and somewhat erratic Henry James urged the identity of Christianity and socialism.[128] Henry James, reared in Presbyte-

---

[126] See Maurice C. Latta, *The Background for the Social Gospel in American Protestantism,* in *Church History,* Vol. V, pp. 256ff.

[127] A very important book in this field, Charles Howard Hopkins, *The Rise of the Social Gospel in American Protestantism, 1865-1915* (Yale University Press, 1940), was published too late to be used in the preparation of this section.

[128] Bliss, *The Encyclopedia of Social Reform,* p. 258.

rianism of the Scotch-Irish tradition and for a time a student at Princeton Theological Seminary, had found spiritual release through Swedenborgianism. He was even more famous as the father of the novelist Henry James and the philosopher and psychologist William James.[129] In 1872 a Christian Labour Union was organized.[130] In 1874-1875 the clergyman founder of this union published in Boston a paper, *Equity*, which really advocated Christian Socialism.[131]

Two volumes of the 1870's and 1880's which were in part the product of Christian idealism contributed to creating an atmosphere favourable to the social gospel. In 1877-1879 Henry George wrote *Progress and Poverty*. Henry George had been reared in Philadelphia in an Evangelical congregation of the Protestant Episcopal Church. From this background and from a life of hardship in California he had come to a passionate desire to rid the earth of poverty and to a great hope.[132] As a programme he proposed the expropriation of the unearned increment by taxation and the abolishment of all imposts except that on land values.[133] He believed profoundly in a Creator who showered gifts on men, more than enough for all.[134] He was confident that in spite of temporary defeats God's will would be done.[135] *Progress and Poverty* brought its author national and international fame. In the late 1880's Edward Bellamy, the son of a New England Baptist parsonage,[136] wrote *Looking Backward*, in which he pictured, in contrast with the industrial and commercial society of his day which he denounced as the embodiment of an anti-Christian spirit, a Utopia, inaugurated by peaceful revolution in the twentieth century, in which Christian principles would prevail.[137] This, too, was widely read.

In these same decades two Congregational clergymen of New England stock, Theodore Thornton Munger and Washington Gladden, were beginning to wrestle with the problems presented by capitalism and industrialism and to present their thinking in print.[138] Gladden especially became prominent in the social gospel movement.[139]

---

[129] *Dictionary of American Biography*, Vol. IX, pp. 577, 578.
[130] Dombrowski, *The Early Days of Christian Socialism in America*, pp. 77ff.; Bliss, *op. cit.*, p. 258; Gabriel, *The Course of American Democratic Thought*, p. 308.
[131] Bliss, *op. cit.*, p. 258; Gabriel, *op. cit.*, pp. 308, 309.
[132] Henry George, Jr., *The Life of Henry George, passim*, especially p. 6; *Dictionary of American Biography*, Vol. VII, pp. 211-215.
[133] Henry George, *Progress and Poverty*, Book VIII, Chap. 2.
[134] Henry George, *op. cit.*, Book X, Chap. 5.
[135] Henry George, Jr., *op. cit.*, p. 502. For further insight into the Christian roots of Henry George's message, see Dombrowski, *op. cit.*, pp. 35ff.
[136] *Dictionary of American Biography*, Vol. II, pp. 163, 164.
[137] Edward Bellamy, *Looking Backward 2000-1887* (Boston, Houghton Mifflin Co., 1890, pp. v, 337), *passim*, especially p. 281.
[138] Gabriel, *op. cit.*, pp. 310-315.
[139] *Dictionary of American Biography*, Vol. VIII, pp. 325-327.

In the 1880's William Dwight Porter Bliss, also of New England Congregational ancestry, but a clergyman of the Protestant Episcopal Church, was the leading spirit in founding the Church Association for the Advancement of the Interests of Labour and the Society of Christian Socialists. The Church Social Union was organized in New York City in 1891, on the lines of the English Christian Social Union, and sent Bliss on a tour to promote interest in it.[140]

In 1885 appeared a book, *Our Country,* which made its author, Josiah Strong, internationally famous. Strong was a Congregational clergyman reared in the New England tradition in the Western Reserve in Ohio. In his various writings, for he had a prolific pen, he argued that Jesus came to found an ideal society, The Kingdom, on earth and that the Church existed to extend this Kingdom. He advocated actively many projects for social amelioration, founded the League for Social Service (later the American Institute for Social Service), and was largely responsible for the campaign for "safety first" in industry and transportation.[141]

In 1892 the Brotherhood of the Kingdom was organized, with a nucleus of Baptist clergymen who were committed to the vision of God's rule being realized in human society. It was largely for reciprocal stimulus. Twenty annual conferences were held.[142] One of this group was Walter Rauschenbusch, a scion of a long line of clergymen and the son of an immigrant who came from Germany with that exodus of idealists who fled their native land after the failure of the abortive liberal revolution of 1848.[143] Later, while a member of the faculty of Rochester Theological Seminary, he wrote several volumes, among them *Christianity and the Social Crisis* and *Christianizing the Social Order,* whose titles gave an indication of their contents.[144] For a time in the first part of the twentieth century he was the outstanding exponent of the "social gospel" and his books had an enormous circulation.

A brilliant but erratic exponent of the social gospel was George Davis Herron (1862-1925). He was particularly prominent in the 1890's. A Congregational clergyman, in common with many American Protestant leaders of the period, he was convinced that the Kingdom of God was imminent. He eloquently proclaimed what he believed to be its message. He had a large part in founding the Rand School of Social Science in New York City. Later he

---

[140] Gabriel, *op. cit.,* pp. 315-318; Bliss, *op. cit.,* p. 275; Dombrowski, *op. cit.,* pp. 96ff.

[141] *Dictionary of American Biography,* Vol. XVIII, pp. 150, 151.

[142] E. H. Hopkins in *Church History,* Vol. VII, pp. 138ff.

[143] *Dictionary of American Biography,* Vol. XV, pp. 392, 393.

[144] Walter Rauschenbusch, *Christianity and the Social Crisis* (New York, The Macmillan Co., 1907, pp. xv, 429); Walter Rauschenbusch, *Christianizing the Social Order* (New York, The Macmillan Co., 1916, pp. xii, 493).

came to the opinion that the teachings of Jesus were not adequate for the social revolution which he envisaged, but by that time his influence in the United States had waned.[145]

A tract in the form of a story, *In His Steps,* by another Congregational clergyman, Charles M. Sheldon, first appeared in 1898 and achieved an enormous circulation in many languages. It sought to apply the test: "What would Jesus do?" Sheldon himself, in a long life in the ministry, endeavoured to follow that principle.[146]

A strong impulse was given to the study of social problems by Richard T. Ely,[147] one of the pioneers in a new American school of economics. Ely had been reared in a Presbyterian manse. He had studied in Germany and there had been moulded by German economists who had an ethical interest. The American Economics Association, in whose founding he was a leading spirit, should, he said, bring science to the aid of Christianity.[148] It had a number of clergymen in its early membership.[149] One of Ely's books, *Social Aspects of Christianity,* appealed to Christians to advocate measures for the betterment of the conditions of labour and against political corruption.[150]

Unlike the campaigns for abolition, peace, and temperance, the social gospel was not made concrete by a single clearly defined objective, nor did it take form in a few nation-wide organizations. In the nature of the case it could scarcely do so. Its results, therefore, could not be so clearly ascertained as could those of these other movements. Moreover, it encountered vigorous opposition in many of the churches and indifference in still more. It was a minority enterprise. Yet the minority was growing. That the social gospel had far-reaching consequences in the life of the country no one who knew the opening decades of the twentieth century could well doubt. Efforts for the alteration of society embodied in some of the legislation of the period, and especially on the eve of 1914 by Woodrow Wilson, owed a debt to it. The struggle for the abolition of child labour, for safeguarding women in industry, and for better conditions for industrial labourers was reinforced by it. After 1914 it contributed to many of the liberal and radical programmes which marked those years.

The Roman Catholic Church did not join in the social gospel movement.

[145] *Dictionary of American Biography,* Vol. VIII, pp. 594, 595; Gabriel, *op. cit.,* pp. 319-321; Dombrowski, *op. cit.,* pp. 171ff.

[146] Charles M. Sheldon, *His Life Story* (New York, George H. Doran Co., 1925, pp. 309. Autobiographical), *passim.*

[147] Dombrowski, *op. cit.,* pp. 50ff.; Gabriel, *op. cit.,* pp. 296-299.

[148] Ely, *Social Aspects of Christianity,* pp. 24, 25.

[149] Dombrowski, *op. cit.,* p. 51.

[150] See the practical programme urged, in Ely, *op. cit.,* pp. 73ff.

That was purely Protestant. It did, however, show concern for the social issues of the day. Due largely to the vigorous advocacy of the head of the American hierarchy, Cardinal Gibbons, Rome did not, as some urged it to do, ban the Knights of Labour in the United States. To Gibbons was attributed some of the influence which induced Pope Leo XIII to endorse labour's claim to the right to organize.[151] Gibbons fought the movement to place *Progress and Poverty* on the index of forbidden books. A New York priest, Edward McGlynn, was among the most ardent advocates of Henry George.[152]

True to its past history, especially in Western Europe, Christianity gave rise to many measures and institutions for the alleviation and healing of physical distress. Many, probably the large majority of churches, made it part of their task to care for the poor among their own members.[153] We hear, too, of organized Roman Catholic help for the indigent. Roman Catholics founded scores of hospitals, homes for the aged, and orphan asylums.[154] Protestants were not so active in the creation of such institutions under ecclesiastical auspices. Here and there were a few, some of them outstanding.[155] Protestants, however, were prominent in initiating secular community enterprises, and, when these were not fully maintained by public taxation, contributed to them from their own purses. The asylums for the insane for whose inauguration Dorothea Dix was so largely responsible were simply a few examples. An institution for the deaf and dumb, at Hartford, Connecticut, incorporated in 1816, arose out of the suggestion of a deeply religious physician who encouraged a clergyman to go to Europe to learn there the latest methods for teaching these unfortunates. Other similar institutions were opened in various parts of the country, mainly with financial support from the state, but at the outset under the direction of men who were pronounced Christians.[156] It may have been indicative of his underlying purpose that S. G. Howe, the husband of Julia Ward Howe, in his pioneering in the education of the blind, stressed placing the Bible in the hands of the blind.[157] The Children's Aid Society of New York City, which sought to assist the underprivileged youth, largely of

[151] Will, *Life of Cardinal Gibbons*, Vol. I, pp. 320-360.

[152] Will, *op. cit.*, Vol. I, pp. 361ff.

[153] For examples of this see Johnson, *Ante-Bellum North Carolina*, pp. 423-426.

[154] In 1920 296 orphan asylums, 45,687 orphans, and 121 homes for the aged were reported, and in 1930 624 hospitals.—*The Official Catholic Directory* (New York, P. J. Kennedy & Sons, 1940, pp. vi, 1108, 157, 197), p. 1108.

[155] For some under the Disciples of Christ, see *Survey of Service*, pp. 270-333.

[156] Baird, *Religion in the United States of America*, pp. 404-406. On the part of a clergyman in inaugurating care for the deaf-mutes in New York, see Schneider, *The History of Public Welfare in New York State 1609-1866*, p. 201.

[157] For a life of Howe, see F. B. Sanborn, *Dr. S. G. Howe, the Philanthropist* (New York, Funk and Wagnalls, 1891, pp. 370).

the foreign-born, through lodging houses, industrial schools, night schools, summer camps, and sanatoria, was founded and long directed by Charles Loring Brace, who had planned to enter the Protestant ministry and engaged in this philanthropy from a deep desire to follow Christ.[158] In the financial depression of the 1890's, Booth-Tucker, of the Salvation Army, planted agricultural colonies of the urban unemployed and so helped them to achieve self-respecting self-support.[159]

It is clear that in moulding the professed ideals of the country, in stimulating attempts to eliminate specific features of the life of the land which were deemed contrary to its principles, and in the relief of unfortunate individuals, Christianity was very potent. One is constrained to inquire, however, the extent to which this influence made itself felt in the general structure of the government, in the laws, and in the political life of the nation. In the official separation of Church and state which characterized the United States, did the state escape the influence of Christianity? The answer must be an emphatic negative. Government was profoundly modified by Christianity.

Separation of Church and state did not mean that government was antagonistic or even lukewarm to the faith which was professed by an increasing proportion of the population. Although full religious freedom was a fundamental principle of national and state governments, and although after the first quarter of the nineteenth century no state gave financial subsidies to churches as churches, in many ways government was interpenetrated by Christianity and accorded support to it. The constitutions of an overwhelming majority of the states made acknowledgment of God. Several contained in the opening paragraph some such phrase as "grateful to Almighty God for our freedom."[160] A few invoked "the favour and guidance of Almighty God" or "His blessing."[161] One declared that morality and piety rightly grounded on evangelical principles would afford the best and greatest security to govern-

---

[158] The Life of Charles Loring Brace Chiefly Told in His Own Letters. Edited by His Daughter (New York, Charles Scribner's Sons, 1894, pp. x, 503), passim; Schneider, op. cit., pp. 330ff.

[159] F. A. Mackenzie, Booth-Tucker (London, Hodder and Stoughton, 1930, pp. xv, 295), pp. 171-173.

[160] California, Idaho, Nebraska, Nevada, New York, Ohio, and Wisconsin. See texts in Kettleborough, The State Constitutions, pp. 120, 351, 848, 876, 970, 1058, 1500.

Phrases with a similar purpose were in the constitutions of Arizona, Arkansas, Connecticut, Florida, Illinois, Indiana, Iowa, Kansas, Kentucky, Louisiana, Maryland, Massachusetts, Michigan, Minnesota, Montana, New Jersey, New Mexico, North Carolina, Pennsylvania, Rhode Island, South Carolina, South Dakota, Utah, Washington, and Wyoming. See texts in Kettleborough, op. cit., pp. 55, 89, 237, 283, 381, 413, 430, 448, 466, 501, 612, 654, 685, 710, 816, 923, 937, 1021, 1174, 1203, 1220, 1256, 1352, 1441, 1540.

[161] Alabama, Georgia, Illinois, Mississippi, Oklahoma, Rhode Island, and Texas. See texts in Kettleborough, op. cit., pp. 12, 310, 381, 738, 1091, 1203, 1312.

ment.[162] One of them, that of Utah, because of the strong feeling in the country at large against Mormonism, had written into it as a condition of admission to the Union, "polygamous and plural marriages are forever prohibited," a striking evidence of the power of Christian standards in the marriage relation.[163] The presence of chaplains in legislative bodies and in the army and navy testifies to the formal regard for Christianity. The setting aside of an annual Thanksgiving Day for services in the churches, partly by decree of various state governors and legislatures, occasionally by action of the national government and, beginning in 1864, regularly by proclamation of the President, is evidence of it. In at least one state Good Friday was officially observed. We hear of fast days set aside by the state legislature.[164] Sunday was marked by the closing of government offices, and in some states laws declared that the day should be kept sacred and that certain amusements should be prohibited on it.[165] The Presidents and some other officials took their oaths of office on the Christian Bible. A frequent form of administering oaths was in the name of God. The commentaries of some of the great jurists, notably Story and Kent, were based in part upon Christianity.[166] Jewish-Christian morality was widely acknowledged by the courts to have helped to shape the common law. Christianity entered largely into the political structure of the nation.

How far Christianity guided the officers who conducted the government it would be impossible to measure with accuracy. The prominence of the clergy in political life in New England may be supposed to have made for the influence of the faith which they professed. That prominence rapidly declined in the fore part of the nineteenth century.[167] So far as one may judge, the Presidents of the later decades of the period were more committed to Christianity than were those of the earlier ones. To be sure, most of the Virginia Presidents of the first forty years of the nation had the connexion of the planter aristocracy with the Protestant Episcopal Church. Even Jefferson, while dissenting from Orthodox Christianity, preserved a respect for much of its ethics, and Madison had had at Princeton a certain amount of theological training.[168] Of the New England Presidents, John Adams had once seriously con-

[162] New Hampshire. Text in Kettleborough, *op. cit.*, p. 904.

[163] Text in Kettleborough, *op. cit.*, p. 1354.

[164] Bond, *The Civilization of the Old Northwest*, pp. 492ff.

[165] Johnson, *The Legal Status of Church-State Relationships in the United States*, pp. 231ff.

[166] Gabriel, *The Course of American Democratic Thought*, p. 389.

[167] In Connecticut, for instance, the constitution adopted in 1818 ended the "Standing Order" and the domination of the Congregational clergy.—Bacon, *Leonard Bacon*, p. 289.

[168] *Dictionary of American Biography*, Vol. XII, p. 184.

sidered entering the ministry,[169] and the courageous and acidulously upright John Quincy Adams was a Unitarian by conviction.[170] Van Buren was a faithful member of the Dutch Reformed Church.[171] Polk drew from his Presbyterian mother firm religious beliefs which contributed to his extreme conscientiousness and not long before his death his predilections led him into the Methodist Episcopal Church.[172] Yet several of the Presidents in the first three-fourths of the century had no formal church membership. Even Lincoln, although deeply influenced by Christianity, profoundly committed to some of its chief teachings, and growing in a religious faith which shaped some of his best remembered utterances and actions, was not a member of any church. Neither was Grant a member of a church, although he was not without a faith based upon Christianity.[173] Of the Presidents in the latter part of the pre-1914 period, three, Arthur, Cleveland, and Wilson, were sons of clergymen and bore clearly the imprint of their rearing. Garfield, whom Arthur succeeded, had been a lay preacher of the Disciples of Christ.[174] Benjamin Harrison, who came between Cleveland's two terms, was for forty years an elder in the Presbyterian Church, was a teacher and superintendent in the Sunday School, and was prominent in the national councils of his denomination.[175] McKinley, who followed Cleveland, was from youth a member of the Methodist Episcopal Church and believed Christianity to be the mightiest factor in the civilization of the world.[176] Theodore Roosevelt, McKinley's successor, was a life-long member of the Dutch Reformed Church. Taft could not conform to the orthodox Congregationalism with which he had been in close contact in youth, but his high sense of duty and his Unitarianism seem to have been interrelated. The most prominent non-President statesman of the closing years of the nineteenth and the opening years of the twentieth century, William Jennings Bryan, was outspokenly Christian,[177] and seems to have been led to his championship of the various political causes which he espoused by convictions drawn largely from his Christian background. All these leaders

[169] Dictionary of American Biography, Vol. I, p. 73.
[170] Dictionary of American Biography, Vol. I, p. 92.
[171] Dictionary of American Biography, Vol. XIX, p. 156.
[172] Dictionary of American Biography, Vol. XV, p. 34.
[173] On Lincoln, see William E. Barton, The Soul of Abraham Lincoln (New York, George H. Doran Co., 1920, pp. 407), passim. On Grant, see Vincent, John Heyl Vincent, pp. 49, 50, 100, 101.
[174] Dictionary of American Biography, Vol. VII, p. 145.
[175] Dictionary of American Biography, Vol. VIII, pp. 332, 335.
[176] Dictionary of American Biography, Vol. XII, p. 109.
[177] The Memoirs of William Jennings Bryan, by Himself and His Wife Mary Baird Bryan (Philadelphia, The John C. Winston Co., 1925, pp. 560), pp. 15-51; Wayne C. Williams, William Jennings Bryan (New York, G. P. Putnam's Sons, 1936, pp. xv, 513), p. 26.

were from the Protestantism of the older American stock and, in general, represented the effect of the radical strain of Protestantism out of which had come so many movements for social and moral reform. That this environment influenced them seems incontestable.

Now and again men came out against political corruption from motives of obviously Christian origin. Thus while a pastor in Brooklyn, T. DeWitt Talmage denounced vigorously the bribery and infamy in that city and in New York.[178] A few years later Charles H. Parkhurst, pastor of the Madison Square Presbyterian Church in New York City, exposed so effectively the corruption in the municipal government that measures were taken for improvement not only there but also in some other urban centres.[179]

In family life, in spite of the prevalence of purely civil ceremonies, the majority of marriages were probably solemnized by the rites of the Church. This must have added a certain sanctity to the marriage tie. It did not, however, prevent the rapid increase of divorces which marked the later years of the era.

It would be difficult to appraise the effect of Christianity upon economic life. That among many Christian faith made for industry and thrift is clear.[180] In some instances, spectacularly in the action of Sheldon Jackson in introducing reindeer to remedy the dwindling food supply of the Alaskan Eskimos,[181] it brought marked economic betterment. That it impelled many to honesty is obvious. However, that it did not restrain some men eminent in the business world from practices which many Christians condemned as unethical was also one of the commonplaces of the history of the time. As a major force in the abolition of slavery Christianity led to a revolution in the economic structure of the South. As a contributory, even though a minor, factor in the development of individualistic *laissez faire* capitalism, Protestant Christianity assisted in the growth of a system which was markedly characteristic of the United States of the nineteenth century. However, Christianity and especially Protestant Christianity registered some progress in curbing features of that capitalism which threatened the human values prized by Christianity. In aiding movements for restrictions on the employment of women and children, for shortening the hours of the working day, and for better labour conditions, and, through minorities, in advocating a socialistically organized economic life, it made itself felt.

One of the striking features of the life of the United States, the vast amounts

---

[178] *T. DeWitt Talmage as I Knew Him* (New York, E. P. Dutton and Co., 1912, pp. viii, 439. An autobiography), *passim.*
[179] Weigle, *American Idealism*, p. 215.
[180] For one instance, see Gingerich, *The Mennonites in Iowa*, p. 205.
[181] Stewart, *Sheldon Jackson*, pp. 386ff.

given for philanthropy by those who had accumulated fortunes in the economic expansion of the country, was due in large part to Christianity. Not all of the great gifts could be traced to that source, but many could. Thus A. A. Hyde, who gave about a million and a half dollars, largely to religious enterprises, felt it to be un-Christian to pile up wealth and kept for himself and his family only enough for their immediate needs.[182] The enormous gifts of John D. Rockefeller began through the channels of the Baptist denomination and were due to the conviction that wealth had come as the gift of God.[183] Another whose donations to charitable and religious enterprises, unobtrusively made, ran into millions of dollars, Daniel Willis James, was moved by purposes of Christian origin.[184] The list might be extended to great length.

Some Protestant Christians suffered from compunctions of conscience over the acceptance by ecclesiastical organizations of money which they believed to have been acquired by unethical means. The most famous instance was the protest against the acceptance by the American Board of Commissioners for Foreign Missions of a gift of $100,000 for its educational enterprises.[185] In general, however, as in this case, the majority believed it to be right to utilize for worthy ends contributions from whatever source, so long as they involved no endorsement of the donors' business practices.

In attitudes towards amusements Christians and churches differed. Many believed dancing and theatre-going to be wrong. Others encouraged them. The majority of churches provided in one way or another for some kind of group recreation for their members. For thousands the churches were centres of social and intellectual life as well as places of worship.

The direct contribution of Christianity to art and music in the United States was marked, but not outstanding. Some church buildings were hideous. Others were beautiful. Many of the chaste structures, with their tall spires, developments from the Georgian "colonial" architecture, which were erected in New England late in the eighteenth and early in the nineteenth century, long remained models of severe good taste. The revivals among the masses gave birth to hundreds of simple hymns, a kind of religious folk music.[186] Numbers of the most famous and widely used of these were in the collections of "Gospel Hymns" used by Moody in his meetings, but there were thousands of others. They were at once the outgrowth and the moulders of much of the Protestant

---

[182] George Irving, *Master of Money, A. A. Hyde of Wichita* (New York, Fleming H. Revell Co., 1936, pp. 157), *passim*.

[183] John T. Flynn, *God's Gold. The Story of Rockefeller and His Times* (New York, Harcourt, Brace and Co., 1932, pp. ix, 520), pp. 303ff., 395.

[184] *Dictionary of American Biography*, Vol. IX, pp. 573, 574.

[185] *The Missionary Herald*, Vol. CI, pp. 227-232, Vol. CXXII, pp. 173, 174.

[186] Jackson, *White Spirituals in the Southern Uplands*, pp. 214ff.

religious life of the land. However, no such great architecture or music arose out of this nineteenth century Christianity of the United States as came out of the European Christianity of the preceding centuries.

Upon the literature of the nineteenth century in the United States Christianity had a varied effect. It seems to have been largely due to its Christian heritage that the New England stock had so outstanding a part in the literary life of the middle of the century. Some of the prominent figures—such as the Quaker John G. Whittier and the Puritan Harriet Beecher Stowe—remained devout Christians and their writings were inspired and moulded by their faith. Some reflected the Unitarian development from New England Puritanism which flourished around Boston—among them Henry Wadsworth Longfellow, Ralph Waldo Emerson, James Russell Lowell, and Oliver Wendell Holmes. Nathaniel Hawthorne bore the impress of his Puritan forebears. William Cullen Bryant, while abandoning much of the New England Calvinism in the midst of which he had been reared, in his editorship of the New York *Evening Post* displayed its moral qualities. Horace Greeley's high moral sense in the editorials which made him one of the forces of the day seems to have come in part from a New England and Scotch-Irish heritage, with a rearing in the Bible and the Shorter Catechism.[187] In Walt Whitman such Christian influence as existed was derived indirectly through an ancestry which had in it traces of Quakerism and from his admiration for Emerson.[188] The stormy, restless, emotionally unstable Vachel Lindsay showed a religious strain which in his youth had been nourished on the revivalism of the Middle West.[189] Some, like Samuel L. Clemens (Mark Twain), became profoundly sceptical. No theologian or theology of first rank issued from the nineteenth century Christianity of the United States. In literature and thought, as in art and music, the Christian faith did not stimulate the American mind to creation of so high a quality as it had helped to produce in earlier and even in contemporary Europe. The main achievements of the United States were in other fields.

[187] On Horace Greeley, see Horace Greeley, *Recollections of a Busy Life* (New York, J. B. Ford & Co., 1868, pp. 624), pp. 17ff., 68-74. He came to be a Universalist in conviction.

[188] On some of these writers, see comments in Gabriel, *The Course of American Democratic Thought, passim,* and in Vernon Louis Parrington, *Main Currents in American Thought. An Interpretation of American Literature from the Beginnings to 1920* (New York, Harcourt, Brace and Co., 3 vols., 1927-1930), *passim.* See also Van Wyck Brooks, *The Flowering of New England 1815-1865* (New York, E. P. Dutton & Co., 1936, pp. 550), *passim,* and Van Wyck Brooks, *New England: Indian Summer 1865-1915* (New York, E. P. Dutton & Co., 1940), *passim.*

[189] Edgar Lee Masters, *Vachel Lindsay* (New York, Charles Scribner's Sons, 1935, pp. ix, 392), *passim.*

In the provision of schools for the country, from elementary to university grade, Christianity had a major, perhaps the major share.

We have already seen the leading place taken by missionaries and the churches in initiating education for Indians and Negroes.

In the promotion of elementary schools and in making effective the dream of at least some education for all, Christianity seems to have been the greatest exciting factor. The Roman Catholic Church, in the endeavour to hold its youth through an education which included instruction in its faith, developed a nation-wide system of parochial schools for the children of its members. Here and there a few Protestant denominations made similar attempts, although not in so thorough-going and persistent a manner. Among these were Old School Presbyterians,[190] Quakers,[191] Lutherans,[192] and Disciples of Christ.[193] Even more important, the initiative and early leadership in the creation of the system of free public schools supported by the state came largely from those who seem to have caught their inspiration from the Protestant wing of Christianity. Horace Mann, who was the great pioneer in organizing public education in Massachusetts and who had a marked influence upon the entire country, had been reared on the preaching of Nathaniel Emmons. While even as a boy he reacted vigorously against much of the latter's Calvinism, the early formed purpose to be of benefit to mankind which impelled him may have come (although without his being conscious of it) from the principle of "universal benevolence" and the pursuit of the public good which Emmons taught as necessary to "a truly unselfish life."[194] Certainly he was deeply religious. Charles Brooks, who helped to bring into existence in Massachusetts what was said to be the first real state board of education in the United States and who did much for the creation of some of the earliest normal schools, was a Unitarian clergyman.[195] Henry Barnard, who promoted

[190] L. J. Sherrill, *Presbyterian Parochial Schools 1846-1870, passim.*

[191] William C. Dunlap, *Quaker Education in Baltimore and Virginia Yearly Meetings With an Account of Certain Meetings of Delaware and the Eastern Shore Affiliated with Philadelphia* (Philadelphia, The Science Press Printing Co., 1936, pp. xi, 574), *passim.*

[192] Maurer, *Early Lutheran Education in Pennsylvania*, p. 199.

[193] Fortune, *The Disciples of Christ in Kentucky*, pp. 177-182.

[194] See quotations from letters and journals of Mann in *Life of Horace Mann by His Wife* (Boston, Walker, Fuller and Co., 1865, pp. 602), pp. 13-15, 49, 50, 71-74. See also *Dictionary of American Biography*, Vol. XII, pp. 240-243; R. B. Culver, *Horace Mann and Religion in the Massachusetts Public Schools* (Yale University Press, 1929, pp. x, 301), p. 5. On Emmons's teachings, see *The Works of Nathaniel Emmons* (Boston, Congregational Board of Publication, 6 vols., 1861-1863), Vol. IV, pp. 498, 499. Note the striking similarity between this passage and Mann's purpose in accepting the secretaryship of the Massachusetts Board of Education, as seen in an extract from Mann's journal in Culver, *op. cit.*, p. 36.

[195] *Dictionary of American Biography*, Vol. III, pp. 74, 75.

public schools in Connecticut and Rhode Island and was the first United States Commissioner of Education, while not a member of any church, had been cradled in New England and was deeply religious.[196] De Witt Clinton, called the most effective force for public education in the history of New York State, was also a vice-president of the American Bible Society and of the Education Society of the Presbyterian Church.[197] Robert J. Breckenridge, who as superintendent of public instruction in Virginia from 1847 to 1851 multiplied ten-fold the school attendance, was a Presbyterian clergyman.[198] So was William H. Ruffner, who was sometimes termed the Horace Mann of the South and who as state superintendent of public schools in Virginia after the Civil War drafted a school law which became a model for other Southern states and, in the face of opposition, advocated the education of Negroes at white expense.[199] John D. Pierce, who went to Michigan as an agent of the American Home Missionary Society, was largely responsible for the section in the constitution of that state which provided for a comprehensive plan for public education and became the first superintendent of the system.[200] Jonathan Baldwin Turner, brother of the pioneer home missionary, Asa Turner, and himself a member of the faculty of Illinois College, founded by home missionaries, lectured widely through Illinois in advocacy of a public school system.[201] It was Samuel Lewis, a lawyer who was also a Methodist local preacher, who as the first superintendent for common schools for Ohio placed the school system of that state upon a solid foundation.[202] Joseph Ward, "the father of Congregationalism in the Dakotas," was the chief author of the education law of South Dakota and had a prominent part in keeping the school lands of the territory out of the hands of Eastern speculators.[203] George H. Atkinson, a leading Congregational home missionary in Oregon, had a large share in inaugurating public schools in that area.[204]

Ecclesiastical organizations also founded a large number of secondary schools. What was said to be the first literary institution in the Mississippi Valley was an academy inaugurated by the Presbyterians.[205] As time passed, public high schools multiplied and absorbed or, by their competition, drove out of existence

[196] *Dictionary of American Biography*, Vol. I, pp. 621-625.
[197] *Dictionary of American Biography*, Vol. IV, pp. 221-225.
[198] *Dictionary of American Biography*, Vol. III, pp. 10, 11.
[199] *Dictionary of American Biography*, Vol. XVI, pp. 218, 219.
[200] Weigle, *American Idealism*, p. 283; Goodykoontz, *Home Missions on the American Frontier*, p. 368.
[201] Magoun, *Asa Turner*, p. 112; Goodykoontz, *op. cit.*, p. 369.
[202] Weigle, *op. cit.*, p. 283.
[203] *Dictionary of American Biography*, Vol. XIX, pp. 429, 430.
[204] *Dictionary of American Biography*, Vol. I, pp. 408, 409.
[205] Posey, *The Development of Methodism in the Old Southwest*, p. 5.

many of the Protestant institutions. Some of those which survived continued by appealing to families of the upper income levels who were able to pay the tuition charges. Several of these acquired fame, among them Groton School, which had for its creator a clergyman of the Protestant Episcopal Church, Endicott Peabody.[206] In contrast with the decrease of private secondary schools under Protestant auspices, those maintained by Roman Catholics continued to grow.[207]

It was in beginning and maintaining colleges and universities that the churches made one of their most outstanding contributions to education in the United States. In the colonial period all the colleges which were established owed their inception to an impulse which was clearly of Christian origin and most of them were largely controlled and staffed by clergymen.[208] As we have seen,[209] colleges and universities were inaugurated in large numbers by the churches on the advancing frontier.[210] This was partly from the purpose of providing leadership for the churches and partly from the desire to help raise the level of culture in the new communities. In the fore part of the nineteenth century revivals again and again swept the campuses of older colleges of the Eastern states. Under their impetus, many of the graduates went out to found colleges in the West which would similarly be centres of education and Christian living.[211] These colleges were, indeed, Christian communities and had a certain kinship to the monasteries which, in the Middle Ages, were so often the pioneers of culture in Northern Europe. Members of the teaching staffs usually served sacrificially from a sense of Christian mission. Children from religious homes tended to be attracted to them. By 1860 about 180 colleges which had an enduring life had been formed under denominational auspices. Of these fourteen were Roman Catholic and the remainder Protestant.[212] Numbers of others were opened which persisted for a time, served their constituencies, and then died.[213] In 1900, of 664 institutions of college or

[206] Frank D. Ashburn, *Fifty Years On. Groton School 1884-1934* (New York, Privately Printed, 1934, pp. xiii, 225), *passim*.
[207] Weigle, *op. cit.*, p. 293.
[208] Vol. III, p. 227.
[209] Vol. IV, Chap. 6.
[210] Tewksbury, *The Founding of American Colleges and Universities Before the Civil War*, pp. 1-5. A few of the many books giving the history of individual colleges and educators are Jonas A. Jonasson, *Bricks Without Straw, the Story of Linfield College* (Caldwell, Idaho, The Caxton Printers, 1938, pp. 215); William Warren Sweet, *Indiana Asbury-De Pauw University 1837-1937* (Cincinnati, The Abingdon Press, 1937, pp. 298); Paul Neff Garber, *John Carlisle Kilgo, President of Trinity College, 1894-1910* (Duke University Press, 1937, pp. xi, 412).
[211] Tewksbury, *op. cit.*, pp. 65-68.
[212] Tewksbury, *op. cit.*, p. 69.
[213] Tewksbury, *op. cit.*, pp. 14-31.

university grade, 403 were under avowedly Protestant and 63 under Roman Catholic auspices.[214] It is significant that the two outstanding universities in the metropolitan centre of the Middle West, the University of Chicago and Northwestern University, were inaugurated, the one by the Baptists, the other by the Methodists, the two denominations which had been especially active in winning the masses of the older American stock in the frontier days of that region. Conversion had borne fruit in higher education. Moreover, many a university supported by the state owed its inception to the Christian forces. Some were built upon the foundations of earlier avowedly Christian institutions. It was a New England clergyman, Manasseh Cutler, extraordinarily versatile in his intellectual interests, who drew up the plan for what eventually became Ohio University, at Athens, Ohio.[215] The state universities of Tennessee and Delaware arose out of Presbyterian colleges.[216] In 1868 the College of California, founded by the Presbyterians and Congregationalists, became the (state) University of California.[217]

The fact that colleges and universities owed so large a debt to Christianity did not ensure their fidelity to that faith. By 1914 a marked movement away from Christianity was in progress. A growing proportion of the members of teaching staffs were either lukewarm towards Christianity or were openly sceptical or even hostile. These attitudes were shared by many of the students. The new knowledge, showing itself in part in the theory of evolution and in the application of historical criticism to the Bible, seemed to many to have made Christianity intellectually untenable. The wave of hostility did not reach such dimensions as it had among the student bodies in the last decade of the eighteenth and the first decade of the nineteenth century. Active voluntary religious organizations on the campuses combated the tendency. Yet the trend, even in the institutions founded under church auspices, was towards secularization.

From the Christian impulse issued, as in preceding centuries in Europe, new methods and types of education. Something in Christianity seemed to stir men and women to embark upon new adventures of the human mind and to seek to provide larger opportunities for education for those heretofore deprived of them.

Education for women, and particularly higher education, in its beginnings and in much of its later development was primarily a fruit of the Christian

[214] Padelford in *Christian Education*, Vol. XIX, pp. 210ff.
[215] Arthur G. Beach, *A Pioneer College. The Story of Marietta* (Privately printed, 1935, pp. xiv, 325), p. 37.
[216] Tewksbury, *op. cit.*, p. 95.
[217] Pond, *Gospel Pioneering*, p. 54.

faith. Thus Thomas Smith Grimké, whom we have met as an advocate of peace and temperance, also favoured higher education for women.[218] Catherine Beecher, daughter of that redoubtable clergyman, Lyman Beecher, shared in the establishment of the Western Female Institute in Cincinnati.[219] The idealistic Christian colony, Oberlin, in the very first circular of its "collegiate institute" announced the purpose of opening the same privileges to women as to men, a promise which it resolutely kept.[220] It was in a school conducted by a clergyman, Joseph Emerson,[221] that Mary Lyon, creator of Mount Holyoke Seminary, had part of her training.[222] Mount Holyoke was a path-breaker in providing college training for women. In its opening years it had a warmly Christian atmosphere and scores of its graduates became missionaries and founded schools and colleges, some of them for Negroes and Indians.[223] Wellesley College owed its existence to Henry F. Durant, who, devotedly Christian, wished to give to girls the same opportunities which Harvard opened to men, and desired all its teachers to be earnest Christians.[224]

A complete list of innovators in education whose impulse came largely from the Christian faith would be a long one. On it would be Amos Bronson Alcott, who through early contact with the Quakers acquired a belief in individual inspiration which was the cornerstone of his life work. His very advanced educational program anticipated later developments.[225] The list would include Jonathan B. Turner, whom we have already met as an early promoter of public schools in Illinois. From what seems to have been religious conviction, he advocated advanced training in agriculture and the mechanical arts that farming and industry might be raised to the level of the traditionally learned professions. He formulated a plan for the financing of this type of education by a large grant of public land by the national government to each of the states. This appears to have been partly responsible for the Morrill Act of 1862, by which Congress set aside lands for that purpose, a step which

[218] *Dictionary of American Biography*, Vol. VII, pp. 635, 636.

[219] Goodykoontz, *Home Missions on the American Frontier*, pp. 369, 370.

[220] Hosford, *Father Shipherd's Magna Charta*, p. 5.

[221] *Dictionary of American Biography*, Vol. VI, pp. 129, 130.

[222] *Dictionary of American Biography*, Vol. XI, pp. 531, 532.

[223] *Centenary of Mount Holyoke College* (Published by the College, South Hadley, Mass., 1937, pp. 195), p. 13. For lives of Mary Lyon, showing her governing Christian purpose and the outstanding place which Christianity was given in the early years of Mount Holyoke, see Edward Hitchcock, Compiler, *The Power of Christian Benevolence, Illustrated in the Life and Labors of Mary Lyon* (Northampton, Hopkins, Bridgman and Co., 1852, pp. viii, 486), containing extensive excerpts from Miss Lyon's own letters and writings, and Beth Bradford Gilchrist, *The Life of Mary Lyon* (Boston, Houghton Mifflin Co., 1910, pp. x, 462).

[224] Moody, *D. L. Moody*, p. 305.

[225] *Dictionary of American Biography*, Vol. I, pp. 139-141.

gave an enormous impetus to the kind of education which Turner had so much at heart.[226] The educational hall of fame would also give high rank to John H. Vincent, a Methodist clergyman. Out of the Chautauqua Sunday School Assembly which was first held in 1874 on the site of a camp-meeting and under the auspices of the Methodists arose, largely under his direction, a nation-wide movement for popular education which sought to reach all ages, and especially youth and adults. Its summer schools seem to have been the first of their kind in the United States. Its home reading courses reached many. It had correspondence courses. It led in developing in the United States the university extension idea by which were carried some of the privileges of the university to all who wished them. Assemblies bearing the Chautauqua name, but without organic connexion with the parent movement, sprang up in many different parts of the country.[227]

That Christianity had a profound effect upon the life of the United States is indubitable. In moulding religion; in creating for the nation its dominant ideals of liberty and equal opportunity; in contributing to the atmosphere of abounding optimism; in stimulating attempts at communities which would embody Christian principles; in calling into existence reform movements which successfully attacked Negro slavery, sought to curb the use of alcoholic beverages, strove to bring about international peace, and advocated greater opportunities for women; in obtaining prison reform and humane treatment of the insane; in arousing efforts to solve the moral and social problems brought by the progress of the industrial revolution; in shaping law, politics, family life, and business; and in stimulating intellectual activity and education—in these and in other ways the Christian faith had a striking influence upon the United States.

Was that influence growing or declining? Was Christianity a waxing or a waning force? Exact measurements are impossible.

To some, especially in intellectual circles, on the eve of 1914 Christianity seemed to be losing its hold. The complexity and drive of industrialized life, particularly in the larger cities, was appearing to wean men's attention from

[226] Edmund J. James, *The Origin of the Land Grant Act of 1862 (the So-Called Morrill Act) and Some Account of its Author, Jonathan B. Turner* (University of Illinois, The University Studies, Vol. IV, No. 1, Nov., 1910, pp. 111), *passim*.

[227] Arthur Eugene Bestor, *Chautauqua Publications. An Historical and Bibliographical Guide* (Chautauqua, N. Y., Chautauqua Press, 1934, pp. 67), pp. 1-10; Jesse Lyman Hurlburt, *The Story of Chautauqua* (New York, G. P. Putnam's Sons, 1921, pp. xxv, 429), *passim*; John H. Vincent, *The Chautauqua Movement* (Boston, Chautauqua Press, 1886, pp. ix, 308), pp. 2-43; Vincent, *John Heyl Vincent, passim*.

the churches. The scientific approach and the knowledge accumulated by it were held by many to render Christianity obsolete.[228] Moreover, by 1914 the radical wing of Protestantism from which the striking influences of Christianity upon the nation's life had chiefly issued was probably proportionately not so strong numerically as formerly. It had drawn largely from the older American stock. With the flood of immigration and the declining birth rate in the families of colonial ancestry which marked the later decades of the period, this stock was no longer so large a segment of the population as it had once been. It was not at all certain that the Christianity of the newer arrivals would be so potent. Quite clearly it had not the same social ideals as the other. In the leadership of the nation the older stock was still dominant and as time passed it was, in general, more nearly committed to this radical Protestantism than in early years. However, when the newer elements rose to power, as they were probably to do, the religious picture and with it the effect of Christianity might be profoundly altered.

On the other hand, impressive evidence seems to support the opposite thesis. The proportion of church members in the population was undoubtedly increasing, both in the older and the newer sections, and among whites, Negroes, and Indians. By the close of the third quarter Negro slavery had been abolished and, so far as the Federal Constitution could accomplish it, the Negroes had been granted citizenship and the franchise. In the latter part of the century the Christian impulse achieved much for the education of the Negro. The fight against liquor experienced successes and failures, but by 1914 the prohibition movement had more nearly eliminated the traffic than at any previous time. Christianity had been important in prison reform and in the care of the blind, the deaf, the dumb, and the insane. In all these directions gains continued to be made. Women were progressively being accorded the same opportunities as men, and so far as Christianity was a contributory cause in this important phase of culture it was moving forward. The Christian conscience had stirred a minority to assist in obtaining better conditions for labourers in farm and industry, and here, too, advances were being registered. The outstanding statesmen of the third of a century which immediately preceded 1914 seem to have been more committed to Christianity than were their predecessors. Although in colleges and universities religious scepticism was prominent and was possibly increasing, never had voluntary Christian organizations of students and faculty been so vigorous, and through the Student Volunteer Move-

---

[228] For an interesting study, with rather an adverse report for the standing of Christianity among intellectuals, see James H. Leuba, *The Belief in God and Immortality. A Psychological, Anthropological and Statistical Study* (Boston, Sherman, French & Co., 1916, pp. xvii, 340), *passim.*

ment for Foreign Missions a growing number of college and university graduates were going to other lands to propagate the Christian faith. Gifts for the spread of Christianity at home and abroad were mounting, evidence partly of the wealth of the land and partly of a widening interest among professing Christians. It was certain that the United States was far from conforming fully to Christian ideals. Yet, in spite of some tendencies in the opposite direction, on the whole Christianity was a growing force in the nation's life.

Chapter XII

THE UNITED STATES OF AMERICA. THE EFFECT OF THE ENVIRONMENT UPON CHRISTIANITY

THE Christianity which developed in the United States was unique. It displayed features which marked it as distinct from previous Christianity in any other land. In the nineteenth and twentieth centuries the Christianity of Canada most nearly resembled it, but even that was not precisely like it. The characteristics peculiar to the Christianity of the United States were due to the environment, if that term be allowed to have its broadest meaning. Some of these qualities we noted in the preceding chapter. To these we must revert and add to them others.

Before the Thirteen Colonies had achieved their independence the Christianity of the country had begun to show itself different.[1] The outstanding qualities of that Christianity persisted into the nineteenth and twentieth centuries. Some of them were accentuated. A few became less prominent. To them others were added. Yet the Christianity of the United States was, in general, the logical outgrowth of that of the colonial period.

Even more than in the days before political independence, the Christianity of the United States presented unprecedented variety. Eventually all of the major and most of the minor kinds of Christianity which had arisen in Asia and Europe were represented. Roman Catholics, not only of the Latin but also of some of the Uniate rites, Greek Orthodox, including those of more than one nation of Europe and Asia, Armenians of the Gregorian Church, Jacobites, Nestorians, and the majority of the branches of Protestants were present. To these imported forms were added several indigenous ones. When the country began an independent life, it is said to have contained twenty-eight denominations, of which eighteen were of foreign and ten of native origin.[2] In 1916 at least one hundred and ninety-two were reported, of which about half were from abroad and about half had sprung up in the United States.[3] The result was a Joseph's coat of many colours.

[1] Vol. III, pp. 229-232.
[2] Douglass, *Church Unity Movements in the United States*, p. 28.
[3] Department of Commerce, Bureau of the Census, *Religious Bodies 1916*, Part II.

The variety was due in part to immigration. The population of the United States was recruited from peoples of many ecclesiastical backgrounds. The diversity was also made possible by two features of the environment which profoundly affected the Christianity of the United States—religious toleration and the separation of Church and state. Both had begun in the colonial period, although then still far from complete, and both displayed a marked growth after the achievement of independence. The constitution of the Federal Government forbade Congress to make any "law respecting an establishment of religion or prohibiting the free exercise thereof."[4] It also provided that "no religious test shall ever be required as a qualification to any office or public trust under the United States."[5] These clauses in the Federal Constitution did not apply to the states. In several of the latter in the early years of the nation a special position was accorded to particular denominations—to the Congregational churches in Massachusetts, Connecticut, and New Hampshire, and to the Church of England in some others. In a number of states religious tests were required of office-holders—in some a belief in the Christian religion, in some an adherence to Protestantism, in some a belief in God, and in some an acknowledgment of the divine inspiration of the Old and New Testaments.[6] By the time that the first third of the nineteenth century had passed, all but one of the states had removed the remnants of a religious establishment.[7] The constitutions of a number of the states provided for religious toleration.[8] One, Utah, forbade the union of Church and state.[9] Two prohibited the levying of a tax for the erection of a house of worship or the support of any church or ministry[10] However, down into the twentieth century eight of the states in their constitutions required of the holders of certain offices a belief in the existence of God and two exacted a belief in a future state of rewards and punishments.[11] It must also be said that, although legal toleration of all religions became the rule, much popular intolerance continued. Since the country was overwhelmingly Protestant by tradition, this was usually directed against the Roman Catholics. At times it became very active.[12] Now and then it broke out against some extreme offshoot of Protestantism. The Mormons

---

[4] Constitution of the United States, first amendment.
[5] Constitution of the United States, Article VI, section 3.
[6] Zollmann, *American Church Law*, pp. 4, 5.
[7] Zollmann, *op. cit.*, pp. 16, 17.
[8] Zollmann, *op. cit.*, pp. 9, 10.
[9] Zollmann, *op. cit.*, pp. 18, 19.
[10] Zollmann, *op. cit.*, p. 19.
[11] Zollmann, *op. cit.*, pp. 6, 7.
[12] For one period of this anti-Roman Catholic agitation, see Ray Allen Billington, *The Protestant Crusade 1800-1860* (New York, The Macmillan Co., 1938, pp. viii, 514), *passim*.

especially were subjected to violence in their early days. With these exceptions, Church and state were separated and religious freedom prevailed. In this environment, it was possible for Christianity to preserve and to take on many different forms. Although in the nineteenth century these conditions ceased to be a novelty and obtained in an increasing number of lands, the United States was the first in which Christianity had experienced them. Never before had Church and state been separated in any land in which Christianity was the dominant faith and never had all forms of Christianity known so near an approach to full toleration.

During most of the nineteenth century, Church and state could be kept separate without much friction. The state's activities were restricted to a relatively few functions and churches seldom sought to influence the government. When Christians felt constrained by their faith to advocate legislative measures they usually acted as individuals or through organizations, such as the anti-slavery societies, created especially for that purpose rather than through ecclesiastical bodies. Only in education did Church and state tend to overlap, and even there conflict was infrequent.

The absence of an established church was accompanied by the presence in the United States of several denominations which in Europe were state churches. The Roman Catholics, the Greek Orthodox, the Anglicans, the Lutherans, and the Presbyterians had all, in one country or another, enjoyed the exclusive support of the state. Each of these groups carried to the United States a certain pride inherited from that Old Country tradition. No one, however, held the numerical preponderance which it had enjoyed in the land or lands where it was established by law, and none had either the social or the political prestige which it had possessed on the other side of the Atlantic.

A feature of the Christianity of the United States which came as a corollary of the separation of Church and state and which had begun to make its appearance in colonial days was voluntaryism. Churches were supported by the gifts of their constituencies and not by public taxation.

A characteristic of the religious situation which arose from the multiplicity of Christian denominations was the usual (although not universal) absence of the parish as a geographical entity. In lands of state churches where one ecclesiastical body had a monopoly or at least was in the ascendant, the country was usually divided into parishes and the people of each parish could be approached by the Church as a group. Where in a single village or rural district several different denominations were represented, as was often the case in the United States, each local congregation sought to reach individuals and families, but could not initiate a programme for the entire community. This handicap, if handicap it was, could easily be exaggerated. It fitted in with the individualism of American life, and in many community enterprises Christians of various denominations co-operated. However, repeatedly the divisions between the churches gave rise to divisions in the community itself.

The religious toleration and the associated separation of Church and state which were outstanding characteristics of the *milieu* in which the Christianity of the United States developed arose in part out of two other features of that Christianity. One was the fact that, due to the history of the original settlements, the Christianity of the United States was predominantly Protestant. To be sure, Roman Catholicism had been present in colonial days and became increasingly important numerically in the nineteenth and twentieth centuries. By 1914 various Eastern churches were added to the religious scene. Yet even in the twentieth century the Roman Catholic Church, while the largest single denomination, had only a minority of the church membership.[13] Even if the Eastern churches were added,[14] as late as 1916 Protestants still constituted fully three-fifths of the church membership. Moreover, as we saw in the last chapter, Protestant Christianity had a much larger share in shaping the culture of the nation than even this numerical strength would have given warrant to expect. The other feature was one to which we also referred in the last chapter, the fact that in this Protestantism the more radical wing was more strongly represented than in Europe.[15] It was radical Protestantism which in colonial days had from their inception made Rhode Island and, to a somewhat lesser extent, Pennsylvania havens of religious toleration. It was these elements which contributed largely to the separation of Church and state in Virginia.[16] The increase in the varieties of Protestantism made for religious toleration and

[13] In 1916 the Roman Catholic Church had approximately 37.7 per cent. and the Eastern churches less than .6 per cent. of the church membership.—U. S. Department of Commerce, Bureau of the Census, *Religious Bodies: 1926,* Part I, pp. 276ff.

[14] *Ibid.*

[15] On the Anglo-Saxon strain in this Protestantism, see Hall, *The Religious Background of American Culture, passim.*

[16] On this development of religious liberty and the separation of Church and state immediately before and after the Revolution, see Sanford H. Cobb, *The Rise of Religious Liberty in America. A History* (New York, The Macmillan Co., 1902, pp. xx, 541), pp. 482ff. The major part of this book deals with the colonial period. Henry R. McIlwaine, *The Struggle of Protestant Dissenters for Religious Toleration in Virginia* (Baltimore, The Johns Hopkins Press, 1894, pp. 67), is almost entirely confined to the colonial era. On the persecution of Baptists in Virginia which helped to precipitate the final and successful battle for religious liberty in that state, see Lewis Peyton Little, *Imprisoned Preachers and Religious Liberty in Virginia* (Lynchburg, Va., J. P. Bell Co., 1938, pp. xix, 534), *passim.* See also for the growth of dissent in Virginia and the achievement of religious liberty the well documented survey, John M. Mecklin, *The Story of American Dissent* (New York, Harcourt, Brace and Co., 1934, pp. 381), pp. 231ff.

the equality of the several churches before the law. Where an established church existed its privileged position was rendered peculiarly difficult by the growth of rival bodies. Some of the more radical groups, moreover, with their emphasis upon the priesthood of all believers and the duty of each Christian to follow his conscience as he felt himself guided by God, were from conviction advocates of toleration, at least of other Protestants, and tended to sever all ties between Church and state. Both of these policies were furthered by some who were not committed to any church but were governed chiefly by the liberal rationalism of the period.

The strength of the radical strains was largely responsible for another characteristic of much of American Protestantism, especially that of the older American stock. A marked tendency existed to ignore the developments which had taken place in Christianity in the Old World after the first century. A widely spread conviction held that these were corruptions of true Christianity and that, since the norm for the latter was to be found in the New Testament, additions were to be spurned. This trend had existed in several of the more extreme Protestant groups in Europe, but always these were small minorities overshadowed by great state churches which were conscious of a continuous history rooted in a long past. In the United States, however, the communions which in Europe were associated with the state were represented by minorities, even though large minorities, and in many quarters were regarded as at least semi-alien and not quite belonging to the American scene. Moreover, in the United States the atmosphere was one of fresh beginnings. All connected with the Old World was suspect. In the United States, so it was held, humanity was making a new start, unhampered by the dead hand of an evil past. Possibly this was in part begotten of radical Protestantism. Certainly it reinforced the latter. As a consequence of these several factors, the Protestant Christianity of the United States was more nearly divorced from what in the broad sense could be called Catholic Christianity, namely, that in which the majority of Christians since New Testament times had been nurtured, than any large body of Christians had ever been. Although the centuries since the New Testament had left traces even on radical Protestantism, in the latter less awareness existed of this long growth, except perhaps as repugnance to what was deemed a perversion of true Christianity, than there ever had been in any extensive segment of Christendom. It was this Christianity which was dominant in the United States.

The absence of a state church and the presence of so many different kinds of Christianity, including several which in Europe were espoused by the state, made it more difficult to speak of sects than in Europe. Unless it was radical

Protestantism, no one strain of Christianity was normative in the United States. No one had a substantial majority. Sects, in the sense of bodies which had split off from the majority church, could not be said to exist. To be sure, the term was occasionally used, but it was somewhat inaccurate when applied to the Christianity of the United States.

In most of the Christianity of the United States the lay element was more prominent than in several of the churches of Europe. In the majority of the churches, laymen shared in the administration. This was partly because of the belief in democracy. In a land in which all were supposed to be equal in the sight of the law and to be competent to share in the government, respect for a special clerical class was hard to maintain. Even in the Roman Catholic Church it was only after a painful struggle that the clergy succeeded in establishing their control. In Protestantism laymen and women became prominent in both national and local organizations. This was characteristic of much of radical Protestantism in Europe. It was emphasized in the United States. The funds for the support of the churches were derived overwhelmingly from the voluntary gifts of the laity. In the United States more than in Europe, the temper of Christianity was set by those who were giving most of their time and energy to non-ecclesiastical pursuits.

The Christianity of the United States tended to be activistic and to devote little attention to profound theological thought. Religious questions were widely debated, for nearly all felt themselves competent to discuss them. However, the trend was towards basing these discussions on concrete human needs rather than upon theological systems arrived at by *a priori* reasoning. There was much endeavour to transform society here and now. Movements for the reform of society flourished. This characteristic was from more than one source. It was in part from the Christianity of Western Europe, which for centuries had been more activistic than the quietistic Christianity of Eastern Europe. It was in part from radical Protestantism, which was inclined to stress the ethical aspects of Christianity. It was partly because, in a new country, men were too engrossed in the task of subduing the wilderness and building new institutions to take time for detached reflection. The life of the scholar could be possible only as wealth began to accumulate and a leisure class became feasible. The Protestant hostility to the monastic life with its emphasis on contemplation was probably also a factor.[17]

Still another feature of much of the Christianity of the United States was its spread and perpetuation by means of the revival. This was especially char-

[17] For a suggestion as to the fashion in which the frontier contributed to activism or "secularization," see Mode, *The Frontier Spirit in American Christianity*, pp. 146ff.

acteristic of the radical Protestantism of the older American stock. Popular mass movements had been seen before, not only in Christianity but also in other religions. In the United States they appear to have been accentuated in part by the frontier[18] and in part by the kind of Protestantism which spread on the frontier. Frontiersmen seem to have been peculiarly susceptible to the kind of group suggestion which accompanied the revivals. The denominations which flourished on the frontier, whether Calvinistic or Arminian, had a message which, with its denunciation of sin and its consequences, its appeal to repentance, and its assurance of joyous conversion, fitted in with this temper of mind.[19]

In the United States, moreover, the frontier spirit made for democracy. It is significant that denominations with a strongly democratic form of government, notably the Baptists and Disciples of Christ, flourished on the frontier. To be sure, the Methodists, with a less democratic type of organization, multiplied in that region. Yet in its organization of local groups and congregations Methodism also embodied much of democracy.

The Protestant churches which were strong on the frontier acquired the tradition of stressing the evil of certain customs which were characteristic of the new settlements, among them gambling, drunkenness, sexual irregularity, profanity, and the non-observance of Sunday. The struggle against these was not confined to the frontier, but the emphasis upon them as particularly heinous seems to have come from pioneer traditions.[20]

As we have earlier noted,[21] in their origin some denominations were peculiar to the frontier.

We must remind ourselves, however, that the frontier in itself did not ensure revivalism, democracy in the churches, activism, the attack on certain kinds of evils, or the emergence of new denominations. Certainly it did not have these consequences in Roman Catholic Latin America or French Canada. It was special types of Protestantism combined with the frontier which produced them.

One of the striking developments in the Protestant Christianity of the United States was the departure from Calvinistic theology in the denominations which were Calvinistic by tradition. Some of the most powerful and numerous bodies, notably the Congregationalists, the Presbyterians, and the large majority of the Baptists, possessed Calvinistic antecedents. Yet long before

[18] Mode, *op. cit.*, pp. 41ff.
[19] On an analysis of the effect of the frontier on religion, see M. E. Gaddis in *Church History*, Vol. II, pp. 152-170.
[20] Douglass, *Church Unity Movements in the United States*, p. 35.
[21] Vol. IV, chap. 6.

the close of the nineteenth century, except for conservative minorities, they had largely abandoned some of the most striking features of that system. In place of the doctrine of election they had substituted free will. From stressing man's total depravity and helpless sinfulness, they tended to believe him to be innately good and competent to achieve upon this planet an ideal human society. From awe before the sovereignty of God they inclined to swing to confidence in the human mind and spirit. The transition did not take place suddenly. In only a minority was it fully accomplished. The large majority still held to the divine initiative and power. A few professed to adhere to strict Calvinism. Yet the drift was away from determinism and towards free will and humanism.

This development was not confined to the United States. It was also found in Europe. Several of the same causes operated on both sides of the Atlantic. Some, however, were of American origin.

The relaxation of Calvinism was partly from the rationalism of the eighteenth century which persisted into the nineteenth century. The Deism which was so prominent in intellectual circles in eighteenth century Europe had repercussions in the United States. It profoundly influenced such leaders in the Revolutionary and early national period as Benjamin Franklin, George Washington, John Adams, Thomas Jefferson, and James Madison. It was not atheistic and had in it much of Christian origin, but it stressed man's competence to find truth and discounted revelation.[22] The modification of Calvinism was to no small degree the product of the optimism which marked the Occident of the nineteenth century. Then, too, in a new country such as the United States where success or failure in material things seemed to depend upon the initiative of the individual, the trend was to believe in man's ability. The departure from Calvinism was, however, to a large extent the outgrowth of the revivals of the eighteenth and nineteenth centuries. It is significant that the most prominent native-born leaders of these revivals, Jonathan Edwards, Charles G. Finney, and Dwight L. Moody, were all from New England or New England ancestry and hence from a background which had once been steeped in Calvinism. Yet strict Calvinism discouraged the kind of preaching which these men, especially the last two, represented. If a man's salvation were determined by the decree of God, if God's grace in effecting the salvation of the elect were irresistible, and if the elect, when saved, were certain to persevere in their new life, as extreme Calvinism declared, then preaching to

---

[22] For a semi-popular, sprightly account of the rise and decline of Deism in the United States, see Ernest Sutherland Bates, *American Faith. Its Religious, Political, and Economic Foundations* (New York, W. W. Norton & Co., 1940, pp. 479), pp. 218ff., 304ff.

induce men to repentance and faith was quite useless. However, some, after extreme anguish of soul, did find peace, seemingly through an act of volition and faith made through their own initiative.[23] The trend of the revivals was towards appealing to men as though all possessed sufficient free will to enable them really to repent and to assure men that God's love wished the salvation of all. Moreover, something in the spirit of the nineteenth century Occident rebelled against the idea of an inscrutable Divine decree which, apparently quite arbitrarily, chose some for salvation and left others, no matter of however great seeming virtue, limed by the universal human taint of sin, to be helplessly engulfed in eternal torment.[24] This appeared to them to be thoroughly unjust and contrary to the God whom they believed they saw in the New Testament. The revolt against some of the sterner features of Calvinism developed in several of the preachers of revivals. Thus, beginning with Edwards, and continuing through his disciple, Samuel Hopkins, and Nathaniel W. Taylor, something of a relaxation progressively occurred in the extreme Calvinistic restriction on the freedom of man's will.[25] Finney, taking up Taylor's ideas, argued for real freedom of the will,[26] called on his hearers "to make themselves a new heart and a new spirit, and pressed the duty of instant surrender to God."[27] Some of the leaders of the camp-meetings in the West who had been nurtured in Presbyterianism, among them Barton W. Stone, a pioneer in the formation of the Christian denomination, slighted or explicitly denied much of the Calvinistic system and acted on the assumption that all might find salvation.[28] For a number of years Transylvania University, prominent in the early educational life of Kentucky, in spite of a strong Presbyterian element in its board of trustees, had presidents who had departed from Calvinism.[29] The majority of Baptists on the frontier, while bearing traces of Calvinism, were inclined to hold that Christ died for all men.[30] Some, indeed, because of their rejection of Calvinism, withdrew from the denomination and joined the Christian movement.[31]

[23] This seems to have been the case in the conversion of the mother of Leonard Bacon, a distinguished Congregational clergyman.—Bacon, *Leonard Bacon*, p. 6.

[24] See *The Moral Argument against Calvinism* in *The Works of William Ellery Channing*, pp. 459ff.

[25] Foster, *A Genetic History of the New England Theology*, p. 247.

[26] Foster, *op. cit.*, p. 252.

[27] *Memoirs of Charles G. Finney*, pp. 189, 190.

[28] Garrison, *Religion Follows the Frontier*, p. 67.

[29] Niels Henry Sonne, *Liberal Kentucky 1780-1828* (New York, Columbia University Press, 1939, pp. ix, 287), *passim*.

[30] Sweet, *Religion on the American Frontier, The Baptists, 1783-1830*, p. 44.

[31] Fortune, *The Disciples of Kentucky*, pp. 67ff.

Much more extreme than the majority of Baptists in their departure from Calvinism, and also arising from revivals, were the Freewill Baptists. These had as their founder Benjamin Randall (1749-1808), who was born and reared in New England, was a convert of the Calvinistic Whitefield and for a time a member of a Congregational church, also Calvinistic. Randall became an indefatigable evangelist, preaching widely, chiefly in Vermont, New Hampshire, and Maine, then largely a frontier. He emphatically rejected the doctrine of election. Other itinerant preachers followed up his labours. True to the fruits of much of the revivalism of the period, the Freewill Baptists were anti-slavery, anti-Masonic, and pro-temperance.[32] Eventually, as the majority of Baptists moved farther away from Calvinism, the two denominations coalesced.

Largely although not entirely out of Calvinism came two denominations, the Unitarians and the Universalists, who departed more rapidly and radically from it than did the leaders of the revivals. Both embodied opinions which had long been represented in the Christian movement on the other side of the Atlantic. Unitarianism was especially strong around Boston. There it took form in the latter part of the eighteenth and the beginning of the nineteenth century. It had as one of its early champions Jonathan Mayhew, from the family which for several generations had been missionaries to the Indians on Martha's Vineyard, and as a slightly later exponent William Ellery Channing, who as a youth had sat under the preaching of Samuel Hopkins. Both were in the stream of that Calvinism which had sought to propagate the Christian faith and so had been confronted with the problem presented by determinism. Unitarianism was also in part a reaction of the well-to-do and educated circles in and around prosperous Boston against the emotional phases of revivalism. It was as well a development from a chronic resentment against a feature of New England Puritanism, the separation of the community into church members, the elect, and non-church members. Some of the Unitarian pioneers believed in the ultimate salvation of all human souls, but the denomination which bore the name of Universalist had its inception chiefly through the preaching of John Murray, English-born and Calvinist-reared, who, after disavowing Calvinism, came to America in 1770 and preached fairly widely. It was in New England that the denomination had its chief hold and it was Hosea Ballou, the son of a New England Baptist clergyman, who was its most eminent and influential preacher. Both denominations spread to other parts of the country, and some in other fellowships shared their views,

---

[32] *Dictionary of American Biography*, Vol. XV, pp. 345, 346; Newman, *A History of the Baptists of the United States*, pp. 269-271, 495-499.

but both drew their chief strength from a constituency which had been nurtured in New England Calvinism.[33]

The majority of the churches of the Standing Order in New England remained in what became orthodox Congregationalism. However, this Congregationalism moved, although more slowly, in the direction taken by the Unitarian and Universalist dissidents.[34] Periodic controversy marked the transition. By the close of the nineteenth century Andover Theological Seminary, which had been founded as a centre of the older views, was manned by a faculty which held liberal positions.[35] Since Unitarianism eventually departed much more widely from the convictions embodied in the main stream of historic Christianity than had its early leaders, orthodox Congregationalism continued to be more conservative, but by 1914 it had travelled much farther from the Calvinism of the fathers than would once have been deemed possible.

Presbyterianism also was affected. The stream of New England liberalism embodied in the New Haven Theology of Nathaniel W. Taylor which entered through co-operation with the Congregationalists and the Plan of Union for winning the frontier brought in a strong element which journeyed far from historic Calvinism. The elements of Scotch and Scotch-Irish ancestry proved more resistant. Strains developed which led for some decades in the middle of the nineteenth century to separation between the two into the Old School and the New School. By the end of the third decade, reunion had been achieved in the northern branch of the denomination. While, in general, partly because of an ecclesiastical structure which was less hospitable to change, Presbyterianism did not depart so decidedly from Calvinism as did Congregationalism, by 1914 large elements in its northern wing had gone a great distance in that direction.

As the decades passed, a minority in several denominations of Calvinist provenance became extreme humanists. They not only abandoned the doctrine of election, but also rejected the sovereignty and even the independent existence of God. To them God became a symbol for the highest human aspirations and without reality apart from the minds of men. Interestingly enough,

---

[33] Joseph Henry Allen and Richard Eddy, *A History of the Unitarians and the Universalists in the United States* (New York, The Christian Literature Co., 1894, pp. ix, 506), *passim*. On one of the leaders in the early struggle against Unitarianism, see James King Morse, *Jedidiah Morse. A. Champion of New England Orthodoxy* (New York, Columbia University Press, 1939, pp. ix, 180), *passim*.

[34] See an account of several of the Congregational leaders of thought, mostly of the latter part of the nineteenth and the opening years of the twentieth century, in John Wright Buckham, *Progressive Religious Thought in America. A Survey of the Enlarging Pilgrim Faith* (Boston, Houghton Mifflin Co., 1919, pp. 352), *passim*.

[35] Frank Hugh Foster, *The Life of Edwards Amasa Park* (New York, Fleming H. Revell Co., 1936, pp. 275), *passim*.

a chief centre of this view was in the University of Chicago, an institution founded by the formerly Calvinistic Baptists, and in the Middle West, the heir of frontier evangelism.

It may also be significant that the two leading pragmatists among the philosophers of the United States, William James and John Dewey, came from backgrounds which had once been permeated with Calvinism. They, too, in part marked a reaction against it, although they were not the founders of religious cults.

It was not only Calvinism which was modified or abandoned as the nineteenth century progressed. The impact of current thought also led to changes in other teachings of the churches. The theory of evolution associated with the name of Charles R. Darwin and hence dubbed Darwinism seemed to negate the traditional beliefs about the creation and early history of man. Geology and biology appeared to render obsolete the Biblical account of the origin of the universe. New methods of handling historical documents when applied to the Scriptures disturbed many by denying cherished convictions concerning the authorship and the accuracy of some of the books in that venerated volume. Anthropology, by tracing the origin of religion and the belief in immortality, seemed to discredit both. Numbers of sensitive, honest souls felt their faith undermined. Many critics rejoiced in new weapons with which to attack Christianity and the churches. Within the leadership of the churches strong differences developed over these views. Some hotly rejected them and elaborated arguments to refute them. Others accepted them in whole or in part and made room for them in their interpretation of the Christian faith.[36]

In general, the religious bodies most permeated by the new thought were those descended from the radical wing of Protestantism, including the ones in which the revolt against Calvinism had occurred. This was the Christianity which had been most potent in shaping the United States. The newer bodies whose strength was in the more recent immigration, notably the Roman Catholics and the majority of the Lutherans, were less flexible and in general maintained their theologies and dogmas unmodified. In any one denomination the elements most affected were usually the best educated and hence of the higher income levels.

To many it seemed that the denominations heretofore dominant in the life of the land were suffering fatal disintegration. A common opinion held that

[36] The history of the struggle, embracing a much longer period than the nineteenth century, but also including the latter, is in Andrew Dickson White, *A History of the Warfare of Science with Theology in Christendom* (New York, D. Appleton Co., 2 vols., 1896), *passim.*

they were being hopelessly weakened by internal dissensions over the new learning and that science was sapping their foundations. That many individuals were perplexed and had their faith unnerved or destroyed was incontestable. On the other hand, it is significant that most of these denominations continued their numerical growth, some of them more markedly than several of the strongest of the ultra-conservative Protestant and non-Protestant bodies.[37] That this growth was accompanied by deep conviction is seen in the phenomenal increase in the support from these churches for the foreign missionary enterprise. It was in the decades immediately before 1914 that the Protestant denominations of the United States, and largely those most penetrated by the new learning, began forging ahead into the leadership of the Protestant foreign missionary enterprise. Moreover, it was from the students, the class most shaped by the new intellectual currents, that this leadership came. The decades in which "Darwinism" and the "higher criticism" were making their chief headway were also those in which the Student Volunteer Movement for Foreign Missions had its phenomenal growth. Some of the reform movements which had their rise and much of their support in this radical Protestantism also flourished as never before—among them that for the abolition of the liquor traffic, the campaign for greater opportunities for women, and the "social gospel." There was in this Protestant Christianity a vitality which might be hampered by the new science but which, at least until 1914, was not held back from amazing and increasing achievements.

The great variety presented by the Christianity of the United States, the absence of a state church, and the presence of legal toleration led to at least three results within that Christianity. It made for the interpenetration of one kind of Christianity by another, to an impatience with the divisions within the Christian body, and to the beginnings of co-operation between denominations. The effects were most conspicuous in the Protestantism of the older stock, partly because it had been longest subjected to the American environment. Yet these three features were not confined to the United States. They were also to be found in Protestant Canada and on the other side of the Atlantic, notably in the British Isles. Here were general movements, particularly strong in Anglo-Saxon circles.

The interpenetration took many forms. In the endless debates, public and

[37] See comparative figures for 1906, 1916, and 1926 in U. S. Department of Commerce, Bureau of the Census, *Religious Bodies: 1926,* Vol. I, pp. 276ff. Thus between 1906 and 1916 the growth of the conservative Missouri Synod (Lutheran) was less than 18 per cent., that of the Roman Catholics about 11 per cent., while (to pick some of the larger denominations most affected by the new views) that of the Congregationalists was about 12.5 per cent., that of the Northern Baptist Convention about 18 per cent., that of the Methodist Episcopal Church about 25 per cent., and that of the Presbyterian Church in the U. S. A. (Northern) nearly 30 per cent.

private, on religious subjects, ideas from one group entered another, sometimes provoking heightened opposition and sometimes issuing in partial
acceptance. Forms of public and private worship, especially in non-liturgical
denominations, tended to display identical patterns. Many of the hymns, with
the ideas which they embodied, were common property and crossed denominational lines. Frequently the same hymnals were utilized in congregations of
several different religious bodies. A single book might contain hymns by
Roman Catholics, Anglicans, Lutherans, Presbyterians, Quakers, Congregationalists, and Baptists. Members of more than one denomination rubbed
shoulders in joint religious and social efforts in such organizations as the Young
Men's and Young Women's Christian Associations, the Young People's Societies of Christian Endeavour, student Christian groups, and various reform
societies. The same Sunday School lessons and often the same commentaries
on the lessons were used in the church schools of congregations of more than
one ecclesiastical affiliation. There was, in consequence, a trend towards a common type of Christianity. To this the Roman Catholics, the Eastern churches,
and the newer Lutheran bodies were more unyielding than were most of the
others.

The unhappiness over the fissiparousness of the Christianity of the land
showed itself in many ways. We have already described the fashion in which
it led to congregations and denominations bearing the name of Christian or
Disciples of Christ which sought to bring all together on a fresh and simple
basis.[38] Such organizations as the American Tract Society, the American Bible
Society, and the American Home Missionary Society, in which members of
several denominations worked together, were also an expression. In 1792
Bishop Madison, of the Protestant Episcopal Church, proposed a plan for a
union of the Methodists with that body.[39] In 1882 a clergyman of the Protestant
Episcopal Church took steps which he hoped would lead to a union with
non-Episcopal churches.[40] In 1838 the liberal Lutheran, Samuel S. Schmucker,
who had enjoyed intimate contacts with more than one denomination, issued
a *Fraternal Appeal to the American Churches, with a Plan for Catholic Union
on Apostolic Principles*,[41] in which he suggested a federation which would not
abolish existing denominations or do violence to doctrines held by any one and

[38] Vol. IV, chap. 6.
[39] Tiffany, *A History of the Protestant Episcopal Church in the United States of
America*, p. 388.
[40] Slosser, *Christian Unity*, p. 337.
[41] S. S. Schmucker, *Fraternal Appeal to the American Churches, with a Plan for Catholic Union on Apostolic Principles* (New York, 2d ed., Gould and Newman, 1839,
pp. 149), *passim*. The preface to the first edition is dated March 26, 1838. See also
S. S. Schmucker, *Overture for Christian Union Submitted for the Consideration of the
Evangelical Denominations in the United States . . . 1838*—text in Sanford, *Origin and
History of the Federal Council of the Churches of Christ in America*, pp. 404-419.

believed by him to be true, but which would be based upon the Apostles' Creed and a *United Protestant Confession* stating the faith common to all orthodox Protestant bodies and among whose members there should be "free sacramental, ecclesiastical, and ministerial communion." Already, in December, 1835, a proposal had been made for a Christian union dedicated to the termination of religious controversy and to combining the efforts of Christians against evil.[42] In 1839, largely in consequence of Schmucker's appeal, a society for promoting Christian union was formed. Schmucker's initiative also contributed to the organization, in 1846, of the English Evangelical Alliance and, in 1867, of the American Evangelical Alliance.[43]

In spite of the recrudescence about the middle of the nineteenth century of strong denominational particularism and inter-denominational competition, the undercurrent, aided by the logic of the multiplicity of denominations, had set too strongly towards co-operation to be checked. An international meeting of the Evangelical Alliance held in New York City in 1873 gave a strong impetus to the movement.[44] In this conference the eminent scholar and church historian, Philip Schaff, German by birth and training but American by adoption, was a leading figure. Through his long advocacy of Christian union he gave marked stimulus to the co-operation of Christians both in the United States and throughout the world.[45] In the 1880's an American Congress of Churches held two annual meetings.[46] Out of a meeting of the state conference of Congregational Churches in 1890 issued the Interdenominational Commission of Maine, in which four denominations joined in the organization and maintenance of churches, partly in the effort to prevent wasteful duplication of effort in the smaller towns.[47] In 1895 came the New York (City) Federation of Churches.[48] In 1899 the Connecticut Bible Society in which, since its inauguration in 1809, members of several denominations had shared, took action favouring a Connecticut State Federation of Churches.[49] In 1894 an interdenominational fellowship, the Open and Institutional Church League, was formed with the comprehensive and ambitious purpose "to save all men, by all means, abolishing so far as possible the distinction between the religious

[42] Harlow, *Gerrit Smith*, p. 197.
[43] Slosser, *op. cit.*, p. 178.
[44] Schaff and Prime, *History, Essays, Orations and Other Documents of the Sixth General Conference of the Evangelical Alliance . . . 1873, passim.*
[45] David S. Schaff, *The Life of Philip Schaff, in Part Autobiographical* (New York, Charles Scribner's Sons, 1897, pp. xv, 526), pp. 252ff.
[46] Sanford, *op. cit.*, p. 113.
[47] Sanford, *op. cit.*, p. 104.
[48] Charles S. Macfarland, *The Progress of Church Federation* (Chicago, Fleming H. Revell Co., 1917, pp. 188), p. 28.
[49] Sanford, *op. cit.*, pp. 104-107.

and the secular, and sanctifying all days and all means to the great end of saving the world for Christ."[50] In 1900, out of a meeting in New York City, sprang the National Committee on Federation of Churches.[51] Later in that same year the Federation of Churches and Christian Workers of the State of New York was organized.[52] By 1901 several city and state bodies were in existence, usually with the name of Evangelical Alliance or Federation of Churches and Christian Workers. In 1901 these sent delegates to a conference in Philadelphia which resulted in the formation of the National Federation of Churches and Christian Workers.[53] From this arose, in 1908, the Federal Council of the Churches of Christ in America.[54] On this latter body the member denominations were officially represented. It was, therefore, an agency through which Protestants of several denominations co-operated, not as individuals, but through delegates appointed by their respective churches. In addition to this central organization of the churches, the home mission societies formed, also in 1908, the Home Missions Council.[55] The foreign mission societies had already, in 1893, come together in the Foreign Missions Conference of North America.[56] Here and there were unions of similar denominations. Thus, in 1858, most of the Associate Synod (Secession) and of the Associate Reformed Synod (Secession and Covenanter), ultra-conservative Presbyterian bodies, fused to form the United Presbyterian Church of North America.[57]

Projects for co-operation and for the dimming of denominational lines were by no means confined to the United States. They were occurring in Protestantism in other lands, notably in those where Christianity was being freshly introduced. However, they were, in general, making more rapid progress in the United States than across the Atlantic. This was in large part because of the environment. The new *milieu*, with its lessened emphasis on tradition, its air of experimentation, and its multiplicity of Christian bodies which were all equal in the eye of the law, greatly favoured them. The movement was gathering momentum and was to proceed even more rapidly after 1914. In comparison with the total church membership of the country, denominations were less numerous in 1916 than in 1906 and were still fewer in 1926.[58]

[50] Sanford, *op. cit.*, pp. 34-37.
[51] Sanford, *op. cit.*, pp. 112-117.
[52] Sanford, *op. cit.*, p. 129.
[53] Sanford, *op. cit.*, p. 146.
[54] Sanford, *op. cit.*, pp. 244ff.
[55] Douglass, *The New Home Missions*, p. 208.
[56] Moss, *Adventures in Missionary Cooperation*, pp. 9, 10.
[57] U. S. Department of Commerce, Bureau of the Census, *Religious Bodies: 1926*, Vol. II, p. 1159.
[58] Douglass, *Church Unity Movements in the United States*, p. 3.

The strong movement towards co-operation and unity did not prevent the emergence of new denominations. These were in part an indication of the abounding vitality of the Protestant Christianity of the United States. They gave evidence that the Christian impulse was a continuing source of fresh conviction which expressed itself in new and original ways. They also were in part the result of the environment. It may be significant that the majority of the new religious bodies which arose in the United States sprang from the Protestantism of the older stock, or, in other words, from that Christianity which had been longest subjected to the American setting. To catalogue fully the many denominations of American origin would needlessly prolong these pages. Several of the most notable, including the outstanding ones which were in part the product of the frontier, the Cumberland Presbyterians, the Christians, the Disciples of Christ, and the Mormons, have already been mentioned.[59] So, too, have some of those which emerged in the course of the transplanting of Lutheranism to the United States, from the contacts of Pietism and Methodism with those of German descent,[60] from the spread of Christianity among the Negroes,[61] and as a protest against the earlier orthodoxy of New England.[62] Here we need only to call attention to a few of the new bodies which thus far have not appeared in our narrative.

One of the most remarkable religious fellowships of American origin was the one bearing the organized name of the Church of Christ, Scientist, and teaching what was called Christian Science.[63] Like so many of the American groups of nineteenth century origin, it was an offshoot of New England. It is a striking fact of religious history that the two largest denominations of American birth which departed the most widely from historic Christianity, Mormonism and Christian Science, sprang from leaders of New England ancestry. The founder of Christian Science was Mary Morse Baker Eddy (1821-1910). Born in New England, reared in a devout home, and in early life a member of a Congregational church, she was surrounded by the atmosphere

[59] Vol. IV, Chap. 6.
[60] Vol. IV, Chap. 7.
[61] Vol. IV, Chap. 9.
[62] See above, in this chapter.
[63] One account, professing to be based upon research in official archives and manuscript material and distinctly favourable to Mrs. Eddy, is Lyman P. Powell, *Mary Baker Eddy. A Life Size Portrait* (New York, The Macmillan Co., 1930, pp. xii, 364). Another account, also professing to be based on extensive research in pertinent sources, but very critical of Mrs. Eddy and damaging to her, is Edwin Franden Dakin, *Mrs. Eddy. The Biography of a Virginal Mind* (New York, Charles Scribner's Sons, 1930, pp. x, 563). Ernest Sutherland Bates and John V. Dittemore, *Mary Baker Eddy. The Truth and the Tradition* (New York, Alfred A. Knopf, 1932, pp. 476, xxxiv), utilizes manuscript material and is, in general, objective. An extensive sketch, somewhat critical, is in *Dictionary of American Biography*, Vol. VI, pp. 7-14.

of New England Christianity. Sensitive, subject to what seem to have been nervous disorders and hysteria, from childhood she was frail and in much of her early womanhood she was for long periods an invalid or semi-invalid. She obtained great relief—indeed, what she believed to be health—through Phineas Parkhurst Quimby. Quimby was also a product of New England and, like Mrs. Eddy, without much formal education.[64] He had familiarized himself with mesmerism and had become a faith-healer. He seems to have been honest, entirely unselfish, and a man of marked beauty of character. Although he held orthodox Christianity in disdain, he developed an elaborate Christology which, in its separation of the divine Christ from the human Jesus, resembled some of the variants of Christianity of the early centuries. Sometimes he termed his system "Science" or "Christian Science." Mrs. Eddy derived many of her basic ideas from him but modified them and added to them. She was probably also much indebted to a pupil of Quimby, Warren Felt Evans, successively a Methodist clergyman, a Swedenborgian, and a faith-healer.[65] She attracted disciples and taught them. She was a voluminous writer, but the core of her system—if it may be called such—was in a volume, *Science and Health,* which was first published in 1875 and which went through many revised editions.[66] In 1875 an informal group of her students termed themselves Christian Scientists. The following year they formed the Christian Scientists' Association. In 1879 the Church of Christ, Scientist, was chartered in Massachusetts. Headquarters, for a time at Lynn in that state, were moved to Boston and remained there. In 1886 the National Christian Science Association was formed. Mrs. Eddy proved an astute and able organizer. She devised a structure for the movement which placed a great amount of authority at the centre. Although long officially in retirement, she remained the directing spirit until the infirmities of old age and prolonged illness made this impossible. The Church of Christ, Scientist, enjoyed a rapid growth. Its chief appeal was its assurance of physical healing. It was almost entirely an urban denomination, and its spread coincided with the great increase in the population of cities at the close of the nineteenth and in the opening decades of the twentieth century. In 1890 it was said to have 8,724, in 1906 about 85,000, and in 1926 about 202,000 members.[67] Its propagation was largely by means of the printed page. Although it attracted much attention, the Church of Christ, Scientist, did not become in

[64] *Dictionary of American Biography,* Vol. XV, pp. 304, 305.

[65] *Dictionary of American Biography,* Vol. VI, p. 213.

[66] What is called the two hundred and first edition is Mary Baker G. Eddy, *Science and Health with Key to the Scriptures* (Boston, Joseph Armstrong, 1900, pp. xii, 663).

[67] U. S. Department of Commerce, Bureau of the Census, *Religious Bodies: 1926,* Vol. II, pp. 348, 349.

numbers a major denomination. Nor did it equal in size that other offspring from the New England stock which was also a striking departure from the main stream of historic Christianity, the Church of Jesus Christ of Latter Day Saints.[68]

It is interesting that a smaller movement, New Thought, stemmed from Quimby through Julius Dresser.[69]

It was also from men of New England birth that there arose another set of movements of distinctly American origin and owing much to the temper of the country, those which looked for the early second coming of Christ. The pioneer was William Miller (1782-1849).[70] He was born in Western Massachusetts and grew to manhood in New York. A farmer, with slight formal education, but an eager student, he rose to positions of trust in his community. After a severe inward struggle he experienced conversion and from long pondering on the Bible became convinced that Jesus was to return in 1843. With compelling sincerity he began preaching to warn his hearers to prepare for the great event. His views were given wide publicity by Joshua Vaughan Himes,[71] who had been born in Rhode Island, had been pastor of one of the Christian churches, and was an abolitionist and an organizer of the Non-Resistance Society. With this radical history it was not surprising that Himes was won by Miller's views. The movement attracted nation-wide attention. When the first date, in 1843, passed uneventfully, October 22, 1844, was fixed. As the hour approached, great excitement prevailed. The second disappointment shook the faith of many but not of all. Miller remained the nominal head of the adventist church which had been formed for his followers.[72]

The largest group of those who had their rise from Miller were the Seventh Day Adventists.[73] They owed their practice of keeping the seventh instead of the first day to contact with Seventh Day Baptists. Their real founder was Mrs. Ellen G. White, a prophetess. Although in 1916 numbering only about eighty thousand,[74] they were ardent missionaries and propagated their views throughout most of the world.

[68] In 1890 the Church of Jesus Christ of Latter Day Saints had 144,352, in 1906, 215,-796, and in 1926, 542,194 members.—U. S. Department of Commerce, Bureau of the Census, *Religious Bodies: 1926*, Vol. II, p. 669.

[69] *Dictionary of American Biography*, Vol. XV, p. 305.

[70] *Dictionary of American Biography*, Vol. XII, p. 641. For a semi-official history of the Adventists, based upon careful research in the records and including an account of Miller, see M. Ellsworth Olsen, *A History of the Origin and Progress of Seventh-Day Adventists, passim.*

[71] *Dictionary of American Biography*, Vol. IX, pp. 60, 61.

[72] See Clark, *The Small Sects of America*, pp. 43ff., for a brief history of the movement and the organized denomination.

[73] Olsen, *op. cit.*, pp. 177ff.; Clark, *op. cit.*, pp. 50ff.

[74] U. S. Department of Commerce, Bureau of the Census, *Religious Bodies: 1926*, Vol. II, p. 18.

The emergence of Mormonism, Christian Science, New Thought, and the Adventists from the stream of the religious life of New England was not an isolated phenomenon. These groups, indeed, were only a small part of the wave of religious, social, and intellectual idealism which issued from that section. To make the picture as well-rounded as the reality, one must recall that it was in New England that the first two large societies formed with the purpose of carrying the Christian message to the non-Christian world had their rise; that from New England came much of the effort for winning the frontier; that the three outstanding leaders of the revival movement, Edwards, Finney, and Moody, were born in New England; that at least three other denominations, Unitarianism, Universalism, and the Free Will Baptists, had their early development largely in New England; that New Englanders took an outstanding part in the creation of many of the societies for social reform, among them those against slavery and war; that several of the progressive movements in education were initiated by New Englanders; and that a disproportionate number of the men and women of letters of the nineteenth century were of New England stock. Something in the New England environment seems to have been responsible for this burst of creative energy. Significantly it showed itself in the realm of the spirit more than in political administration or in business—although it was by no means absent from these latter phases of the nation's life. The source seems chiefly to have been in that religious radicalism of the extreme wing of Protestant Christianity which had so large a part in the settlement of New England, and which, through the structure of the Standing Order, gave form and unity to the cultural pattern of the section. It was not until after the traditional New England was depleted by the vast westward migration and by the influx of the prodigious nineteenth and twentieth century European immigration of quite different racial and religious composition that the stream dwindled.

New denominations came by no means exclusively from the New England environment. The majority of them had other origins. A movement known variously as Jehovah's Witnesses, the International Bible Students' Association, the Watch Tower, and the Russellites was created and at first controlled by Charles Taze Russell (1852-1916).[75] Russell was born in Pittsburgh, Pennsylvania, of Scotch-Irish descent. He revolted against the doctrine of everlasting punishment which he heard preached in the Congregational church in which

[75] Milton Stacey Czatt, *The International Bible Students. Jehovah's Witnesses* (Scottdale, Pa., Mennonite Press, 1933, pp. 44); [C. T. Russell], *Studies in the Scriptures* (Series 1-7, International Bible Students' Association, 1917-1923); [C. T. Russell], *Millennial Dawn* (Pittsburgh, Pa., Zion's *Watch Tower*, 3 vols., 1886-1891); Clark, *op. cit.*, pp. 58ff.; *Dictionary of American Biography*, Vol. XVI, p. 240.

he was reared. On the basis of his own study of the Bible he arrived at the belief that Jesus was to come in invisible form in 1874. His teachings as eventually developed repudiated the Trinity, included no mention of the Holy Spirit, declared that death brings total annihilation but that in the millennium the dead will be recreated and that an evangelistic campaign will be carried on among them, and that since the second coming occurred in 1874 the millennium has already begun. All churches, both Protestant and Roman Catholic, were denounced as rejected by God. Russell travelled and preached widely. In spite of serious charges brought against him of financial and sexual irregularities, about twelve hundred congregations arose, with him as their theoretical pastor, in the United States, Canada, the British Isles, and Europe. The movement spread among the Negroes in Africa and there produced serious political complications.[76] Indeed, Russell prepared the way for these by teaching that since the millennial age and the day of Jehovah had already dawned, very shortly an international revolt of the working classes would occur with the reduction of society to chaos and that this would be followed by the resurrection and the last judgment. After Russell's death the leadership devolved upon J. F. Rutherford who insisted that the final battle between Christ and Satan would soon be fought and that hence "millions now living will never die."

In the course of the nineteenth and twentieth centuries, several small denominations arose which taught the possibility of perfection as part of the essence of the Christian faith. Usually, moreover, they protested against what they deemed the moral laxity of the larger denominations. Finney had preached a type of perfectionism. Methodism, too, had made much of what was termed sanctification. Most of the small groups which stressed the attainment of freedom from sin were offshoots from Methodism. In 1843 the Wesleyan Methodists separated from the parent body from the conviction that a more pronounced attitude should be taken against Negro slavery. Later they stressed "entire sanctification" as cleansing from "all inbred sin."[77] The Free Methodists came into existence in 1860 after a prolonged agitation against what they adjudged as laxity in morals and doctrine and too much autocracy in the Methodist Episcopal Church. They also emphasized salvation from all inward sin.[78] After the Civil War, in part in protest against the moral disintegration which followed that conflict, a Holiness Movement sprang up, largely out of Methodism, which preached a "second blessing" beyond conversion and an

---

[76] *The International Review of Missions*, Vol. XXIX, pp. 216ff.
[77] U. S. Department of Commerce, Bureau of the Census, *Religious Bodies: 1926*, Vol. II, pp. 950, 951.
[78] U. S. Department of Commerce, Bureau of the Census, *Religious Bodies: 1926*, Vol. II, pp. 980-983; Clark, *op. cit.*, p. 85.

ensuing perfection of life. A National Camp Meeting Association for the Promotion of Holiness and then a Holiness Union appeared.[79] Such denominations as the Pentecostal Holiness Church,[80] the Pentecostal Assemblies of the World,[81] the Holiness Methodist Church,[82] the Church of God,[83] the Church of the Nazarene,[84] the Peniel Missions,[85] and the Pilgrim Holiness Church[86] in general embodied these views. The Assemblies of God and the Apostolic Faith Mission made much not only of sanctification but also of divine healing, speaking with tongues, and the early second coming of Christ.[87] Some were highly emotional and in their meetings reproduced phenomena earlier associated with camp-meetings. Several of them, however, far from being rural, began in the third of a century before 1914 and had their following chiefly from among the proletariat in the cities which grew so rapidly in that period.

The Christian Catholic Church in Zion founded in 1896 by a native of Scotland, John Alexander Dowie, taught faith-healing, and was notable for the community established at Zion City, Illinois, in 1901, which it was hoped was to be governed by its ideals.[88]

The Baptists were congregationally organized and, accordingly, readily developed variety. Although by the end of the nineteenth century the overwhelming majority were associated with one of the three larger national bodies—the Northern Baptist Convention, the Southern Baptist Convention, and the National Baptist Convention (made up of Negroes)—smaller numbers existed in other groups bearing the Baptist name.[89] Some of these, such as the Primitive Baptists, had their strength chiefly in rural regions in the South, where conditions perpetuated much of the atmosphere of the frontier. The Primitive Baptists, numerically the second largest of these minorities of American origin, were staunch Calvinists and protested against an educated clergy, Sunday

[79] Clark, op. cit., pp. 92, 93.
[80] U. S. Department of Commerce, Bureau of the Census, Religious Bodies: 1926, Vol. II, pp. 1094, 1095.
[81] U. S. Department of Commerce, Bureau of the Census, Religious Bodies: 1926, Vol. II, pp. 1086ff.
[82] U. S. Department of Commerce, Bureau of the Census, Religious Bodies: 1926, Vol. II, pp. 989, 990.
[83] U. S. Department of Commerce, Bureau of the Census, Religious Bodies: 1926, Vol. II, pp. 367-369.
[84] U. S. Department of Commerce, Bureau of the Census, Religious Bodies: 1926, Vol. II, pp. 388-393.
[85] Clark, op. cit., pp. 102, 103.
[86] U. S. Department of Commerce, Bureau of the Census, Religious Bodies: 1926, Vol. II, pp. 1100-1104.
[87] Clark, op. cit., pp. 134, 135.
[88] Dictionary of American Biography, Vol. V, pp. 413, 414.
[89] For a number of these see U. S. Department of Commerce, Bureau of the Census, Religious Bodies: 1926, Vol. II, pp. 130ff.

Schools, and missionary societies.[90] The largest of the American-born Baptist minorities, the Baptist General Association (later the American Baptist Association), was organized in 1905. They were often dubbed the "Landmarkers." They were extremely conservative. They also claimed that their local associations were directly descended from the time of Christ—a kind of apostolic succession.[91]

A movement which displayed traces of Christian influence but which departed widely from much of traditional Christianity was Spiritualism. Its distinctive belief was the possibility of communication with the dead. It is usually dated as having begun with the Fox sisters in 1848, but the phraseology and underlying principles came chiefly from Andrew Jackson Davis (1826-1910). It taught that growth continues after death and preached social reconstruction as well as spiritual regeneration.[92]

Most of these new bodies arose out of Protestantism. Here and there, however, were a very few which sprang from others of the main branches of Christianity. Of these the largest was the Polish National Catholic Church of America.[93] It came into existence from friction between Polish Roman Catholic immigrants and their ecclesiastical superiors. It began a formal existence in 1904 and its head, a Roman Catholic priest, obtained episcopal consecration through the Old Catholic bishops of Holland.

Although these past few paragraphs must give the impression of a rapid division of organized Christianity under the religious liberty and absence of coercion by the state which existed in the United States, as a matter of fact throughout this period the vast majority of those possessing a church connexion were affiliated with religious bodies which had their origin on the other side of the Atlantic. Even in 1914 it was only a small minority of the total, probably not as many as one-tenth, who belonged to denominations of purely American creation. It was with denominations of European or Eastern birth that the great majority of the Christians of the United States had fellowship.

Yet these transplanted denominations usually departed somewhat from those from which they were sprung. Nearly every one of them presented differences in temper and organization from the parent European bodies.

---

[90] H. L. Poe in *The Chronicle*, Vol. II, pp. 51-64.
[91] U. S. Department of Commerce, Bureau of the Census, *Religious Bodies: 1926*, Vol. II, pp. 224-227.
[92] Weigle, *American Idealism*, pp. 172, 173; *Dictionary of American Biography*, Vol. V, p. 105; U. S. Department of Commerce, Bureau of the Census, *Religious Bodies: 1926*, Vol. II, pp. 1314ff.
[93] U. S. Department of Commerce, Bureau of the Census, *Religious Bodies: 1926*, Vol. II, pp. 1108-1111.

Some generalizations can be made which apply to several of the churches which were carried to the United States.

In the first place, the imported denominations tended to conform to the political framework of the country. Several of them formed national organizations in the days when the Federal Constitution was being framed and the Federal Government initiated.[94] Others did so later. Several, too, developed state organizations within the national structure.

In the second place, several denominations were sectional. Three denominations which had been nation-wide, the Methodists, the Baptists, and the Presbyterians,[95] separated over the question of slavery into Northern and Southern wings. After the Civil War and the abolition of slavery the division continued. During the Civil War the Southern dioceses withdrew from the Protestant Episcopal Church and organized a Confederate Church. Shortly after the war, however, reunion was effected.[96] In general, the Southern denominations, since they were in a region less quickly affected by the new intellectual and social currents which were sweeping the country, remained more conservative theologically than the corresponding ones in the North. A number of other denominations, although in theory national, in membership tended to be sectional. Because relatively few New Englanders moved South, Congregationalism remained almost entirely Northern. Methodists had been particularly active in carrying the Christian message to the frontier. They were, accordingly, stronger west of the Appalachians than in the older sections of the North east. The Disciples of Christ, being chiefly of frontier origin and development, had their stronghold in the West. Baptists were especially numerous in the South, among both whites and Negroes.

A third generalization is that, in general, denominations were inclined to follow racial and national divisions inherited from the other side of the Atlantic.[97] Those of Anglo-Saxon descent were chiefly in certain Protestant denominations which were also strong in Great Britain. Most of the Negro Christians were in denominations peculiarly their own. Lutherans were divided among those of German, Danish, Norwegian, Swedish, and Icelandic descent. There was a Dutch Reformed Church, a German Reformed Church, and a Hungarian Reformed Church. The United Brethren and the Evangelical Association were mainly among those of German ancestry. Methodists, Baptists, and Congregationalists had special organizations among Germans. Swedish Bap-

---

[94] Sweet, *The Story of Religions in America*, p. 9.
[95] On the Presbyterians, see Vander Velde, *The Presbyterian Churches and the Federal Union, 1861-1869, passim*.
[96] Shanks in *Church History*, Vol. IX, pp. 120-140.
[97] Niebuhr, *The Social Sources of Denominationalism*, pp. 106, 107.

tists, Danish Baptists, and Norwegian Baptists possessed their own congregations. The Eastern Orthodox churches organized according to the Old World groupings of their constituencies. Even the strong, comprehensive structure of the Roman Catholics was unable quickly to erase national differences, and in the case of some of the Poles, race proved stronger than the ecclesiastical bond and led to the formation of the Polish National Catholic Church of America.

With this identification of particular denominations with immigrant groups came a fourth difference. In the United States the immigrant churches constituted centres of community life for their respective national groups. They were usually the last strongholds of the mother tongues as against the prevailing English. In most of them the transition from those tongues to English as the language of the sermon or public worship was resisted and precipitated a sharp struggle.[98]

A fifth development was that some denominations which in Europe had been both urban and rural in the United States became predominantly either urban or rural in membership. Thus the Roman Catholic Church, the Protestant Episcopal Church, and the Presbyterian Church in the United States of America, although national in the Old World and drawing indiscriminately from both country and city, in the United States had the majority of their members in the cities. This was notably true of the Roman Catholics. On the other hand, Baptists and Methodists, who in the British Isles were chiefly in the towns and cities, in the South of the United States counted the majority of their members in the farms and country villages.[99]

A sixth modification was the somewhat different class division of denominations in the United States. To be sure, some denominations, such as the Baptists and Methodists, tended, as on the east side of the Atlantic, to be from the middle or lower income levels of society, and Unitarians to be from the intelligentsia. Yet Protestant Episcopalians drew more nearly exclusively from the upper income levels than did the Church of England, the Presbyterians had a somewhat larger proportion from those levels than in Scotland, and the Roman Catholics were much more nearly proletarian than in Europe.

When one comes to individual denominations which were brought over from Europe, a number of departures from the Old World pattern arose.

In the British Isles Congregationalism was Nonconformist, in opposition to the established churches and largely from the urban middle class. In New England it long enjoyed the position of the Standing Order, akin to that of

---

[98] Douglass, Church Unity Movements in the United States, p. 5.

[99] For one of these conflicts, see Weng, The Language Problem in the Lutheran Church in Pennsylvania, 1742-1820, in Church History, Vol. V, pp. 359-375.

a state church. It acquired, therefore, the attitude of a dominant church and tended to draw more extensively from the so-called "better families." Moreover, in the United States it was more aggressive, less on the defensive, and was the source of more new movements, social and religious, than in Great Britain.

The Protestant Episcopal Church differed in a number of respects from the Church of England. It embraced a much smaller proportion of the population. It was much less dependent on endowments. It was organized federally, as was the government of the nation. Each of its dioceses was partly autonomous, like the states. It had a system of representative government. In each parish the members elected the vestry and the vestry chose the rector and controlled the temporal affairs of the parish. Its national convention, like Congress, had two houses, the house of bishops and the house of deputies. Provision was made for lay representation. It had no archbishop and its presiding bishop possessed no special authority. It was completely separated from the state. Its prayer book deviated somewhat from that of the Church of England, omitting the Athanasian Creed and making a slight but important change in the Order for the Administration of the Holy Communion.[100] The name adopted, the Protestant Episcopal Church in the United States of America, was significantly different from that of the Church of England.[101]

The great body of Presbyterians comprised, in the latter part of the nineteenth century, in the Presbyterian Church in the United States (Southern) and the Presbyterian Church in the United States of America (Northern) differed decidedly from the Presbyterianism of Europe, including that of Scotland and Ireland from which came the Scotch-Irish elements which were so strong in America. The Presbyterianism of Scotland had been twice tempered, first by its removal to Ireland and second by transplantation to the New World.[102] There was less emphasis upon the Church as divinely constituted and more upon it as a voluntary society of men. There was much more of revivalism, for Presbyterianism had early been carried by the Scotch-Irish to the frontier, the region where revivals flourished. Theological knowledge was not so great and interest in theology was probably somewhat less marked. The New England element and the revivals made for a departure from strict Calvinism.

The Methodism of the United States was unlike that of Great Britain partly

[100] Tiffany, *A History of the Protestant Episcopal Church in the United States of America*, pp. 360, 380-384; Manross, *A History of the American Episcopal Church*, pp. 196, 200.

[101] Tiffany, *op. cit.*, p. 303.

[102] Vander Velde. *The Presbyterian Churches and the Federal Union 1861-1869*, pp. 10, 11.

in having bishops and partly in being relatively more prominent. Occasionally protests, due in some degree to the democratic spirit of the land, broke out against the centralization of power in the hands of the bishops. Thus in 1792 James O'Kelley led a group which wished to restrain Asbury's domination and which, defeated, withdrew and organized the Republican Methodists.[103] The Methodist Protestant Church sprang from a demand for representation of the laity in the annual and general conferences and from opposition to the episcopacy[104]—both outgrowths of the American democratic environment.

The Lutheranism of the United States tended to have a stronger Pietist strain than that of Europe. This was partly because of the fact that clergy with Pietist convictions had had so large a part in its organization. Conservatism was much more marked and was accentuated by resistance to assimilation to the American atmosphere. Conservatism was particularly pronounced in the groups which had more recently arrived. The older groups slowly conformed to the temper of the prevailing Anglo-Saxon Protestantism. The humanistic liberalism which emanated from the German universities was much less influential than in the Old World. The fact that it was not a state church made the Lutheranism of the United States very different in temper from that of Germany and Scandinavia. It was on the defensive as a church of immigrants of speech and culture different from the majority and was without the prestige which accrues from a state connexion. Moreover, the state could not, as in Europe, where it possessed a voice in church affairs, tie together in one ecclesiastical organization those holding sharply conflicting theological views. There was less emphasis upon beauty in public worship and less theological and literary activity. On the other hand, in the United States Lutherans gave more liberally through their churches to various benevolent enterprises. In organization the Lutheranism of the United States had no bishops. The congregation was the unit and the congregations were associated in synods.

The Baptists of the United States differed from those of Great Britain partly in having a strong rural as well as a large urban constituency. In general, too, American pastors gave less time to preaching and calling and more time to organizations and activities than did their British confreres.

The Friends partly succumbed to contacts with other denominations, especially in the West, where social institutions were more fluid. The American type of evangelism with the accompanying revivals affected Quakerism west of the Alleghenies. Salaried pastors became customary. Church services, with

<hr>

[103] Buckley, *Constitutional and Parliamentary History of the Methodist Episcopal Church,* pp. 70ff.
[104] Buckley, *A History of Methodists in the United States,* p. 368.

music, a stated order of worship, and sermons were usual. Many of the meetings in the Eastern states and a few conservatives in the West retained the old ways, but the drift was towards conformity with other Protestant denominations.[105]

Because of the environment the Roman Catholic Church in the United States took on certain unique characteristics which marked it off from that in Europe. To be sure, in doctrine no schism occurred. The Pope still possessed final authority over the Church and was its acknowledged head. In liturgy no essential deviation developed. Yet in some respects the Roman Catholicism of the land displayed distinct features. It was much more the church of the lower social strata than it had been in any major land in Europe except Ireland. This was because it was composed so largely of immigrants who had been recruited from the poorer classes of Europe. In common with other denominations, it could not boast an official connexion with the state. It had no concordat with Washington such as it possessed with several of the governments of Europe. In contrast with Europe, it had no endowed benefices and no cathedral chapters to nominate bishops. It paid less attention to dignity in the liturgy. Yet, on the whole, in the United States Roman Catholics were more frequent communicants, took their faith more seriously, and had less of the perfunctory in their attitude than did the nominal Roman Catholics who composed so much of the membership in Europe. The activist temper of the land was contagious. More time was given to social problems than in the Old World. The preparation of the clergy was long less exacting intellectually than in Europe.[106] Even in the twentieth century the priesthood in general showed much less interest in theological and philosophical questions than their confreres on the other side of the Atlantic.[107] The clergy were less restrained by canon law and were more autocratic in their parishes.[108] Bishops also were inclined to act arbitrarily in disregard of the canon law. This contributed to Rome's decision to set up a Delegation in Washington to which cases could be referred without the delay of reference to the Papal Curia. However, when the first Plenary Council was called to make uniform laws and regulations to govern the Church in the United States, because of the fear of opposition from non-Roman Catholics no Delegate was sent directly from Rome to preside, but Archbishop Gibbons, of Baltimore, was assigned the task.[109] The creation of the Delegation came later. In the Middle West some Jesuits put in practice

[105] Jones, *The Quakers of Iowa,* pp. 95-102.
[106] O'Connell, *Recollections of Seventy Years,* p. 150.
[107] Krebs, *Um die Erde,* p. 190.
[108] O'Connell, *op. cit.,* pp. 150-154.
[109] O'Connell, *op. cit.,* p. 154.

a plan of itinerant priests to serve the German farmers,[110] a programme which was reminiscent of the Methodist circuit rider, but which probably arose not by deliberate copying but from the necessity of meeting the same conditions that had evoked the Methodist system.

Here and there were outstanding Roman Catholics who were markedly affected by the atmosphere of the land. Thus Edward McGlynn, born in New York City, as a priest proved too independently-minded to achieve the high position in the hierarchy which his intellectual ability forecast, but was friendly to the clergy of other denominations, championed public as against parochial schools, and espoused the cause of Henry George and of organized labour. All of this brought him into controversy with his bishop. For a time he was excommunicated, an action which led many of his followers to leave the Roman Catholic Church. Eventually Rome restored him to the priesthood, averring that he had not taught anything contrary to the doctrines of the Church.[111] Isaac Thomas Hecker, himself a convert, the founder of the Paulists, that body which directed its efforts to the conversion of non-Roman Catholics, believed that the Roman Catholic Church was not out of accord with the fundamental genius of the nation and that, without departing from its basic convictions, it could and should adapt itself to the United States. The methods of the Paulists were somewhat akin to the revivalism which was so prominent in Protestant circles in America. Hecker held that in other ways the Church should acclimatize itself in the land. Largely through an enthusiastic biography of Hecker, these views became known to Roman Catholics in Europe. There, and particularly in France, they provoked vigorous criticism. Their "Americanism" was labelled as dangerously untrue to the Church. It was feared that in the United States a national church would develop which would depart from Roman Catholic tradition. Rome was forced to take account of the storm. In 1899 Pope Leo XIII addressed to Cardinal Gibbons, as the head of the hierarchy in the United States, a long and friendly letter in which he condemned any departure from "the deposit of faith" or toning down of its meaning or suppressing any doctrine belonging to it with the purpose of winning converts, but in which he also heartily endorsed the principle that, when no such compromise was entailed, the rule of life laid down for Roman Catholics might well accommodate itself to the "endowments of mind which belong to the American people."[112]

[110] Garraghan, *The Jesuits of the Middle United States*, Vol. II, pp. 65, 66.
[111] Stephen Bell, *Rebel, Priest and Prophet. A Biography of Dr. Edward McGlynn* (New York, The Devin-Adair Co., 1937, pp. 303), *passim*.
[112] Will, *Life of Cardinal Gibbons*, Vol. I, pp. 544ff.; Gabriel, *The Course of American Democratic Thought*, pp. 58ff. The biography which excited so much comment

Because of the diverse sources of the Roman Catholic immigration to the United States, customs and practices came in from many peoples and gave variety to the Roman Catholicism of the land. Thus with the influx of Mexicans into the South-west, folk cults entered—some for healing[113] and one of *penitentes* who cared for the sick and poor and who in Holy Week inflicted physical torture on themselves with whippings, cross-carrying, and being bound to a cross.[114]

Because of contradictory elements in the environment—on the one hand the many nations from which Roman Catholics were drawn and, on the other, national sentiment in the United States—serious conflicts arose within American Roman Catholicism. Priests, bishops, and congregations of differing nationalities clashed.[115] Sometimes a congregation made up chiefly of members of one racial group quarrelled with their priest who, coming from another background, seemed to them an alien.[116] Dissensions broke out between Roman Catholics of the diverse European backgrounds.[117] Here and there were parishes drawn exclusively from one language group.[118] Efforts were made by some to segregate into separate organizations within the inclusive Church the main national strains from Europe, with a continuation of the languages of the mother lands. The most notable of these movements was one which we mentioned a few chapters back, that associated with the name of Peter Cahensly. It sought to keep apart those of German birth and ancestry and advocated a similar arrangement for Italians, Poles, and other nationalities.[119] Against these attempts a number of American prelates, among them Gibbons, set themselves. To their mind, if the Roman Catholic Church were not to be hopelessly handicapped in its effort to establish itself as an integral part of the life of a country which by tradition was overwhelmingly Protestant, it must achieve a national organization and gradually eliminate the various tongues of Europe, except the ecclesiastical Latin, and adopt English for its vernacular. After a prolonged

was Walter Elliott, *The Life of Father Hecker* (New York, The Columbus Press, 2d ed., 1894, pp. xviii, 428).

[113] Gamio, *Mexican Immigration to the United States,* pp. 81-83.

[114] Alice Corbin Henderson, *Brothers of the Light. The Penitents of the Southwest* (New York, Harcourt, Brace & Co., 1937, pp. 126), *passim.*

[115] Guilday, *The Life and Times of John England,* Vol. I, pp. 164ff., 380-425, 476; Guilday, *The Catholic Church in Virginia (1815-1822),* passim.

[116] Roemer, *The Ludwig-Missionsverein and the Church in the United States (1838-1918),* pp. 17-27.

[117] O'Connell, *op. cit.,* pp. 306-309; O'Brien, *John England,* p. 24.

[118] F. J. Zwierlein in Edward R. Foreman (editor), *Centennial History of Rochester, N. Y.,* Vol. IV (Rochester, 1934, pp. viii, 483), pp. 197, 218.

[119] O'Connell, *op. cit.,* pp. 157, 216; Will, *op. cit.,* Vol. I, pp. 497ff.; Roemer, *op. cit.,* p. 49; Guilday, *The Life and Times of John Carroll,* pp. 291-295; Guilday, *A History of the Councils of Baltimore,* p. 151.

and at times stormy struggle, these Americanizers triumphed.[120] Differences of Old World origin were gradually reduced under a comprehensive hierarchy organized according to the territorial divisions of the land and not according to groupings of European provenance.

Partly as a symbol of the desire to give the church a national unity and partly as a means of its achievement, the Catholic University of America was established at Washington, the capital of the country. The suggestion of such an institution, to give dignity to the presentation of the Roman Catholic position to the intelligentsia of the land and to be a centre of intellectual life for the Church in the United States, was made to the Second Plenary Council of Baltimore, in 1866.[121] At the Third Plenary Council, in 1884, steps were taken to implement the idea, and in 1889 the institution was opened.[122]

In one respect the Roman Catholic Church fought vigorously and successfully against a strong tendency in its environment. It overcame a movement to share the control of the Church with the laity. This concomitant of democracy which had become marked in some other denominations began to show itself in the Roman Catholic fold. As we have seen, it took the form of vesting the legal ownership of church property in the hands of lay trustees. As a corollary, these lay trustees sometimes sought to control the appointment of priests to the local congregations and in other ways to bring pressure on their pastors. The system proved so fraught with difficulties and conflicts that the bishops eventually eliminated it. Before the middle of the nineteenth century it was declining and long before the end of the century it had ceased to be a serious problem.[123]

In many respects the Christianity of the United States differed from that of Europe. This was due in large part to the variety in the Christianity which was brought from the other side of the Atlantic. It was also because of the conditions on the American side which invited that transplanting. Individuals added their contributions by creating new denominations and organizations and by modifying those which had been imported. The frontier made certain changes.

The main respects in which the faith was altered by the conditions in the new land are quickly summarized. Greater diversity existed than in any

[120] Will, op. cit., Vol. I, pp. 517ff.
[121] Guilday, A History of the Councils of Baltimore, pp. 211, 212.
[122] Guilday, op. cit., pp. 236, 237.
[123] Dignan, A History of the Legal Incorporation of Catholic Church Property in the United States (1784-1932), pp. 67-213.

country in which Christianity had previously existed. All the major and many of the minor divisions which had arisen in the Old World were transplanted to the New, and these were augmented by some which sprang from the soil. The main branches of imported Christianity existed in somewhat different proportions than they had in Europe. Particularly prominent was the type of Protestantism which had grown up on the extreme wing of that movement and which had come primarily from Great Britain. It was this radical, Anglo-Saxon Protestantism, with its insistence upon a personal experience of God and its dream of seeing ideal Christian communities established, which had been prominent in colonial days and remained dominant throughout the nineteenth century. The variety of the Christianity of the country was made possible by religious toleration and the separation of Church and state. In general, the lay element had a larger place than in Europe, although the Roman Catholic hierarchy succeeded, after a struggle, in asserting its full authority. In general, the Christianity of the United States was more activistic and paid less attention to profound speculative theology than in Europe. Out of this activism many movements for social betterment arose, primarily from the radical Anglo-Saxon Protestantism, which strove, sometimes with marked success, to alter society. Revivalism was prominent. It sought to win all to a Christian faith and so tended to make Christianity conterminous with the country rather than the possession of minorities. The majority of those of Calvinist background moved away from some of the features of that system towards a confidence in man's free will, in his ability to accept the salvation offered by God, and in his capacity for improvement both individually and collectively. It was largely from those of Calvinistic antecedents that the reform movements and the social gospel sprang. Many individuals went over to an extreme humanism. Dissatisfaction over the numerous divisions among Christians presented by the country gave birth to attempts at co-operation and union. Yet these did not prevent the emergence of new denominations. Each of the denominations imported from Europe was modified by the new environment. They all tended to be confined to certain racial strains and class groups. The temper and organization of several were somewhat altered.

Yet, potent though the environment was, the Christianity which developed in the United States was not basically changed. In its central doctrines, purposes, and ecclesiastical structure it remained about what it had been in Europe. The denominations which were represented both in Europe and in the United States found no very great difficulty in maintaining fellowships which bridged the Atlantic. Presbyterians, Anglicans, Baptists, Lutherans, and Congregationalists formed comprehensive bodies which brought together members of their respective bodies on both sides of the ocean. Roman Catholics remained united with those in the rest of the world. Eastern Orthodox kept in touch with their brethren in Europe. In organizations such as the Evangelical Alliance and various international missionary conferences, although not without some friction and difficulty of reciprocal understanding, Protestants of the United States fraternized with those of Europe. The largest of the denominations of American origin, the Disciples of Christ, was admitted into the co-operative enterprises which the Protestants of other groups developed. Those bodies of American birth, of which the Mormons and the Christian Scientists were the most notable examples, which had departed so far from historic Christianity, as it had taken shape in the Old World, that they were not accepted in Protestant joint enterprises, were a small minority of the whole. The continuing bond was Jesus and the impulse which came from him. Even the Christian Scientists and the Church of Jesus Christ of Latter Day Saints by their very names professed loyalty to him. While in details differing from the European Christianity from which it was sprung, in its main features the Christianity of the United States was far from making a clean break with the past.

Chapter XIII

BY WAY OF SUMMARY AND ANTICIPATION

THE nineteenth century was a time of unequalled expression of the vitality inherent in the Christian faith.

The period had been preceded by one of growing religious apathy and was ushered in by a half century of political revolution and war in the Americas and Europe. In the closing decades of the eighteenth century rationalism was the prevailing temper in the intellectual circles of the Occident. It professed to discern an awe-inspiring but quiescent God disclosed through immutable natural law and discovered by the human mind, in place of a God who, as Christianity had always declared, had actively revealed himself in history, and who through Jesus and his Spirit was continually seeking to transform man. This rationalism with its Deism had even penetrated ecclesiastical circles. Most of the churches were subservient to autocratic monarchical civil governments. The rate of expansion, so marked since the beginning of the sixteenth century, had slowed down. The Roman Catholic Church, which had been the chief channel of that expansion, suffered from a variety of ills. The American War of Independence had brought to a pause hopeful stirrings of life in the Protestantism of the Thirteen Colonies and had been accompanied by a distracting European war. The French Revolution had followed hard on its heels and in turn had given rise to a series of wars more destructive to old institutions in Europe than that continent had known for generations. As a sequel to these wars, most of Spanish America broke away from the mother country and adopted republican forms of government.

Moreover, the nineteenth century did not permit Christianity to go unchallenged. Much of eighteenth century rationalism, in general inimical to the faith, continued. Several of the revolutionary political and social movements which characterized the era, although in part sprung from Christianity, regarded that religion as outworn and the Church which represented it as a hindrance to progress. Much of the knowledge achieved by the scientific advance of the period seemed to discredit the basic beliefs of Christians. The new machines and mechanical inventions brought about a vast accumulation of wealth, multiplied for thousands the comforts of life, and appeared to

457

render Christianity irrelevant. Moreover, for other thousands they brought fresh social evils and aggravated the age-long ills of poverty and overcrowding in such fashion as to present the Christian conscience with additional and extraordinarily difficult problems. Negro slavery, inherited from the preceding period of the expansion of European peoples, in 1789 was as yet unrelieved and was a denial on a colossal scale, and by professedly Christian nations, of Christian ethical ideals. International war, while partly in abeyance between 1815 and 1914, remained a threat to civilization, accentuated by the terrifying means of wholesale destruction introduced by the machine. In Europe hundreds of thousands more or less openly renounced their inherited faith. In the United States, in time the largest of the nations which arose from European migration, the opening of the nineteenth century saw only about one out of fourteen of the population with a formal church connexion. The nineteenth century presented no easy road for Christianity.

Yet the outlook for Christianity was not so bleak as it had been at least twice before in its history. The long, heart-breaking decline from the close of the fifth to the beginning of the eleventh century, with its prodigious losses of territory to Islam and paganism and its decline in the inward morale of the Church was still the darkest age that the faith had known. The recession in the fourteenth and fifteenth centuries, with the parallel corruption in the Church, was much more grave than the situation which Christianity faced in the eighteenth century. Moreover, while by 1789 the rate of territorial advance of Roman Catholic Christianity had slowed down and here and there had become a retreat, and although eighteenth century rationalism had undercut much of religious conviction, a revival was already under way in Protestant Christianity. The close of the seventeenth century had seen the rise of Pietism. Out of Pietism had come movements to spread Christianity, and from it and persecuted remnants of an earlier Protestantism had sprung the Moravians with their phenomenal missionary activity. In the eighteenth century came the Evangelical movement led by John Wesley and Whitefield, and the Great Awakening in the English Thirteen Colonies in America. Although for a time in the last third of the century the tide of religious life ebbed in America, the decline proved only an interlude. By the end of the century the revival gave signs of breaking out afresh. In Great Britain it had no serious pause but continued to mount. Protestant Christianity entered the nineteenth century on a rising tide.

In spite of the serious obstacles presented in the nineteenth century, in that period Christianity had a more extensive and more profound effect upon mankind than ever before. So widely did it spread and such diverse and remarkable results did it have, that we are compelled to devote as much space to that era as to all the preceding eighteen centuries. To confine it even to that compass requires the most rigid compression. This present volume we have devoted to Europe and the United States, the chief centres from which nineteenth-century Christianity expanded.

In Europe, the traditional home of its greatest strength, Christianity enjoyed a remarkable renewal. In the Roman Catholic Church more new orders and congregations appeared than in any preceding period of equal length. Since a new order or congregation was a sign of vigour and conviction, this fact gave indication of abounding vitality. The weakening of the tie between Church and state, a phenomenon apparent in many countries, was accompanied by a lessening of that control by the secular authorities which had been a marked feature of the preceding three centuries and by a strengthening of the authority of the Papacy. Although for many thousands their nominal connexion with the church became increasingly tenuous, the loyalty of other thousands was intensified. Frequent communions were more common. The line between practising and non-practising Roman Catholics became more sharply drawn. More than in any earlier era the Roman Catholic Church tended to become a closely integrated, well organized world-wide community within secular society yet distinct from it and directed by the one head at Rome. Within this renewed Roman Catholic Church many old orders put forth fresh efforts for the propagation of the faith and new societies, orders, and congregations spontaneously sprang into existence to share in that enterprise. As never before, the rank and file of Roman Catholics participated actively in the spread of their faith. Financial support no longer came chiefly from the state, as in the preceding period, or from the nobility, as in some earlier centuries, but was primarily from comparatively small individual gifts by thousands of laymen, women, and children. Never had the Roman Catholic Church had so many professional missionaries. Never had so many from the masses of its membership been active in their maintenance. By 1914 additional aid was beginning to come from Roman Catholics in the United States and other lands outside of Europe.

It was in Protestantism that the nineteenth century awakening in Christianity was most pronounced. Protestantism became less a political and more a religious movement than at any previous time. In many respects the nineteenth century was the Protestant century. The augmented life was especially marked in Anglo-Saxon Protestantism. It was here that the greatest revivals occurred. From it they spread to other branches of Protestantism. New organizations and new denominations multiplied. More than the new orders and congregations in the Roman Catholic fold, they displayed originality of purpose, form, and method, and hence were evidence of creative vitality of an exceptionally high order. Within Protestantism arose hundreds of societies for the propagation of Christianity. Many of these were in Europe. A growing number were in the United States and, to a lesser extent, in other regions to which Europeans had migrated. Like the corresponding Roman Catholic organizations, they were made possible by the voluntary gifts of thousands. This expansion of Protestantism was even less accomplished by the aid of the state than was that of Roman Catholicism.

In the Eastern churches renewal of life was by no means so marked as in Roman Catholicism and Protestantism. In South-eastern Europe, to be sure, some of the Orthodox churches emerged from under the Moslem Turkish rule. In Russia dissenters from the official church multiplied, evidence of mounting life. However, in Russia, where Orthodoxy had its chief stronghold, the state church was so dominated by the government that it was really an arm of the secular authority and had little independent life of its own.

In Europe Christianity achieved some gains among those minorities who had not previously been brought into a formal connexion with it. There were extensive missions to the Jews, particularly by Protestants, but, chiefly because no force was employed, rather fewer conversions occurred than in previous periods. In the extreme North and East pagan cults had survived into the nineteenth century. Some advance was registered against them, especially in Russia through strong inducements offered by the state. Here and there a few Moslems became Christians. As against one another, the main branches of Christianity put forth efforts at conversion, but without achieving extensive shifts of population across ecclesiastical boundaries. In Western Europe the vast cityward drift of population brought by the machine age presented serious problems to the churches. In general, substantial progress was made in following the migrants to the new centres and in providing clerical care and devising fresh methods to match the novel conditions.

In some respects, the civilization of Western Europe was more profoundly moulded by Christianity than at any previous time. The democracy which was so pronounced a trend in governments in large part had a Christian source, particularly Protestantism. Mainly but by no means exclusively from Anglo-Saxon Protestantism sprang movement after movement to meet the social ills of the day. If, as seems probable, the machine itself was to some degree a product of Christianity (for it was by Christianity that that confidence in an orderly and dependable universe had been bred in the European mind on which was based the scientific attitude out of which came the machine), then Christianity was to that extent responsible for the collective evils which followed it. However, there also issued from Christianity, notably in Great Britain where it had had its earliest extensive application, efforts to remedy the sufferings brought by the machine and so to reconstruct society that it would be a blessing and not a curse. Some of these attacked specific problems. Others addressed themselves to a basic remaking of society. Of the latter, several of the most prominent, such as Marxian socialism, were only unconsciously and indirectly indebted to Christianity. In others, the Christian element was more obvious and pronounced. Among the reforms which most clearly caught their inspiration from Christianity were those directed against Negro slavery, for the creation of modern nursing, and for the control and reduction of war and the relief of the sufferings entailed by war.

In the United States of America the gains made by Christianity were even more striking than in Europe. Here arose the largest of the new nations born of the migration of European peoples. Here Christianity was confronted with a combination of challenges—to follow and mould the population on the westward moving frontier, to hold to their traditional religious allegiance the immigrants from Europe, to reach the non-Christian elements among the immigrants, notably the Jews and the Orientals, to protect the Indian and the Negro from exploitation by the aggressive whites and to win them to its faith, and to shape the rapidly changing culture of the land. In meeting this collection of gigantic problems Christianity made really astounding progress. While at the outset of the nation's independent life only about one in twenty had a formal membership in some church, by 1914 more than four out of ten were on the rolls of the churches, and this in spite of the prodigious growth in population. Not much effort was made to reach the Jews, but numbers from the small Oriental enclaves had been touched, and between a third and a half of the Indians and about half of the Negroes had become professedly Christian. Due largely to impulses issuing from Christianity, Negro slavery had been abolished and the Negroes had made enormous strides in education. From the Christian conscience had come many attempts to protect the Indians and to enable them to achieve a successful adjustment to the strange world created by the white man. From Christianity, too, had come major contributions to the ideals of the country, to government, to education, to a different status for women, towards the curbing of the use of alcoholic beverages, to better care of the sick and the insane, to improved prisons, to more tolerable conditions for labourers in mines and factories, and to larger opportunities for the underprivileged in the great cities. As in Europe, most of the programmes for international peace stemmed from Christian idealism. In addition to effecting all these results in the country itself, the Christianity of the United States was increasingly reaching out to other lands and was undertaking a growing share in the world-wide missionary enterprise. In the United States, Protestant Christianity, and especially Anglo-Saxon radical Protestant Christianity, had the outstanding part. However, Protestantism from the continent of Europe had an important place, Roman Catholic Christianity was rapidly rising into prominence, and several of the Eastern communions were represented. It was a variegated Christianity which the United States presented, more so than had heretofore been seen in any land.

In the next volume we are to move on to areas whose story seems logically to follow after that of Europe and the United States. We are to deal with those lands which were dominated by Europeans, in which, as in the United States, the advancing white man and his culture were impinging upon peoples of primitive cultures and in some of which the whites were to form the majority of the population and to build new nations of predominantly European blood and civilization. We are first to tell of the great portions of the Americas which were not included in the United States. Then we are to go to the Pacific, to the many islands of that ocean, and to Australia and New Zealand. Finally, we are to deal with Negro Africa. In the sixth volume we are to carry the story of the nineteenth century spread of the faith into Asia. In both volumes we are to see the further course of that unprecedented expansion of Christianity which made the nineteenth century so outstanding in the history of that religion and of the world. Then in a seventh volume we are to trace the course of Christianity in the thrilling and terrifying world which began to take shape after 1914.

BIBLIOGRAPHY

IN THE present volume the same procedure has been followed in compiling the bibliography as in the preceding one. Items have been listed alphabetically by author, or, when no author is given, by title. Only those books have been included which have been referred to more than once in the footnotes. For those employed only once the appropriate data of place of publication, publisher, date, and number of pages have been given with the citation. This method has considerably shortened the bibliography, for to have included the books used only once would have lengthened the list by about half or two-thirds. The arrangement should increase rather than impair the serviceability of the bibliography, for it makes the latter less unwieldy. A list of books on any subject covered by the volume is quickly obtained by turning to the footnotes of the section in which that topic is treated. If a book is used only once in the volume, the pertinent information is with its citation. If it is utilized more than once, the full information can be had from the bibliography.

Abbott, Edith, *Historical Aspects of the Immigration Problem. Select Documents* (University of Chicago Press, 1926, pp. xx, 881). On the period before 1882.

Abel, Theodore, *Protestant Home Missions to Catholic Immigrants* (New York, Institute of Social and Religious Research, 1933, pp. xi, 143). Scholarly, careful, based largely upon field work.

Addison, James Thayer, *Our Expanding Church* (New York, National Council of the Protestant Episcopal Church, 1930, pp. ix, 117). A popular study book for denominational use by an expert on missions.

Adeney, Walter F., *The Greek and Eastern Churches* (New York, Charles Scribner's Sons, 1928. [Preface, 1908.] Pp. xix, 634). A scholarly survey.

The African Repository and Colonial Journal (Washington, The American Colonization Society, 1826ff.).

Allen, Devere, *The Fight for Peace* (New York, The Macmillan Co., 1930, pp. xi, 740). In large part a history of the peace movement, especially in the United States, based upon laborious research in original sources. The author's bias, that of an earnest pacifist, is apparent.

Allen, Stephen, and Pilsbury, W. H., *History of Methodism in Maine 1793-1886* (Augusta, Charles E. Nash, 1887, pp. xvi, 650).

Allen, W. O. B., and McClure, Edmund, *Two Hundred Years: The History of The Society for Promoting Christian Knowledge, 1698-1898* (London, Society for Promoting Christian Knowledge, 1898, pp. vi, 551). The standard history, based upon records, letter-books, reports, and minutes.

463

Allgemeine Missions-Zeitschrift (Berlin, 1874-1923). A leading Protestant periodical on missions, founded by Gustav Warneck.

The American and Foreign Christian Union (New York, American and Foreign Christian Union, 1850ff.). Succeeded the *American Protestant* and the *Quarterly Paper*; followed by *The Christian World*.

Ninety-ninth Annual Report of the American Baptist Foreign Mission Society 1913 (Boston, 1913, pp. 225).

One-Hundredth Annual Report of the American Baptist Home Mission Society (New York City, 1932, pp. 180).

American Baptist Missionary Union. Eighty-Third Annual Report with the Proceedings of the Annual Meeting . . . (Boston, 1897, pp. 226).

Annual Reports of the American Bible Society (New York, 1838ff.).

Annual Reports of the American Board of Commissioners for Foreign Missions (1810ff.).

The American Historical Review (New York, The Macmillan Co., 1894ff.). The official publication of the American Historical Association.

American Missionary Association Annual Reports (1847ff.).

American Seamen's Friend Society Annual Reports (1829ff.).

Twenty-second Annual Report of the American Tract Society (1847).

Ander, Oscar Fritiof, *T. N. Hasselquist. The Career and Influence of a Swedish-American Clergyman, Journalist and Educator* (Rock Island, Illinois, The Augustana Library Publications, 1931, pp. 260). Based in large part upon manuscript sources and contemporary periodicals.

Anderson, Rufus, *Observations upon the Peloponnesus and Greek Islands, made in 1829* (Boston, Crocker and Brewster, 1830, pp. 334). By a secretary of the American Board of Commissioners for Foreign Missions.

Annales de l'Association de la Propagation de la Foi (Lyon, 1837ff.).

Arens, Bernard, *Handbuch der katholischen Missionen* (Herder & Co., Freiburg i.B., 1920, pp. xix, 418). A second edition, enlarged, was issued in 1925.

Arnold, W. E., *A History of Methodism in Kentucky* (Volume I, 1783 to 1820, Vol. II, 1820-1846. Louisville, Herald Press, 1935, 1936). Based upon extensive research, by a Methodist clergyman.

[Asbury, Francis], *The Heart of Asbury's Journal,* edited by Ezra Squier Tipple (New York, Eaton & Mains, 1904, pp. xii, 712).

Ashton, R. S., *The Christian Travellers Continental Handbook* (London, Elliot Stock, 1886, pp. 72).

Attwater, Donald, *The Catholic Eastern Churches* (Milwaukee, Wis., The Bruce Publishing Co., 1935, pp. xx, 308). By a Roman Catholic. Contains excellent bibliographies.

Attwater, Donald, *The Dissident Eastern Churches* (Milwaukee, Wis., The Bruce Publishing Co., 1937, pp. xviii, 349).

Augustana Historical Society Publications (Rock Island, Illinois, 1931ff.).

Aulard, A., *Christianity and the French Revolution.* Translated by Lady Frazer (London, Ernest Benn, 1927, pp. 164). An excellent summary based upon the sources and wide reading in secondary works, but without footnotes.

Bacon, Theodore Davenport, *Leonard Bacon. A Statesman in the Church.* Edited by Benjamin W. Bacon (New Haven, Yale University Press, 1931, pp. xv, 563). A biography, by a grandson, based largely upon original documents.

Baird, Robert, *Religion in the United States of America. Or an Account of the Origin, Progress, Relations to the State, and Present Conditions of the Evangelical Churches in the United States* (Glasgow, Blackie and Son, 1844, pp. xix, 725). Contains valuable information, but without much indication of the sources.

Baldwin, Alice M., *The New England Clergy and the American Revolution* (Durham, N. C., Duke University Press, 1928, pp. xiii, 222). Scholarly, well documented.

Bancroft, Hubert Howe, *History of Alaska, 1730-1885* (San Francisco, A. L. Bancroft and Co., 1886, pp. xxxviii, 775). Well documented.

Bancroft, Hubert Howe, *History of California* (San Francisco, A. L. Bancroft and Co., 7 vols., 1884-1890). Well documented.

Barnes, Gilbert Hobbs, *The Antislavery Impulse, 1830-1844* (New York, D. Appleton-Century Co., 1933, pp. ix, 298). Based upon careful research.

Barnes, Gilbert H., and Dumond, Dwight L., editors, *Letters of Theodore Dwight Weld, Angelina Grimké Weld and Sarah Grimké 1822-1844* (New York, D. Appleton-Century Co., 2 vols., 1934).

Barr, James, *The United Free Church of Scotland* (London, Allenson and Co., 1934, pp. 302).

Bass, Althea, *Cherokee Messenger* (Norman, Okla., University of Oklahoma Press, 1936, pp. 348). An account of Samuel A. Worcester, based largely upon manuscript files of the American Board of Commissioners for Foreign Missions.

Bassett, John Spencer, *A Short History of the United States* (New York, The Macmillan Co., 1914, pp. xv, 885). A standard handbook.

Bassett, John Spencer, *Slavery in the State of North Carolina* (Baltimore, The Johns Hopkins Press, 1899, pp. 111). Carefully done.

Bates, Ernest Sutherland, *American Faith. Its Religious, Political, and Economic Foundations* (New York, W. W. Norton & Co., 1940, pp. 479). A stimulating interpretation, in sprightly, semi-popular style.

Beach, Harlan P., *A Geography and Atlas of Protestant Missions* (New York, Student Volunteer Movement for Foreign Missions, 1906, 2 vols., 1901, 1906).

Beach, Harlan P., and St. John, Burton, editors, *World Statistics of Christian Missions* (New York, The Committee of Reference and Counsel of the Foreign Missions Conference of North America, 1916, pp. 148).

Beard, Augustus Field, *A Crusade of Brotherhood. A History of the American Missionary Association* (Boston, The Pilgrim Press, 1909, pp. xii, 334). The author was a secretary of the American Missionary Association.

Beardsley, Frank Grenville, *A History of American Revivals* (New York, American Tract Society, 1904, pp. 352). Popularly written.

Bell, Stephen, *Rebel, Priest and Prophet. A Biography of Dr. Edward McGlynn* (New York, The Devin-Adair Company, 1937, pp. 303). Sympathetic.

Benedict, David, *A General History of the Baptist Denomination in America and Other Parts of the World* (New York, Lewis Colby and Co., 1848, pp. 970). Contains a mine of information gleaned from many sources.

Benson, Adolph B., and Hedin, Naboth, editors, *Swedes in America 1638-1938* (Yale University Press, 1938, pp. xvi, 614).

Berg, Ludwig, *Die katholischen Heidenmission als Kulturträger* (Second edition, Aachen, Aachener Missionsdruckerei, 3 vols., 1927). Carefully supported by references to authorities, which as a rule are standard German experts and missionary periodicals. Warmly pro-Roman Catholic and critical of Protestants.

Berger, D., *History of the Church of the United Brethren in Christ* (In *The American Church History Series,* Vol. XII, New York, The Christian Literature Co., 1894, pp. 309-382).

Binns, Leonard Elliott, *The Evangelical Movement in the English Church* (London, Methuen & Co., Ltd., 1928, pp. xv, 171). A fairly objective, semi-popular account by a liberal Evangelical Anglican clergyman.

Binyon, Gilbert Clive, *The Christian Socialist Movement in England. An Introduction to the Study of Its History* (London, Society for Promoting Christian Knowledge, 1931, pp. x, 238). Sympathetic, carefully done.

Bishop, Robert H., *An Outline of the History of the Church in the State of Kentucky during a Period of Forty Years: containing the Memoirs of Rev. David Rice and Sketches of the Origin and Present State of Particular Churches and of the Lives and Labours of a Number of Men who were Eminent and Useful in Their Day* (Lexington, Thomas T. Skillman, 1824, pp. 420). By a teacher in Transylvania University.

Bland, F. E., *How the Church Missionary Society Came to Ireland* (Dublin, Church of Ireland Printing and Publishing Co., 1935, pp. 206). Much of the material was drawn from original sources.

Blegen, Theodore C., *Norwegian Migration to America 1825-1860* (Northfield, Minnesota, The Norwegian-American Historical Association, 1931, pp. xi, 413). Scholarly, well documented.

Bliss, William D. P., *The Encyclopedia of Social Reform* (New York, Funk & Wagnalls Co., 1897, pp. vii, 1439). By a large number of contributors, among them some distinguished scholars.

Bond, Beverley W., Jr., *The Civilization of the Old Northwest. A Study of Political, Social, and Economic Development, 1788-1812* (New York, The Macmillan Co., 1934, pp. ix, 543). Based upon meticulous research.

Bond, Horace Mann, *The Education of the Negro in the American Social Order* (New York, Prentice-Hall, Inc., 1934, pp. xx, 501). Carefully done.

Borrow, George, *The Bible in Spain; or, the Journeys, Adventures, and Imprisonments of an Englishman in an Attempt to Circulate the Scriptures in the Peninsula* (New York, E. P. Dutton & Co., 1906, pp. xiv, 509. Everyman's Library edition). First published, Dec., 1842. The record of journeys of an agent of the British and Foreign Bible Society in Spain and Portugal, 1835-1839.

Bracq, Jean Charlemagne, *The Evolution of French Canada* (New York, the Macmillan Co., 1924, pp. viii, 467). Sympathetic, containing a wealth of factual information.

Brawley, Benjamin, *Doctor Dillard of the Jeanes Fund* (New York, Fleming H. Revell Co., 1930, pp. 151). Sympathetic.

Bready, J. Wesley, *Doctor Barnardo, Physician, Pioneer, Prophet: Child Life Yesterday and To-day* (New York, Fleming H. Revell Co., 1930, pp. 271). Based upon primary first-hand materials.

Bready, J. Wesley, *England: Before and after Wesley. The Evangelical Revival and Social Reform* (London, Hodder and Stoughton, 1938, pp. 463). Enthusiastic concerning the change wrought by the Evangelical Revival. Based upon extensive research. Carefully documented.

Reports of the British and Foreign Bible Society, with Extracts of Correspondence, &c. (Vol. I, 1805-1810, London, pp. xvi, 399†).

Broomhall, Marshall, *The Jubilee Story of the China Inland Mission* (London, Morgan & Scott, 1915, pp. xvi, 386). An official history.

Brosnan, Cornelius J., *Jason Lee, Prophet of the New Oregon* (New York, The Macmillan Co., 1932, pp. x, 348). Scholarly, with extensive footnote references to the sources.

Brown, Arlo Ayres, *A History of Religious Education in Recent Times* (New York, The Abingdon Press, 1923, pp. 282).

Brown, Arthur Judson, *One Hundred Years. A History of the Foreign Missionary Work of the Presbyterian Church in the U. S. A., With Some Account of Countries, Peoples and the Policies and Problems of Modern Missions* (New York, Fleming H. Revell Co., 1937, pp. 1140). An official history by a secretary emeritus of the board.

Brown, William Adams, *A Teacher and His Times. A Story of Two Worlds* (New York, Charles Scribner's Sons, 1940, pp. xiv, 391). An autobiography.

Bruner, C. V., *An Abstract of the Religious Instruction of the Slaves in the Antebellum South* (Nashville, George Peabody College for Teachers, 1933, pp. 7).

Brunner, Edmund deS., *Immigrant Farmers and Their Children* (Garden City, New York, Doubleday, Doran & Co., 1929, pp. xvii, 277). Carefully done.

Buchan, John, and Smith, George Adam, *The Kirk in Scotland 1560-1929* (London, Hodder and Stoughton, 1930, pp. ix, 244). Semi-popular.

Buckley, James M., *Constitutional and Parliamentary History of the Methodist Episcopal Church* (New York, The Methodist Book Concern, 1912, pp. viii, 414).

Buckley, J. M., *A History of Methodists in the United States* (New York, Charles Scribner's Sons, 1903, pp. xix, 714).

Burnett, R. G., *Christ Down East* (New York, Fleming H. Revell Co. [no date, c. 1931], pp. 160). Based upon the work of the East End Mission in London.

Burns, J. A., *The Principles, Origin and Establishment of the Catholic School System in the United States* (Cincinnati, Benziger Brothers, 1912, pp. 415). Based chiefly upon well-known printed material, but in part upon manuscript sources.

Burns, J. A., *The Growth and Development of the Catholic School System in the United States* (Cincinnati, Benziger Brothers, 1912, pp. 421). A continuation of the preceding book, covering the period from about 1840 onward.

Bury, J. B., *History of the Papacy in the 19th Century (1864-1878)*. Edited with a memoir by R. H. Murray (London, Macmillan and Co., 1930, pp. lx, 175). Based upon extensive reading.

Bushnell, Henry, *The History of Granville, Licking County, Ohio* (Columbus, Ohio, Hann & Adair, 1889, pp. x, 372).

Callahan, Adalbert, *Medieval Francis in Modern America. The Story of Eighty Years 1855-1935* (New York, The Macmillan Co., 1936, pp. xiv, 494). A sympathetic, carefully done history of the Franciscans in the United States.

Callan, Louise, *The Society of the Sacred Heart in North America* (New York, Longmans, Green and Co., 1937, pp. xvii, 809). Based largely upon manuscript archives.

Cannon, James, III, *History of Southern Methodist Missions* (Nashville, Cokesbury Press, 1926, pp. 356).

Canton, William, *A History of the British and Foreign Bible Society* (London, John Murray, 5 vols., 1904-1910).

Carey, S. Pearce, *William Carey D.D., Fellow of Linnæan Society* (New York, George H. Doran Co., preface 1923, pp. xvi, 428). By a great-grandson. A standard biography.

Carey, William, *An Inquiry into the Obligations of Christians to use Means for the Conversion of the Heathens. In which the Religious State of the Different Nations of the World, the Success of Former Undertakings, and the Practicability of Further Undertakings, are Considered* (Leicester, Ann Ireland, 1792, pp. 87). Reprinted by photographic reproduction, London, Baptist Missionary Society, 1934.

Carpenter, Niles, *Immigrants and Their Children 1920. Census Monographs VII* (Washington, D. C., U. S. Government Printing Office, 1927, pp. xvi, 431).

Carpenter, S. C., *Church and People, 1789-1889. A History of the Church of England from William Wilberforce to "Lux Mundi"* (London, Society for Promoting Christian Knowledge, 1933, pp. vii, 598). Objective, comprehensive, based upon wide reading.

Carroll, H. K., *Federal Council Year Book. An Ecclesiastical and Statistical Directory of the Federal Council, Its Commissions and Its Constituent Bodies, and of All Other Religious Organizations in the United States, Covering the Year 1915* (New York, Missionary Education Movement of the United States and Canada, 1916, pp. 209).

Cartwright, Peter, *Autobiography of Peter Cartwright, The Backwoods Preacher.* Edited by W. P. Strickland (New York, Hunt & Eaton, 1856, pp. 525).

Catholic Colleges and Schools in the United States. High Schools and Academies, Elementary Schools. National Summary (Washington, D. C., National Catholic Welfare Conference, 1936, pp. 21).

The Catholic Directory of South Africa for the Year 1931. Eighteenth Issue (Cape Town, Salesian Press, pp. xvi, 256).

The Catholic Encyclopedia (New York, 16 vols., 1907-1913). Written for informative and apologetic purposes.

Chadwick, W. Edward, *The Church, the State and the Poor. A Series of Historical Sketches* (London, Robert Scott, 1914, pp. viii, 223). Based upon only moderately extensive reading and only in part on the sources. From a strongly Christian point of view.

Channing, W. E., *The Works of William Ellery Channing, D.D., With an Introduction* (Boston, American Unitarian Association, 1891, pp. v, 1060).

Čapek, Thomas, *The Čechs (Bohemians) in America. A Study of their National, Cultural, Political, Social, Economic and Religious Life* (Boston, Houghton Mifflin Co., 1920, pp. xix, 294). Based upon extensive reading in material in English and Czech.

Cherrington, Ernest Hurst, editor-in-chief, *Standard Encyclopedia of the Alcohol Problem* (Westerville, Ohio, American Issue Publishing Co., 6 vols., 1925-1930). Compiled under forces working for prohibition, to aid in the fight against alcohol.

The Christian Century (Chicago, 1894ff.).

Christian Education (Lancaster, Penna., 1924ff.).

The Christian Missionary (Dayton, Ohio, 1895ff.). The official missionary organ of the Christian Church.

The Christian Science Journal (Boston, 1883ff.).

The Christian World. Magazine of the American and Foreign Christian Union (New York, 1850-1884).

The Chronicle. A Baptist Historical Quarterly (Scottdale, Penna., The American Baptist Historical Society, 1938ff.).

Church History (Chicago, 1932ff.). Official organ of the American Society of Church History.

Clark, Calvin Montague, *History of the Congregational Churches in Maine, Vol. I, History of the Maine Missionary Society 1807-1925* (Portland, The Southworth Press, 1926, pp. xiii, 378). Based upon extensive and careful research, largely in manuscript sources.

Clark, Elmer T., *The Small Sects in America* (Nashville, Cokesbury Press, 1937, pp. 311). Based upon extensive research, often through personal visitation.

Clark, Joseph B., *Leavening the Nation. The Story of American Home Missions* (New York, The Baker & Taylor Co., 1903, pp. 362). An excellent survey.

Clark, Joseph S., *A Historical Sketch of the Congregational Churches in Massachusetts from 1620 to 1858* (Boston, Congregational Board of Publication, 1858, pp. xii, 344).

Clarke, Henry Lowther, *Constitutional Church Government in the Dominions Beyond the Seas and in Other Parts of the Anglican Communion* (London, Society for Promoting Christian Knowledge, 1924, pp. xvi, 543). Contains a large number of documents; by a former Archbishop of Melbourne.

Cleveland, Catherine C., *The Great Revival in the West, 1797-1805* (University of Chicago Press, 1916, pp. xii, 215). Carefully done.

Cohen, Israel, *Jewish Life in Modern Times* (London, Methuen & Co., 1914, pp. xii, 374). Sympathetic, but on the whole objective; based upon travel and wide reading.

Collins, Ross William, *Catholicism and the Second French Republic 1848-1852* (New York, Columbia University, 1923, p. 360).

Colquhoun, John Campbell, *William Wilberforce: His Friends and His Times* (London, Longmans, Green, Reader, and Dyer, 1867, pp. vii, 459).

Commager, Henry Steele, *Theodore Parker* (Boston, Little, Brown & Co., 1936, pp. ix, 339). Based upon the sources.

Commons, John R., *Races and Immigrants in America* (New York, The Macmillan Co., new ed., 1920, pp. xxix, 242). By a distinguished scholar.

Condit, Ira M., *The Chinaman as We See Him and Fifty Years of Work for Him* (New York, Fleming H. Revell Co., 1900, p. 233). From personal experiences on the Pacific Coast.

The Connecticut Evangelical Magazine and Religious Intelligencer (Hartford, Lincoln & Gleason, 1808ff.).

Conybeare, Frederick C., *Russian Dissenters* (Harvard University Press, 1921, pp. x, 370). Based upon standard Russian secondary accounts, not on the sources. Somewhat biased in favour of the Dissenters.

Cooley, Rossa B., *School Acres. An Adventure in Rural Education* (New Haven, Yale University Press, 1930, pp. xxii, 166). An account of the Penn Normal, Industrial and Agricultural School, on St. Helena Island, South Carolina, by its principal.

Coolidge, Mary Roberts, *Chinese Immigration* (New York, Henry Holt and Co., 1909, pp. x, 531). Scholarly.

Corwin, Edward Tanjore, *A Manual of the Reformed Church in America* (New York, Board of Publication of the Reformed Church in America, 1902, pp. viii, 1082).

Corwin, E. T., Dubbs, J. H., and Hamilton, J. T., *A History of The Reformed Church, Dutch, The Reformed Church, German, and The Moravian Church in the United States* (New York, The Christian Literature Co., 1895, pp. xviii, 525). In *The American Church History Series*.

Coste, Pierre, *La Congrégation de la Mission Dite de Saint-Lazare* (Paris, Librairie Lecoffre, J. Gabalda et Fils, 1927, pp. viii, 231). By a Lazarist, based upon standard authorities.

Cromwell, John W., *The Negro in American History. Men and Women Eminent in the Evolution of the Americans of African Descent* (Washington, The American Negro Academy, 1914, pp. xiii, 284).

Crowther, J. G., *British Scientists of the Nineteenth Century* (London, Kegan Paul, Trench, Trubner & Co., 1935, pp. xii, 332).

Cullen, Thomas F., *The Catholic Church in Rhode Island* (North Providence, Rhode Island, The Franciscan Missionaries of Mary, 1936, pp. 482). Based upon a variety of sources, including memories of participants.

Curti, Merle Eugene, *The American Peace Crusade, 1815-1860* (Durham, Duke University Press, 1929, pp. viii, 250). Begun as a doctoral dissertation at Harvard.

Curtiss, John Shelton, *Church and State in Russia. The Last Years of the Empire 1900-1917* (New York, Columbia University Press, 1940, pp. ix, 442). Well documented.

Data Book. Volume I. For the Use of Delegates to the North American Home Missions Congress . . . Washington, D. C., December 1 to 5, 1930 (pp. x, 299).

Davidson, Robert, *History of the Presbyterian Church in the State of Kentucky: with a Preliminary Sketch of the Churches in the Valley of Virginia* (New York, Robert Carter, 1847, pp. xii, 371). Based upon extensive research.

Davies, Noelle, *Education For Life. A Danish Pioneer* (London, Williams & Norgate, 1931, pp. 207). Life of Nicolai Frederik Severin Grundtvig.

Dawson, Christopher, *Progress and Religion: An Historical Enquiry* (London, Longmans, Green and Co., 1929, pp. xvii, 254).

Dawson, William Harbütt, *Bismarck and State Socialism. An Exposition of the Social and Economic Legislation of Germany since 1870* (London, Swan Sonneschein & Co., 1891, pp. xii, 170).

Department of Commerce, Bureau of the Census, *Indian Population in the United States and Alaska* (Washington, Government Printing Office, 1915, pp. 285).

Department of Commerce, Bureau of the Census, *Negro Population, 1790-1915* (Washington, Government Printing Office, 1918, pp. 844).

Department of Commerce and Labor, Bureau of the Census, *Special Reports, Religious Bodies: 1906* (Washington, Government Printing Office, 2 Parts, 1910).

Department of Commerce, Bureau of the Census, *Religious Bodies 1916* (Washington, Government Printing Office, 2 vols., 1919).

Descamps, Baron, *Histoire Générale Comparée des Missions* (Paris, Librairie Plon, 1932, pp. viii, 760). Seven other writers have contributed. A standard survey, by Roman Catholic scholars, of Roman Catholic mission history from the beginning, together with chapters on the spread of Protestantism and of some other religions.

Devas, Dominic, *Mother Mary of the Passion, Foundress of the Franciscan Missionaries of Mary (1839-1904)* (London, Longmans, Green and Co., and Franciscan Missionaries of Mary, 1924, pp. 102).

Dictionary of American Biography (New York, Charles Scribner's Sons, 21 vols., 1928-1937). The standard work. A monument of careful research.

Dictionary of National Biography (London, Macmillan and Co., 63 vols., 1885-1900, 6 supplementary volumes through 1912).

Dignan, Patrick J., *A History of the Legal Incorporation of Catholic Church Property in the United States (1784-1932)* (Washington, D. C., The Catholic University of America, 1933, pp. 289). A doctoral dissertation.

Dilhet, Jean, *État de l'Église Catholique ou Diocèse des États-Unis de l'Amerique Septentrionale.* Translated and annotated by Patrick William Browne (Washington, D. C., The Salve Regina Press, 1922, pp. xxii, 261). A doctoral dissertation. Parallel French text and English translation of a manuscript chiefly valuable for first-hand impressions obtained in a residence from 1798 to 1807.

Dionne, N.-E., *Gabriel Richard Suplicien Curé et Second Fondateur de la Ville de Détroit* (Quebec, Laflamme & Proulx, 1911, pp. xv, 125).

Döring, Heinrich, *Vom Juden zum Ordensstifter. Der Ehrw. P. Libermann und die Gründung der afrikanischen Mission im 19. Jahrhundert* (Neuss, Missionshaus Knechtsteden, 2d ed., 1930, pp. xv, 343). Based upon a fairly extensive bibliography, but apparently entirely of printed material. Popularly written from a Roman Catholic viewpoint.

Doggett, Laurence L., *History of the Young Men's Christian Association* (New York, Association Press, 1922, pp. 405). Based upon careful research.

Dombrowski, James, *The Early Days of Christian Socialism in America* (New York, Columbia University Press, 1936, pp. vii, 208). Carefully documented.

Dorchester, Daniel, *Christianity in the United States from the First Settlement down to the Present Time* (New York, Phillips & Hunt, 1888, pp. 793). Contains a great deal of useful material.

Douen, O., *Histoire de la Société Biblique Protestante de Paris (1818 à 1868)* (Paris, Agence de la Société Biblique Protestante, 1868, pp. 418, 31). By an agent of the society.

Douglass, H. Paul, *The Church in the Changing City. Case Studies Illustrating Adaptation* (New York, George H. Doran Co., 1927, pp. 453).

Douglass, H. Paul, *Church Unity Movements in the United States* (New York, Institute of Social and Religious Research, 1934, pp. xxxviii, 576). Shares the scholarly, objective qualities of the work of this Institute.

Douglass, Harlan Paul, *The New Home Missions. An Account of Their Social Redirection* (New York, Missionary Education Movement of the United States and Canada, 1914, pp. xv, 266). A study manual for Protestants.

Douglass, H. Paul, *The St. Louis Church Survey. A Religious Investigation with a Social Background* (New York, George H. Doran Co., 1924, pp. 327). Carefully and boldly done.

Douglass, H. Paul, *The Springfield Church Survey. A Study of Organized Religion with Its Social Background* (New York, George H. Doran Co., 1926, pp. 445). Carefully and boldly done.

Douglass, R. S., *History of Missouri Baptists* (Kansas City, Mo., Western Baptist Publishing Co., 1934, pp. xxii, 545).

Dowling, Patrick John, *The Hedge Schools of Ireland* (London, Longmans, Green and Co., 1935, pp. xvii, 182). Well documented.

Doyle, Sherman H., *Presbyterian Home Missions. An Account of the Home Missions of the Presbyterian Church in the U.S.A.* (New York, Presbyterian Board of Home Missions, 1905, pp. xiv, 318).

Drach, George, editor, *Our Church Abroad. The Foreign Missions of the Lutheran Church in America* (Philadelphia, The United Lutheran Publication House, 1926, pp. 277). An official description of the missions of the various Lutheran bodies of the United States.

Dubnow, S. M., *History of the Jews in Russia and Poland from the Earliest Times until the Present Day.* Translated from the Russian by I. Friedlaender (Philadelphia, The Jewish Publication Society of America. Vol. I, to 1825, 1916, pp. 413). Apparently carefully done but without references to the sources.

Dunlop, John, *Memories of Gospel Triumphs among the Jews during the Victorian Era* (London, S. W. Partridge & Co., 1894, pp. xxi, 490). Written for purposes of edification.

Drury, A. W., *History of the Church of the United Brethren in Christ* (Dayton, Ohio, United Brethren Publishing House, revised edition, 1931, pp. 832). By one long connected with the church: based upon personal knowledge and extensive research.

Drury, Clifford Merrill, *Henry Harmon Spalding* (Caldwell, Idaho, The Caxton Printers, 1936, pp. 438). Careful, thorough, well documented.

Dubbs, Joseph Henry, *History of the Reformed Church, German* (New York, The Christian Literature Society, 1895, pp. 213-423). In *The American Church History Series.*

Du Bois, W. E. Burghardt, editor, *The Negro Church* (Atlanta, Ga., The Atlanta University Press, 1903, pp. viii, 212).

Du Bois, W. E. Burghardt, *The Philadelphia Negro. A Social Study* (Philadelphia, The University of Pennsylvania, 1899, pp. xx, 520). Scholarly.

[Dwight, E. W.], *Memoirs of Henry Obookiah, a Native of Owhyhee and a Member of the Foreign Mission School. Who Died at Cornwall, Conn., Feb. 17, 1818. Aged 26 Years* (New Haven, 1818, p. 109).

Dwight, Henry Otis, *The Centennial History of the American Bible Society* (New York, The Macmillan Co., 2 vols., 1916). By a secretary of the society.

Earnest, Joseph B., *The Religious Development of the Negro in Virginia* (Charlottesville, Va., The Michie Co., 1914, pp. 233). A doctoral dissertation.

The East and the West. A Quarterly Review for the Study of Missionary Problems (Westminster, The Society for the Propagation of the Gospel in Foreign Parts, 1903-1927).

Eastman, Elaine Goodale, *Pratt. The Red Man's Moses* (Norman, Okla., University of Oklahoma Press, 1935, pp. 285).

Eckhardt, Carl Conrad, *The Papacy and World-Affairs As Reflected in the Secularization of Politics* (University of Chicago Press, 1937, pp. xiv, 310).

Ecumenical Missionary Conference, New York, 1900. Report of the Ecumenical Conference on Foreign Missions, held in Carnegie Hall and Neighboring Churches, April 21 to May 1 . . . (New York, American Tract Society, 2 vols., 1900).

Eisenach, George J., *A History of the German Congregational Churches in the United States* (Yankton, S. D., The Pioneer Press, 1938, pp. xvi, 315). Based upon careful research in manuscript and printed sources and through personal correspondence and questionnaires.

Elliott, Walter, *The Life of Father Hecker* (New York, The Columbus Press, 1894, 2d ed., pp. xvii, 428). Warmly sympathetic.

Elsbree, Oliver Wendell, *The Rise of the Missionary Spirit in America 1790-1815* (Williamsport, Pa., The Williamsport Printing and Binding Co., 1928, pp. 187). Based upon the printed sources, especially of missionary journals and reports of missionary societies.

Ely, Richard T., *Social Aspects of Christianity And Other Essays* (New York, Thomas Y. Crowell & Co., new ed., 1889, pp. x, 161).

Embree, Edwin R., *Brown America* (New York, The Viking Press, 1931, pp. vi, 311). Written in a popular style, but authoritatively.

Emery, Julia C., *A Century of Endeavor 1821-1921. A Record of the First Hundred Years of the Domestic and Foreign Missionary Society of the Protestant Episcopal Church in the United States of America* (New York, The Department of Missions, 1921, pp. xiii, 466). Based upon careful and prolonged research in the sources, but without footnote references.

The Encyclopædia Britannica (London, The Encyclopædia Britannica, 14th ed., 24 vols., 1929).

Encyclopædia of the Social Sciences (New York, The Macmillan Co., 15 vols., 1930-1935).

Engelhardt, Zephyrin, *The Missions and Missionaries of California* (San Francisco, The James H. Barry Co., 4 vols., 1908-1915).

Faris, John T., *The Alaskan Pathfinder. The Story of Sheldon Jackson For Boys* (New York, Fleming H. Revell Co., 1913, pp. 221). Based partly on Stewart's *Sheldon Jackson* and partly on the diaries and other records of Jackson.

Farish, Hunter Dickinson, *The Circuit Rider Dismounts. A Social History of Southern Methodism 1865-1900* (Richmond, The Dietz Press, 1938, pp. 400).

Faust, Albert Bernhardt, *The German Element in the United States with Special Reference to Its Political, Moral, Social, and Educational Influence* (New York, The Steuben Society of America, 2 vols., 1927. Copyrighted 1909). A standard work.

Fergusson, E. Morris, *Historic Chapters in Christian Education in America. A Brief History of the American Sunday School Movement and the Rise of the Modern Church School* (New York, Fleming H. Revell Co., 1935, pp. 192). Based partly on archives and personal recollections.

Fides News Service (Rome, c.1926ff.). A mimeographed set of news release notes on current happenings in Roman Catholic Missions, compiled in close co-operation with the Association for the Propagation of the Faith.

Findlay, G. G., and Holdsworth, W. W., *The History of the Wesleyan Methodist Missionary Society* (London, The Epworth Press, 5 vols., 1921-1924). An official history, based largely upon the manuscript records of the society.

Finley, James B., *Autobiography of Rev. James B. Finley; or Pioneer Life in the West*. Edited by W. P. Strickland (Cincinnati, The Methodist Book Concern, 1854, pp. 455).

Finley, James B., *Sketches of Western Methodism: Biographical, Historical, and Miscellaneous, Illustrative of Pioneer Life*. Edited by W. P. Strickland (Cincinnati, The Methodist Book Concern, 1854, pp. 551). Chiefly biographical and autobiographical sketches.

[Finney, Charles G.], *Memoirs of Charles G. Finney written by Himself* (New York, H. S. Barnes & Co., 1870, pp. xxii, 477).

[Fisher, Ezra], *Correspondence of the Reverend Ezra Fisher, Pioneer Missionary of the American Baptist Home Mission Society in Indiana, Illinois, Iowa and Oregon*. Edited by Sarah Fisher Henderson, Nellie Edith Latourette, and Kenneth Scott Latourette [Portland, Oregon. Privately printed, 1916, pp. 492].

Fleming, J. R., *A History of the Church in Scotland 1843-1874* (Edinburgh, T. and T. Clark, 1927, pp. x, 276).

Fleming, J. R., *A History of the Church in Scotland 1875-1929* (Edinburgh, T. and T. Clark, 1933, pp. x, 338).

Fortune, Alonzo Willard, *The Disciples of Kentucky* (The Convention of the Christian Churches in Kentucky, 1932, pp. 415). Based upon sources sympathetic with the Disciples, but fairly objective.

Foster, Frank Hugh, *A Genetic History of the New England Theology* (The University of Chicago Press, 1907, pp. xv, 568). Critical, but in places sympathetic.

Foster, Robert V., *A Sketch of the History of the Cumberland Presbyterian Church* (New York, The Christian Literature Co., 1894, pp. 258-509). In *The American Church History Series*.

Fox, Columba, *The Life of the Right Reverend John Baptist Mary David (1761-1841), Bishop of Bardstown and Founder of the Sisters of Charity of Nazareth* (New York, The United States Catholic Historical Society, 1925, pp. [4], 240, [3]). Based partly upon manuscript archives.

Fox, Early Lee, *The American Colonization Society 1817-1840* (Baltimore, The Johns Hopkins Press, 1919, pp. 231). Scholarly, inclined to favour the Society.

Frank, Arnold, editor, *Witnesses from Israel. Life-Stories of Jewish Converts to Christianity*. Translated from the German by Mrs. A. Fleming (Edinburgh, Oliphant, Anderson and Ferrier, 1903, pp. 118). Popularly told brief biographies, several of them by the eminent authority J.F.A. de le Roi.

Frere, W. H., *Some Links in the Chain of Russian Church History* (London, Faith Press, 1918, pp. xvi, 200). Scholarly, based upon extensive reading, well written, sympathetic.

Freri, Joseph, *The Society for the Propagation of the Faith and the Catholic Missions* (New York, Press of the Society for the Propagation of the Faith, 1912, pp. 40).

Friesen, P. M., *Die alt-evangelische mennonitische Brüderschaft in Russland (1789-1910) im Rahmen der mennonitischen Gesamtgeschichte* (Halbstadt, Taurien, "Raduga," 1911, pp. xx, 776, 154).

Fry, C. Luther, *The U.S. Looks at Its Churches* (New York, Institute of Social and Religious Research, 1930, pp. xiv, 183).

Gabriel, Ralph Henry, *The Course of American Democratic Thought. An Intellectual History Since 1815* (New York, The Ronald Press Co., 1940, pp. xi, 452).

Galitzi, Christine Avghi, *A Study of Assimilation among the Roumanians in the United States* (New York, Columbia University Press, 1929, pp. 282).

Galpin, W. Freeman, *Pioneering for Peace. A Study of American Peace Efforts to 1846* (Syracuse, The Bardeen Press, 1933, pp. ix, 237). Based upon the sources.

Gamio, Manuel, *Mexican Immigration to the United States* (University of Chicago Press, 1930, pp. xviii, 262). Summarizing a scholarly investigation.

Gammell, William, *A History of American Baptist Missions in Asia, Africa, Europe, and North America* (Boston, Gould, Kendall and Lincoln, 1849, pp. xii, 359).

Garraghan, Gilbert J., *The Jesuits of the Middle United States* (New York, The American Press, 3 vols., 1938). Based upon extensive research by a Jesuit scholar.

Garrison, Winfred Ernest, *Religion Follows the Frontier. A History of the Disciples of Christ* (New York, Harper & Brothers, 1931, pp. xvi, 317). A well written, scholarly book by a Disciple.

The General Education Board. An Account of Its Activities 1902-1914 (New York, General Education Board, 1915, pp. xv, 240).

[George, Henry], *The Writings of Henry George* (New York, Doubleday and McClure Co., 10 vols., 1898-1900). Volumes 1 and 2 contain *Progress and Poverty* (written 1877-1879), and Volume X is *The Life of Henry George* by Henry George, Jr.

Ghéon, Henri, *The Secret of Saint John Bosco*. Translated by F. J. Sheed (New York, Sheed & Ward, 1936, pp. 203). An admiring biography for popular consumption.

Gidney, W. T., *The History of the London Society for Promoting Christianity amongst the Jews, from 1809 to 1908* (London, London Society for Promoting Christianity amongst the Jews, 1908, pp. xxx, 672). A centenary history by a secretary of the Society, based upon the Society's records.

Gidney, W. T., *Missions to Jews. A Handbook of Reasons, Facts, and Figures* (London, London Society for Promoting Christianity amongst the Jews, 10th ed., 1912, pp. 230).

Giles, R. A., *The Constitutional History of the Australian Church* (London, Skeffington & Son, 1929, pp. 320). Scholarly.

Gill, Charles Otis and Pinchot, Gifford, *Six Thousand Country Churches* (New York, The Macmillan Co., 1920, p. xiv, 237). A careful study of Ohio.

Gill, Everett, *Europe and the Gospel* (Richmond, Va., Educational Department, Foreign Mission Board, Southern Baptist Convention, 1931, pp. 174). By a European representative of the Foreign Mission Board of the Southern Baptist Convention.

Gillard, John T., *The Catholic Church and the American Negro* (Baltimore, St. Joseph's Society Press, 1929, pp. xv, 324). A careful survey written from the Roman Catholic standpoint.

Gingerich, Melvin, *The Mennonites in Iowa* (Iowa City, The State Historical Society of Iowa, 1939, pp. 419). Based in part upon rare periodicals and unpublished sources.

Goodell, William, *The American Slave Code in Theory and Practice: Its Distinctive Features Shown by Its Statutes, Judicial Decisions, and Illustrative Facts* (New York, American and Foreign Anti-Slavery Society, 1853, pp. ix, 431). Antislavery, containing many quotations from the laws.

Goodwin, Edward Lewis, *The Colonial Church in Virginia with Biographical Sketches of the First Six Bishops of the Diocese of Virginia and Other Historical Papers together with Brief Biographical Sketches of the Colonial Clergy of Virginia* (Milwaukee, Morehouse Publishing Co., 1927, pp. xxiv, 342). A posthumous work by the historiographer of the (Episcopal) Diocese of Virginia.

Goodykoontz, Colin Brummitt, *Home Missions on the American Frontier. With Particular Reference to the American Home Missionary Society* (Caldwell, Idaho, The Caxton Printers, 1939, pp. 460). Based upon extensive research.

Goyau, Georges, *L'Allemagne Religieuse, Le Catholicisme* (Paris, Perrie et Cie, 4 vols., 1905-1910). Well documented.

Graves, W. W., *Annals of Osage Mission* (St. Paul, Kansas, W. W. Graves, 1935, pp. 489).

Grenfell, Wilfred, *Forty Years For Labrador* (Boston, Houghton Mifflin Co., 1932, pp. viii, 372). A largely rewritten new edition of an autobiography which first appeared in 1919.

Griffin, Joseph A., *The Contribution of Belgium to the Catholic Church in America (1523-1857)* (Washington, D. C., The Catholic University of America, 1932, pp. xvi, 235). A doctoral dissertation, based upon extensive research, largely in printed materials.

Grose, Howard B., *Aliens or Americans* (New York, Young People's Missionary Movement, 1906, pp. 337). A mission study textbook.

Guilday, Peter, editor, *The Catholic Church in Contemporary Europe, 1919-1931. Papers of the American Catholic Historical Association*, Vol. II. (New York, P. J. Kenedy and Sons, 1932, pp. xiv, 354).

Guilday, Peter, *The Catholic Church in Virginia (1815-1822)* (New York, The United States Catholic Historical Society, 1924, pp. xxv, 159). Based chiefly upon manuscript archives.

Guilday, Peter, *A History of the Councils of Baltimore (1791-1884)* (New York, The Macmillan Co., 1932, pp. x, 291).

Guilday, Peter, *The Life and Times of John Carroll, Archbishop of Baltimore (1735-1815)* (New York, The Encyclopedia Press, 1922, pp. xi, 864). The standard life, by a competent Roman Catholic historian.

Guilday, Peter, *The Life and Times of John England, First Bishop of Charleston (1786-1842)* (New York, The American Press, 2 vols., 1927). By an eminent Roman Catholic historian.

Haldane, Alexander, *The Lives of Robert Haldane of Airthrey and of His Brother, James Alexander Haldane* (London, Hamilton, Adams and Co., 3d. ed., 1853, pp. xvi, 706). From first-hand documents and recollections.

Halich, Wasyl, *Ukrainians in the United States* (University of Chicago Press, 1937, pp. xiii, 174). Based upon fairly extensive research and personal knowledge.

Hall, Thomas Cuming, *The Religious Background of American Culture* (Little, Brown & Co., Boston, 1930, pp. xiv, 317). Presenting an interesting thesis.

Hallenback, Wilbur C., *Urban Organization of Protestantism* (New York, Harper & Brothers, 1934, pp. xii, 285). An Institute of Social and Religious Research publication.

Hamilton, Robert, *The Gospel among the Red Men. The History of Southern Baptist Indian Missions* (Nashville, Tenn., Sunday School Board of the Southern Baptist Convention, 1930, pp. 239). The material was drawn from secondary sources and also from reports, from letters and diaries, from government bulletins, from thirty years of observation and fellowship with missionaries to the Indians, from the author's own experience as a missionary, and from what missionaries had told him.

Hanzsche, Wm. Thomson, *The Presbyterians. The Story of a Staunch and Sturdy People* (Philadelphia, The Westminster Press, 1934, pp. 194). A popularly written survey, chiefly of Presbyterianism in the United States.

Harlow, Ralph Volney, *Gerrit Smith, Philanthropist and Reformer* (New York, Henry Holt and Co., 1939, pp. vi, 501). Based upon primary sources, largely in manuscript.

Harris, Abram L., *The Negro as Capitalist. A Study of Banking and Business among American Negroes* (Philadelphia, The American Academy of Political and Social Science, 1936, pp. xii, 205). Based upon careful research.

Harris, John, *A Century of Emancipation* (London, J. M. Dent & Sons, 1933, pp. xv, 287). A popular account of an anti-slavery advocate, based in part upon original documents.

Hastings, John, editor, *Encyclopædia of Religion and Ethics* (New York, Charles Scribner's Sons, 13 vols., 1908-1927).

Hayes, Carlton J. H., *The Historical Evolution of Modern Nationalism* (New York, Richard R. Smith, 1931, pp. viii, 327). A scholarly study written in readable style.

Heimbucher, Max, *Die Orden und Kongregationen der katholischen Kirche* (Paderborn, Ferdinand Schöningh, 2d ed., 3 vols., 1907, 1908). Well documented, with excellent selected bibliographies.

Held, John A., *European Missions in Texas* (Nashville, Tenn., Broadman Press, 1936, pp. 136). Baptist missions in Texas.

Hendrick, Burton J., *The Lees of Virginia. Biography of a Family* (Boston, Little, Brown & Co., 1935, pp. xii, 455).

Hendricks, Robert J., *Bethel and Aurora. An Experiment in Communism as Practical Christianity with Some Account of Past and Present Ventures in Collective Living* (New York, The Press of the Pioneers, 1933, pp. xv, 324).

Hensel, Sebastrian, *The Mendelssohn Family (1729-1847). From Letters and Journals.* Translated by C. Klingemann and an American collaborator (New York, Harper & Brothers, second revised edition, 2 vols. 1882).

Heuss, Theodor, *Friedrich Naumann. Der Mann, das Werk, die Zeit* (Stuttgart, Berlin, Deutsche Verlags-Anstalt, 1937, pp. xii, 751).

Hickey, Edward John, *The Society for the Propagation of the Faith. Its Foundation, Organization and Success (1822-1922)* (The Catholic University of America Studies in American Church History, Vol. III, 1922, pp. x, 195).

Hoffmann, M. M., *The Church Founders of the Northwest. Loras and Cretin and Other Captains of Christ* (Milwaukee, The Bruce Publishing Co., 1937, pp. xiii, 387). Based largely upon archives.

Hole, Charles, *The Early History of the Church Missionary Society for Africa and the East to the End of A.D. 1814* (London, Church Missionary Society, 1896, pp. xxxviii, 677). Very full. Based upon extensive and careful research.

[Hopkins, Samuel], *The Works of Samuel Hopkins, D.D.* (Boston, Doctrinal Tract and Book Society, 3 vols., 1852).

Horsch, John, *The Hutterian Brethren 1528-1931. A Story of Martyrdom and Loyalty* (Goshen, Indiana, The Mennonite Historical Society, 1931, pp. xxi, 168). Sympathetic, based upon careful research.

Hosford, Frances Juliette. *Father Shipherd's Magna Charta. A Century of Coeducation in Oberlin College* (Boston, Marshall Jones Co., 1937, pp. ix, 180).

Houghton, Louise Seymour, *Handbook of French and Belgian Protestantism* (New York, Missionary Education Movement, 1919, pp. viii, 245).

Hudson, Estelle, *Czech Pioneers of the Southwest* (Dallas, Texas, South-West Press, 1934, pp. xv, 418). Popularly and sympathetically done, incorporating much first-hand material.

Hughes, H. L., *The Catholic Revival in Italy, 1815-1915* (London, Burns Oates and Washbourne, 1935, pp. xii, 177). Semi-popular, warmly Roman Catholic in tone.

Hulbert, Archer Butler, and Hulbert, Dorothy Printup, editors, *The Oregon Crusade. Across Land and Sea to Oregon* (The Stewart Commission of Colorado College and The Denver Public Library, 1935, pp. xvi, 301). Chiefly selected documents of the Methodist and American Board Missions to Oregon.

Huonder, Anton, *Der einheimische Klerus in den Heidenländern* (Freiburg im Breisgau, Herdersche Verlagshandlung, 1909, pp. x, 312). Based upon fairly wide reading.

Huxley, Leonard, *Life and Letters of Thomas Henry Huxley* (New York, D. Appleton and Co., 2 vols., 1900).

Ichihashi, Yamato, *Japanese in the United States. A Critical Study of the Problems of the Japanese Immigrants and Their Children* (Stanford University Press, 1932, pp. x, 426). Scholarly, strongly pro-Japanese.

Ikenberry, Charles S., *The Daily Vacation Church School* (Elgin, Ill., The General Sunday School Board, 1920, pp. 176).

The International Review of Missions (London, 1912ff.). The standard Protestant journal on foreign missions.

International Survey of the Young Men's and Young Women's Christian Associations (New York, The International Survey Committee, 1932, pp. vi, 425). A careful, objective study.

Ives, J. Moss, *The Ark and the Dove. The Beginning of Civil and Religious Liberties in America* (New York, Longmans, Green and Co., 1936, pp. xi, 435). Sympathetic with Roman Catholicism.

Jackson, George Pullen, *White Spirituals in the Southern Uplands. The Story of the Fasola Folk, Their Songs, Singings, and "Buckwheat Notes"* (Chapel Hill, University of North Carolina Press, 1933, pp. xiv, 444). Based upon careful research.

James, Henry, *Charles W. Eliot, President of Harvard University 1869-1909* (Boston, Houghton Mifflin Co., 2 vols., 1930). A standard biography made up largely of Eliot's own letters.

Janson, Florence Edith, *The Background of Swedish Immigration, 1840-1930* (University of Chicago Press, 1931, pp. xi, 517). Enlarged from a doctoral dissertation.

The Jewish Era. A Christian Quarterly in Behalf of Israel (The Chicago Hebrew Mission, 1892ff.).

Johnson, Alvin W., *The Legal Status of Church-State Relationships in the United States with Special Reference to the Public Schools* (University of Minnesota Press, 1934, pp. ix, 332).

Johnson, Charles S., *The Negro in American Civilization. A Study of Negro Life and Race Relations in the Light of Social Research* (New York, Henry Holt and Co., 1930, pp. xiv, 538). The synthesis of many studies presented to a national inter-racial conference of agencies for social work among Negroes and the improvement of the relationships between white and coloured.

Johnson, Guion Griffis, *Ante-Bellum North Carolina. A Social History* (Chapel Hill, University of North Carolina Press, 1937, pp. xv, '935). Based upon exhaustive research in sources, manuscript and printed.

Jones, E. K. *The Story of Education in a Welsh Border Parish or The Schools of Cefnmawr, 1786-1933* (Cefnmawr, Wrexham, Alfred Smith, 2d ed., 1934, pp. 138). Based upon careful research in the sources, by a Baptist.

Jones, John G., *A Concise History of the Introduction of Protestantism into Mississippi and the Southwest* (St. Louis, P. M. Pinckard, 1866, pp. 257). By a Methodist descended from early settlers. Undocumented, but fairly carefully done.

Jones, Louis Thomas, *The Quakers of Iowa* (Iowa City, The State Historical Society of Iowa, no date, pp. 360). Based upon extended research.

Jones, Thomas Jesse, editor, *Department of the Interior, Bureau of Education. Negro Education. A Study of the Private and Higher Schools for Colored People in the United States.* Prepared in co-operation with the Phelps-Stokes Fund under the Direction of Thomas Jesse Jones (Washington, Government Printing Office, 2 vols., 1917).

Joseph, Samuel, *Jewish Immigration to the United States from 1881 to 1910* (New York, 1914, pp. 211). A doctoral dissertation prepared for Columbia University.

The Journal of Modern History (Chicago, 1929ff.)

The Journal of Negro History (Lancaster, Pa., and Washington, D. C., The Association for the Study of Negro Life and History, 1916ff.).

Journals of the General Conference of the Methodist Episcopal Church (Vol. I, 1796-1836, New York, Carlton & Phillips, 1855).

Kelly, Mary Gilbert, *Catholic Immigrant Colonization Projects in the United States 1815-1860* (New York, The United States Catholic Historical Society, 1939, pp. ix, 290).

Kelsey, Rayner Wickersham, *Friends and the Indians 1655-1917* (Philadelphia, The Associated Executive Committee of Friends on Indian Affairs, 1917, pp. ix, 291). Carefully done.

Kennedy, William S., *The Plan of Union: or A History of the Presbyterian and Congregational Churches of the Western Reserve; with Biographical Sketches of the Early Missionaries* (Hudson, O., Pentagon Steam Press, 1856, pp. iv, 262). Drawn from original sources.

Kettleborough, Charles, *The State Constitutions and the Federal Constitution and Organic Laws of the Territories and Other Colonial Dependencies of the United States of America* (Indianapolis, B. F. Bowen & Co., 1918, pp. 1644).

King, William R., *History of the Home Missions Council with Introductory Outline History of Home Missions* (New York, Home Missions Council, no date, pp. 64).

Kinney, J. P., *A Continent Lost—A Civilization Won* (Baltimore, The Johns Hopkins Press, 1937, pp. xv, 366). Scholarly history, largely of the Indian land policy of the United States Government.

Krebs, Engelbert, *Um die Erde. Eine Pilgerfahrt* (Paderborn, Bonifacius-Druckerei, 1928, pp. 620). By a German Roman Catholic professor of theology, arising from a journey made in 1926 and 1927.

Krout, John Allen, *The Origins of Prohibition* (New York, Alfred A. Knopf, 1925, pp. 339). Well documented.

Krummacher, Friedrich-Wilhelm, *Gottfried Daniel Krummacher und die niederrheinische Erweckungsbewegung zu Anfang des 19 Jahrhunderts* (Berlin and

Leipzig, Walter de Gruyter & Co., 1935, pp. 304). Carefully based upon the sources.

Kutak, Robert I., *The Story of A Bohemian-American Village. A Study of Social Persistence and Change* (Louisville, The Standard Printing Co., 1933, pp. xvi, 156). A scholarly study of Milligan, a Bohemian town about sixty miles west of Lincoln, Neb.

Lankard, Frank Glenn, *A History of the American Sunday School Curriculum* (New York, The Abingdon Press, 1927, pp. 360).

Latimer, Robert Sloan, *Dr. Baedeker and His Apostolic Work in Russia* (London, Morgan and Scott, 1908, pp. 223). Contains extensive quotations from Baedeker's letters and journals.

Latimer, Robert Sloan, *Under Three Tsars. Liberty of Conscience in Russia 1856-1909* (New York, Fleming H. Revell Co., no date, pp. xii, 244). Popularly written. Strongly Pro-Protestant.

Latimer, Robert Sloan, *With Christ in Russia* (London, Hodder and Stoughton, 1910, pp. x, 239). Drawn from personal observation, warmly sympathetic with Protestantism.

Latourette, Kenneth Scott, *A History of Christian Missions in China* (New York, The Macmillan Co., 1929, pp. xii, 930).

Launay, Adrien, *Histoire Générale de la Société des Missions-Étrangères* (Paris, Pierre Téqui, 3 vols., 1894). By a member of the Society. Based upon the archives.

Lawrence, John, *The History of the Church of the United Brethren in Christ* (Dayton, Ohio, The United Brethren Printing Establishment, 2 vols., 1861, 1868). Largely drawn from an older history by H. G. Spayth.

Laymen's Foreign Missions Inquiry (New York, Harper & Brothers, 7 vols., 1933).

Lemmens, Leonhard, *Geschichte der Franziskanermissionen* (Münster i.W., Aschendorffschen Verlagsbuchhandlung, 1929, pp. xx, 376). Carefully done, by a Franciscan.

Lennox, William G., *The Health and Turnover of Missionaries* (New York, The Advisory Committee and the Foreign Missions Conference, 1933, pp. 217).

Lesourd, Paul, editor, *L'Année Missionaire 1931* (Paris, Desclée de Brouwer et Cie, pp. 667).

Leuba, James H., *The Belief in God and Immortality* (Boston, Sherman, French & Co., 1916, pp. xvii, 340).

Liese, Wilh., *Geschichte der Caritas* (Freiburg i.Br., Caritasverlag, 2 vols., 1922). From a Roman Catholic standpoint, with a warm appreciation of the part of the Church in charity.

Lindquist, G. E. E., *The Red Man in the United States. An Intimate Study of the Social, Economic and Religious Life of the American Indian* (New York, George H. Doran Co., 1923, pp. 461). Scholarly, objective.

Lovett, Richard, *The History of the London Missionary Society 1795-1895* (London, Henry Frowde, 2 vols., 1899).

Ludlum, David M., *Social Ferment in Vermont 1791-1850* (New York, Columbia University Press, 1939, pp. x, 305). Well written. Based upon careful research.

Lübeck, Konrad, *Die Christianisierung Russlands,* (Aachen, Xavieriusverlagsbuchhandlung, 1922, pp. 118). By a Roman Catholic scholar, using a good deal of Russian material, as well as that in Western European languages. Objective, scholarly.

The Lutheran World Almanac and Annual Encyclopedia for 1921 (New York, The Lutheran Bureau, 1920, pp. 966).

McConnell, S. D., *History of the American Episcopal Church from the Planting of the Colonies to the End of the Civil War* (New York, Thomas Whittaker, 1890, pp. xiv, 392). Excellent.

M'Kerrow, John, *History of the Foreign Missions of the Secession and United Presbyterian Church* (Edinburgh, Andrew Elliott, 1867, pp. ix, 518). Drawn largely from the *Missionary Record of the United Presbyterian Church.*

Mackichan, D., *The Missionary Ideal in the Scottish Churches* (London, Hodder and Stoughton, 1927, pp. 238). A semi-popular series of lectures.

McKinney, William Wilson, *Early Pittsburgh Presbyterianism. Tracing the Development of the Presbyterian Church, United States of America, in Pittsburgh, Pennsylvania from 1758-1839* (Pittsburgh, The Gibson Press, 1938, pp. 345).

McLean, Archibald, *The History of the Foreign Christian Missionary Society* (New York, Fleming H. Revell Co., 1919, pp. 444). By a president of the society.

McNamara, William, *The Catholic Church on the Northern Indiana Frontier 1789-1844* (Washington, D. C., The Catholic University of America, 1931, pp. vii, 84). A doctoral dissertation based partly upon manuscript archives.

McNeill, John T., *Christian Hope for World Society* (Chicago, Willett, Clark and Co., 1937, pp. vii, 278). A thoughtful series of lectures by a church historian.

McNemar, Richard, *The Kentucky Revival; or, A Short History of the Late Extraordinary Outpouring of the Spirit of God in the Western States of America, etc.* (New York, Edward O. Jenkins, 1846, pp. 156).

Maes, Camillus P., *The Life of Rev. Charles Nerinckx; with a Chapter on the Early Catholic Missions of Kentucky; Copious Notes on the Progress of Catholicity; in the United States of America, from 1800 to 1825; an Account of the Establishment of the Society of Jesus in Missouri, and an Historical Sketch of the Sisterhood of Loretto in Kentucky, Missouri, New Mexico, etc.* (Cincinnati, Robert Clarke & Co., 1880, pp. xvii, 635). Based largely upon unpublished documents, especially letters of Nerinckx.

Magoun, George F., *Asa Turner. A Home Missionary Patriarch and His Times* (Boston, Congregational Sunday-School and Publishing Society, 1889, pp. 345). By a close friend.

Malcolm, M. Vartan, *The Armenians in America* (Boston, The Pilgrim Press, 1919, pp. xxvi, 142).

Mangano, Antonio, *Sons of Italy. A Social and Religious Study of the Italians in America* (New York, Missionary Education Movement of the United States and Canada, 1917, pp. xii, 234). By an Italian Protestant leader.

Manross, William Wilson, *A History of the American Episcopal Church* (New York, Morehouse Publishing Co., 1935, pp. xvi, 404). By a member of the faculty of General Theological Seminary. Except for Chapters 1, 2, and 8, based upon original sources.

Marie, Élie, *Aux Avant-postes de la Chrétienté. Histoire des Instituts Religieux et Missionnaires* (Paris, P. Lethielleux, 1930, pp. xii, 343). Has useful bibliographies.

Martin, M. Aquinata, *The Catholic Church on the Nebraska Frontier (1854-1885)* (Washington, D. C., The Catholic University of America, 1937, pp. ix, 202). A doctoral dissertation.

The Massachusetts Baptist Missionary Magazine (Boston, 1803ff.).

Masters, Victor I., editor, *The Home Mission Task* (Atlanta, The Home Mission Board of the Southern Baptist Convention, 1912, pp. 331).

Mathews, Basil, *John R. Mott, World Citizen* (New York, Harper & Brothers, 1934, pp. xiii, 469). A warmly appreciative biography by a personal friend, based upon careful research and upon data provided by Dr. Mott.

Mathieson, William Law, *English Church Reform 1815-1840* (London, Longmans, Green and Co., 1923, pp. x, 180). Objective, well documented.

Mattingly, Mary Ramona, *The Catholic Church on the Kentucky Frontier (1785-1812)* (Washington, D. C., The Catholic University of America, 1936, pp. viii, 235). A doctoral dissertation, based partly upon manuscript archives.

Mattoon, C. H., *Baptist Annals of Oregon* (McMinnville, Ore., The Pacific Baptist Press, 2 vols., 1906, 1913). By a pioneer Baptist missionary.

Maurer, Charles Lewis, *Early Lutheran Education in Pennsylvania* (Philadelphia, Dorrance and Co., 1932, pp. xii, 284). Especially good on details of schools in particular regions.

May, Mark A., *The Education of American Ministers* (New York, Institute of Social and Religious Research, Vols. II and III, 1934).

Mays, Benjamin Elijah, and Nicholson, Joseph William, *The Negro's Church* (New York, Institute of Social and Religious Research, 1933, pp. xiii, 321). Scholarly.

Mead, Margaret, *The Changing Culture of an Indian Tribe* (New York, Columbia University Press, 1932, pp. xiv, 313).

Mears, Eliot Grinnell, *Resident Orientals on the American Pacific Coast. Their Legal and Economic Status* (New York, American Group, Institute of Pacific Relations, 1927, pp. xvi, 526). Scholarly.

Meriam, Lewis et alii, *The Problem of Indian Administration* (Baltimore, The Johns Hopkins Press, 1928, pp. xxii, 872). A standard work.

Annual Report of the Board of Foreign Missions of the Methodist Episcopal Church for the Year 1913 (New York, 1913, pp. 674).

The Methodist Forward Movement in the United States. Annual of the Board of Home Missions and Church Extension of the Methodist Episcopal Church for the Year 1907-1908 (Philadelphia, n.d., pp. 236).

The Methodist Magazine (New York, 1818ff.). Continued as the *Methodist Review*.

Meylan, A., *Histoire de l'Evangelisation des Lapons* (Paris, Société des Écoles du Dimanche, 1863, pp. 211). A popular account.

The Millennial Harbinger (Bethany, W. Va., 1830-1870).

Miller, William, *The Ottoman Empire and Its Successors, 1801-1927, with an Appendix, 1927-1934* (Cambridge University Press, revised ed., 1934, pp. xv, 638).

Millis, H. A., *The Japanese Problem in the United States* (New York, The Macmillan Co., 1915, pp. xxi, 334). Carefully done.

Milukow, Paul, *Skizzen russischer Kulturgeschichte. Deutsche vom Verfasser durchgesehene Ausgabe von E. Davidson* (Leipzig, Otto Wigand, 2 vols., 1898, 1901).

Minogue, Anna C., *Pages from A Hundred Years of Dominican History. The Story of the Congregation of Saint Catharine of Sienna* (New York and Cincinnati, Frederick Pustet & Co., 1921, pp. 291). Sympathetic, based upon the records of the Congregation.

Minutes of the Annual Conferences of the Methodist Episcopal Church for the Years 1773-1828 (Vol. I, New York, T. Mason and G. Lane, 1840).

The Missionary Herald (Boston, 1821ff.). An official organ of the American Board of Commissioners for Foreign Missions.

The Missionary Intelligencer. Published Monthly by the Foreign Christian Missionary Society, Cincinnati, Ohio (1888ff.).

Missionary Yearbook 1936. Nineteenth Annual Report Board of Missions, Methodist Episcopal Church, South (Nashville, Tenn., pp. 329).

Missions en Chine et au Congo (Bruxelles, 1899ff.). (Beginning with 1909, the Philippines were added to the title.) Published for the Congregation of the Immaculate Heart of Mary.

Mode, Peter G., *The Frontier Spirit in American Christianity* (New York, The Macmillan Co., 1923, pp. x, 196). A suggestive and scholarly essay.

Moffett, Thomas C., *The American Indian on the New Trail* (New York, Missionary Education Movement of the United States and Canada, 1914, pp. xiii, 302).

Moody, William R., *D. L. Moody* (New York, The Macmillan Co., 1930, pp. 556). A biography by a son, valuable for its intimate recollections and the wealth of quotations from contemporary documents.

Moore, John F., *Will America Become Catholic?* (New York, Harper & Brothers, 1931, pp. x, 252). Objective, by a Protestant.

Moore, John Milton, *The Challenge of Change. What is Happening to Home Missions* (New York, Council of Women for Home Missions and Missionary Education Movement, 1931, pp. xi, 204). A textbook by a clergyman.

Moore, William Thomas, *A Comprehensive History of the Disciples of Christ* (New York, Fleming H. Revell Co., 1909, pp. xiv, 830). By a clergyman, favourable to the Disciples.

Morgan, E. R., *The Catholic Revival and Missions* (Westminster, The Society for the Propagation of the Gospel in Foreign Parts, 1933, pp. vii, 83). An account of the effect of the Oxford Movement on the work of the Anglican Communion overseas, by a specialist on church history.

Morison, John, *The Fathers and Founders of the London Missionary Society with a Brief Sketch of Methodism and Historical Notices of Several Protestant Missions from 1556 to 1839* (London, Fisher, Son & Co., 2 vols., no date).

Morris, Henry, *The Life of Charles Grant Sometime Member of Parliament for Inverness-shire and Director of the East India Company* (London, John Murray, 1904, pp. xviii, 404).

Morse, Hermann N., editor, *Home Missions Today and Tomorrow. A Review and Forecast* (New York, Home Missions Council, 1934, pp. xvi, 419). An official study by the Home Missions Council.

Moss, Leslie B., *Adventures in Missionary Cooperation* (New York, Foreign Missions Conference of North America, 1930, pp. 121).

Mott, John R., *Five Decades and a Forward View* (New York, Harper & Brothers, 1939, pp. 139). Semi-autobiographical.

Moyer, Elgin S., *Missions in the Church of the Brethren. Their Development and Effect upon the Denomination* (Elgin, Ill., Brethren Publishing House, 1931, pp. 301). Scholarly.

Murphy, Du Bose, *A Short History of the Protestant Episcopal Church in Texas* (Dallas, Texas, Turner Co., 1935, pp. ix, 173). Largely from the archives of the diocese.

Newman, A. H., *A History of the Baptist Churches in the United States* (New York, The Christian Literature Co., 1894, pp. xv, 513). In *The American Church History Series*.

The New-York Missionary Magazine and Repository of Religious Intelligence (New York, 1800-1803).

Niebuhr, H. Richard, *The Kingdom of God in America* (Chicago, Willett, Clark & Co., 1937, pp. xvii, 215). A brilliant interpretation of the religious history of the United States.

Niebuhr, H. Richard, *The Social Sources of Denominationalism* (New York, Henry Holt and Co., 1929, pp. viii, 304). Brilliantly written.

Nippold, Friedrich, *The Papacy in the 19th Century. A Part of "The History of Catholicism since the Restoration of the Papacy."* Translated by Laurence Henry Schwab (New York, G. P. Putnam's Sons, 1900, pp. ix, 372). Critical of Roman Catholicism and of the Jesuits.

Nordhoff, Charles, *The Communistic Societies of the United States: From Personal Visit and Observation* (New York, Harper & Brothers, 1875, pp. 439).

Norlie, Olaf Morgan, *History of the Norwegian People in America* (Minneapolis, Augsburg Publishing House, 1925, pp. 602). Packed with information, but without footnote references to the sources.

North, Louise McCoy, *The Story of the New York Branch of the Woman's Foreign Missionary Society of the Methodist Episcopal Church* (New York, The New York Branch, 1926, pp. 340).

Publications of the Norwegian-American Historical Association. Studies and Records (Minneapolis, Norwegian-American Historical Association, 1926ff.).

Noyes, H. E., *Church Reform in Spain and Portugal. A short History of the Reformed Episcopal Churches of Spain and Portugal, from 1868 to the Present Time* (London, Cassell and Co., 1897, pp. xii, 192).

Nutting, M. Adelaide, and Dock, Lavinia L., *A History of Nursing* (New York, G. P. Putnam's Sons, 4 vols., 1907-1912).

O'Brien, Joseph L., *John England—Bishop of Charleston. The Apostle to Democracy* (New York, The Edward O'Toole Co., 1934, pp. xiii, 222). Warmly sympathetic.

O'Connell, William, *Recollections of Seventy Years* (Boston, Houghton Mifflin Co., 1934, pp. ix, 395).

O'Daniel, V. F., *The Father of the Church in Tennessee, or the Life, Times, and Character of the Right Reverend Richard Pius Miles, O.P., the First Bishop of Nashville* (Washington, D. C., The Dominicana, 1926, pp. xiv, 607). Sympathetic. Based upon extensive research.

O'Daniel, V. F., *The Right Rev. Edward Dominic Fenwick, O.P., Founder of the Dominicans in the United States* (Washington, D. C., The Dominicana, 1920, pp. xiv, 473). Based upon careful research in the sources. Warmly sympathetic.

O'Donnell, John Hugh, *The Catholic Hierarchy of the United States 1790-1922* (Washington, D. C., The Catholic University of America, Studies in American Church History, Vol. IV, 1922, pp. xiv, 223). A doctoral dissertation. Contains brief biographies of the bishops and extensive bibliographies.

O'Gorman, Thomas, *A History of the Roman Catholic Church in the United States* (New York, The Christian Literature Co., 1895, pp. xviii, 515). In *The American Church History Series*.

Olmstead, Frederick Law, *A Journey in the Back Country in the Winter of 1853-4* (New York, G. P. Putnam's Sons, 2 vols., 1907, originally published in 1860). Critical of slavery, and therefore tending to give a gloomy picture of Negro life.

Olmstead, Frederick Law, *A Journey in the Seaboard Slave States with Remarks on Their Economy* (New York, Mason Brothers, 1858, pp. xv, 723).

Olsen, M. Ellsworth, *A History of the Origin and Progress of Seventh-Day Adventists* (Washington, D. C., Review and Herald Publishing Association, 3d ed., 1932, pp. 768). Very favourable, based upon official records, by a member of the denomination.

Padelford, Frank W., *The Commonwealths and the Kingdom. A Study of the Missionary Work of State Conventions* (Philadelphia, The Griffith and Rowland Press, 1913, pp. xiii, 209). An authoritative textbook of the home missions of the Northern Baptist state conventions.

Paine, Robert, *Life and Times of William McKendree, Bishop of the Methodist Episcopal Church* (Nashville, Publishing House Methodist Episcopal Church, South, 1922, pp. 549). Based partly upon McKendree's papers, and by a personal friend.

Parker, Edwin Pond, *Historical Discourse in Commemoration of the One Hundredth Anniversary of the Missionary Society of Connecticut* (Hartford, The Case, Rockwood & Brainard Co., 1898, pp. 40).

Pascoe, C. F., *Two Hundred Years of the S.P.G. An Historical Account of the Society for the Propagation of the Gospel in Foreign Parts, 1701-1900* (London, published at the Society's Office, 1901, pp. xli, 1429). Very detailed, by an assistant secretary of the Society.

Paxson, Frederich, *History of the American Frontier 1763-1893* (Boston, Houghton Mifflin Co., 1924, pp. vi, 598).

Peck, William George, *The Social Implications of the Oxford Movement* (New York, Charles Scribner's Sons, 1933, pp. x, 346). By an Anglo-Catholic.

Peers, E. Allison, *Spain, the Church and the Orders* (London, Eyre and Spottiswoode, 1939, pp. xi, 219). By an Anglican. Sympathetic. Derived from long residence and some reading.

Peet, Stephen, *History of the Presbyterian and Congregational Churches and Ministers in Wisconsin. Including an Account of the Organization of the Convention and the Plan of Union* (Milwaukee, Silas Chapman, 1851, pp. 208). By a contemporary leader. Much of the book is drawn from his own experience.

Periodical Accounts Relative to a Society formed among the Particular Baptists for Propagating the Gospel among the Heathen (No date or place given of first issue, but was c. 1794).

Phillips, C. S., *The Church in France 1769-1848: A Study in Revival* (London, A. R. Mowbray and Co., 1929, pp. viii, 315). Scholarly, objective, by an Anglican.

Phillips, C. S., *The Church in France 1848-1907* (London, Society for Promoting Christian Knowledge, 1936, pp. 341).

Pollard, Edward B., and Stevens, Daniel Gurden, *Luther Rice, Pioneer in Missions and Education* (Philadelphia, The Judson Press, 1928, pp. 125). Based largely upon the unpublished diary and journal of Rice.

Pond, William C., *Gospel Pioneering: Reminiscences of Early Congregationalism in California 1833-1920* (Oberlin, The News Printing Co., 1921, pp. 191).

Posey, Walter Brownlow, *The Development of Methodism in the Old Southwest 1783-1824* (Tuscaloosa, Ala., Weatherford Printing Co., 1933, pp. 151). Carefully documented.

One Hundred Twelfth Annual Report Board of Home Missions of the Presbyterian Church in the United States of America, 1914 (New York, Presbyterian Building, 1914, pp. 260).

Priester und Mission Jahrbuch der Unio Cleri pro Missionibus in den Ländern deutscher Zunge. Herausgegeben von der Unio Cleri pro Missionibus in Deutschland, Österreich, Schweiz, Tschechoslowakei (Aachen, Unio Cleri pro Missionibus, 1917ff.).

Proceedings of the Board of Missions of the Protestant Episcopal Church in the United States of America, at their Forty-First Annual Meeting, Held in Philadelphia, October, 1876 (New York, E. S. Dodge Steam Presses, 1876, pp. 258).

Proceedings of the Church Missionary Society for Africa and the East (Vol. I, London, 1805, pp. 479).

Proceedings of the Society for Propagating the Gospel Among the Heathen. Sesqui-Centennial Number . . . 1937 (Published by the Society, Bethlehem, Penn., 1937, pp. 138).

Proceedings of the Union Missionary Convention Held in New York, May 4th and 5th, 1854 (New York, Taylor & Hogg, 1854, pp. 611).

Puckett, Newbell Niles, *Folk Beliefs of the Southern Negro* (Chapel Hill, University of North Carolina Press, 1926, pp. xiv, 644).

Raven, Charles E., *Christian Socialism 1848-1854* (London, Macmillan and Co., 1920, pp. xii, 396). Well written, based upon careful research, and warmly sympathetic.

Raven, Charles E., *Jesus and the Gospel of Love* (New York, Henry Holt and Co., 1931, pp. 452).

Ray, Mary Augustina, *American Opinion of Roman Catholicism in the Eighteenth Century* (New York, Columbia University Press, 1936, pp. 456). Scholarly.

Reid, J. M., *Missions and Missionary Society of the Methodist Episcopal Church.* Revised and extended by J. T. Gracey (New York, Hunt and Eaton, 3 vols., 1895-1896). Based upon manuscript and printed sources, but without footnote references to the authorities.

Rice, Edwin Wilbur, *The Sunday-School Movement 1780-1917 and the American Sunday-School Union* (Philadelphia, American Sunday-School Union, 1917, pp. 501).

Richards, Thomas C., *Samuel J. Mills, Missionary Pathfinder, Pioneer and Promoter* (Boston, The Pilgrim Press, 1906, pp. 275).

Riley, B. F., *History of the Baptists of Alabama from the Time of Their First Occupation of Alabama in 1808 until 1894* (Birmingham, Roberts and Son, 1895, pp. 481). Issued under the auspices of the Alabama Baptist Historical Society.

Robbins, Harry E., editor, *A Hand-Book of the Church's Mission to the Indians* (Hartford, Conn., Church Missions Publishing Co., 1894, pp. 329).

Roemer, Theodore, *The Ludwig-Missionsverein and the Church in the United States (1838-1918)* (Washington, D. C., The Catholic University of America, 1933, pp. xii, 161). A doctoral dissertation by a Capuchin.

Rohne, J. Magnus, *Norwegian American Lutheranism up to 1872* (New York, The Macmillan Co., 1926, pp. xxiv, 271). Carefully documented.

de le Roi, J. F. A., *Die evangelische Christenheit und die Juden unter dem Gesichtspunkte der Mission geschichtlich betrachtet* (Karlsruhe and Berlin, H. Reuther, 3 vols., 1884-1892). A revised edition of the second and third volumes was issued under the title *Geschichte der evangelischen Juden-mission seit Entstehung des neueren Judentums* (Leipzig, J. C. Hinrichs'sche Buchhandlung, 2 vols., 1899). Although lacking in many precise references to the sources, it contains excellent bibliographies.

Rouse, Michael Francis, *A Study of the Development of Negro Education under Catholic Auspices in Maryland and the District of Columbia* (Baltimore, The Johns Hopkins Press, 1935, pp. ix, 125). A doctoral dissertation by a Xaverian Brother long engaged in education.

Ruane, Joseph William, *The Beginnings of the Society of St. Sulpice in the United States (1791-1829)* (Washington, D. C., The Catholic University of America, 1935, pp. x, 266). A doctoral dissertation based largely upon manuscript archives.

Ruppin, Arthur, *The Jews in the Modern World* (London, Macmillan and Co., 1934, pp. xxx, 423). By a Jewish scholar; comprehensive, objective.

Sanford, Elias B., *Origin and History of the Federal Council of the Churches of Christ in America* (Hartford, The S. S. Scranton Co., 1916, pp. xii, 528). By one long officially connected with the Council and with the movements which led up to it.

Schaff, Philip, and Prime, S. Irenaeus, editors, *History, Essays, Orations, and Other Documents of the Sixth General Conference of the Evangelical Alliance Held in New York, Oct. 2-12, 1873* (New York, Harper & Brothers, 1874, pp. iv, 773).

Schlatter, Wilhelm, *Geschichte der Basler Mission 1815-1915* (Basel, Basler Missionsbuchhandlung, 3 vols., 1916). Based especially upon unpublished sources.

Schmeckebier, Laurence F., *The Office of Indian Affairs. Its History, Activities and Organization* (Baltimore, The Johns Hopkins Press, 1927, pp. xiv, 591). A scholarly history of the Indian policy and administration of the Government of the United States.

Schmidlin, Joseph, *Catholic Mission Theory (Katholische Missionslehre im Grundniss)*. A translation by Matthias Braun (Techny, Ill., Mission Press, S.V.D., 1931, pp. xii, 544).

Schmidlin, Joseph, *Katholische Missionsgeschichte* (Steyl, Missionsdruckerei, 1924, pp. xi, 598). A standard work by a distinguished Roman Catholic specialist on missions, with extensive bibliographical notes.

There is an English translation, by Matthias Braun (Techny, Ill., Mission Press, 1933, pp. xiv, 862), which makes additions to the bibliographies, especially of more recent works and works in English, and here and there adds to the text and footnotes. In some portions, therefore, it is fuller and better than the German original.

Schneider, Carl E., *The German Church on the American Frontier. A Study in the Rise of Religion among the Germans of the West Based on the History of the Evangelischer Kirchenverein des Westens (Evangelical Church Society of the West), 1840-1866* (St. Louis, Missouri, Eden Publishing House, 1939, pp. xx, 579). Based upon careful research.

Schneider, David M., *The History of Public Welfare in New York State 1609-1866* (University of Chicago Press, 1938, pp. xix, 395). Well documented. Based upon solid research.

Schonfield, Hugh, J., *The History of Jewish Christianity from the First to the Twentieth Century* (London, Duckworth, 1936, pp. 256). Moderately objective, rather pro-Jewish-Christian, sketchy, with many omissions.

Schrott, Lambert, *Pioneer German Catholics in the American Colonies (1734-1784)* (New York, The United States Catholic Historical Society, 1933, pp. xviii, 144).

Schulze, Adolf, *200 Jahre Brüdermission. II Band, Das zweite Missionsjahrhundert* (Herrnhut, Verlag der Missionsbuchhandlung, 1932, pp. xii, 715). Well documented.

Schwager, Friedrich, *Die katholische Heidenmission der Gegenwart im Zusammenhang mit iher grossen Vergangenheit* (Steyl, Missionsdruckerei, 1907, pp. 446). A standard work.

1914 Year Book of the Seventh-Day Adventist Denomination (Washington, D. C., Review and Herald Publishing Association, 1914, pp. 314).

Shaughnessy, Gerald, *Has the Immigrant Kept the Faith? A Study of Immigration and Catholic Growth in the United States 1790-1920* (New York, The Macmillan Co., 1925, pp. 289). By a Roman Catholic, learned and optimistic.

Shaw, P. E., *American Contacts with the Eastern Churches, 1820-1870* (Chicago, The American Society of Church History, 1937, pp. 208). Based upon the sources; careful and objective.

Shea, John Gilmary, *History of the Catholic Missions among the Indian Tribes of the United States, 1529-1854* (New York, P. J. Kenedy, 1899, pp. 514). By a Roman Catholic, favourable to missions.

Shearer, Donald C., *Pontificia Americana: A Documentary History of the Catholic Church in the United States (1784-1884)* (Washington, D. C., The Catholic University of America, 1933, pp. xi, 413). Contains important documents in the original languages, with introductory comments and summaries in English.

Shedd, Clarence P., *Two Centuries of Student Christian Movements, Their Origin and Intercollegiate Life* (New York, Association Press, 1934, pp. xxii, 466). Covers chiefly the period from 1700 to 1900. Based upon careful research in the sources.

Shepherd, R. H. W., *Literature for the South African Bantu. A Comparative Study of Negro Achievement* (Pretoria, The Carnegie Corporation Visitors' Grants Committee, 1936, pp. 81). Largely a report of a visit by a South African to the United States.

Sherrill, Lewis Joseph, *Presbyterian Parochial Schools, 1846-1870* (Yale University Press, 1932, pp. xv, 261). A doctoral dissertation.

Sims, Mary S., *The Natural History of a Social Institution—the Young Women's Christian Association* (New York, The Woman's Press, 1936, pp. x, 251). Semi-official, objective.

Slosser, Gaius Jackson, *Christian Unity. Its History and Challenge in All Communions, in All Lands* (New York, E. P. Dutton and Co., 1929, pp. xix, 425). A comprehensive account, with the chief emphasis upon the nineteenth and twentieth centuries.

Smirnoff, Eugene, *A Short Account of the Historical Development and Present Position of Russian Orthodox Missions* (London, Rivingtons, 1903, pp. xii, 83). By the chaplain to the Russian Embassy in London; based upon careful study of reports of the Chief Procurator of the Holy Synod and of the various missions.

Smirnov, Jean N., *Les Populations Finnoises des Bassins de la Volga et de la Kama. Études d'Ethnographie Historique Traduites du Russe et Revues par Paul Boyer. Première partie, Groupe de la Volga ou Groupe Bulgare. I. Les Tchérémisses, II. Les Mordves* (Paris, Ernest Leroux, 1898, pp. viii, 486).

Smith, C. Henry, *The Mennonites of America* (Scottdale, Pa., Mennonite Publishing House, 1909, pp. 484). Based upon extensive research by a well trained scholar.

Smith, George A., *The Rise, Progress and Travels of the Church of Jesus Christ of Latter-Day Saints* (Salt Lake City, Deseret News Office, 1872, pp. 71). By a President of the Mormons.

[Snethen, Abraham], *Autobiography of Abraham Snethen, The Barefoot Preacher,* collected and compiled by Mrs. N. E. Lamb, corrected and revised by J. F. Burnett (Dayton, Ohio, Christian Publishing Association, 1909, pp. 296).

Spalding, M. J., *Sketches of the Early Catholic Missions of Kentucky; from Their Commencement in 1787, to the Jubilee of 1826-7* (Louisville, B. J. Webb & Brother, preface 1844, pp. xvi, 308). By a Bishop of Louisville; compiled with the aid of an early missionary, S. T. Badin.

Spreng, Samuel P., *History of the Evangelical Association* (New York, The Christian Literature Co., 1894, pp. 383-439). In *The American Church History Series.*

Spring, Gardiner, *Memoirs of the Rev. Samuel J. Mills, Late Missionary to the South Western Section of the United States and Agent of the American Colonization Society Deputed to Explore the Coast of Africa* (New York, New York Evangelical Missionary Society, 1820, pp. 247). By a friend; in part made up of letters and journals of Mills.

Stead, Francis Herbert, *The Story of Social Christianity* (London, James Clarke and Co., 2 vols., [no date]). Laudatory of the social changes wrought in the world by Christianity throughout the course of its history.

Steiner, Edward A., *The Immigrant Tide. Its Ebb and Flow* (New York, Fleming H. Revell Co., 1909, pp. 370). Popularly written.

Stephen, James, *Essays in Ecclesiastical Biography* (London, Longmans, Green and Co., 2 vols., 1907 [first edition 1849]).

Stephenson, George M., *The Religious Aspects of Swedish Immigration. A Study of Immigrant Churches* (University of Minnesota Press, 1932, pp. viii, 542). Carefully done and based upon sources and an extensive literature.

Stewart, George, *A History of Religious Education in Connecticut to the Middle of the Nineteenth Century* (Yale University Press, 1924, pp. xiv, 402). A definitive work.

Stewart, Robert Laird, *Sheldon Jackson, Pathfinder and Prospector of the Missionary Vanguard in the Rocky Mountains and Alaska* (New York, Fleming H. Revell Co., 2d ed., 1908, pp. 488). Compiled from data provided by Jackson and his family.

Stiansen, P., *History of the Baptists in Norway* (Chicago, The Blessing Press, 1933, pp. xi, 176). Result of careful research in Norway.

Stiansen, P., *History of the Norwegian Baptists in America* (The Norwegian Baptist Conference of America and The American Baptist Publication Society, 1939, pp. 344).

Stirling, Anna Maria Wilhelmina (Pickering), *The Ways of Yesterday. Being the Chronicles of the Way Family from 1307 to 1885* (London, Thornton Butterworth, 1930, pp. 320). Based upon original documents.

Stock, Eugene, *The History of the Church Missionary Society: Its Environment, Its Men, and Its Work* (London, Church Missionary Society, 4 vols., 1899-1916). The standard history, by a secretary of the Society.

Stone, Barton Warren, *The Biography of Eld. Barton Warren Stone, Written by himself: with Additions and Reflections by Elder John Rogers* (Cincinnati, J. A. & U. P. James, 1847, pp. ix, 404).

Stout, John E., *The Daily Vacation Church School. How to Organize and Conduct It* (New York, The Abingdon Press, 1923, pp. 119).

Strack, Hermann L., *Jahrbuch der evangelischen Judenmission. I. Band* (Leipzig, J. C. Hinrichs'sche Buchhandlung, 1906, pp. 124).

Streit, Carolus, *Atlas Hierarchicus* (Typographia Bonifaciana, Paderborn, 1913, pp. 128, 37, 35).

Strong, Josiah, *The Challenge of the City* (New York, Eaton and Mains, 1907, pp. xiv, 332). A mission study textbook.

Strong, William Ellsworth, *The Story of the American Board: An Account of the First Hundred Years of the American Board of Commissioners for Foreign Missions* (Boston, The Pilgrim Press, 1910, pp. xv, 523). A semi-official history.

Students and the Modern Missionary Crusade. Addresses Delivered Before the Fifth International Convention of the Student Volunteer Movement for Foreign Missions, Nashville, Tennessee, February 28—March 4, 1906 (New York, Student Volunteer Movement for Foreign Missions, 1906, pp. xii, 713).

[Sturtevant, Julian M.], *Julian M. Sturtevant, An Autobiography,* edited by J. M. Sturtevant, Jr. (New York, Fleming H. Revell Co., 1896, pp. 346).

Survey of Service. Organizations Represented in International Convention of Disciples of Christ (St. Louis, Christian Board of Publication, 1928, pp. 723). Various authors have contributed, writing from first-hand knowledge, describing the work of the denomination.

Sweet, William Warren, *Circuit-Rider Days Along the Ohio. Being the Journals of the Ohio Conference from its Organization in 1812 to 1826. Edited With Introduction and Notes* (New York, The Methodist Book Concern, 1923, pp. 299).

Sweet, William Warren, *Religion on the American Frontier. The Baptists, 1783-1830, a Collection of Source Material* (New York, Henry Holt and Co., 1931, pp. ix, 652).

Sweet, William Warren, *Religion on the American Frontier. Vol. II, The Presbyterians 1783-1840, a Collection of Source Materials* (New York, Harper & Brothers, 1936, pp. xii, 939).

Sweet, William Warren, *Religion on the American Frontier 1783-1850. Vol. III, The Congregationalists. A Collection of Source Materials* (University of Chicago Press, 1939, pp. xi, 435).

Sweet, William Warren, *The Rise of Methodism in the West. Being the Journal of the Western Conference 1810-1811. Edited, with Notes and Introduction* (New York, The Methodist Book Concern, 1920, pp. 207).

Sweet, William Warren, *The Story of Religions in America* (New York, Harper & Brothers, 1930, pp. vii, 571). An historical survey confined to the United States.

Tamarati, Michel, *L'Église Géorgienne des Origines jusqu'a nos Jours* (Rome, Imprimerie de la Société Typographico-Editrice Romaine, 1910, pp. xv, 710). Based upon extensive research.

Taylor, E. R., *Methodism and Politics 1791-1851* (Cambridge University Press, 1935, pp. xi, 227). Ably written, objective.

Taylor, James B., *Memoir of Rev. Luther Rice, One of the First American Missionaries to the East* (Nashville, Tenn., Boardman Press, 1937, pp. 303). A reprint of a work first issued in 1840 and including many of Rice's letters and making use of his diary.

Tewksbury, Donald G., *The Founding of American Colleges and Universities Before the Civil War. With Particular Reference to the Religious Influences Bearing upon the College Movement* (New York, Bureau of Publications, Teachers College, Columbia University, 1932, pp. x, 254). Based upon extensive reading in primary and secondary sources.

Theophilus (Bishop), *A Short History of the Christian Church and the Ritual of the Eastern Orthodox Church, Its History and Meaning* (San Francisco, Douglass Brothers, 1934, pp. 46). An official statement for a popular audience.

Thompson, A. E., *A Century of Jewish Missions* (New York, Fleming H. Revell Co., 1902, pp. 286). A Protestant work confined to Protestant missions, warmly sympathetic, undocumented.

Thompson, Robert Ellis, *A History of the Presbyterian Churches in the United States* (New York, The Christian Literature Co., 1895, pp. xxxi, 424). In *The American Church History Series.*

Tiffany, Charles C., *A History of the Protestant Episcopal Church in the United States of America* (New York, The Christian Literature Society, 1895, pp. xxiv, 593). In *The American Church History Series.*

Time. The Weekly News-Magazine (New York, 1923ff.).

Timpe, Georg, *Katholisches Deutschtum in den Vereinigten Staaten von Amerika. Ein Querschnitt* (Freiburg im Breisgau, Herder & Co., 1937, pp. xii, 248).

Tolstoi, Lyof N., *My Confession and the Spirit of Christ's Teaching* (New York, Thomas Y. Crowell & Co., 1887, pp. x, 242).

Tow, J. S., *The Real Chinese in America* (New York City, The Academy Press, 1923, pp. 168). By a Chinese.

Townsend, Leah, *South Carolina Baptists 1670-1805* (Florence, S. C., The Florence Printing Co., 1935, pp. 391). A doctoral dissertation.

Toynbee, Arnold J., *A Study of History* (Oxford University Press, Vols. 1-3, 1934, Vols. 4-6, 1939). A mammoth work of correlation and interpretation.

Tracy, Joseph, *History of the American Board of Commissioners for Foreign Missions Compiled chiefly from the Published and Unprinted Documents of the Board* (New York, M. W. Dodd, 2d ed., 1842, pp. viii, 452).

Tupper, Eleanor, and McReynolds, George E., *Japan in American Public Opinion* (New York, The Macmillan Co., 1937, pp. xiii, 465). Objective, based largely upon public opinion as reflected in newspapers and periodicals.

Turner, Frederick Jackson, *The Frontier in American History* (New York, Henry Hall and Co., 1931 [First published 1920], pp. 375).

Tyler, B. B., *History of the Disciples of Christ* (New York, The Christian Literature Co., 1894, pp. 519). In *The American Church History Series.*

Uhlhorn, G., *Die christliche Liebesthätigkeit* (Stuttgart, D. Goudert, 3 vols., 1882-1890).

Underhill, Evelyn, *Worship* (New York, Harper & Brothers, 2d ed., 1937, pp. xxi, 350).

United States Department of Commerce, Bureau of the Census, *Religious Bodies: 1926* (Washington, United States Government Printing Office, 2 vols., 1930).

Vahl, J., *Lapperne og den lapske Mission* (Copenhagen, G.E.C. Gads Voghandel, 1866, pp. 174, 189. Extensive references to pertinent sources and literature.

Vail, Albert, L., *The Morning Hour of American Baptist Missions* (Philadelphia, American Baptist Publication Society, 1907, pp. 477). Without footnotes, but apparently based upon careful research in the sources.

Vander Velde, Lewis G., *The Presbyterian Churches and the Federal Union 1861-1869* (Harvard University Press, 1932, pp. xv, 575). Based upon extensive research into original documents.

Van der Zee, Jacob, *The British in Iowa* (Iowa City, Iowa, The State Historical Society of Iowa, 1922, pp. 340). Well documented.

Vernadsky, George, *A History of Russia* (Yale University Press, Revised edition, 1930, pp. xix, 413). An excellent summary.

Vidler, Alec. R., *The Modernist Movement in the Roman Church: Its Origins and Outcome* (Cambridge University Press, 1934, pp. xiii, 286).

Vincent, Leon H., *John Heyl Vincent. A Biographical Sketch* (New York, The Macmillan Co., 1925, pp. 319). Based chiefly upon Vincent's journal, other private papers, and autobiography.

Visser 't Hooft, W. A., *Anglo-Catholicism and Orthodoxy. A Protestant View* (London, Student Christian Movement Press, 1933, pp. 175).

Wagner, Donald O., *The Church of England and Social Reform Since 1854* (New York, Columbia University Press, 1930, pp. 341). A doctoral dissertation, in general sympathetic with the Church.

Walker, Robert Sparks, *Torchlights to the Cherokees. The Brainerd Mission* (New York, The Macmillan Co., 1931, pp. xii, 339). An account based largely upon the manuscript files of the American Board of Commissioners for Foreign Missions; very favourable to the missionaries and Cherokees.

Walker, Williston, *A History of the Congregational Churches in the United States* (New York, The Christian Literature Society, 1894, pp. xiii, 451). By a competent scholar.

Walsh, James J., *American Jesuits* (New York, The Macmillan Co., 1934, pp. ix, 336). Warmly sympathetic with the Jesuits.

Warburton, Stacy R., *Eastward! The Story of Adoniram Judson* (New York, Round Table Press, 1937, pp. xi, 240). Sympathetic; based upon careful research.

Ware, Charles Crossfield, *Barton Warren Stone, Pathfinder of Christian Union. A Story of His Life and Times* (St. Louis, The Bethany Press, 1932, pp. xiv, 357). Based largely upon printed sources.

Warne, Frank Julian, *The Immigrant Invasion* (New York, Dodd, Mead and Co., 1913, pp. 336). Semi-popular.

Warneck, Gustav, *Abriss einer Geschichte der protestantischen Missionen von den Reformation bis auf die Gegenwart, mit einem Anhang über die katholischen Missionen* (Berlin, Martin Warneck, 10th ed., 1913, pp. x, 624).

Washington, Booker T., *The Story of the Negro. The Rise of the Race from Slavery* (New York, Doubleday, Page & Co., 2 vols., 1909).

Washington, Booker T., *Up From Slavery. An Autobiography* (New York, Doubleday, Page & Co., 1901, pp. ix, 330).

Wayland, Francis, *A Memoir of the Life and Labors of the Rev. Adoniram Judson, D.D.* (Boston, Phillips, Sampson and Co., 2 vols., 1853). Includes extensive excerpts from original documents, including letters of Judson.

Wayland, F., *The Moral Dignity of the Missionary Enterprise* (6th ed., Edinburgh, James Robertson and Co., 1826). A sermon delivered Nov. 4, 1824, before the Boston Missionary Society.

Wearmouth, Robert F., *Methodism and the Working-Class Movements of England 1800-1850* (London, The Epworth Press, 1937, pp. 289). Scholarly, and sympathetic with Methodism and the working class movement.

Webb, Ben. J., *The Centenary of Catholicity in Kentucky* (Louisville, Charles A. Rogers, 1884, pp. v, 594). Based upon personal knowledge, long residence, and careful research: warmly Roman Catholic.

Weber, Herman C., *1933 Edition Yearbook of American Churches* (New York, Round Table Press, 1933, pp. 400).

Weigle, Luther A., *American Idealism* (Yale University Press, 1928, pp. 356). A competent survey, with running commentaries on pertinent illustrations, of the religious history of the United States.

Wentz, Abdel Ross, *The Lutheran Church in American History* (Philadelphia, The United Lutheran Publication Society, 2d ed., 1933, pp. 465). An authoritative survey.

Wesley, Charles H., *Richard Allen, Apostle of Freedom* (Washington, The Associated Publishers, 1935, pp. xi, 300).

Wheeler, W. Reginald, King, Henry H., and Davidson, Alexander B., editors, *The Foreign Student in America* (New York, Association Press, 1925, pp. xxxiv, 329).

White, Andrew Dickson, *A History of the Warfare of Science with Theology in Christendom* (London, Macmillan and Co., 2 vols., 1896).

White, Charles L., *A Century of Faith: . . . Centenary Volume Published for the American Baptist Home Mission Society* (Philadelphia, The Judson Press, 1932, pp. 320).

Wicher, Edward Arthur, *The Presbyterian Church in California 1849-1927* (New York, Frederick H. Hitchcock, 1927, pp. xi, 360). A semi-official history, based upon careful research in original sources, but without footnote references.

Wilder, Robert P., *The Great Commission. The Missionary Response of the Student Volunteer Movements in North America and Europe; Some Personal Reminiscences* (London, Oliphants, 1936, pp. 115).

Will, Allen Sinclair, *Life of Cardinal Gibbons, Archbishop of Baltimore* (New York, E. P. Dutton & Co., 2 vols., 1922). Based upon personal acquaintance and extensive research in the journals and letters of Gibbons.

Williams, Daniel Jenkins, *One Hundred Years of Welsh Calvinistic Methodism in America* (Philadelphia, The Westminster Press, 1937, pp. xxi, 447).

Williams, Michael, with the collaboration of Julia Kernan, *The Catholic Church in Action* (New York, The Macmillan Co., 1934, pp. 358). By a Roman Catholic.

Williams, N. P., and Harris, Charles, *Northern Catholicism. Centenary Studies in Oxford and Parallel Movements* (London, Society for Promoting Christian Knowledge, 1933, pp. xvi, 555). By a number of authors.

Winkworth, Catherine, *Life of Pastor Fliedner of Kaiserswerth*. Translated from the German (London, Longmans, Green and Co., 1867, pp. xiv, 155).

Woodson, C. G., *The Education of the Negro Prior to 1861. A History of the Education of the Colored People of the United States from the Beginning of Slavery to the Civil War* (New York, G. P. Putnam's Sons, 1915, pp. v, 454). Well documented.

Woodson, Carter G., *The History of the Negro Church* (Washington, D. C., The Associated Publishers, 2d ed., 1921, pp. x, 330).

Work, Monroe N., editor, *Negro Year Book. An Annual Encyclopedia of the Negro* (Tuskegee Institute, The Negro Year Book Publishing Co., 1914ff.).

World Missionary Conference, 1910 (Edinburgh and London, Oliphant, Anderson & Ferrier, 9 vols., 1910).

World Unity (New York, 1927-1935).

Wright, Edward Needles, *Conscientious Objectors in the Civil War* (Philadelphia, University of Pennsylvania Press, 1931, pp. vii, 274). A scholarly study, unbiased and well documented.

Zeilinger, G. J., *A Missionary Synod with a Mission. A Memoir of the Seventy-Fifth Anniversary of the Evangelical Lutheran Synod of Iowa and Other States* (Chicago, Wartburg Publishing House, 1929, pp. 115). Published under the authority of the Synod.

Zeitschrift für Missionswissenschaft (Münster, i.W., 1911ff.).

Zollman, Carl, *American Church Law* (St. Paul, West Publishing Co., 1933, pp. xv, 675). Carefully documented.

INDEX

Abernaquis, 316
Abolition movement, in the United States, 345-351
Aborigines Protection Society, 159
Abstinence, total, 157
Abyssinia, 1
Accommodation Plan, 208
Adams, John, 411, 413
Adams, John Quincy, 347, 412
Addams, Jane, 372
Additional Curates Society, 149
Africa, 1, 3, 13, 20, 51, 56, 62, 80, 85, 101
African Episcopal Church of St. Thomas, 338
African Methodist Episcopal Church, 338, 339, 354, 356
African Methodist Episcopal Zion Church, 339, 340, 354, 356
African Union Church, 340
African Union Methodist Protestant Church, 340
Agnosticism, 23
Ahnfelt, Oscar, 276
Aix-la-Chapelle, Congress of, 113
Alabama, 182
Alani, 119
Alaska, 2, 13, 213, 256, 311, 312, 315, 320
Albanians, in the United States, 258
Albertson, Ralph, 391
Albright, Jacob, 287, 288
Alcott, Amos Bronson, 420
Aleutian Islands, 311
Aleuts, 256, 312
Alexander I, 24, 113, 117, 129, 164
Alexander II, 129
Alexander III, 108, 129, 142
Alexander, Michael Solomon, 114
Algeria, 133
Allahabad, 104
Allen, Richard, 338
Allgemeine Missionszeitschrift, 92
Alliance of the Reformed Churches holding the Presbyterian System, 103
Altai mission, 107
Amana Community, 391
Ambrose, Archbishop of Kazan, 121
America, 388
America, Latin, 3, 5, 8, 31, 94, 104

American and Christian Foreign Union, 283
American Baptist Home Mission Society, 88, 289, 360
American Baptist Publication Society, 216
American Bethel Society, 374
American Bible Society, 86, 132, 219
American Board of Commissioners for Foreign Missions, organized, 79-82; 84, 86, 88, 103, 315-319, 350, 414
American Christian Convention, 199
American College at Rome, 246
American College of the Immaculate Conception of the Blessed Virgin Mary, 238, 241
American Colonization Society, 85, 344, 345, 351
American Home Missionary Society, 87, 103, 209-213, 220, 284, 290, 291
American Institute for Social Service, 407
American Missionary Association, 88, 350, 358, 359, 373
American National Baptist Convention, 355
American Peace Society, 398, 399
American Protestant Society, 283
American Seamen's Friend Society, 374
American Society for Meliorating the Condition of the Jews, 293
American Society for Propagating the Gospel among the Indians and Others in North America, 77
American Sunday School Union, 219, 376
American Temperance Society, 393, 394
American Temperance Union, 395
American Tract Society, 86, 87, 220
American Unitarian Association, 291
American Woman Suffrage Association, 402
Amish, 263
Amur, 15
Anderson, Paul, 274
Andover, Illinois, 274
Andover Theological Seminary, 79-81, 96, 211, 434
Ann Arbor, Michigan, 267
Anthony, Susan B., 402
Anthropology, 435
Anti-Masonic movement, 401
Anti-Missouri Brotherhood, 273

Anti-Saloon League, 395
Anti-slavery movement, in the United States, 345-351
Apostolate of Saints Cyril and Methodius, 127
Apostolic Faith Missions, 445
Apostolic Lutheran Synod, 277
Apostolic Society, 58
Aquinas, Thomas, 28
Arabs, in the United States, 257
Aral, 15
Archangel Raphael Society, 244
Arizona, 213, 310
Armenians, in the United States, 258
Armstrong, Samuel Chapman, 359
Art in the United States, 414
Arthur, Chester A., 412
Asbury, Francis, 186-189, 286, 288, 393
Ashmun, Jehudi, 345
Asia, 3, 8
Asmun Institute, 335
Assemblies of God, 445
Associate Reformed Church, 84
Association for the Religious Instruction of Negroes, 335
Association of the Holy Childhood, 57, 58, 60
Assumptionists, 53
Assyrian Christians, in the United States, 259
Astronomy, 9
Atkinson, George H., 211, 417
Atlanta University, 358
Atoms, 9, 18
Augustana Synod, 274, 275
Aurora, Oregon, 263, 391
Australia, 3, 8, 13, 20, 31, 66, 94, 98
Austria, 58, 62
Automobile, 10
Avery, Charles, 335
Avery College, 335
Azores, 2

Baader, Franz von, 165
Baedeker, Friedrich Wilhelm, 142
Bacon, David, 390, 404
Bacon, Leonard, 349
Bacone College, 320
Badin, Stephen Theodore, 234, 305
Bailey, Wellesley C., 101
Baldwin, Theron, 221
Balkan Peninsula, 147
Ballou, Hosea, 391, 433
Baltimore, 231, 234, 235, 244, 328, 329
Banco Popular de Leon XIII, 157
Baptism, instruction for, 50

Baptist Association of the Western States and Territories, 355
Baptist Domestic Missionary Society of the State of New York, 214
Baptist Foreign Mission Convention of the United States, 355
Baptist General Association, 446
Baptist, General Missionary Convention, 83
Baptist General Tract Society, 216
Baptist Missionary Convention of the State of New York, 214
Baptist Missionary Society, British, 66-69
Baptist Missionary Society in Massachusetts, 313
Baptist missions to Indians, 320, 321
Baptist Seaman's Bethel, 289
Baptist Society for Propagating the Gospel in India and Other Foreign Parts, 83
Baptist Society for the Evangelization of the Jews, 294
Baptist World Alliance, 103
Baptist Young People's Union, 37
Baptists, anti-mission, 86; among Germans in the United States, 289; among Scandinavians in the United States, 289; among the Negroes of the United States, 332, 333, 336-338, 345, 347, 354-356; in France, 133; in Germany, 134; in Scandinavia, 135, 136; in Russia, 142; on the frontier of the United States, 181, 182, 186, 193, 214, 215; various groups in the United States, 445, 446
Baraga, Frederic, 305
Barcelona, 242
Bardstown, 233-235, 247
Barmen, 267
Barnard, Henry, 416
Barnardo, Thomas John, 148, 154
Basel, 90-93, 267, 269
Bavaria, 58
Beatty, 241
Beaver Islands, 202
Beecher, Catherine, 420
Beecher, Henry Ward, 348, 387, 402
Beecher, Lyman, 348, 349, 420
Beguines, 238
Belgium, 19, 61, 137, 237, 238
Bellamy, Edward, 406
Bellamy, Joseph, 204
Beloit College, 211, 274
Benedictines, 27, 241, 309, 330
Bengal, 70
Berea College, 335, 358
Berlin, 90, 267
Berlin Missionary Society, 91

Berlin Society for the Promotion of Christianity among the Jews, 114
Berliner Frauenverein für christliche Bildung des weiblichen Geschlechts, 92
Berliner Gesellschaft zur Beförderung des Christenthums unter der Juden, 115
Berliner Missionsgesellschaft, 91
Bethany, West Virginia, 198
Bethel, Missouri, 391
Bethel African Methodist Episcopal Church, 338
Bethlehem Church, Berlin, 90
Bible, historical criticism of, 16, 23, 41, 171; distribution of in the United States, 219; translated into Indian tongues, 322
Bible societies, 72, 84, 86
Bigard, Mme., 59
Biology, 9
Birney, James G., 347
Bishop Hill, Illinois, 270
Bishop Payne Divinity School, 360
Bismarck, 17, 28, 145, 156
Blackfeet, 308
Blanchet, François Norbert, 308, 309
Blind, education of, 409
Bliss, William Dwight Porter, 407
Board of Church Erection, 213
Board of Domestic Missions, 278
Boehm, Henry, 288
Boehm, Martin, 286
Boer War, 12
Boerenbond, 146, 157
Bohemian Catholic Alliance, 245
Bombay, 83
Boniface Society, 146
Book of Mormon, 201
Booth, William, 36
Booth-Tucker, 410
Borneo, 3
Bornheim, 237
Bosco, John, 25, 54, 145
Boston, 233, 234, 246, 441
Bourbons, 24
Boville, R. G., 378
Boyd, Richard Henry, 356
Brace, Charles Loring, 410
Bradley, James, 320
Brainerd, David, 67, 74
Breck, James Lloyd, 320
Breckenridge, Robert J., 417
Brethren, Society of the, 80, 96
British and Foreign Anti-Slavery Society, 159
British and Foreign Bible Society, 72, 92, 131, 132
British Empire, 14

Brook Farm, 252, 391
Brooks, Charles, 416
Brooks, Phillips, 387
Broome, Arthur, 156
Brotherhood of the Kingdom, 407
Brown, David, 70
Brown University, 81
Browning, 166
Brownson, Orestes A., 252
Brunner, Franz Sales, 241
Bryan, William Jennings, 412
Bryant, William Cullen, 415
Buchanan, Claudius, 81
Buffalo, 240, 245, 265
Bulgaria, 42, 127, 128, 141
Bulgarian Uniate Church, 128
Bulgars, in the United States, 257
Burder, George, 71
Bureau of Catholic Indian Missions, 310
Burma, 1, 3, 14, 49, 83
Burritt, Elihu, 165, 398
Bushnell, Horace, 377, 386
Butler, Elizur, 316
Butler, Josephine, 156
Buxton, T. F., 156, 158

Cable, 18
Cadbury, George and Robert, 156
Cahensly, 244
Calcutta, 70, 82
California, 303, 304
Calvinism, departure from in the United States, 430-433
Calvinistic Methodist Church of Wales, 259, 260
Calvinistic Methodists, 72
Cambodia, 54
Cambridge, England, 39, 70, 101
Cambridge Seven, 96, 100
Campbell, Alexander, 198, 199
Campbell, Thomas, 198
Camp-meetings, 191-195
Canada, 8, 31, 64, 66, 94
Cane Ridge, 193
Cane Ridge Church, 347
Canterbury, Archbishop of, 74
Canton Christian College, 102
Cape of Good Hope, 2
Cape Verde Islands, 2
Capers, William, 316, 334
Capitalism, 11
Capuchins, 59
Carey, William, 66-69, 82, 105
Carlsson, Erland, 274
Carlyle, 166

Carmelites, 27
Carnegie, Andrew, 400
Carroll, Daniel, 230
Carroll, James, 230
Carroll, John, 231-234, 240, 305, 328
Cartwright, Peter, 189
Cary, Lott, 345
Cataldo, 309
Catherine of Siena Congregation of Dominican Sisters, 330
Catherine the Great, 264
Catholic Board for Mission Work Among the Coloured People, 330
Catholic Foreign Mission Society of America, 55
Catholic Total Abstinence Union, 394
Catholic Union of Bohemian Men, 245
Catholic University of America, 250, 454
Caucasus, 119, 120
Cayuses, 318
Celebes, 54
Central Missionary Society of the Evangelical Lutheran Church in the United States, 266
Ceylon, 1, 3, 14, 104
Chaldeans, in the United States, 251
Chalmers, Thomas, 154, 156, 168
Champagnot, Benedict, 54
Channing, William Ellery, 348, 387, 398, 403, 433
Chapel-cars, 216
Chappotin, Helene Marie Philippine de, 55
Charity, 152
Charles, Thomas, 72
Charleston, 233, 238
Chase, Philander, 217
Chateaubriand, 24
Chautauqua movement, 421
Chemistry, 9
Cheremis, 121
Cherokees, 305, 314-317, 320
Chesne, Marie-Zoc du, 58, 59
Chevalier, Julius, 53
Cheverus, Jean-Louis Lefebvre, 233, 234, 305
Chicago Hebrew Mission, 294
Chicago Theological Seminary, 211, 290, 291
Chicago, University of, 419, 435
Chickasaws, 316
Children's Aid Society of New York, 409
China, 1, 3, 13, 14, 51, 104
China Inland Mission, 100
Chinese, 225, 226; in the United States, 294, 295
Chippewas, 307, 310, 320

Choctaws, 212, 316
Christadelphians, 399
Christian Alliance, 283
Christian Association, 198
Christian Brothers of Ireland, 146
Christian Commission, United States, 400
Christian Commonwealth Colony, 391
Christian denominations, 196-199
Christian Endeavour, Young People's Society of, 37, 103
Christian Labour Union, 406
Christian nurture, 377, 386
Christian Reformed Church, 279
Christian Science, 40, 138, 440, 441
Christian Social Movement, 161
Christian Social Union, 161
Christian Socialist movement, 161
Christianity, effect on nineteenth century Europe, 150-174; kind of which influenced the United States, 381-385; questions concerning, 8; threats to, 15-17, aids to, 18-21; in the United States, variety of, 424, 425
Church and state, separation of in the United States, 426
Church Association for the Advancement of the Interests of Labour, 407
Church Building Society, 149
Church, disestablishment of, 17
Church membership in the United States, growth of, 177
Church Missionary Society, 39, 70, 71, 81, 90
Church of England, 39, 70, 71; approach to Eastern churches, 131
Church of England Zenana Missionary Society, 98
Church of God, 445
Church of Jesus Christ of Latter Day Saints. See Mormons
Church of Scotland, 39, 40, 74, 150
Church of the Brethren, in Europe, 136; on the frontier of the United States, 185; 399
Church Pastoral Aid Society, 73, 149
Church Peace Union, 400
Church, separation of from the state, 6, 17, 23, 34
Church Social Union, 407
Church Society for Promoting Christianity among the Jews, 293
Chuvash, 122
Cincinnati, 233, 234
Circuit-riders, 188, 189
Cities, growth of, 16; in the United States, adaptation of Christianity to, 369, 370
City mission societies, 370

City missions, 148
Civil War, American, 12, 351, 399, 400
Clapham Sect, 39, 71, 72, 113
Clark, Francis E., 37
Clark, Sidney James Wells, 100
Clausen, Claus L., 273
Clavis, John, 336
Clemens, Samuel L., 415
Clergy, Protestant, in the United States, 387, 388
Cleveland, Aaron, 397
Cleveland, Grover, 412
Clinton, De Witt, 417
Cock-fighting, 404
Coetus of Pennsylvania, 266
Coke, Thomas, 72
Coker, Daniel, 339
Colleges, in the United States, 221, 418
Colonial and Continental Church Society, 73
Colonial Bishoprics Fund, 73
Colorado, 242
Coloured Methodist Episcopal Church, 354, 356, 360
Coloured Methodist Protestant Church, 340
Commerce, 20
Commission for Catholic Missions among the Coloured People and Indians, 330
Commission on Church and Country Life, 372
Committee on Co-operation in Latin America, 104
Commune in Paris, 28
Communion, frequent, 27
Communism, 11, 17
Comte, 22
Concanen, Luke, 233
Concordia Theological Seminary, 264
Conference of Missionary Societies of Great Britain and Ireland, 104
Congo, 49, 54, 61
Congregation for the Propagation of the Faith, 5, 56, 63, 64, 254
Congregation of Daughters of Mary Help of Christians, 54
Congregation of St. Mary Magdalen, 247
Congregation of Saint Scholastica, 241
Congregation of the Immaculate Heart of Mary, 54
Congregation of the Precious Blood, 26
Congregational Home Missionary Society, 210
Congregationalism, British, 70; in the United States, 77, 87; on the frontier, 183-185, 203-213; among the Germans in the United States, 290; and the Negroes, 350, 358, 359, 361; among the

Scandinavians in the United States, 291; peculiarities in the United States, 448
Congress of Churches, American, 438
Connecticut Bible Society, 438
Connecticut Federation of Churches, 438
Connecticut, General Association of, 78, 205
Connecticut, Missionary Society of, 78
Connolly, John, 233
Consolidated American Baptist Missionary Convention, 355
Constantine, 47, 48
Constitutions of states and religion, 410, 411
Cook, Charles, 133
Cook, James, Voyages, 67, 68
Cooper, Anthony Ashley. See Shaftesbury, Lord
Co-operation, among Protestants, 102-105
Cortes of 1812, 24
Costa, Isaac da, 116
Council of Women for Home Missions, 218
Cour d'Alenes, 308
Coventry, 71
Crawford, Isabel, 321
Creeks, 314, 316
Crete, Nebraska, 290
Cretin, 305
Crummell, Arthur, 334
Cumberland Presbyterian Church, 195, 196
Cutler, Manasseh, 419
Czechs, 245, 254

Daily Vacation Bible Schools, 378
Dakota, 211-213
Dakotas, 319
Damascus, 257
Danes, in the United States, 276, 277
Danish Baptist Church, 289
Danish Evangelical Church in North America, 277
Danish Evangelical Lutheran Church in America, 277
Danish-Halle mission to India, 90
Danish Missionary Society, 92
Danish-Norwegian Conference (Methodist), 289
Danske Missionsselskab, 92
Darby, J. M., 133
Darby, John Nelson, 261
Darwinism, 435, 436
David, John Baptist Mary, 235, 247
Davis, Andrew Jackson, 446
Deaconesses, 148, 150, 153
Deaf, education of, 409
Declaration of Independence, 230
Deep Sea Fishermen, Mission to, 149
Deism, 5, 22, 176, 431

Delawares, 314
Delitzsch, Franz, 115
Demers, Modeste, 308
Democracy, 11, 33
Denison University, 215
Denmark, 92, 126, 157
Derrick, William B., 353
De Smet, Pierre-Jean, 307, 308
Detroit, 248
Deutsche Orient Mission, 141, 143
Deutscher Evangelischer Kirchentag, 103
Dewey, John, 435
Dickens, 166
Dietrichson, J. W. C., 272
Dillard, James Hardy, 361
Disciples of Christ, denomination, 40, 136, 138, 196-199
Disraeli, Benjamin, 116
Disruption, of the Church of Scotland, 39, 40
Dix, Dorothea Lynde, 403, 409
Dodge, David Low, 397
Dodge, William E., 395, 399
Domestic and Foreign Missionary Society of the Protestant Episcopal Church, 87, 217
Dominicans, 27, 62, 234, 237
Don, 119
Dostoievski, 166
Douglass, F·ederick, 343
Dow, Neal, 394
Dowie, John Alexander, 445
Dresden, 91
Dresser, Julius, 442
Drexel, Katharine, 309, 330
Drummond, Henry, 35, 171
Dublin, 101
Dubois, John, 235
Dubois, Marie, 56
DuBourg, Louis William Valentine, 57, 235, 236, 243, 306
Dubuque, 306
Duff, Alexander, 74, 103
Dumb, education of, 409
Duncan, William, 321
Dunkers. See Church of the Brethren
Durant, Henry F., 420
Durham University, 168
Dutch, in the United States, 278, 279
Dutch Reformed Church, 84
Dwight, E. W., 84
Dwight, Timothy, 204, 207

East End Mission, 148
East India Company, 70
East India Missionary Institute, Halle, 90

East Indies, 1, 3, 62
Eastern churches, 42; in the United States, 255-259; among the Negroes, 331-332
Eclectic Society, 71
Ecumenical Missionary Conference (1900), 106
Eddy, Mary Baker, 138, 440, 441
Edersheim, Alfred, 117
Edinburgh, World Missionary Conference, 106
Education, 11; in Europe, 167, 168; in the United States, 416-421; for women, 419, 420
Edwards, Jonathan, 78, 79, 204, 431
Egan, Michael, 232
Egypt, 1
Eichstätt, 241
Eielsen, Elling, 271
Einsiedeln, 241
Electricity, 11
Eliot, Charles W., 389
Eliot, John, 67
Elliott, William, 333
Ellis, Harrison, 345
Ely, Richard T., 408
Emerson, Joseph, 420
Emerson, Ralph Waldo, 387, 414
Emigrant Aid Society, 350
Emmanuel House, 293
Emmitsburg, Maryland, 246
Emmons, Nathaniel, 416
Engelberg, 241
England, John, 239, 245, 329
Environment in Europe, effect on Christianity, 170-173
Ephraim, Wisconsin, 271
Epworth League, 37
Equity, 406
Esbjörn, Lars Paul, 274
Eskimos, 213, 320, 413
Eucharistic Congresses, 27
Eudists, 27
Europe, 1, 8; spread of Christianity in, in nineteenth century, 110-174
Evangelical Alliance, 42, 104, 117, 438
Evangelical Association, 40, 287, 288
Evangelical Continental Society, 137
Evangelical Lutheran Conference of America, 265
Evangelical Lutheran Synod of Northern Illinois, 274-276
Evangelical movement, 38, 39, 113
Evangelical Synod of Iowa and Other States, 267
Evangelical Synod of North America, 269
Evangelical Synod of the West, 269

Evangelical Union, 161
Evangelicals, 70-71
Evangelisch-lutherische Mission zu Leipzig, 91
Evangelization of the world in this generation, 97, 102
Evans, Henry, 336
Evans, Warren Felt, 441
Evolution, 11; theory of, 435
Exeter Hall, 105
Expansion of European peoples, 13, 14, 19

Factory system, 11
Faraday, Michael, 169
Fayette, New York, 201
Fayetteville, North Carolina, 336
Federal Council of the Churches of Christ in America, 104, 218, 372, 439
Federation of Churches, New York, 438; Connecticut, 438; National Committee on, 439
Federation of Churches and Christian Workers of the State of New York, 439
Fee, James G., 335
Female Bible and Domestic Missions, 148
Female Missionary Society, 87
Fenwick, Benedict Joseph, 234
Fenwick, Edward Dominic, 234, 237, 305
Fifteenth Amendment, 351
Filipinos, 1
Finland, 93, 119, 137
Finley, Robert, 344
Finney, Charles G., 35, 195, 203, 204, 209, 347-350, 370, 392, 393, 402, 431
Finnish Evangelical Lutheran Church of America, 277
Finnish Evangelical Lutheran National Church, 277
Finnish Missionary Society, 93
Fisher, Ezra, 215, 216
Fisk University, 358
Five Civilized Tribes, 302
Fjellstedt, Peter, 150, 274
Flaget, Benedict J., 233, 234, 305
Flathead Indians, 307, 308, 318
Fleischmann, Conrad Anton, 289
Fliedner, Theodore, 148, 153
Florida, 235
Florissant, 237, 306, 307
Flury, Peter, 290
Folk schools, 167
Forbin-Janson, Charles de, 57
Foreign Evangelical Society, 283
Foreign Missionary Society of the Evangelical Lutheran Church, 88

Foreign Missions Conference of North America, 104, 106, 439
Fort Wayne, Indiana, 267
Fourteenth Amendment, 351
Fox sisters, 446
France, 14, 15, 17, 19, 23, 27, 30; revival of Roman Catholicism in, 24-26; and foreign missions, 47, 48; place in nineteenth century Roman Catholic missions, 60, 61; Protestant missions from, 92
Franciscan Missionaries of Mary, 55, 59, 60
Franciscans, 27, 53, 56, 58, 241, 304, 310
Franco-Prussian War, 12
Franklin, Benjamin, 231, 431
Franklin College, 216
Franson, Frederick, 276
Free African Society, 338
Free Baptists, 40
Free Church of Scotland, 40, 150
Free Churches, 276
Free German Catholic Churches, 284
Free Magyar Reformed Church in America, 279
Free Methodists, 444
Freedmen's Aid Societies, 358
Freewill Baptists, 433
French Bible Society, 92
French Canadians, 226, 236
French Revolution, 5, 7, 23, 24, 65, 176
Friends. See Quakers.
Friends of Mary at the Foot of the Cross, 246
Friends of the Indians, 323
Froebel, 167
Frontier, in the United States, 178-223
Fry, Elizabeth, 155, 156
Fulda, 241

Gallicanism, 29
Gambier Islands, 58
Gambier, Ohio, 217
Garfield, James A., 412
Garrison, William Lloyd, 349
Gaylord, Reuben, 212
General Assembly, Congregationalists represented in, 207, 208
General Council of the Evangelical Lutheran Church in North America, 268
General Synod of the Evangelical Church in the United States, 265, 268
General Theological Seminary, 217
Geology, 9
George, Henry, 406
Georgetown, 232, 328
Georgia (Caucasus), 129
Georgia, 316, 354

German Evangelical Church, 269
German Evangelical Church Diet, 103
German Evangelical Lutheran Synod of Missouri, Ohio, and Other States. See Missouri Synod
German Methodism, 288
German Protestants in the United States, 261-269
German Reformed Church in the United States, 266
German Roman Catholics in the United States, 239-242, 244, 245
Germans, in the United States, 225, 227
Germany, 12, 17, 19, 24; revival of Roman Catholicism in, 25; growth of interest in Roman Catholic missions in, 62; Protestant missionary societies in, 89-92
Gesellenvereine, 242
Gettysburg, 339
Gibbons, James, 244, 245, 330, 409, 451, 452
Gibraltar, Bishopric of, 131
Gilbert's Creek, Kentucky, 181
Gladden, Washington, 406
Gladstone, William Ewart, 162, 165
Glasgow Missionary Society, 74
Gloucester, 38
God, questioned, 16
Going, Jonathan, 215
Gold Coast, 92
Good Friday, 411
Good Templars, Independent Order of, 394
Gospel Hymns, 414
Gossner, Johannes Evangelista, 267
Gossner Missionary Society, 91
Gossnersche Missionsgesellschaft, 91
Grabau, 265
Grant, Charles, 70-72
Grant, U. S., 302, 313, 412
Granville, Massachusetts, 181
Granville, Ohio, 181
Graul, Karl, 91
Gravois Settlement, Missouri, 269
Gray, W. H., 318
Great Awakening, 5, 32, 34, 65, 77, 176, 192
Great Britain, 14, 19, 31, 35; Roman Catholicism in, 31, 63, 124, 125; Protestant missionaries societies formed in, 65-74
Greece, 42, 128, 141
Greek Evangelical Church, 141
Greek Roman Catholics, in the United States, 251
Greeks, in the United States, 257
Greeley, Horace, 415
Green Bay, Wisconsin, 271
Green River, 192
Greenland, 2, 8

Gregory XVI, 64
Grellet, Stephen, 155
Grimké, Angelina Emily, 402
Grimké, Sarah Moore, 402
Grimké, Thomas Smith, 398, 402, 420
Grinnell College, 211
Gros Ventres, 308
Groton School, 418
Grundtvig, Nicolai Frederick Severin, 157, 167, 272, 277
Gurius, Brotherhood of St., 122
Gurley, Ralph Randolph, 345
Guthrie, Thomas, 168
Guyau, 23

Hague Conferences, 164, 165
Haldane, Robert, 131, 133, 198
Halle, 90, 93, 114
Hamilton Missionary Society, 214
Hampton Institute, 320, 358, 359, 362
Hand, Daniel, 359
Hanover, 91
Hardie, J. K., 161
Hare, William Hobart, 320
Harmony, Pennsylvania, 262
Harms, Louis, 91
Harneck, Gustav, 92
Harrison, Benjamin, 412
Hartford, 252
Hartwick, J. C., 265
Harvard, 79, 258, 348
Hasselquist, Tuve Nilsson, 274, 275
Hastings, Thomas, 44
Hauge, Hans Nilsen, 92, 150, 270
Hauge's Norwegian Evangelical Lutheran Synod, 271
Hawaiian Islands, 83, 84
Hawawiny, Ralph, 257
Hawes, Mrs. W. A., 378
Hawthorne, Nathaniel, 415
Haystack Meeting, 80, 100
Heber, Reginald, 44
Hebrew-Christian Alliance, 114
Hecker, Thomas, 252, 452
Hegel, 41, 159, 171
Herder, Johann Gottfried von, 163
Hermannsburg Mission, 91
Herrnhut, 90
Herron, George Davis, 407
Herschell, Ridley Haim, 117
Heydt, Daniel von der, 153
Hibernian Church Missionary Society, 71
Hicks, George W., 320
Higher criticism, 435, 436
Himes, Joshua Vaughan, 442
Hobart, Henry, 319

Holck, A. O., 136
Holiness Methodist Church, 445
Holiness movements, 444, 445
Holland, 55, 61, 64, 65, 89, 125, 126
Holland, Michigan, Classis of, 278
Holmes, Oliver Wendell, 415
Holy Alliance, 164, 165
Holy Childhood, Association of the, 57, 58, 60
Holy Ghost, Congregation of the, 54, 112
Holy Ghost fathers, 5
Holy Heart of Mary, Society of the, 54, 112
Holy Synod, 42, 108, 121, 256
Home Missionary Society of the General Synod, 266
Home Missions Council, 104, 218, 322, 439
Hopedale, Massachusetts, 391
Hopkins, Samuel, 77-79, 81, 204, 346, 348, 432, 433
Howard University, 361
Howe, Julia Ward, 402, 409
Howe, S. G., 409
Hudson Bay Company, 308
Hughes, John Joseph, 239
Humanism, 434
Hungarian Reformed Church in America, 279
Hunter, Timothy Dwight, 185
Hutterian Brethren, 263
Huxley, 23
Hyde, A. A., 414

Icelandic Evangelical Lutheran Synod in North America, 277
Ideals, of the United States, shaped by Christianity, 389, 390
Illinois, 204, 215, 216, 270
Illinois Band, 210, 222
Illinois College, 210, 212
Ilminski, Nicholai Ivanovitch, 121, 122
Immigration, in the United States, 224-298
Imperialism, 19; and foreign missions, 47, 48
In His Steps, 408
India, 1, 3, 14, 49, 51, 68, 70, 74, 75, 78, 94, 104
Indian Rights Association, 323
Indian Territory, 302, 314
Indiana, 199, 215, 241, 314
Indianapolis, 215
Indians, in the United States, 76, 77, 86, 213; missions to in the United States, 299-324
Individualism, 11, 18
Indo-China, 1, 3, 14
Industrial revolution, 10, 19, 66

Infallibility, Papal, 30, 170
Ingersoll, Robert Green, 23
Inner Mission, 147, 148, 153, 267, 277
Insane, care for, 403
Institutum Judaicum, 114
Institutum Judaicum Delitzschianum, 115
International Bible Students' Association, 443, 444
International Lesson Committee, 376
International Missionary Council, 105, 106
International Missionary Union, 105
International Primary Union, 376
International Sunday School Association, 220, 376
International Sunday School Conventions, 376
International Uniform Lesson System, 376
Interpenetration of one kind of Christianity by another in the United States, 436, 437
Interseminary Missionary Alliance, 96
Iowa, 183, 202, 204, 212, 213, 216, 236, 259, 260
Iowa Band, 211
Iowa College, 211
Iowa, Evangelical Synod of, and Other States, 267
Ireland, 238, 239; and Roman Catholic missions, 62; schools in, 168
Ireland, John, 394
Irish, in the United States, 225, 227
Iroquois, 308
Islam, 1, 3, 6, 101, 120-122
Issoudun, Fathers of the Holy Heart of Jesus of, 26, 53
Italy, 12, 19, 27, 61, 139, 140

Jack of Virginia, 336
Jackson, Sheldon, 212, 213, 320, 413
Jacobites, 259
Jänicke, Johann, 90
James, Daniel Willis, 414
James, Henry, 405, 406
James, William, 406, 435
Janson, Eric, 270
Janson, Kristofer Nagel, 291
Janssen, Arnold, 54
Japan, 1, 3, 13, 14, 104
Japanese, 225, 226, 295, 296
Jaricot, Pauline-Marie, 56, 57
Jeanes, Anna T., 361
Jeanes Fund, 361
Jefferson, Thomas, 411, 431
Jehovah's Witnesses, 443, 444
Jerusalem, Bishopric of, 114
Jesuits, 27, 53, 62, 231, 237, 242, 306-309, 329

Jews, missions to in Europe, 110-118; in the United States, 292-294
John Street Methodist Episcopal Church, 339
Johnson, Gisle, 150
Jones, Absalom, 338
Jones, Charles Colcock, 335
Jones, Edward, 260
Joubert, Nicholas, 328
Judson, Adoniram, 80-83

Kaffraria, 74
Kaiserswerth, 148, 153
Kalispels, 308
Kalkar, Chr. H., 117
Kalmyks, 119
Kaloshs, 256
Kamchatka, 256, 312
Kansas, 204, 211, 350
Kansas City, 330
Kazan, 108, 121, 122
Keil, William, 263, 391
Kentucky, 180-183, 189, 190, 192, 193, 196, 197, 207, 217, 233, 235, 246, 335, 347
Kenyon College, 288
Ketteler, Emanuel von, 161
Kettering, 67, 68
Key, Francis Scott, 388
Kickapoo Indians, 306
Kiefer, Frank, 285
Kiev, 257, 258
Kilbuck, John, 315
Kincaide, William, 196
King's College, London, 168
Kingsbury, Cyrus, 315
Kingsley, Charles, 161
Kiowas, 321
Kirchenverein des Westens, 269
Kirghis, 121
Kirtland, Ohio, 202
Knights of Labour, 409
Knights of Peter Claver, 330
Know Nothing movement, 241
Knowledge of the physical universe, 9
Kodiak Island, 311
Kold, Kristen, 167
Kolping, Adolph, 146, 242
Korea, 1, 3
Krüdener, Madame de, 165
Ku Klux Klan, 351
Kulturkampf, 28, 55, 241
Kurile Islands, 312

L. U. P. O. Society, 267
Labarum, 47
Labour Party, 161

Lacordaire, 26
Ladd, William, 398
Ladoga, Lake, 311
Laestadius, Lars Levi, 277
Laissez-faire, 11
Lake Baptist Missionary Society, 214
Lambert, Jeremiah, 190
Lambeth Conferences, 103
Lamennais, 30
Lammers, Gustav Adolf, 136
Lancaster, Pennsylvania, 286
Landmarkers, 446
Lane Theological Seminary, 347
Langenberg, 267
Lapps, 93, 118, 119
Lapwai, 318
La Salle County, Illinois, 289
Latrobe, 241
Lavalle, 54
Lavigerie, 59, 159
Lay element in the Christianity of the United States, 429
Laymen, in missions, 99
Laymen's Missionary Movement, 99
Lazarists, 5, 53, 242
League for Social Service, 407
League of Universal Brotherhood, 399
Leavitt, Joshua, 349
Lee, Jason, 191, 317
Lee, Jesse, 191
Lee, Robert E., 387, 400
Le Grand, Daniel, 155
Leicester, 67
Leipzig, 91
Le Mar, Iowa, 259
Leo XIII, 25, 28, 30, 157, 165, 409, 452
Leopoldina, Archduchess, 58
Leopoldine Association, 58
Leopoldinen-Stiftung, 58
Liberia, 85, 87, 334, 345
Libermann, Franz Maria Paul, 54, 111, 112
Libermann, Simon, 112
Liberty Party, 347
Life insurance, 404
Lincoln, Abraham, 17, 351, 400, 412
Lincoln University, 335
Lindsay, Vachel, 415
Lingnan University, 102
Litchfield County, Connecticut, 79, 214
Literature, in the United States, 415
Little Brothers of Mary, 54
Liverpool, Conference on Missions, 105
Livesay, Joseph, 157
Livingstone, David, 101
Local option, 396
Local preachers, 189

Loehe, Konrad Wilhelm, 267
London, 36
London City Mission, 148
London Methodist Mission, 149
London Missionary Society, 69, 70, 71, 82, 89, 90, 103, 113
London Society for Promoting Christianity amongst the Jews, 113, 114
London, Vicar Apostolic of, 231
Longfellow, Henry Wadsworth, 415
Looking Backward, 406
Loras, 306
Loretto, Kentucky, 246
Loretto, Sisters of, 306, 329
Louisiana, 87, 191, 328
Lourdes, 27
Louvain, 238, 241
Lovejoy, Elijah Parish, 349
Lowell, James Russell, 398, 415
Lowell, Massachusetts, 249
Lucerne, 59
Ludlow, John Malcolm Forbes, 161
Ludwig-Missionsverein, 58, 241, 242
Lumbermen, 374
Lund, 93
Lundy, Benjamin, 349
Luther League, 37
Lutheran Board for Coloured Missions, 361
Lutheran Brethren in America, 273
Lutheran Evangelical Synod of Texas, 267
Lutheran Free Church, 273
Lutheranism, peculiarities in the United States, 450
Luxemburg, 125
Lyon, Mary, 420
Lyons, 56, 57

McAuley, Jerry, 36, 371
McCall Mission, 132, 133
McCall, R. W., 133
McCoy, 321
McGlynn, 409, 452
McGready, James, 192
McKendree, William, 190, 316
McKinley, William, 412
McLoughlin, John, 308, 309
Machines, 10, 11, 14, 16, 18
Madeiras, 2, 139
Madison, James, 411, 431
Madison Square Presbyterian Church, 413
Magyars, 62
Maine, 179, 191, 199, 206; and prohibition, 394
Maine, Interdenominational Commission of, 438
Malaya, 3

Malthus, Thomas Robert, 160
Manchester Guardian, 167
Manchuria, 54
Mann, Horace, 416
Manning, Henry Edward, 31, 124
Marechal, Ambrose, 235
Mariner's Bethel, 136
Mariner's Church, 373
Marists, 26
Mark Twain, 415
Maronites, in the United States, 251
Marquette League, 309
Marranos, 116
Marriage, civil, 28, 29
Martin, Richard, 156
Mary of the Passion, 55
Maryknoll, 55
Maryland, 217, 230-233, 328, 334
Marx, Karl, 116, 159
Masons, 338
Mass modification, 51, 52
Mass movements, 50
Massachusetts Baptist Missionary Society, 78, 214, 215
Massachusetts, General Association of, 79, 81
Massachusetts Missionary Society, 78, 206, 313
Massachusetts Peace Society, 398
Mastery of man's physical environment, 10
Mathew, Theobald, 157, 394
Maurice, John Frederick Denison, 161, 167
Mauritius, 2
Maximilian, Leopold, 58
Mayhew, Jonathan, 433
Mazzini, 17, 163
Meade, William, 334, 345
Melchites, in the United States, 251
Membership of churches in United States, percentage to population, 385
Mendel, David, 116
Mendelssohn-Bartholdy, Jakob Ludwig Felix, 116
Mendelssohn, Moses, 115
Mennonites, 142, 263, 264, 286, 397
Methodism, in France, 133; in Germany, 133, 134; in Scandinavia, 134-136
Methodist Episcopal Church, 40; on the frontier of the United States, 185-191, 193
Methodist Episcopal Church, South, 350, 354, 360
Methodist missions to the Indians, 316, 317
Methodist Protestant Church, 450

Methodists, among Germans in the United States, 286-288; among the Negroes of the United States, 332-334, 338, 341, 346, 354, 355, 357
Methods, Protestant, 107
Metlakahtla, 321
Mexican War, 399
Mexicans, in United States, 284
Mexico, 304
Miamis, 307
Michigan, 204, 207, 267, 279
Micronesia, 3
Milan, 56
Mildmay Park, London, 105, 148
Miles, Richard Pius, 234
Mill Hill, 55, 329
Miller, William, 389, 442
Millerites, 389
Mills, Samuel J., 79-86, 206, 207, 344, 345
Milwaukee, 245
Mining camps, 375
Minneapolis, 258
Minnesota, 212, 320
Mission Friend Movement, 276
Mission to Lepers, 101
Missionary and Bible Society of the Methodist Episcopal Church in America, 87
Missionary Priests of St. Paul the Apostle, 252
Missionary Society of Connecticut, 78, 205, 313
Mississippi, 183, 191
Mississippi Valley, 75, 76, 84, 206, 262
Missouri, 182, 184, 200, 202, 260, 263, 264
Missouri Compromise, 350
Missouri Synod, 264, 265, 267, 273
Mitteleuropa, 161
Mohonk, Lake, 323, 400
Molecules, 9
Mongolia, 54
Monod, Frédéric, 92
Montana, 213
Moody, Dwight L., 35, 96, 99, 149, 172, 276, 371, 431
Morals, effect of Christianity on in the United States, 386, 387
Moravians, 65, 66, 69, 77, 89, 90, 92, 271, 314, 315
Mordvs, 121
More, Hannah, 168
Morehouse College, 362
Mormons, 40, 135, 138, 200-202, 291, 292
The Morning Light is Breaking, 389
Morrill Act, 420
Moscow, Metropolitan of, 256
Mott, John R., 35, 96-99, 106, 143

Mott, Lucretia Coffin, 401
Moulton, 67
Mt. Angel, 241
Mt. Hermon, 95-97
Mount Holyoke Seminary, 420
Mountain whites, 373
Moyë, Jean Martin, 54
Muehlmeier, H. A., 266
Müller, C. G., 133
Müller, George, 154
Münster, 241
Munger, Theodore Thornton, 406
Murray, Ellen, 360
Murray, John, 433
Murray, Orson S., 401

Nagasaki, Vicar Apostolic of, 59
Nancy, 57
Naples, 242; Kingdom of, 24, 27
Napoleon, 5, 23
Napoleon, wars of 5, 7, 23, 24, 65
Nashotah, Wisconsin, 320
Nashville, 224
Nasmith, David, 148
Nast, William, 288
National Baptist Convention, 356
National Baptist Publishing Board, 356
National Christian Convention opposed to Secret Societies, 401
National Educational Convention, 355
National Federation of Churches and Christian Workers, 439
National Indian Association, 321
National Sunday School Conventions, 376
National Temperance Society and Publication House, 395
Nationalism, 12, 17, 162, 163
Natural Law in the Spiritual World, 171
Natural religion, 5, 22
Naumann, Friedrich, 161
Nauvoo, Illinois, 202
Navajos, 310
Nazarene, Church of the, 445
Neale, Leonard, 234
Near East, 14, 49, 51, 53, 59, 75
Nebraska, 212, 213, 260
Nederlandsche Zendelinggenootschap, 89
Negro clergyman, 353
Negroes, 2, 54, 71, 112; in the United States, 76, 77, 85, 325-366; numbers of in the United States, 325; numbers of Christian, 341, 342; effect of Christianity on, 342-344
Nerinckx, Charles, 237, 246, 329
Nestorians, 259
Netherlands, the. See Holland

Netherlands Missionary Society, 89, 90
Neuendettelsau, Mission Institute of, 267
New England, 40, 192, 194, 203, 205; source of denominations, 443
New England Missionary Convention, 355
New England Theology, 78, 204, 205, 208, 377
New Guinea, 3
New Hampshire, 179, 205
New Harmony, Indiana, 262
New Haven Theology, 209, 348, 434
New Jersey, 258
New Mexico, 213, 242, 310
New Orleans, 233, 235, 236, 328
New Thought, 442
New York Baptist Missionary Society, 313
New York City, 85, 233, 235, 238, 240, 242, 249, 258, 260, 262, 286, 293
New York City Anti-Slavery Society, 349
New York City Baptist Mission Society, 378
New York Missionary Society, 78
New York Peace Society, 397
New York Port Society, 373
New York (State), 179, 204, 206, 207
New Zealand, 3, 8, 13, 20, 66, 94, 98
Newfoundland, 64
Newman, John Henry, 31, 124
Newport, 77
Nez Perce Indians, 307, 318
Nicholas, Bishop, 256
Nicholas I, 117
Nicholas II, 126, 165
Nightingale, Florence, 153
Nîmes, 53
Noli, Fan Stylian, 258
Non-Resistance Society, 442
Norddeutsche Missionsgesellschaft, 91
Norelius, Eric, 275
Det Norske Missionsselskab, 92
North Carolina, 181, 182, 199, 334, 336
North German Missionary Society, 91
Northampton, England, 66
Northern Baptist Convention, 350
Northern Missionary Society of the State of New York, 313
Northfield, Minnesota, 213
North-west Coast, 317, 318
Northwestern University, 419
Norway, 126
Norwegian Augustana Synod, 273
Norwegian Baptist Church, 289
Norwegian-Danish Conference, 273, 277
Norwegian Evangelical Lutheran Church in America, 272

Norwegian Lutheran Church in America, 273
Norwegian Lutheran Home Missionary Society, 150
Norwegian Missionary Society, 92
Norwegian Synod, 272
Norwegians, in the United States, 270-273
Notre Dame de Namur, Sisters of, 238
Nottingham, 67
Nova Scotia, 74
Noyes, John Humphrey, 391
Nuremberg, 72
Nursing, 26, 153

Oberlin, Ohio, 209, 347, 390, 402, 420
Oberlin, Pastor, 155
Oblate Sisters of Providence, 328
Oblates of St. Francis de Sales, 53
Oblates of the Immaculate Heart of Mary, 53
Oblates of the Immaculate Virgin Mary, 26
Obookiah, Henry, 84
Occident, main features of in nineteenth century, 9-21
O'Cull, James, 285
Œcumenical Patriarch, 42, 127, 256, 257
L'Œuvre Apostolique, 58
L'Œuvre des Écoles d'Orient, 59
L'Œuvre d'Orient, 59
Ohio, 193, 199, 204, 205, 207, 217, 267, 314
Ohio University, 419
Ojibwas, 313
O'Kelly, James, 196, 450
Okhotsk, 256
Oklahoma, 302, 320
Old Believers, 127, 129, 130
Old Catholic Church, 30
Olsson, Olof, 271
Oncken, J. G., 134, 136
Oneida, New York, 391
Oneida County, New York, 260
Oneidas, 313, 319
Open and Institutional Church League, 438
Optimism, 12, 18
Oregon, 182, 184, 212, 216, 241, 308, 309, 317
Oregon City, 309
Orthodox Church, 42
Orthodox Missionary Society, 107, 122, 312
Ortinsky, Stephan, 251
Osage Indians, 306, 307, 316
Ossetes, 119
Otey, James Hervey, 184, 217
Otsego County, New York, 265
Ottawas, 307, 310
Otterbein, Philip William, 286

Our Lady, Sisters of, 241
Oxford, 101
Oxford Movement, 31, 39, 148, 153, 217, 319
Ozanam, Antoine Frédéric, 26

Pacific University, 212
Paine College, 360
Pallotine Sisters, 242
Pallotti Fathers, 26
Papacy, and supervision of missions, 63; supervision of the Roman Catholic Church in the United States, 253, 254
Paris, 133
Paris Evangelical Missionary Society, 92
Parish, in the United States, 426
Parker, Samuel, 318
Parker, Theodore, 389
Parkhurst, Charles H., 413
Parochial schools, Lutheran, 376
Pascendi, encyclical, 30
Passionists, 252
Pasteur, 169
Paterson, New Jersey, 241, 259
Patten County, Illinois, 289
Patton, W. W., 361
Paul I, 264
Paulers Pury, 66
Paulists, 252
Pavia, 56
Pawnees, 316
Payne, Daniel Alexander, 339
Peabody Education Fund, 361
Peabody, Endicott, 418
Peabody, George, 361
Peace, 12, 19
Peace, movement for, 164, 165, 396-400
Peasants' League, 146
Peck, John Mason, 214, 215, 289
Peerson, Cleng, 270
Peet, Stephen, 211
Peking, 1
Peniel Missions, 445
Penn School, 360
Pennsylvania, 74, 230, 260, 335
Pentecostal Assemblies of the World, 445
Pentecostal Holiness Church, 445
Perpetual adoration of the reserved sacrament, 26
Perry County, Missouri, 264
Persico, Ignatius, 242
Pessimism, 12
Peter and Paul, society of, 56
Petersburg, Virginia, 337
Peyote cults, 322
Phelps-Stokes Fund, 362
Philadelphia, 293, 338

Philadelphia, Synod of, 206
Philippines, 54
Physics, 9
Physiology, 10
Piacenza, 242
Picpus Fathers, 26
Pierce, John D., 417
Pietism, 65, 66, 89, 90, 163, 274, 277, 280, 286
Pilgrim Holiness Church, 445
Pioneer Total Abstinence Association, 157
Pittsburgh, 240
Pittsburgh, Synod of, 88, 207
Pius VII, 27, 235
Pius IX, 61, 246
Pius X, 64, 165
Pius Society of the Missionaries of St. Charles Borromeo, 242
Plan of Union, 207-209
Platon, 258
Plimsoll, Samuel, 155
Plymouth Brethren, 133, 261
Pobiedonostsiev, 42, 122, 129, 147, 171
Poland, 24, 242
Poles, 62
Polish National Catholic Church of America, 254, 446
Polk, Franklin K., 412
Polynesia, 3
Pompey, New York, 214
Pond, Gideon H., 319
Pond, Samuel W., 319
Ponziglione, Paul, 307
Poor Clares, 235, 238
Pope, increase of power of, 29
Portieux, 54
Portugal, 62, 139
Postal systems, 18
Potawatomis, 306, 307
Powell, Joab, 184
Praise houses, 364
Prayer-meeting revival, 371
Precious Blood, Society of the, 240
Premonstratensians, 240
Prentiss, Narcissa, 318
Presbyterian Board of Domestic Missions, 212
Presbyterian Church in the United States of America, 260
Presbyterian Foreign Missionary Society, 88
Presbyterians, among the Negroes, 335, 336, 340, 360, 361; British, 70; in the United States, 78; New School, 87, 88, 209, 210; Old School, 87, 88, 299; on the frontier, 183, 193, 206-213; peculiarities in the United States, 449
Presiding elders, 188

Preuss, A. C., 272
Price, Thomas F., 55
Primitive Baptists, 445
Princeton. 221
Princeton Theological Seminary, 212, 268
Printing press, 18
Prison Discipline Society, 403
Prison reform, 156
Prisoners' Society of Germany, 153
Progress and Poverty, 406
Prohibition of alcoholic beverages, in the United States, 394-396
Prohibition Party, 395
Propaganda. See Congregation for the Propagation of the Faith
Protestant Episcopal Church, 76, 217, 259, 272, 291, 293, 319, 320, 334, 338, 357, 360, 381, 447; peculiarities in the United States, 449
Protestant missions to the Jews in Europe, 112-117
Protestant organization for missions, 64-107
Protestantism, 4, 17, 19; on the frontier in the United States, 178-223; missions for Roman Catholics in the United States, 282-285; missions to the Indians of the United States, 312-324; among the Negroes, 332-365
Protestantism, kind of which influenced the United States, 381-385
Protestantism, radical, in the United States, 427, 428
Protestantism, revival in nineteenth century, 32-44
Protestants, missions among other Christians in Europe, 130-143
Providence Association, 338
Prussia, 27

Quakers, 158, 162, 270, 397, 399; in Tennessee, the North-west Territory, Iowa, 183; among the Indians, 313; among the Negroes, 335, 346, 360; peculiarities in the United States, 450
Queen's College for Women, 167
Quickenborne Charles Felix Van, 237, 306
Quimby, Phineas Parkhurst, 441, 442
Quincy, Illinois, 210

Radstock, Lord, 142
Ragged Schools, 168
Raikes, Robert, 38
Railway, 10, 18
Ramazotti, Angelo, 56
Randall, Benjamin, 433

Ranyard, Mrs., 148
Raphaelsverein, 244
Rapp, Johann Georg, 262
Rappists, 262
Raskolniks, 129, 171
Rationalism, 11, 17
Ratisbonne, Maria Alphonse, 112
Ratisbonne, Maria Theodore, 112
Rauschenbusch, August, 289
Rauschenbusch, Walter, 407
Reconstruction, 351
Red Cross, 164
Redemptorists, 237, 240
Redfield College, 290
Reformed Church in America, 278
Reformed Church in the United States, 266, 279
Reformed Synod of Ohio, 266
Reformed Zion Union Apostolic Church, 355
Reformers, 199
Reindeer, 214, 413
Religious Education, 220
Religious Education Association, 376
Religious Tract Society, 71
Renaissance, 6
Renan, 171
Republican Methodist Church, 196, 450
Rerum Novarum, 25, 157
Rescue Missions, 36, 371
Rese, Frederic, 58, 243
Reunion, 2
Revealed religion, 22
Revivals, 34, 191-195, 429, 430
Revolutionary War, American, 5, 7, 34
Rheinische Missionsgesellschaft, 91
Rheinisch-Westfälische Diakonissen-Verein, 148
Rhenish Missionary Society, 91, 269
Rice, David, 183, 347
Rice, Edmund Ignatius, 146
Rice, Luther, 82, 83, 215
Richard, Gabriel, 248
Richmond, Virginia, 239, 337
Richmond African Baptist Missionary Society, 345
Rigdon, Sidney, 201
Riggs, Mary, 319
Riggs, Stephen R., 319
Rio de Janeiro, 87
Ritschl, 41, 171
Rochester Theological Seminary, 407
Rock Castle, Virginia, 330
Rock Island, Illinois, 289
Rockefeller, John D., 362, 414
The Rocky Mountain Presbyterian, 213

Roe, Walter, 321
Rogerines, 399
Rogers, John A. R., 335
Roman Catholic Christianity, 1, 3, 5, 17
Roman Catholic, organization for missions, 52-64; converts from Protestantism in the United States, 252, 253; missions to Indians in the United States, 303-310
Roman Catholicism, revival of in nineteenth century, 23-33; missions to Jews in Europe, 111, 112; spread among Protestants in Europe, 123-126; among Eastern Orthodox Christians, 126, 127; among the immigrants in the United States, 229-255; peculiarities in the United States, 451-454
Roman Catholics among the Negroes, 327-331
Romanticism, 11, 17, 24, 163
Rome, 5, 56
Rønne, Bone Falch, 92
Roosevelt, Theodore, 412
Rosenius, Carl Olaf, 275
Roumania, 42, 128
Roumanian Baptist Association of North America, 285
Roumanian Uniates, in the United States, 251
Roumanians, in the United States, 256
Ruffner, William H., 417
Rural Problem in the United States, 372
Rush, Benjamin, 404
Russell, Charles Taze, 443, 444
Russell, Howard Hyde, 395
Russia, 12, 14, 15, 27; Jews in, 117, 118; Protestantism in, 142, 143; Mennonites in, 264
Russian American Company, 311
Russian Bible Society, 121
Russian Christianity, 1
Russian Orthodox Church, 4, 42, 107, 171; gains at expense of other Christian churches, 128-130; in the United States, 256
Russian Orthodox missions, 119-123; among Indians of North America, 311, 312
Russian Turkestan, 15
Ruthenian Uniates, 126, 256
Ruthenians, in the United States, 250, 251, 254
Rutherford, J. F., 444
Rymker, F. L., 136

Sacred Heart, Society of, 236
Sacred Hearts of Jesus and Mary, 27
Safety first, 407

St. Chrischona, Pilgrim Mission of, 267
St. Helena Island, 360
St. Joseph's Society, 55
St. Joseph's Society for Coloured Missions, 330
St. Louis, 215, 233, 237, 240, 264, 286, 307
St. Mary's Seminary, 235, 245
St. Mary's University, 235
St. Paul, Minnesota, 306
Saint Scholastica, Congregation of, 241
Saint-Simon, 161
Saint Vincent de Paul, Society of, 26
St. Walburg's Convent, 241
Salem, North Carolina, 314
Salesians of Don Bosco, 25, 26, 54
Salesianum, 245
Salvation Army, 36, 145, 371, 410
San Domingo, 328
San Francisco, 185, 256, 258
Sandell, Lina, 276
Sandemanians, 169, 198
Santa Anna, 304
Sarajevo, 12
Sarajian, Hovsep, 258
Sardinia, 24
Savannah, 242
Scalabrini, 242
Scandinavian Augustana Synod, 273
Scandinavian Evangelical Lutheran Augustana Synod, 275
Scandinavians, in the United States, 226, 227, 269-277
Scepticism, 22, 28
Schaff, Philip, 438
Schervier, Franziska, 244
Scheutveld, 54
Schlatter, Michael, 286
Schlegel, Friedrich von, 24
Schleiermacher, 41, 171
Schmucker, Samuel Simon, 266, 268, 339, 437
Schwenkfelders, 399
Schools, on the frontier, 220-22; Roman Catholic, in the United States, 247-249
Science, 10, 16, 169
Scotch-Irish, 208
Scotch Society for Propagating Christian Knowledge, 74
Scotland, 39, 40; Roman Catholic Church in, 31; missionary societies formed in, 74
Scott, C. P., 167
Scott, George, 134, 135, 274, 276
Scottish Missionary Society, 74
Secession Church, 74
Second coming of Christ, 442, 444, 445

Second Great Awakening, 77, 79, 192, 197, 204

Secret Societies, movement against, 401

Seminaries, Roman Catholic, in the United States, 245, 246

Sepulchre, Holy, 58

Serbia, 42, 128

Serbs, in the United States, 258

Seton, Elizabeth Ann Bayley, 246, 252

Seventh Day Adventists, 40, 134, 135, 442

Seventh Day Baptists, 442

Shaftesbury, Lord, 38, 105, 155, 156, 160

Shakers, 391, 397, 399

Shantung, 55

Sharp, Granville, 70, 72

Sheldon, Charles M., 408

Sheldon, Stewart, 212

Shore, John, 72

Shurtleff College, 215

Siam, 1, 14

Siberia, 1, 13, 15, 108, 311, 312

Sierra Leone, 71, 334, 342

Simeon, Charles, 39, 70

Sioux, 319, 320

Sisterhood of Our Lady of Sion, 112

Sisters of Charity, 246, 248

Sisters of Notre Dame de Namur, 238

Sisters of Our Lady, 241

Sisters of Our Lady of Mount Carmel, 328

Sisters of Providence of Portieux, 54

Sisters of St. Francis of Aachen, 244

Sisters of the Blessed Sacrament for Indians and Negroes, 309, 330

Sisters of the Holy Family, 328

Sitka, 256, 312

Skogsbergh, A. August, 276

Slater, John F., Fund, 361

Slave trade, 326

Slavery, abolition of, 158, 159, 345-351

Slavic Baptist Churches, 284

Slovak Evangelical Synod of America, 278

Slovak Lutheran Synod of Pennsylvania and Other States, 278

Smiley, Albert Keith, 323, 400

Smith, Elias, 196

Smith, Gerrit, 392, 402

Smith, Joseph, 200-202

Smith, Joseph, Jr., 202

Smith, Samuel Francis, 388

Snethen, Abraham, 401

Social gospel movement, 404-408

Social service, 407

Social settlements, 371

Socialism, 11, 17

Société des Missions Étrangères, of Paris, 5, 53, 56

Société des Missions Évangéliques de Paris, 92

Society for Promoting Christian Knowledge, 69, 70, 73

Society for Promoting Collegiate and Theological Education in the West, 221

Society for the Free Instruction of Orderly Blacks and People of Colour, 335

Society for the Preservation of the Faith among Indian Children, 309

Society for the Prevention of Cruelty to Animals, 156

Society for the Prevention of Cruelty to Children, 156

Society for the Propagation of the Faith, 57, 60, 68, 243

Society for the Propagation of the Gospel in Foreign Parts, 69, 70, 73, 101, 216

Society for the Revival of Orthodoxy in the Caucasus, 108

Society of Christian Socialists, 407

Society of Jesus. See Jesuits

Society of Marie-Réparatrice, 55

Society of Mary, 26

Society of St. Catherine of Siena, 247

Society of St. Joseph, 329

Society of St. Peter the Apostle, 59

Society of the Divine Word, 54, 330

Society of the Holy Ghost, 330

Society of the Holy Hearts of Jesus and Mary, 26

Society of the Precious Blood, 240

Society of the Sacred Heart, 236

Society of the Schools of the Orient, 59

Sojourner Truth, 364

Soloviev, Vladimir, 127

Sorbonne, 26

South Africa, 20, 66

South America, 85

South Carolina, 333, 334, 337

South Dakota, 212

South Seas, 78

Southern Baptist Convention, 360

Spain, 24, 28, 62, 139

Spalding, Henry H., 318

Spanish-American War, 400

Speer, Robert E., 99

Speer, William, 295

Spelman College, 360, 362

Spencer, Herbert, 23

Spiritualism, 446

Spirituals, Negro, 364

Spittler, C. F., 267

Spotsylvania County, Virginia, 181

Springfield Presbytery, 197

Stahl, Friedrich Julius, 116

Standing Order, 203
Stanton, Elizabeth Cady, 402
Star Spangled Banner, 388
Stavanger, 270
Steam, 11
Steamship, 10, 18
Stephan, Martin, 264
Stern, Max, 266
Steyl, 55
Stiles, Ezra, 77
Stockfleth, Joakim Christian Vibe, 119
Stockholm, 119, 135
Stokes, Caroline Phelps, 362
Stolberg, Count, 146
Stolberg, Friedrich Leopold, 24
Stone, Barton W., 196-199, 432
Stone, James Kent, 252
Stone, Lucy, 402
Stowe, Harriet Beecher, 348, 415
Straight University, 358
Strang, James Jesse, 202
Strasbourg, 111, 112, 269
Strategic Points in the World's Conquest,
    97
Strauss, 171
Strong, Josiah, 407
Studd, Charles T., 100
Studd, J. E. K., 96
Student Christian Movement of Great
    Britain and Ireland, 97, 138
Student Foreign Missionary Union, 97
Student Volunteer Missionary Union, 97
Student Volunteer Movement for Foreign
    Missions, 44, 95-98, 102, 138, 436
Stundists, 42, 142
Sudan United Mission, 100
Sulpicians, 233, 235, 245, 246, 248
Sunday and Adult School Union, 376
Sunday School Council of Evangelical De-
    nominations, 220
Sunday Schools, 38, 219, 220, 375-378
Suomen Lahetysseura, 93
Suomi Synod, 277
Surinam, 2
Svenska Missionssällskapet, 93
Swabia, 263
Swahlen, John, 288
Sweden, 93, 126, 150
Swedenborgianism, 406
Swedes, in the United States, 274, 275
Swedish Baptist Church, 289
Swedish Episcopalians, 291
Swedish Evangelical Free Church, 276
Swedish Evangelical Lutheran Ansgarius
    Synod, 276

Swedish Evangelical Lutheran Mission
    Synod, 276
Swedish Evangelical Mission Covenant, 276
Swedish Missionary Society, 93
Switzerland, 126
Syllabus of Errors, 30
Syrians, in the United States, 251, 257

Taft, William H., 412
Tahiti, 68
Talladega College, 358
Tallmadge, Ohio, 390, 404
Talmage, T. DeWitt, 413
Tank, Nils Otto, 271
Tappan, Arthur, 393
Tartars, 121, 122
Taylor, Edward T., 36
Taylor, James Hudson, 100
Taylor, Nathaniel W., 204, 209, 432, 434
Taylor, William, 191
Teignmouth, Lord, 72
Telegraph, 10, 18
Telephone, 10
Temperance movement, 157, 393-396
Tennessee, 181, 182, 184, 190, 217
Tennyson, 166
Texas, 179, 217; Lutheran Evangelical
    Synod of, 267
Thanksgiving Day, 411
Theological seminaries, 222
Theology, weakness of, in the United States,
    429
Thirteenth Amendment, 351
Thomas, John, 68
Thornton, Henry, 72
Thornton, Samuel, 71
Thornwell, James H., 390
Tibet, 1
Tiflis, 108
Tikon, 258
Tillotson College, 358
Toleration, religious, in the United States,
    425, 426
Tolstoi, 166
Tongues, speaking with, 445
Toniolo, Guiseppe, 25
Tougaloo University, 358
Towne, Laura M., 360
Toynbee Hall, 154
Tractarian Movement, 39
Transcendental Club, 391
Transylvania, 128, 257
Transylvania University, 432
Trappists, 235, 236
Triennial Convention, Baptist, 83, 215, 315
Tunis, 133

Turin, 145
Turkey, 12, 42, 120
Turner, Asa, 210, 212, 417
Turner, Henry M., 353
Turner, Jonathan Baldwin, 417, 420
Tuscarawas County, Ohio, 263
Tuscaroras, 313
Tuskegee, 362
Tyrol, 241

Ultramontanism, 29
Unalaska, 311
Uncle Tom's Cabin, 348
Uniates, 126-128, 250-252
Union American Methodist Episcopal Church, 340
Union Church of Africans, 340
Union College, 212
Union Missionary Convention (1854), 103, 105
Union Missionary Society, 213
Union of Salesian Co-operators, 54
Union, plans for, of churches in the United States, 437, 438
Unione Popolare, 25
Unitarians, 40, 433
United Brethren in Christ, 40, 134, 286, 287
United Christian Missionary Society, 84
United Danish Evangelical Lutheran Church in America, 277
United Domestic Missionary Society, 87, 209
United Free Church of Scotland, 41
United Norwegian Lutheran Church, 273
United Presbyterian Church of North America, 439
United Presbyterian Church, Board of Freedmen's Missions, 361
United States of America, 8, 12, 14, 15, 19, 23, 55, 163, 175-455; formation of missionary societies in, 75-89; leadership in Protestant foreign missions, 93-98; Protestant missions to Europe, 130-143
United States Temperance Union, 395
Universalists, 391, 433
Universities' Mission to Central Africa, 101
Urban College of the Propaganda, 245, 305
Ursulines, 236, 241
Ussuri, 15
Utah, 200-202
Utrecht, Archbishop of, 239

Valladolid, 62
Van Buren, Martin, 412
Vancouver, Fort, 308
Vanderkemp, John Theodore, 89
Van Quickenborne, Charles Felix, 237, 306

Varick, James, 340
Variety in the Christianity of the United States, 424, 425
Vatican, Council of 1870, 29
Vaudois, 139, 140
Vaughan, Herbert, 55
Veniaminoff, John, 256, 311, 312
Verbist, Theophile, 54
Vermont, 179, 194, 201, 205, 349
Vienna, 240
Vincent, John H., 421
Virginia, 181, 182, 189, 190, 199, 216, 333, 334, 355; Synod of, 207
Volanski, Ivan, 251
Volga, 119, 121
Voltaire, 22
Volunteers of America, 371
Vyatka, 120

Waiilatpu, 318
Waldenses, 139, 140, 279
Wales, 72, 168
Walsh, James A., 55
Walther, Carl Ferdinand Wilhelm, 264
War, 12
Ward, Joseph, 212, 417
Ware, Henry, 348
Washington, Booker T., 330, 362
Washington, George, 431
Washington (State), 211, 212
Washingtonians, 393
Watch Tower, 443, 444
Waterloo, 12
Watts, Isaac, 44
Way, Lewis, 113, 114
Wayland, 19
Weld, Theodore Dwight, 347, 349, 402
Wellesley College, 420
Welsh, in the United States, 259, 260
Wesley, John, 38, 72, 186
Wesleyan Methodist Missionary Society, 73
Wesleyan Methodists, 444
Wesleyan movement, 32, 65
West Indies, 2, 8, 72
Westcott, Brooke Foss, 161
Western Coloured Baptist Convention, 338
Western Female Institute, 420
Western Foreign Missionary Society, 88
Western Missionary Society, 207
Western Reserve, Ohio, 205, 209
Western Seamen's Friend Society, 374
Westminster, Archbishops of, 125
Whipple, Henry Benjamin, 320
White, Mrs. Ellen G., 442
White River, 314

INDEX

hitefield, 38, 404

hitefield, Archbishop of Baltimore, 242

Whitman, Marcus, 318

Whitman, Walt, 415

Whittier, John G., 415

Wichern, J. H., 147

Wieselgren, Peter, 158

Wilberforce University, 335, 339

Wilberforce, William, 38, 71, 72, 156, 159, 160

Wilder, Robert P., 96, 97

Willard, Frances E., 395

Willey, Samuel H., 211

Williams, Archbishop of Boston, 246

Williams College, 80, 100

Williams, Eleazer, 319

Williams, George, 36

Williamson, Thomas S., 319

Wilmington, Delaware, 330, 340

Wilson, Woodrow, 390, 408, 412

Wimmer, Boniface, 241

Winnebagos, 321

Wisconsin, 204, 207, 211, 217, 271, 273, 313, 319, 320

Wiseman, Cardinal, 125

Wishard, Luther D., 99

Wolff, Joseph, 114

Woman's American Baptist Home Mission Society, 360

Woman's Christian Temperance Union, 395

Woman's Home Missionary Association, 213

Woman's Temperance Crusade, 395

Woman's Union Missionary Society for Heathen Lands, 98

Women, in Roman Catholic Church, 26, 27; in foreign missions, 49, 50; in Protestant foreign missions, 98; franchise for, 162

Women's rights, 401, 402

Wood River Association, 338

Woolman, John, 346

Worcester, Massachusetts, 258

Worcester, Noah, 398

Worcester, Samuel A., 316

World Alliance for the Promotion of International Friendship Through the Churches, 400

World culture, 14, 21

World Dominion Movement, 100

World Missionary Conference, Edinburgh, 106

World War of 1914-1918, 7

Worldwide Evangelization Crusade, 100

World's Student Christian Federation, 35, 103

World's Sunday School Association, 38, 103, 376

World's Sunday School Conventions, 38, 376

World's Young Women's Christian Association, 37, 103

Wright, Elizur, 404

Württemberg, 262, 269

Wyandottes, 313

Wyoming, 213

Xaverian Brothers, 238

Yakutsk, 312

Yale, 80, 84, 204, 210, 211, 221, 404

Yale Foreign Missionary Society, 101

Yale in China Association, 101

Yankton College, 212

Young, Brigham, 201, 202

Young, Hall, 320

Young Men's Christian Associations, 36, 37, 96, 99, 103, 137, 145, 371, 379; World's Alliance of, 36, 103

Young People's Society of Christian Endeavour, 37

Young Women's Christian Associations, 37, 98, 103, 145, 371, 379

Zeisberger, David, 314

Zinzendorf, 69

Zion City, Illinois, 445

Zion Union Apostolic Church, 355

Zoar, Ohio, 391

Zoarites, 263